Blazing Trails

TEACHER'S EDITION
LEVEL 11

Margaret Early
G. Robert Canfield
Robert Karlin

Thomas A. Schottman
Sara Krentzman Srygley
Evelyn Wenzel

HBJ BOOKMARK READING PROGRAM Eagle Edition

 Harcourt Brace Jovanovich, Publishers
New York   Chicago   San Francisco   Atlanta   Dallas   *and*   London

Acknowledgments

For permission to reprint copyrighted
material, grateful acknowledgment is
made to the following source:

Harcourt Brace Jovanovich, Inc:
Reprinted from *The HBJ School
Dictionary,* ©1977, 1972, 1968.

HBJ BOOKMARK READING PROGRAM
Level-to-Grade Correspondences

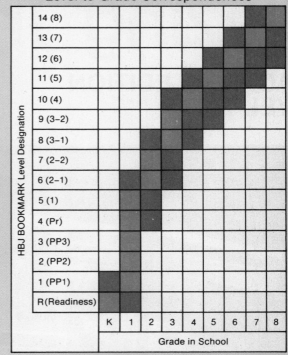

HBJ BOOKMARK Level Designation		
14 (8)		
13 (7)		
12 (6)		
11 (5)		
10 (4)		
9 (3–2)		
8 (3–1)		
7 (2–2)		
6 (2–1)		
5 (1)		
4 (Pr)		
3 (PP3)		
2 (PP2)		
1 (PP1)		
R (Readiness)		

Grade in School: K 1 2 3 4 5 6 7 8

☐ Levels used by a majority of students at each grade

☐ Levels used by some students at each grade

Note: The red blocks indicate the HBJ BOOKMARK
materials used by a majority of children in each grade.
However, children who are using materials from the
levels marked red or gray for their grades are well
within the normal progress range.

A Teacher's Edition is not automat-
ically included with each shipment
of a classroom set of textbooks.
However, a Teacher's Edition will
be forwarded when requested by
a teacher, an administrator, or a
representative of Harcourt Brace
Jovanovich, Inc.

A Teacher's Resource Book is available for
every level of the *HBJ Bookmark Reading
Program, Eagle Edition* (one for levels 2/3).
For information, please contact your sales
representative.

CONTENTS

continued

CONTENTS

Authors of the HBJ Bookmark Reading Program

Margaret Early, senior author, is Associate Dean of Academic Affairs in the School of Education, Syracuse University. She also directs the program in English Education, teaches graduate courses in reading instruction, and is the author of articles and monographs on the teaching of reading. Dr.Early received her Ed.D.from Boston University, where she was a Warren Research Fellow in English. A past president of the National Council of Teachers of English, she has served this organization and the International Reading Association in many capacities.

Elizabeth K. Cooper is a well-known author of children's books, including *Who Is Paddy?, The Fish From Japan, A Tree Is Something Wonderful, The Wild Cats Of Rome,* and the award-winning *Science In Your Own Back Yard.* She is also a coauthor of a widely used science series, published by Harcourt Brace Jovanovich, Inc.
  A former teacher in Cleveland Heights, Ohio; New York, N.Y.; and Los Angeles, California, Dr. Cooper received her doctorate at U.C.L.A., where she taught courses in education, child development, and psychology. She has also served as Director of Elementary Education in the Santa Monica, California, public schools, and as Coordinator of Teacher Training for the University of California.

Robert Karlin is Professor of Education and Coordinator of Graduate Reading Programs at Queens College of the City University of New York. He has been a member of the faculty at Southern Illinois University and at New York University, where he received his Ph.D. Dr. Karlin has written many articles and monographs on reading and is the author of several professional books on the teaching of reading. His *Teaching Elementary Reading: Principles and Strategies* is now in its third edition.

Nancy Santeusanio is currently serving as principal of the South Intermediate School in Lynnfield, Massachusetts and served many years as principal of Center Elementary School in the same district. She is also a visiting lecturer at Salem (Massachusetts) State College, where she has taught courses in reading for administrators, the improvement of reading instruction, early childhood and primary reading, and differentiated instruction. Throughout the country, Dr. Santeusanio continues to conduct workshops to develop strategies for more effective reading instruction. She received her B.A., M.Ed., and Ed.D. from Boston University.

G. Robert Canfield is a professor of education and a former chairman of the Reading Education Department at the State University College in Oswego, New York. He has taught courses in elementary reading instruction, reading in the content areas, and individualizing reading instruction. He has also been the project director for several research grants and currently serves on the College Proficiency Examination Committee for Reading for the State Education Department of New York. Dr. Canfield received his Ed.D. from Syracuse University.

Thomas A. Schottman is the principal of Lincoln Elementary School in Scotia, New York. Formerly, he was an elementary school teacher, a curriculum specialist, and an instructor of corrective and remedial reading at Syracuse University. Mr. Schottman has been President of the New York State Association for Supervision and Curriculum Development. He has also written for professional journals, including the *National Elementary Principal,* which published his "Still Groping in Grouping." Mr. Schottman received his B.A. and M.A. from Cornell University.

continued ▶

Donald Gallo is a professor of English at Central Connecticut State College. Formerly, while on the faculty of the University of Colorado, he was a codirector of the ERIC/CRIER Reading Resources Center and the director of the Denver campus's Urban Education Program. Dr. Gallo, who received his Ph.D. from Syracuse University, has also served as a consultant to the National Assessment of Educational Progress, as a trustee of the National Council of Teachers of English Research Foundation, and as the editor of the *Connecticut English Journal.* He is presently a Director of the Assembly on Literature for Adolescents (NCTE) and a member of the Executive Board of the conference on English Education.

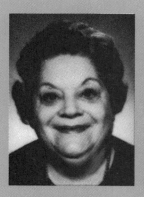

Sara K. Srygley is Professor Emeritus in the School of Library Science, Florida State University. She was formerly the supervisor of school libraries for the Florida State Department of Education and has been a visiting professor at the University of Colorado. Ms. Srygley has also been a guest lecturer at numerous universities, including the University of Chicago, San Jose State University, and the University of Michigan, and has published in library and educational journals. She received her M.S. from Columbia University.

Gwendolyn Kerr is a former seventh- and eighth-grade language arts teacher, as well as a former school librarian. She now lives in Milford, New Jersey, where she is self-employed as a free-lance writer. Ms. Kerr received her bachelor's degree from Skidmore College and her master's degree in education from Rutgers, the State University of New Jersey.

Evelyn L. Wenzel is Professor Emeritus in the College of Education, University of Florida. Dr. Wenzel, who began her career as a classroom teacher in Dayton, Ohio, has taught at the campus laboratory schools of Miami (Ohio) University and Indiana State University. She has also taught graduate and undergraduate courses in reading, children's literature, and elementary language arts. Dr. Wenzel has published *Time for Discovery: Informational Books* and a number of articles. She received her Ed.D. from Teachers College, Columbia University.

Maurine A. Fry chairs the Department of Educational Psychology at Arizona State University. She was formerly an instructor at the University of Iowa, where she received her Ph.D. in educational psychology. Dr. Fry has also been an elementary school teacher and a school psychologist. In addition to contributing articles to several professional journals, she has recently published research in *School Psychology Review* on a developmental perspective towards factors that influence reading.

Jerry D. Harris is Associate Professor of Educational Psychology at Arizona State University. He was formerly a school psychologist and a secondary English teacher. Dr. Harris received his Ph.D. in educational psychology from the University of Minnesota. He is a member of the American Psychological Association and the National Association of School Psychologists and has published a number of articles in professional journals, including *Psychology in the Schools, Psychological Measurement,* and *School Psychology Review.*

Advisory Board

The members of this Advisory Board have been selected for their contributions to the understanding of the teaching of reading. They work closely with the authors and editors in the development of the *HBJ Bookmark Reading Program.*

Shirley M. Byrne, Ed.D.
Associate Professor of
   Education
Eastern Kentucky University
Richmond, Kentucky

John E. Davis, Ed.D.
Professor of Education
Purdue University Calumet
Hammond, Indiana

Gilbert Lamarre, Ed.D.
Reading Consultant
Longmeadow High School
Longmeadow, Massachusetts

Donna Ogle, Ed.D.
Chairperson, Graduate
   Reading and Language Arts
   Department
National College of Education
Evanston, Illinois

Howard H. Schroeder, Ph.D.
Professor of Reading and
   Language Arts
Department of Curriculum and
   Instruction
Mankato State University
Mankato, Minnesota

Julie M. T. Chan, Ed.D.
Co-founder, CompuKids Inc.
Associate Professor of
   Education
California State University
Long Beach, California

Colin Dunkeld, Ph.D.
Professor of Education
Portland State University
Portland, Oregon

Donald R. Lashinger, Ed.D.
Professor of Education
College of William & Mary
Williamsburg, Virginia

Thomas A. Rakes, Ed.D.
Coordinator of Graduate
   Studies
Department of Curriculum and
   Instruction
Memphis State University
Memphis, Tennessee

Pat Tarplee
Parent
Indianapolis, Indiana

Fred Chavez, Ed.D.
Director, Reading Support
   Services Center
Los Angeles Unified School
   District
Los Angeles, California

Gloria Fried, Ed.D.
Professor of Education
Georgian Court College
Lakewood, New Jersey

Nancy B. Livingston, Ed.D.
Specialist, Reading Education
Office of the Utah State Board
   of Education
Salt Lake City, Utah

Edward L. Robbins, Ed.D.
Associate Professor of
   Education and Director of
   Undergraduate Studies
Indiana University – Purdue
   University at Indianapolis

Helen Turner, Ed.D.
Supervising Director, Office of
   Reading
Public Schools of the District of
   Columbia
Washington, D.C.

Bernice E. Cullinan, Ph.D.
Professor of Education, Early
   Childhood and Elementary
   Education
New York University
New York, New York

**Brother Robert J. Kealey,
F.S.C., Ed.D.**
Associate Superintendent of
   Schools / Director of
   Curriculum, Archdiocese of
   New York
Assistant Professor, Manhattan
   College
Riverdale, New York

Edna Minaya
Coordinator of Language Arts,
   Grades 7-12
Metropolitan Public Schools
Nashville, Tennessee

Migdalia Romero
Lecturer
Hunter College
New York, New York

James S. Vacca, Ph.D.
Special Education Supervisor
Albany–Schoharie–
   Schenectady Board of
   Cooperative Educational
   Services
Albany, New York

Critical Readers

Teachers, principals, and curriculum leaders from all parts of the country reviewed and evaluated portions of the *Eagle Edition* of the *HBJ Bookmark Reading Program* prior to its publication. Their commentary was extremely beneficial in refining the new materials and confirming the propriety and practicality of their structure, content, and organization.

Scott Baker
Teacher, Grade 1
Lake Oswego, Oregon

Thomas V. Bennett
Teacher, Grade 4
Evansville, Indiana

Sharon K. Botelle
Reading Consultant
Faribault, Minnesota

George Canney
Associate Professor of Reading
University of Idaho
Moscow, Idaho

Dorothy Degraffenried
Teacher, Grade 3
Cincinnati, Ohio

Robert E. Dennis
Reading Coordinator
Lindenhurst, New York

Sue Fairless
Reading Supervisor
Windsor, North Carolina

Robert A. Fulmer
Reading Coordinator
Lake George, New York

Kay Grate
Teacher, Grade 1
Norwood, Ohio

Arlene Grindstad
Teacher, Grade 2
Phoenix, Arizona

Toni C. Hill
Reading Coordinator
Durham, North Carolina

Corrine Hochgraef
Instructional Specialist
Scottsdale, Arizona

Miriam Hoffman
Reading Specialist
Selden, New York

Carolyn Hughes
Principal
Shaker Heights, Ohio

Sister Donna Innes, C.S.A.
Curriculum Coordinator
Archdiocese of St. Paul
and Minneapolis
St. Paul, Minnesota

Merrillyn Kloefkorn
Library Media Specialist
Jefferson County, Colorado

Judy Lanfrey
Reading Specialist
Newtown, Pennsylvania

Judy Lay
Reading Consultant
Elizabethtown, Kentucky

Judy Long
Professor of Reading
North Georgia College
Dahlonega, Georgia

Trudy B. Matthews
General Supervisor
Wilmington, North Carolina

Barbara McMillin
Instructional Specialist
Alabama State Department
of Education
Montgomery, Alabama

Jean Moody
Supervisor of Reading
Pascagoula, Mississippi

Annie Morgan
Teacher, Grades 3-5
Detroit, Michigan

Grace A. Morse
Reading/Language Arts
Coordinator
Ontario Center, New York

Florence A. Nelson
Professor of Education
University of South Carolina
Columbia, South Carolina

Betty M. Nichols
Reading Coordinator
Statesville, North Carolina

Joan O'Brien
Instructional Specialist
Scottsdale, Arizona

Beverly Peterman
Director of Reading
Stanford, Connecticut

John Poeton
Reading Consultant
Vermont State Department
of Education
Montpelier, Vermont

Margaret Pope
Supervisor, Curricular
Services/Materials
North Little Rock, Arkansas

Bill Rhinehart
Coordinator of Language Arts
and Developmental Learning
Syosset, New York

Sylvia Robbins
Reading Supervisor
Pensacola, Florida

Linda Snyder
Teacher, Grade 4
Richmond, Indiana

Carla Steinforth
Curriculum Consultant
Las Vegas, Nevada

Mary Tierney
Teacher, Grade 1
Middle Village, New York

Shirley Walsh
Reading Coordinator
Watertown, New York

Karolanne D. Wenning
Teacher, Grade 6
Peachtree City, Georgia

HBJ Bookmark Reading Program
EAGLE EDITION

Success in learning to read

Success in reading to learn

Success in reading for pleasure

Please turn the page to see the many benefits you'll find in the *HBJ Bookmark Reading Program, Eagle Edition.*

HBJ Bookmark has everything students need to succeed in reading

★ Materials uniquely matched to essential reading goals

No other program is as carefully structured to match reading needs, from readiness through junior high. As your students' goals mature from learning to read to reading for pleasure and learning, *HBJ Bookmark* is there to meet them with the specific instruction they need.

★ A broadly based approach to reading skills mastery

Oral and written activities systematically develop five major skills strands: decoding (emphasizing phonics, plus context and word structure clues), comprehension, language, study skills, and literature appreciation.

★ The most logical teaching strategy

Skills and vocabulary are thoroughly taught and immediately applied in reading selections. Once introduced, skills are continually reviewed and maintained.

★ Rich provisions for individual differences

Attention to the needs of slower learners and high-achieving students is an integral part of *HBJ Bookmark.* The program offers an exceptionally wide range of activities, teaching strategies, and materials to meet individual pupils' needs.

x

☆ **Active, every-child participation in learning to read**

Teacher-directed lessons involve every child actively and individually. This active participation makes on-the-spot diagnosis simple and effective.

☆ **Vital attention to reading to learn**

High-interest nonfiction, informational articles, and comprehension-building exercises begin at the earliest grades. In-depth lessons in grades 4-8 teach comprehension, vocabulary, and study skills.

☆ **Practical preparation for reading in the content areas**

Actual textbook excerpts help intermediate/junior high students transfer reading skills to other school subjects.

☆ **An exhilarating introduction to reading for pleasure**

Award-winning stories, plays, folktales, poetry, and more encourage young minds to discover the joys of reading.

☆ **Dramatic, colorful art and photographs**

Illustrations entertain, inform, and build reading enthusiasm at every turn of the page.

☆ **Uncommonly thorough Teacher's Editions**

HBJ Bookmark's clear, complete teaching plans give you continual ease of instruction. There is abundant extra practice and enrichment for each lesson, plus ideas, activities, and reproducible worksheets that move beyond the basic plans for individualization.

☆ **Convenient, economical Teacher's Resource Books**

A wealth of copying masters enable you to reproduce classroom quantities of pages from the Reading Skills Workbooks, Duplicating Masters, and Periodic Tests, Form A, for each level.

Components of the HBJ Bookmark Reading Program Eagle Edition

For instruction, practice, and enjoyment at all levels

PUPIL'S EDITIONS (Levels R-14)

Optional, full-color, consumable readiness materials

- *Look, Listen, and Learn,* for developing a broad range of prereading skills
- *Sounds, Symbols, and Sense,* to provide an introduction to sound/symbol correspondences and vocabulary which will be taught in the preprimers

Selections that promote reading for pleasure

- Top-quality traditional and contemporary literature
- Award-winning authors and illustrators
- Outstanding variety, including folktales, plays, fantasy, realistic fiction, poetry, myths, biographies, and more
- "Bonus" selections at the end of each primary level, for independent reading
- In-depth author studies at each intermediate/junior high level

Selections that promote the development of skills required for reading to learn

- Articles packed with information—about the arts, careers, hobbies, animals, life-styles, people, and places
- An exceptional variety of subjects related to the content areas, including science, mathematics, social studies, and language arts
- Actual textbook excerpts that give intermediate/junior high students directed help in applying reading skills to other school subjects

Skills lessons, questions, and activities that teach and reinforce reading skills

TEACHER'S EDITIONS (Levels R-14)

- Clear, easy-to-use lesson plans
- Full-color, annotated pupil pages and, at primary levels, reproduced workbook pages
- Suggestions for evaluation built into each lesson
- Numerous opportunities for additional skills practice
- Enrichment to extend students' interest in the content of the reading selections
- Reading and Resource Centers filled with skills games and (in primary levels) independent learning activities, along with lists of extended reading suggestions and multi-media materials
- Extra practice worksheets and record keeping forms on convenient copying masters
- A complete skills index for easy access to additional activities and materials

TEACHER'S RESOURCE BOOKS
(Levels R-14)

- Helpful materials which teachers are free to reproduce in classroom quantities
- Every page from Reading Skills Workbooks for the appropriate level, in copying master form
- Exercises from the supplementary Duplicating Masters, in copying master form
- Periodic Tests, Form A, in copying master form
- Perforated and three-hole punched

Note: Parent Letters, in both English and Spanish, are included in the Teacher's Editions, Levels 1-9, and in the Teacher's Resource Book for Levels R through 9.

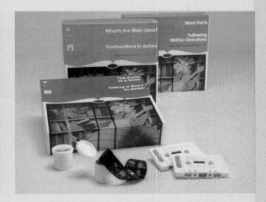

READING SKILLS WORKBOOKS
(Levels 1-14)

- For primary grades, full-color workbooks (also available in duplicating master form) that develop skills and vocabulary before students read selections, and provide follow-up practice after reading
- For intermediate/junior high grades, full-color workbooks that provide additional practice in skills and vocabulary
- Annotated Teacher's Edition for each workbook

DUPLICATING MASTERS (Levels R-14)

- Additional independent written skills practice
- Vocabulary reinforcement exercises
- At-home activities for parents to use with their children (Levels R-9)

BOOKMARK READING FILMSTRIPS
(Levels R-12)

- Six full-color sound filmstrips per grade (© 1980-78) that reinforce and enrich reading skills
- Colorful characters and lively sound tracks that capture children's imaginations

For evaluation and management at all levels

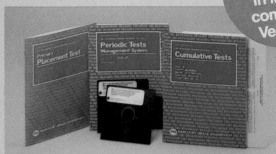

Periodic Tests also available in Microcomputer Version!

PLACEMENT TESTS

- Prereading Skills Inventory (Level R) to identify pupils who need readiness instruction
- Primary and Intermediate/Junior High Placement Tests (Levels 1-9 and 10-14) to determine the best starting point for students new to *HBJ Bookmark*

PERIODIC TESTS/ MANAGEMENT SYSTEM

- Diagnostic/prescriptive tests for ongoing skills assessment
- Forms A and B for pre-, post-, or retesting
- Teacher's Editions with reproducible copies of tests, record forms, and suggestions for reteaching and additional practice

MICROCOMPUTER VERSION/ PERIODIC TESTS/ MANAGEMENT SYSTEM

- Speeds evaluation with Periodic Tests, Levels R-14
- Provides compact, timesaving record-keeping and retrieval
- Diskettes compatible with today's most popular microcomputers

CUMULATIVE TESTS

- End-of-level tests that measure achievement in major skills areas
- Annotated test pages in the Teacher's Edition of the test

INDIVIDUAL PROGRESS FOLDER

- A convenient way to record Periodic and Cumulative Test scores and informal teacher evaluation
- For each child's permanent record

For aiding and supplementing instruction at the primary levels

LANGUAGE ACTIVITY KIT (Level R)

- Colorful, varied components to develop oral language and prereading skills
- Photo cards, art cards, floor games, letters and numerals, storyboards, and more in a shelf-size storage box
- A resource-rich Teacher's Edition with 150 lesson plans and with copying masters to aid in practice and evaluation

TRY THIS BOXES

(Try This, Levels 1-5; Try This Too, Levels 6-7; Now Try This, Levels 8-9)

- Self-directing, self-correcting activity cards that reinforce decoding, comprehension, language, and study skills

THE BOOKMARK LIBRARIES (Levels R-9)

- Four sets of delightful paperbacks for independent reading
- Twelve full-color books per set
- Reinforcement for vocabulary used in the pupil's books

PUPIL RESPONSE CARDS (Levels 1-5)

- Alphabet, number 1-2-3, and yes/no cards for 36 pupils
- Allows for every-child participation in decoding and vocabulary-recognition exercises

WORD SERVICE/ DECODING BOX (Levels 1-5)

- Letter, picture, and phonics key cards to enhance oral decoding lessons and teach sound-letter relationships

VOCABULARY/ LANGUAGE SKILLS BOX (Levels 1-5)

- Word cards for all vocabulary introduced in Levels 1-5 plus inflectional-ending, punctuation, and consonant-substitution cards
- Can be used to teach word structure, phrase construction, and sentence composition

INSTRUCTIONAL CHARTS (Levels 1-9)

- Large, spiral-bound reproductions of chalkboard activities called for in core steps of each teaching unit

TUTORIAL PROGRAMS (Levels 1-9)

- Duplicating masters and Tutor's Guide for each primary grade
- To reinforce skills and vocabulary and provide guided oral reading practice
- For use by aides or nonprofessional instructors

VOCABULARY AND COMPREHENSION PRACTICE BOOK (Levels 4-9)

- Optional independent practice for use following the reading of the selection

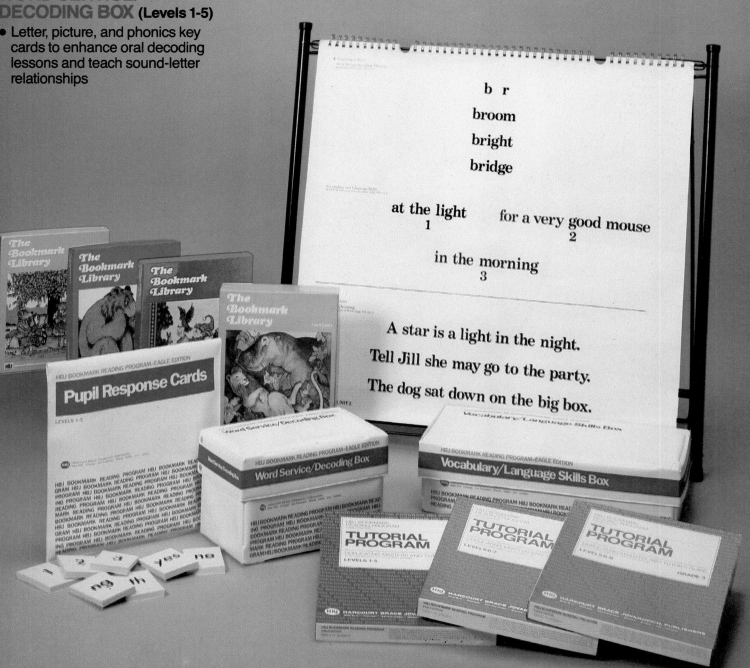

HBJ Bookmark develops a lifelong appreciation for literature in all its forms

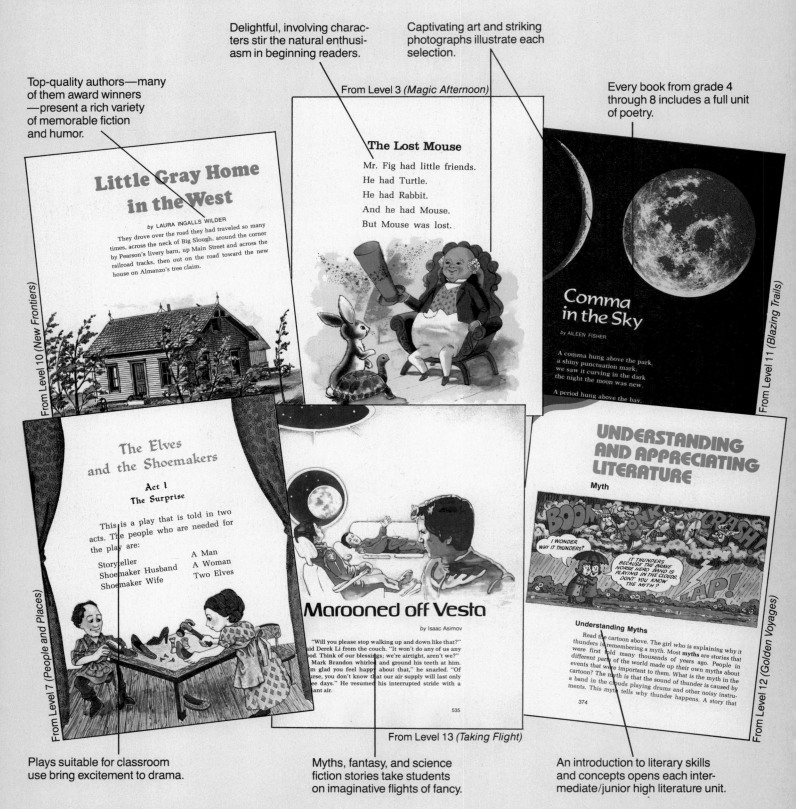

Top-quality authors—many of them award winners —present a rich variety of memorable fiction and humor.

Delightful, involving characters stir the natural enthusiasm in beginning readers.

Captivating art and striking photographs illustrate each selection.

Every book from grade 4 through 8 includes a full unit of poetry.

From Level 3 (Magic Afternoon)

Little Gray Home in the West

by LAURA INGALLS WILDER

They drove over the road they had traveled so many times, across the neck of Big Slough, around the corner by Pearson's livery barn, up Main Street and across the railroad tracks, then out on the road toward the new house on Almanzo's tree claim.

From Level 10 (New Frontiers)

The Lost Mouse

Mr. Fig had little friends.
He had Turtle.
He had Rabbit.
And he had Mouse.
But Mouse was lost.

Comma in the Sky

by AILEEN FISHER

A comma hung above the park,
a shiny punctuation mark,
we saw it curving in the dark
the night the moon was new.

A period hung above the bay.

From Level 11 (Blazing Trails)

The Elves and the Shoemakers

Act 1
The Surprise

This is a play that is told in two acts. The people who are needed for the play are:

Storyteller   A Man
Shoemaker Husband   A Woman
Shoemaker Wife   Two Elves

From Level 7 (People and Places)

Marooned off Vesta

by Isaac Asimov

"Will you please stop walking up and down like that?" said Derek Li from the couch. "It won't do any of us any good. Think of our blessings; we're airtight, aren't we?" Mark Brandon whirled and ground his teeth at him. "I'm glad you feel happy about that," he snarled. "Of course, you don't know that our air supply will last only three days." He resumed his interrupted stride with a ... ant air.

535

From Level 13 (Taking Flight)

UNDERSTANDING AND APPRECIATING LITERATURE

Myth

I WONDER WHY IT THUNDERS?

IT THUNDERS BECAUSE THE BRAVE NORSE HERO BAND IS PLAYING IN THE CLOUDS. DON'T YOU KNOW THE MYTH?

Understanding Myths

Read the cartoon above. The girl who is explaining why it thunders is remembering a myth. Most **myths** are stories that were first told many thousands of years ago. People in different parts of the world made up their own myths about events that were important to them. What is the myth in the cartoon? The myth is that the sound of thunder is caused by a band in the clouds playing drums and other noisy instruments. This myth tells why thunder happens. A story that

374

From Level 12 (Golden Voyages)

Plays suitable for classroom use bring excitement to drama.

Myths, fantasy, and science fiction stories take students on imaginative flights of fancy.

An introduction to literary skills and concepts opens each intermediate/junior high literature unit.

Sample pages reduced. Actual size is 7" x 9⅛."

HBJ Bookmark teaches skills essential for reading to learn

From the earliest levels, high-interest informational articles help students see direction and purpose in their reading.

Thinking and comprehension skills are systematically taught in special skills lessons.

Intermediate/junior high vocabulary study receives in-depth attention.

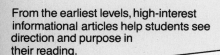

Growing Things

You can see a plant grow.
Just get a seed like this.

Put it in a jar.

Wet the seed.

Soon the seed will grow.

Seeds like this grow until they are big plants.

137

From Level 4 (Sun and Shadow)

SKILLS LESSON

Predicting Outcomes

Look at the picture story above. Can you tell what will happen next? If so, then you are **predicting an outcome.**

When you predict an outcome, you think about what is happening or has already happened. Then you use your powers of reasoning to figure out what is likely to happen next.

472

From Level 10 *(New Frontiers)*

VOCABULARY STUDY

Prefixes

"I was watching a movie down at the bottom of the ocean," said Thaddeus the blue whale. "I have to submerge now."

"Wait! Don't go under!" cried the reporter for *Marine Semimonthly Magazine*. "I need only one more fact for my story about the order, or group, of large fishlike mammals. I've already talked to a dolphin and a porpoise. I just need a few comments from someone in the **suborder** of whales."

"The prefix *sub-* means 'under.' So a suborder is a division under an order of living things."

"Yes," agreed the reporter. "Please come back. Just swim in a **semicircle** back to me so we can talk."

"The prefix *semi-* means 'half.' So you don't want me to swim all the way around your ship—just halfway around?"

"Yes, Thaddeus. Now here's my question. How long have whales been on the Earth?"

"Since **prehistory**," answered Thaddeus. "The prefix *pre-* means 'before.' We've been around since *before* humans first wrote histories thousands of years ago. Now I really must get back to my movie. I left just at the part where Moby Dick meets Son of Flipper."

Word Play

Match each word on the left with its meaning on the right. Then use each word in a sentence.

semimonthly
suborder
prefix
semicircle
submerge
prehistory

a. half a circle
b. go under the water
c. before history was written
d. happening every half month
e. a division under an order (group) of living things
f. a word part added before a root word

From Level 12 (Golden Voyages)

From Level 11 *(Blazing Trails)*

TEXTBOOK STUDY

Recognizing To...

Since textbooks ar... generally arranged to... ideas of paragraphs. ... stated.

Think about each... main idea. Use the si...

Recognizing Topic...

Some kind of plant w... anywhere on the earth... the spaces between t... sidewalks. They gr... boxes in cities. You wo... time finding a place ... not grow. Some plant... soil; some in deserts... ponds and streams, wh... in the ocean. Plants... mountaintops and in ... Arctic.

Plants can grow on... objects. Perhaps you h... growing on rocks an... even grow on old sho... mals. Where else have ... growing?

—Understanding...

From Level 11 (Blazing Trails)

TEXTBOOK STUDY

Recognizing Important Details

Which details in textbooks are important? The answer depends on your purpose in reading. If you have specific questions to answer, you will need to pay close attention to details that will help you answer those questions. If your purpose is to remember generally what a textbook selection is about, you will need to look for main ideas. The important details, then, would be those that can help you understand the main ideas.

As you read the following selections, refer to the side-notes. They will help you focus on main ideas and important details.

Recognizing Important Details in Social Studies

Tame animals work for people. The ox and the donkey may have been the first animals trained to carry and pull loads in northern Africa and western Asia. In India and China, people tamed water buffalo at a very early time. These slow, gentle animals still give much of the animal power in India and Southeast Asia. The water buffalo have sometimes been called the "living tractors of the East."

This is the main idea. The next two sentences give important details about which animals were tamed and where.

From Level 12 (Golden Voyages)

Actual textbook excerpts help students apply their reading skills to other subject areas.

In this selection, you'll find many details in the graphic aids. Th... ...aphic aids and the text may help ...h how to learn about the ...your town or city.

...town or city have a ...et? If it does, you can ...about your local his-...find the answer to ...on . . .

...tever ...pened to ...n Street?

...Weitzman

As you read this selection, look for the kinds of information you would be likely to include in a set of notes.

They enjoy sunshine, exercise, and the sweet smell of the good earth. The men and women in agricultural careers are . . .

People Who Love the Land

by Sarah Splaver

436

In the 1800's, more than 50 percent of the American people had agricultural jobs. Today, the number has dropped to less than 5 percent. In the last century, the average farmer supplied food for only about five people. Today, a single farmer can meet the food needs of forty-five people. Despite these statistics, farming still offers many career opportunities for people who love the land.

A number of young people who are attracted to farming grew up around barns, silos, and fields. Others either spent summer vacations on farms, enjoy working outdoors, or love the independence that can only be found on a farm.

From Level 14 (Widening Pathways)

Nonfiction selections focus on science, art, nature, sports, and famous personalities, enhancing skills instruction with real-life experience.

HBJ Bookmark gives effective teaching help in the most efficient way

Every lesson plan follows a three-step approach to reading skills mastery. Skills and vocabulary are introduced, immediately applied in reading selections, and continually maintained through oral and written activities.

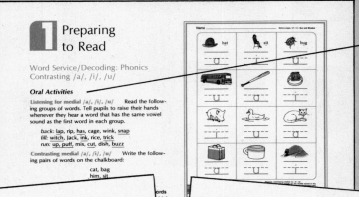

Thorough oral and written activities develop skills in decoding, comprehension, language, content area study, and literature appreciation.

1 Preparing to Read

Word Service/Decoding: Phonics
Contrasting /a/, /i/, /u/

Oral Activities

Listening for medial /a/, /i/, /u/ Read the following groups of words. Tell pupils to raise their hands whenever they hear a word that has the same vowel sound as the first word in each group.

back: lap, rip, has, cage, wink, snap
fill: witch, Jack, ink, rice, trick
run: up, puff, mix, cut, dish, buzz

Contrasting medial /a/, /i/, /u/ Write the following pairs of words on the chalkboard:

cat, bag
him, sit

Call attention to the second sentence. The new word in this sentence is a color. When a traffic light is this color, it is safe to go. What is the new word? (green) Read the sentence silently, and underline the new word. Write the word green on the writing line. Have the sentence read aloud.

Have pupils look at the third sentence. The new word in this sentence means "in a short time," and it rhymes with moon. Read the sentence silently, and underline the new word. What is the new word? (soon) Trace the word soon on the writing line. Have the sentence read aloud.

Call attention to the fourth sentence. The new word in this sentence begins with the same sounds as grass and green. Read the sentence silently, and underline the new word. What is the new word? (grow) Have pupils say the new word and trace it on the writing line. Have the sentence read aloud.

Using new words Direct pupils' attention to the exercise at the bottom of the page. Tell pupils to read each sentence silently and underline the word that makes sense in the sentence. Have the completed sentences read aloud.

✓ See "Providing for Individual Differences" for additional practice with these skills.

2 Reading and Discussing

Summary
"Growing Things" is an informational selection about how plants grow. First, pupils learn how to sprout a seed in a jar. Then the cycle of a tomato plant's growth—from seed to plant to fruit and back to seed—is shown. After pupils read the selection, you may wish to encourage them to grow plants in the classroom.

Setting Purposes for Reading
Have pupils recall the previous selection. What were Victor and Jack doing in the last story? (planting) What did they grow? (peas, carrots, tomatoes, and potatoes) How did they care for their garden? (They watered their garden and pulled weeds from it.) Today we will learn some new facts about how plants grow. Open your books to page 137.

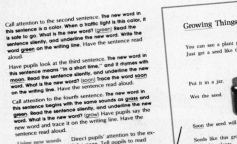

Growing Things

You can see a plant grow.
Just get a seed like this.

Put it in a jar.
Wet the seed.

Soon the seed will grow.

Seeds like this grow until they are big plants.

137

Comprehension

Directed Silent Reading
Direct pupils' attention to the first photograph on page 137, and ask them what is in the child's hand. (a seed) Tell pupils the seed is a lima bean seed.

Read page 137 to find out what happens to the seed.

Page 137
1. What two things were done to the seed? (It was put in a jar with soil and was watered.) LITERAL
2. How did the seed change? (It began to grow.) INFERENTIAL

Read page 138 to find out what else most plants need in order to grow.

T252   Sun and Shadow and Reading Skills 4 Teacher's Edition

3 Maintaining Skills

Comprehension Skills

Recognizing multiple meanings of words Display word cards like, plant, and light, and have them read. Discuss with pupils the various meanings of each word.

like: to enjoy or be fond of; the same as
plant: something that grows; to put a seed in earth to grow
light: not dark; not heavy; something that gives off brightness

Then read the following sentences, and have pupils tell which word makes sense in the sentence. Read the completed sentence aloud.

A feather is very _____. (light)
My notebook is just _____ yours. (like)
Let's _____ the flower seeds today. (plant)
When the sun comes up, it gets _____. (light)
Your _____ is beginning to grow. (plant)
When it gets dark, the _____ will come on. (light)
I _____ green peppers better than red ones. (like)

Have pupils use each word in a sentence to illustrate each meaning.

Direct pupils to page 106 of Reading Skills 4.

Reading Skills 4, Page 106

Recognizing cause and effect Direct pupils' attention to the pictures at the top of the page. Be sure pupils understand the cause-and-effect relationship depicted.

Have pupils read the first sentence on the left—the cause—and find a sentence on the right that tells the effect. Ask them to draw a line between the two sentences. Have pupils complete the page independently. When pupils are finished, have the cause-and-effect statements read aloud.

✓ See "Providing for Individual Differences" for additional practice with this skill.

Recognizing time relationships Discuss with pupils the time it takes for most plants to grow. Usually we plant tomato seeds in the spring and pick tomatoes in the late summer. How many months is it from early spring to late summer? (about five months) Help pupils count the months from March to August.

Discuss the fact that sometimes growth and change can occur quickly, but other times they occur slowly. Have pupils compare the following activities and decide whether each requires a long or a short time. Also, you wish to discuss why some things only seem to

take a longer or shorter time than they really do.

painting a picture
making a cat mask
making your bed
the school year
growing tomatoes
making tomato soup
riding to school
growing up
grocery shopping
one birthday to another

Literature Appreciation

Comparing and contrasting selections Have pupils open their books to the table of contents. Review the theme of each section, and discuss the various selections in Sun and Shadow. You may wish to use the following questions:

How many sections or groups of stories have we read in our book so far? (5)

In which group were all the selections make-believe? ("On the Magic Hill")

Which group told about life in the city? ("In the City")

In which group did the selection take place at night? ("After Dark")

Sun and Shadow and Reading Skills 4 Teacher's Edition

Reduced pupil edition pages are reproduced in full color. At the primary levels, workbook pages are also reproduced.

New vocabulary is identified the first time it appears in context in the pupil's book.

Uncommonly clear organization lets you find specific information at a glance.

Sample Teacher's Edition pages reduced. Actual size is 9" x 11¼."

HBJ Bookmark includes rich provisions for individualized instruction

"Enrichment" follows and extends each reading selection and suggests activities to integrate reading with other subject areas.

"Reading Centers" at the primary levels and "Resource Centers" for grades 4-8 are packed with activities, bibliographies, suggested audio/visual aids, and other helpful ideas for students and teachers.

"Providing for Individual Differences" offers optional instruction and practice at the end of each teaching unit.

Teaching plans give references to additional practice and optional components where appropriate.

Enrichment

Language Experience

Have pupils make up their own riddles, and have the others guess what is being described. Remind pupils that a riddle gives clues about the object it describes without naming the object. If pupils have difficulty choosing objects, tell them to begin with things in the classroom.

Listening to Poetry

Write the title of the following poem on the board. Ask pupils to listen carefully as you read the poem so they will be able to answer the question that is the poem's title. (a bunny rabbit)

What Is It?

Tall ears,
Twinkly nose.

Related Materials

More riddles for pupils' enjoyment may be found in the following books:

Riddle Giggles by Helen Hoke contains illustrations filled with funny people and weird animals and riddles about them.

Nailheads and Potato Eyes by Cynthia Basil is a beginners' book that children will enjoy.

Who Am I? by Lois Raeback is a collection of activity songs for children.

What? A Riddle Book by Jane Sarnoff and Reynold Ruffins contains over five hundred riddles and humorous illustrations.

Too Funny for Words, compiled by Charles Keller, is a fun-filled activity book. It includes photographs of children presenting jokes from American folklore.

HBJ BOOKMARK Related Materials

Words and Their Opposites is a ten-minute filmstrip which may be used at this time to extend the skill of re...

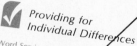
THE READING CENTER

Setting Up a Reading Center

To enhance enthusiasm for reading, set up a reading center where pupils can read independently and reinforce their reading skills through a variety of reading-related activities.

The reading center may be an area in your classroom with a rug, couch, or soft chairs, or it can be just a nook furnished with carpet tiles, oversized pillows, and a large collection of library books. You may wish to add a bulletin board to which activity packets and other reading materials are attached. Use tables, baskets, and brightly decorated cartons for storing and exhibiting books. Display the books so that the covers are visible and will attract readers.

After you have read a book to pupils, add it to the reading center collection. Pupils enjoy browsing through books that have been read to them, even if they cannot read the text.

Provide as wide a variety of books as possible, gathered from your school or public library, and change the books at regular intervals throughout the year. Provide a selection of alphabet books, picture books, and story books ranging from easy to more challenging.

Each week, post in the reading center an idea related to the story the pupils have just completed. Able pupils may write and illustrate a story related to the theme. Others may create stories by dictating them to you or to an aide or by recording them on a cassette. All stories on the same theme may be bound together, with a decorative cover added, and placed in the reading center.

Books related to the stories in *Sun and Shadow* are suggested in the "Enrichment" section of each Teaching Unit. A cumulative list of these books, as well as films and filmstrips, records and tapes, and study prints, appears in the Media List at the end of this unit.

The following materials, designed to supplement the core components of the HBJ BOOKMARK READING PROGRAM, will provide valuable skills reinforcement for individual pupils using the reading center:

THE BOOKMARK LIBRARY: BLUE—twelve full-color, soft-cover books that pupils can read independently. These books are carefully designed to reinforce vocabulary taught in HBJ BOOKMARK.

TRY THIS—a box of 100 self-directing, self-correcting reading activities that provide additional practice in decoding, comprehension, language, and study skills taught in HBJ BOOKMARK.

BOOKMARK READING FILMSTRIPS: BLUE—colorful filmstrips with entertaining story lines that reinforce skills and concepts taught in the core components.

Skills Games and Activities

Before placing a game in the reading center, provide thorough instruction for playing it. The following steps are suggested:

Play each game yourself before introducing it to pupils.

Tell pupils the name of the game. Demonstrate the game thoroughly, so that pupils can learn to play independently.

You may wish to have one or more pupils demonstrate the game to a small group.

Appoint one pupil to be "Game Leader." The Game Leader explains the game's rules to new players and checks daily to see that game pieces are put away properly. (Rotate this job among pupils.)

The following activities reinforce and extend the reading skills taught in *Sun and Shadow* and *Reading Skills 4*, and they encourage pupils to read and to work independently.

Kinesthetic Letters

Recognizing, naming, and making letters and words are skills that can be practiced in the reading center.

Letters like those found in the *Pupil Response Cards* and the *Word Service/Decoding Box* may be cut from cardboard or sandpaper or purchased commercially.

Using clay, pupils can practice constructing and recognizing letters. Show pupils how to roll clay into thin strips and how to shape letters. Display a small chart of letters for pupils to copy.

Another medium for Kinesthetic Letters is a box of sand or salt. Put the sand or salt into a box approximately four inches deep, twelve inches wide,

The Reading Center **T1**

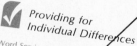
Providing for Individual Differences

Word Service/Decoding

Additional Practice

Listening for initial and medial /a/ Read each pair of words below. Have pupils repeat the word or words that have the same first sound as *ax*.

apple, after	antler, inch
arrow, under	attic, yellow
add, antelope	anchor, act

Read the words below. Have pupils raise their hands and repeat each word that has the same vowel sound as *bat*.

dog, bill, fat, last, pin, fan, rug, tan, pig, sack, take, mat, bell, bag, cut, sand, wag, hum

■ **Relating initial and medial /a/ to a** Have each pupil number a piece of paper from 1 through 10 and draw two blanks next to each number. Say each of these words: tag, bat, hat, act, fan, ant, pat, nap, ask, fat. Have pupils repeat the word and listen. If the sound represented by a is the first sound in the word, have them write a in the first blank. If the sound represented by a comes in the middle of the word, have them write a in the second blank. This activity can be adapted to be used in the listening station, described in "The Reading Center," by recording the words on a cassette and having pupils use the sheet provided to record their answers. Include an answer key so that pupils can correct their responses.

DM This skill is reinforced using *Duplicating Masters 4*, page 21. Pictured items are: ax, bed, anchor; fish, mask, lamp; flag, fan, book.

■ ▶ **Identifying words using context and initial and medial /a/** Distribute copies of the worksheet on page T274 of this Teacher's Edition. Have pupils read each sentence and then complete it by writing the word that has the same vowel sound as *hat* and ax and makes sense in the sentence.

DM This skill is further reinforced using *Duplicating Masters 4*, page 22. Pictured items are: sack, box, anchor; mask, doctor, ambulance; bats, apples, balloons; ant, key, map; pen, hat, astronaut.

■ **Recognizing a as a symbol for more than one sound** Refer to the Box Grid, described in "The Reading Center," for directions on how to proceed with this activity. Choose from the following list of words to insert in the grid pockets, making sure to include words that represent more than one sound represented by a. Use the words *back* and *Fay* as the key words, having pupils vary the card representing the

sound for which the others should listen. Words to choose from are: am, and, dad, past, as, that, gray, Mack, last, Jack, play, splash, day, game, save, chair, Stan, sat, can, Pat, swam, at.

■ **Recognizing vocabulary** *Sun and Shadow* Wheels and Word Ladders, described in "The Reading Center," provide additional reinforcement of vocabulary introduced and reviewed in this unit.

Comprehension Skills

Additional Practice

■ **Recognizing sequence** Provide independent practice for this skill by preparing sentence strips for the sentences below, using paper of a different color for each group and writing the number indicated on the back of each strip. Place each group of strips in a separate envelope. Pupils may work individually or in pairs to arrange these sentences to match the sequential order of "The Game."

Ant went down into the pond. (1)
Wet Ant went away. (2)
Bug went back to sleep. (3)

But Ant called, "You are a silly bug." (1)
Bug said, "I am as bright as a bug." (2)
Ant said, "I am as bright as you." (3)

■ **Recognizing cause and effect** Write each of the following sentences on a strip of oaktag, numbering the back of each strip as indicated below:

The dog was not clean. (1)
The boy washed his dog. (1)
The ant needed some sleep. (2)

It sat down and went to sleep. (2)
The boy saw lightning in the dark sky. (3)
He went into his house. (3)

Refer to the Pocket Sorting Chart, described in "The Reading Center," for directions on how to proceed with this activity.

DM Use *Duplicating Masters 4*, page 23, for further reinforcement of this skill.

Language Skills

Additional Practice

■ **Recognizing descriptive words** Remind pupils that some words help to describe, or tell about, something. Display the sentences that follow. Have pupils underline the descriptive words in each sentence.

Cats have bright eyes.
The little gray cat is on a big hill.
The girl had a funny magic hat.
We had fun playing the silly game.

Teaching Unit 8 **T97**

For a more detailed explanation of how an intermediate/junior high teaching unit works, please see page xxvi.

HBJ Bookmark Reading Program
Eagle Edition

READING SKILLS CHART

Word Service/Decoding Skills columns:
1. Vocabulary Development: Oral and Written
2. Letter Names
3. Auditory Memory and Discrimination
4. Visual Memory and Discrimination
5. Initial Consonants
6. Final Consonants
7. Medial Consonants
8. Consonant Clusters
9. Consonant Digraphs
10. Variant Consonant Spellings
11. Phonograms (Vowels)
12. Short Vowels
13. Long Vowels
14. r-Controlled Vowels
15. Variant Vowel Sounds and Spellings
16. Using Context and Knowledge of Phonics
17. Syllabication
18. Structural Analysis

Comprehension Skills columns:
19. Multiple Meaning
20. Figurative Language
21. Classification
22. Sequence
23. Main Idea
24. Details
25. Cause and Effect
26. Predicting Outcomes
27. Drawing Conclusions
28. Making Judgments
29. Making Generalizations
30. Distinguishing Fact and Opinion
31. Recognizing Author's Purpose
32. Recognizing Slanted Writing
33. Comparisons and Contrasts
34. Other Literal Comprehension Skills
35. Other Inferential Comprehension Skills
36. Other Critical (Evaluative) Skills

Word Service/Decoding Skills

Level	1	2	3	4	5	6	7	8	9	10	11	12	13	14	15	16	17	18
Kindergarten/Readiness																		
Language Activity Kit	•	•	•	•														•
Level R Look, Listen, and Learn	•	•	•	•	•	•										•		
Level R Sounds, Symbols, and Sense	•	•	•	•	•	•					•							
Primary																		
Level 1 Sun Up	•	•	•	•	•						•					•		•
Level 2 Happy Morning	•			•	•	•			•	•						•		•
Level 3 Magic Afternoon	•		•	•	•	•	•		•	•	•					•		•
Level 4 Sun and Shadow	•		•	•	•	•	•	•	•	•		•		•	•	•		•
Level 5 Together We Go	•		•	•	•	•	•	•	•	•	•		•			•		•
Level 6 World of Surprises	•		•	•	•	•	•	•	•	•	•	•	•	•		•	•	•
Level 7 People and Places	•		•		•	•	•	•	•	•	•	•	•	•	•	•	•	•
Level 8 Widening Circles	•		•										•		•	•	•	•
Level 9 Ring Around the World	•		•													•		•
Intermediate/Junior High																		
Level 10 New Frontiers	•			•	•	•	•	•	•		•	•			•	•	•	
Level 11 Blazing Trails	•			•	•	•				•					•	•	•	
Level 12 Golden Voyages	•			•	•	•				•			•		•	•	•	
Level 13 Taking Flight	•												•			•		•
Level 14 Widening Pathways	•										•				•		•	

Comprehension Skills

Level	19	20	21	22	23	24	25	26	27	28	29	30	31	32	33	34	35	36
Kindergarten/Readiness																		
Language Activity Kit			•	•														
Level R Look, Listen, and Learn			•	•	•											•	•	•
Level R Sounds, Symbols, and Sense			•	•	•	•	•	•										
Primary																		
Level 1 Sun Up			•	•	•	•	•	•								•	•	•
Level 2 Happy Morning	•		•	•	•	•	•	•								•	•	•
Level 3 Magic Afternoon	•		•	•	•	•	•	•	•						•	•	•	•
Level 4 Sun and Shadow	•		•	•	•	•	•	•	•	•					•	•	•	•
Level 5 Together We Go	•		•	•	•	•	•	•	•	•					•	•	•	•
Level 6 World of Surprises	•		•	•	•	•	•	•	•	•	•	•			•	•	•	•
Level 7 People and Places	•		•	•	•	•	•	•	•	•	•				•	•	•	•
Level 8 Widening Circles	•		•	•	•	•	•	•	•	•	•	•			•	•	•	•
Level 9 Ring Around the World	•		•	•	•	•	•	•	•	•	•	•	•		•	•	•	•
Intermediate/Junior High																		
Level 10 New Frontiers	•	•	•	•	•	•	•	•	•	•	•	•	•		•	•	•	•
Level 11 Blazing Trails	•	•	•	•	•	•	•	•	•	•	•	•	•		•	•	•	•
Level 12 Golden Voyages	•	•	•	•	•	•	•	•	•	•	•	•	•		•	•	•	•
Level 13 Taking Flight	•	•	•	•	•	•	•	•	•	•	•	•	•	•	•	•	•	•
Level 14 Widening Pathways	•	•	•	•	•	•	•	•	•	•	•	•	•	•	•	•	•	•

This chart provides a general overview of skills in the HBJ BOOKMARK READING PROGRAM, Eagle Edition. A more detailed scope and sequence of skills may be found at the back of each Teacher's Edition.

Scope and Sequence Chart

	Literature Appreciation											Language Skills																		Study Skills													
	Realism and Fantasy	Elements of Humor	Imagery	Forms of Writing	Story Elements: Plot, Characterization, and Setting	Point of View	Mood	Theme	Elements of Poetry	Relating Author's Life to Works	Fact and Fiction	Abbreviations	Pronouns and Antecedents	Mechanics (Capitalization, Punctuation, etc.)	Usage	Inflectional Endings	Root Words	Prefixes and Suffixes	Contractions	Compound Words	Etymologies	Understanding Phrases and Sentences	Homographs and Homophones	Synonyms and Antonyms	Descriptive Words	Singular and Plural Nouns	Possessive Forms	Language Experience	Composition: Oral and Written	Listening	Alphabetical Order	Following Directions	Parts of a Book	Typographical Signals	Using Illustrations	Using Maps, Charts, Graphs, and Diagrams	Using the Dictionary and Glossary	Using the Library and Reference Books	Skimming and Scanning	Outlining	Reading for a Purpose	Adjusting Reading Rate	Summarizing and Taking Notes
Kdg./R																																											
LAK																												●	●	●		●											
Lev. R																														●	●	●	●										
Lev. R														●							●					●		●	●	●	●	●	●		●							
Primary																																											
Lev. 1	●										●			●	●	●				●		●			●	●	●	●		●	●	●	●								●		
Lev. 2	●										●	●	●	●	●	●	●			●		●		●		●	●	●	●	●	●	●	●	●							●		
Lev. 3	●										●	●	●	●	●	●			●	●		●		●		●	●	●		●	●	●	●	●							●		
Lev. 4	●		●	●	●						●	●	●	●	●	●	●	●		●		●		●	●	●	●	●	●	●	●	●	●	●							●		
Lev. 5	●		●	●	●				●		●	●		●	●	●	●	●		●		●		●	●	●	●	●	●	●	●	●	●	●							●		
Lev. 6	●	●	●	●	●		●		●		●	●	●	●	●	●	●	●		●		●		●	●	●	●	●	●	●	●	●	●	●			●		●		●		
Lev. 7	●	●	●	●	●		●		●		●	●	●	●	●	●	●	●		●	●	●		●	●	●	●	●	●	●	●	●	●	●	●		●		●		●		
Lev. 8	●	●	●	●	●		●		●		●	●	●	●	●	●	●	●		●	●	●		●	●	●	●	●	●	●	●	●	●	●	●		●		●	●	●		●
Lev. 9	●	●	●	●	●		●		●		●	●	●	●	●	●	●	●		●	●	●		●	●	●	●	●	●	●	●	●	●	●	●		●		●	●	●		●
Inter./JH																																											
Lev. 10	●	●	●	●	●		●		●	●	●	●	●	●	●	●	●	●		●	●	●		●	●	●			●	●	●	●	●	●	●	●	●	●	●		●		●
Lev. 11	●	●	●	●	●		●	●	●	●	●	●	●	●	●	●	●	●		●	●	●		●	●	●			●	●	●	●	●	●	●	●	●	●	●	●	●		●
Lev. 12	●	●	●	●	●		●	●	●	●	●	●	●	●	●	●	●	●		●	●	●		●	●	●			●	●	●	●	●	●	●	●	●	●	●	●	●	●	●
Lev. 13	●	●	●	●	●	●	●	●	●	●	●	●	●	●	●	●	●	●		●	●	●		●	●	●			●	●	●	●	●	●	●	●	●	●	●	●	●	●	●
Lev. 14	●	●		●	●	●	●	●	●	●	●	●	●	●	●	●	●	●	●	●	●	●		●	●	●	●	●	●	●	●	●	●	●	●	●	●	●	●	●	●	●	●

HBJ Bookmark Reading Program
Eagle Edition

PROGRAM MATERIALS

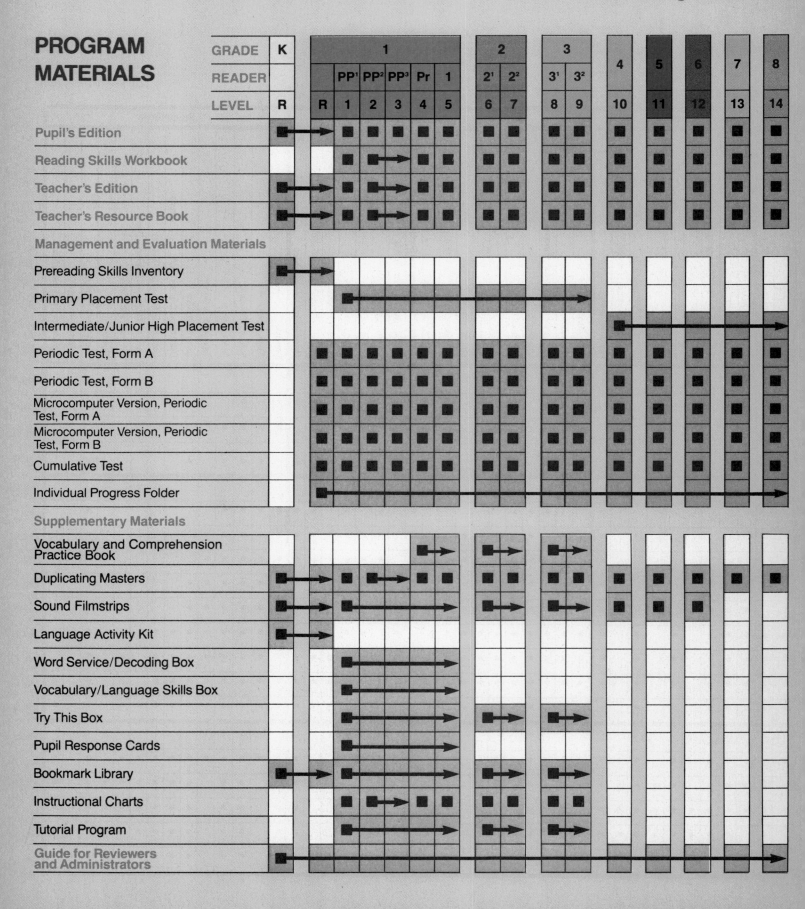

GRADE / READER / LEVEL key:

GRADE	K	1						2		3		4	5	6	7	8
READER			PP¹	PP²	PP³	Pr	1	2¹	2²	3¹	3²					
LEVEL	R	R	1	2	3	4	5	6	7	8	9	10	11	12	13	14

Material	K(R)	R	1	2	3	4	5	6	7	8	9	10	11	12	13	14
Pupil's Edition	■→	■	■	■	■	■	■	■	■	■	■	■	■	■	■	■
Reading Skills Workbook			■	■→	■	■	■	■	■	■	■	■	■	■	■	■
Teacher's Edition	■→	■	■	■→	■	■	■	■	■	■	■	■	■	■	■	■
Teacher's Resource Book	■→	■	■	■	■	■	■	■	■	■	■	■	■	■	■	■

Management and Evaluation Materials

Material	K(R)	R	1	2	3	4	5	6	7	8	9	10	11	12	13	14
Prereading Skills Inventory	■→															
Primary Placement Test		■→									→					
Intermediate/Junior High Placement Test												■→				→
Periodic Test, Form A		■	■	■	■	■	■	■	■	■	■	■	■	■	■	■
Periodic Test, Form B		■	■	■	■	■	■	■	■	■	■	■	■	■	■	■
Microcomputer Version, Periodic Test, Form A		■	■	■	■	■	■	■	■	■	■	■	■	■	■	■
Microcomputer Version, Periodic Test, Form B		■	■	■	■	■	■	■	■	■	■	■	■	■	■	■
Cumulative Test		■	■	■	■	■	■	■	■	■	■	■	■	■	■	■
Individual Progress Folder		■→														→

Supplementary Materials

Material	K(R)	R	1	2	3	4	5	6	7	8	9	10	11	12	13	14
Vocabulary and Comprehension Practice Book					■→			■→		■→						
Duplicating Masters	■→	■	■	■→	■	■	■	■	■	■	■	■	■	■	■	■
Sound Filmstrips	■→	■	■→					■→		■→		■	■	■		
Language Activity Kit	■→															
Word Service/Decoding Box			■→													
Vocabulary/Language Skills Box			■→													
Try This Box			■→					■→		■→						
Pupil Response Cards			■→													
Bookmark Library	■→							■→		■→						
Instructional Charts			■	■→		■		■	■	■	■					
Tutorial Program			■→					■→		■→						
Guide for Reviewers and Administrators	■→															→

Features of the Program at the Intermediate and Junior High Grades, Levels 10 through 14

★ Reading to Learn
★ Reading for Pleasure

The goal of the HBJ BOOKMARK READING PROGRAM, EAGLE EDITION for the intermediate/junior high grades is to develop reading skills that enable students *to read to learn* and *to read for pleasure.* All five areas of skills development—decoding, comprehension, language skills, study skills, and literature appreciation—are treated in Levels 10 through 14. Major emphasis, however, is placed on comprehension, language skills, study skills, and literature appreciation.

The Intermediate-Grades Reading Gap

As students move into the intermediate grades, they suddenly find that a majority of the reading required of them is in textbooks, reference materials, library books, magazines, and newspapers—materials that differ greatly from their primary reading books. For many students, even for very good readers, there is often a gap between what they are *expected* to read and understand in content-related materials and textbooks and what they *can* read and understand. This intermediate-grades reading gap is a serious problem in the elementary school curriculum.

Bridging the Gap

HBJ BOOKMARK, EAGLE EDITION is committed to helping students bridge the intermediate-grades reading gap by identifying the real reading needs of intermediate/junior high students, establishing well-defined instructional objectives, and appropriately organizing materials that clearly match these objectives.

Intermediate/Junior High Materials That Match Objectives

The intermediate/junior high reading program has two major objectives:

1. To teach the vocabulary, comprehension, and study skills required for *reading to learn*—skills that will prepare students for the kinds of reading required throughout the upper elementary and high school years and beyond.
2. To develop further the skills and understanding that promote a lifelong interest in *reading for pleasure* and personal enrichment.

Specialized skills require specialized materials. Content-area reading skills, those skills required in reading to learn, cannot be developed through literature (plays, poetry, fictional narratives). Neither can students learn to appreciate the beauty of literature by reading science articles or mathematics textbooks. Characterization and plot are not relevant to science and mathematics. In turn, one cannot apply map-reading skills when reading poetry.

Each Pupil's Edition from Level 10 through Level 14 of HBJ BOOKMARK, EAGLE EDITION features two different kinds of reading matter, organized into two distinct parts: Reading to Learn and Appreciating Literature.

Reading to Learn

The skills needed to acquire information are taught in Reading to Learn parts which contain skills instruction, informational articles, and excerpts from textbooks.

Appreciating Literature

The skills and understanding needed to read for pleasure are taught in Appreciating Literature parts which contain high-quality children's literature. Poetry, plays, folktales, and short stories are some of the genres students will encounter.

Only HBJ BOOKMARK, EAGLE EDITION offers this rich variety in reading instruction. By providing materials that precisely match learning objectives and a program that is paced especially for intermediate and junior high students, HBJ BOOKMARK, EAGLE EDITION bridges the intermediate-grades reading gap while instilling in students a lifelong enjoyment of reading.

Pupil's Edition

Each Pupil's Edition for Levels 10 through 14 consists of eight parts: four Reading to Learn parts and four Appreciating Literature parts.

Reading to Learn

Parts 1, 3, 5, and 7 focus on basic reading skills and study skills instruction. Skills taught in the primary levels are maintained, extended, and applied to

Continued

content-area reading, with emphasis in comprehension and vocabulary skills.

Each Reading to Learn part consists of a Skills Lesson, a Vocabulary Study, one or more Reading Selections, and a Textbook Study.

Skills Lesson

The Skills Lesson teaches, in language students can understand easily, an important reading or study skill, or a cluster of related skills. Among the skills treated are these: recognizing main ideas; identifying cause and effect; drawing conclusions; reading maps, charts, and graphs; using the dictionary, reference books, and library catalogues; and recognizing biased writing.

Each Skills Lesson concludes with "Try This" activities in which students apply the skill just taught.

Vocabulary Study

A Vocabulary Study follows the Skills Lesson. Each Vocabulary Study is designed to entertain as well as to instruct. Vocabulary-building skills, essential to the mature reader, are developed. These include: using synonyms and antonyms, recognizing multiple meanings, using context clues, and identifying root words and affixes. Many of the words studied are drawn from the unit reading selections.

Each Vocabulary Study concludes with "Word Play" activities in which students practice the skill treated.

Reading Selections

After completing a Skills Lesson and a Vocabulary Study, students are prepared to read one or more nonfiction selec-

tions. Students now apply their newly learned reading or study skill to high-interest reading material.

After reading each selection, students may complete the "Understanding What You've Read" section, either in writing or in discussion. This section focuses on comprehension at the *literal, inferential,* and *critical* levels. *Literal* comprehension questions require students to understand and recall material actually stated in the selection; *inferential* comprehension questions require students to make inferences about the content of the selection; *critical* comprehension questions require students to make judgments and evaluations, and to think creatively.

In the section "Applying the Skills Lesson," students complete activities in which they apply the skill taught in the Skills Lesson to the content of the selection they have just read.

Textbook Study

After completing skills and vocabulary instruction and reading one or more selections, students come to the Textbook Study. This section helps students apply their new or expanded skills to reading brief excerpts from current textbooks in mathematics, social studies, science, language arts, and other curriculum areas.

Each Textbook Study section concludes with "Building Skills" activities that require students to apply the skill taught in the Skills Lesson to the textbook selections.

Appreciating Literature

In parts 2, 4, 6, and 8 of the

Pupil's Edition, the focus is on reading literature for pleasure.

Understanding and Appreciating Literature

This brief, frequently humorous section presents a literary concept, such as plot, characterization, or theme, or discusses a literary genre. This section concludes with "Try This" activities and optional writing activities.

Reading Selections

After completing the Understanding and Appreciating Literature section, students read one or more works of literature. The literary concept presented in Understanding and Appreciating Literature is evident in each selection.

Selections include fantasy, plays, folktales and myths, biography, historical fiction, and humor. One entire part of each level is devoted to poetry, and in each level there is an Author Study, a section in which students read a biographical sketch about an author and then read selections by that author.

Each selection is followed by an "Understanding What You've Read" section in which students answer comprehension questions about the selection. An optional "Writing" section offers creative writing activities in which students can demonstrate their understanding of the literary concepts presented in the reading selections and the Understanding and Appreciating Literature lesson.

Any portion of the Appreciating Literature parts may be done independently, since their focus is on reading for pleasure. Students will not be formally tested on this material.

The Teacher's Edition

The Teacher's Edition parallels the structure of the Pupil's Edition, with four Reading to Learn parts that alternate with four Appreciating Literature parts. Each of the eight parts is divided into Teaching Units that correspond to the sections in the Pupil's Edition.

Resource Center and Overview

A Resource Center at the beginning of the teaching plans for each part lists enrichment materials and activities appropriate to that part that require advance planning by the teacher. A bibliography for students and one for the teacher lists books related to the selections in that part. Appropriate films, filmstrips, records, and tapes are also listed.

An Overview of each part lists skills objectives, and describes the theme of the part.

Core Steps

The teaching plans for Levels 10 through 14 are similar to the primary plans. Where appropriate, the same core and optional steps are employed.

There is one important difference. In the primary levels, a Teaching Unit is a relatively brief block of instruction, and a single teaching plan covers the entire unit. In the intermediate/junior high levels, a Teaching Unit is considerably longer and consists of separate but related sections. Each of these unit sections has its own separate Teaching Plan.

Each Teaching Unit in the Reading to Learn parts consists of four separate sections: Skills Lesson, Vocabulary Study, Reading Selection(s), and Textbook Study. Therefore, four separate teaching plans make up each Reading to Learn Teaching Unit. In the Appreciating Literature parts, each Teaching Unit consists of two sections: Understanding and Appreciating Literature, and Reading Selections. Therefore, two separate teaching plans make up each Appreciating Literature Teaching Unit.

The Teaching Plans for each reading selection include three core steps:

- Preparing to Read
- Reading and Discussing
- Maintaining Skills (Reading to Learn selections only)

Optional Steps

"Providing for Individual Differences" and "Enrichment" offer suggestions and activities for meeting a wide range of instructional needs and interests.

Instructional Strategies

Relevant skills are taught and new vocabulary is introduced before students read the selections so that they approach each reading selection with confidence. As students proceed through the program, skills are carefully maintained. In addition, there are ample provisions for assessment, reinforcement, enrichment, and remediation.

Reading Skills Workbooks

Reading Skills Workbooks at the intermediate/junior high level are optional. They provide additional follow-up practice with the skills covered in the Skills Lessons, the Vocabulary Studies, and the Understanding and Appreciating Literature sections.

Duplicating Masters

Duplicating Masters are also optional. They provide written practice with selection vocabulary plus skills practice following the reading of the selections.

A Sample Teaching Unit: Reading to Learn

Teaching Units and the corresponding Pupil's Edition pages are clearly identified.

Each Teaching Unit begins with a list of the unit's contents. Teacher's Edition page numbers are listed for the teacher's convenience.

Additional Materials lists optional components of the HBJ BOOKMARK READING PROGRAM, EAGLE EDITION that may be useful during instruction. These materials have been prepared solely for the teacher's convenience; their use is by no means essential to instruction.

The **Key to Symbols for skills objectives** appears here.

The **Key to Symbols used on reduced Pupil's Edition pages** appears here.

A **Resource Center,** located at the beginning of each of the eight parts of the Teacher's Edition, lists enrichment materials and activities that require advance planning.

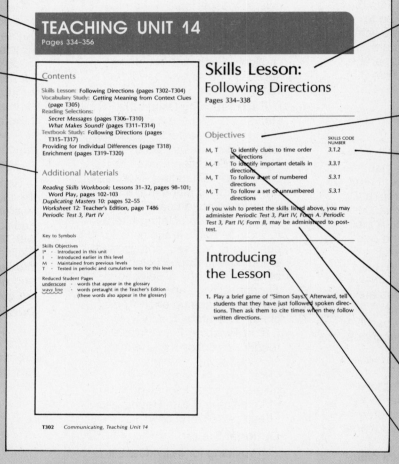

TEACHING UNIT 14
Pages 334–356

Contents

Skills Lesson: Following Directions (pages T302–T304)
Vocabulary Study: Getting Meaning from Context Clues (page T305)
Reading Selections:
  Secret Messages (pages T306–T310)
  What Makes Sound? (pages T311–T314)
Textbook Study: Following Directions (pages T315–T317)
Providing for Individual Differences (page T318)
Enrichment (pages T319–T320)

Additional Materials

Reading Skills Workbook: Lessons 31–32, pages 98–101; Word Play, pages 102–103
Duplicating Masters 10: pages 52–55
Worksheet 12: Teacher's Edition, page T486
Periodic Test 3, Part IV

Key to Symbols

Skills Objectives
I* – Introduced in this unit
I – Introduced earlier in this level
M – Maintained from previous levels
T – Tested in periodic and cumulative tests for this level

Reduced Student Pages
underscore – words that appear in the glossary
wavy line – words pretaught in the Teacher's Edition (these words also appear in the glossary)

T302   *Communicating, Teaching Unit 14*

Skills Lesson:
Following Directions
Pages 334–338

Objectives

		SKILLS CODE NUMBER
M, T	To identify clues to time order in directions	3.1.2
M, T	To identify important details in directions	3.3.1
M, T	To follow a set of numbered directions	5.3.1
M, T	To follow a set of unnumbered directions	5.3.1

If you wish to pretest the skills listed above, you may administer *Periodic Test 3, Part IV, Form A. Periodic Test 3, Part IV, Form B,* may be administered to post-test.

Introducing the Lesson

1. Play a brief game of "Simon Says." Afterward, tell students that they have just followed spoken directions. Then ask them to cite times when they follow written directions.

A **Skills Lesson** begins each Teaching Unit. The title of the Skills Lesson indicates the skill that will be taught. Later in the unit, students will apply this skill when reading the selection(s).

Objectives for each teaching plan are defined clearly.

HBJ Skills Code Numbers serve as a reference guide for locating additional instruction and practice in each skill. In the Skills Index at the back of the Teacher's Edition, each skill is listed by skills code number and major skills category.

Symbols identify whether a skill is **introduced** at this level or **maintained** from a previous level, and whether it is **tested** in this level.

This note tells the teacher when **Periodic Tests** may be given.

The **Teaching Plan** for the Skills Lesson contains two steps: **Introducing the Lesson** provides skills instruction before reading; **Developing the Skill** gives instruction for reading and comprehending the Skills Lesson.

An **Overview,** which follows each Resource Center, explains how to use the Management System, previews the part, and lists the objectives.

The **Try This** activities that follow Developing the Skill may be completed orally or as written activities.

All sample Teacher's Edition pages are from Level 10 (*New Frontiers*
Sample Teacher's Edition pages reduced. Actual size is 9" x 11¼."

A **Vocabulary Study** follows each Skills Lesson and provides practice with vocabulary acquisition skills, such as synonyms, antonyms, multiple meanings, and homophones.

Developing the Skill provides instruction for reading and comprehending the vocabulary lesson in the Pupil's Edition.

In both Reading to Learn and Appreciating Literature Teaching Units, **all activities preceded by the symbol ✔ are optional.** These include **Reading Skills Workbook pages** and **Duplicating Masters.** Other optional activities for reviewing, reinforcing, and extending skills are suggested in the **Providing for Individual Differences** section at the end of the Reading to Learn Teaching Unit.

Vocabulary Study:
Getting Meaning from Context Clues
Page 339

Objective

		SKILLS CODE NUMBER
M	To use context clues to determine word meaning	3.0.2

Developing the Skill

1. Tell students that the *Vocabulary Study* they are about to read has three riddles. Ask them if they know what riddles are and, if so, to give some examples. (Example: What has four "eyes" but cannot see? Answer: Mississippi)

2. Explain that in this *Vocabulary Study* the riddles are sets of context clues. Ask students what context clues do. (help you figure out the meanings of words)

3. Have students read the *Vocabulary Study* and do the *Word Play* activities at the bottom of the page.

Answers to *Word Play*

1. Answers will vary. Sample definitions are as follows: *aquarium:* a tank that holds live fish; *code:* a secret message in which letters, numbers, or other symbols stand for letters or words; *pantomime:* a way of communicating through gestures rather than speech.
2. Responses will vary.

✔ Use *Reading Skills Workbook,* Lesson 32, page 101. See *Providing for Individual Differences,* page T318, for additional practice.

Each page of the Pupil's Edition is reproduced in the Teacher's Edition.

A Sample Teaching Unit: Reading to Learn (continued)

Reading Selection(s) follow the Skills Lesson and Vocabulary Study. Skills previously taught in the unit are applied immediately as students read the selection(s). Thorough preparation enables students to read successfully—to understand, enjoy, and discuss what they read.

The **Teaching Plan** for the Reading Selection(s) contains three core steps that provide essential instruction: **Preparing to Read, Reading and Discussing,** and **Maintaining Skills.**

Step 1, Preparing to Read, provides prereading instruction.

The **Summary** is a brief synopsis of the selection provided for the teacher's information.

Background provides further information on the subject of the selection.

Books for teachers, which provide additional background information, are listed.

A **red line** under a word indicates that the word appears in the Pupil's Edition glossary.

Reading Selection:
Secret Messages
Pages 340–345

Objectives

		SKILLS CODE NUMBER
M, T	To follow a set of unnumbered directions	5.3.1
M	To draw conclusions based on given information	3.4.1
M	To identify word parts: root words, prefixes, and suffixes	4.1

1 Preparing to Read

Summary

This selection discusses the difference between a *code* and a *cipher.* In a code, one letter, number, word, or sign stands for a whole word or a group of words. In a cipher, one letter, number, or sign stands for each letter of the alphabet. In popular usage, however, the word *code* refers to both systems, and the author recognizes this fact by referring to both codes and ciphers as "codes." Three codes are introduced, and readers are asked to *decode* and *encode* several messages.

Background

Cryptography, or putting messages into code or cipher, comes from Greek words meaning *hidden* and *writing.* Cryptography goes back to the time of the ancient Greeks. Cryptanalysis is the art of breaking codes without a key. While there are many skills involved in cryptanalysis, notably perseverance, luck is also a factor. Cryptologists are aware of each language's unique characteristics. For example, the most frequently used letters in the English language are *A, E, I, O, N, R, S,* and *T.*

The following book will provide you with additional background information.

Kohn, Bernice. *Secret Codes and Ciphers.* An introduction to codes and ciphers: their histories, uses of different types, and deciphering.

T306 *Communicating, Teaching Unit 14*

Developing Vocabulary and Concepts

position: the place occupied by something
count: matter; to be important

1. **a.** Write the following sentences on the board and underline the new vocabulary.

   In my phone number—648-3840—there is an 8 in the third position and in the fifth position.
   In doing puzzles, it's having fun that counts.

   b. Ask a student volunteer to read the first sentence and explain what *position* means. (Accept *place* as a synonym.) Ask another student to read the second sentence. Ask for a synonym for *counts.* (Sample answer: matters)

2. Write the following on the board.

   1 = M   2 = A   3 = D   4 = P
   5 = N   6 = L   7 = C

   Tell students to decode the following message.

   2 125, 2 4625, 2 72526—425212

   (The answer is *A man, a plan, a canal—Panama,* a group of words that is the same whether it's spelled forward or backward.)

   ✓ Use *Duplicating Masters 10,* page 52.

Developing Vocabulary and Concepts focuses on new vocabulary words and concepts that students will encounter in the selection.

New vocabulary words appear in boldfaced type, and definitions are given.

Concepts needed to understand the selection are introduced and discussed.

The **Duplicating Master** listed here provides more practice with vocabulary. **All activities preceded by the symbol ✓ are optional.** These include Duplicating Masters, Reading Skills Workbook pages, and activities suggested in the Providing for Individual Differences section.

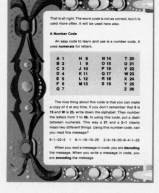

2 Reading and Discussing

Have students read the selection. Most students will be able to complete it in one sitting. If you prefer, the selection may be read in two parts, breaking before the heading "A Position Code" on page 343.

NOTE: The questions that appear in the student's text at the end of the selection focus on comprehension of selection content and on application of the *Skills Lesson* to the selection. Answers to these questions begin on page T308.

Communicating, Teaching Unit 14 **T307**

Setting Purposes

Skills

Have students read the skills note at the top of page 340. Ask them why it is important to follow directions when writing a secret code message.

Content

Have students read the lead-in to the title. Explain that they will now read about several different ways to write secret messages.

Setting Purposes helps students focus on specific skills and content related to the selection.

Students note that the **skill** taught in the Skills Lesson will be applied to the Reading Selection.

Content discussion encourages interest in the selection's subject.

Step 2, Reading and Discussing, concentrates on the selection in the Pupil's Edition. Thorough preparation in the Skills Lesson and Step 1, Preparing to Read, enables students to read successfully. Step 2, Reading and Discussing, helps them understand, enjoy, and discuss what they read.

Sample Teacher's Edition pages reduced. Actual size is 9" x 11¼."

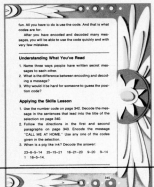

A **wavy red line** indicates a new vocabulary word that appears in the glossary and is pretaught in the Teacher's Edition.

A **straight red line** indicates that a word appears in the glossary.

Questions in **Understanding What You've Read** concentrate on the development of **literal, inferential,** and **critical** comprehension skills. **Literal** questions require students to recall specific facts. **Inferential** questions require students to derive meaning that is implied in the selection. **Critical** questions require students to make judgments and evaluations, to think creatively, and to relate the selection to other reading materials and concepts, as well as to their own experiences.

Suggested answers are provided for all questions except those for which there are many acceptable answers. The skill reflected in each question is identified.

Questions preceded by a bullet are additional questions and appear in the Teacher's Edition only. The other questions appear in the student's text after the selection.

Understanding What You've Read

1. *Name three ways people have written secret messages to each other.* (People have used invisible ink, covered up letters or added words to messages to mix them up, and used codes or ciphers.) page 340) LITERAL   Recalling specific details

• *What is the difference between a code and a cipher?* (In a code, one letter, number, word or sign stands for a whole word or a group of words. In a cipher, one letter, number, or sign stands for one letter of the alphabet.   page 340) INFERENTIAL   Contrasting ideas

2. *What is the difference between encoding and decoding a message?* (When you write a message in code, you are encoding the message. When you read a coded message, you are decoding the message.   page 342) LITERAL   Recalling stated information

• *What three different kinds of ciphers are mentioned in the selection?* (sign code, page 341   number code, page 342   position code, page 344; also accept word code, page 340) LITERAL   Recalling specific details

T308   *Communicating, Teaching Unit 14*

Numbered questions appear in the Pupil's Edition.

Questions preceded by a bullet appear in the Teacher's Edition only. These questions provide for extended discussion of the selection.

Applying the Skills Lesson requires students to apply the skill taught in the Skills Lesson directly to the selection.

• *What is a sign code? What is a number code? What is a position code?* (Sign code: a sign, not a letter or number, stands for a letter of the alphabet.   page 341   Number code: a numeral stands for a letter of the alphabet.   page 342   Position code: the position of the letters is what counts.   page 344) LITERAL   Recalling stated information

3. *Why would it be hard for someone to guess the position code?* (It is necessary to know what diagram was used in order to decode a message.   page 344) LITERAL   Recalling stated information

• *Which code mentioned in the selection would be easiest to "break"? Why?* (Perhaps the number code, since breaking it would involve only testing various correspondences of numbers to letters. Accept any other choices that students can substantiate.) CRITICAL   Drawing conclusions

Applying the Skills Lesson

1. *Use the number code on page 342. Decode the message in the sentences that lead into the title of the selection on page 340.* (I HAVE A SECRET.)   Following directions

• *Read the first two paragraphs on page 343 again. These paragraphs are a set of directions on how to encode a message. What materials do you need?* (ruled paper and sharp pencils)   Following directions

• *Find the time clues in the second paragraph, page 343.* (first; when you have finished writing the message)   Identifying time clues

• *The following steps are not in the right order. Put them in the correct order as stated in the second paragraph, page 343.*
   1. *Leave a space of four lines.*
   2. *Write each code numeral under each letter in the message.*
   3. *Copy the message on your paper.*
   (Correct order: 3, 1, 2)   Following directions

2. *Follow the directions in the first and second paragraphs on page 343. Encode the message "CALL ME AT HOME." Use any one of the codes given in the selection.*

(Sign Code:

□□▽▽ ▽⊞ □│ △⊖▽⊞

Position Code:

└ ⅃<<   ∧□   ⅃⅂   □Ч∧□

Number Code:

3–1–12–12   13–5   1–20   8–15–13–5)

Following directions

• *Encode your name in all three codes. Then pass your codes to a partner to check them.* (Answers will vary.)   Following directions

3. *When is a pig like ink? Decode the answer:*
23–8–5–14 25–15–21 16–21–20 9–20 9–14 1 16–5–14
(WHEN YOU PUT IT IN A PEN—Refer students to the number code, page 342.)   Following directions

• *What has eyes but cannot see? Decode the answer:*

① ⊖ │ □ │ ⊖ ⊞ │

(POTATOES—Refer students to the sign code, page 341.)   Following directions

• *What room can no one enter? Decode the answer:*

⅃ ∧⌐⊏□ └Ч∧

(A MUSHROOM—Refer students to the position code, page 344.)   Following directions

 Use *Duplicating Masters 10*, page 53. See *Providing for Individual Differences*, page T318, for additional practice.

3 Maintaining Skills

Comprehension Skills

Drawing conclusions   Morse code, Braille, shorthand, and sign language are kinds of codes that students may have heard about. Read each of the following paragraphs and ask students to determine what kind of code is being described, based on what they just learned about codes from reading the selection. (NOTE: In *Enrichment*, Morse code and Braille are illustrated.)

1. Louis Braille was a blind musician who lived in France. In 1825, he developed a code using raised dots that people could read by running their fingers over them. Two sizes of dots are placed in six possible positions. Each set of six dots stands for a letter of the alphabet.

Ask what kind of code Braille is—sign, number, or position. (It is both a sign code and a position code because the position of the dots is what counts.)

2. In 1844, Samuel Morse, the man who invented the telegraph, sent the first message using Morse code. In Morse code, each letter of the alphabet is represented by a dot or a dash or a combination of dots and dashes in certain positions.

Step 3, Maintaining Skills, reviews and maintains previously taught skills.

Skills are maintained systematically in four instructional strands: Word Service/Decoding, Comprehension, Language, and Study Skills.

Communicating, Teaching Unit 14   **T309**

A Sample Teaching Unit: Reading to Learn
(continued)

Ask what kind of code Morse code is—sign, number, or position. (It is both a sign code and a position code because the position or sequencing of the dots and dashes is what counts.)

3. In 1888, J. R. Gregg invented a system of shorthand. In Gregg shorthand, symbols stand for words or sounds.

Ask what kind of a code shorthand is—sign, number, or position. (It is a sign code because it uses signs to stand for words or sounds.)

Language Skills

Identifying word parts: root words, affixes Have students identify the root word in each word below and tell the meaning of each prefix or suffix.

decode   encode   invisible   arrival

(Root words: code, code, visible, arrive; Prefixes: *de-* = remove or reverse, *en-* = put into, *in-* = not; Suffix: *-al* = noun ending)

Tell students that *decode* means to break a code. Ask them if they can think of a word meaning "to break a cipher." (decipher)

★ For additional resources and curriculum-related activities, see *Enrichment,* page T319.

Enrichment, an optional step at the end of the Teaching Unit, suggests a variety of activities, books, and other media to extend students' interest in the content or theme of the selection. The symbol ★ appears with each reference to Enrichment.

Textbook Study:
Following Directions
Pages 352–355

Objectives

		SKILLS CODE NUMBER
M, T	To identify clues to time order in directions	3.1.2
M, T	To identify important details in directions	3.3.1
M, T	To follow a set of unnumbered directions	5.3.1

Applying the Skill

1. Before students read the selections, you may wish to write the vocabulary word on the board and discuss it or have students look it up in the glossary.

   Language Arts Selection:
   sturdy: strong

2. Have students read the introduction and the two selections. You may wish to have them read the selections on their own and then do *Building Skills.* Or you may wish to direct students, using the following procedure.

Following Directions in Science

1. Have students read the paragraph and the sidenote on page 352. What common sounds in the classroom do they think they'd record if they were performing this experiment? Write five or six of their answers on the board.

In the **Textbook Study,** students apply the skill presented in the Skills Lesson to excerpts from actual textbooks.

The Teaching Plan for the Textbook Study contains one core instructional step: **Applying the Skill.**

Excerpts are from current textbooks in five areas: Science, Social Studies, Health, Mathematics, and Language Arts.

Each Textbook Study includes activities called **Building Skills.** These exercises may be completed as written activities or may be used for group discussion.

---

xxx

Sample Teacher's Edition pages reduced. Actual size is 9″ x 11¼.″

Providing for Individual Differences, the first optional step in the Teaching Plan, suggests alternative methods and materials, as well as additional activities to accommodate individual learning needs and to reinforce unit skills.

Additional Practice activities are provided for students who need reinforcement of previously taught skills.

Full-size, reproducible Worksheet Masters may be found at the back of the Teacher's Edition.

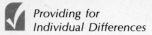

Providing for Individual Differences

Skills Lesson

Additional Practice

Worksheet 12, Teacher's Edition, page T486

Vocabulary Study

Additional Practice

■ **Using context to determine meaning**   Read the following paragraph aloud. Have students choose the best definition for *mongoose* after you read the paragraph.

Have you ever read Rudyard Kipling's story about Riki-Tiki-Tavi? If so, you may know something about the behavior of mongooses. These animals live in parts of Asia and Africa. They are about three feet long, including the tail. Snakes—even the most poisonous—are terribly afraid of mongooses. These fast-moving little animals are just about the best snakehunters in the world. For this reason, some people who live where there are poisonous snakes keep mongooses as pets.

1. a kind of snake kept as a pet
2. a small animal of Asia or Africa that preys on snakes
3. the best snakehunter in the world
(Answer: 2)

Challenge Activity

■ **Determining meaning from context**   Read the following paragraphs aloud. After you read the paragraphs, have students give a definition for *mangrove*. Have them check their answers in a dictionary.

What should you do if you find yourself in a warm marsh during a hurricane? One way to protect yourself might be to stay among the spider-like roots of a mangrove. These roots are really branches that take root and form a cagelike tangle.

Mangroves grow in marshy regions in warm parts of the world. The thick, leathery leaves of these evergreens fall into the water and rot. As they rot, they are eaten by small animals like crabs and worms. These small animals are, in turn, eaten by larger sea creatures and birds.

(Sample definition of *mangrove*: an evergreen tree that grows in warm, marshy regions, having thick, leathery leaves and branches that take root and form a cagelike tangle)

T318   *Communicating, Teaching Unit 14*

Reading Selection: Secret Messages

Additional Practice

■ **Using time order to follow directions**   Have students "unscramble" this recipe for scrambled eggs. Tell them to identify the time clues and put the steps in the correct order.

1. Finally, cook the eggs over a low flame for a few minutes until they are the way you like them. (Finally; for a few minutes)
2. Then break two eggs into a bowl. Add milk and salt and pepper. (Then)
3. First melt a pat of butter in a frying pan. (First)
4. Pour the mixture into the greased pan.
5. Now beat the egg mixture. (Now)
(Correct order: 3, 2, 5, 4, 1)

Challenge Activity

Using time clues in directions   Direct students to an experiment in their science textbooks. Tell them to find all the time clues in the experiment's directions.

Reading Selection: What Makes Sound?

Additional Practice

Recognizing clues to time order   To follow a set of unnumbered directions requires careful reading and rereading and skill in recognizing clues to time order. Sometimes the author gives sequencing clues without using numbers. Refer students to an experiment in their science textbook. Have them find out how many steps are in the directions and list the time-clue words.

Challenge Activity

■ **Using time order to follow directions**   Have students make a string telephone following the directions given on pages 348–349 of the selection.

Evaluation

Periodic Test 3, Part IV, Form A or *Form B,* may be administered after this unit to test skills marked **T**. If you have pretested using *Form A,* administer *Form B.*

To posttest all the skills marked **T** in the four teaching units in "Communicating," Part 5, use *Periodic Test 3, Parts I–IV.*

A red box ■ indicates an activity that is suitable for an aide or volunteer to direct.

Challenge Activities provide reinforcement and extension of skills for students who have mastered the basic concepts and are able to apply these skills to more complex projects.

The **Evaluation** section lists **Periodic Tests** that may be given at the completion of each Reading to Learn Teaching Unit or after every four Reading to Learn units. The **Cumulative Test** is listed at the end of Teaching Unit 19 to remind the teacher that this test may be administered at the end of the level.

Enrichment, the second optional step in the Teaching Plan, suggests a variety of activities, books, and other media to expand students' interest in the content or theme of the selection.

The **Bibliography** section lists books related to the selection.

Books are identified for teachers as **easy, average,** or **challenging.**

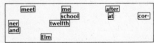

Enrichment

Secret Messages

Bibliography

The following books are about codes and ciphers.

Average

Epstein, Sam. *First Book of Codes and Ciphers.* (59 pages) All types of codes; how to break a cipher; and more.

Yerian, Cameron. *Codes and Mystery Messages.* (46 pages) Information on how to create different kinds of codes.

Challenging

Rothman, Joel. *Secrets with Ciphers and Codes.* (32 pages) Ten secret codes, with directions for sending and receiving them.

Films and Filmstrips

NOTE: For more information, see *Resource Center.*

Guidance Assocs. *Using Your Reading Skills Series.* Reading and following directions are important for a magic act in the Part II filmstrip of "Skim, Scan, or Study?"

Curriculum Coordination

Language Arts

1. Explain that Cardinal Richelieu, a famous figure in French history, invented a code. He cut holes into a piece of paper and laid the paper over a blank sheet of paper. Inside each hole, he wrote a word to form a real message, as shown below. Then he wrote a misleading message around the real message. Explain the Richelieu code to students and allow them to use the code to send messages to each other.

meet		me		after	
		school		at	cor-
ner		twelfth			
and					
	Elm				

The meeting will immediately begin after the bell rings. Come to the schoolhouse on Saturday. A corner seat in the twelfth row has been saved for you, and I'm sure you'll like the play. We're putting on "Under the Elms."

2. Obtain a chart of Braille and the Morse code or reproduce the following charts for students on activity cards. Then ask students to compose various messages, using these codes. When students are finished, have them exchange papers and decode the messages.

— Braille Alphabet and some words —

A B C D E F G
H I J K L M N
O P Q R S T U
V X Y Z and for of
the with ch gh sh th wh
ed er ou ow W will

— Morse Code —

A ·—   J ·———   S ···   2 ··———
B —···   K —·—   T —   3 ···——
C —·—·   L ·—··   U ··—   4 ····—
D —··   M ——   V ···—   5 ·····
E ·   N —·   W ·——   6 —····
F ··—·   O ———   X —··—   7 ——···
G ——·   P ·——·   Y —·——   8 ———··
H ····   Q ——·—   Z ——··   9 ————·
I ··   R ·—·   1 ·————   0 —————

Science

1. Perhaps you could borrow a chemical model of a molecule such as sugar. Such models show the elements in different shapes and/or colors. Tell students what elements the shapes or colors represent. Then have them try to "decode" the chemical formula. (High school students frequently make such models; high school or college chemistry departments often have such models or kits for making them. A chemistry teacher might be willing to help you in this activity.)

2. Ethologists—scientists who study animal behavior—"decode" such things as the "dances" of bees, birds, and fish. Students may enjoy researching and reading about the work of ethologists such as Karl von Frisch or Konrad Lorenz.

Communicating, Teaching Unit 14   **T319**

The **Films and Filmstrips** section lists audiovisual materials related to the selection.

The **Resource Center,** located at the beginning of each part in the Teacher's Edition, suggests activities and materials that require advance planning.

Enrichment suggestions include **curriculum-coordinated activities** for language arts, science, social studies, mathematics, and career education.

A Sample Teaching Unit: Appreciating Literature

Teaching Units and the corresponding Pupil's Edition pages are clearly identified.

Each Teaching Unit begins with a list of the unit's contents. Teacher's Edition page numbers are listed for the teacher's convenience.

Additional Materials lists optional components of HBJ BOOKMARK, EAGLE EDITION that may be useful during instruction. These materials have been prepared solely for the teacher's convenience; their use is by no means essential to instruction.

The **Key to Symbols for skills objectives** appears here.

The **Key to Symbols used on reduced Pupil's Edition pages** appears here.

Reading Selections follow Understanding and Appreciating Literature. The literary skills and concepts discussed aid students in understanding and enjoying the selections and help students develop an appreciation of literature.

The **Teaching Plan** for the Reading Selections contains two core steps: **Preparing to Read** and **Reading and Discussing.** New vocabulary words and concepts that students will encounter in the selection are introduced. Then comprehension questions—those from the Pupil's Edition plus additional questions that appear only in the Teacher's Edition—help students understand, enjoy, and discuss what they have read. Optional Writing activities are also suggested.

The **Summary** is a brief synopsis of the selection.

Understanding and Appreciating Literature, which begins each Literature Teaching Unit, introduces literary skills and concepts that will aid students in reading the selections.

The title indicates the literary skill, concept, or genre to be discussed.

Objectives for each Teaching Plan are defined clearly.

HBJ Skills Code Numbers serve as a reference guide for locating additional instruction and practice in each skill. In the Skills Index at the back of the Teacher's Edition, each skill is listed by skills code number and major skills category.

The Teaching Plan for Understanding and Appreciating Literature contains two steps: **Introducing the Lesson** provides a basis for discussion of the skill, concept, or genre; **Developing the Skill** gives a framework for guiding students through the lesson.

Background provides biographical information about the author and gives other pertinent information about the selection.

All activities preceded by the symbol ✔ are **optional.**

The symbol ★ appears with each reference to **Enrichment,** an optional step at the end of the Teaching Unit, which suggests a variety of activities, books, and other media to extend students' interest in the content or theme of the selection.

TEACHING UNIT 5
Pages 96–136

Contents

Understanding and Appreciating Literature: Plot (pages T92–T94)
Reading Selections:
The Princess and the Admiral (pages T95–T103)
Stone Soup (pages T104–T109)
Two Fables by Aesop (pages T110–T114)
Enrichment (pages T115–T117)

Additional Materials

Reading Skills Workbook: Lesson 11, pages 34–36;
Word Play, page 37
Duplicating Masters 10: pages 15–18

Key to Symbols

Skills Objectives
I* - Introduced in this unit
I - Introduced earlier in this level
M - Maintained from previous levels

Reduced Student Pages
underscore - words that appear in the glossary
wavy line - words pretaught in the Teacher's Edition (these words also appear in the glossary)

Understanding and Appreciating Literature:
Plot
Pages 96–99

Objectives

		SKILLS CODE NUMBER
I*	To identify plot in fiction	6.11
I*	To recognize the elements of plot	6.11.1
I*	To recognize plot development	6.11.2
I*	To identify plot in a literature selection	6.11

Introducing the Lesson

Have students name favorite stories and briefly tell what happened in each one. When they have finished, tell students that they have just told you the plot of each story. Explain that the plot is what happens in a story. Write the word *plot* on the board.

Reading Selection:
The Princess and the Admiral
Pages 100–118

Objectives

		SKILLS CODE NUMBER
I*	To identify plot in literature	6.11
I*	To recognize the elements of plot	6.11.1
M	To identify forms of writing: folktale	6.4.3
M	To identify sequence and time order	3.3.7; 3.3.7.1

1 Preparing to Read

Summary

As the Tiny Kingdom is about to celebrate one hundred years of peace, the ruler, Princess Mat Mat, learns that warships are approaching. As a defense, she orders that huge spikes be hammered into the river bed at low tide. The enemy warships are lured into the river at high tide and become lodged on the spikes. The Admiral of the enemy fleet is taken ashore, but the Princess does not execute him. Instead, she teaches him a lesson by telling him a fable that expresses the peaceful philosophy of her people and by giving him and his troops provisions with which to return home. The Admiral leaves, and the Tiny Kingdom celebrates almost a hundred years of peace.

Background

This folktale comes from Vietnam, a small country located in Southeast Asia. This traditional tale emphasizes the wisdom of achieving peace. In 1975 the author, Charlotte Pomerantz, received the Jane Addams Children's Book Award for her version of this story. The award is presented for a book with literary merit that stresses themes of dignity, equality, peace, and social justice.

Folktales are traditional stories that were told for hundreds of years before they were ever written down. Many tales contain elements of magic, cleverness, or trickery. In two stories in this unit, the main characters use their wits instead of force to defeat their adversaries.

The following books will provide you with additional background information on folk literature.

Bettelheim, Bruno. *The Uses of Enchantment: The Meaning and Importance of Fairy Tales.* An examination of folklore and its relationship to children's needs and feelings.
Cullinan, Bernice E. *Literature and the Child.* Chapter 5 provides an excellent presentation of the origin and role of folklore in children's literature.
Huck, Charlotte S. *Children's Literature in the Elementary School.* Chapter 4 provides a good overview of folk literature for children.
Rudman, Masha K. *Children's Literature: An Issues Approach.* Interesting discussion of sex-role stereotypes found frequently in folktales.
Sutherland, Zena, and May Hill Arbuthnot. *Children and Books,* 5th ed. Chapters 6, 7, and 15 cover folklore, fables, and the art of storytelling.

The following books are about making paper decorations and puppets.

Color Crafts. *Working with Paper.* Instructions for making paper kites in the Asian tradition--hanging fish, snakes, dragons, and others.
Denzer, Ann Wiseman. *Making Things: The Hand Book of Creative Discovery.* Instructions for making puppets. A good general reference for many craft projects.
Lewis, Shari, and Lillian Oppenheimer. *Folding Paper Masks.* Making and decorating origami masks.
Ross, Laura. *Hand Puppets: How to Make and Use Them.* Directions for making different kinds of puppets from paper bags, papier-mâché, and rods.

Developing Vocabulary and Concepts

advisers: persons who give advice, as to a ruler
flit: to move or fly rapidly
slither: to slide or slip
writhe: to twist the face or body
astrology: the study of the stars and planets and their supposed effects on people and their future
furl: to roll up and fasten
primitive: not modern; in or as if in a very early time
bailing: taking water out of something, such as out of a boat with a pail
ebb: the flowing of the tide back to the ocean
skirmish: a small, short fight, not as important as a battle

Tell Me a Story, Teaching Unit 5 **T95**

Sample Teacher's Edition pages reduced. Actual size is 9" x 11¼."

Blazing Trails

HBJ BOOKMARK READING PROGRAM, EAGLE EDITION

Margaret Early

G. Robert Canfield

Robert Karlin

Thomas A. Schottman

Sara Krentzman Srygley

Evelyn L. Wenzel

Level 11

Blazing Trails

HARCOURT BRACE JOVANOVICH, PUBLISHERS

New York Chicago San Francisco Atlanta Dallas and London

ACKNOWLEDGMENTS: For permission to reprint copyrighted material, grateful acknowledgment is made to the following sources:

ADDISON-WESLEY PUBLISHING COMPANY: Adapted from *501 Balloons Sail East* (titled "The Wind Watchers") by Edith Battles. © 1971 by Edith Battles, a Young Scott Book.
ISAAC ASIMOV: Adapted from "Benjamin Franklin Changes the World" by Isaac Asimov from *Cricket Magazine*, 1976.
ATHENEUM PUBLISHERS: "The Whales Off Wales" from *One Winter Night in August and Other Nonsense Jingles* by X. J. Kennedy (a Margaret K. McElderry Book). Copyright © 1975 by X. J. Kennedy. "The Dream Woman" from *The Apple Vendor's Fair* by Patricia Hubbell. Copyright © 1963 by Patricia Hubbell.
BRANDT & BRANDT LITERARY AGENTS, INC.: "Nancy Hanks" from *A Book of Americans* by Rosemary & Stephen Vincent Benét. Copyright 1933 by Rosemary & Stephen Vincent Benét. Copyright renewed © 1961 by Rosemary Carr Benét.
COWARD, MCCANN & GEOGHEGAN, INC.: Adapted from *Mary's Monster* (titled "Curiosities from the Cliffs") by Ruth Van Ness Blair. Copyright © 1975 by Ruth Van Ness Blair. Illustrations by Richard Cuffari, reprinted by permission from *Mary's Monster.* Illustration copyright © 1975 by Richard Cuffari. "The Temper of Tempe Wick" from *This Time, Tempe Wick?* by Patricia Lee Gauch. Copyright © 1974 by Patricia Lee Gauch. Adapted from *The Little Riders* by Margaretha Shemin. Copyright © 1963 by Margaretha Shemin. Adapted from *The Cabin Faced West* (titled "Hamilton Hill: September 18, 1784") by Jean Fritz. Copyright © 1958 by Jean Fritz.
THOMAS Y. CROWELL, PUBLISHERS: An adaptation of the text from pages 10 to 20 of *Maria Tallchief* (titled "Truly a Ballerina") by Tobi Tobias. Copyright © 1970 by Tobi Tobias. Based on text excerpts from *Ghost Towns of the American West* (titled "Golden Ghosts") by Robert Silverberg. Copyright © 1968 by Robert Silverberg. Text adaptation of "The Seeing Stick" by Jane Yolen. Text copyright © 1977 by Jane Yolen.
CURTIS BROWN, LTD.: Adapted from "The Peddler's Pack" by Charlotte MacLeod. Copyright © 1976 by Charlotte MacLeod.
DOUBLEDAY & COMPANY, INC.: "He Reached for the Stars" and "The Secret of the Sea" adapted from *Pioneers and Patriots* by Lavinia Dobler and Edgar A. Toppin. Copyright © 1965 by Doubleday & Company, Inc. Adapted from *The Camels: Ships of the Desert* (titled "The Ship of the Desert") by George Laycock. Copyright © 1976 by George Laycock. "I Go Forth to Move About the Earth" by Alonzo Lopez from *The Whispering Wind,* edited by Terry Allen. Copyright © 1972 by the Institute of American Indian Arts.
E. P. DUTTON: Adapted from *Little Rascal* (titled "A Boy and a Raccoon") by Sterling North. Copyright © 1965 by Sterling North.
AILEEN FISHER: "Comma in the Sky" from *In the Woods, In the Meadow, In the Sky* by Aileen Fisher. Scribners, New York, 1965.
BARTHOLD FLES LITERARY AGENCY: Adapted "Light My Fire" (titled "Feliciano!") from *Challenged by Handicap: Adventures in Courage* by Richard B. Lyttle. Copyright © by Richard B. Lyttle.
FOLLETT PUBLISHING COMPANY: "A Modern Dragon" from *Songs from Around a Toadstool Table* by Rowena Bennett. Copyright © 1967 by Rowena Bastin Bennett.
FOUR WINDS PRESS, A DIVISION OF SCHOLASTIC MAGAZINES, INC.: *Petronella* by Jay Williams. Text copyright © 1973 by Jay Williams.
GOLDEN GATE JUNIOR BOOK DIVISION OF CHILDRENS PRESS, CHICAGO: Adapted from *A Tree Is Something Wonderful* (titled "Giants in the Earth") by Elizabeth K. Cooper and Padraic Cooper. © 1972. Adapted from *Living Lights – The Mystery of Bioluminescence* (titled "Living Lights in Our World") by Alvin and Virginia Silverstein. © 1970.
GREENWILLOW BOOKS (A DIVISION OF WILLIAM MORROW & CO.): "The Snoop on the Sidewalk" from *The Snoop on the Sidewalk and Other Poems* by Jack Prelutsky. Copyright © 1976, 1977 by Jack Prelutsky.
GROSSET & DUNLAP, INC.: "Glory, Glory . . ." from *Twenty-Six Ways of Looking at a Black Man* by Raymond R. Patterson. Copyright 1969 by Raymond R. Patterson.
HARCOURT BRACE JOVANOVICH, INC.: Excerpts on pp. 90 and 91; 201–03; 368 and 369 (text and art); 450 and 451; and diagrams on pp. 325 and 326; from *Concepts in Science,* Newton Edition (Purple) by Paul F. Brandwein et al. Copyright © 1975 by Harcourt Brace Jovanovich, Inc. Excerpts on pp. 248 and 249; 298 and 299; from *Language for Daily Use,* Explorer Edition (Purple) by Mildred A. Dawson et al. Copyright © 1978 by Harcourt Brace Jovanovich, Inc. Excerpts on pp. 47 and 48; 344 and 345 (text and art); 452 and 453; 497–99; from *Balance in Your Life* (Purple) by Sam F. Seeley et al. Copyright © 1977 by Harcourt Brace Jovanovich, Inc. Excerpts on pp. 370 and 371 (text and art) from *Growth in Mathematics* (Purple) by David W. Wells et al. Copyright © 1978 by Harcourt Brace Jovanovich, Inc. Entries on pp. 51–54; 66; 67; taken from (or adapted from) *HBJ School Dictionary.* Copyright © 1977, 1972, 1968 by Harcourt Brace Jovanovich, Inc.
HARCOURT BRACE JOVANOVICH, INC., AND THE BODLEY HEAD: Adapted from "The Oba Asks for a Mountain" in *Olode the Hunter and Other Tales from Nigeria* (British title: *Ijapa the Tortoise and Other Nigerian Tales*) by Harold Courlander with Ezekiel Aderogba Eshugbayi. Copyright © 1968 by Harold Courlander.
HOLT, RINEHART AND WINSTON, PUBLISHERS: Adapted from *Poor Richard in France* by F. N. Monjo. Copyright © 1973 by Ferdinand Monjo and Louise L. Monjo.
HOUGHTON MIFFLIN COMPANY: Excerpts on pp. 45 and 46; 198–200; 249–51; 319; 434 and 425; from *Windows on Our World: The United States* by Anderson and King. Copyright © 1976 by Houghton Mifflin Company. *The Toothpaste Millionaire,* by Jean Merrill. Copyright © 1972 by Houghton Mifflin Company.
HOUGHTON MIFFLIN COMPANY AND GEORGE ALLEN & UNWIN LTD.: From "Oliphaunt" from *The Adventures of Tom Bombadil* by J. R. R. Tolkien. Copyright © 1962 by George Allen & Unwin Ltd.

iv

LAIDLAW BROTHERS, A DIVISION OF DOUBLEDAY & COMPANY, INC.: Excerpts on pp. 20 and 21; 220 and 221; 472 and 473; from *Exploring Science*, Level Five. Copyright © 1976 by Laidlaw Brothers, Publishers. Excerpts on pp. 320 and 321 (text and art); 426–28; 494–96 (text and art); from *Discovery in English* (5). Copyright © 1975 by Laidlaw Brothers, Publishers.
J. B. LIPPINCOTT: "Pencil and Paint" from *Eleanor Farjeon's Poems for Children*. Originally published in *Joan's Door* by Eleanor Farjeon. Copyright 1926, 1954, by Eleanor Farjeon.
LITTLE, BROWN AND COMPANY: Adapted from *Whatever Happened to Main Street?* from *My Backyard History Book* by David Weitzman. Copyright © 1975 by David Weitzman.
LOTHROP, LEE & SHEPARD CO. (A DIVISION OF WILLIAM MORROW & CO.): Adapted from *Creative Shellcraft* (titled "Shell Treasures") by Katherine N. Cutler. Copyright © 1971 by Katherine N. Cutler. "On Our Bikes" from *The Sidewalk Racer and Other Poems* by Lillian Morrison. Copyright © 1977 by Lillian Morrison.
MACMILLAN PUBLISHING CO., INC.: Glossary excerpt on pp. 68 and 69 from Macmillan Mathematics, Series m, Level 5. Copyright © 1976 Macmillan Publishing Co., Inc.
MACMILLAN PUBLISHING CO., INC., AND CASSELL LTD.: Excerpts on p. 229 from *The New Cassell's French Dictionary* by Denis Girard et al. Copyright © 1962, 1963, 1964, 1965, 1966, 1968, 1969, 1970, 1971, 1972, 1973 by Cassell & Co., Ltd.
MACMILLAN PUBLISHING CO., INC., MRS. IRIS WISE; MACMILLAN LONDON AND BASINGSTOKE: "Check" from *Collected Poems* (British title: *The Rocky Road to Dublin*) by James Stephens. Copyright 1915 by Macmillan Publishing Co., Inc., renewed 1943 by James Stephens.
MCINTOSH AND OTIS, INC.: Adapted from *Some Went West* (titled "Sod-Shanty Pioneers") by Dorothy M. Johnson. Copyright © 1965 by Dorothy M. Johnson.
EVE MERRIAM C/O INTERNATIONAL CREATIVE MANAGEMENT: "Autumn Leaves" from *There Is No Rhyme for Silver* by Eve Merriam. Copyright © 1962 by Eve Merriam.
JULIAN MESSNER, A SIMON & SCHUSTER DIVISION OF GULF & WESTERN CORPORATION: Adapted from *Black on White and Read All Over* (titled "Gifts from China") by Albert Barker. Copyright © 1971 by Albert Barker.
CYNTHIA DE NARVAEZ: Adapted from *My Dear Dolphin* (titled "Dolphin Days") by Cynthia de Narvaez. Copyright © 1969 by Cynthia de Narvaez.
THE NEW AMERICAN LIBRARY, INC., NEW YORK, NY: Adapted from *Rising Voices* (titled "Daniel Villanueva: The Idea is to Care") by Al Martinez. Copyright © 1974 by Carnation Company.
PLAYS, INC., PUBLISHERS, BOSTON, MA 02116: "The Book That Saved the Earth" from *Plays and Programs for Boys and Girls* by Claire Boiko. Copyright © 1967 by Plays, Inc. This play is for reading purposes only. For permission to produce this play, write to Plays, Inc., 8 Arlington St., Boston, MA 02116.
READ MAGAZINE, PUBLISHED BY XEROX EDUCATION PUBLICATIONS: "Foul Shot" by Edwin A. Hoey from *Read Magazine* dated January 1962. Copyright © 1962 by Xerox Corporation.
KARLEEN S. SABOL: Adapted from "So You Want to Start a Theatre" (titled "Start Your Own Theater") by Karleen Schart Sabol from *Cricket Magazine*, 1976.
SCOTT, FORESMAN AND COMPANY: Excerpts on pp. 181; 342 and 343; from *Mathematics Around Us*, Book 5, by L. Carey Bolster et al. Copyright © 1978, 1975 by Scott, Foresman and Company.
CHARLES SCRIBNER'S SONS: Excerpts from *Explorers and Penguins* (titled "Penguin Paradise") by Edna M. Andreas. Copyright © 1950 by Edna M. Andreas.
SILVER BURDETT COMPANY: Excerpts on pp. 22 and 23; 92 and 93; 222 and 223; 473–74; from *Silver Burdett Social Science: People in the Americas* © 1976 by Silver Burdett Company. Excerpts on pp. 179 and 180; 297; from *Science: Understanding Your Environment* (Level 5). © 1975 by General Learning Corporation.
VIKING PENGUIN, INC.: "Nothing New Under the Sun (Hardly)" from *Homer Price* by Robert McCloskey. Copyright 1943. © renewed 1971 by Robert McCloskey. "Skiing" from *From Summer to Summer* by Rose Burgunder. Copyright © 1965 by Rose Styron.
WESTERN PUBLISHING CO., INC.: "Open Range" from *Cowboys and Indians* by Kathryn Ann Jackson. Copyright © 1968, 1948 by Western Publishing Company, Inc.
THE WESTMINSTER PRESS: Excerpts from *The Way It Was—1876* (titled "'Modern' America in the 1880's") by Suzanne Hilton. Copyright © 1975 by Suzanne Hilton.

PHOTO CREDITS:

Key: L–Left; R–Right; C–Center; T–Top; B–Bottom.

Cover, Keith Gunnar/Bruce Coleman, Inc. Title page, Bradley Smith/Animals Animals.
Page 1, TL, HBJ Photo; TC, Jen & Des Bartlett/Bruce Coleman, Inc.; CL, Olen S. Hanson/NAS/Photo Researchers; BL, HBJ Photo; BR, Keith Richardson/Shostal Associates; inset, George Leavens/Photo Researchers; 2, B, Kenneth W. Fink/Photo Researchers; 5, Angermayer/Photo Researchers; 6, Oxford Scientific Films/Bruce Coleman, Inc.; 29, Russ Kinne/Photo Researchers; 32–33, C. Haagner/Bruce Coleman, Inc.; 34, The Bettmann Archive; 35–36, Guy Mannering/Bruce Coleman, Inc.; 38, Bruce Coleman, Inc.; 40, Ivan Polunin/Bruce Coleman, Inc.; 42, T, Stephen Dalton/Photo Researchers; B, W. E. Ruth/Bruce Coleman, Inc.; 43, Jane Burton/Bruce Coleman, Inc.; 45, George H. Harrison; 47, T and B, 48, Runk/Schoenberger/Grant Heilman, Inc.; 56, Jane Burton/Bruce Coleman, Inc.; 57, 58, 61, 62, 63, 65, Copyright © 1969, 1976, 1980, Jerry Greenberg. All rights reserved; 71, Robert Weinreb/Bruce Coleman, Inc.; 73, Dr. E. R. Degginger; 74, Grant Thompson/Photo Researchers; 76, Permanent Collection, Berkshire Museum, Pittsfield, Massachusetts; 79, T, Len Rue, Jr./Bruce Coleman, Inc.; B, Verna Johnston/Photo Researchers; 84–85, Norman Myers/Bruce Coleman, Inc.; 85 (inset), Norman Owen Tomalin/Bruce Coleman, Inc.; 86, TR, Leonard Lee Rue III/Bruce Coleman, Inc.; BL, Norman Owen Tomalin/Bruce Coleman, Inc.; 88, Courtesy of the American Museum of Natural History; 91, Karen Collidge; 95, Edward Lettau/Photo Researchers; 129, 130, Viking-Penguin; 150, TL, Bill Hamilton/Shostal Associates; CL, HBJ Photo, San Francisco; CR, HBJ Photo, San Francisco; BL, Richard Hutchings/Photo Researchers; BR, HBJ Photo, San Francisco; 162, TL, Michael and Barbara Reed/Animals, Animals; TR, N. Reinhard/Bruce Coleman, Inc.; BL, Jerry Cooke/Animals, Animals; BR, Aqua Set Industries/Taurus Photos; 175, Courtesy of José Feliciano, Burl Hechtman Management; 177, © 1969, Children's Television Workshop. Reprinted by permission; 183, Smithsonian Institution No. 77-7845; 184, Smithsonian Institution No. 72551AD; 185, William A. Graham/Photo Researchers; 190, HBJ Photo; 191, 192, 194B, 195, 196, 197, D. Micolupp; 194T, 201, 202, 203, HBJ Photo; 209, T and B, Division of Tourism, State of Missouri; CL, James Lester/Photo Researchers; CR, R. B. Keene/Shostal Associates; 211, TL, Wayne Miller/Magnum; TR, Joseph Martin/Scala, EPA, Inc.; BL, Michael Philip Mannheim/Photo Researchers; BR, Erich Hartmann/Magnum; 221, Jerome

Wexler/Photo Researchers; 229, HBJ Picture Library; 231, L, The Bettmann Archive; 7C, Bradley Smith/Animals, Animals; BC, Paolo Koch/Photo Researchers; R, Paul Keel/Photo Researchers; 234–242, Copyright © 1979 by United Press Syndicate, Inc. All rights reserved. Based on excerpts from PEANUTS JUBILEE: MY LIFE AND ART WITH CHARLIE BROWN AND OTHERS by Charles M. Schulz (Copyright © 1975 by United Feature Syndicate, Inc.) Used by permission; 243, 245, Alfred Eisenstaedt/LIFE Magazine © 1954 TIME Inc.; 246, Martha Swope; 250, John J. Bagma/Photo Researchers; 253, August Upitis/Shostal Associates; 259, HBJ Photo; 263, National Aeronautics and Space Administration; 267, Norm Clasen/Focus on Sports; 279, TL, Catherine Ursillo/Photo Researchers; CL, Judi Benvenuti; CR, Ed Cooper/Shostal Associates; BL, Judi Benvenuti; BR, Bookcraft Projects; 297, Bruce J. Nelson/Shostal Associates; 322, Yale University Library; 324, Library of Congress; 330–331, 332, 334, 335, 338, 339, The Bettmann Archive; 333, Brown Brothers; 336, 7, Montgomery Ward and Company; B, New York State Historical Association, Cooperstown; 340, Otis Elevator Company; 366, T, Margot Gayle, Friends of Cast Iron Architecture; 7C, Linda Keil, Friends of Cast Iron Architecture; BC, B. Jan Lukas/Photo Researchers; 373, Marc and Evelynne Bernheim/Woodfin Camp Associates; 407, TL, Jim Carter/Photo Researchers; CL, David S. Strickler/Monkmeyer Press Photos; CR, HBJ Photo, San Francisco; BL, HBJ Photo; BR, Henry Deters/Monkmeyer Press Photos; 408, Sperry Corporation; 415, 417, 418, 419, 421, 422, 433, Florence M. Harrison; 444, The Bettmann Archive; 452, TL, TR, Courtesy of Loren Miller Homes, San Francisco, California; 467, The Granger Collection; 470, Courtesy Tri Arts Press, New York; 472, Tom Stack; 479, Wally McNamee/Woodfin Camp Associates; 487, 488, Maryland Historical Society, Baltimore; 489, Richard Hewitt; 490, UPI; 491, 492, SIN National Spanish Television Network; 497, L, HBJ Photo; TR, Steve McCutcheon; BR, Courtesy of Loren Miller Homes, San Francisco, California; 501, Judi Benvenuti.

ART CREDITS: The artists in this book and the pages on which their work appears are as follows:

Richard Amundsen: pp. 11–18; Nava Atlas: 468, 469; Richard Bennett: 447, 448; Mark Brown: 100–111; Gil Cohen: 268–269, 507–511; Olivia Cole: 214–218; Peter Cross: 2–4, 24, 26, 28, 49, 50, 53, 70, 160, 165, 182, 187, 204–207, 224, 228, 230, 280–284, 300–302, 327, 346, 408, 409, 411, 412, 430, 431, 433, 454–456, 476–478; Ray Dallasta: 256–260, 482–485; Creston Ely: 258; Max Gerhard: 306–311; Ethel Gold: 362–365; John Hamberger: 80–82; Denman Hampson: 460–466; Jeanette Kehl: 276–277; Gordon Laite: 378–382; Robert Lapsley: 263, 354–359; Ken Longtemps: 260–261; Bonnie Gordon Lucas: 275–278; Robert McCloskey: 135–156; Susan Spellman Mohn: 265; Sal Murdocca: 393–404; Meredith Nemirof: 384–391; Michael O'Reilly: 292–295; Ruth Sanderson: 526–547; Bob Shore: 312–316; Don Silverstein: 271–272; Deborah Sims: 96, 97, 98, 254, 374, 502; Jerry Smath: 113–127; Steve Stroud: 266; Kyuzo Tsugami: 166–173; George Ulrich: 514–526.

Maps: Richard Bennett: pp. 347, 348; Howard Friedman: 360, 443.

HBJ maps and charts: pp. 87, 349, 350, 351, 367, 368, 370, 371.

Glossary art: Denman Hampson: pp. 552–574, except for Graphic Arts International: pp. 554, 559 (l), 569 (br).

Vocabulary pages were designed by Kaeser & Wilson Design, Ltd; illustrated by Guy Smalley: pp. 9, 30–31, 55, 75, 166–167, 188–189, 213, 232–233, 285, 305, 328–329, 353, 414–415, 434–435, 458–459, 480–481.

Contents

To the Reader

Blazing Trails—that is what you will be doing as you explore this book. Like a pioneer, you will be traveling new roads, discovering new ideas, and learning skills. You will learn about some of nature's mysteries. You will enjoy stories that will make you laugh. You will read about people and the different ways they express themselves through music, the arts, science, poems, and folktales. You will read articles and stories about America's past. You will learn about discoveries and ideas that have made our lives today richer and better. You may even learn about your own hometown.

Your book, *Blazing Trails*, is divided into eight parts. In Parts 1, 3, 5, and 7, you will learn to improve your reading skills through Skills Lessons, Vocabulary Studies, and Textbook Studies. The reading selections are yours to enjoy as you explore new information. In Parts 2, 4, 6, and 8, you will discover ways to understand and appreciate literature. The selections and poems are yours to enjoy as you laugh and dream with the characters and writers.

When you read, you often follow new roads in new directions. You are a pioneer discovering new territory and learning new skills. So lead the way—discover *Blazing Trails*.

xvi

Part 1
Learning About Living Things

RESOURCE CENTER

The following list identifies materials that you may wish to gather before reading the selections in "Learning About Living Things." The list also suggests optional activities that require advance planning. The *Enrichment* section at the end of each Teaching Unit explains how to employ these resources. The *Enrichment* section also gives suggestions for additional activities that do not require advance preparation.

Enrichment Materials and Activities

A Boy and a Raccoon
Pages 10–19

Enrichment Materials:
Information about wildlife from:
  National Wildlife Federation
  1412 16th St., NW
  Washington, DC 20036
Information about veterinary careers from:
  Animal and Plant Health Inspection Service
  Personnel Division
  12th and Independence Avenue, SW
  Washington, DC 20250
                    or
  American Veterinary Medical Association
  930 N. Meacham Road
  Schaumburg, IL 60172
  (Send self-addressed stamped business envelope.)

Activity Needing Advance Planning:
A trip to a zoo or animal farm

Guest Speakers:
A wildlife specialist
A veterinarian

Penguin Paradise
Pages 32–37

Activity Needing Advance Planning:
A trip to a zoo or an aquarium

Guest Speaker:
A representative of one of the U.S. Armed Forces

Living Lights in Our World
Pages 38–44

Activities Needing Advance Planning:
Growing molds in Petri dishes
A trip to a natural history museum

Dolphin Days
Pages 56–66

Activities Needing Advance Planning:
A trip to an aquarium
A trip to a natural history museum

Giants in the Earth
Pages 76–83

Enrichment Materials:
Literature from:
  Sierra Club
  530 Bush Street
  San Francisco, CA 94108

Activities Needing Advance Planning:
A fund-raising activity to buy trees to plant
A visit to a tree nursery

Guest Speaker:
A naturalist or botanist

Bibliography

For Students

NOTE: For more information about these books, see the *Enrichment* section at the end of each Teaching Unit.

Adamson, Joy. *Elsa*. Pantheon, 1963.
Allison, Linda. *The Reasons for Seasons*. Little, 1975.
Anderson, Margaret J. *Exploring City Trees and the Need for Urban Forests*. McGraw-Hill, 1976.

Budlong, Ware, and Mark H. Fleitzer. *Experimenting with Seeds and Plants.* Putnam, 1970.

Chapin, Henry. *The Remarkable Dolphin.* Addison-Wesley, 1962.

Cosgrove, Margaret. *Wonders of the Tree World.* Dodd, 1969.

Eberle, Irmengarde. *Pandas Live Here.* Doubleday, 1973.
_____. *Penguins Live Here.* Doubleday, 1975.

Foster, Virgil. *Close-up of a Honeybee.* Addison-Wesley, 1960.

Hogner, Dorothy Childs. *Sea Mammals.* T. Y. Crowell, 1979.

Hutchins, Ross E. *This Is a Tree.* Dodd, 1964.

Kieran, John. *An Introduction to Birds.* Doubleday, 1974.

Kipling, Rudyard. *Just So Stories.* Doubleday, 1972.

Leen, Nina. *Cats.* Holt, Rinehart & Winston, 1980.

Lubell, Winifred. *In a Running Brook.* Rand McNally, 1968.

Malone, Margaret Gay. *Dolly the Dolphin.* Messner, 1978.

McClung, Robert M. *Aquatic Insects and How They Live.* Morrow, 1970.

Matheu, Martha F. *Whales, Sails, and Scrimshaw.* Addison-Wesley, 1963.

Milne, Lorus J. *Gifts from the Sky.* Atheneum, 1967.

Mizumura, Kazue. *Emperor Penguins.* T. Y. Crowell, 1969.

Moffett, Martha, and Robert Moffett. *Dolphins.* Watts, 1971.

National Geographic World. "Dolphins: The Smart Animals?" Number 21, May 1977, pages 12–17.

North, Sterling. *Little Rascal.* Dutton, 1965.

Patent, Dorothy Hinshaw. *Bears of the World.* Holiday, 1980.

Pitt, Valerie, and David Cook. *A Closer Look at Deserts.* Watts, 1975.

Quilici, Folco. *Great Deserts.* McGraw, 1969.

Ricciuti, Edward R. *Plants in Danger.* Harper & Row, 1979.

Simon, Hilda. *Living Lanterns: Luminescence in Animals.* Viking, 1971.

Simon, Seymour. *Killer Whales.* Lippincott, 1978.
_____. *Projects with Plants.* Watts, 1972.

Tinbergen, Niko. *Animal Behavior.* Young Reader's Library, Silver Burdett Co., 1977.

Tyler, Margaret. *Deserts.* John Day, 1970.

Weber, William J. *Wild Orphan Babies (Mammals and Birds): Caring for Them and Setting Them Free,* 2nd ed. Holt, Rinehart & Winston, 1978.

Zim, Herbert S. *Golden Guide to Mammals.* Golden Press, Western Pub., 1955.

For Teachers

NOTE: For more information about these books, see the *Background* section that precedes the reading selections.

Burt, William H. *A Field Guide to the Mammals.* Houghton Mifflin, 1976.

Cousteau, Jacques-Yves, and Philippe Diole. *Dolphins.* Doubleday, 1975.

Guiness, Alma, ed. *The Joy of Nature.* Reader's Digest, 1977.

Hegner, Robert W. *Parade of the Animal Kingdom.* Macmillan, 1967.

Herriot, James. *All Things Wise and Wonderful.* St. Martin, 1977.

Honders, John, ed. *The World of Mammals.* Peoples Press, 1975.

Hutchins, Ross E. *Insects and Their Young.* Dodd, 1975.

Leopold, A. Starker. *Desert.* Time-Life, 1961.

Orr, Robert T. *Mammals of North America.* Doubleday, 1970.

Peterson, Roger T. *Birds.* Time-Life, 1968.

Petrides, George A. *A Field Guide to Trees and Shrubs.* Houghton Mifflin, 1973.

Tweedie, Michael. *Insects: World of Miniature Beauty.* Crescent Books, 1971.

Films and Filmstrips

Sources related to specific skills

Guidance Assocs. *The Reading Skills Series.* Titles: "Working with Prefixes," "Working with Suffixes." Teacher's guide for each title. Two programs, each with record (#9A–302 065) or cassettes (#9A–302 073, #9A–302 099).

Guidance Assocs. *Using Your Reading Skills Series.* Titles: "Getting the Main Idea," "Charts, Tables, Maps, and Graphs," "Finding Word Clues," "Skim, Scan, or Study?" Discussion guide and spirit duplicating masters for each title. Four programs with records (#9A–305 068) or cassettes (#9A–305 076).

Sources related to reading selections

Coronet Instructional Media. *Trees.* Titles: "The Different Kinds," "Their Structure," "Flowers, Fruits, and Seeds," "How They Grow," "Their Products," "Their Importance." Six filmstrips with records (#S116) or cassettes (#M116).

Ealing Films. *The Yearling: Reading Skills Kit.* Three color strips with three cassettes, ten student reading scripts, fifteen activity cards (#8R2-047-0).

Guidance Assocs. *World of the Sea Series.* Titles: "World of the Sea—Group One," "World of the Sea—Group Two." Teacher's guide with scripts for each title. Spanish version also. Two programs, six parts with cassettes (#9A-306 397).

Prentice-Hall Media. *Desert Life.* Titles: "What Is a Desert?" "How Desert Plants Survive," "How Desert Animals Survive," "Balance of Life in a Desert." Teacher's guide for each title. Four captioned filmstrips with cassettes (#HAC3450).

Valiant Instructional Materials Corp. *The Animal Kingdom.* Titles: "Birds," "Lions," "Sharks," "Bears," "Elephants," "Monkeys and Apes," "Whales," "Ecology." Ten filmstrips (#FS226).

OVERVIEW

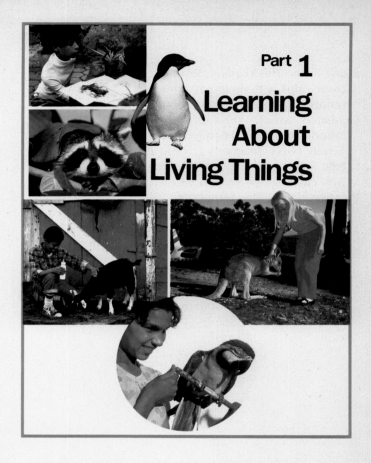

Part 1

Learning About Living Things

The skills focus of "Learning About Living Things" covers language skills: using context clues in sentences to find word meanings; using root words, prefixes, and suffixes as clues to word meanings; using the dictionary; and identifying relationships of ideas within and between sentences. The selections give interesting facts about plants and animals. For example, several selections tell about the habits and remarkable abilities of such animals as raccoons, dolphins, penguins, and camels. One selection tells about the history of trees and describes unusual trees that still grow after thousands of years on earth.

Using the Management System

Periodic Test 1, Forms A and B, covers the tested skills in "Learning About Living Things." The test may be administered in parts preceding and/or following instruction in each Teaching Unit. Or, Parts I through IV may be administered together for pretesting and/or post-testing all the tested skills in "Learning About Living Things." For full information on administering tests, see the Teacher's Edition of *Periodic Tests, Level 11.* In addition, the following activities within the student's text may be used as part of your ongoing assessment of students' progress.

> *Try This* sections of the *Skills Lessons*
> *Applying the Skills Lesson* activities following each selection
> *Building Skills* sections of *Textbook Studies*

Previewing "Learning About Living Things"

Have students turn to the table of contents in their text. Tell students that their book is divided into eight parts, four of which emphasize reading to learn and four of which emphasize appreciating literature. Part 1, "Learning About Living Things," stresses reading to learn. Point out that each of the Reading to Learn parts contains four sections. Each section contains a *Skills Lesson,* a *Vocabulary Study,* one or more *Reading Selections,* which are indicated in boldfaced type, and a *Textbook Study.*

Have students examine the photographs on page 1. Ask them to share any facts they know about the animals or other living things pictured. Explain that some of the selections in this part of the book give interesting information on the history, habits, and abilities of some animals; other selections tell about plant life. Ask students to examine the pictures and titles of the selections for a few minutes and then discuss the specific living things they will read about.

Objectives

The following list of objectives is provided to help you plan your teaching of "Learning About Living Things." All the objectives listed under *Maintained and Tested* are for skills presented in the four *Skills Lessons* of "Learning About Living Things" in the student's text. *Applying the Skills Lesson* sections following each selection in the student's text, as well as the *Try This* activities within the *Skills Lessons,* informally assess students' progress with these skills. *Periodic Test 1* may be used for more formal evaluation.

The objectives listed under *Maintained* are for skills presented in the *Maintaining Skills* sections in this Teacher's Edition.

The symbols I*, I, M, and T are used throughout the Teacher's Edition. The symbol I* indicates skills introduced for the first time in the program. The I indicates skills introduced earlier in Level 11. The M indicates skills taught at earlier levels and maintained in Level 11. The T indicates a skill that is taught for mastery and tested. The italicized numbers following the objectives are part of a code developed by the HBJ School Department to facilitate the correlation of skills within and between programs. See page T499.

Maintained and Tested

These skills have been introduced in earlier levels of the HBJ BOOKMARK READING PROGRAM, EAGLE EDITION. They are further developed in Level 11 and tested in *Periodic Test 1.*

	SKILLS CODE NUMBER
To identify and use context clues to determine word meaning	3.0.2
To identify definitions in context	3.0
To identify and use synonyms as context clues	3.5.4; 3.0
To identify and use antonyms as context clues	3.5.3; 3.0
To identify sound-letter relationships	2.1; 2.2
To identify the number of syllables in a word	2.6
To identify word parts: root words, prefixes, and suffixes	4.1
To identify base words in compound words	4.2.1
To locate dictionary and glossary entries	5.6.4; 5.6.6
To use a dictionary or glossary to find pronunciation and meaning	5.6.4; 5.6.6
To use a dictionary or glossary to find meanings of multiple-meaning words	5.6.4; 5.6.6
To identify cause-and-effect relationships	3.3.3
To identify words that signal cause-and-effect relationships	3.3.3.1

Maintained

Each of these skills was previously taught in the HBJ BOOKMARK READING PROGRAM, EAGLE EDITION. None of them is tested in *Periodic Test 1.* In planning your teaching, select those exercises from the *Maintaining Skills* sections that best meet your students' specific needs for maintaining skills presented earlier in the program.

	SKILLS CODE NUMBER
To determine the correct sequence for a set of events	3.3.7.4
To distinguish between fact and opinion	3.6.3
To draw conclusions based on given information	3.4.1
To identify reference materials	5.11
To identify the topic and stated main idea of a paragraph	3.3.8
To identify details that support the stated main idea of a paragraph	3.3.1; 3.3.8.3
To scan a selection for specific information	5.9
To use a dictionary pronunciation key	5.6.5
To identify an author's purpose	3.6.4
To predict outcomes based on given information and personal knowledge	3.4.2
To interpret information from a picture	5.4.5
To interpret information from a map	5.4.3

Vocabulary

The following skills are practiced on the *Vocabulary Study* pages in the student's text for "Learning About Living Things." These skills are also covered in the *Skills Lessons* and are tested in *Periodic Test 1.*

	SKILLS CODE NUMBER
To identify base words in compound words	4.2.1
To identify and use synonyms as context clues	3.5.4; 3.0

The following skills are not tested in *Periodic Test 1.*

To use context clues to determine the meanings of multiple-meaning words	3.5.5; 3.0.2
To distinguish between homophones	3.5.1

Contents

Additional Materials

Reading Skills Workbook: Lessons 1–2, pages 1–8
Duplicating Masters 11: pages 1–2
Worksheet 1: Teacher's Edition, page T480
Periodic Test 1, Part I

Key to Symbols

Skills Objectives
I* — Introduced in this unit
I — Introduced earlier in this level
M — Maintained from previous levels
T — Tested in periodic and cumulative tests for this level

Reduced Student Pages
underscore — words that appear in the glossary
wavy line — words pretaught in the Teacher's Edition
          (these words also appear in the glossary)

Skills Lesson:
Using Context Clues to Find Word Meaning
Pages 2–7

Objectives

		SKILLS CODE NUMBER
M, T	To identify and use context clues to determine word meaning	3.0.2**
M, T	To identify definitions in context	3.0
M, T	To identify and use synonyms as context clues	3.5.4; 3.0
M, T	To identify and use antonyms as context clues	3.5.3; 3.0

If you wish to pretest the skills listed above, you may administer *Periodic Test 1, Part I, Form A. Periodic Test 1, Part I, Form B*, may be administered to posttest.

** Skills code numbers are used in the Skills Index in the back of this Teacher's Edition.

Introducing the Lesson

1. **a.** Write the word *forgo* on the board and pronounce it for the class. Ask students if they can tell you its meaning. (Your students will probably not be familiar with this word.)

   b. Next, write the following sentence on the board:

   Poor health forced him to <u>forgo</u> rough sports.

Using Context Clues to Find Word Meaning

What would you think if you saw the sign above on the left? You probably wouldn't know what to think. But suppose you saw the sign on the right? Now you would know that an ibex is an animal you can find at the zoo. In fact, an ibex is a wild goat that looks like the animal below.

2

You were able to tell that an ibex is an animal when you saw it on the sign with other animal names. The word *ibex* was used in a context that gave you a clue to its meaning.

Context means "the words or sentences around a certain word." Writers often tell you what a new word means by defining it in context. Here is an example:

- Snakes and turtles are reptiles—cold-blooded animals that have no legs or very short legs.

In the sentence above, the word *reptiles* is defined in context. The context often helps to explain a word even if a definition is not given. Read this sentence:

- Tigers usually hunt their prey at night.

Perhaps you know what *prey* is. If you don't, you can tell from the context that prey is something that is hunted. If you wanted to know the word's exact meaning, you could check a dictionary. You would find that *prey* means "any animal taken by another for food."

3

Ask students to guess what *forgo* means. (to give up; to go without)

c. Ask why they had a better idea of the meaning of the word when they saw it in a sentence. (The sentence gave a clue to its meaning, since poor health would probably cause someone to give up or go without rough sports.)

2. Now ask students to turn to page 2. Have them read the paragraph and examine the illustrations. Point out that, just as with the word *forgo*, seeing the sign with the word *ibex* alone doesn't give a clue to its meaning. However, when the word *ibex* is listed on the sign with other animal names, it is in a *context* that gives a clue to its meaning.

Developing the Skill

A. *Writers often tell you what a new word means by defining it in context.*

Have students read the first two paragraphs on page 3 and the example sentence. Ask what word is defined in context. (reptiles)

B. *The context often helps to explain an unfamiliar word even if a definition is not given.*

Have students read the explanatory paragraph and the example sentence about tigers. Ask students to guess what the word *prey* means in the context. (something that is hunted) Then have students read the explanatory paragraph at the bottom of page 3.

Synonyms

Synonyms

The clue to a word you don't know may be a **synonym**—a word that has the same or nearly the same meaning as another word. Thinking about what you are reading helps you to see such clues. Read this sentence:

● I called my dog "Rascal" because he was such a mischief.

If you know the meaning of the word *mischief,* you may be able to figure out the meaning of the name "Rascal." If you know what *rascal* means, you may be able to figure out that a mischief is a person or animal that teases or is naughty.

4

Antonyms

Antonyms

Sometimes when you come to a word you don't know, there will be an **antonym**—a word with an opposite meaning—in the same context. Read the sentence below. Think about the meaning of the word *immense.*

● We had expected all the tigers to be little, but one of them was immense.

If you do not know what *immense* means, what clue will help you? The word *but* signals an opposite idea. You might, therefore, reason that *immense* must have an opposite meaning from *little.*

5

Synonyms

The clue to a word you don't know may be a synonym.

1. Have students read the explanatory paragraph and the example sentence on page 4. Explain that the two synonyms in this sentence are *Rascal* and *mischief.* Ask if students know the meaning of either of these words, and if they do, ask them to use the meaning of one word to figure out the meaning of the other. (*mischief:* a person or animal that teases or is naughty; *rascal:* a playfully naughty child or animal)

2. Have students read the explanatory paragraph at the bottom of the page.

Antonyms

The clue to a word you don't know may be an antonym. .

1. Have students read the explanatory paragraph and the example sentence on page 5. Ask students what clue in the sentence would help readers who don't know the meaning of *immense.* (The word *but* signals an idea that is the opposite of *little.*)

2. Have students read the explanatory paragraph at the bottom of the page.

Try This

Read the sentences below. Using clues in the context to help you, figure out the meaning of each word in italics. Then make up a sentence using each word.

1. Bees are able to *transmit* their knowledge of the location of honey to other bees by a "dance" that is full of messages.
2. Although people may not be able to *interpret* the bees' messages, other bees can easily tell what the dance means.
3. It appears that bees don't have to learn the "steps" of the dance. They know what the "steps" mean by *instinct*.

6

The Larger Context

Clues to the meaning of a word are often right in the sentence that contains the word. But sometimes you need to look further. Read the two sentences below.

● All kinds of stones come out of a volcano. Pumice is one kind.

You know from the two sentences above that *pumice* is one kind of volcanic stone. The larger context of the paragraph tells you even more about *pumice:*

● Pumice looks like a sponge. It is the lightest stone in the world. It's so light that if you put it in water, it will float. That's because it's filled with gas bubbles. The lava was thrown out with such force that the gas in it couldn't escape.

Now you know quite a bit about *pumice.* The full paragraph explained it. Remember to look for *all* the information you can find about a new word.

Try This

Read the following paragraph. Then, in one sentence, explain what *diatoms* are.

Algae are simple plants that grow in water or damp places. They lack true roots, stems, or leaves. One kind, the *diatom,* is a major food source for animals that live in the sea. They also produce much of the earth's oxygen. Diatoms make up the slippery coatings on the stems of large water plants and on rocks.

7

Try This

Have students complete *Try This.*

Answers to *Try This*

1. *transmit:* send or pass on from one person or place to another; Context clue: "messages"; **2.** *interpret:* explain; Context clue: "tell"; **3.** *instinct:* a natural tendency that causes animals to act in characteristic ways; Context clue: "don't have to learn." Sentences will vary.

The Larger Context

Clues to the meaning of an unfamiliar word may appear in a sentence that comes before or after the sentence that contains the unfamiliar word.

Have students read the rest of the lesson, stopping before *Try This.* Ask them to define *pumice* in one sentence. (Sample answer: Pumice is a very light, volcanic stone filled with gas bubbles.)

Try This

Have students complete *Try This.*

Answers to *Try This*

Sample answer: Diatoms are algae that serve as a major food source for animals that live in the sea; diatoms also produce much of the earth's oxygen.

 Use *Reading Skills Workbook,* Lesson 1, pages 1–7. See *Providing for Individual Differences,* page T24, for additional practice.

Vocabulary Study:
Multiple Meanings

Pages 8–9

Objective

M   To use context clues to determine the meanings of multiple-meaning words

SKILLS CODE NUMBER
3.5.5; 3.0.2

Developing the Skill

1. Tell students that the *Vocabulary Study* they are about to read is about a dribbling perch. Ask if anyone can guess what a dribbling perch might be. If possible, elicit a few answers. Explain that the *Vocabulary Study* will give them various meanings for *dribbling*, *perch*, and *litter*.

2. Have students read the *Vocabulary Study* and do the *Word Play* activities.

Answers to *Word Play*

1. **a.** a freshwater fish; **b.** a high resting place; **c.** bouncing a ball; **d.** drooling; **e.** rubbish; **f.** the young that were born at one time; **2.** Sentences will vary.

 Use *Reading Skills Workbook*, Lesson 2, page 8. See *Providing for Individual Differences*, page T24, for additional practice.

VOCABULARY STUDY
Multiple Meanings

"I have here a very unusual item, ladies and gentlemen. What am I bid for this *dribbling perch* that comes with its own *litter?*"

"Excuse me, please. What do you mean by **perch**? Is that thing a *freshwater fish*, or is it a *high resting place*, such as for a bird?"

"The answer to your questions, madam, is yes. Now, who will start the bidding for the *dribbling perch?*"

"Hold it! What do you mean by **dribbling**? Is that perch thing *drooling*, or is it *bouncing or kicking a ball very quickly?*"

"The answer to your questions, sir, is yes. Now, come on folks. Let's get this auction under way. First, we have the *dribbling perch* and its *litter*. . . . Do I hear fifty dollars?"

"No. Not until you tell us what the **litter** is. Is it a *group of puppies or other young that were born at one time*, or is it *rubbish?*"

"The answer to that question is also yes! YES! YES! YES! Now please, ladies and gentlemen, I beg you. Give me a bid."

"I wouldn't give you two cents for that thing!"

"*I* wouldn't give you a quarter!"

"A quarter! The lady in blue says a quarter. Do I hear fifty cents?"

"Yes! Fifty cents!"

"One dollar!"

"Twenty dollars!"

"Do I hear twenty-five dollars? No? Going once . . . going twice . . . SOLD to the gentleman for twenty dollars! An excellent buy, sir. Will you pay for it with cash or a check?"

"You know, I like the idea of words having more than one meaning. I think I'll write you a check!"

8

Word Play

1. What do *perch*, *dribbling*, and *litter* mean in the sentences below?

   a. The first time I went fishing, I caught a **perch**.
   b. I looked up and saw the bird on its **perch**.
   c. Basketball players do a lot of **dribbling** during a game.
   d. The monster was **dribbling** water from its mouth.
   e. We cleaned up the **litter** on the sidewalk.
   f. That kitten is the cutest in the **litter**.

2. Look up *check* in a dictionary. Make up a sentence for each different meaning of the word.

9

Reading Selection:
A Boy and a Raccoon

Pages 10–19

Objectives

		SKILLS CODE NUMBER
M, T	To identify and use context clues to determine word meaning	3.0.2
M, T	To identify definitions in context	3.0
M, T	To identify and use synonyms as context clues	3.5.4; 3.0
M, T	To identify and use antonyms as context clues	3.5.3; 3.0
M	To determine the correct sequence for a set of events	3.3.7.4
M	To distinguish between fact and opinion	3.6.3

 # Preparing to Read

Summary

NOTE: The summary is included for the teacher's convenience and should not be read to students.

One happy summer when the author was a boy, he and a motherless young raccoon played and explored the countryside together. "Rascal" was partly a pet and, remarkably, was partly a friend. Through the narration of delightful incidents, the author shows that an animal may display many seemingly human traits yet still remain true to the nature of the wild.

Background

Raccoons are omnivorous mammals that are native to North and Central America. They usually live in wooded swamps or in forests near streams or lakes. Raccoons are generally nocturnal, but also hunt during the day. In the north, raccoons stay in their nests in a state of semi-hibernation during the coldest parts of the year. Raccoons, like most other wild animals, generally do *not* make good pets and will bite if approached by humans.

The following books will provide you with additional background information.

Herriot, James. *All Things Wise and Wonderful.* Continuation of the story of a veterinary surgeon. Sequel to *All Things Bright and Beautiful* and *All Creatures Great and Small.*

Honders, John, ed. *The World of Mammals.* The characteristics of mammals from aardvark to zebu.

Developing Vocabulary and Concepts

curiosity: a desire to learn or know
yelped: made a sharp, high-pitched cry or bark
shallow: not deep; shallows: a shallow place in a body of water
companion: one who shares in what another is doing
demon: a person having great energy or skill
tackle: equipment or gear for a particular use
active: busy or lively
coves: small bays

1. **a.** Read aloud the following sentences or write them on the board. If you read them aloud, write the underlined vocabulary on the board.

   Many wild animals seem to have a lot of <u>curiosity</u> about human beings. They seem to want to learn more about the humans.

   The dog <u>yelped</u> loudly at the burglar, who ran away at the dog's bark.

   The raccoon dropped his food into the <u>shallow</u> water. Because the water in the <u>shallows</u> was not deep, the raccoon could easily fish the food out again.

   When the boy went fishing, the raccoon was his <u>companion</u>. They enjoyed being together.

   The raccoon became a speed <u>demon</u> and enjoyed fast bicycle rides.

   Raccoons don't need fishing <u>tackle</u>—their claws are all the equipment they need for catching fish.

   Raccoons are usually <u>active</u> at night, but they are also busy looking for food during the day.

   The boy explored the <u>coves</u>—or bays—along the shore.

   b. Ask students to give the meaning of each vocabulary word. Remind them to use the context clues in the sentences to help them.

2. Encourage students to tell about pets they would like to have. Ask if anyone has ever cared for an unusual pet. Let students describe some of the personality traits and abilities of their pets.

 Use *Duplicating Masters 11,* page 1.

Summertime can be wonderful for . . .

A Boy and a Raccoon

by Sterling North

How do you feed a baby raccoon that weighs less than one pound?

Some people feed them with a medicine dropper or a doll's bottle. But I fed my tiny raccoon through a clean wheat straw. I took warm milk in my mouth. Then I tilted the <u>hollow</u> straw downward to his mouth and watched him suck eagerly.

I called my raccoon "Rascal" because he was such a <u>mischief</u>. He had shining black eyes, a mask like a little bandit, and five black rings around his fluffy tail. His whispered <u>trills</u> were full of wonder and curiosity. High up in the wide-spreading oak tree behind our house, there was a hole. The hole made a good home for Rascal. Here he dreamed away his first two months, sleeping happily between feedings.

10

11

Setting Purposes

Skills

Have students read the skills note at the top of page 10. Remind them of the kinds of context clues they often find in their reading. (definitions given in context; the general context of a sentence and the larger context of a paragraph; synonyms and antonyms) Before they read, have students look at the second sentence in the third paragraph on page 10. Ask them to find the context clue to the meaning of the word *bandit*. (a mask)

Content

Have students read the lead-in to the title. Ask what things a small-town boy might do in the summertime. Could a pet do any of those things with him? Explain that they are going to read a *true* story about a boy with a very unusual pet.

Reading and Discussing

Have students read the selection. Most students will be able to complete it in one sitting. If you prefer, the selection may be read in two parts, breaking before the heading, "Rascal the Speed Demon" on page 16.

NOTE: The questions that appear in the student's text at the end of the selection focus on comprehension of selection content and on application of the *Skills Lesson* to the selection. Answers to these questions begin on page T19.

At the foot of this great tree lay my big Saint Bernard, Wowser. He was a dependable watchdog who protected all my pets.

Wowser was a handsome animal weighing 170 pounds. Only a brave dog or a foolish person would have tried to disturb Wowser's new friend, my little raccoon, Rascal.

One day in June, Wowser and I heard a trill at the hole in the tree. A moment later, we saw two bright eyes shining from a small, black mask. Rascal was peeking out at the world below from the door of his home. Soon he began backing down the tree like a little bear, tail first.

Wowser was worried. He yelped a question or two and looked up to see what I thought about this new problem. I told my dog not to worry, but to watch what happened.

I had a shallow minnow pool not far from the tree. Rascal hurried to the little pond and started fishing. His hands searched the shallows, while his eyes gazed far away, as though he were thinking of something else entirely. Soon his clever little hands caught a minnow. He began washing it back and forth, as raccoons do with almost everything they eat. Rascal carried his minnow to the edge of the pool, very pleased with himself. He began eating the small fish in polite, little bites. Then he started exploring the back yard around the oak tree.

Having explored his little world, my raccoon climbed the tree and disappeared into his safe home in the hollow of the oak. Wowser sighed with relief. Rascal was again safely in his nest. He had not hurt himself in any way.

13

14

The Mystery of the Disappearing Sugar

My father and I lived together in a little town in Wisconsin. He let me keep any number of pets and let me wander as free as the wind over meadows and hills. I knew that he would not mind having Rascal eat with us. From the attic I carried down the family high chair, last used when I was a baby.

At breakfast the next morning I put a shallow bowl of warm milk on the tray of the high chair. Rascal stood in the chair, placing his hands on the edge of the tray. He could reach the milk easily. He drank the milk, hardly dribbling a drop. In fact, his table manners were better than those of many children. My father smiled at our new breakfast companion. I was delighted at Rascal's good behavior.

All went well until I offered Rascal a lump of sugar. He took it between his two hands and began washing it back and forth in his milk, just as he had washed the fish. In a moment or two, of course, it melted entirely away. You could not imagine a more surprised little raccoon!

First he felt all over the bottom of the bowl to see if he had dropped it. Then he looked in his right hand. No sugar lump! Next he looked in his left hand. No sugar lump there either!

Finally he turned to me and shrilled a sharp question: Who had stolen his lump of sugar?

When I stopped laughing, I gave him a second lump. He thought about washing it, but then a look came into his shining eyes. He took the sugar directly into his mouth and chewed it happily.

15

Rascal was a very bright raccoon. When he learned a lesson, he learned it for life. Never again did he try to wash a lump of sugar.

Rascal, the Speed Demon

A boy, a bicycle, a little raccoon! Imagine the adventures we had! Rascal had become a speed demon. He liked nothing better than whizzing down a steep hill. This lovable little animal had the heart of a lion. He liked to stand in the basket of my bicycle with his feet wide apart and his hands holding the front rim of the basket. His natural goggles made him look like a racing driver. His small button of a nose pointed straight into the wind, and his whiskers blew back nearly to his ears as his long tail streamed out behind.

Sometimes he shared the bicycle basket with bunches of radishes that I raised in my garden and sold to the grocery stores. Other times, when we went to the river to fish, Rascal shared the basket with my box of fishing tackle.

Summer Fun

Summer passes all too quickly for an active boy of eleven. Rascal and I often went fishing below the dam in the river. I fished for big, fighting silver catfish in my favorite hole, below a pleasant sand-bar. Rascal, meanwhile, fished in the shallows along the edge of the bar. He often grabbed a crayfish—those little monsters that look so much like small, freshwater lobsters. These he washed and ate, tail first, with great delight.

16

Even with mowing lawns and working in my garden, I always found time to read. I would lie in the hammock and listen to all the sounds of summer.

Sometimes my father would hang a sign on the office door: GONE FOR THE DAY.

Then, I'd fill a picnic basket with sandwiches and a few bottles of soda. My father and Rascal and I would climb happily into the front seat of our car, with the top back and the windshield down. All three of us wore goggles—Rascal's being natural, of course. He liked to perch between us on the back of the seat. He looked joyfully ahead as we headed up the road toward Lake Koshkonong.

17

Here we hunted for arrowheads, searched a nearby cave, or swam in the cold water. Rascal was a fine swimmer, dog-paddling along beside us until he grew tired. He thought of me as his protector when we were in deep water. He would climb on my shoulder or my head for a rest. Often I would float on my back and raise my chest above the water. This gave him a better resting place. As soon as he had caught his breath, he would dive in again. Then he would paddle along bravely through the little waves as we explored the coves and grassy points along the sandy shore.

Sterling North is a well-known author of books for young people. This selection comes from his book **Little Rascal.** Even as a boy in 1918, Mr. North believed that wild animals should not be kept as pets. Though he enjoyed Rascal's visits, he knew that the raccoon belonged in its natural home—the forest. He showed how much he truly loved Rascal when he encouraged the raccoon to return to the wild at the end of the summer.

18

Understanding What You've Read

1. How old was Rascal when the boy first found him?
2. How did the boy know that his father would not mind having Rascal in the house?
3. What things showed that Rascal was bright?
4. Why did the boy let the raccoon sleep in a tree, fish for minnows, and swim in the lake?
5. What might have happened if the boy had not encouraged the raccoon to return to the wild?

Applying the Skills Lesson

What is the meaning of each of the words in italics below? Choose one of the meanings given below the sentences. What words in the context give you clues to the meanings of the words?

1. Rascal carried his *minnow* to the edge of the pool. . . . He began eating the small fish in polite, little bites.

    a. a small, freshwater fish   b. a kind of rock

2. All three of us wore *goggles*—Rascal's being natural, of course.

    a. tall hats   b. large eyeglasses, with side guards

3. His whispered *trills* were full of wonder and curiosity.

    a. warbling sounds   b. movements

19

washing it.   page 15   He knew he could rest on the boy's body if he grew tired of swimming.   page 18   Accept other reasonable answers.) INFERENTIAL <u>Drawing conclusions</u>

● *The author says, "When he (Rascal) learned a lesson, he learned it for life." Why does the author believe this?* (Rascal never washed a sugar cube again. page 16) INFERENTIAL   <u>Drawing conclusions</u>

● *What do you think Rascal had the most fun doing? Why do you think so?* (Let students discuss their choices. They may explain their answers by finding passages in the selection to read aloud.) INFERENTIAL <u>Making judgments</u>

4. *Why did the boy let the raccoon sleep in a tree, fish for minnows, and swim in the lake?* (He believed that wild animals should not be kept as pets and that Rascal belonged in his natural home.   page 18) INFERENTIAL   <u>Identifying cause-and-effect relationships</u>

5. *What might have happened if the boy had not encouraged the raccoon to return to the wild?* (Accept all reasonable answers.) CRITICAL   <u>Predicting outcomes</u>

Questions preceded by a bullet are additional questions and appear in the Teacher's Edition only. The other questions appear in the student's text after the selection.

Understanding What You've Read

1. *How old was Rascal when the boy first found him?* (He was a tiny baby, probably just born.   page 10) INFERENTIAL   <u>Drawing conclusions</u>

● *Name one or two ways in which the baby raccoon was like a very young human baby.* (He had to be fed warm milk; he slept most of the time.   page 10) INFERENTIAL   <u>Making comparisons</u>

2. *How did the boy know that his father would not mind having Rascal in the house?* (In the past the father had let the boy keep a lot of pets.   page 15) INFERENTIAL   <u>Predicting outcomes</u>

● *What things did the boy and the raccoon do together?* (ate together; rode a bicycle; fished; picnicked; swam   pages 15–18) LITERAL   <u>Recalling stated information</u>

3. *What things showed that Rascal was bright?* (Possible answers: Rascal drank milk from a bowl.   page 15   Rascal ate the second sugar cube instead of

Applying the Skills Lesson

What is the meaning of each of the words in italics below? Choose one of the meanings given below the sentences. What words in the context give you clues to the meanings of the words? (The words the students are to determine meanings for are underlined.)
1. *Rascal carried his <u>minnow</u> to the edge of the pool. . . . He began eating the small fish in polite, little bites.*
a. *a small, freshwater fish*   b. *a kind of rock*
2. *All three of us wore <u>goggles</u>—Rascal's being natural, of course.*
a. *tall hats*   b. *large eyeglasses, with side guards*
3. *His whispered <u>trills</u> were full of wonder and curiosity.*
a. *warbling sounds*   b. *movements*
(1. a;   Clue: "the small fish";   2. b;   Clue: "Rascal's being natural";   Point out that the picture also acts as a context clue.   3. a;   Clue: "whispered") <u>Identifying and using context clues to determine word meaning</u>

● *In the last paragraph on page 16, Rascal catches a crayfish. How does the author help you understand what a crayfish is?* (In the same sentence, the author says that crayfish are "those little monsters that look so much like small, freshwater lobsters.")   <u>Identifying definitions in context</u>

- *What synonym helps you understand the meaning of curiosity in the sentence "His whispered trills were full of wonder and curiosity"? Explain what curiosity means.* (Synonym: wonder; Meaning: a desire to learn or know) <u>Identifying and using synonyms as context clues</u>

 Use *Duplicating Masters 11*, page 2. See *Providing for Individual Differences*, page T24, for additional practice.

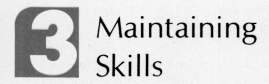 # Maintaining Skills

Comprehension Skills

Determining the correct sequence for a set of events
Explain that a story can be difficult to understand if events are not told in the order in which they happened. Write the following sentences on the board. Ask students to read them and decide whether the order of the events makes sense. (They do not make sense because the sequence is incorrect.) Have students put the events into the right time order. Allow them to refer to the selection.

1. Rascal was greatly surprised.
2. Rascal washed a lump of sugar in his milk.
3. Rascal ate the sugar without trying to wash it.
4. The boy put Rascal into a high chair and gave him a bowl of milk.
5. The lump of sugar melted away.
6. Rascal had learned a lesson for life.
7. The boy gave Rascal another lump of sugar.
(Correct order: 4, 2, 5, 1, 7, 3, 6)

Distinguishing between fact and opinion Remind students that a fact is something known to be true, but an opinion is only what someone believes. Read aloud the following sentences. Ask students to identify each sentence as a fact or an opinion.

Wowser weighed 170 pounds. (fact)
Wowser was a handsome animal. (opinion)
Rascal was a mischief. (opinion)
He had shining black eyes, a mask like a little bandit, and five black rings around his fluffy tail. (fact)
In a moment or two, of course, the sugar lump melted entirely away. (fact)
You could not imagine a more surprised little raccoon. (opinion)

 For additional resources and curriculum-related activities, see *Enrichment*, page T25.

Textbook Study:
Using Context Clues
Pages 20–23

Objectives

		SKILLS CODE NUMBER
M, T	To identify definitions in context	3.0
M, T	To identify and use context clues to determine word meaning	3.0.2

Applying the Skill

Have students read the introduction and the two selections. You may wish to have them read the selections on their own and then do *Building Skills*. Or you may wish to direct students, using the following procedure.

Using Context Clues in Science

1. Have students read the first paragraph and answer the question in the sidenote on page 20. Point out that the heading *Scattering* is in boldfaced type. Ask students what *scattering* means. (separating and going in many directions)

TEXTBOOK STUDY

Using Context Clues

Whenever you read a textbook, use all your skills to understand the meanings of new words. Look for context clues that may help you. Notice any words printed in boldface or italic type. They may be defined in context, or they may be found in the glossary of your textbook.

As you read the following textbook selections, use the sidenotes to help you find clues to the meanings of new words.

Using Context Clues in Science

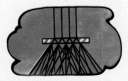

Words in headings like this will usually be explained. What is *scattering*?

SCATTERING. When light passes through things, it does not always travel in the same way. For example, when light passes through some things, such as frosted glass, it scatters. That is, the light separates and goes in many directions. If you were to look at this kind of glass, you could see light shining through it. However,

20

you could not see objects very well through the glass.

Things which you cannot see through very well, such as frosted glass, are *translucent*. Thin cloth and thin paper are such things. When do you think it is important to have something that scatters light?

[sidenote] A word in italics is often explained or defined in context. What does this word mean?

PASSING STRAIGHT THROUGH. Light can pass through some things in another way. It can pass straight through these things. Such things are *transparent*. Some transparent things are clear glass, air, and water. Because light can pass straight through transparent things, you can see through them clearly. What other transparent things can you think of? When might you want to be able to see through something?

[sidenote] Very often, examples are given to help you understand a new word. What examples are given to help you understand the word transparent*?*

— *Exploring Science: Green Book*
Laidlaw Brothers

21

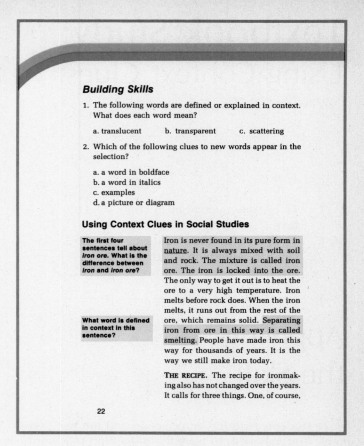

Building Skills

1. The following words are defined or explained in context. What does each word mean?

   a. translucent   b. transparent   c. scattering

2. Which of the following clues to new words appear in the selection?

   a. a word in boldface
   b. a word in italics
   c. examples
   d. a picture or diagram

Using Context Clues in Social Studies

[sidenote] The first four sentences tell about iron ore*. What is the difference between* iron *and* iron ore*?*

Iron is never found in its pure form in nature. It is always mixed with soil and rock. The mixture is called iron ore. The iron is locked into the ore. The only way to get it out is to heat the ore to a very high temperature. Iron melts before rock does. When the iron melts, it runs out from the rest of the ore, which remains solid. Separating iron from ore in this way is called smelting. People have made iron this way for thousands of years. It is the way we still make iron today.

[sidenote] What word is defined in context in this sentence?

THE RECIPE. The recipe for ironmaking also has not changed over the years. It calls for three things. One, of course,

22

2. Have students read the first full paragraph on page 21 and the first sidenote. Point out that the word *translucent* is in italics. Ask what *translucent* things are. (things which you cannot see through very well)

3. Have students read the text after the heading *Passing Straight Through* and answer the question in the last sidenote. (clear glass, air, water)

4. Have students complete *Building Skills.*

Answers to *Building Skills* Science Selection

1. **a.** allowing light to pass through but without giving clear view; **b.** allowing light to pass through and giving clear view; **c.** light separating and going in many directions; 2. All items listed were context clues.

Using Context Clues in Social Studies

1. Have students read the first paragraph in the selection and answer the question in the first sidenote. (Iron ore is a mixture of iron, soil, and rock; iron is one of the elements in iron ore.)

2. Have students answer the question in the second sidenote. (smelting)

is iron ore. Another is a fuel that can make a fire hot enough to melt iron. The third is a mineral called lime-stone. When iron is melted out of the ore, it is not really pure. There are still bits of rock, dirt, and other things mixed with it. Limestone helps get them out. It melts along with the iron and mixes with these other things. Together, they float to the top. That floating stuff is called slag. The slag is then skimmed off. What remains is pure iron.

Limestone may be a new word to you. The context tells you what it is (a mineral), and what it does. What does *limestone* do in ironmaking?

Slag is defined in context. What is *slag*?

—*People in the Americas*
Silver Burdett

Building Skills

Not every new word in the selection is defined in con-text. See if you know what each word below means. Match each word in column 1 with its meaning in column 2.

1	2
1. skimmed	a. any natural substance, such as coal, that is not a plant or animal
2. mineral	b. removed floating matter from the sur-face of a liquid
3. recipe	c. a type of mineral, such as marble, that contains calcium
4. fuel	d. a set of directions or a way to get a desired result
5. limestone	e. something that produces energy

23

3. Have students read the text after the heading *The Recipe* and answer the question in the first sidenote on page 23. (Limestone helps get the bits of rock, dirt, and other impurities out of the iron ore.)

4. Have students answer the question in the last side-note. (Slag is the rock, dirt, other impurities, and limestone that float to the top of the melted iron.)

5. Have students complete *Building Skills*.

Answers to *Building Skills*
Social Studies Selection

1. b; 2. a; 3. d; 4. e; 5. c

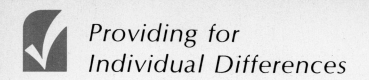

Providing for Individual Differences

NOTE: The exercises in this section are optional. They reinforce skills that have already been taught in this unit. Take into account individual needs when deciding which exercises to use.

Additional Practice activities reinforce the skills at the level of difficulty at which they were initially presented. Challenge Activities are designed for students who have mastered the basic concepts. A complete explanation of this section is in the Sample Teaching Unit at the front of this Teacher's Edition.

Skills Lesson

Additional Practice

Worksheet 1, Teacher's Edition, page T480

Vocabulary Study

Additional Practice

■ **Using context clues to determine meaning**
Write the following four words on the board. Then read aloud the sentences and have students give the meaning of each word according to its use in the sentence.

> bid   buy   quarter   litter

> I made the highest *bid* for the drooling fish. (offer of money for an item)
> And now it's time to *bid* goodnight. (give a greeting or farewell)
> Tom told me why he was late, but I don't *buy* his excuse. (believe)
> At twenty-five dollars, the perch was an excellent *buy.* (bargain)
> The lady in blue paid a *quarter* for the fish. (twenty-five cents)
> There are many empty lots in that *quarter* of the city. (section or area)
> The farmer made a *litter* of straw for the animals to lie on. (bedding of straw, hay, or leaves used by animals)
> When David broke his leg, he had to be carried on a *litter.* (stretcher)

Reading Selection: A Boy and a Raccoon

Additional Practice

■ **Using synonyms to determine meaning**   Remind students that synonyms are words with the same or nearly the same meaning and that antonyms are words with opposite meanings. Explain that an author often uses a synonym or an antonym to help explain another word. Then write the following sentences on the board or read them aloud. Ask students to find the synonyms in each sentence.

> A very young animal often looks clumsy and awkward when it walks. (clumsy, awkward)
> The two babies cried a great deal, as infants often do. (babies, infants)
> The girl rode happily along, looking joyfully ahead. (happily, joyfully)
> Maria was always kind and considerate to people who were in need of help. (kind, considerate)

Ask students to find the antonyms in each of the following sentences.

> Harry happily looked forward to the journey, but Mary thought about it gloomily all day. (happily, gloomily)
> After all the noise we had heard, we could hardly believe there was silence at last. (noise, silence)
> The going was very rough until we got back on the smooth pavement. (rough, smooth)
> After carrying the heavy suitcase all day, she found the shopping bag to be very light. (heavy, light)

Challenge Activity

■ **Identifying context clues**   Read aloud the following sentences and write the italicized words on the board. Have students tell what they think each word means. Also have them identify the context clues that helped them.

> After Jane begged and *pleaded* to go on the trip, her parents agreed. (asked earnestly for help; Clue: synonym "begged")
> The movie was so confusing, he was unable to *comprehend* it. (understand; Clue: "confusing")
> Cats and dogs are *carnivorous*—eating or living on meat. (meat-eating; Clue: definition in context)

Evaluation

Periodic Test 1, Part I, Form A or *Form B,* may be administered after this unit to test skills marked **T.** If you have pretested using *Form A,* administer *Form B.*

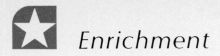

Enrichment

A Boy and a Raccoon

Bibliography

The following books are about unusual pets.

Easy

Adamson, Joy. *Elsa.* A short version of *Born Free*—the true story of a lioness raised by people who taught her to stalk and kill so that she could be set free in the jungle.

Average

Milne, Lorus J. *Gifts from the Sky.* The true story of a mute swan that came to live in the author's home-town.

North, Sterling. *Little Rascal.* An eleven-year-old catches a raccoon kit, raises it, and then sets it free.

Zim, Herbert S. *Golden Guide to Mammals.* Pictures and descriptions of 218 American animals.

Challenging

Weber, William J. *Wild Orphan Babies (Mammals and Birds): Caring For Them and Setting Them Free,* 2nd ed. A handbook offering instruction on the housing, feeding, and general care of orphaned wild animal babies and how to prepare them for life in the wild.

Films and Filmstrips

NOTE: For more information, see *Resource Center.*

Skills

Guidance Assocs. *Using Your Reading Skills Series.* "Finding Word Clues": Part I, context clues to word meanings in mathematics, science, social studies, and language arts.

Selection content

Ealing Films. *The Yearling: Reading Skills Kit.* A young boy in the Florida backwoods raises a young deer as a pet.

Curriculum Coordination

Language Arts

1. Other sections of Rascal's story (see *Bibliography*) may be read aloud to the class. You may also want to have a copy of the book kept in the classroom so that students may have the opportunity to read it.

2. Have students write a poem about a creature or creatures of the wild.

3. Have students prepare and give short talks about their own pets.

Science

1. Schedule a trip to a zoo or an animal farm to see raccoons and other animals of the raccoon family (ringtail cats, kinkajous, Australian "honey bears," coatimundis).

2. If a wildlife specialist or expert on the outdoors lives in or near your community, invite him or her to talk with students about the value of studying wildlife and how students can study wildlife in their own community. Interested students can write to the National Wildlife Federation. (See *Resource Center.*)

3. Integrate a lesson on ecology with this selection. For example, since raccoons feed on rodents and insects as well as on other foods, what could happen to crops if all the raccoons left an area where there were many rodents and insects?

Career Education

Some students may want to do research on career opportunities in veterinary medicine. You might ask a veterinarian to be a guest speaker. Students can also check various encyclopedias for information. Perhaps your school or public library has a special section for career information. Students can also write for information about veterinary medicine as a career. (See *Resource Center.*)

Contents

Additional Materials

Reading Skills Workbook: Lessons 3–4, pages 9–14
Duplicating Masters 11: pages 3–6
Worksheet 2: Teacher's Edition, page T481
Periodic Test 1, Part II

Key to Symbols

Skills Objectives
I* — Introduced in this unit
I — Introduced earlier in this level
M — Maintained from previous levels
T — Tested in periodic and cumulative tests for this level

Reduced Student Pages
underscore — words that appear in the glossary
wavy line — words pretaught in the Teacher's Edition
          (these words also appear in the glossary)

Skills Lesson:
Clues to Word Meaning
Pages 24–29

Objectives

		SKILLS CODE NUMBER
M, T	To identify sound-letter relationships	2.1; 2.2
M, T	To identify the number of syllables in a word	2.6
M, T	To identify word parts: root words, prefixes, and suffixes	4.1
M, T	To identify base words in compound words	4.2.1

If you wish to pretest the skills listed above, you may administer *Periodic Test 1, Part II, Form A. Periodic Test 1, Part II, Form B,* may be administered to posttest.

Introducing the Lesson

1. **a.** On the board, write a sentence that contains a word that students will not know, such as:

   The play is so confusing, it is easy to <u>misconstrue</u> the plot.

   Ask them how they would go about figuring out the meaning of the word *misconstrue* (which means "to misunderstand or interpret wrongly").

Clues to Word Meaning

You find new words everywhere. You find them in your textbooks and in the books you read for fun. You find them when you talk with people or when you watch TV. What are some other places in which you find new words?

Suppose you meet a new word in your reading. What are some of the things you can do to learn what it means?

24

Look at the following list of things you can do to learn new words.

• You can use what you know about sound–letter relationships. You can try to divide the word into syllables. When you can say the word, you often find that you have heard it before. It may not really be a "new" word after all.
• You can look for clues to meaning within the word. Is it a compound word? Is there a prefix or suffix? Does the word have a root within it?
• You can look for clues in the context. Other words in the same sentence or in other sentences may give you help.
• You can look up the word in a glossary or dictionary.

Do you need to do all these things with every new word? Of course not. Often, however, you will use two or three clues to help you find the meaning of a new word.

Using Sound–Letter Relationships

You know what sounds letters stand for. So you can **decode** most words that you've never seen in print before. When you do so, you often find that they're words you know "by ear." Perhaps the word *squid* is one that you have not seen before. You can pronounce it because you know what sounds its letters stand for. Once you have said the word, you may know that a squid is a sea animal with many arms.

Syllables Help in Pronouncing Words

Knowing about sound–letter relationships can help you pronounce a word like *squid*. But how do you tackle a long,

25

---

b. Let students discuss the different methods they would use to determine the meaning. These may include dividing the word into syllables to decode it (*mis·con·strue*), looking for familiar prefixes, suffixes, and root words (the prefix *mis-* means "bad" or "wrong"), and looking for context clues to its meaning. (In the example sentence, the context clue is *confusing*.) As a final check, students might look up the word in the dictionary.

2. Have students turn to page 24, examine the illustration, and read the introductory paragraphs. Have them name other places in which they have come across new words.

Developing the Skill

When you meet a new word in your reading, there are several things you can do to learn what the word means.

1. Have students read the first sentence on page 25 and the following list. Ask students which of these methods were used when the class was trying to figure out the meaning of *misconstrue*. (all four methods)

2. a. Have students read the paragraph under the list. Then write the following sentence on the board.

The scientist had studied geology, so she knew what kind of rock she'd found.

Ask students to define *geology*. (the study of the earth)

b. Ask students to find two context clues in the sentence you wrote. ("scientist" and "what kind of rock")

c. Ask students the meanings of the Greek word parts *geo-* (earth) and *-logy*. (study of)

d. Finally, you may want the class to check their glossaries for the meaning of *geology*.

Using Sound-Letter Relationships

When you see a word you don't know, you should try to pronounce it.

1. Have students read the explanatory paragraph below the heading. Ask them to relate instances when they've found that they know a word "by ear."

2. a. Write the following words on the board. Tell students that they should be able to pronounce the words even if they have never seen them before.

collateral   lode   tolerable
dissonant   roan   proscription

unfamiliar word? Dividing a word into syllables can help you say it. Look at this sentence:

● The scientist studying the *bacteria* had a *fabulous* idea.

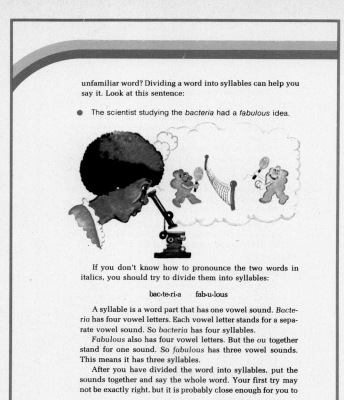

If you don't know how to pronounce the two words in italics, you should try to divide them into syllables:

bac·te·ri·a   fab·u·lous

A syllable is a word part that has one vowel sound. *Bacteria* has four vowel letters. Each vowel letter stands for a separate vowel sound. So *bacteria* has four syllables.

Fabulous also has four vowel letters. But the *ou* together stand for one sound. So *fabulous* has three vowel sounds. This means it has three syllables.

After you have divided the word into syllables, put the sounds together and say the whole word. Your first try may not be exactly right, but it is probably close enough for you to

26

recognize each word. Say the words *bacteria* and *fabulous*. Now do you know that bacteria are tiny living things? Did you recognize that *fabulous* means "wonderful"?

Try This

Read the sentences below. If the words in italics are new to you, try to decode them. Break them into syllables and try to say them. Once you say them, you may find you know what they mean. Match each word with one of the meanings listed below the sentence. Then look up the words in a dictionary.

1. The tiny animal could be seen only under a *microscope*.

   a. a mountain filled with caves
   b. a large animal that does not cast a shadow
   c. an instrument used to magnify very small things

2. Mopsy is just an *ordinary* dog.

   a. brown   b. common   c. fat

Word Parts Help with Meaning

Words are made up of units of meaning. The word *glowworm* has two units of meaning: *glow* and *worm*. Notice that each of these units of meaning is a whole word. These two words, when put together, form a **compound** word.

In some compound words (like *glowworm*), it is easy to see how the meaning of each word helps you understand the meaning of the compound word. In other compound words, however, the meaning of the whole word cannot be found by

27

---

b. Explain that students were able to pronounce these words because they used two of their reading skills: They figured out what sounds the letters stand for, and they figured out the number of vowel sounds (syllables) in each word.

Syllables Help in Pronouncing Words

Dividing a long, unfamiliar word into syllables can help to pronounce it.

1. Have students read the paragraph below the heading on page 25 and the example sentence on page 26. Have them try to pronounce the words in italics.

2. Have students read the next four explanatory paragraphs and examine the syllabicated words.

3. **a.** Have students identify the number of syllables in each word that you listed on the board. (*collateral:* four; *dissonant:* three; *lode:* one; *roan:* one; *tolerable:* four; *proscription:* three)

   b. Ask students in which of these words two vowel letters stand for one sound. (*roan; proscription*)

Try This

Have students complete *Try This*.

Answers to *Try This*

1. c; **2.** b

Word Parts Help with Meaning

The meaning of a compound word may or may not be determined by combining the meaning of its shorter words.

Have students read the explanatory paragraphs and the three compound words. Ask which compound words have meanings that can be determined by combining the meanings of the separate words. (*buttonhole; headache*)

simply combining the meanings of the separate words. You may have to use your imagination to figure out what the compound word means. Look at the compound words below. In which ones can you find the meaning simply by combining the meanings of the separate words?

buttonhole   skyscraper   headache

You can find the meaning of *buttonhole* and *headache* by combining the meanings of the separate words. But a skyscraper is not something that scrapes the sky. It is a very tall building.

Prefixes, Suffixes, and Root Words

Prefixes are units of meaning added to the beginnings of words. **Suffixes** are units of meaning added to the ends of words. Prefixes and suffixes are not whole words. They must be added to whole words. The unit of meaning to which a prefix or suffix is added is called the **root word**.

28

How many units of meaning are there in *unhelpful?* If you said three, you're right. You recognized the root word *help*, the prefix *un-*, and the suffix *-ful*. *Un-* means "not," and *-ful* means "full of." So you know that the whole word means "not full of help." Find the units of meaning in each of these three words.

unhappy   helpless   successful

Try This

1. Read the sentences below. Try to pronounce each of the words in italics. Notice the units of meaning. Separate the root word from its suffix or prefix. What does each whole word mean?

   a. A mineral is a *nonliving*, natural thing.
   b. John helped the baby until she could walk *unaided*.
   c. The *courageous* girl defended her sister.
   d. The tank held a *hammerhead* shark.
   e. Daisy is *unusually* late today.

2. Combine each root word in Column A with a prefix or suffix in Column B to make a new word. Then combine the words in Column A with other words to make as many compound words as you can.

A	B
cycle	-ing
set	bi-
soft	-y
sun	re-
motor	-en
total	-ly
dress	un-

Prefixes, Suffixes, and Root Words

Prefixes, suffixes, and root words are units of meaning in words.

Have students read the explanatory paragraphs. Then ask what the units of meaning are in *unhappy, helpless,* and *successful.* (*unhappy: un- + happy; helpless: help + -less; successful: success + -ful*)

Try This

Have students complete *Try This.*

Answers to *Try This*

1. a. *non-* + *living* = "not living"; **b.** *un-* + *aided* = "not aided"; **c.** *courage* + *-ous* = "full of courage"; **d.** *hammer* + *head* = "a shark with a head resembling a hammer"; **e.** *un-* + *usual* + *-ly* = "not in the usual manner"; **2.** Sample answers: *cycling, recycle, reset, resetting, setting, soften, softening, softly, sunny, sunning, motoring, totally, undress; motorcycle, sunset, sundress, motorboat.*

 Use *Reading Skills Workbook,* Lesson 3, pages 9–13. See *Providing for Individual Differences,* page T44, for additional practice.

Vocabulary Study:
Compound Words
Pages 30–31

Objective

		SKILLS CODE NUMBER
M, T	To identify base words in compound words	4.2.1

Developing the Skill

1. Tell students that the *Vocabulary Study* they are about to read contains several compound words. Ask students what a compound word is. (two or more shorter words combined to make a new word)

2. Ask students if they can figure out the meanings of the following compound words by combining the meanings of the shorter words that each is made from: *mushroom* (no); *typewriter* (yes); *backache* (yes); *butterfly* (no).

3. Have students read the *Vocabulary Study* and do the *Word Play* activity.

Answers to *Word Play*

eyesight: the power of seeing; vision; *windshield:* the front window of a car; *eyelashes:* hairs growing on the edges of the eyelids; *breathtaking:* very beautiful, taking one's breath away. Sentences will vary.

✓ Use *Reading Skills Workbook*, Lesson 4, page 14. See *Providing for Individual Differences*, page T44, for additional practice.

Reading Selection:
Penguin Paradise
Pages 32–37

Objectives

		SKILLS CODE NUMBER
M, T	To identify sound-letter relationships	2.1; 2.2
M, T	To identify the number of syllables in a word	2.6
M, T	To identify word parts: root words, prefixes, and suffixes	4.1
M	To draw conclusions based on given information and personal knowledge	3.4.1
M	To identify reference materials in which specific information may be found	5.11

 # Preparing to Read

Summary

Antarctic penguins are birds, but they cannot fly and really don't act like birds at all. The selection describes Admiral Richard E. Byrd's account of one of his expeditions to Antarctica and includes many incidents involving the birds. It also gives descriptions of the Adélie and emperor penguins, their extreme curiosity, general fearlessness, and love of "fun and games."

Background

Penguins do not live only in the Antarctic. When the author says that they are found "only in the southern part of the world" (page 33), she means only in the Southern Hemisphere. Penguins can be found in coastal areas of the Southern Hemisphere as far north as the equator. One breed (the Humboldt penguin) lives on islands off the west coast of South America and is known as far north as Peru. The penguin is not the only flightless bird—the ostrich is one that may be familiar to students, and there are a number of others.

The following book will provide you with additional background information.

Peterson, Roger T. *Birds*. A comprehensive study of the lives and habits of all birds, from prehistoric times to the present.

Developing Vocabulary and Concepts

rear admiral: in the U.S. Navy, an officer ranking just above a captain and just below a vice-admiral
respectfully: politely
squawk: a shrill, harsh cry

1. **a.** Read aloud the following sentences or write them on the board. If you read them aloud, write the underlined vocabulary on the board.

   Jane Gibbs is an officer, a <u>rear admiral</u>, in the United States Navy.
   The polite penguin bowed <u>respectfully</u> to the members of the crew.
   The penguin cried out with a loud <u>squawk</u> to show its anger at the dogs.

   b. Ask students to give the meaning of each vocabulary word. Remind them to use the context clues in the sentences to help them.

2. **a.** Introduce the idea of the Antarctic by asking if anyone knows which very cold part of the world is a home of penguins. (Students may answer "the South Pole.") Have someone find the south polar regions on a map or globe, and identify the continent of Antarctica.

   b. Explain that the region around the North Pole is called the Arctic, and the *opposite* region, around the South Pole, is the Antarctic. (Explain that *ant-*, as in *antonym*, means "against" or "opposite.") Tell students that the selection they will read describes some of the penguins that a great explorer encountered when he was in Antarctica.

3. Explain to students that there are several ranks in the U.S. Navy. Ask them if they know what any of these are. Then write *rear admiral* on the board and explain that this is a rank just above captain.

 Use *Duplicating Masters 11,* page 3.

To pronounce any words that are new to you, use what you know about sound–letter relationships. Breaking new words into syllables may help you say them. Look for units of meaning in any word that is new to you.

Travelers to the southernmost part of the world enjoy watching the strange birds in . . .

32

PENGUIN PARADISE

by Edna M. Andreas

When people first sailed far south to Antarctica, they met a bird that walked like a human, swam like a fish, and acted like a busybody. It didn't seem to be a bird at all until it became sleepy. Then, like every other bird in the world, it tucked its bill under its wing and went to sleep.

This strange bird was a penguin. It is found only in the southern part of the world. It shows no fear of people and sometimes is quite friendly.

Rear Admiral Richard E. Byrd made his first trip to Antarctica in 1928. Day by day, he kept a record of all that happened. On December 17, he wrote the story of his first meeting with live penguins.

33

Setting Purposes

Skills

Have students read the skills note at the top of page 32. Remind them that prefixes, suffixes, and root words can give them clues to the meanings of new words. Write *southern* and *southernmost* on the board. Help students recognize the root word *south* and the change in the pronunciation of *south* in the words *southern* and *southernmost*.

Content

Have students read the lead-in to the title. Ask them to read to find out why penguins would be fun to watch. Ask them to look for ways in which penguins are like other birds as well as ways in which they are different.

2 Reading and Discussing

Have students read the selection. Most students will be able to complete it in one sitting. If you prefer, the selection may be read in two parts, breaking before the heading "The Adélies" on page 35.

NOTE: The questions that appear in the student's text at the end of the selection focus on comprehension of selection content and on application of the *Skills Lesson* to the selection. Answers to these questions begin on page T34.

Meeting an Emperor

The Admiral's ship was sailing through the ice pack. This is a ring of floating ice which circles Antarctica. Suddenly, on some ice near the ship, Admiral Byrd spied an emperor penguin. He knew that Antarctica couldn't be very far away.

The emperor is the largest of all penguins. The one Byrd saw was nearly four feet tall. It was a handsome bird. Its back

Admiral Byrd and friends.

34

was gleaming black. Its chest feathers were the color of rich cream. On each side of its neck was a patch of golden yellow feathers. On its beak were bright orange lines. The beak was so long and the body so large that the emperor's head looked very small indeed.

The bird stood on its two feet. It looked quietly at the men as if to say, "I own this great land of ice and snow!" And this is almost true, for the emperor spends more of its life on Antarctica's shores than any other living thing. In fact, before the humans came to Antarctica, these birds had 6 million square miles of land all to themselves every winter. Other animals leave when winter and darkness come. But that is the very time the emperors raise their young!

Admiral Byrd was surprised to see how much this huge penguin looked like a person. In its fancy "coat" and "shirt," it seemed to be dressed for a grand party. Because the emperor looked so proud, the Admiral thought he should speak to it respectfully. But the penguin didn't want to speak to Byrd. It just bowed a little. Then the penguin turned and walked away.

The Adélies

Later, Byrd met another kind of penguin, the Adélie [ə-dā′lē]. These birds are smaller than the emperors. They are also more friendly. Whatever they do, they seem to have fun.

Many of the birds came near the Admiral's ship. Some came sliding down small hills of ice on their fat, round stomachs. Some of the sailors jumped onto the ice and played with the penguins. No one knew who had more fun—the sailors or the birds.

The Adélies swam like fish behind the ship. Now and then, a bird would race across the ice on its stomach. By pushing with its flippers, the Adélie could travel as fast as a person could walk.

A penguin's wings are not like other birds'. They are not built to lift the penguin's plump body off the ground. And they

Adélie feeding two chicks. The chicks will soon be old enough to leave for the sea.

35

are not usually called wings. They're called flippers.

A penguin's strong flippers are useful in many ways. They help to balance the bird when it walks. They serve as clubs during a fight. They help the bird glide over the snow. And, used as paddles, flippers make the penguin one of the world's best swimmers.

Who's Afraid? Not an Adélie!

As the sailors unloaded the ships, they were never alone. The Adélies followed them everywhere. The birds came close and stared with their funny round eyes. The white rings around their eyes made them look wide-awake and very wise.

Admiral Byrd soon learned that the Adélies were too curious and too fearless for their own good. Adélies are afraid of only three things in the world. They fear the leopard seals and killer whales that gobble penguins in the sea. They are also afraid of the skua [skyōō′ə] gulls that steal eggs and eat baby penguins. Nothing else can frighten an Adélie.

The birds showed that they had no fear of the great ships

nearby, or of the noisy people at work. They were not even afraid of the barking dogs that pulled the sleds.

In his book *Little America,* Admiral Byrd told about one brave Adélie. It came heading straight toward a team of nine sled dogs. The Admiral knew that it would take only one husky to kill an Adélie.

There was no stopping the noisy penguin. On and on it came. When it reached the team, it started to fight with all nine dogs at once. The nine dogs barked. The penguin squawked. The dogs tried to bite with their sharp, strong

36

Questions preceded by a bullet are additional questions and appear in the Teacher's Edition only. The other questions appear in the student's text after the selection.

Understanding What You've Read

1. *What is this selection chiefly about?*
   a. funny things Admiral Byrd saw a penguin do
   b. life in Antarctica
   c. penguins in general, and a few individual ones
   (Answer: c) INFERENTIAL   Identifying main idea

● *What is the name of the largest kind of penguin?* (the emperor penguin   page 34) LITERAL   Recalling specific details

● *What does the author think about emperor penguins?*
   a. They are unfriendly.
   b. They are proud and quiet.
   c. They are very friendly.
   (Answer: b   page 34) LITERAL   Identifying an author's conclusions

● *Name the different ways in which a penguin's flippers are useful.* (They help balance the penguin when it walks; they serve as clubs during a fight; they help the penguin glide over snow; they are used as paddles when the penguin swims, thus making the penguin an excellent swimmer.   page 36) LITERAL   Recalling stated information

2. *Why can't penguins fly?* (Their wings are not built for flying—they can't lift the penguin's body off the ground.   page 35) LITERAL   Identifying cause-and-effect relationships

● *What facts from the selection tell how fearless the Adélie penguins are?* (They were not afraid of the big ships, the noisy people at work, or the barking dogs.   page 36) LITERAL   Recalling specific details

3. *What are the only things Adélie penguins are afraid of? Why are they afraid?* (They are afraid of leopard seals and killer whales because they eat penguins, and of skua gulls because they steal eggs and eat baby penguins.   page 36) LITERAL   Identifying cause-and-effect relationships

4. *Why did Admiral Byrd rescue a penguin? How did the penguin seem to feel about being rescued?* (The penguin was trying to fight nine dogs at once and it would only take one husky to kill the penguin. The penguin seemed to be angry that Admiral Byrd had not let it finish the fight.   page 37) LITERAL   Recalling specific details

● *How do you think penguins might feel if they saw an airplane on the ground? How might they feel if they saw a plane flying low or about to land?* (Accept all reasonable answers. Penguins would probably be curious about a plane on the ground or might even try to fight with it. They might think a plane low in the air was a great skua gull or other great bird and would be frightened.) CRITICAL   Predicting outcomes

5. *Before people went to Antarctica, the penguins had the land to themselves. What effects do people have on an animal when they move into the animal's environment?* (Accept all reasonable answers.) CRITICAL   Predicting outcomes

Applying the Skills Lesson

How many syllables are there in each of the words below? Pronounce each word. What does each one mean?
1. Antarctica   4. admiral   7. emperor
2. plump   5. fearless   8. penguin
3. gleaming   6. Adélie   9. squawking
(1. four syllables; "a continent including the South Pole, almost totally within the Antarctic Circle, largely covered with ice. The word *Antarctic* means at the opposite part of the globe from the Arctic."
2. one syllable; "slightly fat or rounded"
3. two syllables; "shining"
4. three syllables; "in the U.S. Navy, an officer of the second highest rank"
5. two syllables; "without fear; not at all afraid"
6. three syllables; "a species of small penguin found in the Antarctic"; pronounced /ə•dā′lē/

7. three syllables; "the largest species of penguin found in the Antarctic"

8. two syllables; "a black-and-white swimming bird of the Antarctic"

9. two syllables; "giving a shrill, harsh cry")   Identifying sound-letter relationships/Identifying the number of syllables in a word

- *How many syllables are there in each of the words below? Pronounce each word and tell what it means.*
  1. tucked   3. stomach
  2. southern   4. husky
  (1. one syllable; "put or pressed into a close or hidden place"
  2. two syllables; "toward or in the south"
  3. two syllables; "a pouch in the digestive tract that receives food when it is swallowed, partially digests it, and passes it on to the intestines"
  4. two syllables; "a large, strong dog with thick fur, used by Eskimos and others to pull sleds")   Identifying sound-letter relationships/Identifying the number of syllables in a word

- *Identify the root word and suffix in each of the following words. Then use each unit of meaning to tell what the whole word means.*
  1. smaller   3. fearless
  2. useful   4. thankful
  (1. Root word: *small*; Suffix: -er; "more small"
  2. Root word: *use*; Suffix: -ful; "having use"
  3. Root word: *fear*; Suffix: -less; "without fear"
  4. Root word: *thank*; Suffix: -ful; "full of thanks")
  Identifying word parts: root words and suffixes

 Use *Duplicating Masters 11*, page 4. See *Providing for Individual Differences*, page T44, for additional practice.

3 Maintaining Skills

Comprehension Skills

Drawing conclusions   Review the difference between making a decision based on facts and "jumping to conclusions"—deciding something without really considering the facts. Explain that if students make sure they understand the facts, they will be on their way to a correct conclusion. Remind them that they often reason in this way when working out a mathematics problem.

Then ask the class to decide which numbered statement is the right conclusion for each of the following groups of facts. You may wish to write the possible conclusions on the board and read aloud the facts.

Other animals leave the Antarctic when winter comes. But that is the time the emperor penguins raise their young.

1. Other animals are smarter than emperor penguins.
2. The penguins are smarter than other animals.
3. Emperor penguins are suited to a very cold climate.
(Answer: 3)

A penguin does not fly. Its wings are not built to lift its body off the ground. The wings are called flippers. The birds use their flippers for balance when they walk and as paddles when they swim.

1. A penguin cannot really be a bird.
2. A penguin's wings are different from those of most other birds.
3. Since it is a bird, a penguin is bound to be able to fly.
(Answer: 2)

Study Skills

Using reference sources   Review some of the major uses of a dictionary, an encyclopedia, and an atlas. Then have students select from these three reference sources the best place or places to look for the following information:

the meaning of the word *squawk* (dictionary)
something about Admiral Byrd's life and exploration (encyclopedia)
the shape of Antarctica (atlas or encyclopedia)
facts about the Antarctic "ice pack" (encyclopedia)
how long penguins may live (encyclopedia)
how to pronounce the word *admiral* (dictionary)
a map of the region around Antarctica (atlas or encyclopedia)

For additional resources and curriculum-related activities, see *Enrichment*, page T46.

Reading Selection:
Living Lights in Our World
Pages 38–44

Objectives

		SKILLS CODE NUMBER
M, T	To identify base words in compound words	4.2.1
M, T	To identify word parts: root words, prefixes, and suffixes	4.1
M	To identify the stated main idea of a paragraph	3.3.8.3
M	To identify details that support the stated main idea of a paragraph	3.3.1; 3.3.8.3
M	To scan a selection for specific information	5.9

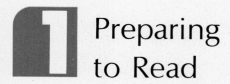

Preparing to Read

Summary

Fascinating and beautiful "living lights" exist in both the plant and animal kingdoms. Fireflies and glowworms are some of these. In the oceans there are microscopic organisms as well as larger sea creatures that sparkle, flash, or glow. All these living lights are "cold" lights in which no energy is lost as heat. Scientists hope that learning how living lights work may someday teach people how to make cold lights.

Background

The technical term for "living lights" is *bioluminescence.* The lumination is produced in a special body organ by the burning of a chemical called luciferin. The burning is triggered by an enzyme (luciferase) that the animal or plant secretes when it is properly stimulated. Several species of fish are bioluminescent and use their own lights to find their way in the dark.

The following books will provide you with additional background information on insects and bioluminescence.

Guiness, Alma, ed. *The Joy of Nature.* A reference book with projects for school and family. Also includes color photos of bioluminescent creatures.

Hutchins, Ross E. *Insects and Their Young.* The prehistory, development, habits, and characteristics of insects, with a section on bioluminescence. Illustrated, with index.

Tweedie, Michael. *Insects: World of Miniature Beauty.* Growth, self-protection, flight, senses, etc., of insects. With photographs.

Developing Vocabulary and Concepts

species: a group of animals or plants that have certain common characteristics and whose members can interbreed
perched: sat or placed on
grotto: a cave
burrows: holes made in the ground by certain animals
squid: a ten-armed sea animal

1. **a.** Read aloud the following sentences or write them on the board. If you read them aloud, write the underlined vocabulary on the board.

   There are several different species, or kinds, of fireflies.
   The fireflies perched on the branches of the tree before flying away.
   When the group walked into the grotto, or cave, they saw the lights of the glowworm.
   Fireworms live in burrows, or holes, at the bottom of the sea.
   Like an octopus, a squid is a many-armed sea animal.

   b. Ask students to give the meaning of each vocabulary word. Remind them to use the context clues in the sentences to help them.

2. Introduce the idea of "living lights" by asking if anyone has ever seen or caught an insect that had a "built-in flashlight." What was it? When they have identified fireflies (or "lightning bugs"), ask what might be a good expression with which to describe living things that flash or glow. ("living lights") Explain that the selection they are going to read tells of many other amazing "living lights" in the world besides the familiar firefly.

 Use *Duplicating Masters 11,* page 5. See *Providing for Individual Differences,* page T44, for additional practice.

38

In this selection, you will find many compound words. The separate units of meaning in a new word may give you a clue to the meaning of the whole word. Try to pronounce any word you find that is new to you.

On a summer evening, in a boat or on land, you may be able to see some of the lovely . . .

LIVING LIGHTS IN OUR WORLD

by Alvin and Virginia Silverstein

Tiny <u>flashes</u> of light are sprinkled through the summer evenings. These <u>winking</u> lights are made by living creatures called fireflies.

The firefly is not a fly. It is a dark-colored little beetle, about half an inch long. The male has four large wings and can fly swiftly through the air. But in many <u>species</u>, the female cannot fly.

Both male and female fireflies have something which most other beetles do not have. At the very end of its body, each firefly carries a light that it can turn on and off whenever it wants. This is no ordinary light. It is a living light.

How Living Lights Work

How does the firefly's light go on and off? Threadlike nerves reach deep into the firefly's body. Messages are carried along these nerves from the firefly's brain. This sets off a chemical <u>reaction</u> that makes a light flash on.

People love to watch the winking lights of the fireflies in the summer, nighttime sky. But did you know that the fireflies really use their lights as signals? They <u>flash</u> them on and off to signal other fireflies.

39

The firefly is a living light.

How often a firefly lights up <u>depends</u> on a number of things. First of all, it depends on the kind of firefly it is. One kind lights up every two seconds. Other kinds of fireflies light up at different rates.

You might want to signal to a firefly with a flashlight. You will have to signal at just the right time and at just the right speed — just as though you were a firefly. Some people have been able to fool fireflies with small lights. As long as the rate is right, the firefly will come toward the light.

There are more than sixty kinds of fireflies in the United States. Many other kinds of fireflies are found in different parts of the world. Some of them have very strange ways.

In Burma and in Thailand, hundreds or even thousands of fireflies may gather on a certain kind of tree growing near the water. <u>Perched</u> so thickly on branches that they may nearly cover the tree itself, they all light up together. No one has figured out why the Asian fireflies act in this strange way. Whatever the reason, these living lights are a <u>breathtaking</u> sight.

40

Setting Purposes

Skills

Have students read the skills note at the top of page 39. Review that a compound word is made up of two or more words and that the separate word meanings can often be put together to give the meaning of the compound word.

Content

Have students read the lead-in to the title. Ask them if they have ever seen any "living lights."

 # Reading and Discussing

Have students read the selection. Most will be able to complete it in one sitting. If you prefer, the selection may be read in two parts, breaking before the heading "Living Lights in the Sea" on page 41.

NOTE: The questions that appear in the student's text at the end of the selection focus on comprehension of selection content and on application of the *Skills Lesson* to the selection. Answers to these questions begin on page T39.

Glowworms

Some glowworms live in caves in <u>New Zealand</u>. They hang from the ceilings of the caves and spin sticky "fishing nets." These "nets" are similar to spider webs. Small insects that live in the caves see the bright lights and fly up to them. On the way, they are caught in the glowworms' "fishing lines." The successful glowworms pull in their sticky threads, gobble up their <u>prey</u>, and then lower their fishing lines again.

The tiny glowworms, grouped together in thousands on the ceilings of the caves, are a beautiful sight. About 50,000 tourists a year now visit the great Glowworm <u>Grotto</u> in New Zealand. There they are treated to a wonderful show.

Visitors enter the Glowworm Grotto in boats. They are carried along by an underground river. The tunnel entrance opens up into a huge cave, lighted by twinkling lights of tiny glowworms hanging from the ceiling. There are so many glowworms that their light is bright enough to read a book by. But if anyone should suddenly make a loud noise, every single light in the cave goes out. For a moment, there is darkness. Then,

slowly, one by one, the tiny lights wink on again.

Most glowworms glow only one color. But one large beetle, which lives in South America, has two different sets of colored lights. This is the railroad worm. When it is resting, a pair of bright red lights glows from its head. But when this strange creature begins to crawl, a row of bright green lights on each side of its body winks on. It looks like a little railroad train, with red headlights and green lights shining out the windows of the cars.

Living Lights in the Sea

Sometimes a ship plowing through the sea on a warm summer night may seem to <u>set</u> the water on fire. The <u>wake</u> of the ship sparkles and flashes. Floating and swimming along in the ocean <u>currents</u> are countless numbers of tiny creatures. Each is so small that you wouldn't be able to see it without a microscope. But together they make a dazzling show. When they are disturbed by a passing ship or a large fish, they begin to sparkle. Then, when the water is quiet again, their lights wink out, and all around them it is dark once more.

41

Above, glowworm with lights on.

Below, thousands of glowworms drop their "fishing lines" (sticky threads) to catch insects.

42

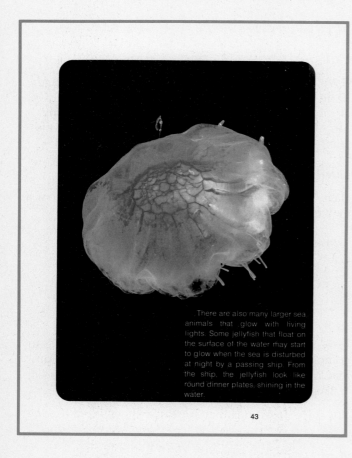

There are also many larger sea animals that glow with living lights. Some jellyfish that float on the surface of the water may start to glow when the sea is disturbed at night by a passing ship. From the ship, the jellyfish look like round dinner plates, shining in the water.

43

Questions preceded by a bullet are additonal questions and appear in the Teacher's Edition only. The other questions appear in the student's text after the selection.

Understanding What You've Read

1. *Why do fireflies light up?* (Messages are carried along the nerves from the firefly's brain. This sets off a chemical reaction that makes a light flash on. page 39) LITERAL __Identifying cause-and-effect relationships__

● *What would you have to do in order to fool a firefly by using a flashlight?* (You would have to signal at just the right time and speed.   page 40) LITERAL __Recalling stated information__

2. *What is meant by "living lights"?* (light given off by living things) INFERENTIAL __Identifying the main idea of a selection__

● *What are some kinds of living lights besides fireflies?* (glowworms; some sea life; some jellyfish; fireworms; some shrimps, clams, and squids.   pages 41, 43, and 44) LITERAL __Recalling specific details__

3. *Where does the railroad worm get its name?* (It has two sets of lights, one set green and one set red, that make it look like a tiny railroad train.   page 41) LITERAL __Recalling stated information__

● *In what way is one kind of glowworm like a spider?* (It spins sticky threads, similar to spider webs, to catch small insects.   pages 41 and 42) INFERENTIAL __Making comparisons__

Applying the Skills Lesson

1. *Look for units of meaning in the words below. What is the meaning of each word?*
flashlight   railroad   glowworm
(*flash* + *light:* "a small, battery-powered light that can be flashed on and off"
rail + *road:* "a road having steel rails that form a track for trains to travel on"
glow + *worm:* "a worm-shaped larva, or young form, of a beetle that glows"
Refer students to the glossary.)   __Identifying base words in compound words__

● *Look for two separate words in the following compound words. Then tell what each word means.*
nighttime   starlight   sunlight
(*night* + *time:* "the time from sunset to sunrise" or "when it is night"
star + *light:* "the light given off by a star"
sun + *light:* "the light of the sun")   __Identifying base words in compound words__

● *Identify the root word and the prefix or suffix in each of the following words. Then use each unit of meaning to tell what the compound word means.*
wonderful   countless   unlike
(*wonderful*—Root: *wonder;* Suffix: *-ful;* Meaning: "causing a person to be full of wonder"
countless—Root: *count;* Suffix: *-less;* Meaning: "without count"
unlike—Root: *like;* Prefix: *un-;* Meaning: "not like")   __Identifying word parts: root words, prefixes, and suffixes__

2. *What is the root word of each word below? What is the meaning of each whole word?*
suddenly   successful   darkness
(*suddenly*—Root: *sudden;* Meaning: "quickly"
successful—Root: *success;* Meaning: "having a favorable result"
darkness—Root: *dark;* Meaning: "the state of being without light")   __Identifying word parts: root words and suffixes__

 Use *Duplicating Masters 11,* page 6. See *Providing for Individual Differences,* page T44, for additonal practice.

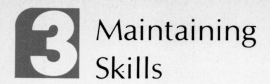

3 Maintaining Skills

Comprehension Skills

Identifying the stated main idea and supporting details of a paragraph   Review with the class the idea that the details in a paragraph often support the main idea and help the reader to understand it better. Point out also that details are related to each other, as well as to the main idea.

Have students read the second paragraph of the selection on page 39. Ask them to identify the main idea. ("The firefly is not a fly.") Then have them find the details that support the main idea. (It is a beetle; not all fireflies can fly.)

Have students identify the main idea of the second paragraph on page 44. ("Many other creatures of the deep sea carry their own lights.") Ask them to name creatures that are given as examples to support this main idea. (shrimps, clams, squids)

Study Skills

Scanning a selection for specific information   Have students scan to find out how many sections there are in the selection. (four: the opening and three other sections, as indicated by three headings within the selection) Also have them scan to find the location of the glowworms that spin what the authors call "fishing lines." (caves in New Zealand; first paragraph, page 41)

Next, have students scan the selection and answer the following questions.

How long is the section on glowworms? (four paragraphs, page 41)

Where does the railroad worm live? (South America; fourth paragraph, page 41)

Where can you find a description of how the firefly's light works? (On page 39, the first paragraph under the heading "How Living Lights Work." Some students may describe this paragraph as the one that begins with the question "How does the firefly's light go on and off?")

What heading guides you to information about sea life? On what page is the heading found? ("Living Lights in the Sea," page 41)

What kind of living lights can be seen in Burma and Thailand? (fireflies that gather on trees, described on page 40, last paragraph)

★ For additional resources and curriculum-related activities, see *Enrichment*, page T46.

Textbook Study:
Understanding New Words

Pages 45–48

Objectives

		SKILLS CODE NUMBER
M, T	To identify base words in compound words	4.2.1
M, T	To identify word parts: root words, prefixes, and suffixes	4.1

Applying the Skill

Have students read the introduction and the two selections. You may wish to have students read the selections on their own and do *Building Skills*. Or you may wish to direct students, using the following procedure.

TEXTBOOK STUDY

Understanding New Words

When you come to a new word in your textbooks, use what you know about sounds and letters to help you pronounce it. Use what you know about word parts for more help in figuring out its meaning.

The sidenotes for the first selection will help you to understand some of the words you may not know. Refer to them as you read. Try to answer the questions in them.

Understanding New Words in Social Studies

For years, people looked at <u>wetlands</u> and thought only of the ways in which such land might be put to work. So they drained them and built

Two words make up this compound word. Why is this word a good name for land that is covered by water most of the time?

45

Understanding New Words in Social Studies

1. Have students read the first paragraph and answer the question in the first sidenote. (The meaning of *wetlands* is apparent from the combined meanings of the two words.)

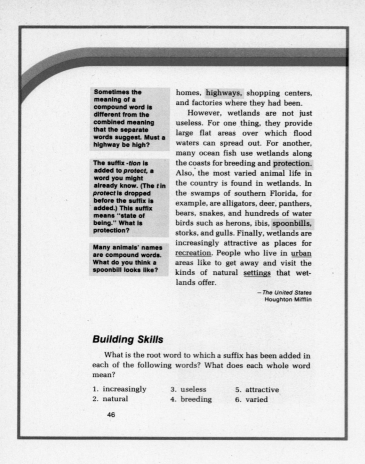

Sometimes the meaning of a compound word is different from the combined meaning that the separate words suggest. Must a highway be high?

The suffix *-tion* is added to *protect*, a word you might already know. (The *t* in *protect* is dropped before the suffix is added.) This suffix means "state of being." What is protection?

Many animals' names are compound words. What do you think a spoonbill looks like?

homes, highways, shopping centers, and factories where they had been.

However, wetlands are not just useless. For one thing, they provide large flat areas over which flood waters can spread out. For another, many ocean fish use wetlands along the coasts for breeding and protection. Also, the most varied animal life in the country is found in wetlands. In the swamps of southern Florida, for example, are alligators, deer, panthers, bears, snakes, and hundreds of water birds such as herons, ibis, spoonbills, storks, and gulls. Finally, wetlands are increasingly attractive as places for recreation. People who live in urban areas like to get away and visit the kinds of natural settings that wetlands offer.

—The United States
Houghton Mifflin

Building Skills

What is the root word to which a suffix has been added in each of the following words? What does each whole word mean?

1. increasingly
2. natural
3. useless
4. breeding
5. attractive
6. varied

46

Understanding New Words in Health

There are no sidenotes for this selection. Read it and then answer the questions that follow.

Animals that live off other animals are called **parasites.** Some parasites, like fleas, are a bother to the animals they live on. But they are not really harmful. Others can cause much harm.

The picture at the bottom of the page also shows parasites. But these parasites do not live *on* an animal or a person. They live *inside* an animal's or a person's body. They are so small that you can't see them without a special **microscope.** They are **microorganisms.** Sometimes people call them microbes for short.

47

Understanding New Words in Health

1. Have students read the introductory paragraph. Point out that there are no sidenotes. Then have students read the selection.

2. Have students answer the question in the sidenote at the top of page 46. (no)

3. Have students read the paragraph on page 46 and answer the question in the next sidenote. (the state of being protected or safe)

4. Have students answer the question in the last sidenote. (a bird with a spoon-shaped bill)

5. Have students complete *Building Skills.*

Answers to *Building Skills*
Social Studies Selection

1. *increase,* "more and more often"; 2. *nature,* "of or having to do with nature"; 3. *use,* "without use"; 4. *breed,* "producing young"; 5. *attract,* "likely to or tending to attract"; 6. *vary,* "of several kinds"

As they live inside your body, some of these microorganisms harm your body cells. Some of them give off poisons. The result is disease.

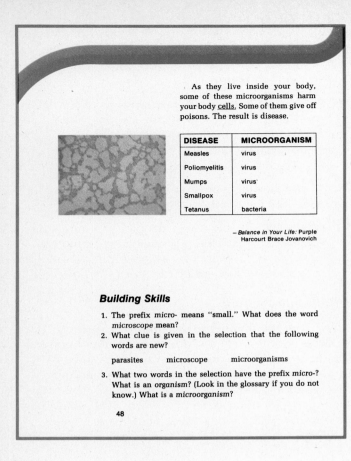

DISEASE	MICROORGANISM
Measles	virus
Poliomyelitis	virus
Mumps	virus
Smallpox	virus
Tetanus	bacteria

— Balance in Your Life: Purple
Harcourt Brace Jovanovich

Building Skills

1. The prefix *micro-* means "small." What does the word *microscope* mean?
2. What clue is given in the selection that the following words are new?

   parasites   microscope   microorganisms

3. What two words in the selection have the prefix *micro-*? What is an *organism*? (Look in the glossary if you do not know.) What is a *microorganism*?

48

2. Have students complete *Building Skills.*

Answers to *Building Skills*
Health Selection

1. "an instrument, usually consisting of a combination of lenses, used to magnify objects too small to be seen or clearly observed by the naked eye"; **2.** They are in boldfaced print. **3.** *microscope, microorganisms,* and *microbe; organism:* a plant or animal composed of parts and organs; *microorganism:* an organism so small that it can be seen only through a microscope

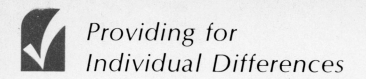

Providing for Individual Differences

Skills Lesson

Additional Practice

Worksheet 2, Teacher's Edition, page T481

Vocabulary Study

Additional Practice

■ **Identifying base words in compound words**
On the board, draw the following diagram for a puzzle. Then give students the clues and have them complete the puzzle on the board or on their papers. Explain that each answer is a compound word.

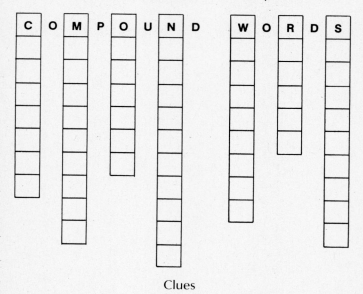

Clues

C free from cares or worries (carefree)

M the most important spring in a clock or watch (mainspring)

O a porridge made from oats rolled into meal or flakes (oatmeal)

N able to see only things that are near (near-sighted)

W something put on a wall instead of paint (wall-paper)

R the strip of ground that airplanes run along during takeoff and landing (runway)

S the time of year when trees and flowers bloom (springtime)

Reading Selection: Penguin Paradise

Additional Practice

■ **Identifying sound-letter relationships and syllables**
Remind students that each syllable has one vowel sound. Also remind them that after they divide a word into separate syllables, they should put the sounds together and say the whole word.

Write the following words on the board and have students identify the number of syllables in each.

hopes (1)	able (2)	people (2)	automatic (4)
hoping (2)	unable (3)	single (2)	auto (2)
hopeful (2)	ability (4)	syllable (3)	activity (4)
repeated (3)	defend (2)	adviser (3)	protector (3)

Challenge Activity

Identifying the number of syllables in a word Have students look through a textbook or another book from the classroom library and list ten words of three or more syllables that are new to them. (Remind them that words in italics or boldface are usually new.) Have them try to pronounce the new words. They may check their results with the dictionary. Students may enjoy starting a "vocabulary bank," a notebook of new words they are adding to their vocabularies.

Reading Selection: Living Lights in Our World

Additional Practice

■ **Recognizing compound words (Identifying parts)**
Read aloud or write on the board the sentences below. If you read them aloud, write the underlined words on the board. Explain that all the underlined words are compound words. Ask students to find the two words that make up each compound word somewhere else in the sentence. Also ask them to write a short definition for each compound word.

That boy likes school better than any other school-boy I know. (*boy; school;* a boy who attends school)

It's best to use a bookmark when you want to mark your place in a book. (*mark; book;* an object, such as a ribbon or a piece of paper, put in a book to mark a place)

In the summertime you will have time to swim and fish and enjoy the long summer days. (*time; summer;* the time of the summer season)

The light made by the sun on the leaves was the most beautiful sunlight I ever saw. (*light; sun;* the light of the sun)

When the snowstorm started, the snow fell lightly, but after a while it turned into a storm. (*snow; storm;* a storm with a heavy fall of snow)

Challenge Activity

Recognizing compound words   Ask students to
make a list of all the compound words they can think
of and to decide how they would define each one.
They may make another list, if they have time, of words
that use prefixes and suffixes, such as *un-, re-, -less,*
and *-ful,* as units of meaning, and define these as well.
If students are keeping a vocabulary notebook as suggested in the *Challenge Activity* for "Penguin Paradise"
(page T44), these word lists can become part of the
notebook.

Evaluation

Periodic Test 1, Part II, Form A or *Form B,* may be administered after this unit to test skills marked **T.** If you
have pretested using *Form A,* administer *Form B.*

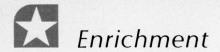 *Enrichment*

Penguin Paradise

Bibliography

The following books are about penguins and other birds.

Easy

Eberle, Irmengarde. *Penguins Live Here.* A simple history of the lives of the Adélie penguins.

Mizumura, Kazue. *Emperor Penguins.* A straightforward description of the emperor penguin and its habits, with lovely wash drawings.

Average

Hogner, Dorothy Childs. *Sea Mammals.* Includes physical characteristics, habits, environment, and life cycle of whales, dolphins, porpoises, sea cows, seals, walruses, sea otters, and polar bears.

Kieran, John. *An Introduction to Birds.* Picture, description, habits, and habitat of each bird.

Films and Filmstrips

NOTE: For more information, see *Resource Center.*

Skills

Guidance Assocs. *The Reading Skills Series.* Both filmstrips in the series are appropriate. Meanings of prefixes, suffixes, and whole words through humor and word games.

Guidance Assocs. *Using Your Reading Skills Series.* "Finding Word Clues" in Part II; word meanings through prefixes and suffixes.

Selection content

Valiant Instructional Materials Corp. *The Animal Kingdom.* "Birds" is especially appropriate.

Curriculum Coordination

Language Arts

Have students write a story about an imaginary adventure with penguins while exploring Antarctica or a story about "the penguin that thought it was a person."

Science

1. Students may be interested in writing to the zoos and aquariums closest to your area to find out if any penguins live there and, if so, some facts about them and their life at the zoo. If such a zoo is nearby, plan a visit to see the penguins.

2. Visit a natural history museum that has exhibits on the Arctic and Antarctic regions.

Social Studies

Integrate a lesson on the cold regions and climates of Earth with this selection. Does anything grow in Antarctica? How have explorers learned to survive there? How much wildlife is there? What can be found out about the geography of the land lying under ice?

Art

Drawings, paintings, or craft representations of penguins will have a special appeal at this time.

Career Education

Remind students that Admiral Byrd was a member of the U.S. Armed Forces. Invite a representative from one of the Armed Forces to discuss the career training and job and travel opportunities now available.

Living Lights in Our World

Bibliography

The following books are about bioluminescent and non-bioluminescent insects and other animals.

Easy

Foster, Virgil. *Close-up of a Honeybee.* Photographic book in which the author shares his experience in observing and studying bees on his own and with the help of a beekeeper.

McClung, Robert M. *Aquatic Insects and How They Live.* The types of insects that can be found around a pond or stream: dragonflies, mayflies, caddisworms, water beetles, etc.

Average

Tinbergen, Niko. *Animal Behavior.* Facts about various animals.

Challenging

Simon, Hilda. *Living Lanterns: Luminescence in Animals.* Bioluminescence, from fireflies to flightless land animals and underwater life, is explored in this technical synthesis of historical material and studies made by scientists in the field. Many color illustrations by the author.

Films and Filmstrips

NOTE: For more information, see *Resource Center.*

Skills

Guidance Assocs. *The Reading Skills Series.* Both programs in this series are appropriate.
Guidance Assocs. *Using Your Reading Skills Series.* "Finding Word Clues" in Part II; prefixes and suffixes.

Curriculum Coordination

Language Arts

1. Have students find, memorize, and share with the class a poem about fireflies or other insects.

2. Have students write poems about "lights in the night," or a story about a mysterious light, with a surprise ending.

Science

1. Have students research (using library books or encyclopedias) and report on glowing mushrooms or molds. Such reports can then be integrated with a lesson on plant life or a project on molds. (Molds can be grown simply in a Petri dish or a jar. Many biology books have references to this and other experiments with molds.)

2. A visit to a natural history museum can be an exciting follow-up to the reading of this selection. Check beforehand, or have students write a letter, to find out what exhibits would be of particular interest.

Art

In combination with the poetry- and story-writing described above, students may want to use paint, chalk, bits of paper, or other media to create a picture about the subject of their poem or story.

Career Education

The selection tells students about how living lights work. Invite an electrician or electrical engineer to tell the class how "hot" electric light works, where it gets its energy, and what materials are needed to make a light bulb light up. Students may also be interested in learning about "cold" electric light.

TEACHING UNIT 3
Pages 49–69

Contents

Additional Materials

Reading Skills Workbook: Lessons 5–6, pages 15–21
Duplicating Masters 11: pages 7–8
Worksheet 3: Teacher's Edition, page T482
Periodic Test 1, Part III

Key to Symbols

Skills Objectives
I* –   Introduced in this unit
I   –   Introduced earlier in this level
M   –   Maintained from previous levels
T   –   Tested in periodic and cumulative tests for this level

Reduced Student Pages
underscore – words that appear in the glossary
wavy line   – words pretaught in the Teacher's Edition
                (these words also appear in the glossary)

Skills Lesson:
The Dictionary
Pages 49–54

Objectives

		SKILLS CODE NUMBER
M, T	To locate dictionary and glossary entries	5.6.4; 5.6.6
M, T	To use a dictionary or glossary to find pronunciation and meaning	5.6.4; 5.6.6
M, T	To use a dictionary pronunciation key	5.6.5
M, T	To use a dictionary or glossary to find meanings of multiple-meaning words	5.6.4; 5.6.6

If you wish to pretest the skills listed above, you may administer *Periodic Test 1, Part III, Form A. Periodic Test 1, Part III, Form B,* may be administered to post-test.

Introducing the Lesson

1. Write the following words on the board: *filone, simoom, pother, batib.* Explain to the class that two of the words are real words and the other two have been made up. Ask students to guess which are actually words. (*Simoom* and *pother* are real words.)

2. Next, ask students how they can find out which are the real words. (by looking the words up in a dictionary) Then have students look up the words and tell the meanings of the real words. (*simoom:* a hot, dry wind of the deserts of northern Africa and southwest Asia, full of sand and dust; *pother:* fuss and commotion)

The Dictionary

Finding the Entry Word

Have you ever looked for a word in a dictionary and not been able to find it? Perhaps it was there but was not listed among the **entry words.** Entry words are the words printed in boldface type at the left-hand side of each column in a dictionary.

Many times the word you need is related to an entry word but has a different form. Its spelling may have been changed by adding a prefix or suffix. When this is the case, you must know the root word and look for it as an entry word.

49

Suppose you do not understand the word in italics in the following sentence:

● This weather makes the cabin seem *mustier* than ever.

You look, but you don't find *mustier* among the entry words in a dictionary. What do you do next? Look for the root word. You can guess that it is *musty.* The suffix -er has been added to the root. (Most words ending in *y* change the *y* to *i* before adding a suffix.) When you find the word *musty* in a dictionary, you will see that *mustier* is part of the entry:

* **must·y** [mus′tē] *adj.* **must·i·er, must·i·est**
1 Having a moldy odor or taste. **2** Stale or old:
musty humor. — **must′i·ness** *n.*

You can see that it is often important to know the root of a word in order to find it in a dictionary. However, remember that many words with prefixes or suffixes added to them *are* listed as entry words in most dictionaries.

* From the *HBJ School Dictionary.* © 1977 by Harcourt Brace Jovanovich, Inc. Reprinted and reproduced by permission of the Publisher.

50

---

3. Have students turn to page 49 and examine the cartoon. Ask why two of the people may be angry. (The third person has made up a word for a word game and can't find it in the dictionary. Accept other reasonable interpretations.) Point out that not all dictionaries contain all words, since there are 500,000 words in the English language but only about 100,000 are useful to most people. The other 400,000 are archaic, technical, or otherwise outside the basic vocabulary of most people.

Developing the Skill

Finding the Entry Word

A. *Sometimes, when the spelling of a word has been changed by the addition of a prefix or suffix, you must look for the root word as the entry word.*

1. Have students read page 49 and the paragraph and example sentence that appear on page 50. Point out that *mustier* cannot be found among the entry words in a dictionary, and ask the class how they would find its meaning. (by looking for the entry for its root word—*musty*)

2. Remind students that most words ending in *y* change the *y* to *i* before adding a suffix. Then have students read the explanatory paragraph and examine the entry.

B. *Some words with prefixes or suffixes added to them are listed as entry words.*

Have students read the last paragraph on page 50. Then write the following words on the board:

semicircle	expression
defrost	international
transplant	irregular

Try This

What entry word in a dictionary would help you find each word below? Find each word in a dictionary and use it in a sentence.

1. resembled   3. silliest   5. unavailable
2. mysteriously   4. successful   6. disloyal

Using the Pronunciation Key and Accent Marks

How do you pronounce the word *amphibian*? If you don't know, a dictionary can help you. Here is the first part of a dictionary entry for this word:

* am·phib·i·an [am-fib′ē·ən]

The letters and symbols in brackets [ ] are the **phonetic respelling** of *amphibian*. A phonetic respelling shows you how to pronounce a word. To understand what the symbols in a phonetic respelling mean, use the **pronunciation key.**

* add, āce, câre, pälm; end, ēqual; it, īce; odd, ōpen, ôrder; tŏŏk, pōōl; up, bûrn; ə = a in *above*, e in *sicken*, i in *possible*, o in *melon*, u in *circus*; yōō = u in *fuse*; oil; pout; check; ring; thin; this; zh in *vision.*

Pronunciation keys are not all the same. But some symbols like the schwa (ə) appear in most of them. Once you get used to the symbols in a dictionary, you will be able to say many of the phonetically respelled words without having to look at the key. Of course, the pronunciation key is always there when you need it for reference. Look for it at the bottom of the dictionary page or in the front of the dictionary.

* From the *HBJ School Dictionary.* © 1977 by Harcourt Brace Jovanovich, Inc. Reprinted and reproduced by permission of the Publisher.

51

When you are working out the pronunciation of words that have two or more syllables, you have to know which syllable to **accent,** or say with the greatest force. A mark like this ′ shows which syllable should be said with the most force. What syllable has the greatest force in am·fib′ē·ən?

In some long words, like *revolution*, two syllables are accented. This mark ′ shows which syllable is said with the greatest force. This mark ′ shows which syllable is said with lesser force. Which syllable is said with the greatest force in rev′ə·lōō′shən? Which syllable is said with lesser force?

Try This

* add, āce, câre, pälm; end, ēqual; it, īce; odd, ōpen, ôrder; tŏŏk, pōōl; up, bûrn; ə = a in *above*, e in *sicken*, i in *possible*, o in *melon*, u in *circus*; yōō = u in *fuse*; oil; pout; check; ring; thin; this; zh in *vision.*

Use the pronunciation key above to match each respelling in the column on the left with a word in the column on the right. Then say each word. Use a dictionary to check your work.

1. kāk   a. alphabetical
2. rek′lis   b. celebration
3. sel·ə·brā′shən   c. cake
4. al′fə·bet′i·kəl   d. reckless

Finding the Definition That Fits the Sentence

If a dictionary gives only one definition for a word, that definition is usually right for any sentence. But sometimes you must choose among several definitions. When you find one

* From the *HBJ School Dictionary,* © 1977 by Harcourt Brace Jovanovich, Inc. Reprinted and reproduced by permission of the Publisher.

52

Explain that each of these words is listed as an entry word in most dictionaries, even though each word contains a prefix and/or a suffix. Therefore, it is not necessary to look up the root word.

Try This

Have students complete *Try This.*

Answers to *Try This*

(Answers will vary according to dictionary used.) **1.** resemble; **2.** mysterious; **3.** silly; **4.** successful; **5.** available; **6.** disloyal. Sentences will vary.

Using the Pronunciation Key and Accent Marks

A. *Use the pronunciation key to understand what the symbols in a phonetic respelling mean.*

1. Have students read the first explanatory paragraph under the heading and examine the phonetic respelling of *amphibian* and the pronunciation key. Point out how the symbols in the pronunciation key correspond to the symbols in the phonetic respelling of *amphibian.*

2. Have students read the next explanatory paragraph and locate the schwa symbol ə in the pronunciation key. Ask a student to pronounce the sound that /ə/ stands for. (uh)

B. *Accent marks show which syllable in a word is said with the most force and which syllables are said with less force.*

1. Have students read the first paragraph on page 52. Ask which syllable in *amphibian* has the greatest force. (the second syllable)

2. Have students read the next paragraph. Point out that the lighter accent mark shows that the syllable is said with some force, but not the greatest force. Then ask which syllable is said with the greatest force in *revolution.* (the third syllable) Which syllable is said with some but not the greatest force? (the first syllable)

Try This

Have students complete *Try This.*

Answers to *Try This*

1. c; **2.** d; **3.** b; **4.** a

Finding the Definition That Fits the Sentence

A. *When a dictionary gives more than one definition for a word, check all the definitions given and choose the one that best fits the sentence you are reading.*

that seems right for a sentence, try using it in place of the word in the sentence. If the sentence makes sense, you have probably chosen the right definition.

Let us find the meaning for *apt* and fit it into this sentence:

● At that moment, Henry made an apt remark.

Suppose you find the following dictionary entry for *apt*. Which meaning is the right one for the sentence above?

* **apt** [apt] *adj.* **1** Having a natural tendency; likely: Fish are *apt* to be biting then. **2** Quick to learn: an *apt* pupil. **3** To the point; fitting: an *apt* suggestion. — **apt′ly** *adv.* — **apt′ness** *n.*

Which meaning from the entry could have been used in place of *apt*? If you use the meaning from definition 1 or 2, would the sentence make sense? No. Try the meaning in definition 3: At that moment, Henry made a *fitting* remark.

When you check an entry in a dictionary, it is usually a good idea to check all the definitions given. Then choose the one that best fits the sentence you are reading.

* From the *HBJ School Dictionary*, © 1977 by Harcourt Brace Jovanovich, Inc. Reprinted and reproduced by permission of the Publisher.

53

Sometimes there are two or more words that have exactly the same spelling but are different words with different meanings. A dictionary puts a number next to each of these entry words. When you see a word marked ¹, remember that the following entry word or words will also have numbers. These entries are spelled the same way, but they are different words. Be sure to check all numbered entries to find the meaning that you want.

Try This

From each dictionary entry given, choose the definition that best fits the word in italics in each sentence below. Make up a sentence using each different meaning given.

1. The yard was covered with *concrete*.

* **con·crete** [kon′krēt *or* kon-krēt′] **1** *n.* A hard substance formed of cement, sand, gravel, and water, used as a building and paving material. **2** *adj. use:* a *concrete* floor. **3** *adj.* Actually existing; real: A chair is *concrete*, but a dream is not. **4** *adj.* Specific; particular: Give me a *concrete* example. — **con·crete′ness** *n.*

2. I knew he was *sensitive*, so I didn't tease him.

* **sen·si·tive** [sen′sə-tiv] *adj.* **1** Capable of feeling, reacting, appreciating, etc., quickly or easily: The ear is *sensitive* to sound; a *sensitive* thermometer; a film *sensitive* to light. **2** Easy to upset or make angry; touchy. **3** Extremely or abnormally susceptible: *sensitive* to changes in diet. **4** Tender or painful: a *sensitive* spot on the skin. — **sen′si·tive·ness** *n.*

* From the *HBJ School Dictionary*, © 1977 by Harcourt Brace Jovanovich, Inc. Reprinted and reproduced by permission of the Publisher.

54

Have students read from the last paragraph on page 52 through the example sentence and the dictionary entry for *apt* on page 53. Ask them which of the meanings is the right one for the example sentence. (definition 3) Then have students read the two explanatory paragraphs.

B. *When there are two or more words that have the same spelling but different meanings, check all the numbered entries to find the word you want.*

Have students read the paragraph on page 54. Have them turn to page 67 and look at entry words *hale¹* and *hale²* to illustrate this point.

Try This
Have students complete *Try This*.

Answers to *Try This*

1. definition 1; **2.** definition 2.   Sentences will vary.

 Use *Reading Skills Workbook*, Lesson 5, pages 15–20. See *Providing for Individual Differences*, page T62, for additional practice.

Vocabulary Study:
Homophones
Page 55

Objective

M   To distinguish between homophones

SKILLS CODE NUMBER

3.5.1

Developing the Skill

1. Tell students that the *Vocabulary Study* they are about to read uses words that sound alike but are spelled differently. Remind students that such words are called *homophones,* and ask students to give examples of homophones. (Sample answers: sail—sale, tail—tale, beech—beach)

2. Have students read the *Vocabulary Study* and do the *Word Play* activity.

Answers to *Word Play*

burrow: a hole in the ground that an animal lives in; *burro:* a small donkey; *prey:* any animal taken by another for food; *pray:* to express words of thanks or appeal to God or an idol; *current:* air that flows in a definite direction; *currant:* a small berry used to make jelly. Sentences will vary.

 Use *Reading Skills Workbook,* Lesson 6, page 21. See *Providing for Individual Differences,* page T62, for additional practice.

VOCABULARY STUDY

Homophones

Van: Rabbits live in **burrows.**
Stan: Did you say rabbits live in *burros*?
Van: Not in burros, "the little donkeys." I'm talking about burrows, "holes in the ground that animals live in." *Burrow* and *burro* are *homophones.* They sound the same but aren't spelled the same. They don't mean the same thing, either. Rabbits live in burrows!
Stan: Oh, those! Why didn't you say so?
Van: I did. Anyway, many small animals hide in burrows when birds of **prey** fly overhead.
Stan: Birds *pray*?
Van: No. They fly down, catch animals, and eat them. *Prey* means "any animal taken by another for food."
Stan: Oh, prey, not pray. Why didn't you say so?
Van: I did. Anyway, birds of prey are often carried high up in the air by **currents.**
Stan: Little *currants* can do that?
Van: Listen carefully, Stanley. *You're* talking about currants, "little berries you use to make jelly." I'm talking about wind currents, "air that flows in definite directions."
Stan: Oh, those! Why didn't you say so?

Word Play

Give a definition for *burrow, burro, prey, pray, current,* and *currant.* Then use each word in a sentence.

55

Reading Selection:
Dolphin Days
Pages 56–66

Objectives

		SKILLS CODE NUMBER
M, T	To locate dictionary entries	5.6.4
M, T	To use a dictionary to find meanings of multiple-meaning words	5.6.4; 5.6.6
M, T	To use a dictionary or glossary to find pronunciation	5.6.4; 5.6.6
M	To identify an author's purpose	3.6.4
M	To determine the correct sequence for a set of events	3.3.7.4

 **Preparing to Read**

Summary

The selection is a diary account of a family's vacation, during which they played and swam with some dolphins. The account gives facts about these remarkable creatures. They can be taught to play games and do tricks, are very affectionate, and enjoy the companionship of human beings. Although dolphins' sense of smell is weak, their senses of hearing, sight, and taste are excellent. They have vocal organs that enable them to "speak" in a variety of humanlike sounds. Some scientists who work with them think that dolphins are as smart as—or even smarter than—humans.

Background

The dolphin is an aquatic mammal related to the whale and the porpoise. (The dolphin's snout is beak-shaped, whereas the porpoise's is rounded.) Dolphins live in all the Earth's seas, but the greatest numbers are found in warm, tropical waters. In North American waters, there are about twelve species, including the nine-to-twelve-foot-long bottlenose dolphins (those mentioned in the selection). Dolphins swim by moving their tails. They use their flippers to steer and balance themselves.

The following books will provide you with additional background information.

Cousteau, Jacques-Yves, and Philippe Diole. *Dolphins.* The result of some of the most significant work Cousteau did over twenty-five years. Gives observations, experiments, and encounters with dolphins.

Honders, John, ed. *The World of Mammals.* The characteristics, habitats, etc., of mammals. Alphabetically arranged from aardvark to zebu.

Developing Vocabulary and Concepts

gasped: caught the breath suddenly; struggled for breath with one's mouth open
immense: very large; huge
mammal: any of the vertebrate animals, the females of which produce milk for their young
porpoise: a sea mammal, similar to a small whale, mostly blackish with a blunt snout
fielded: caught or picked up (a ball)
challenge: an invitation or a dare to do something, usually something difficult or dangerous
intruder: an unwelcome person
twittered: uttered light, chirping notes, like a bird
snaked: moved, wound, or crawled like a snake

1. **a.** Read aloud the following sentences or write them on the board. If you read them aloud, write the underlined vocabulary on the board.

   The children gasped in surprise as they watched the dolphin's breathtaking trick.
   Dolphins from the deep sea are immense, although not as large as some kinds of whales.
   Although dolphins look like fish, they are really mammals and feed their young with milk.
   The porpoise is a mammal that lives in the sea. It is related to the dolphin.
   The dolphin easily fielded the basketball by bouncing it off its beak.
   Ninu dared me to jump into the dolphin's pool. I accepted the challenge and jumped.
   The dolphin was worried about the strange intruder who was swimming in its pool.
   The dolphin made happy noises and twittered like a bird at the little girl.
   As the dolphin moved, it snaked around each person, trying to play.

   b. Ask students to give the meaning of each vocabulary word. Remind them to use the context clues in the sentences to help them.

2. Ask students if they have ever seen any movies or TV shows about dolphins or seen any perform in a water show at an entertainment park. Let them share first-hand observations they have had and any facts they know about dolphins. Have students turn to page 57 to see what a dolphin looks like. Ask if they know that the dolphin is a relative of the whale. Then explain that the selection they will read tells why this animal is one of the most remarkable in the world and describes what it's like to play water games with a dolphin twice your own size.

 Use *Duplicating Masters 11,* page 7.

Setting Purposes

Skills

Have students read the skills note at the top of page 56. Remind them that a dictionary entry may give a number of meanings for a word, and that when they look up an unfamiliar word, they must choose the meaning that fits the sentence in which the word appears. Suggest that they also look up familiar words if the words are used in an unfamiliar way.

Content

Have students read the lead-in to the title. Ask what a *diary* is (a personal record, kept day to day, of what happens to one or what one thinks about) Explain that this selection is a diary account that tells the experiences a family had with some dolphins. Ask students to try to picture the individual personalities of the various dolphins as they read. Ask them also to look for ways in which dolphins may be smarter than other animals.

2 Reading and Discussing

Have students read the selection. Most students will be able to complete it in one sitting. If you prefer, the selection may be read in two parts, breaking before the heading "March 17, Sunday" on page 59.

NOTE: The questions that appear in the student's text at the end of the selection focus on comprehension of selection content and on application of the *Skills Lesson* to the selection. Answers to these questions begin on page T57.

If you have trouble figuring out the meaning of some words in this selection, the glossary or a dictionary can help you.

This selection is a diary account of a family's . . .

by Cynthia de Narvaez

March 15, Friday

Today was clear and cool. The sun sparkled off the blue-green water. It danced on the red and yellow toys that were spread out along the side of the pool. We waited excitedly. Suddenly a fin knifed up through the water. A gleaming gray body rolled over with a puff . . . and was gone. "There's one! There's one! Where did it go?"

A dolphin at last! Ninu, Cynta, Claudia, Felito, and I, their mother, had never seen live dolphins before.

56

The dolphin rose again! It gasped--and
so did we. The animal was much larger than
we had imagined. It moved as though it
were oiled. We had expected to see
dolphins like those in the movies or on
TV--cute and small. But this animal from
the deep sea was immense, strange, and
beautiful.

A man in white pants and a red-and-
white-striped shirt walked out onto the
dock. He introduced himself as Michael,
the trainer, and welcomed us. He greeted

57

Pete, the dolphin in the pool, and gave us
a short talk on dolphins. Michael told us
that they are mammals, not fish. They use
their mouths mostly for eating. They
breathe and speak through the blowhole at
the top of their heads. They can drown if
water enters the blowhole. Not only is the
blowhole the dolphin's "nose," but in it
are organs like our lips, vocal cords, and
tongue. The "tongue" serves to close the
blowhole when the dolphin dives.

The permanent "smiling" expression on a
dolphin's face seems to show that it is
joyful and friendly. In fact, dolphins are
well known for saving people's and other
dolphins' lives. Though they are usually
gentle, they are always ready to protect

58

themselves. They are expert shark-killers.
But they will never hurt someone who has
not hurt them.

There are about thirty kinds of
dolphins. The bottlenose is one of the
largest. Bottlenoses are often called
porpoises. This is a mistake. Porpoises
are smaller animals that are relatives of
dolphins.

Michael told us that a dolphin's skin is
very sensitive. Dolphins have good
eyesight both in the air and under the
sea. They can hear sounds ten miles away
through the water. Their sense of taste
makes up for their lack of a sense of
smell.

When Michael finished talking, Pete
squawked and shook his flippers as if to
say, "That was great. Thank you. But now
let's get on with it!"

Telling him to mind his manners, Michael
threw him a basketball. Pete fielded it
neatly on his beak. He swam through the
pool toward a basket that hung nine feet
above the water. Then he tossed the ball
and scored a perfect goal. We glowed with
pride, as if he had been a member of our
own family.

March 17, Sunday

Yesterday, it rained. But at eight
o'clock Sunday morning we went once again
to the pool. At the end of the show,

59

Michael invited us to swim with Pete. We
all accepted at once. Ninu ran to the
dock, but when she came face to face with
the huge animal lying in the water, she
stopped. She turned to look at me, and
took a few steps back.

"Swim to the end of the pool and wait,"
ordered Michael, unaware of her fear.

"Go on, Ninu," I said. "If you don't, I
will!"

That was a real challenge. She jumped
into the water, swam across the pool, and
waited. Pete stayed near the dock and
watched her. He seemed a bit worried about
the intruder in his pool.

Michael said quietly, "Go get her,
Pete!" Pete then vanished soundlessly
underwater.

"Where is he?" Ninu called, searching
the pool around her. Pete's big fin rose
right in front of her face.

"Take hold of his fin and hang on
tight," Michael called.

She did, and Pete, swimming through the
water, pulled her straight to the dock.

Ninu climbed out, gasping and happy.
Just then, Claudia pushed Cynta in. In
great fear, Cynta swam across the pool.
But Pete was waiting for her at the other
side. He dived and slowly came up to
tickle her. Then he presented his fin and
returned her to the dock. He let her hug
him. Then he twittered at her, nodding
his head.

60

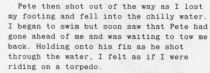

Pete then shot out of the way as I lost my footing and fell into the chilly water. I began to swim but soon saw that Pete had gone ahead of me and was waiting to tow me back. Holding onto his fin as he shot through the water, I felt as if I were riding on a torpedo.

Next we visited with Dove. She did no tricks but was everybody's pet. As I entered the water in her pen, she slid under my arm to be hugged. Happy to have company, she <u>snaked</u> around each one of us. She floated on her back, turning around and smiling. Each time one of us swam

62

toward the side of her pen to get out, Dove moved between the edge and the swimmer. She wanted all of us to stay. She made noises as if to say, "How could you desert me?"

Later we learned some interesting facts about dolphins. Some trainers who work with them think dolphins are as smart as—or even smarter than—people. They believe this because of the shape and size of dolphins' brains and also because dolphins learn so easily.

Dolphins use their hearing to "see" what is around them in the water. In the darkest waters, they are aware of a shark—its distance, its size, and how hungry it is—long before they can see it. A mother dolphin can use her hearing to

63

tell if there are uncomfortable <u>air pockets</u> in her baby's stomach. She knows just where to give the baby a gentle poke with her beak to "bubble" it. Blindfolded, a dolphin can easily jump through hoops in the air or find a fish in the water.

March 18, Monday

When we arrived at the pool this morning, we found that Pete had been joined by Simo [sē′mo] and Beau Brummell [bō′ brum′əl], the two high jumpers. They played with a ball for a long while. Afterwards they swam to the dock and looked at us, showing us all their teeth. Sometimes one would sit up in the water and nod and talk to us. They would not let us touch them, but they came very close. Soon Ninu, Cynta, and I joined them in the water. This scared them. They tore around the pool at high speed. However, they soon decided that we were safe and came closer, circling each one of us. At long last, they let us touch them.

The dolphins seemed to <u>prefer</u> the children to me. Michael told me this was always true at first, but that one of them would soon adopt me. He made it clear that I had no choice which one it would be. The choice is always theirs. I felt like a puppy in a litter up for sale.

They delighted in playing tricks on us. They kept talking excitedly. <u>Rough</u> as they

64

were among themselves, they were never too rough with us. As I was watching them play with the children today, I felt a blow on the top of my head. Then a great weight settled on my shoulder. Simo had bounced the ball on my head. With his head and neck resting on my shoulder, he was looking around into my face. I burst out laughing and hugged him. Then he made a sound so exactly like my laugh that I was surprised. How happy I was that this one seemed to have adopted me!

65

Understanding What You've Read

1. What is this selection chiefly about?

   a. the many things dolphins do
   b. how remarkable dolphins are
   c. a family's vacation

2. Why do some trainers think that dolphins may be smarter than people?
3. What does the author mean in saying that dolphins "speak" and "talk"?

Applying the Skills Lesson

1. What entry word would you look for to find the meaning of each word below? Remember—entry words are usually root words, but not always.

   a. circling   b. soundlessly   c. unaware
   d. snaked   e. intruder   f. uncomfortable

2. Which meaning of *litter* fits the sentence below?

   * **lit·ter** [lit′ər] **1** *n.* Scraps or other things strewn about; clutter. **2** *v.* To make untidy or unsightly with litter: to *litter* the sidewalk with trash. **3** *n.* The young brought forth at one birth by a mammal normally having several offspring at a time. **4** *v.* To give birth to (young). **5** *v.* To have a litter. **6** *n.* Straw, hay, etc., spread as bedding for animals. **7** *n.* A stretcher for carrying sick or wounded persons. **8** *n.* A vehicle consisting of a couch on two poles carried by men or animals.   Litter

   I felt like a puppy in a *litter* up for sale.

   * From the *HBJ School Dictionary*, © 1977 by Harcourt Brace Jovanovich, Inc. Reprinted and reproduced by permission of the Publisher.

66

Questions preceded by a bullet are additional questions and appear in the Teacher's Edition only. The other questions appear in the student's text after the selection.

Understanding What You've Read

1. *What is this selection chiefly about?*
   a. *the many things dolphins do*
   b. *how remarkable dolphins are*
   c. *a family's vacation*
   (Answer: b) INFERENTIAL   Identifying main idea

● *Which of the dolphin's senses is the most remarkable: sight, touch, hearing, smell, or taste?* (The dolphin's sense of hearing. Students should draw this conclusion from information on page 59 and page 63.) INFERENTIAL   Drawing conclusions

2. *Why do some scientists think that dolphins may be smarter than people?* (Some scientists think that dolphins may be smarter than people because of the shape and size of their brains and also because they learn so easily.   page 63) LITERAL   Recalling stated information

● *What is the attitude of dolphins toward people?* (They are usually very friendly toward people.   page 58) INFERENTIAL   Generalizing

3. *What does the author mean in saying that dolphins "speak" and "talk"?* (Dolphins make all kinds of sounds and seem to imitate humans.   pages 58, 59, and 64) CRITICAL   Interpreting figurative language

● *How does the author feel about dolphins?* (Accept answers that reflect the fact that the author obviously likes dolphins, enjoyed playing with them, and was amazed by their capabilities. You may want students to find passages in the selection to support their answers.) INFERENTIAL   Determining an author's unstated opinion

Applying the Skills Lesson

1. *What entry word would you look for to find the meaning of each word below? Remember—entry words are usually root words, but not always.*
   a. *circling*　　b. *soundlessly*　　c. *unaware*
   d. *snaked*　　e. *intruder*　　f. *uncomfortable*
   (Answers may vary according to dictionary used. a. circle; b. soundless; c. unaware; d. snake; e. intrude; f. uncomfortable)　　Locating dictionary entries

● *What entry word would you look for to find the meaning of each word below? Check your dictionary to be sure.*
   a. *sparkled*　　b. *usually*　　c. *largest*
   d. *suddenly*　　e. *striped*　　f. *mostly*
   (Answers may vary according to dictionary used. a. sparkle; b. usual; c. large; d. sudden; e. striped; f. mostly)　　Locating dictionary entries

2. *Which meaning of* litter *fits the sentence below?*

> ✽**lit·ter** [lit′ər] **1** *n.* Scraps or other things strewn about; clutter. **2** *v.* To make untidy or unsightly with litter: to *litter* the sidewalk with trash. **3** *n.* The young brought forth at one birth by a mammal normally having several offspring at a time. **4** *v.* To give birth to (young). **5** *v.* To have a litter. **6** *n.* Straw, hay, etc., spread as bedding for animals. **7** *n.* A stretcher for carrying sick or wounded persons. **8** *n.* A vehicle consisting of a couch on two poles carried by men or animals.

Litter

   I felt like a puppy in a litter *up for sale.*
   (Definition 3)　　Using a dictionary to find the meanings of multiple-meaning words

● *Which meaning of* litter *is the right one for the following sentence? Be sure to put clean* litter *in the barn.* (Definition 6)　　Using a dictionary to find the meanings of multiple-meaning words

● *Which of the entries given for the word* desert *has a meaning that would fit the following sentence?*

> ✽ **des·ert**¹ [dez′ərt] **1** *n.* An extremely dry region, often covered with sand, where few or no plants will grow: the Gobi *Desert.* **2** *adj.* Of or like a desert; barren or remote.
> **de·sert**² [di·zûrt′] *v.* **1** To leave a person, place, or thing, especially if one has a duty to stay; abandon: to *desert* one's family. **2** To leave one's military duty or post without leave and without intending to return. **— de·sert′er** *n.*
> **de·sert**³ [di·zûrt′] *n.* (*often pl.*) Reward or punishment that is deserved, especially in the phrase **just deserts**: They got their *just deserts.*

   She made noises as if to say "How could you desert *me?"* (Entry 2)　　Using a dictionary to find the meanings of multiple-meaning words

● *Which of the entries given for the word* desert *has a meaning that would fit the following sentence? The hot sun baked the* desert *sand.* (Entry 1)
Using a dictionary to find the meanings of multiple-meaning words

● *Are the three entry words for* desert *pronounced the same?* (Pronunciation for entry 1 is different from that of entries 2 and 3).　　Using a dictionary to find pronunciation

 Use *Duplicating Masters 11,* page 8. See *Providing for Individual Differences,* page T62, for additional practice.

3 Maintaining Skills

Comprehension Skills

Identifying an author's purpose　　Explain to students that they can better understand what they read if they recognize the author's reason for writing it. To do this, it is helpful to think about the *kind* of material they are reading. For example, ask students what the author's purpose is if the material is mainly information or a collection of facts. (to teach something or to give information)

If the material presents an argument or a point of view, what would be the author's purpose? (to persuade— that is, to encourage the reader to believe or to think in a certain way) What is the author's purpose if the material is a story or an event from the author's or someone else's life? (to tell a story or to share a personal experience)

Have students reread the second paragraph on page 57 (beginning "A man in white pants . . ."). Ask them to think about the author's purpose as they read. Then have them choose one of the following as the purpose.

   1. to persuade the reader to like dolphins
   2. to give information
   3. to make the reader laugh
   (Answer: 2)

Next, have students turn to the heading "March 17, Sunday" on page 59. Ask them to read up to the end of page 60. Then have them choose one of the following as the author's purpose for this material.

   1. to tell a good story
   2. to teach the reader something
   3. to give general information about dolphins
   (Answer: 1)

Finally, ask students to decide on the author's two *main* purposes for writing the selection "Dolphin Days." Let them discuss their choices and give their reasoning. (The general idea should be that the author probably wanted to share an interesting and enjoyable experience and also wanted to give information about dolphins.)

Determining the correct sequence for a set of events
The following events, taken from "Dolphin Days," are in mixed-up time order. Have students organize these events in their proper time sequence, referring to the selection if necessary.

1. Michael, the trainer, introduced himself and welcomed the family.
2. The family played with Dove.
3. Simo and Beau Brummel at first preferred the children to their mother.
4. Michael invited the family to swim with Pete.
5. Ninu, Cynta, Claudia, Felito, and their mother went to see the dolphins.

(Correct order: 5, 1, 4, 2, 3)

⭐ For additional resources and curriculum-related activities, see *Enrichment,* page T63.

Textbook Study:
Using Dictionaries and Glossaries

Pages 67–69

Objectives

		SKILLS CODE NUMBER
M, T	To use a dictionary or glossary to find meanings of multiple-meaning words	5.6.4; 5.6.6
M, T	To use a dictionary or glossary to find pronunciation and meaning	5.6.4; 5.6.6
M, T	To locate dictionary and glossary entries	5.6.4; 5.6.6

Applying the Skill

Have students read the introduction and examine the two selections. You may wish to have them read the selections on their own and then do *Building Skills*. Or you may wish to direct students, using the following procedure.

Using a Dictionary

1. Have students read the first sidenote. Ask them to identify the names of places and people among the entries. (Haiti and Nathan Hale)

2. Have students answer the question in the second sidenote. (The word *halcyon* came from myths.)

3. Have students read the third sidenote and compare the illustration of *halberd* with its definition.

4. Have students answer the question in the fourth sidenote. (The sentence uses the word in context.) Ask them to substitute the word *nearly* in the sentence.

TEXTBOOK STUDY

Using Dictionaries and Glossaries

You have found that many new words in your textbooks are explained in context. But sometimes you find new words that are not explained and that you cannot decode. In such cases, you need to turn to a dictionary or to a glossary. Study the dictionary and glossary entries that follow. Refer to the sidenotes. They will help you understand some of the entries.

Using a Dictionary

* **Hai·ti** [hā′tē] *n.* **1** A country in the western part of the West Indian island of Hispaniola. **2** A former name of Hispaniola. — **Hai·ti·an** [hā′tē-ən *or* hā′shan] *adj., n.*
hake [hāk] *n., pl.* **hake** or **hakes** A food fish related to the cod.
hal·berd [hal′bərd] *n.* A weapon used about 400 years ago, with a spear point and an ax blade on a long shaft.
hal·cy·on [hal′sē-ən] *adj.* Calm; peaceful. ✦ In myths, the *halcyon* was a bird supposed to build its nest in the water and make the winds become calm while it was nesting.
hale¹ [hāl] *v.* **haled, hal·ing** To compel to go: to *hale* into court.
hale² [hāl] *adj.* **hal·er, hal·est** Vigorous and healthy; robust: He felt *hale* and hearty.
Hale [hāl], **Nathan,** 1755–1776, American patriot, hanged as a spy by the British.
half [haf] *n., pl.* **halves** [havz] **1** *n.* Either of two equal or almost equal parts into which a thing may be divided, or a quantity equal to such a part: Give me *half*. **2** *adj.* Having half of a standard value: a *half* teaspoon. **3** *adj.* Not complete; partial. **4** *adv.* To the extent of a half; partially. **5** *adv.* Nearly: I was *half* inclined to refuse. **6** *adv. informal* To any extent at all: not *half* good enough.

Halberd

Each word and all the information listed about it is called an *entry*. Notice that this dictionary also lists places and people.

Sometimes, a dictionary tells you where a word comes from. Where did the word *halcyon* come from?

Pictures or diagrams in dictionaries help you to understand meanings.

How does the sentence help you to understand this meaning of *half*?

* From the *HBJ School Dictionary*, © 1977 by Harcourt Brace Jovanovich, Inc. Reprinted and reproduced by permission of the Publisher.

67

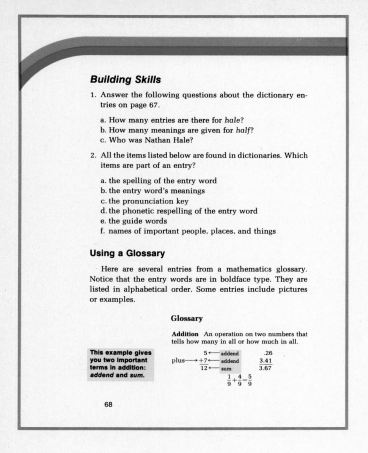

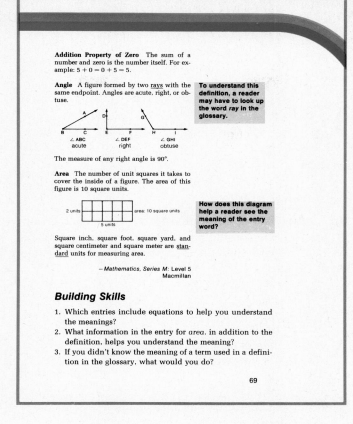

5. Have students complete *Building Skills.*

Answers to *Building Skills*
Dictionary Selection

1. a. two; **b.** six; **c.** an American patriot; **2. a, b, d, f**

Using a Glossary

1. Have students read the introductory paragraph and the sidenote on page 68. Tell them to find the terms *addend* and *sum* in the first entry. Have students read the first sidenote on page 69 and the definition of *angle*. Explain that an unfamiliar term in a definition should be looked up.

2. Have students examine the entry for *area* and answer the question. (The diagram illustrates the ten square units that make up the area of the figure.)

3. Have students complete *Building Skills.*

Answers to *Building Skills*
Glossary Selection

1. Addition; Addition Property of Zero; **2.** the diagram and the information that follows the diagram; **3.** Look up the term in the glossary or in a dictionary.

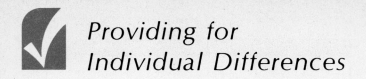

Providing for Individual Differences

Skills Lesson

Additional Practice

Worksheet 3, Teacher's Edition, page T482

Vocabulary Study

Additional Practice

■ **Distinguishing homophones**   Write each group of homophones on the board and then read aloud the sentences. Have students identify which word is used in each sentence.

> *I'll   aisle   isle*
>
> Short-tailed Manx cats come from the *Isle* of Man, which is in the Irish Sea.
> Judy's theater seat was next to the *aisle*.
> *I'll* do it if you won't.
>
> *beech   beach*
>
> If it's hot tomorrow, let's go to the *beach*.
> The bark of a *beech* is smooth and gray.
>
> *raze   raise*
>
> The house is in such bad shape, we'll have to *raze* it.
> My mother received a large *raise* and a job promotion.
>
> *style   stile*
>
> To get into the ride at the amusement park, you have to pass through a *stile*.
> I like the color of the suit, but not the *style*.

Reading Selection: Dolphin Days

Additional Practice

■ **Using the dictionary to find meanings of multiple-meaning words**   Write the following pairs of sentences on the board or read them aloud. If you read them aloud, write the underlined words on the board. Have students use their dictionaries to find the meaning that fits the context for each underlined word.

The baseball player caught the <u>fly</u>. (a baseball batted high over the field)
Have you ever noticed the color of the wings on a <u>fly</u>? (a flying insect)

I hate to see the holidays <u>fly</u> by. (move fast)
It was exciting to <u>fly</u> in an airplane. (travel by air)

My dad is the <u>senior</u> officer of his company. (highest in rank)
My sister will be a <u>senior</u> next fall. (in the last year of school)

Does this restaurant <u>serve</u> food after eight o'clock? (provide)
Will John <u>serve</u> as chairperson this year? (perform a duty)

Challenge Activity

Assign a few pages in a social studies text. Ask students to look up the meanings of words they are not sure of and then to write another sentence using each word *in the same way* as their text uses it.

Evaluation

Periodic Test 1, Part III, Form A or *Form B,* may be administered after this unit to test skills marked **T.** If you have pretested using *Form A,* administer *Form B.*

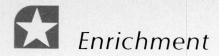

Enrichment

Dolphin Days

Bibliography

The following books are about aquatic mammals.

Average

Malone, Margaret Gay. *Dolly the Dolphin*. The true story of a Florida family that adopted a dolphin.

Matheu, Martha F. *Whales, Sails, and Scrimshaw*. Discusses whaling hunts of the early settlers and the recent progress people have made in studying and preserving the lives of whales.

Moffett, Martha, and Robert Moffett. *Dolphins*. A good survey of dolphins—physical traits, language, intelligence, relatives, current research, etc.

National Geographic World. "Dolphins: The Smart Animals?" No. 21, May 1977, pp. 12–17. A magazine article giving solid, scientific facts about dolphins' behavior, echolocation system, etc., in easy-to-understand language. Beautiful full-color photographs and diagrams.

Challenging

Chapin, Henry. *The Remarkable Dolphin*. A comprehensive study of dolphins. Illustrated with charts, diagrams, and drawings.

Films and Filmstrips

NOTE: For more information, see *Resource Center*.

Selection content

Guidance Assocs. *World of the Sea Series*. "World of the Sea/Group Two" in Part III, adaptations for life in the sea.

Curriculum Coordination

Language Arts

1. A valuable addition to your classroom or school library would be a subscription to *National Geographic World*. You might have students send a business letter inquiring about the price of a year's subscription (twelve issues) to National Geographic Society, 17th and M Street, NW, Washington, DC 20036. This and several other children's magazines are particularly useful for students who need motivation to read on their own.

2. Have students find magazine articles or books in their library on any of the cetaceans (whales, dolphins, seals). Have them explain how they found the materials—did they use the card catalogue, *Readers' Guide to Periodical Literature*, or another index?

3. Have students write a short story or composition from a *dolphin's point of view* about its meeting with the de Narvaez family or about its training.

4. Have students write a light, happy poem about the friendly and playful dolphin.

Science

1. Coordinate this selection with a lesson on animal life. Incorporate a brief study-report project to learn which other marine animals are classed as mammals (seals, whales) and which familiar water animals are *not* mammals (fish, water snakes, frogs, turtles). Be sure students understand why reptiles, fish, amphibians, birds, etc., are not classified as mammals.

2. If there is an aquarium in your area where a live dolphin may be seen, schedule a class visit.

3. A natural history museum may have exhibits that will enable students to compare dolphins with their relatives in the whale family, with seals, and with large fish.

Contents

Additional Materials

Reading Skills Workbook: Lessons 7–8, pages 22–25;
  Word Play, page 26
Duplicating Masters 11: pages 9–12
Worksheet 4: Teacher's Edition, page T483
Periodic Test 1, Part IV

Key to Symbols

Skills Objectives
I* — Introduced in this unit
I   — Introduced earlier in this level
M   — Maintained from previous levels
T   — Tested in periodic and cumulative tests for this level

Reduced Student Pages
underscore — words that appear in the glossary
wavy line   — words pretaught in the Teacher's Edition
                (these words also appear in the glossary)

Skills Lesson:
Recognizing Cause-and-Effect Relationships
Pages 70–74

Objectives

		SKILLS CODE NUMBER
M, T	To identify cause-and-effect relationships	3.3.3
M, T	To identify words that signal cause-and-effect relationships	3.3.3.1

If you wish to pretest the skills listed above, you may administer Periodic Test 1, Part IV, Form A. Periodic Test 1, Part IV, Form B, may be administered to posttest.

Introducing the Lesson

1. Show the class a blown-up balloon and a pin. Break the balloon with the pin. Ask students what happened. (The balloon popped.) Ask what *caused* it to pop. (sticking the pin into it)

Recognizing Cause-and-Effect Relationships

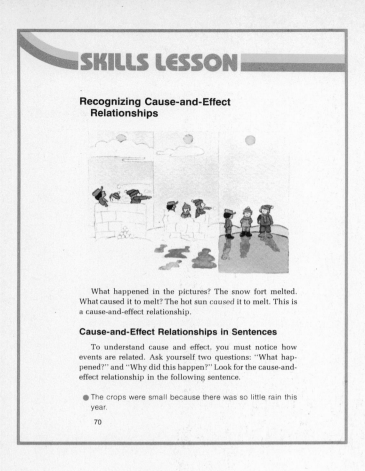

What happened in the pictures? The snow fort melted. What caused it to melt? The hot sun *caused* it to melt. This is a cause-and-effect relationship.

Cause-and-Effect Relationships in Sentences

To understand cause and effect, you must notice how events are related. Ask yourself two questions: "What happened?" and "Why did this happen?" Look for the cause-and-effect relationship in the following sentence.

● The crops were small because there was so little rain this year.

70

What happened to the crops? Your answer is an *effect*: They were small. Why did this happen? Your answer is a *cause*: There was so little rain this year.

Sometimes sentences contain word clues that show cause and effect. Look for such word clues in the two sentences below.

● 1. The cold winter caused the supply of heating fuel to be used up quickly.
2. As a result of the gas and oil shortages, people looked for ways to use energy from the sun.

Using the sun's energy. The heat of the sun warms the water in the bottles. The bottles hold that warmth for a long period of time and warm the air.

71

---

2. Ask what happened in the pictures on page 70. (The snow fort melted.) Ask what caused it to melt. (the sun) Have the class read the first paragraph.

Developing the Skill

Cause-and-Effect Relationships in Sentences

A. *To understand cause and effect, ask yourself, "What happened?" and "Why did this happen?"*

1. Have students read the explanatory paragraph and the example sentence at the bottom of page 70. Ask students what happened to the crops. (They were small.) Ask why this happened. (There was so little rain this year.) Point out that their answer to "What happened?" is the *effect* and their answer to "Why did this happen?" is the *cause*.

2. Have students read the explanation at the top of page 71.

B. *Sometimes sentences contain word clues that signal a cause-and-effect relationship.*

1. Have students read the paragraph on page 71 and the two example sentences. Tell students to identify word clues that show cause and effect in each sentence. (1. caused; 2. As a result) Have students identify the cause and effect in each sentence. (1. Cause: the cold winter; Effect: The supply of heating fuel was used up quickly. 2. Cause: gas and oil shortages; Effect: People looked for ways to use energy from the sun.)

In sentence 1 on page 71, *caused* is a clue word. What happened? The supply of heating fuel was used up. This is the effect. Why did this happen? It happened because of the cold winter. The cold winter is the cause. In sentence 2 on page 71, *As a result* is the clue. That people looked for ways to use energy from the sun is the effect. The cause is the gas and oil shortages.

Cause-and-Effect Relationships Between Sentences

Sometimes separate sentences show cause-and-effect relationships. Again, word clues can often help you see these relationships. Look for the clues to cause and effect in each pair of sentences below.

● 1. In northern states, food for birds becomes scarce in the winter. Therefore, geese and ducks fly south in search of food.

2. In one area, where wolves depended on deer for food, the number of deer decreased. So, the number of wolves in that area also decreased.

In the first pair of sentences above, *Therefore* shows a cause-and-effect relationship. In the second pair of sentences, *So* is the word clue. Sometimes, however, there is a cause-and-effect relationship between sentences that do not have word clues such as *therefore* or *so*. Read the following pair of sentences. There are no word clues in them. Try to find the cause and the effect. Ask yourself "What happened?" and "Why did this happen?"

72

● The giraffe is the tallest living four-legged animal. Giraffes are able to use the leaves of tall trees for their food supply.

You can clearly understand the relationship between these sentences if you ask yourself: What happened? (effect) Why did it happen? (cause)
● (effect)→Giraffes are able to use the leaves of tall trees for their food supply.
(cause)→The giraffe is the tallest living four-legged animal.

73

2. Have students read the text above the heading on page 72.

3. NOTE: You may wish to discuss the cause-and-effect relationship described in the caption below the photo on page 71. Ask what causes the water in the bottles to become warm. (the heat of the sun) Then ask what effect the warm bottles have on the air. (The bottles make the air warmer.)

Cause-and-Effect Relationships Between Sentences

A. *Sometimes separate sentences show cause-and-effect relationships. Word clues can often help you see these relationships.*

1. Remind students that words such as *because* and *as a result* signal a cause-and-effect relationship between sentences. Tell students that the words *so, and so, so that, therefore, since, that is why,* and *for this reason* may also signal a cause-and-effect relationship. Have students read the explanatory paragraph and the two pairs of example sentences. Ask them to identify the word clues that signal cause-and-effect relationships.

2. Now have students identify the cause and the effect in each pair of sentences. (1. Cause: first sentence; Effect: second sentence; 2. Cause: first sentence; Effect: second sentence)

B. *Sometimes there is a cause-and-effect relationship between sentences that do not have word clues.*

1. Have students read up to the end of page 73. Point out that it is easier to identify the cause-and-effect relationship by pretending that the word *because* comes between the sentences.

2. Explain to students that questions which begin with the word *why* usually signal a cause-and-effect relationship. Have students look at questions 2, 3, and 4 on page 37. Point out that each question gives an effect and asks students to identify the cause.

Try This

1. In each sentence below, find the cause and the effect. Use the word clues to help you.

   a. Dad failed to shut the freezer door tightly, so the bag of ice turned to water.
   b. Because several power lines were not working in my town, we found ourselves without electricity.

2. In each pair of sentences below, find the cause and the effect. There are no word clues to help you.

   a. Camels can store enough food and water in their bodies to last them for several days. They can travel long distances in the desert.
   b. As bees gather nectar from flowers, they fertilize the flowers. Bees help both the flowers they visit and the people who enjoy honey as a food.
   c. Ants recognize the other ants that live in their nest by their odor. The ability of ants to recognize the members of their "family" helps them to protect the nest from enemies.

Try This

Have students complete *Try This*.

Answers to *Try This*

1. a. Cause: Dad failed to shut the freezer door tightly. Effect: The bag of ice turned to water.
b. Cause: Several power lines were not working in my town. Effect: We found ourselves without electricity.
2. a. Cause: Camels can store enough food and water in their bodies to last them for several days. Effect: They can travel long distances in the desert.
b. Cause: Bees gather nectar from flowers. Effect: They fertilize the flowers. Bees help both the flowers they visit and the people who enjoy honey as a food.
c. Cause: Ants recognize the other ants that live in their nest by their odor. Effect: The ability of ants to recognize the members of their "family" helps them to protect the nest from enemies.

 Use *Reading Skills Workbook*, Lesson 7, pages 22–24. See *Providing for Individual Differences*, page T82, for additional practice.

Vocabulary Study:
Synonyms
Page 75

Objective

		SKILLS CODE NUMBER
M, T	To identify and use synonyms as context clues	3.5.4; 3.0

Developing
the Skill

1. Tell students that the *Vocabulary Study* they are about to read has two reports in which they will find pairs of synonyms. Ask for a definition of the word *synonym*. (a word that means the same or nearly the same as another word)

2. Have students read the *Vocabulary Study* and do the *Word Play* activities.

Answers to *Word Play*

1. *goggles:* eyeglasses; *grotto:* cave; *disturbed:* bothered; *vanished:* disappeared; *entirely:* totally;
2. Reports will vary.

 Use *Reading Skills Workbook,* Lesson 8, page 25. See *Providing for Individual Differences,* page T82, for additional practice.

VOCABULARY STUDY

Synonyms

The Larsen twins were in an exploring group. They each wrote a report. They didn't want to say exactly the same thing. So, to be different, they used some *synonyms,* words that have the same or nearly the same meanings. Here are parts of their reports.

. . . I put on my **goggles** and went into the **grotto**. Once inside, most of the light disappeared. But the dark never **disturbed** me. Inside we did much climbing and walking. By the time we got outside, I was totally out of breath.

. . . I put on my special eyeglasses and went into the cave. Once inside, most of the light **vanished**. But the dark never bothered me. Inside we did much climbing and walking. By the time we got outside, I was **entirely** out of breath.

Word Play

1. What synonyms in the reports above help you to know the meaning of *goggles, grotto, disturbed, vanished,* and *entirely?*
2. Write a short report about your favorite hobby. Then rewrite your report, replacing some of the words with synonyms.

75

Reading Selection:
Giants in the Earth

Pages 76–83

Objectives

		SKILLS CODE NUMBER
M, T	To identify cause-and-effect relationships	3.3.3
M, T	To identify words that signal cause-and-effect relationships	3.3.3.1
M	To predict outcomes based on given information and personal knowledge	3.4.2
M	To interpret information from a picture	5.4.5

 Preparing to Read

Summary

As far as we know, Earth is the only planet with trees. A tree can live and keep growing as long as it gets the right kind of soil, good air, good water, and sunlight. Every kind of climate has its own kinds of trees. City trees, usually brought to the city from tree farms, must be planted, tended, and protected if they are to live. To grow a big tree, it is best to get a young tree from a plant nursery, rather than try to grow a tree from seed.

Background

There are two kinds of sequoia trees—the redwood and the giant sequoia. The redwood is an important timber tree of the west coast of the United States, found from southern Oregon to about 100 miles south of San Francisco. It grows to a height of 200 to 364 feet and has a long life span; many redwoods are over 1,000 years old.

The giant sequoia is found along the western slopes of the Sierra Nevada in California. These trees grow slowly, and they usually reach a height of 275 feet, although some grow taller. Their wood, unlike that of the redwood, is not of great commercial value.

The following book will provide you with additional background information.

Petrides, George A. *A Field Guide to Trees and Shrubs.* Covers all trees, shrubs, and woody vines in the central and northeastern United States. Includes information on their growth, habitats, and importance to wildlife.

Developing Vocabulary and Concepts

survive: to remain alive
nevertheless: but; however
bored: made a hole in or through, as with a drill
curiosity: something strange, rare, or unusual
environment: the conditions and surroundings that have an effect on the development of a person, animal, or plant
nature: the basic qualities and characteristics of a thing or person

1. **a.** Read aloud the following sentences or write them on the board. If you read them aloud, write the underlined vocabulary words on the board.

   A few trees have managed to <u>survive</u> for thousands of years. However, most trees do not live that long.
   Some trees are not pretty to look at. <u>Nevertheless,</u> they are interesting to study.
   The scientist used a special drill when she <u>bored</u> a hole into the tree.
   The tree was a <u>curiosity</u> because it was 4,000 years old. People were interested in seeing such an unusual tree.
   Some trees can live and grow in a city <u>environment</u>. Other trees do not grow well in city conditions.
   A tree grows in its characteristic way, according to its own <u>nature</u>.

   b. Ask students to give the meaning of each vocabulary word. Remind them to use the context clues in the sentences to help them.

2. Ask students to imagine a tree that is taller than a twenty-story building. Ask if anyone has seen the redwoods or the giant sequoia trees that grow in California. Tell the students that some living trees are over 4,000 years old.

 Use *Duplicating Masters 11,* page 9.

What causes city trees to die? Why was a 4,000-year-old tree called "Pine Alpha"? For the answers to these questions, look for cause-and-effect relationships in this selection.

Long before the first humans or any other animal walked on this planet, the land was filled with great, silent . . .

GIANTS IN THE EARTH

by Elizabeth K. Cooper

The moon has no trees. No trees grow on Mars. As far as we know, only one planet—Earth—has trees.

Trees are alive, just as you are. But most of them are bigger than you are, and many years older. A tree can live and keep growing as long as it gets all the things that it needs.

Every tree needs food, which it makes in its own green leaves. To make its own food, a tree needs good air, good water, and sunlight. A tree also needs the right kind of soil.

Hot lands and cold lands, high places and low ones, wet areas and dry—they all have their own kinds of trees. It is amazing how some trees manage to sur<u>vive</u> where they live.

The First Trees

Millions of years ago, strange trees and tall, treelike plants lived in the green forests. No birds sang. No bees buzzed. No rabbits, squirrels, or chipmunks ran through the leaves. Such animals had not yet begun to live on Earth. Even the dinosaurs had not yet arrived.

In time, some of the <u>ancient</u> trees disappeared from the Earth forever. Other kinds lived on. They changed slowly, as the Earth changed through the ages. Some of the old trees were <u>ancestors</u> of our pines and other <u>cone-bearing</u> trees.

Giant trees once grew in great forests in many parts of the world. Now most of the giants are gone, but one kind—the sequoias—live on. Most of them are in California.

77

Setting Purposes

Skills

Have students read the skills note at the top of page 77. Remind them to look for word clues to cause-and-effect relationships, such as *because* or *therefore*. Also point out that there can be cause-and-effect relationships between sentences that do not have word clues.

Content

Have students read the lead-in to the title. Ask them what the word *giants* in the title refers to. By now they should have guessed that it refers to *trees*. Ask students to name some of the trees in their community.

2 Reading and Discussing

Have students read the selection. Most students will be able to complete it in one sitting. If you prefer, the selection may be read in two parts, breaking before the heading "City Trees" on page 80.

NOTE: The questions that appear in the student's text at the end of the selection focus on comprehension of selection content and on application of the *Skills Lesson* to the selection. Answers to these questions begin on page T72.

Sequoia trees are named for Sequoyah, a Cherokee who invented a written language for his people.

There are two kinds of sequoia trees in California— redwoods and giant sequoias. Earth's tallest tree is a giant sequoia.

The Oldest Trees

The 3,500-year-old General Sherman is a giant tree in Sequoia National Park. It is one of the best-known trees in the world. It is 310 feet tall and more than 32 feet around. But its cones are small, with seeds just a quarter of an inch long. What a miracle that a giant tree can grow from so small a seed!

Not very long ago, some much older trees were discovered. They, too, are in California.

The Pine Alpha is not tall or wide or handsome. Nevertheless, it is a very interesting tree.

It lives high on the steep, rocky side of a mountain. It leans out over miles of wide, empty valley. In the morning it catches the first rays of sunrise. In the evening it is touched by the last glow of sunset.

78

Pine Alpha's trunk and branches have been peeled and cut and shaped by angry winds and blasts of sand and ice. The tree looks more dead than alive, and it is. Nine-tenths of Pine Alpha is dead. Yet the tree is still growing. It still holds live seeds that can grow into new trees. This is amazing, because Pine Alpha is 4,300 years old!

Pine Alpha's age was discovered by a scientist in 1956. With a special tool, he bored into the heart of the tree and drew out a long, thin core of wood. Then he counted the tree's growth rings —one for each year of the tree's life.

Pine Alpha is the first living tree to be dated at more than 4,000 years old. Therefore, it was named *Alpha*, after the first letter in the Greek alphabet.

Pine Alpha is not just a curiosity. It is important to scientists who study our weather. As Pine Alpha grew, its growth rings made records of weather conditions for more than 4,000 years. The U. S. Weather Service's records go back little more than 100 years. Pine Alpha's records cover a period more than forty times that long.

79

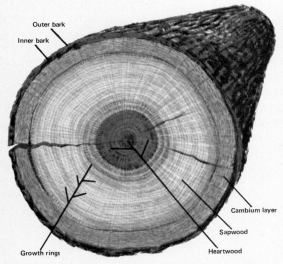

Outer bark
Inner bark
Cambium layer
Sapwood
Heartwood
Growth rings

Other trees have been studied and dated. One has been named *Methuselah,* for the oldest man in the Bible. He is said to have lived for 969 years. The Methuselah tree has been alive and growing for 4,600 years!

It is not an easy thing to visit these ancient trees. They live high above cities and towns.

They are more than 10,000 feet up—on rocky slopes where few other things can grow.

City Trees

In forests and on deserts, trees grow by themselves. They spring up from seeds that fall. No one waters them when they are

80

young. No one watches over them as they grow. Each one grows—if it gets all the things it needs. Otherwise, it dies.

City trees are different. They are brought to the city—often from tree farms—and planted by people. They are like pets. They depend on people for care and protection.

It is not always easy to keep city trees alive. Some get too hot. Many get too dry. Some are planted in poor soil. Some are bumped into by cars. And a few are hurt by people or animals. Those that live and grow are the tough ones. They are the trees that can get along in the city environment.

Plant a Tree

You can grow a real tree in a jar or even in a bottle of water. After you eat an avocado, save the seed. Put one toothpick on each side of the seed. Then put the wide end of the seed in water. The toothpicks will keep the whole seed from slipping into the jar. Watch the roots grow down. Watch the green stems grow up. Watch the green leaves grow and unfold.

When the seedling has about a dozen large leaves, it can be planted in a flowerpot filled with good soil. Of course, it can also be planted outdoors.

If you try to grow a big tree from a seed, you will almost surely be disappointed. You are better off planting a healthy, young tree that has had a head start. You can get one at a plant nursery in your own neighborhood.

The tree you plant today will grow fast or slowly, in its own way. It will grow tall and slender, or round and spreading, according to its own nature. It may live for 100 years or more.

If you plant a tree and look after it, you will feel proud, knowing you have helped a living thing to grow.

82

Understanding What You've Read

1. Why is "Giants in the Earth" a good title for this selection?
2. What trees mentioned in the selection have special names?
3. What have scientists learned by studying the growth rings of the giant sequoia trees?
4. Why is it not always easy to keep city trees alive?
5. What do you think people can do to help trees live longer and healthier lives?

Applying the Skills Lesson

1. In the following sentence, what is the cause? What is the effect?

   A tree can live and keep growing as long as it gets all the things that it needs.

2. Which of the two sentences below gives a cause?

   Pine Alpha is the first living tree to be dated at more than 4,000 years old. Therefore, it was named *Alpha*, after the first letter in the Greek alphabet.

3. Read the following paragraph. Which sentence gives the effect? How many causes are given for this effect?

   It is not always easy to keep city trees alive. Some get too hot. Many get too dry. Some are planted in poor soil. Some are bumped into by cars. And a few are hurt by people or animals.

83

Questions preceded by a bullet are additional questions and appear in the Teacher's Edition only. The other questions appear in the student's text after the selection.

Understanding What You've Read

1. *Why is "Giants in the Earth" a good title for this selection?* (Accept all reasonable answers.) CRITICAL Drawing conclusions

• *What does a tree need in order to make its own food?* (good air and water, sunlight, and the right kind of soil   page 77) LITERAL Recalling stated information

2. *What trees mentioned in the selection have special names?* ("General Sherman"; "Pine Alpha"; and "Methuselah"   pages 78 and 80) LITERAL Recalling specific details

• *Where do we get the name for the sequoia tree?* (Sequoia trees are named for Sequoyah, a Cherokee who invented a written language for his people. page 78) LITERAL Recalling specific details

3. *What have scientists learned by studying the growth rings of the giant sequoia trees?* (Scientists have learned how old trees are by counting the growth rings—one for each year of the tree's life. They have also learned about weather conditions in the past by studying the growth rings.   page 78) LITERAL Recalling stated information

• *Do you think it would be safe to say that most people have not seen the ancient trees described in the selection? Why?* (Yes, because it is not easy to visit these trees. They live high above cities and towns—more than 10,000 feet up on rocky slopes—and most are found only in California.   pages 77 and 80) INFERENTIAL Drawing conclusions

4. *Why is it not always easy to keep city trees alive?* (Some trees get too hot, some are planted in poor soil, and some are bumped into by cars. Many trees get too dry, and a few are hurt by people or animals.   page 81) LITERAL Identifying cause-and-effect relationships

5. *What do you think people can do to help trees live longer and healthier lives?* (Accept all reasonable answers that show consideration of information in the selection.) CRITICAL Making judgments

Applying the Skills Lesson

1. *In the following sentence, what is the cause? What is the effect?*
A tree can live and keep growing as long as it gets all the things that it needs.
(Cause: It gets all the things that it needs; Effect: A tree can live and keep growing.) <u>Identifying cause-and-effect relationships</u>

● *In the following sentences, what is the cause? What is the effect?*
It is not easy to visit these ancient trees. They live high above cities and towns.
(Cause: They live high above cities and towns; Effect: It is not easy to visit these ancient trees.) <u>Identifying cause-and-effect relationships</u>

2. *Which of the two sentences below gives a cause?*
Pine Alpha is the first living tree to be dated at more than 4,000 years old. Therefore, it was named Alpha, after the first letter in the Greek alphabet.
(Cause: Pine Alpha is the first living tree to be dated at more than 4,000 years old.) <u>Identifying cause-and-effect relationships</u>

● *Name the word clue that helps you to see the cause-and-effect relationship in the sentence pair in question 2.* (Therefore) <u>Identifying words that signal cause-and-effect relationships</u>

3. *Read the following paragraph. Which sentence gives the effect? How many causes are given for this effect?*
It is not always easy to keep city trees alive. Some get too hot. Many get too dry. Some are planted in poor soil. Some are bumped into by cars. And a few are hurt by people or animals.
(The first sentence gives the effect. Five causes are given in the remaining five sentences.) <u>Identifying cause-and-effect relationships</u>

✔ Use *Duplicating Masters 11*, page 10. See *Providing for Individual Differences*, page T82, for additional practice.

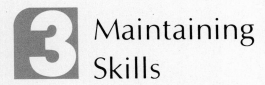

3 Maintaining Skills

Comprehension Skills

Predicting outcomes   Have students apply their own knowledge to the facts in the following paragraphs in order to predict the most likely outcomes.

A tree was planted on a city sidewalk where it didn't get much light. Soon after, a car bumped into the tree and tore off part of the bark. Little children came and carved their names in the tree's bark. The tree will probably . . .
1. grow tall and green
2. die
3. leave the city   (Answer: 2)

Yoshiro put an avocado seed in water. After several weeks, green stems sprouted and leaves grew. When the seedling had about a dozen large leaves, Yoshiro planted it in the back yard. After a month passes, Yoshiro's plant will . . .
1. become a large tree
2. become a little bigger
3. disappear completely   (Answer: 2)

In my yard is a tree that is twenty feet tall. This tree is very old, weak, and heavy. In my yard there is also a younger, stronger tree. Tonight there is a terrible hurricane. The winds are so strong that our house is shaking. The large tree will . . .
1. enjoy the wind and rain
2. protect the smaller tree from the wind
3. fall   (Answer: 3)

Study Skills

Interpreting information from a picture   Have students look at the pictures of trees in the selection. Ask students what information, if any, is given in the pictures that is not given in the text. (Accept reasonable answers.)

Have students look at the picture at the top of page 79 and answer each of the following questions:

What color is the tree? (brown)
How old is the tree? (information not in picture)
How tall is the section of the tree that is shown, compared with the person sitting next to it? (about ten times taller)
What special name does the tree have? (General Sherman)

★ For additional resources and curriculum-related activities, see *Enrichment*, page T83.

Reading Selection:
The Ship of the Desert
Pages 84–89

Objectives

		SKILLS CODE NUMBER
M, T	To identify words that signal cause-and-effect relationships	3.3.3.1
M, T	To identify cause-and-effect relationships	3.3.3
M	To identify the topic and stated main idea of a paragraph	3.3.8
M	To interpret information from a map	5.4.3

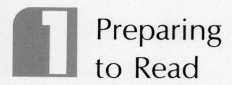 Preparing
to Read

Summary

Camels have walked the hot desert sands for thousands of years, carrying people and goods. Without them, people would not have been able to live or work in the desert. The one-humped Arabian camels live in the Middle East, India, and North Africa. (The dromedary is a type of Arabian camel used for riding.) The two-humped Bactrian camels make their home in the Gobi Desert of northeastern Asia.

The camel is well designed for life in hot, dry regions. Its long legs keep its body away from the hot sands; its hump is filled with fat to provide energy when food is scarce; its body can conserve water for long periods; and its temperature can change to adapt to the weather.

Background

Camels have served humans as beasts of burden longer than any other animal has. Only the Bactrian is still found in a wild state. (However, the descendants of some Arabian camels brought to the Australian Outback in the 1800's have reverted to a wild state.) The Arabian camel has been fully domesticated. It is interesting to note that camels are among the hardiest of animals in captivity; they actually seem to thrive in zoos.

The following book will provide you with additional background information.

Leopold, A. Starker. *Desert.* Characteristics of the desert, its uses, and the plants, animals, and people that inhabit it.

Developing Vocabulary and Concepts

caravan: a group of traders traveling together, especially through a desert
designed: planned for a certain purpose

1. **a.** Read aloud the following sentences or write them on the board. If you read them aloud, write the underlined vocabulary on the board.

   Traders crossing a desert usually join a <u>caravan</u>, a group of traders, rather than travel alone.
   The camel's body is well <u>designed</u> for life in the desert. Its legs keep it far from the hot sands. Its hump is filled with fat that it can live off for long periods.

   b. Ask students to give the meaning of each vocabulary word. Remind them to use the context clues in the sentences to help them.

2. Ask students if they have ever seen a camel. Do they think the camel is a strange-looking animal? Why? (because of its hump[s], very long legs, droopy eyelids, etc.) Tell the class that some of the camel's unusual physical features are very helpful to it in the desert environment and that the selection they will read explains how.

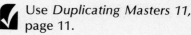 Use *Duplicating Masters 11,* page 11.

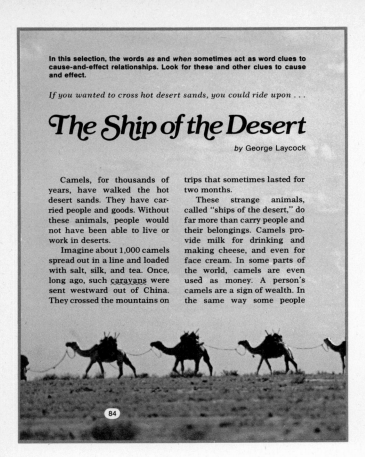

In this selection, the words *as* and *when* sometimes act as word clues to cause-and-effect relationships. Look for these and other clues to cause and effect.

If you wanted to cross hot desert sands, you could ride upon . . .

The Ship of the Desert

by George Laycock

Camels, for thousands of years, have walked the hot desert sands. They have carried people and goods. Without these animals, people would not have been able to live or work in deserts.

Imagine about 1,000 camels spread out in a line and loaded with salt, silk, and tea. Once, long ago, such <u>caravans</u> were sent westward out of China. They crossed the mountains on trips that sometimes lasted for two months.

These strange animals, called "ships of the desert," do far more than carry people and their belongings. Camels provide milk for drinking and making cheese, and even for face cream. In some parts of the world, camels are even used as money. A person's camels are a sign of wealth. In the same way some people

84

save money, some camel owners try to keep all the camels they can get.

Kinds of Camels

There are two different kinds of camels. You can tell the two kinds apart by the number of humps on their backs. The *Arabian* camels have only one hump. Arabian camels live in the Middle East, India, and North Africa.

85

Setting Purposes

Skills

Have students read the skills note at the top of page 84. Remind them that sometimes cause-and-effect relationships may be expressed without the use of specific word clues.

Content

Have students read the lead-in to the title. Suggest that they take note, as they read, of the many things that make the camel a very special animal. Tell them also to think about why the camel is called "the ship of the desert."

2 Reading and Discussing

Have students read the selection. Most students will be able to complete it in one sitting. If you prefer, the selection may be read in two parts, breaking before the heading "Desert Life" on page 88.

NOTE: The questions that appear in the student's text at the end of the selection focus on comprehension of selection content and on application of the *Skills Lesson* to the selection. Answers to these questions begin on page T77.

The other kind of camel—the one with two humps—is the *Bactrian.* Its home country is the Gobi Desert of northeastern Asia. The Bactrian has shorter legs and longer wool than the one-humped camel. It also has stronger, more rugged feet. This is important because instead of having sand to walk on, the Bactrian camels live in rough and rocky parts of the world.

Sometimes people talk about another kind of camel, the *dromedary.* The dromedary is really a special racing model

of the one-humped camel. It is bigger than the average Arabian one-humped camel and can walk faster. The dromedaries are the riding camels.

Camel History

The camel's family history goes back millions of years. And strangely, the camel story leads back to North America. The first kind of camel was small and humpless. Another kind of camel came later. It stood fifteen feet high—almost twice as high as present-day

86

camels. These North American animals were the ancestors of modern camels. They are believed to have spread out in two directions. One branch of the family slowly moved southward. It ended up in South America. The South American llama is a present-day cousin of the camel.

Another branch of the camel family moved northwestward, toward Alaska. Scientists believe that a belt of land once connected North America and Asia. The camels crossed over this land bridge and spread to Asia and Africa. They later died out in North America.

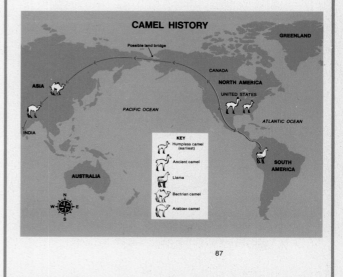

87

Desert Life

Scientists have studied the camel carefully to find out how it can live where many other animals would die. They have found some strange answers. It is well designed for its life in the hot, dry, sandy parts of the world.

Its long legs may help it in more than walking. The hottest part of the desert is right at ground level. Up on those long legs, away from the scorching hot sands, the temperature is somewhat cooler for the camel's body.

Many people have looked at the hump on the camel's back and said, "Ah, there's the answer. The beast simply packs extra water in that hump on its back." But they are wrong about that. The camel's hump is not a big leather bag filled with water. Actually, the hump is filled with fat. There may be eighty pounds or more of fat in the hump, depending on the camel's size.

The fat provides energy to keep the camel going when there is not enough food for it to eat. If hard times last long enough, the camel's hump almost disappears. Owners can tell by the hump if the animal is in good enough condition to make a long journey.

In addition, the camel does a better job than most animals of saving water in its body. Even in the hottest places in the world, a camel gets along fine without doing much sweating at all. A camel's body temperature can also change. As the weather becomes hotter, the camel's body temperature goes up. The camel stays as comfortable as ever. And the

88

Questions preceded by a bullet are additional questions and appear in the Teacher's Edition only. The other questions appear in the student's text after the selection.

Understanding What You've Read

1. *What is contained in a camel's hump?* (fat   page 88) LITERAL   Recalling specific details

● *If you saw a camel without a hump, what could you conclude?* (You could conclude that the camel had not eaten for a long time.   page 88) INFERENTIAL Drawing conclusions

2. *Why do a camel's long legs prove useful in the desert?* (Its long legs keep the camel's body away from the hot sands and enable it to be cooler.   page 88) LITERAL   Identifying cause-and-effect relationships

● *What effect do a camel's long eyelashes have?* (They help shade the camel's eyes.   page 89) LITERAL Identifying cause-and-effect relationships

● *Name some differences between the Arabian camel and the Bactrian camel.* (The Bactrian camel has two humps, shorter legs, longer wool, and stronger, more rugged feet than the Arabian. Bactrians come from the Gobi Desert of northeastern Asia, while Arabians live in the Middle East, India, and North Africa. pages 85 and 86) INFERENTIAL   Identifying contrasts

3. *Describe the two kinds of camels that lived in North America long ago.* (The first kind of camel was small and humpless. The kind that came later stood fifteen feet high—almost twice as high as present-day camels.   page 86) LITERAL   Recalling stated information

● *Do people who use camels for riding usually ride a camel with one hump or with two humps?* (Dromedaries are the riding camels; they have one hump. page 86) LITERAL   Recalling specific details

4. *Why do people call camels "ships of the desert"?* (because they carry people and goods across the desert   page 84) INFERENTIAL   Identifying comparisons

● *Why do you think the author said, "If they thought about it, camels might feel proud of themselves"?* (Accept reasonable answers; however, the general idea should be that camels have been extremely helpful to people, enabling them to live and work in the desert, and that because of the camels' physical features, no other animal could do their work as well as they do.) CRITICAL   Drawing conclusions

Applying the Skills Lesson

In each sentence below, there is a cause-and-effect relationship. Which words tell the cause? Which words tell the effect?
1. If hard times last long enough, the camel's hump almost disappears.
2. As the weather becomes hotter, the camel's body temperature goes up.
3. When the wind blows sand into a camel's face, the animal closes its nostrils.
(1. Cause: hard times last long enough; Effect: the camel's hump almost disappears; 2. Cause: the weather becomes hotter; Effect: the camel's body temperature goes up; 3. Cause: the wind blows sand into a camel's face; Effect: the animal closes its nostrils.)   Identifying cause-and-effect relationships

● *Find the word clue in each sentence in the preceding question that signals a cause-and-effect relationship.* (1. If; 2. As; 3. When)   Identifying words that signal cause-and-effect relationships

 Use *Duplicating Masters 11,* page 12. See *Providing for Individual Differences,* page T82, for additional practice.

3 Maintaining Skills

Comprehension Skills

Identifying the topic and stated main idea of a paragraph   Remind students that the *topic* of a paragraph is a word or group of words that tells what the paragraph is about, and the *main idea* is the most important thing said about the topic. Have students read the last paragraph on page 84. Ask them which of the following choices is the topic of the paragraph.

1. what camels look like
2. the importance of camels
3. how to ride a camel
4. how camels are like ships
(Answer: 2)

Then ask students which sentence states the main idea. (First sentence: "These strange animals, called 'ships of the desert,' do far more than carry people and their belongings.")

Now refer students to the first paragraph on page 86. Ask students which of the following choices is the topic of that paragraph.

1. the Gobi Desert
2. the Bactrian camel
3. the importance of strong feet
4. the importance of shorter legs
(Answer: 2)

Now have students read the third paragraph on page 88. Have them identify the topic of the paragraph and find the sentence that states the main idea. (Topic: the camel's hump; Main idea: "Actually, the hump is filled with fat." Also accept the last sentence as the stated main idea.)

Study Skills

Interpreting information from a map   Have students use the map on page 87 to find the answers to the following questions.

What does the map show? (the routes of the ancient camels to South America and Asia)
Where was the earliest camel found? (North America)
Are both Bactrian and Arabian camels found in Asia? (yes)
Through what parts of North America did the early camels travel in order to reach the Alaskan land bridge? (western U.S., western Canada, Alaska)
In what directions did the route to Asia take them? (north, west, and south)

 Use *Reading Skills Workbook,* Word Play, page 26, for vocabulary review.

 For additional resources and curriculum-related activities, see *Enrichment,* page T83.

Textbook Study:
Understanding Cause-and-Effect Relationships

Pages 90–93

Objectives

		SKILLS CODE NUMBER
M, T	To identify cause-and-effect relationships	3.3.3
M, T	To identify words that signal cause-and-effect relationships	3.3.3.1

Applying the Skill

Have students read the introduction and the two selections. You may wish to have students read the selections on their own and then do *Building Skills*. Or you may wish to direct students, using the following procedure.

TEXTBOOK STUDY

Understanding Cause-and-Effect Relationships

When you read a textbook, look for cause-and-effect relationships. Word clues like *because, so, therefore,* and *as a result* will sometimes help you see these relationships. Remember, cause-and-effect relationships are often written without these word clues. You can still see the relationships, however, if you look for them.

As you read the following selections, refer to the sidenotes. They will help you to notice the cause-and-effect relationships.

Understanding Cause-and-Effect Relationships in Science

Heating and Cooling Rock

What word clue helps you see a cause and an effect in this sentence?

By day, the energy of the Sun acts on the bare rock of the young mountains. How does the Sun's energy heat the rock? Heat causes rock to expand. As you might expect, the outside of the rock is heated more than the inside.

By night, the rock cools and contracts—but the outside of the rock cools faster than the inside. Day and night the rock expands and contracts, expands and contracts, again and

90

Understanding Cause-and-Effect Relationships in Science

1. Have students read the first paragraph and answer the question in the sidenote. (causes)

again. Cracks begin to show in the rock.

Water from rain and snow runs into the cracks. The water changes the rocks as they get hotter and cooler. Sometimes, when water freezes in a crack, the crack widens. If the crack widens enough, the rock may split. In time, a rock may be worn down into a handful of sand.

The breaking down of rock by weather is called weathering. Watching a mountain for a million years or so, you would see the sharp edges and pointed peaks of the young mountain being worn by weathering. You would see the edges and peaks becoming round and smooth, as the forces of weathering worked on them.

—Concepts in Science: Purple
Harcourt Brace Jovanovich

What causes this to happen? The cause can be found in the sentence before this one.

This sentence shows a cause and an effect. What is the effect of the water's freezing?

This is an effect. What causes the mountain to become round and smooth?

Building Skills

There is a cause-and-effect relationship in each of the sentences below. Part of each sentence is shown in italics. Is the part in italics a cause or an effect?

1. By night, the rock cools and *contracts*.
2. *If the crack widens enough*, the rock may split.
3. Watching a mountain for a million years or so, you would see the sharp edges and pointed peaks of the young mountain being worn by *weathering*.

Understanding Cause-and-Effect Relationships in Social Studies

What caused the farmers to work differently? The first sentence states the two causes.

Forests and wilderness were another important part of the American environment. They, too, forced farmers to work differently. In England, as elsewhere in Europe, farmers had hitched their plows to animals and turned over the soil. Then they raked it to break up the lumps, and planted seed. Most often their crop was wheat. In America, the settlers found few open spaces where they could start to farm. First they had to chop down the trees. Then they cleared a small spot of land where the sunshine could break through. The Eastern Woodland Indians had done the same things in the same environment for thousands of

This part of the sentence is an effect. Why was the sunshine now able to break through?

---

2. Have students read the second paragraph and answer the question in the sidenote at the top of page 91. (Cracks are caused by the expansion and contraction that take place day and night.)

3. Have students read the next paragraph and answer the question in the second sidenote on page 91. (The crack widens.)

4. Have students read the last paragraph and answer the question in the last sidenote. (weathering)

5. Have students complete *Building Skills*.

Answers to *Building Skills* Science Selection

1. effect ("Rock cools" is the cause.); 2. cause; 3. cause

years. The settlers' plows and animals were of little use as long as there were tree stumps and roots in the ground. So they cultivated the soil by poking holes in it. When they had trouble growing wheat, they switched over to the Indian crop, corn.

These two sentences show a cause-and-effect relationship. There are actually one cause and two effects. The cause is there were tree stumps and roots in the ground. What are the two effects?

— People in the Americas
Silver Burdett

Building Skills

1. In the sentence below, find a cause and an effect.

   When they had trouble growing wheat, they switched over to the Indian crop, corn.

2. In the sentence below, which is told first, the cause or the effect?

   The settlers' plows and animals were of little use as long as there were stumps and roots in the ground.

93

Books About Living Things

Exploring City Trees and the Need for Urban Forests by Margaret J. Anderson. McGraw, 1976. This book is about the importance of city trees and the birds and animals that live in them.

Pandas Live Here by Irmengarde Eberle. Doubleday, 1973. You'll meet a family of pandas at home in the wilds of Tibet.

Cats by Nina Leen. Holt, Rinehart & Winston, 1980. The various types and behavior patterns of wild and house cats are described, with photographs, in this book.

Dolly the Dolphin by Margaret Gay Malone. Messner, 1978. This is the true story of a Florida family that adopted a dolphin.

The Emperor Penguins by Kazue Mizumura. T.Y. Crowell, 1969. The habits of these unusual birds of the Antarctic are explained in words and pictures.

Bears of the World by Dorothy Hinshaw Patent. Holiday House, 1980. This illustrated book provides information on the ways of life of seven species of bear.

A Closer Look at Deserts by Valerie Pitt and David Cook. Watts, 1976. You'll explore the world of the desert and meet many of the different kinds of plants, animals, and people who live there.

Killer Whales by Seymour Simon. Lippincott, 1978. You'll read about one of the world's largest, smartest, and most misunderstood animals.

94

Understanding Cause-and-Effect Relationships in Social Studies

1. Have students read the first two sentences and answer the question in the first sidenote. (forests and wilderness)

2. Have students read the selection up to and including the sentence "Then they cleared a small spot of land where the sunshine could break through." Now have them answer the question in the second sidenote. (The settlers had cleared the land [chopped down the trees].)

3. Have students read the remainder of the selection and answer the question in the last sidenote. (Effects: The settler's plows and animals were of little use.... They cultivated the soil by poking holes in it.)

4. Have students complete *Building Skills*.

Answers to *Building Skills*
Social Studies Selection

1. Cause: they had trouble growing wheat; Effect: they switched over to the Indian crop, corn; 2. The effect is told first.

If students have not already read these books, you may wish to recommend them at this time. Bibliographic information about these and other books for students is given in the *Resource Center.*

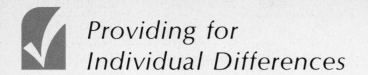

Providing for Individual Differences

Skills Lesson

Additional Practice

Worksheet 4, Teacher's Edition, page T483

Vocabulary Study

Additional Practice

■ **Identifying and using synonyms as context clues**
Write the following italicized words on the board and read aloud each sentence. Have students identify the synonym in each sentence.

humorous—You may think the joke is humorous, but I don't find it amusing. (amusing)

reduce—You can reduce the time it takes to bake this cake if you decrease the amount of each ingredient in the recipe. (decrease)

consolation—Mother always gives me sympathy when I need her consolation. (sympathy)

atrocious—You may not consider it dreadful to put sugar in a salt shaker, but I think it's atrocious. (dreadful)

protest—Some people will object even when there's nothing to protest. (object)

mute—Try to be as silent as a giraffe or as mute as a swan. (silent)

Challenge Activity

■ **Identifying synonyms** Read aloud each sentence or write the sentences on the board. Have students identify the synonyms in each sentence.

Although Ed treated my work with contempt, I don't believe it was worthy of scorn. (contempt, scorn)

Greek is beyond my ken, but I have some knowledge of Latin. (ken, knowledge)

Peggy's report was incomprehensible because her handwriting is unintelligible. (incomprehensible, unintelligible)

Mom wanted to sell her bric-a-brac at the flea market, but apparently no one liked her knick-knacks any more than I do. (bric-a-brac, knick-knacks)

If you think conceited people look in the mirror a lot, then you'll agree that Pat is vain. (conceited, vain)

The small drill won't penetrate the hard wood, but the larger drill will easily pierce it. (penetrate, pierce)

Reading Selection: Giants in the Earth

Additional Practice

■ **Identifying words that signal cause-and-effect relationships** Have students identify the words that signal the cause-and-effect relationships in the sentences below.

1. I got sleepy, so I went to bed. (so)
2. Marie passed the test because she had studied very hard. (because)
3. As a result of my foolishness, I lost two dollars. (As a result)
4. My baby sister wears a bib, so she doesn't get food on her clothing. (so)

Challenge Activity

■ **Identifying cause-and-effect relationships** Have students replace each word clue to the cause-and-effect relationship in the sentences in the preceding activity with another word clue to cause and effect. (Sample answers: 1. therefore; 2. since; 3. Because; 4. therefore)

Reading Selection: The Ship of the Desert

Additional Practice

Identifying cause-and-effect relationships Write the following sentence pairs on the board or read them aloud. Ask students to find a cause and an effect in each sentence pair.

My little sister was soaking wet. (effect) She forgot to take her raincoat with her to school. (cause)

Today was the day we were going on a big trip. (cause) I checked my bag to see if we had everything we needed. (effect)

Tabitha and I saved all our pennies for a while. (cause) Before we knew it, we had several dollars. (effect)

Evaluation

Periodic Test 1, Part IV, Form A or *Form B*, may be administered after this unit to test skills marked **T.** If you have pretested using *Form A*, administer *Form B*.

To posttest all the skills marked **T** in the four Teaching Units in "Learning About Living Things," Part 1, use *Periodic Test 1, Parts I–IV*.

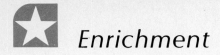

Enrichment

Giants in the Earth

Bibliography

The following books are about trees and plants.

Average

Allison, Linda. *The Reasons for Seasons.* Numerous experiments and interesting stories in "everyday science."

Anderson, Margaret J. *Exploring City Trees and the Need for Urban Forests.* The importance of city trees and the birds and animals that live in them.

Budlong, Ware, and Mark H. Fleitzer. *Experimenting with Seeds and Plants.* Sixty-eight experiments, ranging from very easy to difficult.

Cosgrove, Margaret. *Wonders of the Tree World.* An informal book full of interesting facts and ideas about trees—how to recognize various trees, how to take leaf prints, and things to make from trees. Includes descriptions of unusual trees, such as the banyan, baobab, sequoia, and Joshua.

Simon, Seymour. *Projects with Plants.* Projects that reveal facts about plants.

Challenging

Hutchins, Ross E. *This Is a Tree.* Characteristics of all types of trees.

Ricciuti, Edward R. *Plants in Danger.* Discusses plant species that are in danger of extinction.

Films and Filmstrips

NOTE: For more information, see *Resource Center.*

Selection content

Coronet Instructional Media. *Trees.* The structure, growth, and importance of trees.

Curriculum Coordination

Language Arts

1. Interested students can write letters to the Sierra Club for information about tree conservation. (See *Resource Center* for address.)

2. Have students write a paragraph, poem, or composition entitled "The Life of a Tree" about their impressions of how trees change through the seasons.

Science

1. Integrate this selection with a science lesson on plant life.

2. Invite a naturalist or botanist to take a walk with the class through your community and to point out and discuss the different trees that are seen.

Social Studies

1. With school approval, students can organize a garage sale or carnival to raise funds to buy a tree for the school grounds or community.

2. Students might research countries with few trees. They can share information with the class about how this affects the land.

Art

Students can draw or paint pictures of trees at various stages of growth and during the different seasons for display in the classroom.

Career Education

Arrange for the class to visit a tree nursery.

The Ship of the Desert

Bibliography

The following books are about life in the desert.

Easy

Tyler, Margaret. *Deserts.* The desert world and how animals, plants, and people have adjusted to its harsh conditions.

Average

Pitt, Valerie, and David Cook. *A Closer Look at Deserts.* Different aspects of the desert—its plant life, animal life, and human life.

Challenging

Quilici, Folco. *Great Deserts.* The deserts of the world—their histories and inhabitants, with beautiful pictures.

Films and Filmstrips

NOTE: For more information, see *Resource Center.*

Selection content

Prentice-Hall Media. *Desert Life.* "How Desert Animals Survive" is especially appropriate.

Curriculum Coordination

Language Arts

1. Have students take turns reading about Kipling's "How the Camel Got His Hump" (from the *Just So Stories*). Even though it was written for younger children, intermediate students appreciate and enjoy the humor, imagination, and language used in this story. Encourage them to try to imagine the characters as they read. Have them prepare a joint reading or a dramatization of the story to entertain students in the primary grades.

2. Have students write a story or poem of their own about how the camel got its hump.

3. Have students reread the second paragraph of the selection and then write a poem about a camel caravan. Ask them to describe the land as well as the caravan.

Science

1. Have students do research on plant and animal life in the desert. Perhaps different types of cactuses can be brought into the classroom for students to observe.

2. Students might enjoy a trip to a local zoo where desert animals are kept in their natural habitat. Encourage students to notice the characteristics of these animals that helped them survive the desert environment.

Social Studies

Integrate this selection with a lesson on one or more of the lands where camels are in common use.

Art

1. Students can draw or paint pictures of desert scenes under different weather conditions.

2. Students might make dioramas showing plant and animal life in the desert and share them with the class.

Part 2
You Can't Help Laughing

RESOURCE CENTER

The following list identifies materials that you may want to gather in advance of reading the selections in "You Can't Help Laughing." The list also suggests optional activities that require advance planning. The *Enrichment* section at the end of each Teaching Unit explains how to employ these resources. The *Enrichment* section also gives suggestions for additional activities that do not require advance preparation.

Enrichment Materials and Activities

The Toothpaste Millionaire
Pages 100–112

Enrichment Materials:
Magazines that students may cut up
At least five different brands of toothpaste

Guest Speakers:
An advertising copywriter, art director, account executive, or producer
A scientist involved in the development of new products

The Book That Saved the Earth
Pages 113–128

Enrichment Materials:
Magazines for students to cut, construction paper, art supplies

Activity Needing Advance Planning:
A class excursion to a play

Guest Speaker:
A person involved with local theater: a playwright, an actor, a prop specialist, a scenic designer, or a lighting specialist

Author Study: Robert McCloskey: An Artist with Words and Pictures
Pages 129–133

Guest Speaker:
A writer of fiction

Nothing New Under the Sun (Hardly)
Pages 134–157

Enrichment Materials:
A tape recorder
Drawing paper and pencils
Letter-writing materials

Guest Speaker:
A writer of fiction or a newspaper reporter

Bibliography

For Students

NOTE: For more information about these books, see the *Enrichment* section at the end of each Teaching Unit.

Aiken, Joan. *The Mooncusser's Daughter.* Viking Press, 1974.
Amazing Life Games Company. *Good Cents: Every Kid's Guide to Making Money.* Houghton Mifflin, 1974.
Armstrong, Louise. *How to Turn Lemons into Money: A Child's Guide to Economics.* Harcourt Brace Jovanovich, 1976.
Baumann, Kurt. *The Pied Piper of Hamelin.* Methuen, 1978.
Boiko, Claire, and Sandra Novick. *Who's Afraid of the Big Bad W-H-H-A-A-T?* Childrens, 1977.
Bradley, Alfred, and Michael Bond. *Paddington on Stage: Plays for Children.* Houghton Mifflin, 1977.
Brenner, Barbara. *Ostrich Feathers.* Parents Magazine Press, 1978.
Bunting, Anne Eve. *The Big Cheese.* Macmillan, 1977.
Carlson, Bernice Wells. *Funny-Bone Dramatics.* Abingdon, 1974.
Catling, Patrick Skene. *The Chocolate Touch.* Morrow, 1979.
Cleary, Beverly. *Ramona and Her Father.* Morrow, 1977.
Cone, Molly. *Call Me Moose.* Houghton Mifflin, 1978.
Hicks, Clifford. *Alvin's Swap Shop.* Holt, Rinehart & Winston, 1976.

Hooks, William. *The Seventeen Gerbils of Class 4A.* Coward, 1976.

Hughes, Ted. *The Tiger's Bones and Other Plays for Children.* Viking Press, 1974.

Kalb, Jonah. *The Goof That Won the Pennant.* Houghton Mifflin, 1976.

Korty, Carol. *Silly Soup: Ten Zany Plays.* Scribner, 1977.

McCloskey, Robert. *Blueberries for Sal.* Viking Press, 1948.

————. *Burt Dow, Deep-Water Man.* Viking Press, 1963.

————. *Centerburg Tales.* Viking Press, 1951.

————. *Homer Price.* Viking Press, 1943.

————. *Lentil.* Viking Press, 1940.

————. *Make Way for Ducklings.* Viking Press, 1963.

————. *One Morning in Maine.* Viking Press, 1952.

————. *Time of Wonder.* Viking Press, 1957.

Merrill, Jean. *Maria's House.* Atheneum, 1971.

————. *The Pushcart War.* Addison-Wesley, 1964.

Newell, Crosby. *The Goodbye Summer.* Morrow, 1979.

O'Conner, Jane. *Yours Till Niagara Falls, Abby.* Hastings, 1979.

Olfson, Lewy. *You Can Act!* Sterling, Oak Tree Press, 1971.

Peck, Richard. *Monster Night at Grandma's House.* Viking Press, 1977.

Sharmat, Marjorie. *Maggie Marmelstein for President.* Harper & Row, 1975.

Shearer, John. *The Case of the Sneaker Snatcher.* Delacorte, 1977.

Smith, Moyne Rice. *Seven Plays and How to Produce Them.* Walck, 1968.

Winther, Barbara. *Plays from Folktales of Africa and Asia.* Plays, Inc., 1976.

For Teachers

NOTE: For more information about these books, see the *Background* section that precedes the reading selections.

Baring-Gould, William, and Ceil Baring-Gould. *The Annotated Mother Goose.* Potter, 1962.

Huck, Charlotte S. *Children's Literature in the Elementary School.* Holt, Rinehart & Winston, 1976.

McCloskey, Robert. *Horn Book Magazine.* August 1958.

Parker, Elizabeth Ann. *Teaching the Reading of Fiction.* Teachers College, 1970.

Sebesta, Sam L., and William J. Iverson. *Literature for Thursday's Child.* Science Research, 1975.

Sutherland, Zena, and May Hill Arbuthnot. *Children and Books,* 6th ed. Scott, Foresman, 1981.

Tiedt, Sidney W., and Iris M. Tiedt. *Language Arts Activities for the Classroom.* Allyn, 1978.

Way, Brian. *Development Through Drama.* Humanities, 1972.

Films and Filmstrips

BFA. *The Pied Piper of Hamelin.* Film (#10789).

Encyclopaedia Britannica. *American Legendary Heroes: Rip Van Winkle.* Filmstrip (#7420).

Learning Corp. of America. *The Case of the Elevator Duck.* 16mm color film. Order by title.

Multimedia, Viking Press. Titles: "Blueberries for Sal": eight pupil books, a cassette, and a teacher's guide (#0–670–17593–5); "One Morning in Maine": filmstrip and cassette (#0–670–90586–0); "Make Way for Ducklings": eight pupil books, a cassette, and a teacher's guide (#0–670–45151–7); "Hattie the Backstage Bat": sound filmstrip or filmstrip and cassette (#0–607–90510–0).

Weston Woods. Titles: "Blueberries for Sal": super-8 sound film, or filmstrip with record or cassette (#41); "The Case of the Cosmic Comic": 16mm live-action film or videocassette (#420); "Lentil": film or filmstrip with record or cassette (#14); "Make Way for Ducklings": super-8 sound film, or filmstrip with record or cassette (#3); "Robert McCloskey": film (#403); "Time of Wonder": 16mm film, videocassette, or filmstrip with record or cassette (#31).

Records and/or Tapes

NOTE: Recordings may also be available on other labels.

"Henry Reed, Inc." (Multimedia, Viking Press 0–670–36798–2; cassette 0–670–36799–0)

"Homer Price Stories" (Weston Woods cassette WW 400C)

"The Pied Piper of Hamelin" (Caedmon Records TC 1075; cassette CDL 51075)

OVERVIEW

Part **2**
You Can't Help Laughing

The skills focus of "You Can't Help Laughing" is on identifying elements of humor: the unexpected, exaggeration, and word play. The selections in Part 2 include "The Toothpaste Millionaire," a humorously narrated tale about ambitious friends; "The Book That Saved the Earth," a play involving outrageous characters and fantastic events; and the down-home chuckles of a Robert McCloskey story, "Nothing New Under the Sun (Hardly)."

Previewing "You Can't Help Laughing"

Have students turn to the table of contents in their text. Tell students that their book is divided into eight parts, four of which emphasize reading to learn and four of which emphasize appreciating literature. Part 2, "You Can't Help Laughing," stresses appreciating literature. Point out that each of the Appreciating Literature parts contains an *Understanding and Appreciating Literature* lesson and one or more *Reading Selections,* which are indicated in boldfaced type.

Have students examine the title and the photograph on page 95. Ask students to describe the photograph. (The photograph shows a clown on an elephant.) Ask students to tell what they think Part 2 might be about. (The title and the photograph suggest fun and laughter.)

Have students read the title of each selection and examine the illustrations on pages 96–156. Ask them to think about how the illustrations make them feel. (happy, amused, surprised) Explain to students that in Part 2 they will learn about several types of humor that authors use.

Objectives

The following list of objectives is provided to help you plan your teaching of "You Can't Help Laughing." The objective listed under *Introduced* is for a skill presented for the first time in the HBJ BOOKMARK READING PROGRAM, EAGLE EDITION. All the objectives listed under *Maintained* are for skills previously taught in the HBJ BOOKMARK READING PROGRAM, EAGLE EDITION and reinforced either in

the *Understanding and Appreciating Literature* section in the student's text or in the *Developing the Skill* sections in this Teacher's Edition. Since the emphasis in these lessons is on appreciating literature, the literature skills introduced and maintained in Teaching Unit 5 are not tested.

The symbols I*, I, and M are used throughout this Teacher's Edition. The symbol I* indicates skills introduced for the first time in this program. The I indicates skills introduced earlier in Level 11. The M indicates skills taught at earlier levels and maintained in Level 11. The italicized numbers following the objectives are part of a code developed by the HBJ School Department to facilitate the correlation of skills within and between programs. See page T499 for more information.

Introduced

This skill is introduced for the first time at Level 11 in the HBJ BOOKMARK READING PROGRAM, EAGLE EDITION.

	SKILLS CODE NUMBER
To recognize surprise endings or the unexpected in humor	6.6.5.1

Maintained

These skills have been introduced in earlier levels of the HBJ BOOKMARK READING PROGRAM, EAGLE EDITION and are further developed or refined in Level 11.

	SKILLS CODE NUMBER
To recognize humor in fiction	6.6.5
To recognize word play as an element of humor	6.6.6.7
To recognize exaggeration as an element of humor	6.6.6.6
To recognize humor in illustrations	3.7
To identify techniques of characterization: characters' words and actions	6.9.3.3

Contents

Additional Materials

Reading Skills Workbook: Lesson 9, pages 27–29; Word Play, page 30

Duplicating Masters 11: pages 13–16

Key to Symbols

Skills Objectives
I* — Introduced in this unit
I — Introduced earlier in this level
M — Maintained from previous levels

Reduced Student Pages
underscore — words that appear in the glossary
wavy line — words pretaught in the Teacher's Edition
(these words also appear in the glossary)

Understanding and Appreciating Literature:
Humor
Pages 96–99

Objectives

		SKILLS CODE NUMBER
M	To recognize humor in fiction	6.6.5
M	To recognize word play as an element of humor	6.6.6.7
M	To recognize exaggeration as an element of humor	6.6.6.6
I*	To recognize surprise endings or the unexpected in humor	6.6.5.1

Introducing the Lesson

1. Write the following riddle on the board:

   What kind of paper can you tear?

   Let students volunteer answers before writing the answer:

   Terrible paper!

2. This answer may elicit some giggles from your students. Ask students why they thought this riddle was funny. Encourage them to explain that they didn't expect the answer.

UNDERSTANDING AND APPRECIATING LITERATURE

Humor

Humor is anything that is funny. Cartoons and stories can be humorous in many different ways.

Understanding Humor in Exaggeration and the Unexpected

Humor can come from a surprise twist that you don't expect. Read the cartoon. What is the funny surprise? You don't expect the "cat" to be a tiger. The humor comes from the **unexpected.** When you expect something normal, a cartoon or story can catch you off guard and make you laugh.

96

Many cartoons are funny because they show something that is hard to believe. Look at the cartoon at the right. It is funny because it exaggerates how quickly the plants are growing. **Exaggeration** makes a cartoon or story funny by showing something that is hard to believe.

Read the following story by Alvin Schwartz. Notice how the unexpected and exaggeration make the story funny.

Mule McSneed Captures a Squonk

The squonk is an animal that is so sad about the way it looks that it cries all the time. A famous hunter named Mule McSneed once caught a squonk by following its teardrops. Then he stuck the squonk in a sack and took it home. But the squonk had cried so hard that when he opened the sack, nothing was left of it but a puddle.*

What examples of exaggeration and the unexpected are humorous in the story? The first example of exaggeration is that the squonk cries *all* the time. And that Mule McSneed is able to follow and catch a squonk just by following its trail of tears is also a funny exaggeration. Then, when the author tells us that the squonk turns into a puddle by crying so hard, the author is using the unexpected to help make the story humorous.

Understanding Humor in Word Play

Some authors play on words to make a story humorous. One kind of **word play** is called a *pun.* A pun creates humor by confusing two meanings for the same word. Read the following story.

97

---

3. Tell students that humor is anything someone finds funny, and explain that different types of humor appeal to different types of people. Just as some people like certain foods or kinds of music, some people like certain kinds of humor that others may not like.

4. Have students volunteer to tell other funny riddles or jokes that they know.

Developing the Skill

A. *Humor may come from the unexpected, such as surprise endings.*

1. Have students read the first two paragraphs on page 96.

2. Have students identify what was unexpected in the cartoon. (The cat turned out to be a tiger.)

3. Ask students to tell why they found the cartoon funny. (Students may point out that a huge tiger is so unlike a house cat that the very thought that the boy would call it a cat is funny.)

B. *Humor may come from deliberate exaggeration on the part of an author.*

1. Have students read the first paragraph on page 97. Have them identify the source of humor in this cartoon. (exaggeration) Ask them to tell what is being exaggerated. (Plants growing so fast is an exaggeration.)

2. Ask students to read through the fourth paragraph on page 97. Have them identify the source of humor in the story about the squonk. (exaggeration) Ask them to give examples of exaggeration in the story. (The squonk is described as an animal that is so upset about its appearance that it cries all the time. The squonk is described as having cried itself into a puddle. These are exaggerated events.)

3. Ask students to tell other things that they think are humorous about this story. (Accept all reasonable answers. Students may find the names "squonk" and "Mule McSneed" funny.)

One day a black ant crawled up the side of a cracker box to the top. Here the ant saw a brown ant running as fast as it could around the top edge of the box.

"Why are you running around like that?" the black ant asked.

The brown ant paused and, nearly out of breath, said, "It says, 'To open this box, tear along the dotted line.'"

Why is this story funny? It is funny because of the pun on the word "tear." One meaning for "tear" is "to run hurriedly," as the ant is doing. Another meaning is "to rip or cut open." When the author includes the wrong meaning for "tear," the result is a humorous pun.

Humorous nonsense words are another type of word play. Nonsense words are not real words. "Squonk" is a nonsense word.

Nonsense words may also be mixed-up real words. Read these sentences.

"I stepped in a puddle," said Wilfred, "and my weet got fet. I mean, I stepped in a puddle and my feet got wet."

What are the funny nonsense words? "Weet" and "fet" are nonsense words. What real words did the author mix to make the nonsense words? The sounds at the beginning of the words "feet" and "wet" have been mixed.

Authors create humor in many ways. The unexpected, exaggeration, and word play are all used to create humor. Puns—words that sound the same but have different meanings—and nonsense words are two kinds of humorous word play. No matter how authors create humor, they all have the same goal—they want to make you laugh.

98

Try This

Read the story below. Look for word play, exaggeration, and the unexpected.

Ollepump Possum lived high in a flim-flam tree. He was always happy. If someone told him a joke, Ollepump would laugh for a week. He was a possum who saw the bright side of everything.

One day his friend Pessy warned, "Something terrible will happen someday. What will you say then? Will you *still* see the bright side?"

Just then, Ollepump's branch broke. As Ollepump tumbled past each of his friends, he smiled. "So far, everything's OK!"

Write one sentence from the story to show an example of each of the following kinds of humor:

1. word play   2. exaggeration   3. the unexpected

Writing

1. Use each of the following nonsense words in a funny sentence.

   a. bleeple (animal)   c. Streat Street (place)
   b. floober (bird)   d. fiesel-dueled engine (thing)

2. Write your own humorous paragraph about an imaginary animal called a squoodle. Use exaggeration to make your paragraph funny. You may begin with this sentence:

   The squoodle is so shy that it hides under a rock every time the wind whistles.

As you read "You Can't Help Laughing," look for the different ways humor is created in each story.

99

C. *Some humor is based on word play.*

1. Have students read the last paragraph on page 97 and the first four paragraphs on page 98. Ask students to name the word that is used incorrectly in the context of the story about the ant. (tear) Have students identify the name of this kind of humor. (word play: pun)

2. Have students read through the next-to-last paragraph on page 98. Ask students to name another type of word play. (nonsense words)

3. Ask students to explain what nonsense words are. (They are funny words that are not real words, or they can be mixed-up real words.)

4. Ask students to read the final paragraph on page 98. When they have finished, ask them to give examples from the passages they have just read of each kind of humor. (Something unexpected happens in the cartoon about the tiger; exaggeration appears in the cartoon about the plant and the story of the squonk; word play appears in the story of the squonk and the story about the ant; nonsense words appear in the story about the squonk and the puddle; confusion of meaning is in the story about the ant.)

Try This

Have students complete *Try This*.

Answers to *Try This*

Sentences will vary. **1.** word play: Ollepump Possum lived high in a flim-flam tree. **2.** exaggeration: If someone told him a joke, Ollepump would laugh for a week. **3.** the unexpected: When the branch broke, instead of crying out, Ollepump smiled as he tumbled past each of his friends and said, "So far, everything's OK!"

Writing

(Optional) Have students complete one or both of the *Writing* activities on page 99, using the following procedures:

1. You may wish to write the following titles on the board to help students get started.

   The Day I Met a Strange Animal
   The Bird That Came to Visit
   My Favorite Street
   Henry Brown and His Red Racer

2. Tell students to list or outline their ideas before they begin writing. For students who need help with *Writing* activity 1, suggest that they consider the following: (a) tell what a bleeple looks like, what it eats, or whether it is friendly or unfriendly; (b) tell what a floober looks like—does it fly? What sound does it make?; (c) tell what stores, people, and events you might encounter on Streat Street; (d) tell how this engine is different from others—is it larger or smaller? Does it use more or less fuel? For students who need help with *Writing* activity 2, suggest that they consider the following: (a) tell about the day you brought home a squoodle; (b) tell what a squoodle looks like; (c) tell about the first time you saw a squoodle; (d) tell how you would care for a squoodle as a pet.

3. Encourage students to share their finished work with the class.

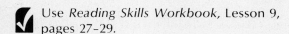 Use *Reading Skills Workbook,* Lesson 9, pages 27–29.

Reading Selection:
The Toothpaste Millionaire

Pages 100–112

Objectives

		SKILLS CODE NUMBER
M	To recognize humor in fiction	6.6.5
M	To recognize exaggeration as an element of humor	6.6.6.6
M	To identify techniques of characterization: characters' words and actions	6.9.3.3

Preparing to Read

Summary

Rufus had big plans to earn his first million dollars making and selling toothpaste, and Kate was going to help. As Rufus saw it, everyone used toothpaste. If 200 million people, approximately the population of the United States, each bought a jar of toothpaste a month, Rufus would be a millionaire in no time! Kate suggested that Rufus go on the Joe Smiley talk show to get some free advertising. While the show-host talked about the fantastic toothpaste, Rufus told the viewers how they could make his toothpaste very easily. Rufus's straightforward approach seemed to work, because the orders began coming in. Although it didn't make them millionaires, Rufus and Kate thought it was a good start.

Background

"The Toothpaste Millionaire," by Jean Merrill, was adapted from a book by the same name. The author has been a writer with the Bank Street College of Education and has written many books for children, including *The Pushcart War* and *Maria's House.*

The following books will provide you with additional background information on humor in children's literature.

Parker, Elizabeth Ann. *Teaching the Reading of Fiction.* A general resource on literary theory; includes discussion of ways to help students develop an appreciation of literature.

Sebesta, Sam L., and William J. Iverson. *Literature for Thursday's Child.* Creative techniques for exploring literature (Part III), and humor as part of the literary experience.

Tiedt, Sidney W., and Iris M. Tiedt. *Language Arts Activities for the Classroom.* Includes teaching literature concepts (Chapter 8) and a resource guide for the teacher (Chapter 10).

Developing Vocabulary and Concepts

curry: a sauce or powder made of finely ground spices and used to season food

census: an official count of all the people in an entire country, a district, or a city, with additional information as to each person's age, sex, occupation, etc.

1. a. Read aloud the following sentences or write them on the board. If you read them aloud, write the underlined vocabulary on the board.

The curry powder added to my food is too hot and spicy for my taste.

Official population figures from the 1980 census show that there are more women than men living in the United States.

b. Ask students to give the meaning of each vocabulary word. Remind them to use context clues in the sentences to help them.

2. Ask students to imagine that they are going to invent a product that will make them millionaires. Ask them to tell what they would invent and why they think such a product might make them millionaires. (Provide time for students to suggest some possible inventions. Ask them to consider whether the invention would appeal to many people, what it would cost to make, and other practical matters.)

3. After students have decided on some products, ask students to consider how they would let people know about their product so that it would sell.

 Use *Duplicating Masters 11,* page 13, Part A.

The Toothpaste Millionaire

by JEAN MERRILL

One afternoon I stopped by my friend Rufus's house to borrow his bike pump. He had about fifty bowls and pans scattered around the kitchen.

"What are you making?" I asked.

"I already made it," Rufus said.

He handed me a spoon and a bowl with some white stuff in it. I took a spoonful.

"Don't eat it," Rufus said. "Just taste it. Rub a little on your teeth. It's toothpaste."

I tried a little.

"How does it taste?" Rufus asked.

"Not bad," I said. "Better than the kind my mother buys in the pink-and-white striped tube. How'd you get it to taste so good?"

"A drop of peppermint oil," Rufus said. "But I've got other flavors, too."

101

He pushed three other pots across the table. The first one had a spicy taste.

"Clove-flavored," Rufus said. "You like it?"

"I don't know," I said. "It's interesting."

"Try this one."

The next sample had a sweet taste. "Vanilla," I guessed.

"Right," Rufus said.

"I like vanilla," I said. "In milkshakes. Or ice cream. But it doesn't seem quite right in toothpaste. Too sweet."

"This one won't be too sweet," Rufus said, handing me another sample.

"*Eeegh*," I said and ran to the sink to wash out my mouth. "What did you put in *that*?"

"Curry powder," Rufus said. "You don't like it? I thought it tasted like a good shrimp curry."

"Maybe it does," I said, "but I don't like curry."

Rufus looked disappointed. "I don't suppose you'd like it almond-flavored, either," he said. "I made some of that, too, but I decided not too many people would take to almond."

"What flavor is in that big plastic pan?" I asked. "You've got enough of that kind to frost twenty-seven cakes."

"That's no kind yet," Rufus said. "That's just seventy-nine cents worth of the stuff that goes in the paste. I didn't want to flavor it till I figured out the best taste."

"What does it taste like plain?" I asked.

"Well," Rufus said, "mostly you taste the bicarb."

"Bicarb!" I said. "You mean all this stuff I've been tasting has got <u>bicarbonate of soda</u> in it?"

102

Setting Purposes

Skills

Remind students to look for elements of humor in "The Toothpaste Millionaire." Ask them to look for exaggeration and humorous descriptions.

Content

Tell students that they are going to read a story about a boy and his partner who think they have invented something that will make them millionaires. Ask students to look for the characters' humorous actions in this story.

2 Reading and Discussing

Have students read the selection. Most students will be able to complete it in one sitting.

NOTE: The questions that appear in the student's text at the end of the selection focus on comprehension of selection content and on understanding humor. Answers to these questions begin on page T97.

Rufus grinned. "Yeah," he said. "It's probably good for your stomach as well as your teeth."

"You must have enough for ten tubes in that plastic bowl," I guessed.

"More, I bet," Rufus said.

"Why don't you squeeze the toothpaste in the tube into a measuring cup and then measure the stuff in the bowl," I suggested.

"That would be a waste of toothpaste," Rufus said. "We couldn't get it back in the tube." Rufus hates to waste anything.

"I have a better idea," he said. "I'll pack into a square pan the toothpaste I made. Then I can figure out how many cubic inches of toothpaste we have. And you can figure out how many cubic inches of toothpaste are in the tube."

"But the tube is round, Rufus," I said. "I can't measure cubic inches unless something is cube-shaped."

Rufus thought a minute. "Maybe we can squeeze the tube into a cube shape," he said.

I thought that was brilliant. But then I had another idea.

"Rufus," I said. "It says on the tube that it contains 3.25 ounces of toothpaste. Why couldn't we just weigh your paste and divide by 3.25 to see how many tubes it would make?"

"Hey—we could!" Rufus said. "You are *smart*, Kate. I'm always doing things the hard way."

That's what is really so nice about Rufus. It's not just that he gets great ideas like making toothpaste. But if *you* have a good idea, he says so.

I was pleased that I had thought of a simpler way of measuring the toothpaste, but I told Rufus, "I wish I was smart enough even to *think* of a hard way of doing something."

I *never* would have thought of measuring toothpaste in cubic inches. Partly because I never can remember exactly how to figure cubic inches. And I certainly wouldn't have thought of making a round tube cube-shaped. Would you?

Anyway it turned out Rufus had made about forty tubes of toothpaste for seventy-nine cents.

Before I finished breakfast the next morning, there was a knock on the door. It was Rufus. He was very excited.

"Kate!" he said. "Do you know what the population of the United States is?"

"No," I said. I never know things like that.

104

My father looked up from his paper. "According to the most recent census—over 200,000,000," he said to Rufus. My father always knows things like that.

"You're right," Rufus said. "And by now, it must be even bigger."

"Probably," my father said.

"Mr. MacKinstrey," Rufus said. "I was thinking that everybody in the United States probably uses about one tube of toothpaste a month."

"Probably," my father said.

"And if they do," Rufus said, "how many tubes of toothpaste are sold in a year?"

My father thought for a second. "Roughly two-and-a-half billion tubes."

"Right!" Rufus said.

I hate people who can multiply in their heads. Except that my father and Rufus are two of the people I like best in the world. How do you explain that?

I really don't like math at all, even when I have a paper and pencil and all the time in the world to figure something out.

And at the same time I look forward every day to Mr. Conti's math class. And how do you explain that, since that's the class where I'm always getting in trouble?

For example, the same day my father answered Rufus's population question, Mr. Conti said in math class:

"Kate MacKinstrey, would you please bring me that note."

"Well, it isn't exactly a note, Mr. Conti."

"I see," says Mr. Conti. "I suppose it's another math problem."

105

"It looks like a math problem, Mr. Conti."

The message from Rufus that Mr. Conti got to read that day said:

If there are 2½ billion tubes of toothpaste sold in the U.S. in one year, and 1 out of 10 people switched to a new brand, how many tubes of the new brand would they be buying?

The right answer is 250 million. It took the class a while to figure that out. Some people have trouble remembering how many zeros there are in a billion.

Then there was a second part to the note:

If the inventor of the new toothpaste made a profit of 1¢ a tube on his toothpaste, what would his profit be at the end of the year?

And it turns out that the inventor of this new toothpaste would make a two-and-a-half million dollar profit!

Well, that's how Rufus's toothpaste business started. Rufus figured out that if he sold the toothpaste for only a penny more than it cost him to make—it cost him about two cents a tube—he'd soon have millions of customers.

106

He had to start in a small way, of course. When he started his business, Rufus packed the toothpaste in baby food jars. A baby food jar holds about as much as a big tube, and the jars didn't cost him anything.

People with babies were glad to save jars for Rufus, as nobody had thought of a way of instantly recycling baby food jars before. When Rufus put a sign on the bulletin board at school saying that he could use the jars, kids brought us hundreds of them.

We sterilized and filled the jars. When we had about five hundred jars, Rufus and I stuffed our saddlebags with as many as they would hold and rode our bikes around the neighborhood selling the toothpaste.

think Rufus's way of advertising the toothpaste would sell toothpaste, either.

Joe Smiley is the kind of guy who is always saying things are the "greatest" thing he ever heard of. Or the most "fantastic." If a girl comes on his show in a pink coat that Joe thinks is attractive, he'll say, "That's the most fantastic coat!" There's nothing that special about the coat. He just means it's nice.

What I mean is, he exaggerates. And everybody Joe has on his show is one of the greatest people he ever met or has done the most fantastic thing.

We sold quite a few jars. At only three cents a jar, most people felt they could afford to give it a try, and most of the customers said it was good toothpaste.

Still, I could not see how Rufus was going to get rich on three-cent toothpaste unless millions of people knew about it. Then I had this idea about how he could get some free advertising.

Everybody in Cleveland watches a program called "The Joe Smiley Show." On the show, Joe interviews people who have interesting hobbies.

I wrote Joe Smiley a letter telling him I had this friend who had a hobby of making toothpaste and could make about two years' supply for the price of one tube. And Joe Smiley called up Rufus to ask if he would be on the show.

Rufus was very good on the show, though I was afraid that he never would get around to talking about the toothpaste. I was worried because when Joe Smiley asked Rufus how he had learned to make toothpaste, Rufus started telling about his Grandmother Mayflower.

He not only told about how she made scrapbook paste, but about how his Grandma Mayflower had made her own furnace out of two 100-gallon oil barrels. Joe Smiley was so interested in that furnace that it was hard to get him off the subject of Rufus's grandmother.

Rufus told about his grandmother taming raccoons, woodchucks, mice, chipmunks, and catbirds. And, of course, about her brushing her teeth with plain baking soda. You wouldn't think all that stuff about Rufus's grandmother would sell toothpaste. But then, as my father pointed out, you wouldn't

So when Joe does get to Rufus's toothpaste, he naturally gives it this big build-up. Which is what I was counting on. And what does Rufus do?

The conversation went something like this:

JOE: Now, Rufus, this fantastic toothpaste you make—I suppose it has a special, secret formula.

RUFUS: No. It's made out of stuff anybody can buy for a few cents and mix up at home in a few minutes.

JOE: Fantastic! And, of course, it's much better than the kind you buy at the store.

RUFUS: I don't know about that. But it tastes pretty good. And for about two cents you can make as much as you get in a seventy-nine cent tube.

JOE: Fantastic! And where can people get some of this great toothpaste?

RUFUS: If they live in East Cleveland, I'll deliver it to them on my bike. Three ounces cost three cents—it costs me two cents to make and I make one cent profit. If anyone outside East Cleveland wants some, I'll have to charge three cents plus postage.

JOE: Fantastic! And what do you call this marvelous new product?

RUFUS: TOOTHPASTE.

JOE: Just toothpaste? It doesn't have a name like SPARKLE or SHINE or SENSATION or

WHITE LIGHTNING or PERSONALITY PLUS?

RUFUS: No, it's just plain TOOTHPASTE. It doesn't do anything sensational such as improve your smile or your personality. It just keeps your teeth clean.

Who would have thought that telling people toothpaste wouldn't do one thing for their personality would sell toothpaste?

But three days after Rufus was on "The Joe Smiley Show," he got 689 orders for TOOTHPASTE. One came all the way from Venice, California, from a man who happened to be telephoning his daughter while the show was watching the show in Cleveland. The daughter said, "There's a kid here who's selling toothpaste for three cents a jar." And her father ordered three dozen jars.

Fantastic!

Understanding What You've Read

1. How did Kate like the taste of the peppermint toothpaste? How did she feel about the curry-flavored toothpaste?
2. Find the word *curry* in a dictionary. Why might curry be an unusual flavor for a toothpaste?
3. In the TV interview between Joe Smiley and Rufus on pages 109–111, what are some of the words that Joe Smiley uses to exaggerate what Rufus says about toothpaste?
4. In the TV interview with Joe Smiley, what does Rufus say that helps you know he's a very honest person? Find sentences to support your answer.

Writing

1. Write one or more sentences describing a new toothpaste. Give your toothpaste a funny name. Tell about all the wonderful things this toothpaste will do for the people who use it. Use exaggeration to make your sentences humorous.
2. Write a few sentences or a paragraph that tells what happened to Rufus after he sold a million jars of toothpaste. Use unexpected events to make your sentences or paragraph funny.

112

Questions preceded by a bullet are additional questions and appear in the Teacher's Edition only. The other questions appear in the student's text after the selection.

Understanding What You've Read

1. *How did Kate like the taste of the peppermint toothpaste? How did she feel about the curry-flavored toothpaste?* (Kate liked the peppermint toothpaste. She did not like the curry-flavored toothpaste. pages 101 and 102) LITERAL <u>Recalling stated information</u>

● *What are some of the other toothpaste flavors Rufus experimented with? What flavors would you make?* (Clove-flavored, vanilla, almond-flavored. page 102 Accept all reasonable answers.) LITERAL/CRITICAL <u>Recalling specific details</u>

2. *Find the word* curry *in a dictionary. Why might curry be an ususual flavor for a toothpaste?* (The *Harcourt Brace Jovanovich School Dictionary* gives this definition for *curry*: A sauce or powder made of finely ground spices and used to season food. Encourage students to recognize that most people like to have a fresh taste in their mouth when they have finished brushing their teeth, not a strong, spicy taste. Accept all reasonable answers.) INFERENTIAL <u>Drawing conclusions</u>

● *What does Rufus say and do in this story that lets you know what kind of person he is? Support your answers.* (Accept all reasonable answers. Encourage students to realize that he is an honest and direct person.) CRITICAL <u>Identifying techniques of characterization: characters' words and actions</u>

3. *In the TV interview between Joe Smiley and Rufus on pages 109–111, what are some of the words that Joe Smiley uses to exaggerate what Rufus says about toothpaste?* (fantastic toothpaste; special secret formula; it's much better than the kind you buy at the store; great toothpaste, marvelous new product) CRITICAL <u>Recognizing exaggeration as an element of humor</u>

4. *In the TV interview with Joe Smiley, what does Rufus say that helps you know he's a very honest person? Find sentences to support your answer.* (He does not make any claims for a secret formula. He does not claim that it tastes better than toothpaste available in stores. He reveals that "for about two cents you can make as much as you get in a seventy-nine cent tube." He says that it doesn't do anything sensational such as improving your smile or your personality. He only claims that it keeps your teeth clean. pages 110 and 111) INFERENTIAL <u>Making judgments</u>

Writing

(Optional) Have students complete one or both of the *Writing* activities on page 112. Or ask students to choose one of the writing activities under *Additional Writing Activity*.

1. *Write one or more sentences describing a new toothpaste. Give your toothpaste a funny name. Tell about all the wonderful things this toothpaste will do for the people who use it. Use exaggeration to make your sentences humorous.*   Writing sentences

   Tell students to list or outline their ideas before they begin writing. If students need help with the *Writing* activity, suggest that they consider the following: (a) exaggerate what the toothpaste will do for people: tell about how it tastes, what it does for the teeth, and how people will be different because of the new toothpaste; (b) choose a flavor for the toothpaste that is unusual, one you wouldn't expect in a toothpaste; (c) tell whether the toothpaste is soft, hard, sweet, sour, or foamy, and tell whether people have to use a little of it or a lot to get their teeth clean.

   You may wish to write the following opening sentences on the board:

   > My new toothpaste is called Purple Sludge.
   > A new toothpaste has hit the market direct from the experimental laboratories of Dynamite Cleansers, Inc.

   Have students write their own opening sentence or choose one from the board and then start writing.

2. *Write a few sentences or a paragraph that tells what happened to Rufus after he sold a million jars of toothpaste. Use unexpected events to make your sentences or paragraph funny.*   Writing a paragraph

   Tell students to list or outline their ideas before they begin writing. If students need help with the *Writing* activity, suggest that they consider the following: (a) tell what Rufus did with his profits from selling a million jars of toothpaste; (b) tell about an important person who wanted to hire Rufus; (c) tell about a trip Rufus took around the world; (d) tell about another "useful" product Rufus invented.

   You may wish to write the following opening sentence on the board:

   > Rufus was scarcely off the air from his TV interview with Joe Smiley when he received a mysterious telephone call.

Additional Writing Activity (Optional)

- *Imagine that you are one of the viewers who saw Rufus on "The Joe Smiley Show." Write Rufus a letter about his appearance on the show and what you thought about it.*   Writing a letter

- *Write a brief conversation between Kate and Rufus that might have taken place the day before the talk show, as they were planning what Rufus would say to advertise his toothpaste.*   Writing a dialogue

Have students list or outline their ideas before they begin writing. Tell students to be sure to include the characters' different opinions.

⭐ For additional resources and curriculum-related activities, see *Enrichment*, page T121.

Reading Selection:
The Book That Saved the Earth

Pages 113–128

Objectives

		SKILLS CODE NUMBER
M	To recognize humor in fiction	6.6.5
M	To recognize word play as an element of humor	6.6.6.7
I*	To recognize the unexpected as an element of humor	6.6.5.1

1 Preparing to Read

Summary

A historian in the twenty-sixth century takes her audience at the Museum of Ancient History back into antiquity to the Martian invasion of Earth in 1988. At that time, a group of Martians with large, egg-shaped heads had landed on Earth, prepared to take over the planet of tiny-headed Earthlings. But upon deciphering a mysterious code in a book they found, the Martians decided to beat a hasty retreat. What was the book that saved the Earth? A book of Mother Goose rhymes, which the Martians took literally—especially the grim rhyme of egg-headed Humpty Dumpty, which convinced them that the Earthlings were aware of the Martians' existence and were preparing to invade Mars.

Background

"The Book That Saved the Earth" is one of many plays Claire Boiko has written for children. This play is for reading purposes only. For permission to produce the play, write to: Plays, Inc., 8 Arlington Street, Boston, MA 02116. Should you decide to produce the play, running time is approximately twenty minutes. Additional scripts can be obtained from Plays, Inc.

The following books will provide you with additional background information on humor and dramatics in children's literature.

Baring-Gould, William, and Ceil Baring-Gould. *The Annotated Mother Goose.* A collection of well-known nursery rhymes.

Huck, Charlotte S. *Children's Literature in the Elementary School.* Discusses humor as it relates to fantasy, realistic stories, poetry, etc. Also discusses drama and creative dramatics.

Way, Brian. *Development Through Drama.* A guide for teachers producing plays with students.

Developing Vocabulary and Concepts

intellectually: of or having to do with the intellect
riffling: turning pages impatiently
iota: the ninth letter of the Greek alphabet; a small amount
omega: the last letter of the Greek alphabet; the end, the last
intently: with great attention
frequency: station or tuning location on a radio
contrary: determined to disagree

1. **a.** Read aloud the following sentences or write them on the board. If you read them aloud, write the underlined vocabulary on the board.

   She was intellectually gifted, and her excellent marks showed her high level of mental ability.
   The nervous professor was riffling through the papers on his desk to find the one he had misplaced.
   There wasn't an iota of evidence against him, so he was released after the trial for lack of evidence.
   She recited the Greek alphabet all the way from alpha, the first letter, to omega, the last.
   The wild bird looked at the boy intently, as if it were trying to memorize his face, and then it flew away.
   Because the radio is set on the wrong frequency, we are not getting the right station.
   My cousin is stubborn and contrary—he always disagrees with me.

   b. Ask students to give the meaning of each vocabulary word. Remind them to use context clues in the sentences to help them.

   c. Students may be interested to know that the word for "big" is from the Greek *mega.* The word *omega* literally means "big o." The Greek word *mega* is found in some English words, such as *megaphone,* which means "big sound."

2. Ask students to turn to page 113 and read the title of the next selection. Ask them to think about how a book could possibly save the Earth. Provide time for a short discussion.

3. Ask students to notice the play form of the next selection. Ask students what the differences are between a play and a story such as "The Toothpaste Millionaire." (Students should understand that a story is written to be read silently or possibly aloud. A play is written to be read aloud or performed, and includes directions for setting, action, and a cast of characters. A play usually has a list of characters and a description of the setting at the beginning, as this one does.)

4. Call attention to the dialogue format of the play. Ask students to tell why they think a character's name appears before each part of dialogue. (Students' answers should include that this format makes it possible for characters to keep track of and to read their parts more easily than they could if the dialogue were in paragraph form.)

5. Ask students to notice the illustration on page 113. Ask them what clues this illustration gives to the context of the play they will read. For example, is the play set in the past or the future? How can they tell? Will the play be factual or fanciful? What makes them think so? (Students should notice that the sign in the illustration refers to a Museum of Ancient History and that this is the Department of the Twentieth Century—the century in which we presently live. This should tell students that the play will be set in the future and that it will be fanciful rather than factual.)

 Use *Duplicating Masters 11,* page 13, Part *B.*

Setting Purposes

Skills

Have students watch for word play used for humorous effect. Also ask them to watch for any funny, unexpected events.

Content

Have students discuss the role of the Historian, who is introduced on page 113. Explain that the Historian is the narrator. You may wish to review with students the function of a narrator, which is often to establish where and when the play is taking place. Ask students to be aware of the function of the Historian as they read the play. Ask them to look for funny character traits.

The Book That Saved the Earth

by CLAIRE BOIKO

Characters

HISTORIAN
GREAT AND MIGHTY THINK-TANK
APPRENTICE NOODLE
CAPTAIN OMEGA
LIEUTENANT IOTA
SERGEANT OOP
OFFSTAGE VOICE

BEFORE RISE: *Spotlight shines on* HISTORIAN, *who is sitting at table down right, on which is a movie projector. A sign on an easel beside her reads:* MUSEUM OF ANCIENT HISTORY: DEPARTMENT OF THE TWENTIETH CENTURY. *She stands and bows to audience.*

HISTORIAN: Good afternoon. Welcome to our Museum of Ancient History, and to my area—things of the good old, far-off twentieth century. The twentieth century was often called the Age of the Book. In those days, there were books about everything from ants to <u>zo-ology</u>. Books taught people how to, and when to, and where to, and why to. But the strangest thing a book every did was to save the Earth. You haven't heard

113

2 Reading and Discussing

Have students read the selection. Most students will be able to complete it in one sitting.

NOTE: The questions that appear in the student's text at the end of the selection focus on comprehension of selection content and on understanding humor. Answers to these questions begin on page T105.

about the Martian invasion of 1988? Really, what *do* they teach children today? Well, you know, Mars never did take over the Earth, because a single book stopped it. What was that book, you ask? A great encyclopedia? A book about rockets and missiles? A secret file from outer space? No, it was none of these. It was—but here, let me turn on the historiscope. I'll show you what happened many, many years ago, in 1988. *(She turns on projector and points it left. Spotlight on* HISTORIAN *goes out and comes up down left on* THINK-TANK, *who is seated on a raised box, arms folded. He has a huge, egg-shaped head, and he wears a long robe decorated with stars and circles.* APPRENTICE NOODLE *stands beside him at an elaborate switchboard. A sign on an easel reads:* MARS SPACE CONTROL. GREAT AND MIGHTY THINK-TANK, COMMANDER-IN-CHIEF. BOW LOW BEFORE ENTERING.*)*

NOODLE *(Bowing)*: O Great and Mighty Think-Tank, most powerful and intelligent being, what are your orders?

THINK-TANK: You left out something, <u>Apprentice</u> Noodle. Go over the whole thing again.

NOODLE: It shall be done, sir. *(In a singsong)* O Great and Mighty Think-Tank, Ruler of Mars and her two moons, most powerful and intelligent being—*(Out of breath)* what-are-your-orders?

THINK-TANK: That's better, Noodle. I wish to talk with our space probe to that silly little world we are going to put under our great rulership. What do they call it again?

NOODLE: Earth, your Intelligence.

114

THINK-TANK: Earth—of course. You see how <u>insignificant</u> the place is? But first, something important. My mirror. I wish to consult my mirror.

NOODLE: It shall be done, sir. *(She hands* THINK-TANK *a hand mirror.)*

THINK-TANK: Mirror, mirror, in my hand. Who is the most fantastically <u>intellectually</u> gifted being in the land?

OFFSTAGE VOICE *(After a pause)*: You, sir.

THINK-TANK *(Smacking mirror)*: Quicker. Answer quicker next time. I hate a slow mirror. *(He admires himself.)* Ah, there I am. Are we Martians not handsome? So much better looking than those ugly Earthlings with their tiny heads. Noodle, keep on using your mind. Someday you may have a balloon brain just like mine.

115

NOODLE: Oh, I hope so, Mighty Think-Tank. I hope so.

THINK-TANK: Now, call the space probe. I want to take over that ball of mud called Earth before lunch.

NOODLE: It shall be done, sir. *(She twists knobs and adjusts levers on switchboard. Electronic buzzes and beeps are heard as the curtains open.)*

*   *   *

SETTING: *The Centerville Public Library*

AT RISE: CAPTAIN <u>OMEGA</u> *stands at center, opening and closing card catalogue drawers in a puzzled fashion.* LIEUTENANT <u>IOTA</u> *is up left, counting books in a bookcase.* SERGEANT OOP *is at right, opening and closing a book, turning it upside down, shaking it, and then* <u>riffling</u> *the pages and shaking his head.*

NOODLE *(Adjusting knobs)*: I can see the space crew, sir. *(*THINK-TANK *puts on a pair of huge goggles and turns toward the stage to watch.)* They seem to have gone into some sort of Earth building.

THINK-TANK: Very good. Make voice contact.

NOODLE *(Speaking into a microphone)*: Mars Space Control calling the crew of Probe One. Mars Space Control calling the crew of Probe One. Come in, Captain Omega. Give us your location.

CAPTAIN OMEGA *(Speaking into a disc which is on a chain around his neck)*: Captain Omega to Mars Space Control. Lieutenant Iota, Sergeant Oop, and I have landed on Earth without any trouble. We are now in this *(Indicates room)*—this square place. Have you any idea where we are, Lieutenant Iota?

117

IOTA: I can't figure it out, Captain. *(Holding up a book)* I've counted two thousand of these odd things. This place must be some sort of storage barn. What do you think, Sergeant Oop?

OOP: I haven't a clue. I've been to seven galaxies, but I've never seen anything like this. Maybe they're hats. *(He opens a book and puts it on his head.)*

OMEGA *(Bowing low)*: Perhaps the Great and Mighty Think-Tank will give us his thoughts on the matter.

THINK-TANK: Very simple, my dear Omega. Hold one of the items up so that I may view it closely. *(OMEGA holds a book on the palm of his hand.)* Yes, yes. I understand now. Since Earthlings are always eating, the place in which you find yourselves is surely a refreshment stand.

OMEGA *(To IOTA and OOP)*: He says we're in a refreshment stand.

OOP: Well, the Earthlings certainly have strange taste.

THINK-TANK: That item in your hand is called a sandwich.

IOTA *(Nodding)*: A sandwich.

OOP *(Taking book from his head)*: A sandwich?

THINK-TANK: Sandwiches are an important part of the Earth diet. Look at it closely. *(OMEGO squints at book.)* There are two slices of what is called "bread" and between them there is some sort of filling.

OMEGA: That is correct, sir.

THINK-TANK: To show that I am right, I order you to eat it.

118

OMEGA *(Gulping)*: Eat it?

THINK-TANK: Do you doubt the Mighty Think-Tank?

OMEGA: Oh, no, no. But poor Lieutenant Iota has not had her breakfast. Lieutenant Iota, I order you to eat this —this sandwich.

IOTA: Eat it? Oh, Captain! It's a very great honor to be the first Martian to eat a sandwich, I'm sure, but— but how can I eat before my sergeant does? *(Handing OOP the book; brightly)* Sergeant Oop, I order you to eat the sandwich.

OOP *(Making a face)*: Who, Lieutenant? Me, Lieutenant?

IOTA and OMEGA *(Slapping their chests in a salute)*: For the glory of Mars, Oop!

OOP: Yes, Captain. At once, Lieutenant. *(He opens his mouth wide. OMEGA and IOTA watch him breathlessly. He bites down on a corner of the book, and pantomimes chewing and swallowing, while making terrible faces.)*

OMEGA: Well, Oop?

IOTA: Well, Oop? *(OOP coughs. OMEGA and IOTA pound him on the back.)*

THINK-TANK: Was it not delicious, Sergeant Oop?

OOP *(Slapping his chest in salute)*: That is right, sir. It was *not* delicious. I don't know how the Earthlings can get those sandwiches down without water. They're as dry as Martian dust.

NOODLE: Sir, sir. Great and Mighty Think-Tank. I beg your pardon, but something just floated into my mind about those sandwiches.

119

THINK-TANK: It can't be worth much but go ahead. Give us your tiny bit of data.

NOODLE: Well, sir, I have seen our films of those sandwiches. I noticed that the Earthlings did not *eat* them. They used them as some sort of communication device.

THINK-TANK *(Haughtily)*: Of course. That was my next point. These are communication sandwiches. Think-Tank is never wrong. Who is never wrong?

OMEGA, IOTA, and OOP *(Together; saluting)*: Great and Mighty Think-Tank is never wrong.

THINK-TANK: Therefore, I order you to listen to them.

OMEGA: Listen to them?

IOTA and OOP *(To each other; puzzled)*: Listen to them?

THINK-TANK: Do you have rocks in your ears? I said, listen to them. *(OMEGA, IOTA, and OOP bow very low.)*

OMEGA: It shall be done, sir. *(They each take two books from the case and hold them to their ears, listening intently.)*

IOTA *(Whispering to OMEGA)*: Do you hear anything?

OMEGA *(Whispering back)*: Nothing. Do you hear anything, Oop?

OOP *(Loudly)*: Not a thing! *(OMEGA and IOTA jump in fright.)*

OMEGA and IOTA: Sh-h-h! *(They listen again.)*

THINK-TANK: Well? Well? Tell me. What do you hear?

OMEGA: Nothing, sir. Perhaps we are not on the correct frequency.

120

IOTA: Nothing, sir. Perhaps the Earthlings have sharper ears than we do.

OOP: I don't hear a thing. Maybe these sandwiches don't make sounds.

THINK-TANK: What? What? Does someone think that the Mighty Think-Tank has made a mistake?

OMEGA: Oh, no sir. No, sir. We'll keep listening.

NOODLE: Please excuse me, your Brilliance. A cloudy piece of information is rolling around in my head.

THINK-TANK: Well, roll it out, Noodle, and I will clarify it for you.

NOODLE: I seem to remember that the Earthlings did not listen to the sandwiches. They opened them and watched them.

THINK-TANK: Yes, that is quite correct. Captain Omega, those sandwiches are not for ear communication. They are for eye communication. Now, Captain Omega, take that large, bright-colored sandwich over there. It looks important. Tell me what you see. (OMEGA *picks up a very large copy of* MOTHER GOOSE, *holding it so that the audience can see the title.* IOTA *looks over his left shoulder, and* OOP *looks over his right shoulder.*)

OMEGA: It seems to contain pictures of Earthlings.

IOTA: And there seems to be some sort of code.

THINK-TANK (*Sharply interested*): Code? Code? I told you this was important. Tell me about it.

OOP: It's little lines and circles and dots. Thousands of them, next to the pictures.

122

THINK-TANK: Code. Perhaps the Earthlings are not as stupid as we have thought. We must break the code. We must.

NOODLE: Forgive me, your Cleverness, but did not we give our crew pills to increase their intelligence?

THINK-TANK: Stop! A thought of great brilliance has come to me. Space crew, we have given you pills to increase your intelligence. Take them and then watch the sandwich. The meaning of the code will slowly unfold before you.

OMEGA: It shall be done, sir. Remove pill. (*Crew take pills from boxes on their belts.*) Present pill. (*They hold pills out in front of them, stiffly.*) Swallow pill. (*They pop the pills into their mouths and gulp simultaneously. They open their eyes wide, and they put their hands to their foreheads.*)

THINK-TANK: Excellent. Now, break that code.

OMEGA, IOTA, *and* OOP (*Together*): It shall be done, sir. (*They frown over the book, turning the pages.*)

OMEGA (*Brightly*): Aha!

IOTA (*Brightly*): Oho!

OOP (*Bursting into laughter*): Ha, ha, ha.

THINK-TANK: What does it say? Tell me this minute. Read, Omega.

OMEGA: Yes, sir. (*He reads with great seriousness.*)

Mistress Mary, quite contrary,
How does your garden grow?
With cockle shells and silver bells
And pretty maids all in a row.

OOP: Ha, ha, ha. Think of that. Pretty maids growing in a garden.

THINK-TANK (*Alarmed*): Stop! This is no time for laughing. Don't you see that this is serious? The Earthlings have found a way to combine farming and mining. They can actually grow crops of rare metals such as silver. And cockle shells. They can grow high explosives, too. Noodle, call our invasion ships.

NOODLE: They are ready to go down and take over Earth, sir.

THINK-TANK: Tell them to hold. Tell them new information has come to us about Earth. Iota, go on reading.

IOTA: Yes, sir. (*She reads very gravely.*)

Hey diddle diddle! The cat and the fiddle,
The cow jumped over the moon,
The little dog laughed to see such sport,
And the dish ran away with the spoon.

OOP (*Laughing*): The dish ran away with the spoon!

THINK-TANK: Stop laughing. This is more and more alarming. The Earthlings have reached a high level of civilization. Didn't you hear? They have taught their animals music and space flight. Even their dogs have a sense of humor. Why, at this very moment, they may be starting an interplanetary attack of millions of cows! Call our ships. No invasion today. Oop, read the next code.

OOP: Yes, sir. (*Reading*)

Humpty Dumpty sat on the wall,
Humpty Dumpty had a great fall;
All the king's horses and all the king's men
Couldn't put Humpty together again.

125

Oh, look, sir. Here's a picture of Humpty Dumpty. Why, sir, he looks like—he looks like—(*He turns a large picture of* HUMPTY DUMPTY *toward* THINK-TANK *and the audience.*)

THINK-TANK (*Screaming and holding his head*): It's me! It's my Great and Mighty Balloon Brain. The Earthlings have seen me. They're after me. "Had a great fall!"—That means they plan to take Mars and me! It's an invasion of Mars! Noodle, get a spaceship for me. I must escape at once. Space crew, you must leave Earth right now. But be sure to hide all trace of your visit. The Earthlings must not know that I know—(OMEGA, IOTA, *and* OOP *rush about, putting books back.*)

NOODLE: Where shall we go, sir?

THINK-TANK: A hundred million miles away from Mars. Order the invasion ships to leave. We are heading for Alpha Centauri, a hundred million miles away. (OMEGA, IOTA, *and* OOP *run off right as* NOODLE *helps* THINK-TANK *off left and the curtain closes. Spotlight shines on* HISTORIAN *down right.*)

HISTORIAN (*Chuckling*): And that's how one dusty old book saved the world from a Martian takeover. As you all know, in the year 2488, five hundred years after all this happened, we Earthlings resumed contact with Mars. And we even became very friendly with the Martians. By that time, Great and Mighty Think-Tank had been replaced by a very clever Martian—the Wise and Wonderful Noodle! Oh, yes, we taught the Martians the difference between sandwiches and books. We taught them how to read, too. We set up a library in the city of Marsopolis. But, as you might expect, there is still one book that the Martians can never bring themselves to read. You've guessed it—MOTHER GOOSE! (*She bows and exits right.*)

127

Questions preceded by a bullet are additional questions and appear in the Teacher's Edition only. The other questions appear in the student's text after the selection.

Understanding What You've Read

1. *Which names of characters are humorous?* (Great and Mighty Think-Tank, Apprentice Noodle, Omega, Iota, and Oop) CRITICAL   Recognizing word play as an element of humor

● *On page 115, when Think-Tank consults his mirror, what does he ask it? This speech is a take-off on a speech by another fictional character. Do you know where it came from? Why do you think it is funny?* (Think-Tank asks his mirror who's the most fantastically intellectually gifted being in the land. This speech is a take-off on the wicked queen from "Snow White," in which the queen asks her mirror who's the fairest of them all. Students may find this take-off humorous. Students may also find Think-Tank's version of the speech funny because he has already said enough to establish that he is not too bright.) LITERAL/CRITICAL   Making analogies

2. *Why didn't the Martians know what libraries and books were?* (The Martians had never seen books or libraries.) INFERENTIAL   Drawing conclusions

● *What did Think-Tank first suggest that the library was? What did he think the books were?* (He thought that the library was a refreshment stand and that the books were sandwiches.   page 118) LITERAL   Recalling specific details

● *Think-Tank confused books with sandwiches. How are these two items similar enough to be confusing?* (The covers of the books are like the bread of sandwiches and the pages between the covers are like some sort of filling.   page 118) INFERENTIAL   Making comparisons

3. *What would you expect someone to do with a book? What unexpected events make the scene on pages 118–119 funny?* (Students should expect that someone would read a book. It is unexpected and funny when Think-Tank orders Omega, who orders Iota, who orders Oop, to eat a book.) CRITICAL   Recognizing the unexpected as an element of humor

● *When Noodle says that he thinks Earthlings use the "sandwiches" as some kind of communication device, how does Think-Tank misinterpret what Noodle says?* (Think-Tank orders his officers to listen to the books, misinterpreting the kind of communication that Noodle is referring to.   page 120) CRITICAL   Recognizing humor in fiction

● *Noodle is very careful not to offend the great Think-Tank when he suggests an idea. How does Noodle phrase his statements on pages 119 and 122 so as not to offend Think-Tank?* (He says, "Something just floated into my mind about those sandwiches" and "A cloudy piece of information is rolling around in my head.") CRITICAL   Recognizing humor in fiction

4. *What was unexpected and funny about the Martians' understanding of the Mother Goose rhymes?* (Accept all reasonable answers. Students should recognize that the Martians interpreted the rhymes literally.) CRITICAL   Recognizing the unexpected as an element of humor

● *Which rhyme terrified Think-Tank? Why did it bother him so much?* ("Humpty Dumpty" scared him because Humpty Dumpty came to such a dismal end and because in the picture in the book, he looked just like Think-Tank.   page 126) INFERENTIAL   Recalling specific details

● *Reread the two speeches of the Historian on pages 113–114 and 127. How would the play have been different without her?* (Accept reasonable answers. Encourage students to recognize that she sets up the story in her first speech and that she ties the story up at the end, thus bringing it to a conclusion.) CRITICAL   Making judgments

Writing

(Optional) Have students complete one or both of the *Writing* activities on page 128. Or ask students to choose one of the writing activities under *Additional Writing Activity.*

1. *Write two sentences that tell what unexpected things might have happened if the Martians had landed in a playground, a zoo, or a supermarket. What might they see? What might they do?* <u>Writing sentences</u>

Tell students to list or outline their ideas before they begin writing. If students need help with the *Writing* activity, suggest that they consider the following: (a) tell what you saw when the Martians landed; (b) tell what the Martians said to you or others; (c) tell how the Martians acted when they left their spaceship and stepped onto the Earth; (d) tell what the Martians reported when they returned home.

2. *Pretend that you are a Think-Tank. Write a funny paragraph to explain one of the following rhymes:*

What Are Little Boys Made Of?
What are little boys made of?
Snips and snails, and puppy dogs' tails;
And that's what little boys are made of.

A Candle
Little Nancy Etticoat
In a white petticoat
And a red nose;
The longer she stands
The shorter she grows.

<u>Writing a paragraph</u>

Tell students to list or outline their ideas before they begin writing. If students need help with the *Writing* activity, suggest that they consider the following: (a) as a Martian, tell how you think an Earth person would use snips, snails, and tails to make a boy; tell about seeing a Martian looking at children and asking, "Where are the snails? Where are the puppy dogs' tails?"; (b) as a Martian, tell how you spent your time looking for someone with a red nose, dressed in white; explain how one or two of the people you found were not Little Nancy Etticoat.

Additional Writing Activity (Optional)

● *Write a paragraph telling about meeting with the Martians. In the first sentence, state a problem involving the Martians' visit. In the next two or three sentences, tell the steps that you would take to solve the problem. In the last sentence, tell what solution you came up with to solve the problem stated at the beginning of the paragraph.* <u>Writing a paragraph</u>

You may wish to suggest the following problems to help students get started:

Where will the Martians stay while visiting Earth? What might be some difficulties for the family that might entertain them?

● *Pretend that the Martians invited you to look over the spacecraft. Write a paragraph telling what you saw in the spacecraft.* <u>Writing a paragraph</u>

Tell students to list or outline their ideas before they begin writing. You may wish to write the following questions on the board to help students get started:

How did the spacecraft compare with what you know about American spacecraft?
What were the living quarters like?
What was the command center like?
How do you think the Martians will get back to their own planet?

⭐ For additional resources and curriculum-related activities, see *Enrichment,* page T122.

Author Study:
Robert McCloskey:
An Artist with Words and Pictures

Pages 129–133

Ask students to read the two paragraphs on page 129. Explain to students that this *Author Study* will tell them about the life of Robert McCloskey and will present background information for the story they are about to read. Have students read the rest of the *Author Study* (pages 130–133).

Author Study:

Robert McCloskey:
An Artist with Words and Pictures

by SARA KRENTZMAN SRYGLEY

The World He Lives In

An author-artist worth knowing is Robert McCloskey. He has written eight books for young people and illustrated them with his drawings and paintings.

Telling about himself in *The Junior Book of Authors*, Mr. McCloskey said, "It is just sort of an accident that I write books. I really think up stories in pictures and just fill in between the pictures with a sentence or a paragraph or a few pages of words." Probably it isn't quite that easy. A look at his life and the books he has produced shows us that his stories and pictures are more carefully planned than Mr. McCloskey suggests.

129

Robert McCloskey with two of his puppets

Robert McCloskey was born in Hamilton, Ohio, in 1914. This was his home until he was a young man. He enjoyed growing up in a small Midwestern town like Hamilton. Robert played in the parks; visited the barber shop, the stores, and the public library; and went to school. He was interested in music. He learned to play the oboe, drums, and harmonica. His favorite instrument was the harmonica. He even taught his friends how to play it. He also enjoyed building model airplanes and all sorts of mechanical contraptions. He is still good at tinkering with machinery and inventing new gadgets. Recently he has been working on developing a new kind of puppet.

Very early in his life, Robert McCloskey knew that he wanted to be an artist. This ambition was encouraged when, as a high school student, he won his first national award for a calendar illustrated with woodcuts.

An art career was his dream, but it became a reality only after years of hard work. He studied art for three years in Boston and for two more years in New York. In the summers, he often went to Cape Cod and painted.

For a while he had a job drawing cartoon strips, but that work did not satisfy him. He liked to draw old Spanish ships, fierce dragons, or heroic characters from Greek and Roman myths. He knew that he wanted to illustrate books.

When he was studying in New York, Mr. McCloskey had taken some of his work to an editor of children's books, May Massee. When Miss Massee had looked carefully at his drawings, she gave him some good advice. She urged him to stop drawing things he knew little about and to concentrate on things that were familiar to him.

Mr. McCloskey took her advice. When he called again on Miss Massee, he had in his portfolio what was to become his first book. *Lentil* is about a boy growing up in a small town in Ohio. Miss Massee was enthusiastic about

the book, and it was published in 1940. Robert McCloskey had begun a successful career as an author and illustrator.

Lentil was followed by other books both written and illustrated by Mr. McCloskey. In addition, he illustrated books written by other authors. Some of his books are picture books in which the pictures and the words are of equal importance in telling the story.

McCloskey was the first illustrator to win the Caldecott Medal twice. This medal is awarded every year for "the most distinguished American picture book for children." In accepting that honor for *Time of Wonder*, he said:

> With everyone clamoring for more scientists, I should like to clamor for more artists and designers. I should like to clamor for the teaching of drawing and design to every child, right along with reading and writing. I think it is most important for everyone really to see and evaluate pictures and really to see and evaluate his surroundings.[1]

The World He Imagines

As you will see, some of Robert McCloskey's own experiences are reflected in his books. The Centerburg in which Homer Price grows up is probably like Mr. McCloskey's hometown. But if he had written and drawn everything as it happened, we would not have had stories — we would have had reports of Robert McCloskey's life.

When Robert McCloskey began to think about the stories of life in the little town of Centerburg, he had to make up names for his characters. The name Homer Price recalls the ancient Greek poet Homer. He was one of the earliest storytellers we know about, and one of the greatest. His

[1] *Horn Book*, August 1958, page 245. Used by permission.

poems tell of adventures of a wandering hero, Ulysses, who left his home to fight in the Trojan War. In one of his adventures, Ulysses saved himself and his companions from evil sirens, or enchanters. He stopped up the ears of his companions so they could not hear the magic song the sirens used to get people to follow them. Robert McCloskey, at the end of "Nothing New Under the Sun (Hardly)," makes Homer Price a modern-day Ulysses.

In Mr. McCloskey's books, Homer Price and Uncle Ulysses are not great heroes — they are just ordinary people in an ordinary town. But perhaps Mr. McCloskey wanted to remind his readers of those famous, ancient men and to suggest that the adventures of ordinary people today are also worth writing books about.

When he wrote the story that follows, "Nothing New Under the Sun (Hardly)," Mr. McCloskey also had some other works of literature in mind. As you will see, the mysterious stranger reminds the people of Centerburg of two famous fictional characters. Have you heard about Rip Van Winkle, the character created by the writer Washington Irving? One day Rip Van Winkle fell asleep in the Catskill Mountains and slept for twenty years. When he woke up, he was an old man with a long beard and old-fashioned clothes. He returned to his village, but of course no one knew him.

Another fictional character that is important in McCloskey's story is the Pied Piper. He was a traveling musician. The mayor of Hamelin, Germany, hired the Pied Piper to rid the town of rats. The Piper played so well that the rats followed him in a swarm. But all the children of the town followed him too — never to return home. When you read "Nothing New Under the Sun (Hardly)," you will see why the people of Centerburg thought the mysterious stranger might be Rip Van Winkle or the Pied Piper.

Reading and Discussing

1. *When did Robert McCloskey know what he wanted to be? What was it? How was his dream encouraged?* (Very early in his life, McCloskey knew he wanted to be an artist. He was encouraged when he won a national art award as a high school senior.   page 131) LITERAL   Recalling specific details

2. *What was the good advice that Miss Massee gave Robert McCloskey? Why do you think it was good advice?* (She told him to draw things that were familiar to him. Students should include the suggestion that familiar things are things that a person knows the most about; they can therefore be portrayed most convincingly to others.   page 131) LITERAL/CRITICAL   Making judgments

3. *What is the Caldecott Medal?* (This medal is awarded every year to an illustrator for "the most distinguished American picture book for children." page 132) LITERAL   Recalling specific details

4. *What school subject did Robert McCloskey point out in his Caldecott Medal acceptance speech as one that he thought every child should be taught?* (He thought drawing and design should be taught along with reading and writing in school. He felt that this would help children to see and evaluate pictures and their surroundings. Some students may agree and others may disagree with this suggestion. Encourage students to support their answers.   page 132) CRITICAL   Making judgments

5. *Where did Robert McCloskey get the names for some of his characters?* (From ancient literature: Homer Price is named for the ancient Greek poet Homer, and Uncle Ulysses is named for one of Homer's greatest characters, Ulysses.   page 133) LITERAL   Recalling specific details

6. *Why do you think Robert McCloskey chose these names for his characters?* (Accept all reasonable answers. The text says that "perhaps Mr. McCloskey wanted to remind his readers of those famous, ancient men and to suggest that the adventures of ordinary people today are also worth writing books about."   page 133) CRITICAL   Drawing conclusions

7. *How do the stories about Centerburg reflect Robert McCloskey's childhood in a small town in Ohio? In what ways has he made the stories different?* (*Lentil* is about a boy growing up in a small town in Ohio, which is like McCloskey's life. He has made the stories different by adding things from his own imagination, things that did not actually happen to him.   pages 131, 132, and 133) INFERENTIAL   Making comparisons

8. *What two fictional characters did Robert McCloskey intend his readers to think of in his story "Nothing New Under the Sun (Hardly)"?* (Rip Van Winkle and the Pied Piper of Hamelin   page 133) LITERAL   Recalling specific details

9. *What kind of person do you think Robert McCloskey is?* (Allow students to express their own views. It is to be hoped that they will have a positive impression of the writer. If students seem eager to know more about this artist and writer, show the film "Robert McCloskey," which can be ordered from Weston Woods. See page T86.) CRITICAL Making judgments

10. *If you wrote a book using experiences you have had, what might you include? If you wanted to honor any book characters that you have particularly liked, which ones would they be? How would you mention these characters in your story?* (Give students a chance to respond on their own. You might then suggest that not only can their characters be named for favorite characters they have read about, but in a description, they might say that a certain character looked, for example, like Fern in *Charlotte's Web*.) CRITICAL   Making judgments

Reading Selection:
Nothing New Under the Sun (Hardly)
Pages 134–157

Objectives

		SKILLS CODE NUMBER
M	To recognize humor in fiction	6.6.5
M	To recognize word play as an element of humor	6.6.6.7
I*	To recognize surprise endings or the unexpected in humor	6.6.5.1
M	To recognize humor in illustrations	3.7

Summary

When a stranger with a long beard and some "strange business" on his car comes into town, it becomes Homer's job to find out what he is up to. Homer reports to his Uncle Ulysses that the man has a musical mousetrap that can rid Centerburg of mice. Homer and his uncle convince the mayor to pay the stranger thirty dollars to do the job. When the stranger starts his machines, the mice come running from every direction.

Everything is going smoothly until the mayor pays the thirty dollars. Then the sheriff charges the stranger thirty dollars for a new license plate for his car. As the stranger drives out of town, the children of the town follow him, and suddenly the grown-ups of Centerburg fear that they may lose their children, Pied Piper–style, along with the mice. It turns out that the children have foreseen the possible enticement of the music and have had the local doctor put cotton in their ears. Everything turns out all right in the end, except that when the mice are released they head straight back to Centerburg.

Background

Robert McCloskey is a well-known author and illustrator of books for children. He was born in Hamilton, Ohio, in 1914 and lived there until he was a young man. McCloskey uses the rich period of his boyhood in many of his stories. He played in parks; visited the barber shop, town stores, and library; and, of course, attended school. He was interested in music and played the oboe, drums, and harmonica. He also enjoyed building model airplanes and tinkering with all sorts of mechanical contraptions.

The following books will provide you with additional background information on humor and on Robert McCloskey.

Huck, Charlotte S. *Children's Literature in the Elementary School.* Extensive information on Robert McCloskey as an author and illustrator, along with general information about humor as it relates to fantasy and realistic stories.

McCloskey, Robert. *Horn Book Magazine.* August 1958. McCloskey's Caldecott Medal acceptance speech for *Time of Wonder.*

Sutherland, Zena, and May Hill Arbuthnot. *Children and Books,* 6th ed. Information on McCloskey as an author and illustrator.

Developing Vocabulary and Concepts

crusade: to fight for a cause or against evil
speculate: to form theories; to imagine possible reasons or answers for something
antique: something very old, made at an earlier time
individualist: a person who believes in or lives his or her own way, no matter what other people think
amnesia: loss of memory caused by sickness, shock, or a hard blow to the head
gaiters: coverings, as of cloth or leather, for the lower legs or ankles
deduction: a conclusion based on reasoning
incorporated: combined, brought together; included as part of something else
spiral: winding or curving like a cone-shaped coil
flustered: confused; embarrassed; upset
pixied: cast a spell over

1. **a.** Read aloud the following sentences or write them on the board. If you read them aloud, write the underlined vocabulary on the board.

Our class at school is going to <u>crusade</u> against cruelty to animals.
I like to <u>speculate</u>, or form theories, about what the weather will be like on the following day.
The rocking chair, which once belonged to my great-grandmother, is old enough to be an <u>antique</u>.
She speaks her mind as an <u>individualist</u>, never caring what others may think.
After he was hit on the head, the man developed <u>amnesia</u> and could not remember his own name or where he lived.
Over his shoes he wore old-fashioned <u>gaiters</u> that covered his ankles.
The detective based her <u>deduction</u> about the crime on the evidence she had gathered.
We have <u>incorporated</u> a bird-watching station into our wildlife recreation center.

I felt dizzy as I climbed up the long, winding <u>spiral</u> staircase.

I was so <u>flustered</u> and embarrassed when it was my turn to speak that I forgot what I wanted to say.

It seemed as though someone had cast a spell over, or <u>pixied</u>, the cat to make it jump in circles.

b. Ask students to give the meaning of each vocabulary word. Remind them to use context clues in the sentences to help them.

2. Ask students to think about the meaning of the title of the next story they will read: "Nothing New Under the Sun (Hardly)." Ask them to tell how the word *hardly* in parentheses changes the meaning of the title. (Students may say that the title means that not much new is happening. They should recognize that the word *hardly* changes the meaning slightly to mean that there is *almost* nothing new happening under the sun.)

3. Since it is important to students' understanding of this story to know stories about Rip Van Winkle, the Pied Piper, and Ulysses and the Sirens, you may wish to play a recording, show a film or filmstrip, or read a book (see *Resource Center*) of each of the stories before asking students to read "Nothing New Under the Sun (Hardly)."

4. Ask students if they have ever heard the saying "If you build a better mousetrap, all the world will beat a path to your door." Ask students to tell what they think this saying means. (Students should recognize that the saying can be interpreted to mean that if someone builds something a little better or has a better idea than someone else, people will want to give it a try.) You may wish to tell students that this saying has become something of a slogan for enterprising businesses.

 Use *Duplicating Masters 11,* pages 14 and 15.

Setting Purposes

Skills

Before students read this next section, remind them to watch for ways in which Robert McCloskey uses word play to create funny situations. Also ask them to look for an unexpected turn of events in this story that changes everything at the last minute.

Content

Ask students to look for ways in which McCloskey's life, growing up in a small town, might have influenced him in writing this story. Also ask them to look for ways in which books that McCloskey read might have influenced him.

2 Reading and Discussing

Have students read the selection. Most students will be able to complete it in one sitting. If you prefer, the selection may be read in two parts, breaking before the first paragraph on page 148.

NOTE: The questions that appear in the student's text at the end of the selection focus on comprehension of selection content and on understanding humor. Answers to these questions begin on page T118.

Nothing New
Under the Sun (Hardly)

by ROBERT McCLOSKEY

After the County Fair, life in Centerburg eases itself back to normal. Homer and the rest of the children concentrate on arithmetic and basketball, and the grownups tend to business and running the town in a peaceful way. Election time still being a month away, the Democrats and the Republicans are still speaking to each other. The Ladies' Aid hasn't anything to crusade about at the moment, and Uncle Ulysses hasn't bought any new-fangled equipment for his lunchroom recently. There is nothing for people to gossip about, or speculate on, or argue about.

There's always the weather, the latest books and movies, and ladies' hats. But, of course, that doesn't provide nearly enough to talk and think about for a whole month until election time. Uncle Ulysses, the sheriff, and the men around the barbershop usually run out of things to talk about toward the middle of the month. Sometimes during the mornings the conversation is lively. Like today, the sheriff came in beaming and said, "Well, I put on long ullen wonderwear—I mean woolen underwear, this morning."

"Soo?" said Uncle Ulysses. "Guess I'll have to get mine out of mothballs this week."

"Humph," said the barber, "I wouldn't wear woolen underwear for anything on earth. It *itches!*"

135

Well, that was something to argue about for almost an hour. Then the subject changed to woolen socks, to shoes, to overshoes, to mud, to mud in roads, to mud in barnyards, barns, and chicken coops. Then there was a long pause. Only ten-thirty by the town hall clock, and conversation had already dwindled to nothing at all. Nothing to do but look out of the barbershop window.

"There goes Doc Pelly," said the barber, "I wonder who's sick?"

"Colby's wife is expectin' a baby," said Uncle Ulysses. "I'll ask Aggy this noon. She might know about it."

"There's Dulcey Dooner," said the sheriff.

"He hasn't worked for three years," added the barber disapprovingly.

A few children came into view. "School's out for lunch," pronounced the sheriff.

The door opened, and Homer came in saying, "Hello, everybody. Uncle Ulysses, Aunt Aggy sent me over to tell you to stir yourself over to the lunchroom and help serve blue-plate specials."

Uncle Ulysses sighed and prepared to leave. The sheriff cupped a hand behind his ear and said, "What's that?" Uncle Ulysses stopped sighing, and everybody listened.

The noise (it was sort of a rattle) grew louder, and then suddenly an old car swung into the town square. The sheriff, the barber, Uncle Ulysses, and Homer watched it with gaping mouths as it rattled around the town square once—twice—and on the third time slowed down and shivered to a stop right out front of Uncle Ulysses' lunchroom.

It wasn't because this car was old, old enough to be an antique; or because some strange business was built onto

136

it; or that the strange business was covered with a large canvas. No, that wasn't what made Homer and the sheriff and Uncle Ulysses and the barber stare so long. It was the car's driver.

"Gosh, what a beard!" said Homer.

"And what a head of hair!" said the barber. "That's a two-dollar cutting job if I ever saw one!"

"Could you see his face?" asked the sheriff.

"Nope," answered Uncle Ulysses, still staring across the square.

They watched the stranger untangle his beard from the steering wheel and go into the lunchroom.

Uncle Ulysses promptly dashed for the door, saying, "See you later."

"Wait for me!" the sheriff called. "I'm sort of hungry."

Homer followed, and the barber shouted, "Don't forget to come back and tell me the news!"

"O.K., and if I bring you a new customer, I get a commission."

The stranger was sitting at the far end of the lunch counter, looking very shy and embarrassed. Homer's Aunt Aggy had already served him a blue-plate special and was eyeing him with suspicion. To be polite, Homer and Uncle Ulysses pretended to be busy behind the counter, and the sheriff pretended to study the menu—though he knew every single word on it by heart. They just glanced in the stranger's direction once in a while.

Finally Uncle Ulysses' curiosity got the best of him, and he sauntered down to the stranger and asked, "Are you enjoying your lunch? Is everything all right?"

The stranger appeared to be very embarrassed, and you could easily tell he was blushing underneath his beard and all his hair. "Yes, sir, it's a very good lunch," he replied with a nod. When he nodded a stray wisp of

137

139

beard accidentally got into the gravy. This made him more embarrassed than ever.

Uncle Ulysses waited for the stranger to start a conversation but he didn't.

So Uncle Ulysses said, "Nice day today."

The stranger said, "Yes, nice day," and dropped a fork. Now the stranger *really was* embarrassed. He looked as though he would like to sink right through the floor.

Uncle Ulysses quickly handed the man another fork, and eased himself away, so as not to embarrass him into breaking a plate, or falling off his stool.

After he finished lunch, the stranger reached into the pocket of his ragged, patched coat and drew out a leather money bag. He paid for his lunch, nodded good-bye, and crept out of the door and down the street with everyone staring after him.

Aunt Aggy broke the silence by bouncing on the marble counter the coin she had just received.

"It's good money," she pronounced, "but it looks as though it had been *buried* for *years!*"

"Shyest man I ever laid eyes on!" said Uncle Ulysses.

"Yes!" said the sheriff. "My as a shouse, I mean, shy as a *mouse!*"

"Gosh what a beard!" said Homer.

"Humph!" said Aunt Aggy. "Homer, it's time you started back to school!"

By midafternoon every man, woman, and child in Centerburg had something to gossip about, speculate on, and argue about.

Who was this stranger? Where did he come from? Where was he going? How long was his beard and his hair? What was his name? Did he have a business? What could be on the back of his car that was so carefully covered with the large canvas?

140

Nobody knew. Nobody knew anything about the stranger except that he parked his car in the town parking space and was spending considerable time walking about town. People reported that he paused in his walking and whistled a few bars of some strange tune, a tune nobody had ever heard of. The stranger was shy when grownups were near, and he would cross the street or go around a block to avoid speaking to someone. However, he did not avoid children. He smiled at them and seemed delighted to have them follow him.

People from all over town telephoned the sheriff at the barbershop asking about the stranger and making reports as to what was going on.

The sheriff was becoming a bit uneasy about the whole thing. He couldn't get near enough to the stranger to ask him his intentions, and if he *did* ask, the stranger would be too shy to give him an answer.

As Homer passed by the barbershop on his way home from school, the sheriff called him in. "Homer," he said, "I'm gonna need your help. This stranger with the beard has got me worried. You see, Homer, I can't find out who he is or what he is doing here in town. He's probably a nice enough fellow, just an individualist. But, then again, he might be a fugitive, in disguise or something." Homer nodded. And the sheriff continued, "Now, what I want you to do is gain his confidence. He doesn't seem to be afraid of children, and you might be able to find out what this is all about. I'll treat you to a double raspberry sundae."

"It's a deal, Sheriff!" said Homer. "I'll start right now."

At six o'clock Homer reported to the sheriff. "The stranger seems like a nice person, Sheriff," Homer began. "I walked down Market Street with him. He wouldn't tell

141

me who he is or what he's doing, but he did say he'd been away from people for a great many years. He asked me to recommend a place for him to stay, and I said the Strand Hotel, so that's where he went just now when I left him. I'll have to run home to dinner now, Sheriff, but I'll find out some more tomorrow. Don't forget about that raspberry sundae," said Homer.

"I won't," replied the sheriff, "and, Homer, don't forget to keep me posted on this fellow."

After Homer had gone, the sheriff turned to the barber and said, "We don't know one blessed thing about this fellow except that he's shy, and he's been away from people for quite a spell. For all we know he might be a fugitive, or a lunatic, or maybe one of these amnesia cases.

"If he didn't have so much hair I could tell in a second what kind of a fellow he is," complained the sheriff. "Yep! Just one look at a person's ears and I can *tell!*"

"Well," said the barber, "I judge people by their *hair*, and I've been thinking. This fellow looks like somebody I've heard about, or read about somewhere. Like somebody out of a book, you understand, Sheriff?"

"Well, yes, in a way, but I could tell you definite with a good look at his ears!" said the sheriff. "Here comes Ulysses. Let's ask him what *he* thinks."

Uncle Ulysses considered a second and said, "Well, *I* judge a person by his *waistline* and his *appetite*. Now I'm not saying I'm right, Sheriff, because I couldn't tell about his waistline under that old coat, but judging from his appetite, I'd say he's a sort a person that I've read about somewhere. I can't just put my finger on it. Seems as though it must have been in a book."

"U-m-m," said the sheriff.

Just then Tony the shoe-repair man came in for a haircut. After he was settled in the barber chair, the sheriff

142

asked him what he thought about the mysterious stranger!

"Well, Sheriff, I judge everybody by their *feet* and their *shoes*. Nobody's worn a pair of gaiters like his for twenty-five years. It seems as though those shoes must have just up and walked right out of the pages of some old dusty book."

"There!" said the sheriff. "*Now*, we're getting somewhere!"

He rushed to the phone and called Mr. Hirsh of the Hirsh Clothing Store, and asked, "Say, Sam, what do *you* think about this stranger? . . . Yes, the one bith the weard, I mean beard! . . . uh-huh . . . storybook clothes, eh? . . . Thanks a lot, Sam, good night."

Then he called the garage and said, "Hello, Luke, this is the sheriff talking. What do you make of this stranger in town . . . Yes? . . . literature, eh? Durned if I kin see how you can judge a man by the car he drives, but I'll take your word for it. Good night, Luke, and thanks a lot."

The sheriff looked very pleased with himself. He paced up and down and muttered, "Getting somewhere! Getting somewhere at last!" Then he surprised everyone by announcing that he was going over to the *library*!

In a few minutes he was back, his mustache twitching with excitement. "I've solved it!" he shouted. "The librarian knew right off just what book to look in! It's *Rip Van Winkle*! It's Rip Van Winkle this fellow's like. He must have driven up into the hills some thirty years ago and fell asleep, or got amnesia, or something!"

"Yeah! That's it!" agreed the barber along with Uncle Ulysses and the shoemaker.

Then Uncle Ulysses asked, "*But how about that* 'what-ever-it-is' underneath the canvas on the back of his car?"

143

"Now look here, Ulysses," shouted the sheriff, "you're just trying to complicate my deduction! Come on, let's play checkers!"

Bright and early the next morning the Rip-Van-Winklish stranger was up and wandering around Centerburg.

By ten o'clock everyone was referring to him as "Old Rip," and remarking how clever the sheriff was at deducing things.

The sheriff tried to see what was under the canvas, but couldn't make head or tail of what it was. Uncle Ulysses peeked at it too and said, "Goodness only knows! But never mind, Sheriff. If anybody can find out what this thing is, Homer will do the finding!"

That same afternoon after school was dismissed, Uncle Ulysses and the sheriff saw Homer strolling down the street with "Old Rip."

"Looks like he's explaining something to Homer," said the sheriff.

"Homer'll find out!" said Uncle Ulysses proudly. Then they watched through the barbershop window while the stranger took Homer across the square to the parking lot and showed him his car. He lifted one corner of the canvas and pointed underneath while Homer looked and nodded his head. They shook hands and the stranger went to his hotel, and Homer headed for the barbershop.

"Did he talk?" asked the sheriff the minute Homer opened the door.

"What's his name?" asked Uncle Ulysses.

"What is he doing?" asked the barber.

"Yes, he told me everything!" said Homer. "It sounds just like a story out of a book!"

144

"Yes, son, did he get amnesia up in the hills?" asked the sheriff.

"Well, no, not exactly, Sheriff, but he did *live* in the hills for the past thirty years."

"Well, what's he doing here now?" the barber demanded.

"I better start at the beginning," said Homer.

"That's a good idea, son," said the sheriff. "I'll take a few notes just for future reference."

"Well, to begin with," Homer started, "his name is Michael Murphy—just plain Michael Murphy. About thirty years ago he built himself a small vacation cabin out in the hills, some place on the far side of the state forest reserve. Then, he liked living in the cabin so much he decided to live there all of the time. He packed his belongings on his car and moved out to the hills."

"He cided ta be a dermit?" asked the sheriff.

"Not exactly *a hermit*," Homer continued. "But yesterday was the first time that he came out of the hills and saw people for thirty years. That's why he's so shy."

"Then he's moving back to civilization," suggested Uncle Ulysses.

"That comes later," said Homer. "I've only told as far as twenty-nine years ago."

"Can't you skip a few years, son, and get to the point?" demanded the sheriff.

"Nope! Twenty-nine years ago," Homer repeated firmly, "Mr. Murphy read in an almanac that if a man can make a better mousetrap than anybody else, the world will beat a path to his house—even if it is way out in the hills.

"So-o-o he started making *mousetraps*."

There was a pause, and then the sheriff said, "Will you repeat that again, son?"

145

"I said, Mr. Murphy started making *mousetraps*. He made good ones too, the very best, and when one of Mr. Murphy's traps caught a mouse, that was the end of that mouse for all time."

The sheriff forgot all about taking notes as Homer continued, "But nobody came to buy the traps. But that was just as well, you see, because twenty-eight years ago Mr. Murphy began to feel *sorry* for the mice. He came to realize that he would have to change his whole approach. He thought and thought and finally he decided to build mousetraps that wouldn't hurt the mice.

"He spent the next fifteen years doing research on what was the pleasantest possible way for a mouse to be caught. He discovered that being caught to music pleased mice the most, even more than cheese. Then," said Homer, "Mr. Murphy set to work to make a *musical* mousetrap."

"That wouldn't hurt the mice?" inquired Uncle Ulysses.

"That wouldn't hurt the mice," Homer stated. "It was a long, hard job too, because first he had to build an organ out of reeds that the mice liked the sound of, and then he had to compose a tune that the mice couldn't possibly resist. Then he incorporated it all into a mousetrap. . . ."

"That wouldn't hurt the mice?" interrupted the barber.

"That wouldn't hurt the mice," Homer went on. "The mousetrap caught mice, all right. The only trouble was, it was too big. What with the organ and all, and sort of impractical for general use because somebody had to stay around and pump the organ."

"Yes, I can see that wouldn't be practical," said Uncle Ulysses, stroking his chin. "But with a small electric motor. . . ."

146

"But he solved it, Uncle Ulysses! The whole idea seems very practical after you get used to it. He decided since the trap was too large to use in a house, he would fasten it onto his car, which he hadn't used for so long anyway. Then, he could drive it to a town, and make a bargain with the mayor to remove all the mice. You see he would start the musical mousetrap to working, and drive up and down the streets and alleys. Then all of the mice would run out of the houses to get themselves caught in this trap that plays music that no mouse ever born can possibly resist. After the trap is full of mice, Mr. Murphy drives them past the city limits, somewhere where they can't find their way home, and lets them go."

"Still without hurting them?" suggested the barber.

"Of course," said Homer.

The sheriff chewed on his pencil, Uncle Ulysses stroked on his chin, and the barber ran his fingers through his hair.

Homer noticed the silence and said, "I guess the idea *is* sort of startling when you first hear about it. But, if a town has a water truck to sprinkle streets, and a street-sweeping truck to remove dirt, why shouldn't they, maybe, just hire Mr. Murphy's musical mousetrap once in a while to remove mice?"

Uncle Ulysses stroked his chin again and then said, "By gum! This man Murphy is a genius!"

"I told Mr. Murphy that *you* would understand, Uncle Ulysses!" said Homer with a grin. "I told him the mayor was a friend of yours, and you could talk him into anything, even hiring a musical mousetrap."

"Whoever heard of a *misical moostrap!*" said the sheriff.

"That doesn't hurt the *mice!*" added the barber, as

Homer and Uncle Ulysses went off arm in arm to see the mayor.

It scarcely took Uncle Ulysses and Homer half an hour to convince the mayor that Mr. Murphy's musical mousetrap should be hired to rid Centerburg of mice. While Uncle Ulysses chatted on with the mayor, Homer dashed over to the hotel to fetch Mr. Murphy.

Homer came back with the bearded inventor and introduced him to the mayor and to Uncle Ulysses. The mayor opened a drawer of his desk and brought out a bag of jelly beans. "Have one," he said to Mr. Murphy, to sort of break the ice and to make his shy visitor feel at home. Mr. Murphy relaxed and answered the mayor's questions without blushing too much.

"How do we know this *thing of a jig* of yours will do what you say it will?" asked the mayor.

Mr. Murphy just whistled a few bars, "*Tum tidy ay dee,*" and a couple of mice jumped right out of the mayor's desk!

"Of course," Homer explained, "the mice come *quicker*, and get *removed* when the mousetrap plays that tune through the streets. Mr. Murphy guarantees to remove every single mouse from Centerburg for only thirty dollars."

"It's a bargain!" said the mayor. "I wondered where my jelly beans were disappearing to!" And he shook hands with Mr. Murphy. Then he proclaimed Saturday as the day for de-mousing Centerburg. By this time everyone knew that the shy stranger's name was Michael Murphy, but people still spoke of him as Rip Van Winkle (Rip for short), because of the sheriff's deduction. Everybody talked about the musical mousetrap (that didn't hurt the mice) and the mayor's de-mousing proclamation.

The children, especially, were looking forward to the great event. They watched with interest while Mr. Murphy went over his car and his musical trap to be sure everything was in perfect working order. Homer and Freddy and most of the other children were planning to follow the trap all around town Saturday and see the mice come out and get caught in Michael Murphy's musical trap.

"Gosh, Homer," said Freddy, "let's follow him until he lets them loose out in the country! That *will* be a sight, seeing all those mice let loose at once!"

"Well, Freddy, I've been thinking it might not be a good idea to follow the mousetrap past the city limits," said Homer, to Freddy's surprise.

"You know, Freddy, I've been over at the library reading up on mice and music—music can do funny things sometimes. It can soothe savage beasts and charm snakes and *lots* of things. If we're going to follow this musical trap till the mice are let loose, we better make some plans."

Homer and Freddy spent all Friday recess period making plans. They decided that all the children should meet in the schoolyard before the de-mousing started on Saturday. They arranged a signal, thumbs up, if everything was going along all right; and thumbs down if anyone was in trouble.

"It's just to be on the safe side," Homer explained.

Saturday dawned a beautiful crisp fall day, fine weather for the grand de-mousing of Centerburg. Mr. Michael Murphy came forth from the Strand Hotel, and after carefully slinging his long gray beard over his shoulder, he cranked his car and warmed up the engine. He carefully removed the canvas covering from the musical mousetrap and ever so painstakingly arranged the spiral ramps and runways so that no mouse, no matter how careless, could stub a toe or bump a nose. He then climbed behind the steering wheel, and the musical mousetrap was under way!

A loud cheer arose from the crowd of children as Mr. Murphy yanked a lever and the reed organ started to play. Even before the cheering stopped the mice began to appear!

Through the streets of Centerburg rolled Mr. Michael Murphy and his musical mousetrap. The mice came running from every direction! Fat, doughnut-fed mice from Uncle Ulysses' lunchroom, thin mice from the churches, ordinary mice from houses and homes, mice from the stores, and mice from the town hall.

They all went running up the ramps and runways and disappeared in Michael Murphy's musical mousetrap. The children followed behind enjoying the whole thing almost as much as the mice.

After traveling down every street in town, the procession came to a stop in front of the town hall, and the mayor came out and presented Mr. Murphy with his thirty-dollar fee—thirty bright, crisp new one-dollar bills.

Just as the mayor finished counting out the bills into Mr. Murphy's hand, the sheriff stepped up and said, "Mr. Murphy, I hope this won't embarrass you too much, in fact, I hate to mention it at all, but this here misical moostrap, I mean mousetrap of yours, has got a license plate that is thirty years old . . . A *new* license will cost you just exactly thirty dollars."

Mr. Murphy blushed crimson under his beard. "It's the law, you know, and *I* can't help it!" apologized the sheriff.

151

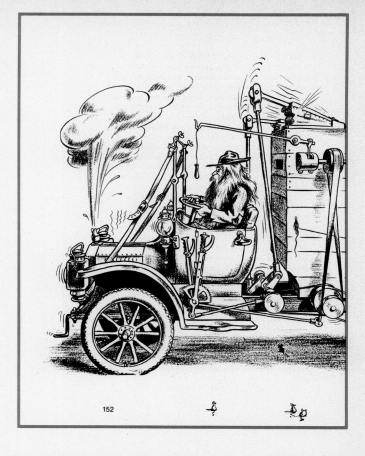

152

Poor Mr. Murphy, poor *shy* Mr. Murphy! He handed his thirty dollars to the sheriff, took his new license plates, and crept down the city hall steps. He climbed into his car and drove slowly away toward the edge of town, with the musical mousetrap playing its reedy music. The children followed along to see Mr. Murphy release all of the mice.

"I really hated to do that, Mayor," said the sheriff as the procession turned out of sight on Route 56A. "It's the law you know, and if I hadn't reminded him, he might have been arrested in the next town he visits."

There's no telling how this de-mousing would have ended if the children's librarian hadn't come rushing up shouting, "Sheriff! Sheriff! Quick! *We guessed the wrong book!*"

"What?" shouted the sheriff and the mayor and Uncle Ulysses.

"Yes!" gasped the children's librarian, "not *Rip Van Winkle*, but *another* book, *The Pied Piper of Hamelin!*"

"And almost every child in town is followin' him this very minute!" the sheriff yelled.

The sheriff and the librarian and the mayor and Uncle Ulysses all jumped into the sheriff's car and roared away after the procession. They met up with the children just outside the city limits. "Come back! Turn around, children!" they shouted.

"I'll treat everybody to a doughnut!" yelled Uncle Ulysses.

The children didn't seem to hear, and they kept right on following the musical mousetrap.

"The music must have affected their minds," cried the librarian.

"Sheriff, we can't lose all these children with election

154

time coming up next month!" mourned the mayor. "Let's give Murphy another thirty dollars!"

"That's the idea," said Uncle Ulysses. "Drive up next to him, Sheriff, and I'll hand him the money."

The sheriff's car drew alongside the musical mouse-trap, and Uncle Ulysses tossed a wad of thirty dollar bills onto the seat next to the shy Mr. Murphy.

"Please don't take them away!" pleaded the librarian.

"Come, Murphy, let's be reasonable," shouted the mayor.

Mr. Murphy was very flustered, and his steering was distinctly wobbly.

Then the sheriff got riled and yelled at the top of his lungs, "Get 'em low! Get 'em go! Let 'em go!"

And that's exactly what Mr. Murphy did. He let them go. He pulled a lever, and every last mouse came tumbling out of the bottom of the musical mousetrap. And such a sight it was, well worth walking to the city limits to see. The mice came out in a torrent. The reedy organ of the musical mousetrap stopped playing, and the squeaking of mice and the cheering of children filled the air.

The torrent of mice paused, as if sensing direction, and then each Centerburg mouse started off in a straight, straight line to his own Centerburg mousehole. Mr. Murphy didn't pause. He stepped on the gas, and the musical mousetrap swayed down the road. The mayor, the children's librarian, the sheriff, Uncle Ulysses, and the children watched as it grew smaller and smaller and finally disappeared.

Then Uncle Ulysses remembered the children. He turned around and noticed them grinning at each other and holding their thumbs in the air. They paid no attention whatever when they were called!

155

"That music has pixied these children!" he moaned.

"No, it hasn't, Uncle Ulysses," said Homer, who had just come up. "There's not a thing the matter with them that Doc Pelly can't cure in two shakes! Just to be on the safe side, Freddy and I asked Doc Pelly to come down to the schoolyard this morning and put cotton in all the children's ears. You know, just like Ulysses, not you, Uncle Ulysses, but the ancient one—the one that Homer wrote about. Not me but the ancient one."

"You mean to say Doc Pelly is mixed up in this?" asked the mayor.

"Yes, he thought it was awfully funny, our being so cautious."

Uncle Ulysses laughed and said, "Round 'em up, and we'll all go down to the lunchroom for doughnuts and milk."

"Sheriff," said the mayor, "with election time coming next month *we* gotta put our heads together and cook up a good excuse for spending sixty dollars of the tax-payers' money."

156

Questions preceded by a bullet are additional questions and appear in the Teacher's Edition only. The other questions appear in the student's text after the selection.

Understanding What You've Read

1. *Many authors bring humor to their stories by having their characters use silly or exaggerated ways of speaking. Find sentences spoken by the sheriff that show such use of humor.* (The sheriff mixes up the beginning sounds of different words. Examples are as follows: "long ullen wonderwear"; "My as a shouse, I mean, shy as a *mouse*!"; "He cided ta be a dermit?"; "Whoever heard of a misical moostrap!" pages 135, 140, 145, 147) CRITICAL   Recognizing word play as an element of humor

- *How is the conversation at the barbershop described on pages 135 and 136? What is the author trying to tell you by describing it in this way?* (The conversation begins with woolen underwear and then covers all sorts of not very interesting things, such as shoes, and mud in chicken coops. Students should be aware that the author is saying that not much is happening and that there isn't much to talk about in Centerburg.   page 136) LITERAL/CRITICAL   Recognizing humor in fiction

- *How does the barbershop conversation prepare you for the excitement about the stranger driving into town?* (Accept all reasonable answers. Encourage students to realize that since there was not much happening in Centerburg, the appearance of a stranger was a big event—particularly such an odd-looking stranger in a weird vehicle.   page 137) CRITICAL   Making judgments

- *Why did the sheriff ask Homer to find out about the stranger for him?* (The sheriff realized that he couldn't get close enough to the stranger to ask him questions, but that a boy Homer's age could.   page 141) LITERAL   Recalling stated information

- *The sheriff says he judges people by their ears. How do the other folk of Centerburg judge people? Do you think this is humorous?* (The barber judges people by their hair; Uncle Ulysses, who owns a lunch counter, judges people by their appetites; the shoe-repair man judges people by their feet and shoes; the clothing store owner judges people by their clothes; the man at the garage judges people by their cars. Some students may find this judging-by-profession funny because it exaggerates the way people judge others from their own viewpoints. pages 142 and 143) LITERAL/CRITICAL   Recognizing humor in fiction

2. *Why did everyone call the stranger "Old Rip"?* (Because of the sheriff's deduction that the stranger was like Rip Van Winkle, who disappeared into the hills and fell asleep for such a long time. "Old Rip" was short for Rip Van Winkle.   pages 143 and 144) LITERAL   Recalling specific details

- *What old saying did Michael Murphy read when he was up in the hills? What did this lead him to do?* (He read that "if a man can make a better mousetrap than anybody else, the world will beat a path to his house." This led him to design and make very good mousetraps.   page 145) LITERAL/INFERENTIAL Identifying cause-and-effect relationships

- *What made Michael Murphy change his mind about his mousetrap? What did he decide to do instead?* ("Michael Murphy began to feel *sorry* for the mice . . . he decided to build mousetraps that wouldn't hurt the mice."   page 146) LITERAL   Recalling specific details

- *What is funny about the scene where the mayor meets Michael Murphy?* (Accept all reasonable answers. The idea of a mayor offering a visitor jelly beans may strike some students as funny.   page 148) CRITICAL   Recognizing humor in fiction

- *What was Homer thinking when he cautioned Freddy not to follow the mousetrap past the city limits?* (Some students who are familiar with the story of the Pied Piper of Hamelin will suspect that Homer, too, knows the story, and that the stranger reminds him not of Rip Van Winkle, but of the Pied Piper. Accept all reasonable answers.) CRITICAL Making judgments

3. *What did the Pied Piper of Hamelin do for the city of Hamelin, Germany? What did the people of Centerburg expect Mr. Murphy to do for them? How was what happened in the story unexpected?* (The people of Hamelin expected the Pied Piper to rid their town of rats. The people of Centerburg expected Mr. Murphy to rid their town of mice. The sheriff's asking Mr. Murphy to pay his thirty dollars for a new license plate was unexpected. Accept reasonable answers that students can justify.   page 151) LITERAL/INFERENTIAL/CRITICAL   Recognizing the unexpected as an element of humor

- *In the story of the Pied Piper, after the Piper rid the town of rats, the townspeople got greedy and decided not to pay him, for the rats had all drowned in the river and he could hardly bring them back. What similar event took place in Centerburg?* (After the mayor of Centerburg paid Michael Murphy his thirty dollars for getting rid of the mice, the sheriff stepped up and charged Michael Murphy thirty dollars for a new license plate. As a result of this, Michael Murphy did not get his money either.   page 151) CRITICAL   Making an analogy

- *What are some of the details of Robert McCloskey's illustration of the musical mousetrap on pages 152 and 153 that you find humorous?* (Accept all reasonable answers. Students may find the signs "Watch Your Step," "Welcome," and "Enter, Friend" funny. Some students may find the design of the machine itself funny, with all its levers, pipes, whistles, and connections. Some students may also think that mice running into the machine is funny.) CRITICAL Recognizing humor in illustrations

- *What might you suspect about Robert McCloskey's childhood that would lead you to think he enjoyed "inventing" this unique musical mousetrap?* (He was creative and enjoyed tinkering with mechanical devices.) CRITICAL   Recognizing the relationship between a writer's life and work

4. *The humor in a story can depend on a misunderstanding by one character of something another one said. What did the sheriff mean on page 155 when he said, "Let 'em go"? What did Mr. Murphy think he meant?* (The sheriff thought Mr. Murphy was leading away the children of Centerburg just as the Pied Piper led away the children of Hamelin, and he said "Let 'em go!" meaning "let the children go." Mr. Murphy thought the sheriff wanted him to let the mice go.) CRITICAL   Recognizing humor in fiction

5. *How is the ending of this story different from the ending of* The Pied Piper of Hamelin? *How does this add to the humor of the story?* (Accept all reasonable answers. In the story *The Pied Piper of Hamelin*, the Piper led the children through the door that opened in a mountain. In this story, the children were afraid of being led away, so they had the doctor put cotton in their ears so they wouldn't be able to hear the music. This is funny because the children were aware of the similarity between Mr. Murphy and the Pied Piper, but the grown-ups didn't catch on.) CRITICAL   Recognizing humor in fiction/Making comparisons

- *What is funny about the mayor's decision to give Michael Murphy another thirty dollars?* (He says, "Sheriff, we can't lose all these children with election time coming up next month!" Here McCloskey is making fun of the mayor, suggesting that if election time weren't so near, he would go ahead and let Michael Murphy lure away the children.   pages 154 and 155) CRITICAL   Recognizing humor in fiction

Writing

(Optional) Have students complete one or both of the *Writing* activities on page 157. Or ask students to choose one of the writing activities under *Additional Writing Activity.*

1. *Use word play to rewrite the following sentences as the sheriff might say them.*
   a. *Come back! Come back!*
   b. *A stitch in time saves nine.*
   c. *Homer, my boy, you really saved the day.*
   Writing sentences using word play

   Tell students to list or outline their ideas before they begin writing. If students need help with the *Writing* activity, suggest that they consider the following: (a) reverse the initial consonants of some words; (b) reverse the order of key words in the sentences; (c) think up additional statements the sheriff might say, and use word play to rewrite the statements.

2. *Pretend you are a reporter for the Centerburg newspaper. Write a humorous paragraph in which you tell what happened the day Michael Murphy drove his musical mousetrap through Centerburg.*
   Writing a humorous paragraph

Tell students to list or outline their ideas before they begin writing. If students need help with the *Writing* activity, suggest that they consider the following: (a) plan an interview with Michael Murphy to obtain information about his mousetrap; (b) plan an article for the newspaper's science page that describes Mr. Murphy's mousetrap; (c) write an article for the newspaper that tells about the events that took place in Centerburg from Mr. Murphy's point of view.

Additional Writing Activity (Optional)

- *Pretend that you are a reporter for a Centerburg radio station. Write an interview in dialogue format that you conducted with the sheriff in which he explains what happened from his point of view.*
  <u>Writing a dialogue</u>

  Tell students to list or outline their ideas before they begin writing. You may wish to tell students to include the sheriff's funny speech patterns in their interviews or suggest that since the sheriff will be up for re-election in a month, he might want to do some campaigning. You may wish to have students read aloud their dialogues.

- *Write a short sequel to "Nothing New Under the Sun (Hardly)" in which you tell what happened to Michael Murphy after he left Centerburg.*
  <u>Writing a short story</u>

  Tell students to list or outline their ideas before they begin writing. You may wish to suggest that students consider the following: (a) describe where Michael Murphy went next; (b) describe how the people in a new town or city reacted to him; (c) describe what happened when he tried to use his musical mousetrap.

 Use *Duplicating Masters 11,* page 16.
Use *Reading Skills Workbook,* Word Play, page 30, for vocabulary review.

 For additional resources and curriculum-related activities, see *Enrichment,* page T123.

More Books to Make You Laugh

Paddington on Stage: Plays for Children by Michael Bond and Alfred Bradley. Houghton Mifflin, 1977. Some of the funniest adventures of the popular bear called Paddington are presented here in play form.

McBroom and the Great Race by Sid Fleischman. Little, 1980. Here's an exaggerated tale of a race between a rooster and a jackalope.

Centerburg Tales by Robert McCloskey. Viking, 1951. Here are more stories about Uncle Ulysses, the sheriff, and Homer's other friends.

Lentil by Robert McCloskey. Viking, 1968. When the town finds itself in an embarrassing situation, Lentil and his harmonica save the day.

Homer Price by Robert McCloskey. Viking, 1971. This book follows Homer through several adventures, including a holdup.

Ghosts I Have Been by Richard Peck. Viking, 1977. Blossom finds that she has supernatural powers that upset life in her hometown.

Black and Blue Magic by Zilpha Keatley Snyder. Atheneum, 1966. Marco is clumsy, so when he receives the gift of wings, it leads to black and blue magic.

158

If students have not read these books, you may wish to recommend them at this time. Bibliographic information about other books for students is given in the *Resource Center.*

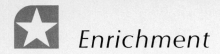

Enrichment

The Toothpaste Millionaire

Bibliography

The following books are humorous realistic fiction or humorous stories.

Easy

Catling, Patrick Skene. *The Chocolate Touch*. When John Midas acquires the "chocolate touch," he is deliriously happy—until practical problems pop up.

Cleary, Beverly. *Ramona and Her Father*. The story of a little girl, her family, and the humor found in everyday life.

Peck, Richard. *Monster Night at Grandma's House*. At night, Toby was sure that he heard the prowlings of a monster.

Sharmat, Marjorie. *Maggie Marmelstein for President*. Maggie finds out that politics can be very complicated.

Shearer, John. *The Case of the Sneaker Snatcher*. The star basketball player's sneakers mysteriously disappear.

Average

Bunting, Anne Eve. *The Big Cheese*. A tale that abounds in word play in the form of proverbs and old sayings.

Cone, Molly. *Call Me Moose*. A funny, touching story of a young girl's awkward attempts at finding her place in the world.

Hooks, William. *The Seventeen Gerbils of Class 4A*. Taking care of a pair of gerbils turns out to be far more complicated than class 4A anticipated.

Kalb, Jonah. *The Goof That Won the Pennant*. A humorous story about a losing baseball team that comes under the direction of a supportive and patient coach.

O'Connor, Jane. *Yours Till Niagara Falls, Abby*. Abby's adventures at Camp Pinecrest humorously related in her letters home.

Challenging

Hicks, Clifford. *Alvin's Swap Shop*. Humor combined with mystery, as Alvin helps Pim elude some criminals.

Newell, Crosby. *The Goodbye Summer*. Allie hates to say goodbye until an unusual friend helps her learn that some things can't be lost.

Films and Filmstrips

NOTE: For more information, see *Resource Center*.

Learning Corp. of America. *The Case of the Elevator Duck*. Gilbert is adopted by a duck—and the fun begins.

Records and/or Tapes

NOTE: Recordings may also be available on other labels.

Multimedia, Viking Press. "Henry Reed, Inc." Henry Reed initiates a series of hilarious business ventures.

Curriculum Coordination

Language Arts

1. Have students dramatize the talk-show scene in "The Toothpaste Millionaire," showing the contrast between Joe Smiley and Rufus.

2. Have students improvise the scene that might have taken place between Kate and Rufus the day before the talk show. Let students demonstrate their different opinions.

3. Have students plan an advertising campaign for a product of their choice. Tell students to make a poster of the product and write some "advertising copy" that they think would sell their product in a radio or TV ad.

Social Studies

Have students collect samples of different kinds of advertising and categorize them by the techniques used to sell the products. Some categories you might suggest are:

glamour—beautiful people shown using the product
get on the band wagon—everyone is buying this product, don't be left out!
down home—the appeal of good old folks getting you to try a product

Also have students look for ads that are straightforward and that present useful information to consumers.

Science

Many products, like toothpaste, can be made from simple ingredients. Have students check at least five brands of toothpaste sold in a local store and then answer the questions at the top of page T122.

How many list their ingredients?
If ingredients are listed, what are they?
Are the individual ingredients things you can buy easily?

Have students report their findings to the class. Have the class decide whether or not it would be possible to make their own toothpaste. You may wish to have interested students try making toothpaste "from scratch." Have them check with a chemistry teacher or local pharmacist for a recipe.

Career Education

1. Invite a guest speaker from the advertising field to speak to your class about the role of advertising in our culture.

2. Invite a scientist to speak to your class about the development of new products.

The Book That Saved the Earth

Bibliography

The following books contain humorous plays.

Easy

Boiko, Claire, and Sandra Novick. *Who's Afraid of the Big Bad W-H-H-A-A-T?* Because of their mutual fears, children and forest animals miss the chance to become friends.

Brenner, Barbara. *Ostrich Feathers.* A fresh approach to play format, in which characters' lines appear in speech bubbles within the illustrations.

Carlson, Bernice Wells. *Funny-Bone Dramatics.* A book that will help students to recognize and build the skills necessary for play production; includes a number of short skits and slapstick plays.

Korty, Carol. *Silly Soup: Ten Zany Plays.* Plays based on noodlehead stories and themes found in folk literature.

Average

Bradley, Alfred, and Michael Bond. *Paddington on Stage: Plays for Children.* Some popular adventures of Paddington the bear, presented in play form.

Olfson, Lewy. *You Can Act!* Suggestions for plays, puppet shows, and pantomime. Encourages students to use creativity in playing a part.

Smith, Moyne Rice. *Seven Plays and How to Produce Them.* Seven plays with simple texts, clear directions, and suggestions for production.

Winther, Barbara. *Plays from Folktales of Africa and Asia.* Adventure plays from the folk literature of Africa and Asia.

Challenging

Aiken, Joan. *The Mooncusser's Daughter.* A play about a family that lives in a lighthouse.

Hughes, Ted. *The Tiger's Bones and Other Plays for Children.* A collection of humorous plays for children.

Films and Filmstrips

NOTE: For more information, see *Resource Center.*

Multimedia, Viking Press. "Hattie the Backstage Bat." Based on the book by Don Freeman about a bat-in-residence at the Lyceum Theater.

Curriculum Coordination

Language Arts

1. Have students practice reading aloud "The Book That Saved the Earth" in groups until each group feels that it has the characters' lines and personalities mastered. Then, if a tape recorder is available, let each group take a turn recording the play.

2. Arrange for the class to attend a play. Use the play as a basis for discussion. Compare it to "The Book That Saved the Earth." Ask students to note any elements of humor in the play.

3. If possible, obtain a copy of *The Annotated Mother Goose* (see *Resource Center*) and read some of the origins of our nursery rhymes to students. They may be interested to know, for example, that "Humpty Dumpty" is actually a riddle nursery rhyme, the answer being *an egg*. This explains why, once he fell to the ground and broke, he could not be put together again.

Social Studies

Ask students to imagine that they are sending a scrapbook from the "good old twentieth century" to be displayed by the Historian in her Museum of Ancient History. Have each student contribute two to four pages to the scrapbook. Students may wish to write descriptions of what life in the 1980's was like, or to draw pictures or cut out of magazines pictures of objects that represent the 1980's. Ask students to try to represent our age to future ages in a kind of "time capsule" scrapbook.

Art

1. Have interested students design a play program for "The Book That Saved the Earth." They may wish to include the following information in their programs.

   a list of characters
   the names of the performers
   biographical information about the performers
   a list of the scenes
   the setting of each scene

   Then have them make actual copies of the program, using construction paper and illustrations.

2. Have interested students make a bulletin board display of costumes that the Martians in "The Book That Saved the Earth" might wear. Have them look through the play for descriptions of the characters and what they wore.

Career Education

Invite someone from a professional theater or an amateur theater group to talk about what he or she does and about the different jobs involved in putting on a play. Some suggestions are:

playwright
actor
prop specialist
scenic designer
lighting specialist

Nothing New Under the Sun (Hardly)

Bibliography

The following books are by Robert McCloskey.

Easy

McCloskey, Robert. *Blueberries for Sal*. The adventure of a little girl and her mother and a little bear and his mother.

_____. *Lentil*. Lentil becomes such a good harmonica player that he saves the day when the town band can't play.

_____. *Make Way for Ducklings*. A family of ducks in search of a home. Caldecott Medal winner.

_____. *One Morning in Maine*. A story about the McCloskey family and the day Sally loses her first tooth.

Average

McCloskey, Robert. *Burt Dow, Deep-Water Man*. A tall tale about a sea captain who is swallowed by a whale and escapes by painting his way out.

_____. *Centerburg Tales*. Homer Price and his Centerburg friends in action again.

_____. *Homer Price*. Homer's zany adventures involve bank robbers and a doughnut machine.

_____. *Time of Wonder*. A story about the end of the summer and a fall hurricane on a Maine island told through a poetic text and beautiful water-color illustrations. Caldecott Medal winner.

Films and Filmstrips

NOTE: For more information, see *Resource Center*.

BFA. *The Pied Piper of Hamelin*. A short film version of the classic tale.

Encyclopaedia Britannica. *American Legendary Heroes: Rip Van Winkle*. The classic story of Rip Van Winkle, who wakes after a twenty-year sleep to find everything changed.

Multimedia, Viking Press. "One Morning in Maine." Filmstrip of the McCloskey family, using art from the book.

Weston Woods. "Blueberries for Sal." While picking berries, Sal and Little Bear get lost.

_____. "The Case of the Cosmic Comic." Homer Price and his friend Freddy help Super-Duper disentangle himself from a wire fence.

_____. "Lentil." Young Lentil practices his harmonica everywhere, and his talent saves the day when the town's most important citizen returns.

_____. "Make Way for Ducklings." Mother and Father duckling find a perfect home for their family in Boston's Charles River.

_____. "Robert McCloskey." McCloskey talks about the various people and places that have influenced his work.

_____. "Time of Wonder." A poetic story of life on an island off the coast of Maine—from early spring through summer, ending with a fall hurricane.

Records and/or Tapes

NOTE: For more information, see *Resource Center*.

Caedmon Records. "The Pied Piper of Hamelin." Read by Boris Karloff. The flip side presents Lewis Carroll's "The Hunting of the Snark."

Weston Woods. "Homer Price Stories." Robert McCloskey reads from *Homer Price*, including "The Doughnuts," "The Case of the Cosmic Comic," and "Nothing New Under the Sun (Hardly)."

Curriculum Coordination

Language Arts

1. Ask students to write a short descriptive paragraph about someone who would be an interesting character in a short story. Assist interested students in developing their paragraphs into stories.

2. Have interested students write letters to Mr. McCloskey in reaction to the *Author Study* and the story they have just read. Students may wish to ask Mr. McCloskey questions about the various influences on his work. They may write to him in care of his publisher, Viking Press.

3. Have interested students practice reading aloud sections of "Nothing New Under the Sun (Hardly)" or any other McCloskey stories that may be available in your classroom or school library. Students may wish to make a tape recording of the reading of several stories and put the tape in a classroom listening center. They may also wish to lend it to other classes for their listening centers.

4. Have a group of several students act out the scene in "Nothing New Under the Sun (Hardly)" from the point at which Michael Murphy first drives into town to the end of the scene in Uncle Ulysses's lunchroom.

Art

Have interested students draw a picture of a new invention. It might be a "better mousetrap" or any other useful kind of invention. Make a bulletin board display of the pictures. Encourage students to write an accompanying paragraph explaining the special features of their inventions.

Music/Science

Have interested students research the effects of music on animals, people, and plants and report their findings to the class.

Social Studies

Invite a speaker who can talk to the class about earlier days in a small town.

Career Education

Invite a writer or a newspaper reporter to talk to your class about the influences on his or her work, both from life experience and from books read, movies seen, or other influences.

Part 3
Expressions

RESOURCE CENTER

The following list identifies materials that you may want to gather in advance of reading the selections in "Expressions." The list also suggests optional activities that require advance planning. The *Enrichment* section at the end of each Teaching Unit explains how to employ these resources. The *Enrichment* section also gives suggestions for additional activities that do not require advance preparation.

Enrichment Materials and Activities

A Street of Games
Pages 168–174

Enrichment Material:
A world map

Feliciano!
Pages 175–178

Enrichment Materials:
A "talking book" from an institute for the blind
A book of songs in Spanish with English translations

Activities Needing Advance Planning:
Observation of a school band or orchestra rehearsal
A visit to a local institute for the blind

Guest Speaker:
A music teacher, musician, or songwriter

Start Your Own Theater
Pages 214–219

Guest Speaker:
An actor or director

Life with the Li'l Folks
Pages 234–242

Activity Needing Advance Planning:
A trip to the local public library

Truly a Ballerina
Pages 243–247

Guest Speaker:
A dancer or dance teacher

Bibliography

For Students

NOTE: For more information about these books, see the *Enrichment* section at the end of each Teaching Unit.

Bruun-Rasmussen, Ole, and Grete Peterson. *Make-up, Costumes, and Masks for the Stage*. Sterling, 1976.

Cole, Ann. *Backyard Vacation: Outdoor Fun in Your Own Neighborhood*. Little, Brown, 1980.

Collier, James Lincoln. *Making Music for Money*. Watts, 1976.

Comins, Jeremy. *Chinese and Japanese Crafts and Their Cultural Background*. Lothrop, 1978.

Cummings, Richard. *Make Your Own Comics for Fun and Profit*. Walck, 1976.

De Leeuw, Adele. *Maria Tallchief: American Ballerina*. Dell, 1975.

Ferretti, Fred. *The Great American Book of Sidewalk, Stoop, Dirt, Curb, and Alley Games*. Workman Pub., 1975.

Fitcher, George S. *American Indian Music and Musical Instruments*. McKay, 1978.

Gallagher, Rachel. *Games in the Street*. Four Winds, Schol. Book Serv., 1976.

Glubok, Shirley. *The Art of the Comic Strip*. Macmillan, 1979.

Goldreich, Gloria, and Esther Goldreich. *What Can She Be? A Newscaster*. Lothrop, 1973.

Graham, Ada. *Foxtails, Ferns, and Fish Scales: A Handbook of Art and Nature Projects*. Four Winds, Schol. Book Serv., 1976.

Gridley, Marion E. *Maria Tallchief*. Dillon Press, 1973.

Hamilton, David. *La Danse*. Morrow, 1974.

Haskins, James. *The Story of Stevie Wonder*. Dell, 1979.

Hawkinson, John, and Martha Faulhaber. *Rhythms, Music and Instruments to Make*. Whitman, 1970.

Horn, George F. *Cartooning*. Davis Publishers, 1965.

Jacobs, Linda. *Stevie Wonder: Sunshine in the Shadow*. EMC Corp., 1976.

Jessel, Camilla. *Life at the Royal Ballet School*. Methuen, 1979.

Kay, Sophie. *I Can Cook Cookbook*. Ideals Publishing/Good Friends, 1980.

Kelly, Elizabeth Y. *The Magic If: Stanislavski for Children*. National Ed. Press, 1973.

Kendall, Alan. *The World of Musical Instruments*. Hamlyn/America, 1972.

Kohn, Bernice. *Beachcombers' Book*. Penguin, 1976.

Krementz, Jill. *A Very Young Dancer*. Knopf, 1976.

Langstaff, John, and Carol Langstaff. *Shimmy Shimmy Coke-Ca-Pop! A Collection of City Children's Street Games and Rhymes*. Doubleday, 1973.

Levine, Jack. *Understanding Musical Instruments: How to Select Your Instrument*. Warne, 1971.

Lincoln, Eric. *Backyard Games*. Galahad, 1973.

Meyer, Charles R. *How to Be a Clown*. McKay, 1977.

Nuttall, Kenneth. *Your Book of Acting*. Transatlantic, 1972.

Olfson, Lewy. *You Can Put On a Show*. Sterling, 1975.

Pratson, Frederick J. *The Special World of the Artisan*. Houghton Mifflin, 1974.

Swope, Martha. *The Nutcracker: The Story of the New York City Ballet's Production*. Dodd, 1975.

Wehrum, Victoria. *The American Theatre*. Watts, 1974.

Wheelock, Warren H. *Carmen Rosa Maymi: To Serve American Women; Roberto Clemente: Death of a Proud Man; José Feliciano: One Voice, One Guitar*. EMC Corp., 1976.

Zaidenberg, Arthur. *How to Draw Cartoons: A Book for Beginners*. Vanguard, 1959.

For Teachers

NOTE: For more information about these books, see the *Background* section that precedes the reading selections.

Baird, John F. *Make-Up: A Manual for the Use of Actors, Amateurs and Professionals*. Samuel French, 1957.

Breger, Dave. *How to Draw and Sell Cartoons*. Putnam, 1966.

Brinson, Peter, and Clement Crisp. *International Book of the Ballet*. Stein & Day, 1970.

Cornberg, Sol, and Emanuel L. Gebauer. *A Stage Crew Handbook*. Harper & Row, 1957.

Crescent Books. *Sea Shells: How to Identify and Collect Them*. Crescent, 1973.

Denzer, Ann Wiseman. *Making Things: The Hand Book of Creative Discovery. Book I: 1973, Book II: 1975*. Little, Brown.

Garland, Phyl. *The Sound of Soul*. Regnery, 1969.

Hoff, Syd. *The Art of Cartooning*. Stravon, 1973.

Janson, H. W. *History of Art*. Harcourt Brace Jovanovich, 1977.

Orlick, Terry. *The Cooperative Sports and Games Book: Challenge Without Competition*. Pantheon, 1978.

Peters, Joan. *Making Costumes for School Plays*. Plays, 1971.

Terry, Walter. *The Ballet Guide*. Dodd Mead, 1976.

Time Magazine. "U.S. Ballet Soars." May 1, 1978. Vol. III, No. 18.

Films and Filmstrips

Sources related to skills

Harcourt Brace Jovanovich. *Bookmark Reading Filmstrips*. "The Structure of a Book," "Outlines That Work," "What's What in the Library."

Guidance Assocs. "The Library: What's in It for You?" Teacher's guide. Two filmstrips with records (#9A-503 381) or cassettes (#9A-503 399).

Sources related to reading selections

BFA. *Learning to Look*. Titles: "Trees," "Lumber," "Plants," "Desert Flowers," "Desert Textures," "Desert Soil, Sand, Stone." Six filmstrips with records (#VR65000) or cassettes (#VR9000).

Guidance Assocs. *Career Discoveries Series*. Titles: "People Who Create Art," "People Who Make Things," "People Who Work in Science," "People Who Influence Others," "People Who Help Others," "People Who Organize Facts." Discussion guide for each title. Six programs, twenty-four parts with records (#9A-302 909) or cassettes (#9A-302 917).

Guidance Assocs. *Cross-Cultural Studies Series*. Titles: "A World Nearby: Canada," "A World Nearby: The Netherlands," "A World Nearby: Czechoslovakia," "A World Nearby: Ghana," "A World Nearby: Egypt," "A World Nearby: India," "A World Nearby: Hong Kong," "A World Nearby: New Zealand," "A World Nearby: Mexico," "A World Nearby: Brazil." Teacher's guide for each title. Ten programs, thirty parts with records (#9A-304 822) or cassettes (#9A-304 830).

Harcourt Brace Jovanovich. *Self-Expression and Conduct: The Humanities Sound Filmstrips*. "The Dramatic Experience." Teacher's manual. Filmstrip with record (#373378-0) or cassette (#373379-9).

International Arts, Inc. *Don Quixote*. Four filmstrips.

Prentice-Hall Media. *Famous Artists at Work*. Titles: Set One: "Elsa Schmid (Mosaic)," "Seymour Lipton (Sculpture)." Two filmstrips with records (#HAR226) or cassettes (#HAC226). Set Two: "Richard Lytle (Oil on Canvas)," "Esteban Vicente (Collage)." Two filmstrips with records (#HAR227) or cassettes (#HAC227). Set Three: "Hank Ketcham (Cartoon)," "Alton Toby (Mural)." Two filmstrips with records (#HAR228) or cassettes (#HAC228). Set Four: "Peter Hurd (Watercolor)," "Ugo Mochi (Outline)." Two filmstrips with records (#HAR229) or cassettes (#HAC229). Teacher's guide for each set.

Prentice-Hall Media. *Music Stories*. Titles: "Peter and the Wolf," "Hansel and Gretel," "The Nutcracker," "Peer Gynt," "The Firebird," "The Sorcerer's Apprentice." Six filmstrips with records (#HAR1750) or cassettes (#HAC1750).

Prentice-Hall Media. *The Ballet*. Titles: "The Background," "The Training," "The Performance." Teacher's guide. Three filmstrips with records (#HAR723) or cassettes (#HAC723).

Prentice-Hall Media. *Once Upon a Sound*. Titles: "Mu, the Horn Blower (Brass)," "The Pipes of Pan (Woodwinds)," "Jubal and the Twanging Strings (Strings)," "Bangalore and Stump Drum (Percussion)," "American Music-Makers." Teacher's guide and eight spirit-master skill sheets. Five filmstrips with records (#HAR5520) or cassettes (#HAC5520).

Scholastic. "Creative Dramatics." One filmstrip with board game, activity skill cards, and cassette (#6279).

Records and/or Tapes

NOTE: Recordings may also be available on other labels.

"Coppelia Suite" by Leo Delibes (Columbia Records MS-6508)

"Firebird Suite" by Igor Stravinsky (Columbia Records MG-30269)

"Folksongs of Woody Guthrie" by Woody Guthrie (Folkways Records 2483)

"John Denver's Country" by John Denver (Pickwick 3515)

"My Favorite Spanish Encores" by Andrés Segovia (RCA Records ARL 1-0485)

"Rodeo" by Aaron Copland (Columbia Records MS-6175)

"The Voice and Guitar of José Feliciano" (RCA Records LPM 3358)

"West Side Story" by Leonard Bernstein (Columbia Records MS-6251)

OVERVIEW

Part 3
Expressions

The skills focus of "Expressions" is on study skills. The selections describe various forms of expression; for example, a selection on street games identifies similarities among children's games from different cultures around the world. Other modes of expression described include dance, music, and theater.

Using the Management System

Periodic Test 2, Forms A and *B,* covers the tested skills in "Expressions." The test may be administered in parts preceding and/or following instruction in each Teaching Unit. Or, Parts I through IV may be administered together for pretesting and/or posttesting all the tested skills in "Expressions." For full information on administering tests, see the Teacher's Edition of *Periodic Tests, Level 11.* In addition, the following activities within the student's text may be used as part of your ongoing assessment of students' progress:

  Try This sections of the *Skills Lessons*
  Applying the Skills Lesson activities following each selection
  Building Skills sections of *Textbook Studies*

Previewing "Expressions"

Have students turn to page 159. Ask what they think "Expressions" means. (feelings or ideas shown in words or gestures) Have students examine the photographs on page 159 and describe the different ways people are expressing themselves. Explain that people use various means of expression—such as music, drawing, painting, sculpting, and dancing. Allow students to look at the titles of the selections and the illustrations from page 168 to page 246 and tell what means of expression they expect to read about in the selections in Part 3.

Objectives

The following list of objectives is provided to help you plan your teaching of "Expressions." All the objectives listed under *Introduced and Tested* and *Maintained and Tested* are for skills presented in the four *Skills Lessons* of "Expressions" in the student's text. *Applying the*

Skills Lesson sections following each selection in the student's text, as well as the *Try This* activities within the *Skills Lessons,* informally assess students' progress with these skills. *Periodic Test 2* may be used for more formal evaluation.

The objectives listed under *Maintained* are for skills presented in the *Maintaining Skills* sections in this Teacher's Edition

The symbols I*, I, M, and T are used throughout the Teacher's Edition. The symbol I* indicates skills introduced for the first time in the program. The I indicates skills introduced earlier in Level 11. The M indicates skills taught at earlier levels and maintained in Level 11. The T indicates a skill that is taught for mastery and tested. The italicized numbers following the objectives are part of a code developed by the HBJ School Department to facilitate the correlation of skills within and between programs. See page T499 for more information.

Introduced and Tested

These skills are introduced for the first time in Level 11 of the HBJ BOOKMARK READING PROGRAM, EAGLE EDITION. They are tested in *Periodic Test 2*.

	SKILLS CODE NUMBER
To use a bibliography	5.5.6
To describe the purpose of an introduction	5.5.1
To identify topical organization	5.10.1
To identify introductory paragraphs	5.10.2
To identify summary paragraphs	5.10.3
To write a topical outline	7.1.5.1
To write a title for a topical outline	7.1.5.1.1

Maintained and Tested

These skills were introduced earlier in the HBJ BOOKMARK READING PROGRAM, EAGLE EDITION. They are developed in Level 11 and tested in *Periodic Test 2*.

	SKILLS CODE NUMBER
To identify parts of a book where specific information may be found	5.5
To use a table of contents	5.5.3
To use an index	5.5.8
To use a glossary to find pronunciation and meaning	5.6.6
To locate and use library catalogue cards	5.11.2
To identify and use reference materials in which specific information may be found	5.11

Maintained

Each of these skills was previously taught in the HBJ BOOKMARK READING PROGRAM, EAGLE EDITION. None are tested in *Periodic Test 2*. In planning your teaching, select those exercises from the *Maintaining Skills* sections that best meet your students' specific needs for maintaining skills presented earlier in the program.

	SKILLS CODE NUMBER
To identify base words in compound words	4.2.1
To scan a selection for specific information	5.9
To identify the number of syllables in a word	2.6
To identify and use context clues to determine word meaning	3.0.2

	SKILLS CODE NUMBER
To distinguish between fact and opinion	3.6.3
To follow a set of written directions	5.3.1
To identify word parts: root words, prefixes, and suffixes	4.1
To identify definitions in context	3.0
To use a dictionary to find meanings of multiple-meaning words	5.6.4
To identify clues to time-order relationships	3.1.2
To determine the correct sequence for a set of events	3.3.7.4
To draw conclusions based on given information and personal knowledge	3.4.1
To identify cause-and-effect relationships	3.3.3

Vocabulary

The following skills are practiced on the *Vocabulary Study* pages in the student's text for "Expressions." These skills are not tested in *Periodic Test 2*.

	SKILLS CODE NUMBER
To identify and use antonyms as context clues	3.5.3; 3.0
To use etymologies to determine word meaning	4.4.1
To identify and use context clues to determine word meaning	3.0.2
To use context clues to determine meanings of multiple-meaning words	3.5.5; 3.0.2

Contents

Additional Materials

Reading Skills Workbook: Lessons 10–11, pages 31–39
Duplicating Masters 11: pages 17–20
Bookmark Reading Filmstrips: Purple: "The Structure of a Book"
Worksheet 5: Teacher's Edition, page T484
Periodic Test 2, Part I

Key to Symbols

Skills Objectives
I* — Introduced in this unit
I — Introduced earlier in this level
M — Maintained from previous levels
T — Tested in periodic and cumulative tests for this level

Reduced Student Pages
underscore — words that appear in the glossary
wavy line — words pretaught in the Teacher's Edition
(these words also appear in the glossary)

Skills Lesson:
Understanding the Parts of a Book
Pages 160–165

Objectives

		SKILLS CODE NUMBER
M, T	To identify parts of a book where specific information may be found	5.5
M, T	To use a table of contents	5.5.3
M, T	To use an index	5.5.8
I*, T	To use a bibliography	5.5.6
I*, T	To describe the purpose of an introduction	5.5.1
M, T	To use a glossary to find pronunciation and meaning	5.6.6

If you wish to pretest the skills listed above, you may administer *Periodic Test 2, Part I, Form A. Periodic Test 2, Part I, Form B,* may be administered to posttest.

Introducing the Lesson

1. **a.** Show students an unopened nonfiction book that is unfamiliar to them. The book should have a somewhat ambiguous title. Ask them to guess what the book is about. Ask what clues they have regarding the book's *content.*

   b. After students have made some guesses, discuss the clues they used. (the title; the author; perhaps a picture on the cover) Point out that it is often not possible to know what a book is about just by looking at its shape, size, and cover. Even the title may not be helpful.

Understanding the Parts of a Book

Suppose you want to find breakfast cereal in a supermarket. You can walk through the whole store looking for the cereal. Or you might look for signs that tell you what is on the shelves. These signs can help you find your way to the breakfast cereals.

A book, like a supermarket, is laid out in an orderly way. Most nonfiction books have guides to help you know what is in them. This lesson will tell you about the useful guides you can find in most books.

160

Using a Table of Contents

In the beginning of most books there is a **table of contents.** This is a list of the major topics—by chapter—that appear in the book. It shows the page on which each chapter begins. It also shows how the writer has organized the major ideas. Look at this table of contents from the book *A Book for Dog Lovers.*

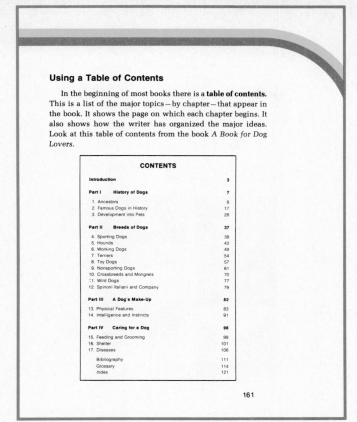

161

c. Open the book to the table of contents and have a student read the chapter titles. Point out how this part of the book gives much better clues about the content of the book.

2. Have students turn to page 160 of *Blazing Trails* and read the two paragraphs. Ask them to describe how a book is organized. (Accept all reasonable answers.)

Developing the Skill

Using a Table of Contents

The table of contents shows the organization of the major ideas in the book, including chapter topics and chapter page numbers.

1. Have students read the paragraph on page 161. Point out that each chapter in *A Book for Dog Lovers* is about dogs. Have students name some of the breeds of dogs mentioned in the table of contents. (sporting dogs, hounds, working dogs, terriers, toy dogs, nonsporting dogs, etc.)

2. a. Have students name the four parts of the table of contents on page 161. (History of Dogs, Breeds of Dogs, A Dog's Make-Up, Caring for a Dog)

b. Ask how many chapters are in the book. (seventeen) How many chapters are in Part II? (nine)

3. a. Discuss the topical organization of the parts and chapters of the book, noting how each large topic is broken down into smaller topics.

b. Ask students on what pages they'd look for information about famous dogs in history. (pages 17–27)

4. Refer students to the listing of Chapter 12 in Part II of *A Book for Dog Lovers.* Point out that chapter titles may not be fully understood until the chapter is actually read. "Spinoni Italiani and Company" actually refers to a miscellaneous breed of dogs.

As you can see from this table of contents, the author has organized the book into four *parts*. What are these four parts? Within each part, there are *chapters*. The numerals on the right are the page numbers on which each chapter begins. How is this book, *Blazing Trails*, organized? Check its table of contents. How is your science book organized?

Which chapter in *A Book for Dog Lovers* tells you about famous dogs? Most of the time, you can tell what a chapter is about from its title. But sometimes you can't. What do you think Chapter 12 in Part II of *A Book for Dog Lovers* is about? You can't tell if you don't already know that the spinoni Italiani is a miscellaneous breed of dog.

162

Using an Index

The table of contents tells you that Chapter 5 is about hounds. But suppose you want to know only one thing about hounds—what a bloodhound looks like. The **index** can help you now.

An index is an alphabetical list of names and *topics*. It is much more detailed than a table of contents. Sometimes there are *subtopics* under each topic. These are listed in alphabetical order, too.

Look at the entry for *Bloodhound* in the first column of the index below. On the first line are listed all of the pages on which *bloodhound* is mentioned in a general way. You might find the answer to your question about what a bloodhound looks like on one of those pages. But perhaps you can find an answer more quickly by looking at the subtopics. Read down the list of subtopics under *Bloodhound* until you come to the line that says *"description of, 45."* That entry shows where to find the answer to your question—on page 45.

163

---

5. Have students read the two explanatory paragraphs on page 162 and look at the table of contents for *Blazing Trails* (page vii) and the table of contents for their science or social studies textbook. Discuss how these tables of contents compare with the table of contents for *A Book for Dog Lovers*.

Using an Index

An index is an alphabetical list of names, topics, and subtopics and the page numbers on which they appear.

1. Have students read the paragraphs on page 163 and examine the sample index. Point out that there are ten major entries, and have a student tell what they are. (Balto; Barry; Basset Hound; Beagle; Behavior of dogs; Bloodhound; Boston terrier; Breeds of dogs; Brushing; Brussels Griffon) Elicit from students that these entries are in alphabetical order.

2. Have students look at the subtopics under "Breeds of dogs" in the index. Ask how many subtopics are listed and have a student name them. (ten; crossbreeds; hounds; miscellaneous; mongrels; nonsporting; sporting; terriers; toys; wild; working) Explain that the term "breeds of dogs" means different kinds of dogs.

Using a Bibliography

Another useful part of many books is a **bibliography.** This is a list of books and their authors. Some bibliographies include magazines, newspapers, and other sources, as well as books. In some books there is only one bibliography. It comes near the end of the book before the index. In other books, you may find a bibliography at the end of each part or chapter.

Some bibliographies list only the sources from which information or articles included in the book were taken. Other bibliographies list books suggested for further reading. The bibliographies in this book are of this type. You'll find one on page 94. What are all the books listed there about? The title *Books About Living Things* tells you what all the books are about. Which books do you think you'd like to read?

The Introduction and the Glossary

THE INTRODUCTION   Some books have an **introduction.** It comes just before the first chapter of the book. Sometimes an introduction is titled "To the Reader." It may tell you about the purpose of the book or why or how the author wrote the book. It may explain special things you will find in the book. Turn to page xvi of this book. What does the introduction **To the Reader** tell you?

THE GLOSSARY   In addition to a table of contents, an index, and a bibliography, many books contain a **glossary.** A glossary is a special dictionary. Words that are used in the book and that may be new to you are listed here. The glossary usually appears near the end of the book. Look at page 551 in this book. Notice how a glossary is like a dictionary.

164

Try This

1. In what part of a book will you find each of the things below?

   a. a list of books you might like to read
   b. an alphabetical list of topics and subtopics
   c. a list of the chapter titles in the book
   d. an explanation of the purpose of the book
   e. an alphabetical list of special words and their meanings

2. Will you find each of the following parts of a book in the front or the back of a book?

   a. glossary   c. table of contents
   b. index   d. introduction

3. Answer the following questions about *Blazing Trails.*

   a. On which page does a Skills Lesson about using the library begin?
   b. What is the general topic of all the selections in the first part of *Blazing Trails?*
   c. Where in *Blazing Trails* can you look to learn how to pronounce *Sacajawea?*

4. In what ways are the glossary for *Blazing Trails* and a dictionary alike? In what ways are they different?

5. Look at the table of contents for *Blazing Trails.* How many bibliographies are listed? On what page is the bibliography for this unit? What kinds of information are given in this bibliography?

165

Using a Bibliography

A bibliography is a list of books or other printed materials.

1. Have students read the first two paragraphs on page 164 and then turn to the bibliography on page 94 and read aloud some of the titles. (page T81)

2. Ask students how they would find these books in their library. (The author and title of each book are given so that students might look these up.)

The Introduction and the Glossary

A. *An introduction in a book gives special information, such as the author's reason for writing the book.*

1. Have students read the paragraph about the introduction on page 164 and *To the Reader* on page xvi. (page T4) Ask them if an introduction is always important. (no) Describe the times when an introduction may be important.

2. Have students look at some of their other books. What information do their introductions provide?

B. *A glossary is a special dictionary of terms used in a book. A glossary usually appears near the end of a book.*

Have students read the paragraph about the glossary on page 164. Then ask them what a jet stream is.

Have them turn to the glossary at the back of their books, and have one student read aloud the definition of *jet stream.* Have students discuss why a glossary is useful to a reader. (It gives the meaning of the word as it is used in the book. A glossary may also give the pronunciation and other information.)

Try This

Have students complete *Try This.*

Answers to *Try This*

1. **a.** bibliography; **b.** index; **c.** table of contents; **d.** introduction; **e.** glossary; **2. a.** back; **b.** back; **c.** front; **d.** front; **3. a.** page 224; **b.** "Learning About Living Things"; **c.** glossary; **4.** Sample answers: the two are alike in that they both list words alphabetically, show pronunciations, show parts of speech, and have guide words. The two are different in that a glossary doesn't give all definitions of a word, and a dictionary may contain more information in addition to definitions; **5.** eight; page 252; book's title, author, publisher, copyright year, and short description of the book

 Use *Reading Skills Workbook,* Lesson 10, pages 31–38. See *Providing for Individual Differences,* page T146, for additional practice.

Vocabulary Study:
Antonyms
Pages 166–167

Objective

SKILLS CODE NUMBER

M   To identify and use antonyms   3.5.3; 3.0
as context clues

Developing
the Skill

1. Ask students what the antonym for the word *synonym* is. (antonym) Remind students that antonyms are often context clues to word meaning. Tell them to look for antonyms in the *Vocabulary Study* they are about to read.

2. Have students read the *Vocabulary Study* and do the *Word Play* activities.

Answers to *Word Play*

1. *serious*   joking   sincere; not joking
   create   destroy   make; invent
   calm   excited   peaceful; quiet

2. Sample answers: **a.** sob; **b.** true; **c.** frown; **d.** sad; **e.** cry. Sentences will vary.

✔ Use *Reading Skills Workbook*, Lesson 11, page 39. See *Providing for Individual Differences*, page T146, for additional practice.

VOCABULARY STUDY

Antonyms

"I've done it, Dr. Lens!"
"You're joking."
"No. I'm quite **serious**."
"Can I touch it?"
"Well, OK, but be careful. One false move and you'll destroy what it took me years to **create**."
"Ooo. It tickles."
"It's supposed to tickle. It's a smile-maker, remember? I'm calling it Chuckle-O."
"Chuckle-O! Ha ha ha ha ha ha ha . . . . That's a good one! Ha ha ha ha ha ha. . . . Funniest thing . . . ha ha ha . . . I ever . . . ha ha ha . . . heard . . . ha ha ha ha ha."
"Dr. Lens! Please! You're too excited. **Calm** yourself."
"Aw, come on, Dr. Mirror. Let yourself go. Touch Chuckle-O. Ha ha ha ha! It's fantastic! Ha ha ha ha!"
"You're going to wear it out if you keep this up. Give me back my Chuckle-O!"
"Never! Ha ha ha ha. You'll have to fight me for it!"
"How can we fight if you're laughing?"

166

"We'll fight when the battery runs down. Hee hee hee hee. By the way, why did you invent Chuckle-O?"
"Because we fight too much, and I don't like to fight."
"Gee. Neither do I. Are you thinking what I'm thinking?"
"Yes. I think I'll get another battery for Chuckle-O."

Word Play

1. Match each word in Column 1 with its antonym, or opposite, in Column 2 and its correct definition in Column 3.

1	2	3
serious	destroy	make; invent
create	excited	sincere; not joking
calm	joking	peaceful; quiet

2. Give an antonym for each of the words below. Then make up sentences using the antonyms.

a. chuckle   b. false   c. smile   d. funny   e. laugh

167

Reading Selection:
A Street of Games
Pages 168–174

Objectives

		SKILLS CODE NUMBER
M, T	To identify parts of a book where specific information may be found	5.5
M	To identify base words in compound words	4.2.1
M	To scan a selection for specific information	5.9

Preparing to Read

Summary

On an imaginary street, modern children, children from ancient times, and children from several countries gather to play street games. Readers are shown that although rules and details of play may vary, many popular street games have been played in the same basic form around the world for centuries.

Background

Street games are only one part of a rich and fascinating folklore specific to children. Children's folklore also includes chants, jokes, songs, riddles, and autograph-book inscriptions. Many of the rituals and variations are part of an oral tradition passed on from parent to child, from sibling to sibling, and from peer to peer. Some children's games are believed to have originated in association with ancient religious ceremonies and social customs. Others were played by both adults and children in those times before childhood was viewed as a distinct period of life (generally before the seventeenth century). Most children's games and verbal folklore grew out of an attempt to imitate adults.

The following book will provide you with additional background information on games.

Orlick, Terry. *The Cooperative Sports and Games Book: Challenge Without Competition.* Lists over one hundred brand-new games based on cooperation, not competition.

Developing Vocabulary and Concepts

Forum: the public marketplace in ancient Rome
lacrosse: a team game, played with a ball and long-handled rackets
generation: those people at one step or stage in the history of a family, such as children, parents, or grandparents

1. **a.** Read aloud the following sentences or write them on the board. If you read them aloud, write the underlined vocabulary on the board.

   Two thousand years ago, children played games in the Forum, or marketplace, of ancient Rome. Lacrosse, a ball game, was first played by teams of South American Indians hundreds of years ago. Children of every generation enjoy games. My parents enjoyed them. I enjoy them. I suppose my children will enjoy games, too.

   b. Ask students to give the meaning of each vocabulary word. Remind them to use the context clues in the sentences to help them.

2. Introduce the topic of games by asking students to name games that they play with their friends. After several games have been named, ask students to tell how they learned the games. Ask students if they think children in other parts of this country or in other countries play the same games. Explain that the selection will tell them more about the kinds of games that have been played by children around the world for thousands of years.

 Use *Duplicating Masters 11,* page 17.

Setting Purposes

Skills

Have students read the skills note at the top of page 168. Ask a volunteer to answer each question. (*pages about marbles:* the index; *a chapter on games in ancient Rome:* the table of contents)

Content

Have students read the lead-in to the title. Ask them to watch for games played in their neighborhood as they read the selection. Discuss briefly what games they think people of earlier times might have played. What games might children in ancient Rome have played? What games might early South American Indians have played? Explain that as students read the selection, they will find out how accurate their guesses were.

Suppose you had a book on games. What part of the book would guide you to the pages about marbles? How would you find out if the book had a chapter on games played in ancient Rome?

How are the games you play like those played in other countries or long ago? Take a walk along . . .

A STREET OF GAMES

by Dina Brown Anastasio

Close your eyes and picture a street. It can be any kind of street, anywhere in the world. It must, however, be big enough for many groups of children to gather and play. All of a sudden the street begins to come alive. Children of all ages form small groups in the middle of the street.

Who are these children? Well, since we are pretending anyway, let us pretend that they are children from different parts of the world. We might even carry our pretending one step further and say that some of these children also lived a long, long time ago.

What a gathering we have imagined! In front of an old red building, a group of very young children are trying to decide what to play. The group includes a child who lived in ancient Rome, one who lived in England a long time ago, a child from China, and several children who live in the United States today. They seem to be trying to find a game that they all know. At last they decide. They will play hopscotch. They all know this game.

They begin by drawing the diagram, and already there is disagreement. Most of the children agree that the diagram should look somewhat like a ladder.

One of the American children <u>prefers</u> that it look like a snail. But he is outvoted.

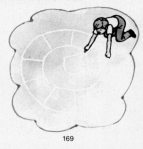

169

They begin to <u>draw</u> the ladder. But how many squares? Most of the Americans agree that there are eight squares in hopscotch.

"No, it's nine," says the girl from Rome. "I am the oldest, and I say that there are nine squares. If you don't believe me, look in the old <u>Forum</u> in Rome. The diagram is still there, scratched into the pavement."

"That's wrong," says a boy from England, who is also very old, but not quite as old as the girl from Rome. "There are twelve squares in hopscotch."

They argue for a little while. Then they decide to try it each way. They play the first game using eight squares.

"Now add a 'HOME,' " says a girl from Maine. "You have to have a place to rest before heading back to 'START.' "

Most of the Americans agree. But the others do not. The boy from England wants to rest in "LONDON." The girl from China wants to rest in the "PUBLIC HOUSE." And the girl from ancient Rome doesn't want to rest at all.

The arguments continue, and the players begin to wonder if they'll ever play. After they have chosen their stones, they argue about what to call them. "It's a tor!" "A potsie!" "A puck!" "A dump!" "A scotch!" "A pick!"

"Oh, what does it matter?" says a boy from Chicago. "Call it whatever you like! Let's just play!"

And so they begin. Some throw their stones into the squares, and some kick it. But it is hopscotch just the same.

170

2 Reading and Discussing

Have students read the selection. Most students will be able to complete it in one sitting. If you prefer, the selection may be read in two parts, breaking before the first paragraph on page 171.

NOTE: The questions that appear in the student's text at the end of the selection focus on comprehension of selection content and on application of the *Skills Lesson* to the selection. Answers to these questions begin on page T138.

Down the street, a tug of war is taking place. There are no arguments this time, for everyone plays the game the same way. However, when you ask the children to tell you the reason for the game, you get many different answers.

For instance, the Eskimo boy tells you that it is a contest to find out whether there will be a mild or a cold winter. When winter is approaching in an Alaskan town, he says, everyone who has a summer birthday takes one end of the rope. Those with winter birthdays pull the other end. If the summer birthdays win, the winter will be mild.

The Korean and Japanese children tell you that a tug of war is not a game. They tell you that it is a very serious contest indeed. One village pulls against another. It is believed that the winning village will have the best harvest.

In the middle of the block, three children are talking. One is a cave boy. The other boy lived near the Amazon River

171

long before Christopher Columbus was born. The girl is from Kansas City. She is throwing a rubber ball up in the air.

"I could teach you how to play ball," she is telling the others. "And then we could play something, maybe baseball, basketball, lacrosse, or even just catch."

The boy from the Amazon reminds her that it was his people who invented the ball.

"They took some gum from the rubber tree," he says, "and formed it into a ball. Lacrosse and basketball?" he adds. "Why, we were playing those games long before the English came to America."

The cave boy laughs and says, "Baseball indeed! We were playing baseball with a stick and a rock before either of you were born."

Farther down the block some older children are playing marbles in the dirt next to the street. A boy from ancient Rome tells the others that he used to use nuts instead of marbles. "Later," he says, "my parents bought me marbles

made of glass." Someone else says that she played the game with beans.

Each of the children seems to want to play a different marble game. A boy from Africa wants to play marble golf. He makes four small holes in the ground. Then he uses a stick to roll his marbles from behind a starting line toward the holes. Other players, in turn, do the same. And the player who fills the most holes is the winner.

A girl from Denver then shows the others how she plays marbles. She draws a circle in the dirt with a stick. Then she puts a marble in the center. Everyone else adds a marble to the center of the circle.

The girl then places her knuckles on the ground outside the circle and shoots another marble, called a "shooter." She tries to shoot some of the marbles out of the circle. If she misses, she leaves her shooter where it is and shoots it from that spot on her next turn. If she shoots some marbles out of the circle, she keeps them.

Or does she? A boy from Paris doesn't seem to agree.

"It's all for fun," he says. "You can't keep my marbles."

173

At the far end of the block, a boy from Spain watches a sewerball game. He guesses that the players are from a city, for it is <u>rare</u> to find three sewer covers on the same corner anywhere else.

The boy wonders if other children play sewerball in Paris, or Rome, or Tokyo. He watches carefully. He is trying to learn the rules so that he can teach them to his friends back in Madrid, Spain.

And this is perhaps the way most of us learn how to play the games of childhood. A sister or brother shows us how to jump hopscotch squares without stepping on the lines. A friend teaches us sewerball and stickball. We pass the rules from one person to another, from one country to another, and from <u>generation</u> to generation. Yes, we make some changes. But the games themselves never really change.

Understanding What You've Read

1. Why do the players disagree about hopscotch?
2. Why do the Korean and Japanese children say that tug of war is not a game?
3. How do we learn to play games?

Applying the Skills Lesson

In which part of a book about sports would you find each of the following items? (Refer to the Skills Lesson if you need help.)

1. an entry that gives the way to pronounce *lacrosse* and a definition of this word
2. the page number on which a chapter on different ball games begins
3. a list of books about sports and games

174

Questions preceded by a bullet are additional questions and appear in the Teacher's Edition only. The other questions appear in the student's text after the selection.

Understanding What You've Read

1. *Why do the players disagree about hopscotch?* (Each child played the game with slightly different rules and thinks his or her way of playing the game is the best one.   pages 169–170) INFERENTIAL <u>Drawing conclusions</u>

● *What details do the children playing hopscotch argue about?* (the shape of the diagram; the number of squares; the name of the resting place; and the name given to the stone   pages 169–170) LITERAL <u>Recalling specific details</u>

2. *Why do the Korean and Japanese children say that tug of war is not a game?* (They believe it is a serious contest in which the winning village will have the best harvest.   page 171) INFERENTIAL <u>Identifying cause-and-effect relationships</u>

● *Suppose a group of Alaskan Eskimo children who have winter birthdays win a tug of war. What might they believe about the coming winter?* (It will be harsh.   page 171) INFERENTIAL <u>Drawing conclusions</u>

● *How do you play games differently from the way children in the selection play them?* (Accept all reasonable answers.) CRITICAL <u>Contrasting ideas</u>

● *Which object would allow the children to play the most games—a rope, a bag of marbles, a ball, or a stone?* (Accept all reasonable answers. A ball might allow children to play the most games.) CRITICAL <u>Drawing conclusions</u>

3. *How do we learn to play games?* (We learn from brothers, sisters, other relatives, and friends.   page 174) LITERAL <u>Identifying the author's conclusions</u>

● *Why are games important to people all over the world?* (Accept reasonable answers. Students' opinions will vary, but most students will conclude that games provide fun, companionship, competition, and exercise.) CRITICAL <u>Drawing conclusions</u>

Applying the Skills Lesson

In which part of a book about sports would you find each of the following items? (Refer to the Skills Lesson if you need help.)
1. an entry that gives the way to pronounce lacrosse and a definition of this word
2. the page number on which a chapter on different ball games begins
3. a list of books about sports and games
(1. glossary; 2. table of contents; 3. bibliography) <u>Identifying the parts of a book</u>

● *In which part of a book about ancient Rome would you find each of the following items?*
1. a list of books about the Roman Empire
2. the page number on which a chapter about the Forum begins
3. the page numbers that show where you can find information about games played by children in ancient Rome
4. an entry that gives the way to pronounce the word Colosseum
(1. bibliography; 2. table of contents; 3. index; 4. glossary)   <u>Identifying the parts of a book</u>

 Use *Duplicating Masters 11*, page 18. See *Providing for Individual Differences*, page T146, for additional practice.

3 Maintaining Skills

Language Skills

Identifying base words in compound words   Ask students how the words *outvoted* and *stickball* are alike. (They are each made up of two shorter words.) Ask students the name for words like these. (compound words) Ask students to define the words. (*outvoted*: losing in a vote; *stickball*: baseball adapted for play in small areas, using a stick and a light ball)

Have students look for other compound words in the selection. (Additional compounds include *baseball, basketball, outside, everyone, anywhere, sewerball, birthday,* and *hopscotch*. You may want to point out that each line used to form the diagram of a hopscotch game is called a *scotch*.)

Have students recall other compounds they know from games or sports.

Study Skills

Scanning a selection for specific information   Ask students to think of the names of some of the games they read about. Then have them scan the selection rapidly to locate the names of *all* the games. Have a volunteer write the names of the games on the board. Students might be divided into teams to compete in identifying the total number of games in the shortest time. (Nine games are mentioned: hopscotch, tug of war, baseball, basketball, lacrosse, catch, marbles, sewerball, and stickball.)

 For additional resources and curriculum-related activities, see *Enrichment*, page T148.

Reading Selection:
Feliciano!
Pages 175–178

Objectives

		SKILLS CODE NUMBER
M, T	To identify parts of a book where specific information may be found	5.5
M	To identify the number of syllables in a word	2.6
M	To identify and use context clues to determine word meaning	3.0.2
M	To distinguish between fact and opinion	3.6.3

 Preparing to Read

Summary

This selection is a short biography of José Feliciano, a blind singer born in Puerto Rico and raised in New York City, who rose to the top in the popular music field. The selection tells about José's childhood, high school years, and early years as a struggling professional musician. It emphasizes the courage and determination that enabled José to overcome the limitations of his blindness.

Background

The selection mentions that José Feliciano first learned music "by ear." Many professional and amateur musicians learn to make an association between sounds they hear and the positions on a musical instrument that produce those sounds. Thus, "reading" music is not always necessary in order to play music. There is a braille system of musical notation for blind musicians who first "read" the notes with their fingers, then play the corresponding tones on their instruments.

The following book will provide you with additional background information.

Garland, Phyl. *The Sound of Soul.* The development of soul music is described. Index, discography, illustrations.

Developing Vocabulary and Concepts

native: born in a particular area
tongue: language
mimic: one who copies the sounds or actions of others
critic: a person who judges the value of books, music, art, etc.
review: an article discussing a book, musical work, etc.
released: presented to the public for the first time

1. **a.** Read aloud the following sentences or write them on the board. If you read them aloud, write the underlined vocabulary on the board.

   One singer could copy, or <u>mimic</u>, the voices of several stars.
   The music <u>critic</u> for our local newspaper wrote a good <u>review</u> of the new record album. In her judgment, this was the musician's best album.
   José made an album in May. It was <u>released</u> for sale in June and was favorably received by the public.

   b. Ask students to give the meaning of each vocabulary word. Remind them to use the context clues in the sentences to help them.

2. **a.** On a classroom map, point out Puerto Rico. Explain that José Feliciano is a *native* of Puerto Rico. Write *native* on the board and ask students to define this word.

   b. Ask students what language is spoken in Puerto Rico. (Spanish) Write the following sentence on the board and have students try to rephrase it. Help them understand that *tongue* means "language."

   José's native tongue is Spanish.
   (The first language José spoke was Spanish.)

3. If possible, play a recording of one of José Feliciano's songs. Tell students that José Feliciano is the performer and ask if anyone can identify the instrument he is playing and the style of music.

 Use *Duplicating Masters 11,* page 19.

Setting Purposes

Skills

Have students read the skills note at the top of page 175. Ask for volunteers to answer the question. (index and table of contents)

Content

Have students read the lead-in to the title. Ask how they think Feliciano might have shown courage. Tell them to read the selection to find out.

Suppose you had a book about musicians. What two parts of the book would guide you to pages giving information about José Feliciano?

A guitar, a song—and an adventure in courage. Here is . . .

Feliciano!

by Richard B. Lyttle

175

José Feliciano is the second of eight sons born to a family of farmers in Puerto Rico. When José was five, his family moved to New York City.

The Feliciano children were full of spirit and good fun. But because José was blind, his parents overprotected him, so he was cut off from much of the fun. He had to learn to amuse himself. Very early in life, the radio and its music became important to him. When he was six, he learned how to play the concertina.

Popular singers were José's heroes. He saw the life of a singer as a way to become independent. But because he was blind, José could not read music. He had to learn by ear. And he did have a natural talent. By the age of nine, he had learned to play the guitar. He made his first public appearance before he was ten years old.

Later, in high school, José was an expert mimic. He delighted his classmates by copying the styles and voices of well-known singers. But these performances did not satisfy him. If he was to become independent, he would have to start singing for pay.

With his guitar in a large paper sack, José began making the rounds of the coffee houses in New York. After entering a coffee house, he would ask the manager if he could play a few songs. Most managers said they had no time to listen to José.

José would then ask if he could at least tune his guitar before leaving. Even the busiest manager could not turn down that request. Of course, the guitar would always be in fine tune. José would pull it out from the paper sack. Then he would play so well that the manager and all of the customers were at once delighted.

176

José was seventeen when he took his first paying job in a Detroit nightclub. When he returned to New York, a music critic for the *New York Times* wrote that everyone who wanted to see the birth of a star should watch Feliciano.

In July 1964, he appeared on national TV for the first time. At about the same time, RCA released his first album. It seemed he was really on his way.

Most of his reviews were good. But one critic said José's voice sounded too much like the voices of other singers. José agreed. His high school performances as a mimic had slowed the development of a style that was all his own.

In 1966, José went on tour in Latin America. There he sang his songs in Spanish. He was a great success. Better still, the songs in his native tongue proved to be just what he needed to build a special style.

Pictures and stories about Feliciano appeared in magazines. José wore success well and lost nothing of his touch in working with an audience.

He continues to work hard and is now widely known in the United States and other countries.

Photograph © 1969 Children's Television Workshop, reprinted by permission.

177

---

2 Reading and Discussing

Have students read the selection. Most students will be able to complete it in one sitting. If you prefer, the selection may be read in two parts, breaking before the first paragraph on page 177.

NOTE: The questions that appear in the student's text at the end of the selection focus on comprehension of selection content and on application of the *Skills Lesson* to the selection. Answers to these questions begin on page T142.

Besides playing the guitar and singing on TV, he has acted on many TV shows.

Of course, José thinks of music as an ideal career for the blind.

"If you are blind," he says, "and have talent as a musician, you probably can make it if you really give it everything you've got and make sure that it is the only thing on your mind."

Anyone who has heard José Feliciano knows he gives his music everything he's got.

Understanding What You've Read

1. Why did José Feliciano make music his career?
2. How did José learn music?
3. How did José feel when a music critic said that his voice sounded too much like the voices of other singers?
4. How do you think José's success might have affected his relationships with other people?

Applying the Skills Lesson

In which part of a book about music and musicians would you find information on the items below? (Refer to the Skills Lesson if you need help.)

1. whether the book had information on José Feliciano
2. whether the book had a chapter on guitar music
3. how to pronounce *concertina* and a description of this instrument
4. a list of books from which the author got information
5. why the author wrote the book

178

Questions preceded by a bullet are additional questions and appear in the Teacher's Edition only. The other questions appear in the student's text after the selection.

Understanding What You've Read

1. *Why did José Feliciano make music his career?* (Music had been very important to him as a child; popular singers were his heroes; he saw music as a way to become independent.   page 176) INFERENTIAL   Identifying cause-and-effect relationships

● *What kind of hard work did José have to do in order to become a good musician?* (Students should conclude that José practiced singing and playing in order to become good at these skills. They might also cite details from the selection: He listened to and mimicked other performers, which helped him learn more about music. In addition, he played and sang for other people in order to learn how to be comfortable and convincing before an audience. page 176) INFERENTIAL   Drawing conclusions

2. *How did José learn music?* (He learned music "by ear."   page 176) LITERAL   Recalling specific details

● *How did José trick some coffee-house managers into letting him play and sing?* (He would ask if he could tune his guitar. When a manager gave permission, José would play and sing instead.   page 176) LITERAL   Identifying the main idea

3. *How did José feel when a music critic said that his voice sounded too much like the voices of other singers?* (José agreed. He did not feel that he had yet developed a singing style of his own.   page 177) LITERAL   Recalling specific details

● *What does the author mean when he says that "José wore success well and lost nothing of his touch in working with an audience"?* (that success didn't change José as a person or performer) INFERENTIAL Interpreting figurative language

4. *How do you think José's success might have affected his relationships with other people?* (Accept all reasonable answers.) CRITICAL   Predicting outcomes

Applying the Skills Lesson

In which part of a book about music and musicians would you find information on the items below? (Refer to the Skills Lesson if you need help.)
1. *whether the book had information on José Feliciano*
2. *whether the book had a chapter on guitar music*
3. *how to pronounce* concertina *and a description of this instrument*
4. *a list of books from which the author got information*
5. *why the author wrote the book*
(1. index; 2. table of contents; 3. glossary; 4. bibliography; 5. introduction)   Identifying parts of books where specific information may be found

● *In which part of a book about Puerto Rico would you find information about the items below?*
1. *whether the book had a chapter about the culture of Puerto Rico*
2. *a list of other books about Puerto Rico and Puerto Ricans*
3. *why the author wrote the book*
4. *how to pronounce* borinqueña *and the definition of this word*
(1. table of contents; 2. bibliography; 3. introduction; 4. glossary)   Identifying parts of books where specific information may be found

 Use *Duplicating Masters 11*, page 20. See *Providing for Individual Differences*, page T146, for additional practice.

3 Maintaining Skills

Word Service/Decoding

Identifying the number of syllables in a word   By this time, most students have probably learned how to pronounce the name José Feliciano. Review the use of the accent mark and its use in the name José. Ask students how many syllables the name has and on which syllable the accent falls. (two; second) Point out that occasionally words of more than three syllables have two accents—primary and secondary. The primary accent receives the most stress, but it may come after the secondary stress. Have students pronounce the name Feliciano [fe•lē'sē•ä'nō] and count the number of syllables. (five syllables) Write the name on the board and have students determine where the primary and secondary accents fall.

Give students the following list of words from the selection. Have students identify the number of syllables in each word, as well as the syllable or syllables that receive an accent. Students should check their work in the glossary at the back of their books.

> Puerto Rico (2 each word: Puer'to Ri'co)
> mimic (2: mim'ic)
> concertina (4: con'cer•ti'na)
> independent (4: in'de•pen'dent)

Comprehension Skills

Using context clues   Write the words *overprotected, independent,* and *request* on the board. Then have students read the following sentences from the selection. Tell them to define each word you listed on the board and identify the context clues that helped them. Also remind them that they should look for root words in the words.

> Page 176, second paragraph: But because José was blind, his parents *overprotected* him, so he was cut off from much of the fun. (protected too much; Clue: But because José was blind; Root word: protect)
> Page 176, fourth paragraph: If he was to become *independent,* he would have to start singing for pay. (self-supporting; Clue: for pay; Root word: depend)
> Page 176, last paragraph: José would then ask if he could at least tune his guitar before leaving. Even the busiest manager could not turn down that *request.* (asking for a favor; Clue: ask; Root word: quest[ion])

Have students read the last three paragraphs in the selection and tell what the word *ideal* means. (perfect)

Distinguishing between fact and opinion   Review with students the difference between fact and opinion. Something that is true or capable of being proved is a fact; something that represents a belief or a judgment is an opinion.

Have students identify the following sentences as facts or opinions.

> José's guitar playing is better than his singing. (opinion)
> José enjoys his success more than most people do. (opinion)
> José plays guitar, piano, banjo, and organ. (fact)
> *Feliciano!* was the best album of 1968. (opinion)

★ For additional resources and curriculum-related activities, see *Enrichment,* page T148.

Textbook Study:
Understanding the Parts of a Textbook
Pages 179–181

Objectives

		SKILLS CODE NUMBER
M, T	To use a table of contents	5.5.3
M, T	To use an index	5.5.8

Applying the Skill

1. Before students examine the textbook selections, you may wish to list the vocabulary words on the board and discuss them or have students look them up in the glossary.

   Science Selection
   matter: anything that has weight and takes up space
   atoms: the building blocks of elements; **atom:** the smallest part of an element that can take part in a chemical reaction
   reproduction: the process by which animals and plants produce new life

   Mathematics Selection
   evaluation: an examination, a check-up, or a test

2. Have students read the introduction and examine the two selections. You may wish to have students examine the selections on their own and then do *Building Skills*. Or you may wish to direct students, using the following procedure.

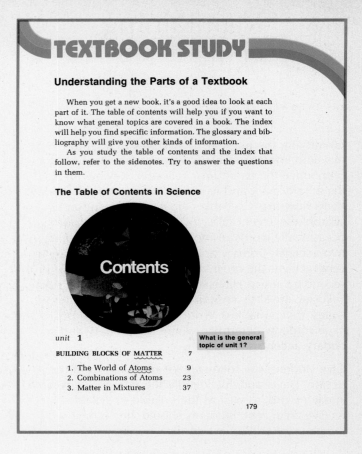

The Table of Contents in Science

1. Have students look at the part of the table of contents shown on page 179. Have them examine the different sizes and styles of type. Ask students to identify how the book is divided. (into units and chapters)

2. Have students answer the question in the first sidenote. (Building Blocks of Matter) Point out that the general topic is what the whole unit is about.

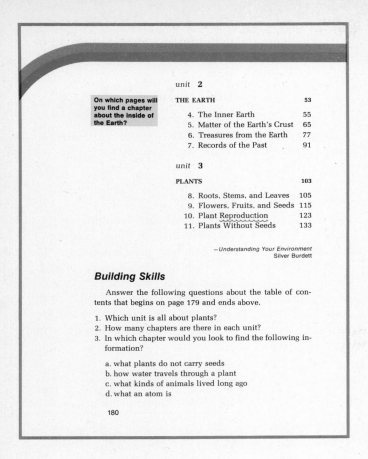

—Understanding Your Environment
Silver Burdett

On which pages will you find a chapter about the inside of the Earth?

Building Skills

Answer the following questions about the table of contents that begins on page 179 and ends above.

1. Which unit is all about plants?
2. How many chapters are there in each unit?
3. In which chapter would you look to find the following information?

   a. what plants do not carry seeds
   b. how water travels through a plant
   c. what kinds of animals lived long ago
   d. what an atom is

180

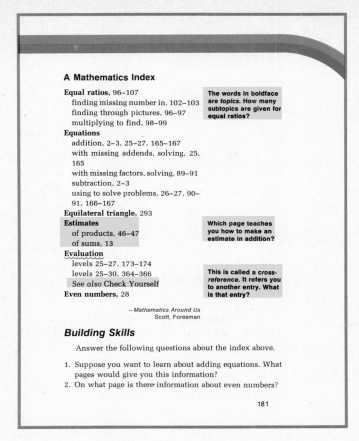

A Mathematics Index

Equal ratios, 96–107
  finding missing number in, 102–103
  finding through pictures, 96–97
  multiplying to find, 98–99
Equations
  addition, 2–3, 25–27, 165–167
  with missing addends, solving, 25, 165
  with missing factors, solving, 89–91
  subtraction, 2–3
  using to solve problems, 26–27, 90–91, 166–167
Equilateral triangle, 293
Estimates
  of products, 46–47
  of sums, 13
Evaluation
  levels 25–27, 173–174
  levels 25–30, 364–366
  See also Check Yourself
Even numbers, 28

The words in boldface are *topics*. How many subtopics are given for equal ratios?

Which page teaches you how to make an estimate in addition?

This is called a *cross-reference*. It refers you to another entry. What is that entry?

—Mathematics Around Us
Scott, Foresman

Building Skills

Answer the following questions about the index above.

1. Suppose you want to learn about adding equations. What pages would give you this information?
2. On what page is there information about even numbers?

181

---

3. Have students name the three chapter titles in Unit 1. (The World of Atoms; Combinations of Atoms; Matter in Mixtures) Point out that each chapter is about a special part of the general topic.

4. Have students answer the question in the sidenote at the top of page 180. (pages 55–64; also accept pages 77–90.)

5. Have students complete *Building Skills*.

Answers to *Building Skills*
Table of Contents in Science
Selection

1. Unit 3; 2. Unit 1: three chapters; Unit 2: four chapters; Unit 3: four chapters; 3. a. Chapter 11, Plants Without Seeds; b. Chapter 8, Roots, Stems, and Leaves; c. Chapter 7, Records of the Past; d. Chapter 1, The World of Atoms

A Mathematics Index

1. Have students answer the question in the first sidenote. (three) Point out the use of the prefix *sub-*, meaning "under," in the word *subtopics*. You may wish to check students' understanding by asking the number of subtopics under *Equations*. (five)

2. Have students answer the question in the second sidenote. (page 13) Ask students to explain how they found out what page taught how to make an estimate in addition. (*Estimates* was listed as a major topic, and *of sums* was listed as a subtopic below it.) You may wish to check students' understanding by asking what pages would teach them how to make an estimate in multiplication. (pages 46–47)

3. Have students answer the question in the third sidenote. (Check Yourself)

4. Have students complete *Building Skills*.

Answers to *Building Skills*
A Mathematics Index
Selection

1. 2–3, 25–27, 165–167; 2. 28

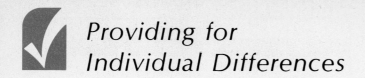

Providing for Individual Differences

Skills Lesson

Additional Practice

Worksheet 5, Teacher's Edition, page T484

Vocabulary Study

Additional Practice

■ **Identifying antonyms**   On the board, write each word at the left; then read aloud the sentence. Have students identify the antonym in each sentence.

earnest — Although Mom thought I was being *earnest,* I was really pretending. (pretending)

destitute — Before I bought the new book, I felt rich, but now I feel *destitute.* (rich)

anonymous — The letter to the famous artist was written by someone who is *anonymous.* (famous)

defiant — It's easier to work with someone who is cooperative than with someone who is always *defiant.* (cooperative)

Challenge Activity

■ **Identifying antonyms**   On the board, write each of the following italicized words. Read aloud the three choices at the right and have students identify the antonym.

earnest	sincere	joking	serious	(joking)
incompetent	unskilled	able	unable	(able)
conceal	hide	disguise	show	(show)
mania	craziness	sanity	madness	(sanity)
erect	destroy	build	raise	(destroy)
defective	flawed	perfect	broken	(perfect)
feeble	strong	weak	faint	(strong)

Reading Selection: A Street of Games

Additional Practice

■ **Identifying parts of a book where specific information may be found**   Assign one or more textbooks or other nonfiction books. Have students examine these books and locate the book parts studied in the *Skills Lesson.* Have them list the name of each book and the names of the parts they find in it. (This could be done in groups of two or three.)

■ **Using the Index**   Have students list the following names of games in the order in which they would be found in an index.

stickball   catch   soccer
tug of war   basketball   marbles
hopscotch   lacrosse

(Correct order: basketball, catch, hopscotch, lacrosse, marbles, soccer, stickball, tug of war)

Challenge Activity

■ **Identifying parts of a book and recognizing specific types of books**   Have students examine many different kinds of books in the classroom or in the library to find out which ones have some or all of the following parts: table of contents, index, glossary, bibliography, and introduction. Students should chart their results (as shown in the following chart) and determine why some of these parts are missing in certain types of books.

Sample Chart

Title	Table of Contents	Index	Glossary	Bibliography	Introduction
Science book	X	X	X	X	
Heidi	X				X
Sports	X	X	X	X	X
Blazing Trails	X	X	X	X	X

Reading Selection: Feliciano!

Additional Practice

■ **Using the table of contents**   Have students locate the table of contents in *Blazing Trails* and identify the page on which each of the following selections begins: "A Street of Games" (page 168); "Shell Treasures" (page 190); "Start Your Own Theater" (page 214).

Challenge Activity

■ **Matching information to specific parts of books**

Write the following two columns on the board. Have students match the information in column 1 with the appropriate book part in column 2.

1. pages on which to find information about Puerto Rico
2. a chapter on electric guitars
3. the meaning of *album*
4. a list of books about music
5. an explanation by the author of the reasons for writing the book

a. table of contents

b. introduction

c. bibliography

d. glossary

e. index

(1. e; 2. a; 3. d; 4. c; 5. b)

Evaluation

Periodic Test 2, Part I, Form A or *Form B,* may be administered after this unit to test skills marked **T.** If you have pretested using *Form A,* administer *Form B.*

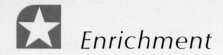

Enrichment

A Street of Games

Bibliography

The following books are about street games.

Average

Gallagher, Rachel. *Games in the Street.* Descriptions of stickball, blindman's bluff, kick-the-can, and many other games, with their histories.

Langstaff, John, and Carol Langstaff. *Shimmy Shimmy Coke-Ca-Pop! A Collection of City Children's Street Games and Rhymes.* Tag games, action games, jump-rope, hand-clapping games—some very old, some new.

Lincoln, Eric. *Backyard Games.* Classic and new games to play in the park, in the street, and on the lawn.

Challenging

Ferretti, Fred. *The Great American Book of Sidewalk, Stoop, Dirt, Curb, and Alley Games.* Rules and descriptions of equipment for more than sixty old games that are played today.

Films and Filmstrips

NOTE: For more information, see *Resource Center.*

Skills

Harcourt Brace Jovanovich. *Bookmark Reading Filmstrips.* "The Structure of a Book."

Selection Content

Guidance Assocs. *Cross-Cultural Studies Series.* Games as part of the lives and experiences of children in various cultures.

Curriculum Coordination

Language Arts

1. Allow students to teach the class a new game. Some students may know a card game or a word game with which the rest of the class is unfamiliar. Before explaining the games, students should make notes that they may use during their presentations.

2. Students might interview adults to find out what types of games they played when they were young. Students' findings could be charted and compared with predictions they made before initiating the survey or with a list of the most popular games among students themselves.

Social Studies

1. As part of the previous activity, students might find out where adults they interviewed lived when they were children. Then the class might discuss which games seem unique to certain locations and which seem to be universally, or nationally, familiar.

2. Place a world map on a large corkboard. Have students place map pins to indicate the places named in the selection: Korea; Maine; Amazon River; England; Rome, Italy; China; Chicago, Illinois; Kansas City, Missouri; Africa; Paris, France; Denver, Colorado; Madrid, Spain; Tokyo, Japan; Alaska

Physical Education

Students could be encouraged to use the books from the bibliography on this page to learn and play a game with which they're not familiar.

Art/Social Studies

Have students make drawings or puppets of children described in the selection, wearing costumes that reflect their nationalities and eras.

Feliciano!

Bibliography

The following books are about music, José Feliciano, and other musicians.

Average

Hawkinson, John, and Martha Faulhaber. *Rhythms, Music and Instruments to Make.* How to make instruments—some easy, some difficult—including guitars, drums, violins, xylophones, and reed pipes.

Jacobs, Linda. *Stevie Wonder: Sunshine in the Shadow.* A clear, readable biography of the blind singer, musician, and composer, and the story of how he achieved great success.

Levine, Jack. *Understanding Musical Instruments: How to Select Your Instrument.* The methods of playing many instruments.

Challenging

Collier, James Lincoln. *Making Music for Money.* Helpful tips about becoming a professional musician—equipment needed, rehearsals, publicity, and how to find jobs.

Kendall, Alan. *The World of Musical Instruments.* An illustrated history of musical instruments.

Wheelock, Warren H. *Carmen Rosa Maymi: To Serve American Women; Roberto Clemente: Death of a Proud Man; José Feliciano: One Voice, One Guitar.* Three short biographies.

Films and Filmstrips

NOTE: For more information, see *Resource Center.*

Skills

Harcourt Brace Jovanovich. *Bookmark Reading Film-strips.* "The Structure of a Book."

Guidance Assocs. *Career Discoveries Series.* "People Who Create Art": interviews with artists, including a drummer.

Prentice-Hall Media. *Once Upon a Sound.* Sounds and appearances of orchestral instruments.

Curriculum Coordination

Language Arts

1. Have students report on famous people who had physical disabilities: Ludwig van Beethoven (deaf composer), Helen Keller (deaf and blind lecturer and writer), Homer (blind author of the *Iliad* and the *Odyssey*), Joseph Pulitzer (blind publisher and congressman), James Thurber (blind writer).

2. Obtain a copy of a "talking book" and have students listen to it in class.

3. Use a book of songs in Spanish with their English translations to teach a song to students in both languages.

Science

Invite a musician who uses amplifiers to demonstrate and explain how electric instruments and amplifiers work.

Music

1. Invite a music teacher or students to explain and demonstrate instruments they play. If your school or a local high school has a band or an orchestra, perhaps they will allow your class to observe a rehearsal.

2. Play for the class samples of different kinds of guitar music. Play selections from Feliciano, Andrés Segovia, Julian Bream, country and western music, folk, etc. (See *Resource Center.*)

Career Education

1. Arrange for students to visit a local institute for the blind. Instructors can explain how a blind person learns to get around. Career counselors can explain how blind people learn to perform their jobs and the many jobs blind people do. Reading instructors can give a lesson in braille.

2. Encourage interested students to learn more about careers in music by making a survey of local music schools and their curricula or by interviewing musicians and/or songwriters, one of whom you might invite to class.

Contents

Additional Materials

Reading Skills Workbook: Lessons 12–14, pages 40–47
Duplicating Masters 11: pages 21–22
Worksheet 6: Teacher's Edition, page T485
Periodic Test 2, Part II

Key to Symbols

Skills Objectives
I* – Introduced in this unit
I – Introduced earlier in this level
M – Maintained from previous levels
T – Tested in periodic and cumulative tests for this level

Reduced Student Pages
underscore – words that appear in the glossary
wavy line – words pretaught in the Teacher's Edition
(these words also appear in the glossary)

Skills Lesson:
Understanding Topical Organization
Pages 182–187

Objectives

		SKILLS CODE NUMBER
I*, T	To identify topical organization	5.10.1
I*, T	To identify introductory paragraphs	5.10.2
I*, T	To identify summary paragraphs	5.10.3

If you wish to pretest the skills listed above, you may administer *Periodic Test 2, Part II, Form A. Periodic Test 2, Part II, Form B,* may be administered to posttest.

Introducing the Lesson

1. **a.** Ask students to make a list of their favorite breakfast foods. Then have them list the foods that would make up their favorite lunches. Finally, have them make a list of their favorite dinner foods.

   b. Explain that students could call the *major topic* of their lists "My Favorite Foods." Ask them into what three topics their list could be divided. (breakfast, lunch, dinner) Explain that the individual foods they listed are details of the three topics. Then, if you wish, ask students to name some of the sections—or topics—into which a restaurant's menu might be organized.

2. Write the term *topical organization* on the board. Explain that the lists students have made are "topically organized." Also explain that many books or articles are topically organized. Ask students why they think a writer would organize an article into topics. (so the reader could easily follow the writer's ideas)

Understanding Topical Organization

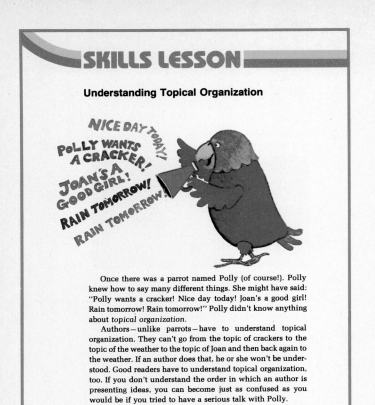

Once there was a parrot named Polly (of course!). Polly knew how to say many different things. She might have said: "Polly wants a cracker! Nice day today! Joan's a good girl! Rain tomorrow! Rain tomorrow!" Polly didn't know anything about *topical organization.*

Authors—unlike parrots—have to understand topical organization. They can't go from the topic of crackers to the topic of the weather to the topic of Joan and then back again to the weather. If an author does that, he or she won't be understood. Good readers have to understand topical organization, too. If you don't understand the order in which an author is presenting ideas, you can become just as confused as you would be if you tried to have a serious talk with Polly.

182

Finding Topics

You know that a table of contents shows the organization of the major topics in a book. Like a book, a chapter or an article may be organized by topics.

The title of a chapter or article sometimes gives you an idea about its major topic. But sometimes the title alone is not enough. Here is the title of an article. You would need to look at the article itself to find out that it is about the Smithsonian Institution.

"America's Attic"

Smithsonian Institution Building, Washington, D.C. Sometimes called The Castle.

183

---

3. a. Have students look at the picture on page 182 and read the first paragraph. Ask what is meant by the last sentence in the paragraph. (Polly skipped from one topic to another.)

b. Have students read the next paragraph.

Developing the Skill

Finding Topics

A. *The title of an article or chapter is often a good clue to the topic of the selection. However, sometimes a title may be misleading.*

1. Have students read the first two paragraphs on page 183. Ask if an article with the title "America's Attic" might be thought to be about attics. About Alaska? Point out that an article titled "America's Attic" could be about almost anything—such as roofing or Alaska or the Smithsonian Institution.

2. Discuss the idea that the author probably chose "America's Attic" to state the topic cleverly and to catch the reader's interest. Use this example to point out that some titles do *not* immediately identify the major topic of a selection for the reader.

B. *Previewing the title and headings may give the reader an idea of the topical organization of the selection.*

Within many chapters and articles, you will see **headings**. These words are usually printed in boldfaced type. When you are reading or studying a chapter or an article, it's a good idea to look at the title and the headings before you begin to read. This is called **previewing**. Previewing gives you an idea of the topics that will be covered. Previewing also helps you see how the topics relate to one another. If you previewed the headings in the article titled "America's Attic," here is what you would find:

title —————→ "America's Attic"
heading ———→ The Museum of History and Technology
heading ———→ The National Air and Space Museum
heading ———→ The Art Museums
heading ———→ The Natural History Museum
heading ———→ The Rest of the Museum

How is the article organized? As you can see from the headings, the article is organized according to the different museums that make up the Smithsonian Institution.

Milestone Hall, National Air and Space Museum

184

When There Are No Headings

Not every chapter or article has headings. But you can be sure that the author has organized his or her ideas in some way. Read the following article in which there are no headings. The sidenotes will help you see how the author has organized the topics of the article.

The Arlington Symphony Orchestra, Arlington, Virginia

The Orchestra

The orchestra is made up of a group of musicians playing together. Most orchestras are large and have many people playing different instruments. The instruments are grouped by "families." There is the *string* family, the *woodwinds*, the *brass*, and the *percussion*. There are also *keyboard* instruments that belong to more than one family.

This paragraph introduces the article. What topics do you think will be covered later in the article?

185

Have students read page 184. Discuss the question "How is the article organized?" (Each of the headings under the title "America's Attic" is related to the main topic. Each heading identifies a museum within the Smithsonian Institution.)

When There Are No Headings

Not every chapter or article has headings, but a careful reading should reveal how the author has organized the material.

1. Have students read page 185. Have them answer the question in the sidenote. (the string, woodwind, brass, and percussion families, and keyboard instruments)

What is the first topic covered in this article?

The strings are the largest family in the orchestra. They make up more than half of it. The family members are the violin, the viola, the cello, and the bass. They are played by the drawing of a bow across their strings.

The topic changes here.

The woodwind family is made up of the flute, the oboe, the clarinet, and the saxophone. This family is only a small part of the orchestra.

What topic is the author dealing with now?

The brass family is known for the brilliance of its sound. Among its family members are the trumpet, the trombone, and the French horn. They are not heard as often as the strings, but you know they're "alive" when you hear them!

The topic of this paragraph is the *percussion family*.

What do you think the members of the percussion family are? Its members are all instruments that are played by being "struck." This includes the drums and many others.

This paragraph and the next have the same topic. The topic of both paragraphs is *keyboard instruments*.

What about the piano? To which family does it belong? It belongs really to both the percussion and the string families. It is a keyboard instrument with felt hammers that strike metal strings to make its sounds.

The organ is also a keyboard instrument. It sometimes joins the orchestra. However, the organ is not used as often as the piano.

186

It is truly a wonderful experience to hear all these families of the orchestra working together.

The last paragraph summarizes or ties all the topics together.

Try This

1. Below is a list of five topics covered in the article you just read. The order of topics is mixed up. Put them in the same order as they appeared in the article.

   a. the brass family   d. the woodwind family
   b. the string family   e. the percussion family
   c. keyboard instruments

2. The following headings are for an article titled "How to Improve Your Writing." The headings are out of order. Put them in the order that would make sense in the article.

   a. Handing In the Perfect Paper   d. Locating the Facts
   b. Editing Your Writing   e. Typing a Clean Copy
   c. Getting It All Down Quickly

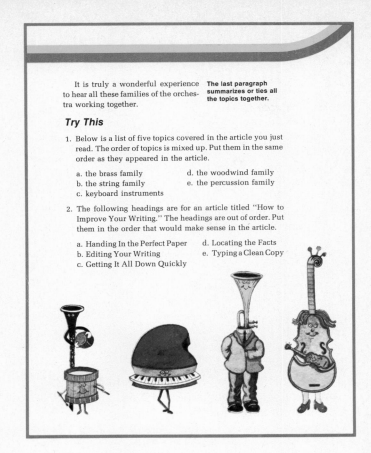

2. Have students read the first paragraph on page 186 and answer the question in the top sidenote. (the string family)

3. Have students read the second paragraph on page 186 and the sidenote next to it.

4. Have students read the third paragraph on page 186 and answer the question in the sidenote. (The topic that the author is dealing with here is the brass family.)

5. Have students read the fourth paragraph on page 186 and the sidenote next to it.

6. Have students read the last two paragraphs on page 186 and the bottom sidenote.

7. Have students read the paragraph on page 187 and the sidenote. Point out that not all articles have summary paragraphs. Also explain that an author might use more than one paragraph to summarize an article.

Try This

Have students complete *Try This*.

Answers to *Try This*

1. Correct order: b, d, a, e, c; 2. Correct order: d, c, b, e, a

 Use *Reading Skills Workbook*, Lesson 12, pages 40–43. See *Providing for Individual Differences*, page T165, for additional practice.

Vocabulary Study:
Etymologies

Pages 188–189

Objective

M   To use etymologies to determine word meaning

SKILLS CODE
NUMBER
4.4.1

Developing
the Skill

1. Tell students that the *Vocabulary Study* they are
about to read is about imported word kits. Ask for a
definition of *imported*. (brought from one country
into another country)

2. Explain that many words that students use in their
everyday speech come from other languages. Ask if
they can give examples of such words. (Examples:
coffee—Turkish; orange—Persian; hurricane—West Indian) Also explain that many English words come
from Latin and Greek.

3. Have students read the *Vocabulary Study* and do the
Word Play activities.

Answers to *Word Play*

1. *ballerina:* a female ballet dancer; *mime:* use gestures
and actions rather than words; *original:* not existing before; new; first; 2. Sentences will vary.

 Use *Reading Skills Workbook,* Lesson 13,
page 44. See *Providing for Individual Differences,*
page T165, for additional practice.

VOCABULARY STUDY

Etymologies

"Do you sell sentences?"

"No, not finished sentences. But we do
sell sentence kits. You can make your own
<u>original</u> sentences. We're having a sale on
imported word kits. I'll give you a good
price on a starter kit—with three terrific words."

"Only three words? What can I do with
three words?"

"Plenty. See for yourself. Each word kit
comes with its own etymology. An etymology
is the history, or origin, of a word. Here's the
French word **ballet**. It originally came from
the Italian *ballo*, meaning 'dance.' "

"Ballet is a dance form using gestures
and actions to tell a story, isn't it? I can make
a nice sentence with the word *ballet*. What
else is in the kit?"

"The word **mimic**, meaning 'to imitate,'
from the Greek word for actor—*mimos*."

"Gee, I don't know. Is it possible to imitate
something in a ballet?"

"Sure. In *Firebird*, a ballerina imitates the
movements of a bird. The kit also contains a
nice Latin word."

"I knew it. Here's the catch!"

"No! The word is **origin**, meaning 'parent-
age.' *Origin* comes from the Latin *originis*,
meaning 'that in which something has its
beginning.' You'll make many original sentences with this kit. By the way, what are you
planning to do with the sentences?"

"They're for a display rack in our dad's
store. He sells punctuation. Here, have a
comma with our compliments."

188

Word Play

1. Each of the words below is related to one of the words in
boldface in the story. Match each word with its meaning.

ballerina	use gestures and actions rather than words
mime	not existing before; new; first
original	a female ballet dancer

2. The Greek word *geo* means "earth." Look up three words
beginning with *geo-* in a dictionary and use each one in
a sentence.

189

Reading Selection:
Shell Treasures
Pages 190–197

Objectives

		SKILLS CODE NUMBER
I*, T	To identify topical organization	5.10.1
I*, T	To identify introductory paragraphs	5.10.2
I*, T	To identify summary paragraphs	5.10.3
M	To identify word parts: root words, prefixes, and suffixes	4.1
M	To identify base words in compound words	4.2.1
M	To follow a set of written directions	5.3.1

Preparing to Read

Summary

Shellcraft, the art of using shells to make decorative items, is described from the collection stage through the construction stage. The selection provides information on two types of mollusks—bivalves and univalves—and offers tips on collecting shells at the beach or obtaining them by other means. Finally, it describes and illustrates shell projects that students might want to complete.

Background

Shells vary enormously in size and weight as well as in shape and pattern. The estimated 100,000 different kinds of mollusk shells range from the tiny vitrinellid, which is about the size of a grain of sand, to the giant clam of the South Pacific, which can be up to 1.2 meters (four feet) long and weigh as much as 230 kilograms (500 pounds). The patterns in a shell are determined by the kinds of minerals the mollusk eats and by the colors added to the shell by special glands. In the past, shells were valued and exchanged as money on nearly every continent of the world.

The following books will provide you with additional background information.

Crescent Books. *Sea Shells: How to Identify and Collect Them.* Beautiful color photographs of shells, with descriptions and information on how to collect them.

Denzer, Ann Wiseman. *Making Things: The Hand Book of Creative Discovery.* Two volume set, excellent for teachers and parents. Stresses the need to allow children the freedom to explore their creativity. Describes over 100 activities, from paper making to jewelry making.

Developing Vocabulary and Concepts

spiral: a curve that looks like the thread of a screw
ridged: having raised strips on the surface
hinge: a joint on which something turns
descriptive: telling what a person or thing is like
crescent: anything having the curved shape of the quarter moon
draw: pull or drag
drift: something piled up by wind or water
coral: a stony substance made up of the many "skeletons" of tiny sea animals

1. **a.** Read aloud the following sentences or write them on the board. If you read them aloud, write the underlined vocabulary on the board.

   The clam shell's surface was no longer <u>ridged</u>. The sand and water had rubbed off the raised strips on it.
   I asked Mark to give a <u>descriptive</u> report about the shell. So he wrote several sentences telling what the shell looks like.
   <u>Draw</u> or drag the tiny shell across a puddle of glue so that one side becomes covered with the glue.
   The wind made huge <u>drifts</u> of sand that were like small hills.

   b. Ask students to give the meaning of each vocabulary word. Remind them to use the context clues in the sentences to help them.

2. Write the word *coral* on the board and ask students if they know what this word means. Have students look the word up in the glossary and tell the three meanings listed for this word. If there is a coral-colored (pinkish or yellowish red) object in the classroom, point it out to students. Explain that coral, like shells, is made of lime.

3. a. Ask students to describe shells. Guide the discussion to include these facts: Shells are homes for clams, oysters, snails, scallops, and other edible or inedible sea animals; shells come in many shapes, sizes, and colors (there are over 100,000 kinds); shells are made of a white substance called lime, which is used to make many things, such as whitewash; in many places around the world, shells have been used as money.

b. Ask students if they have anything at home that is decorated with shells. If so, invite them to bring the objects to school to show the class.

c. Ask students to describe some of the shapes of shells. Write the words *crescent* and *spiral* on the board and ask volunteers to describe these shapes or draw them on the board. If students need help, draw a crescent on the board and ask them to think of things that have this shape. (the moon, a partially eaten cookie, etc.) For *spiral*, ask if anyone has ever seen a circular staircase. Then have students offer examples of other spiral-shaped things. (the thread of a screw; wire that binds notebooks; a tornado; etc.)

d. Ask students to describe clam or oyster shells. Ask what allows these kinds of shells to open and close. If no one offers the word *hinge*, write it on the board and have a volunteer show the hinges on a classroom door.

 Use *Duplicating Masters 11,* page 21.

Setting Purposes

Skills

Have students read the skills note at the top of page 190. Encourage them to preview the selection by reading the title and headings before they read the selection itself. Point out that knowing the topical order in advance will help them understand and remember the information.

Content

Have students read the lead-in to the title. Ask students to suggest what kinds of "treasures" might be made from shells. Explain that the selection will describe how to turn shells into "shell treasures."

As you read, notice how the author has organized the different topics in this selection. The headings will help you to understand this organization.

Some sea animals make beautiful homes that you can turn into . . .

Shell Treasures

by Katherine N. Cutler

Shellcraft is the art of using shells to make many attractive things. The first step in this popular hobby is finding sea shells to work with. The second step is turning these objects of <u>nature</u> into objects of art.

2 Reading and Discussing

Have students read the selection. Most students will be able to complete it in one sitting. If you prefer, the selection may be read in two parts, breaking before the heading "Gluing the Shells" on page 193.

NOTE: The questions that appear in the student's text at the end of the selection focus on comprehension of selection content and on application of the *Skills Lesson* to the selection. Answers to these questions begin on page T159.

Animal Houses

What is a sea shell? It is the house of a soft-bodied animal called a mollusk. The animal has built the shell to protect itself. (You may not realize that shells you've found once held living animals.)

How does the mollusk make its shell? Wrapped around the body of the animal is a sac called a mantle. Inside the mantle are cells that make lime. The shell is made from this lime.

Each kind of mollusk makes its house in a different shape. Some shells are round; some are spiral. Some are smooth and glossy. Others are rough and ridged.

From earliest times people have admired these animal houses. That is why collecting shells has been popular through the ages.

Different Kinds of Shells

Some shells are found only in certain parts of the world. Other shells seem to be everywhere. The warmer the water in which a shell is found, the brighter its color seems to be. Shells from calm waters are thinner than those found where there are high seas and a pounding surf.

Most of the shells you find fall into two classes. They are called *bivalves* and *univalves*.

Bivalves are shells that have two parts joined together by a hinge. (The prefix *bi-* means "two.") Clams and oysters are examples of these. Sometimes you will find only one half of a bivalve. You can recognize it by the hinge mark.

Scallop

Univalves are made in one piece. (The prefix *uni-* means "one.") Cones, sundials, and cowries are some kinds of univalves.

Cone

191

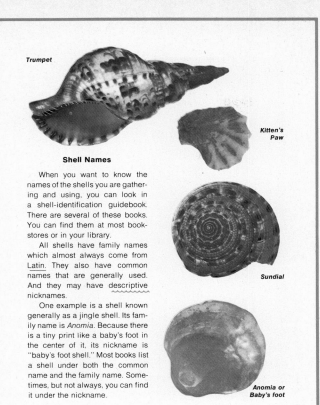

Trumpet

Kitten's Paw

Sundial

Anomia or Baby's foot

Shell Names

When you want to know the names of the shells you are gathering and using, you can look in a shell-identification guidebook. There are several of these books. You can find them at most bookstores or in your library.

All shells have family names which almost always come from Latin. They also have common names that are generally used. And they may have descriptive nicknames.

One example is a shell known generally as a jingle shell. Its family name is *Anomia*. Because there is a tiny print like a baby's foot in the center of it, its nickname is "baby's foot shell." Most books list a shell under both the common name and the family name. Sometimes, but not always, you can find it under the nickname.

192

Collecting Shells

You can make many things with shells that you collect. When you are looking for shells, try not to take ones that house live animals. The animals inside may have come into shallow water to breed, and you would be destroying more than the parent animal.

While it is fun to look for shells at any time, it is best when the tides are at their highest and lowest. This happens when the moon is either crescent or full. High tides bring in more shells. Low tides show greater areas of beach.

As you start out to gather shells, take a good-sized bag to hold your treasures. Wear sneakers or beach shoes, for it is easy to cut a bare foot on a piece of glass or broken shell. To avoid a sunburn, wear a hat and a thin shirt.

Shells are not always lying on the open beach. Sometimes you find the ones you treasure most by poking in the dry seaweed at the tide line. You might turn over a broken plank or move a small rock. Replace rocks you turn over so that sea life will not be disturbed.

You may say, "But how can I make things with shells? I don't live near any beaches where there

are shells." This shouldn't trouble you, for there are many ways to get them. There are many interesting snails in inland ponds and rivers. If you let people know you are interested in shells, you will find that friends will bring some home to you after they go to beaches. They may also give you shells they have at home. Often there are boxes of shells for sale in gift shops and craft shops. There you can buy little packages of shells.

Gluing the Shells

You will need very little equipment. The most important thing is the proper glue. Be sure it is safe to use and clear enough to see through when it dries. It should also be easy to wipe up without causing any damage if it spills. Besides glue, you will need a water-color paintbrush and some tweezers.

To glue single small shells, make a puddle of glue on a piece of paper. Use the tweezers to draw the shell through the glue, and put the shell in place. When you want to cover a large space with shells, paint glue over all of the space. Then stick the shells directly on the glue.

193

Things You Can Make

Here are some ideas for things you may want to make from shells. Of course, you'll also want to make your own shell designs.

Underwater Scene in a Jar: You will need a jar with a top. Put sand in the bottom of the jar. Shake it so that the sand forms drifts. Place different shells and pieces of coral in the sand. (A piece of coral, if you have one, makes a good center of interest.) When you have finished, fill the jar

with water. Add two tablespoons of laundry bleach. This will keep the water clear. Replace the jar top.

194

195

Mobile: Shells on a mobile are balanced so that they move gently in the slightest draft. You can enjoy their beauty from all sides as they turn. Use driftwood or whatever else you like for the bar. Thin wire, heavy thread, or nylon fishing line can be tied to the middle of the bar and fastened to something so that it balances.

Choose shells of different shapes and colors. Make a small hole in each, then thread them to the bar.

Owl: Use a pine cone with a firm, pointed stem end for the owl's body and head. On the top end, glue round, white shells for the eyes and pointed shells for the ears and beak. Make the owl look alive by putting tiny, dark, round shells in the center of the "eyes" for the pupils. Make the back and folded wings by overlapping the shells. Glue two small shells to the stem end for the feet.

Then make a puddle of glue on a branch and hold the owl in place until the glue takes hold.

Shell Display: Make a wall decoration for your room. Find a piece of driftwood or weathered wood that has an interesting shape. Glue shells to it, following the shape of the wood.

Anyone who becomes interested in shells will have many hours of pleasure. It is not only great fun to use shells imaginatively, but it also gives pleasure to your family and friends when you share these things with them.

196

Understanding What You've Read

1. What is a sea shell?
2. When is the best time to collect shells at the beach? Why?
3. How can a shell-identification guidebook be useful?

Applying the Skills Lesson

1. Find a paragraph in the selection that *introduces* the topics that will be covered. Find a paragraph that *summarizes* or ties together all the topics.
2. Below is a list of the topics of some paragraphs covered in this selection. In what order did the topics appear?

   a. how to collect shells
   b. what shells are
   c. what you can make with shells
   d. how shells are named
   e. bivalves and univalves
   f. how to glue shells

197

Questions preceded by a bullet are additional questions and appear in the Teacher's Edition only. The other questions appear in the student's text after the selection.

Understanding What You've Read

1. *What is a sea shell?* (the house of a mollusk   page 191) LITERAL   Identifying the main idea

● *How do mollusks make their own shells?* (Around their bodies is a sac called a mantle, which contains cells that make lime. The shell is made from this lime.   page 191) LITERAL   Recalling stated information

● *Refer to the fifth paragraph on page 191. Why do mollusks that live where there are high seas and a pounding surf have thicker shells than do mollusks that live in calm water?* (The shells must be thicker to be strong enough to withstand the pounding of the seas. Accept any other answers students can justify.) INFERENTIAL   Drawing conclusions

2. *When is the best time to collect shells at the beach? Why?* (When the tide is highest and when the tide is lowest. High tides bring in more shells, and low tides leave a wider beach area on which to find shells.   page 193) LITERAL   Identifying cause-and-effect relationships

3. *How can a shell-identification guidebook be useful?* (It can help you name and describe shells.   page 192) LITERAL   Recalling specific details

● *What would happen if people caught most of the mollusks of a certain kind whenever those mollusks come into shallow water to breed?* (Accept reasonable answers. Students should understand that those mollusks would diminish in number or be eliminated.) CRITICAL   Predicting outcomes

● *What other materials besides those mentioned in the selection might you use to make "shell treasures"?* (Accept all reasonable answers.) CRITICAL   Drawing conclusions

Applying the Skills Lesson

1. *Find a paragraph in the selection that introduces the topics that will be covered. Find a paragraph that summarizes or ties together all the topics.* (First paragraph in selection introduces the topics; last paragraph in selection summarizes the topics.   pages 190 and 196)   Identifying introductory and summary paragraphs

● *Which topic headings in this selection describe mollusks and their shells?* (The topic headings are "Animal Houses," "Different Kinds of Shells," and "Shell Names.")   Identifying topical organization

2. *Below is a list of the topics of some paragraphs covered in this selection. In what order did the topics appear?*
   a. *how to collect shells*
   b. *what shells are*
   c. *what you can make with shells*
   d. *how shells are named*
   e. *bivalves and univalves*
   f. *how to glue shells*
   (b, e, d, a, f, c)
   Identifying topical organization

 Use *Duplicating Masters 11,* page 22. See *Providing for Individual Differences,* page T165, for additional practice.

3 Maintaining Skills

Language Skills

Identifying word parts: root words, prefixes, and suffixes   Write *univalve* and *bivalve* on the board; ask students to state the meanings of the prefixes *uni-* and *bi-*. (*uni-* means "one"; *bi-* means "two") Explain that *valve* is the root of each word. Have students find the meaning of *valve* in the glossary. (half of the shell of an oyster, clam, etc.) Ask students to think of other words that contain the prefixes *uni-* and *bi-*. List their words and any you supply under *univalve* and *bivalve*. Discuss the meaning of each whole word that is listed.

Write the following words from the selection on the board. Have volunteers circle the roots of the words. Then have them draw a line under each prefix and suffix and give the meaning of each whole word.

(identifi)cation (the action of knowing or naming)

(equip)ment (gear; things needed to do or make something)

(tweez)ers (small pliers-like tool, used to pull something out of an object)

re(place) (substitute)

(imagin)atively (creatively; done with imagination)

Identifying base words in compound words   Write on the board the following list of compound words taken from the selection. Have students identify the shorter words in each compound word and give the meaning of the compound word.

sundial (sun + dial; a device that uses shadows to show the time of day)

guidebook (guide + book; a book that is a guide to something)

sunburn (sun + burn; the burning of the skin by the sun)

seaweed (sea + weed; a plant that grows in the ocean)

tablespoon (table + spoon; a measure equal to three teaspoons)

driftwood (drift + wood; wood that is washed onto a shore)

overlap (over + lap; to come over the edge of something)

Study Skills

Following directions   Remind students that when they follow directions, they should pay attention to the steps so that what they make will turn out right. Read aloud the following paragraphs and have students check the selection to determine the answers.

Susan wanted to make a shell mobile like the one described on page 196. She used heavy thread to hang shells from a bar of driftwood. When she tied the mobile to a hook, it leaned to one side. What detail of the directions did Susan forget to follow? (She forgot to balance the mobile.)

Willy tried to make a shell owl by following the directions on page 196. On a pine cone, he glued round white shells for eyes and pointed shells for the ears and beak. He made the owl look alive by putting tiny, dark, round shells in the center of the "eyes." He glued overlapping shells for the back and wings, and he glued two small shells to the stem for feet. Finally, he placed the owl in a puddle of glue on a branch, but it kept falling over. What detail in the directions did Willy ignore that caused the owl to fall over? (After he made a puddle of glue, he forgot to hold the owl in place until the glue took hold.)

 Use *Reading Skills Workbook,* Lesson 14, pages 45–47.

★ For additional resources and curriculum-related activities, see *Enrichment,* page T166.

Textbook Study:
Understanding Topical Organization

Pages 198–203

Objective

SKILLS CODE NUMBER

I*,T   To identify topical organization   *5.10.1*

Applying
the Skill

1. Before students read the textbook selections, you may wish to list the vocabulary words on the board and discuss them or have students look them up in the glossary.

Social Studies Selection

metropolitan: of or related to a large, important city area

abundance: more than enough; an overflowing quantity

irrigation: supplying land with water by artificial means

Science Selection

igneous rocks: rocks formed by the activity of a volcano

TEXTBOOK STUDY

Understanding Topical Organization

Textbooks usually organize information by topics. As you read the following selections from textbooks, look for ways in which the author organizes the information. Sometimes headings may help you to see the organization more clearly. The sidenotes will also help you. Refer to them as you read.

Understanding Topical Organization in Social Studies

Look at the headings. Into how many parts is this selection divided?

In the Northeast

Much of the land in the Northeast is taken up by cities and metropolitan areas. In its northern and western parts are much forest and woodland. These regions are used for lumbering and recreation. The rest of the section has mixed pasture and farmland. Farmers here grow fruits and vegetables and keep dairy cattle.

In the South

Notice that this paragraph talks about the land and products of the South. What is the topic of the paragraph on the Northeast? What is the topic of the paragraph on Alaska and Hawaii?

More people live in this part of the United States than in any other region. The mixture of land here is much like that of the Northeast. There is some little-used mountain and woodland here. The rest is mixed farmland and pasture, but this section produces a

198

---

2. Have students read the introduction and the two selections. You may wish to have them read the selections on their own and then do *Building Skills.* Or you may wish to direct students, using the following procedure.

Understanding Topical Organization in Social Studies

1. Have students answer the question in the first sidenote. (five parts) Ask students what the five parts are about. (areas of the United States)

2. Have students read the entire selection and then answer the questions in the second sidenote. (Northeast: land and products of the Northeast; Alaska and Hawaii: land and products of Alaska and Hawaii)

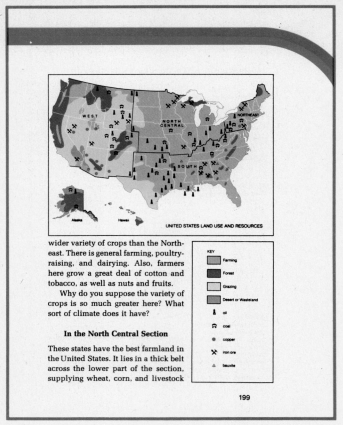

UNITED STATES LAND USE AND RESOURCES

wider variety of crops than the Northeast. There is general farming, poultry-raising, and dairying. Also, farmers here grow a great deal of cotton and tobacco, as well as nuts and fruits.

Why do you suppose the variety of crops is so much greater here? What sort of climate does it have?

In the North Central Section

These states have the best farmland in the United States. It lies in a thick belt across the lower part of the section, supplying wheat, corn, and livestock

KEY

▨ Farming

■ Forest

▨ Grazing

▨ Desert or Wasteland

⬥ oil

⌂ coal

● copper

✕ iron ore

△ bauxite

199

in abundance. Just above this is an area of rich dairyland and general farming. The northernmost part is unfarmed forest.

In the West

Along the Pacific Coast there is much rainfall in the north, and less in the south. But in the valleys, especially the Valley of California and the Willamette River Valley, there is excellent soil. Every kind of farming is found here, even cotton growing. Otherwise, in this region, crops are grown in very tight areas where water is available for irrigation. But cattle are raised everywhere.

In Alaska and Hawaii

Alaska has mostly forest land and frozen plain, but some cattle are raised in the south. The long summer, too, allows some vegetables to be grown. Hawaii has lots of mountains and forest, but some grasslands, where cattle are raised. Along the coasts are strips of farmland as good as that in any other part of the United States. Sugar cane and fruits grow in Hawaii.

—The United States
Houghton Mifflin

200

3. Point out to students that each heading was not complete in identifying the topic of each paragraph. Ask what words must be added to each heading to indicate each topic accurately. (land and products)

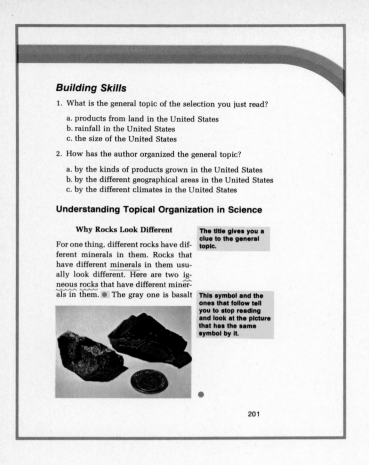

Building Skills

1. What is the general topic of the selection you just read?

   a. products from land in the United States
   b. rainfall in the United States
   c. the size of the United States

2. How has the author organized the general topic?

   a. by the kinds of products grown in the United States
   b. by the different geographical areas in the United States
   c. by the different climates in the United States

Understanding Topical Organization in Science

Why Rocks Look Different

For one thing, different rocks have different minerals in them. Rocks that have different <u>minerals</u> in them usually look different. Here are two igneous rocks that have different minerals in them. ● The gray one is basalt

> The title gives you a clue to the general topic.

> This symbol and the ones that follow tell you to stop reading and look at the picture that has the same symbol by it.

201

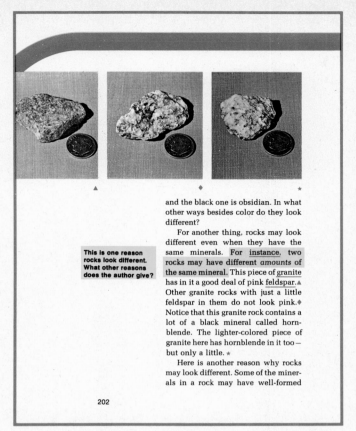

and the black one is obsidian. In what other ways besides color do they look different?

For another thing, rocks may look different even when they have the same minerals. For instance, two rocks may have different *amounts* of the same mineral. This piece of <u>granite</u> has in it a good deal of pink <u>feldspar</u>.▲ Other granite rocks with just a little feldspar in them do not look pink.◆ Notice that this granite rock contains a lot of a black mineral called hornblende. The lighter-colored piece of granite here has hornblende in it too— but only a little. ★

Here is another reason why rocks may look different. Some of the minerals in a rock may have well-formed

> This is one reason rocks look different. What other reasons does the author give?

202

---

4. Have students complete *Building Skills*.

Answers to *Building Skills*
Social Studies Selection

1. a; **2.** b

Understanding Topical Organization in Science

1. Have a student read aloud the title and the first sidenote. Point out that there are no headings *within* the selection. Remind students that they should try to determine the topic of each paragraph. This will help them understand how the selection is organized.

2. Have students read the first paragraph and the second sidenote. Ask them what other symbols appear in the selection. (a triangle, a diamond, a star, and a diamond within a diamond)

3. Have students read the rest of the selection and answer the question in the sidenote on page 202. (Rocks that have different minerals in them look different. Rocks that have crystal faces look different.)

crystal faces. For example, this is the mineral <u>quartz</u>. ◈ A crystal of quartz has eight sides. Each of these sides is a crystal face. <u>Observe</u> the crystal faces.

—Concepts in Science: Purple
Harcourt Brace Jovanovich

◈

Building Skills

1. What is the general topic of the selection you just read?

   a. igneous rocks
   b. why rocks look different
   c. minerals in rocks

2. Below are two lists of topics. Which one shows how the author organized this selection?

1	2
Rocks that have different minerals in them	Basalt and obsidian
Rocks that have different amounts of the same minerals in them	Three kinds of granite
Rocks that have crystal faces	Quartz

203

4. Have students complete *Building Skills*.

Answers to *Building Skills*
Science Selection

1. b; **2.** List 1; list 2 contains examples that illustrate the main idea of each topic.

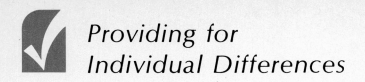

Providing for Individual Differences

Skills Lesson

Additional Practice

Worksheet 6, Teacher's Edition, page T485

Vocabulary Study

Additional Practice

■ **Using etymologies to determine meaning**   Write the following Latin and Greek words and their English meanings on the board. Then write the three columns of English words on the board or read the words aloud. Have students list each English word under the Latin or Greek word from which it is derived. If you wish, have students define each English word and check their answers in a dictionary.

> *memoria* = Latin, "memory"
> *mechanikos* = Greek, "machine"
> *generare* = Latin, "produce"

remember	memorial	mechanize
mechanical	regenerate	memorize
generation	memorable	mechanic
degenerate	mechanism	generator

(*memoria*	*mechanikos*	*generare*
remember	mechanical	generation
memorial	mechanism	degenerate
memorable	mechanize	regenerate
memorize	mechanic	generator)

Reading Selection: Shell Treasures

Additional Practice

■ **Scanning to identify topics**   Have students scan the selection beginning on page 39 and identify the general topic. (living lights) Then write the following list of topics on the board. Have students identify the topics that are found in the selection. Finally, have them put the list in the order in which the topics appear in the selection.

1. living lights in the sea
2. molds and bacteria
3. fireflies
4. sponges
5. glowworms
6. living lights in outer space

(Correct order: 3, 5, 1. Topics 2, 4, and 6 do not appear in the selection.)

Challenge Activity

■ **Identifying topical organization**   Direct students to the selection "The Ship of the Desert" on pages 84–89. Write the following list of topics on the board and ask students which of the topics are covered in the section under the heading "Kinds of Camels." Have students list the topics that are covered in the order in which they appear in the selection.

1. ancient camel
2. Bactrian camel
3. dromedary camel
4. Arabian camel
5. North American camel

(Correct order: 4, 2, 3. Topics 1 and 5 are in another part of the selection.)

Write the following list on the board. Ask students which topics are covered in the section under the heading "Desert Life." Have students list the topics that are covered in the order in which they appear in the selection.

1. long legs
2. body temperature
3. droopy eyelids
4. color
5. hump
6. skin and hair

(Correct order: 1, 5, 2, 3. Topics 4 and 6 do not appear in the selection.)

Evaluation

Periodic Test 2, Part II, Form A or *Form B,* may be administered after this unit to test skills marked **T.** If you have pretested using *Form A,* administer *Form B.*

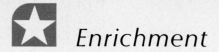 *Enrichment*

Shell Treasures

Bibliography

The following books are about crafts and hobbies.

Average

Graham, Ada. *Foxtails, Ferns, and Fish Scales: A Handbook of Art and Nature Projects.* Driftwood mobiles, woven-grass wall hangings, "weed prints," and other projects using materials from nature.

Kohn, Bernice. *Beachcombers' Book.* A "how-to" book, with projects using materials found at the beach, such as shells, flowers, and driftwood.

Pratson, Frederick J. *The Special World of the Artisan.* A potter, a woodcarver, a glassblower, an instrument maker, and a weaver explain their work and tell of their feelings about their crafts.

Films and Filmstrips

NOTE: For more information, see *Resource Center.*

Selection content

BFA. *Learning to Look.* Beauty in natural objects.

Curriculum Coordination

Language Arts

1. If any students have hobbies such as weaving, model making, or coin collecting, they might explain their hobbies to the class and show samples of their work or collection.

2. If your community has crafts fairs, suggest that students visit them. They might interview artists to find out what the crafts are called, what materials are used, etc., and then write a report of their interviews.

3. Have students use the library to find guidebooks about shells, like those mentioned in the selection. You may also wish to have students find other nature guidebooks on such topics as flowers, trees, insects, and plants.

4. Students may wish to find or write poems about sea shells and share them with the class.

Science

Study of the selection might be coordinated with a science project in which students collect, identify, and classify mollusks.

Social Studies

Interested students might wish to do research on how shells were used in ancient times and how they are used in different parts of the world today.

Art

Students might make objects from sea shells, macaroni shells, pebbles, etc., and display their handicrafts in class.

Career Education

1. Students might explore careers in various handicrafts, such as making and selling objects made from driftwood, shells, and other natural materials. Specific things to investigate include availability of materials, possible items that can be made, market identification, and where the items would be sold.

2. You might wish to invite a marine biologist to discuss his or her training and work.

Contents

Additional Materials

Reading Skills Workbook: Lessons 15–16, pages 48–54
Duplicating Masters 11: pages 23–24
Worksheet 7: Teacher's Edition, page T486
Bookmark Reading Filmstrips: "Outlines That Work"
Periodic Test 2, Part III

Key to Symbols

Skills Objectives
I* — Introduced in this unit
I — Introduced earlier in this level
M — Maintained from previous levels
T — Tested in periodic and cumulative tests for this level

Reduced Student Pages
underscore — words that appear in the glossary
wavy line — words pretaught in the Teacher's Edition
(these words also appear in the glossary)

Skills Lesson:
Using Outlines to Help You Read
Pages 204–212

Objectives

		SKILLS CODE NUMBER
I*, T	To write a topical outline	7.1.5.1
I*, T	To write a title for a topical outline	7.1.5.1.1

If you wish to pretest the skills listed above, you may administer *Periodic Test 2, Part III, Form A. Periodic Test 2, Part III, Form B,* may be administered to post-test.

Introducing the Lesson

1. Show students a variety of items typically found in a teacher's desk. The items might include thumbtacks, paper clips, erasers, pencils, paper, rubber bands, and books.

2. Ask students to suggest ways to group the items so that they could be located easily in a desk. Suggest, if necessary, that one way to group them might be according to the way each item is used or what each item does. Write the name of each item on the board in the group suggested by the students. The lists might resemble the three below.

Things Used in Writing	Things Used to Hold Other Things Together	Books
pencils	thumbtacks	textbooks
paper	rubber bands	roll book
erasers	paper clips	dictionary

Using Outlines to Help You Read

Suppose you are going camping. There are many things you'll need to take along on your trip. When it comes time for you to start packing, how will you remember all the things you wanted to take? One way is to list them. Your list might look like the one on page 205.

204

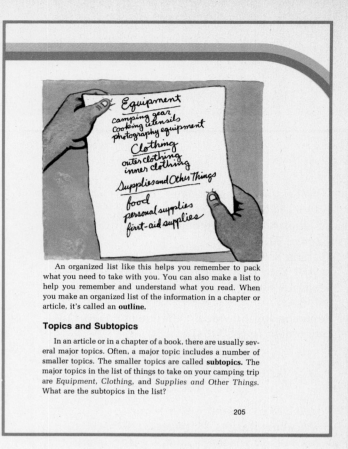

An organized list like this helps you remember to pack what you need to take with you. You can also make a list to help you remember and understand what you read. When you make an organized list of the information in a chapter or article, it's called an **outline**.

Topics and Subtopics

In an article or in a chapter of a book, there are usually several major topics. Often, a major topic includes a number of smaller topics. The smaller topics are called **subtopics**. The major topics in the list of things to take on your camping trip are *Equipment, Clothing,* and *Supplies and Other Things.* What are the subtopics in the list?

205

---

3. Discuss the fact that authors often organize the topics in a selection just as students organized the items in a teacher's desk. An organized list of topics from a selection is called an *outline*. It is a description of the organization of the author's ideas—what they are and how they go together. Explain that good readers often outline what they read. Outlining helps them see how ideas are related, and it helps them remember information.

4. If necessary, review the meaning of the terms *topic* and *subtopic*. Have students identify the general topic (things in a teacher's desk) and the subtopics (headings in step 2) of the lists they made.

Developing the Skill

Points to Discuss

An organized list of information in a chapter or article is called an outline.

Have students look at the picture on page 204 and read the lesson up to the heading on page 205. Ask students what else they make lists of. (Sample answers: things to buy; homework assignments; people to invite to a party; etc.) Ask them the major reason they make lists. (to remember something) Explain that outlining what they have read serves the same purpose.

Topics and Subtopics

A major topic often includes several smaller topics called subtopics.

1. Have students read the last paragraph on page 205. Ask what the subtopics of the major topic *Equipment* are. (camping gear, cooking utensils, photography equipment) Ask what details might be added to the subtopic *photography equipment.* (film, camera, flash bulbs)

2. Ask how many subtopics are covered under the major topic *Clothing* (two) and under the major topic *Supplies and Other Things.* (three) Ask what *details* might be on a list of first-aid supplies. (bandages, antiseptics, etc.)

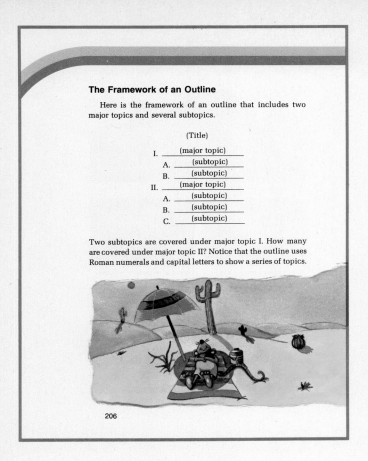

The Framework of an Outline

Here is the framework of an outline that includes two major topics and several subtopics.

(Title)

I. _____ (major topic)
  A. _____ (subtopic)
  B. _____ (subtopic)
II. _____ (major topic)
  A. _____ (subtopic)
  B. _____ (subtopic)
  C. _____ (subtopic)

Two subtopics are covered under major topic I. How many are covered under major topic II? Notice that the outline uses Roman numerals and capital letters to show a series of topics.

206

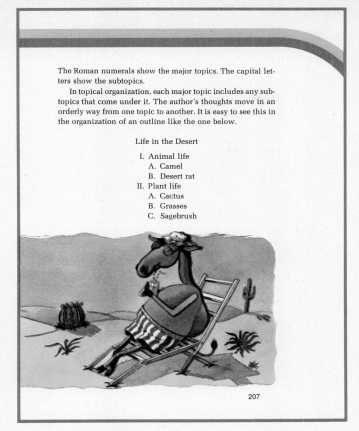

The Roman numerals show the major topics. The capital letters show the subtopics.

In topical organization, each major topic includes any subtopics that come under it. The author's thoughts move in an orderly way from one topic to another. It is easy to see this in the organization of an outline like the one below.

Life in the Desert

I. Animal life
  A. Camel
  B. Desert rat
II. Plant life
  A. Cactus
  B. Grasses
  C. Sagebrush

207

The Framework of an Outline

A. *An outline uses Roman numerals and capital letters to show a series of ideas.*

1. Have students read the first paragraph on page 206 and study the framework. Point out that in this framework the title is centered over the body of the outline, the Roman numerals are at the left, and the letters are indented. Explain that this way of numbering, lettering, and spacing is the standard way to make an outline.

2. Have students read the paragraph under the framework and answer the question. (three subtopics under major topic II)

B. *Each major topic in an outline may include two or more subtopics.*

Have students read the paragraph on page 207 and study the outline of "Life in the Desert." Point out that there are two subtopics under *Animal Life* and three subtopics under *Plant Life*. Explain that there can be two or more subtopics under a major topic.

C. *Sometimes a major topic may have no subtopic.*

Stress the point that in an outline there is never a I without a II or an A without a B. Ask students to imagine that the article on desert life discusses only one form of plant life—grasses. Have a student show how such an article should be outlined by writing the outline on the board.

Answer:
Life in the Desert
  I. Animal life
    A. Camel
    B. Desert rat
  II. Grasses

Making an Outline

You can make an outline to help you understand and remember.

Making an Outline

Read the following article. Think about how you would make an outline from it.

● Some Places of Historical Interest in America

New York City has many places of historical interest. In the Wall Street area of lower Manhattan, you'll find narrow cobblestone streets. These streets were first used over three hundred years ago. Wall Street itself was almost as busy—and as well known—during colonial days as it is today.

Brooklyn Heights and the Battery are two places in New York City that were important during the Revolutionary War. You can still see why if you visit them. Each gives a wonderful view of the harbor, Staten Island, and New Jersey.

Not more than a few hours' drive from Manhattan is Valley Forge, Pennsylvania. Millions of people have visited here over the years to see the place where Washington's troops spent their unforgettable, terrible winter.

Missouri, too, has some places of historical interest. In St. Joseph you can see the stables that housed the Pony Express horses. Hannibal, Missouri, is remembered as the place where Mark Twain's fictional characters, Tom Sawyer, Becky Thatcher, and Huckleberry Finn, grew up.

What are the major topics covered in the article? Three places are mentioned. Here is what your outline of only the major topics will look like:

● I. New York City
   II. Pennsylvania
   III. Missouri

208

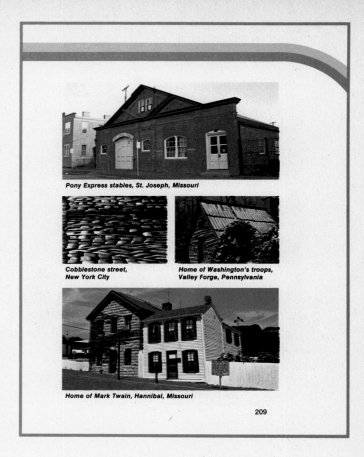

Pony Express stables, St. Joseph, Missouri

Cobblestone street, New York City

Home of Washington's troops, Valley Forge, Pennsylvania

Home of Mark Twain, Hannibal, Missouri

209

Have students read the article "Some Places of Historical Interest in America" on page 208. Then help them make an outline of the article (see the model in the next column), using the following procedure.

1. Have students identify the three major topics. (New York City; Pennsylvania; Missouri) Write the three major topics and the Roman numerals on the board, leaving space between them.

2. Have students tell what subtopics are covered under the topic *New York City*. (Wall Street area; Brooklyn Heights and the Battery) Point out that the article treats Brooklyn Heights and the Battery together, so they should be treated as one subtopic. Add these places to the outline on the board and have volunteers show where A and B should be inserted.

3. Point out that only one place in Pennsylvania—Valley Forge—is described in the article. Erase *Pennsylvania* from your outline on the board and substitute *Valley Forge, Pennsylvania,* for major topic II. Again, stress the point that an outline never has a Roman numeral I without a Roman numeral II or an A without a B.

4. Have volunteers list the two places in Missouri on the outline.

Model outline:

   Some Places of Historical Interest
                in America

   I. New York City
      A. Wall Street area
      B. Brooklyn Heights and the Battery
   II. Valley Forge, Pennsylvania
   III. Missouri
      A. St. Joseph
      B. Hannibal

5. Now have students read the discussion that follows the article.

What subtopics were covered in the paragraphs about New York City? You can list them in this way:

- I. New York City
     A. The Wall Street area
     B. Brooklyn Heights and the Battery

How many places in Pennsylvania are mentioned in the article? Only one—Valley Forge—is talked about. So *Valley Forge* is a separate major topic.

- II. Valley Forge, Pennsylvania

How many places in Missouri are mentioned? Can you see why the next stage of your outline will look like this?

- III. Missouri
     A. St. Joseph
     B. Hannibal

Now you can put the pieces of the outline together. Remember to write the title—*Some Places of Historical Interest in America*—above the whole outline.

How do you choose a title for your outline? The title should state the *general topic* of the chapter or article that you are outlining. Sometimes the title of the chapter or article may be the same as the title of your outline. Other times you may have to make up a title for your outline.

Try This

Read the article on pages 211 and 212. Then outline it. Your outline should show two major topics. One of the major topics has three subtopics. The other has four subtopics. Remember to give a title to your outline.

210

Sculpting is the art of shaping or arranging things in space. There are a number of different methods of sculpting. One of them, *carving*, is cutting away pieces of something from a large piece. Wood, stone, marble, ivory, and bone can be carved into beautiful shapes. If you want to try carving, a large bar of soap would be a good material to try first.

Wood   Ivory

Snow   Stone

211

Try This

Have students complete *Try This*.

Answers to *Try This*

Sample answer:
    Sculpting
 I. Methods of sculpting
     A. Carving
     B. Modeling
     C. Constructing
 II. Visual qualities
     A. Mass
     B. Plane
     C. Color
     D. Texture

 Use *Reading Skills Workbook,* Lesson 15, pages 48–53. See *Providing for Individual Differences,* page T182, for additional practice.

Modeling means making a model from something soft. Clay, wax, and some kinds of soft plastic can be modeled. To model something, artists use their hands and fingers and perhaps some simple tools. Often the clay or wax shape that an artist makes is not finished art. A plaster mold may be made around the shape. Then hot metal is poured by the artist into the mold. After that, the metal is left to cool in the shape of the mold. The cooled, hard metal shape is called a "casting."

Constructing is a third kind of sculpting. This means putting things together. A piece of metal may be attached to other pieces of metal to make a design. Glass, wood, wire, and other things can also be used in constructing.

Artists sometimes talk about a sculpture's "visual qualities": mass, plane, color, and texture. *Mass* means how light or heavy a piece appears to be. Some light pieces *look* heavy. Some heavy pieces *look* light. Mass is not the same thing as real weight.

Plane has to do with curved surfaces and flat surfaces on a piece. Think of a sculpted figure of a person with a body that looks like a box (flat planes). Now think of a snowman (all curves). Think of a real person (a mixture of curves and flat surfaces).

Color is important in creating a mood. Think of a sculpture of a horse painted purple. Now think of a horse sculpted in white marble. How does color affect the "moods" of the two sculptures?

Texture means how rough or smooth something is. Think of a tiger carved in hard, smooth stone. You may get feelings of the tiger's beauty and speed. Now think of a tiger constructed from rusty old car parts. You may get feelings of the tiger's strength and fierceness.

212

Vocabulary Study:
Getting Meaning from Context Clues

Page 213

Objective

		SKILLS CODE NUMBER
M	To identify and use context clues to determine word meaning	3.0.2

Developing the Skill

1. Tell students that the *Vocabulary Study* they are about to read is about Professor Crum's diary. Have a student tell what a diary is. If necessary, point out that "Dolphin Days," pages 56–65, is written in diary form. Explain that Professor Crum always uses context clues in his diary.

2. Have students read the *Vocabulary Study* and do the *Word Play* activities.

Answers to *Word Play*

1. *customers:* people who come to buy; *section:* part (of the store); *arguments:* fights. Sentences will vary.
2. Sentences will vary.

✔ Use *Reading Skills Workbook,* Lesson 16, page 54. See *Providing for Individual Differences,* page T182, for additional practice.

VOCABULARY STUDY

Getting Meaning from Context Clues

The evil Professor Crum sat in the glow of a flickering candle and wrote in his diary.

Dear Diary,
There hasn't been much to do between evil deeds, so I've taken a part-time job. I work in a health food store. It's a popular place. We get a lot of **customers**. Most of the people who come to buy are good and kind, so you can imagine why I feel uncomfortable.
I'm in charge of the juice **section**. It's the busiest part of the store. All day long I have to squeeze avocados and mangos to make fruit drinks. I try hard to start **arguments** with the people by squirting them. But instead of fights, all I get is smiles. I didn't realize there were so many nice people in the world. I may have to raise my rates on evil deeds, or I'll never make a living.

Word Play

1. Find the words or phrases in the diary that tell you what the boldfaced words mean. These words or phrases are context clues. Make up a sentence using each of the boldfaced words.
2. Look up *avocado* in the glossary. Then write a sentence using the word with context clues to show its meaning.

213

Reading Selection:
Start Your Own Theater

Pages 214–219

Objectives

			SKILLS CODE NUMBER
I*, T		To write a topical outline	7.1.5.1
I*, T		To write a title for a topical outline	7.1.5.1.1
M		To identify definitions in context	3.0
M		To identify word parts: root words and suffixes	4.1
M		To use a dictionary to find meanings of multiple-meaning words	5.6.4

 **Preparing to Read**

Summary

The selection provides suggestions and guidelines for starting a neighborhood theater. It explains technical vocabulary used in the theater and identifies the personnel, equipment, and facilities needed, and the steps to follow in getting a production ready.

Background

Theatre was the usual spelling of the word until Noah Webster compiled his American-language dictionary in the early 1800's and "standardized" the spelling with an *er* ending. His spelling was not recognized by all Americans as preferable; either spelling is correct for any sense of the word as long as it is used consistently within a piece.

Most historians trace the origin of modern theater to Greece during the fifth century B.C. Thespis, a Greek actor, won the first contest for tragic acting in 534 B.C. His name survives today in the word *thespian,* which is a synonym for *actor.*

The following books will provide you with additional background information.

Baird, John F. *Make-Up: A Manual for the Use of Actors, Amateurs and Professionals.* The history of stage make-up, including techniques of applying make-up and the use of wigs and beards.

Cornberg, Sol, and Emanuel L. Gebauer. *A Stage Crew Handbook.* Technical aspects of theater production.

Peters, Joan. *Making Costumes for School Plays.* Patterns, styling, cutting, sewing, jewelry—all aspects of costuming. Includes many illustrations.

Developing Vocabulary and Concepts

théater: the building in which plays are performed
set: the scenery in a play
technical: having to do with mechanical skills
technician: a person skilled in the use of electrical equipment or machinery
donation: contribution; gift
apprentice: a person who learns a skill by working for another person who has mastered that skill

1. **a.** Read aloud the following sentences or write them on the board. If you read them aloud, write the underlined vocabulary on the board.

   The <u>set</u> for the play's first act was a forest; the scenery for the second was a gingerbread house.
   During the play, I took care of the <u>technical</u> work, such as the lighting and sound machines.
   We needed two <u>technicians</u> for our play—one to take care of the sound machines and one to work the lights.
   We received <u>donations</u> from neighbors. Some gave us old clothes to use as costumes.
   The <u>apprentice</u> was learning from the more experienced technicians.

   b. Ask students to give the meaning of each vocabulary word. Remind them to use the context clues in the sentences to help them.

2. **a.** Introduce the topic of the theater by asking students about plays they have seen in a theater, on television, or at school. Write *theater* on the board, and discuss the things students know about theaters, such as the stage, make-up, and costumes.

   b. If you wish, read aloud the first paragraph of *Background* in the first column on this page.

   c. Ask students if they've ever acted in a play or helped to put on a play. Allow them to describe the experiences they had. Explain that the selection they are about to read will tell them what they would have to do to start a theater of their own.

 Use *Duplicating Masters 11,* page 23.

As you read, think about how you would outline this selection. Notice that it tells you about three groups of theater workers: people who give directions to others; people in charge of things used in a play; people who perform.

It's fun to be in an audience watching a play. Think what it would be like to . . .

START YOUR OWN THEATER

by Karleen Schart Sabol

One of my friends is twelve years old. She and her friends started a theater in her barn. You can start your own theater, too. You don't need a barn, of course, but you do need a play.

Go to the library and get several books of plays. Pick out one that you like. If the book says anything about *royalties*, you may have to pay to put the play on. The royalty is the money that you pay to the author, or playwright, for the right to use his or her play. There are lots of plays, however, for which you don't need to pay royalties. These are said to be "in public domain." You can ask your librarian to help you find one of these. (Or better still, you can write your own play.) When you do decide on the play you want, make enough copies of it so that everyone working on the play can have one. These copies are called *scripts*.

Your play will need a *producer*. This person organizes the whole thing. He or she makes sure you have a place where you can present your play. This can be almost anywhere. My friend's barn is great, but you can also use a garage, a cellar, or a room that nobody uses much. Even a lawn or sidewalk will do. Just make sure you have enough space for the actors to move around (the stage). You'll also need a place where the actors can get ready or wait when they aren't acting. And, of course, you'll need room for the audience to sit.

The producer also chooses some of the other people who work to put on the play. And if you need any money to put on your play, he or she thinks of ways to earn it. In other words, the producer is the boss. So make sure you get someone who will stick with the job.

A *director* is needed to stage your play. At rehearsals, he or she tells the actors when and where and how to sit, stand, and move while they're on the stage. This is called giving them their *blocking*. The director also helps the actors figure out the best ways to say their lines so the parts they're playing will seem real.

You need a *stage manager* to help the director. The stage manager keeps what is called a master script. In it, he or she writes all the instructions given by the director. This means that every actor's blocking is marked. Every *entrance cue* (when an actor

215

comes onstage) and *exit cue* (when an actor goes offstage) is marked. All the technical cues (when the lights go on or off, when it's time for a sound effect, and so on) are marked. Then, if any questions come up during a rehearsal, the stage manager has the answers ready in the master script. During the actual performances, the stage manager runs the show.

A *set designer* is also needed. This person first reads the play. Then he or she decides what the set should look like. Whatever your play is about, the set should show where the action is taking place. This can be done very simply. But it is a good idea to check the library for books about how to build sets.

What about the wardrobe for your play? Someone is needed to be in charge of the wardrobe. This person gets together all the clothes, or costumes, to be worn in your play. Sometimes, if you put on a modern play, you can wear your own clothes. But even if you do, you'll need someone to make sure they are just right for the play. If your play calls for old-fashioned clothing, the wardrobe

216

Setting Purposes

Skills

Have students read the skills note at the top of page 214. Ask them to watch for examples of the three groups of theater workers as they read the selection.

Content

Have students read the lead-in to the title. Ask students to describe some things they might need and what they would have to do to start their own theater.

 **Reading and Discussing**

Have students read the selection. Most will be able to read it in one sitting. If you wish, the selection may be read in two parts, breaking before the paragraph beginning "A *set designer* . . ." on page 216.

NOTE: The questions that appear in the student's text at the end of the selection focus on comprehension of selection content and on application of the *Skills Lesson* to the selection. Answers to these questions begin on page T177.

person finds out what kind of clothes to make, buy, rent, or borrow. There are books in the library that show what kinds of clothes people have worn in different times and places. If the costumes get ripped and need to be sewn, the wardrobe person is the one to repair them. If they get dirty, the wardrobe person has to clean them. He or she must make sure that all costumes are ready before the play goes on.

Technicians are needed to get lights and sound effects for your play. The lighting can be very simple. The most important thing is having enough light so the audience can see what's happening onstage.

The sound can be handled in a number of ways. You can check your library for records of sounds (train whistles, thunder, screams). Or you can use a tape recorder to record your own sounds. If you have enough people in your theater group, you can let someone stand offstage, banging pans or doing bird calls or making any other sounds that might be needed.

The stage manager tells the lighting and sound technicians

217

when any effects are needed. But it's up to the technicians to figure out the best ways to get these effects. (A warning: Don't touch any electrical wiring if you aren't sure what you're doing. Find a grown-up who knows about electricity to help you.)

A _property_ (or _prop_) person also is important for your play. A sofa on the stage is a prop. So is a telephone, a picture on the wall, a handkerchief, or anything else used in the play. The prop person decides (with the director's help) what is needed. Then he or she makes, borrows, or buys all the props. The person in charge of

getting props works closely with the set designer. Together they make sure that large pieces of furniture match the set. The prop person must also check before each performance to make sure all props are where they belong on the stage.

Now that you know about the producer, director, stage manager, and others, can you guess who is still missing? It is the people to act in your play! You should hold tryouts. At a tryout, everyone who wants to be in your play reads some of the lines of the part he or she wants to play. Then the director and producer, and sometimes

218

Questions preceded by a bullet are additional questions and appear in the Teacher's Edition only. The other questions appear in the student's text after the selection.

Understanding What You've Read

1. *What is a royalty?* (money paid to an author, or playwright, for the use of his or her play   page 215) LITERAL   Recalling specific details

● *What is a script?* (a copy of a play   page 215) LITERAL   Recalling specific details

2. *What are some of the jobs of the producer?* (Sample answers: organizing the play's production; finding a place to present the play; choosing other people to help put on the play; and thinking of ways to earn money to put on the play   page 215) LITERAL Recalling stated information

● *Which worker would help an actor who forgot when to enter or leave the stage?* (the stage manager page 215) INFERENTIAL   Drawing conclusions

● *What might happen if the stage manager didn't record the entrance and exit cues and blocking on the master script?* (Actors might enter or exit at the wrong time or stand in the wrong places. Accept other reasonable answers.) INFERENTIAL   Drawing conclusions

3. *What are two things the author suggests you can do if you want to learn more about the theater?* (The author suggests starting your own theater or becoming an apprentice at a professional or community theater.   pages 215 and 219) LITERAL   Recalling stated information

● *Why does the author say you might need three weeks to a month for rehearsals?* (Students should conclude from the number of jobs described that it would take that long to have the whole production fit together smoothly.) INFERENTIAL   Drawing conclusions

● *Which job described would you most enjoy? Explain your answer.* (Accept all reasonable answers.) CRITICAL Making judgments

Applying the Skills Lesson

Make an outline of the selection you have just read. Your outline should show three major topics. (Hint: See the skills note at the top of page 214.) The subtopics are the different jobs mentioned in the selection. Remember to give your outline a title that states the general topic of the selection. (Answers may vary and should be discussed. Sample answer:)

    People Who Work in a Theater
I. People who give directions to others
  A. Producer
  B. Director
  C. Stage manager
II. People in charge of things used in a play
  A. Set designer
  B. Wardrobe person
  C. Lighting technicians
  D. Sound technicians
  E. Property person
III. People who perform in a play—actors
Writing a topical outline

● *Arrange this list of topics and subtopics in an outline. Use Roman numerals and capital letters to indicate the topics and subtopics. Then decide on a title for your outline. (Copy this list onto the board.)*
    Major Topics
Where to get plays
Things to look for in plays
    Subtopics
Number of characters
Kinds of props
Books
Kinds of sets
Special costumes
Magazines
Write your own play

Sample answer:

    Deciding on a Play

I. Where to get plays
  A. Books
  B. Magazines
  C. Write your own play
II. Things to look for in plays
  A. Number of characters
  B. Kinds of props
  C. Kinds of sets
  D. Special costumes   <u>Writing a topical outline</u>

 Use *Duplicating Masters 11,* page 24. See *Providing for Individual Differences,* page T182, for additional practice.

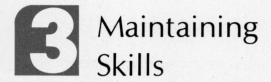

3 Maintaining Skills

Comprehension Skills

Identifying definitions in context   Remind students that authors often give *definitions in context* for new words or words that have special meanings. Have students find the four words or terms in the second paragraph in the selection that are defined in context. (*royalty:* the money that you pay the author for the use of his or her play: *playwright:* the author; *in public domain:* for which you don't need to pay royalties; *scripts:* copies of a play)

Now have students scan the selection for the following words, which are defined in context. Have them write a definition for each word. (Remind students that words defined in context are often italicized.)

    blocking (when, where, and how the actors sit, stand, and move on the stage; page 215, fifth paragraph)

    entrance cue (when an actor comes onstage; page 215, last line)

    exit cue (when an actor goes offstage; page 216, line 1)

    technical cues (when the lighting should change; when it's time for a sound effect; when the curtain should be opened or closed; page 216, line 3)

    property *or* prop (a sofa, telephone, picture, handkerchief, or anything else used in the play; page 218, first paragraph)

Language Skills

Identifying word parts: root words and suffixes   Review with students the fact that with the addition of *-er* or *-or,* some words can be changed in form to mean "someone or something that performs an action." Have students scan the selection for words ending in *-er* or *-or* that follow this principle. Also ask students to identify the root of each word they find. *(producer— produce; actor—act; director—direct; manager—manage; designer—design; recorder—record)*

Study Skills

Using a dictionary   Write the following groups of sentences on the board, or read them aloud and write the underlined words on the board. Have students use a dictionary to find the correct meaning of each underlined word to fit the context of each sentence.

    I <u>set</u> the book on the shelf. (placed)
    We used a huge painting of the Eiffel Tower in the <u>set</u>. (scenery)
    Because we held our play outdoors without lights, we had to put it on before the sun <u>set</u>. (went below the horizon)

    Shirley opened the <u>wardrobe</u> door. (a cabinet or closet)
    The <u>wardrobe</u> for the play needs to be sewed and ironed. (a collection of costumes)

    The playwright received a <u>royalty</u> of $10,000. (money paid to an author for the use of his or her work)
    Our beautiful costumes made us look just like <u>royalty</u>. (royal people: kings, queens, etc.)

    <u>Prop</u> the couch up with a few books so it won't fall over. (use a solid object to support or hold something up)
    We used a couch as a <u>prop</u> for our play. (an item used on stage during a performance)

For additional resources and curriculum-related activities, see *Enrichment,* page T183.

Textbook Study:
Outlining Information
Pages 220-223

Objective

		SKILLS CODE NUMBER
I*, T	To write a topical outline	7.1.5.1

Applying the Skill

1. You may wish to list the following vocabulary words on the board and discuss them or have students look them up in the glossary.

   Science Selection
   minerals: natural substances, neither vegetable nor animal, that are important for nutrition in living things
   cell: the basic unit of any living thing

2. Have students read the introduction and the two selections. You may wish to have them read the selections on their own and then do *Building Skills*. Or you may wish to direct students, using the following procedure.

TEXTBOOK STUDY

Outlining Information

Sometimes you will find it easier to remember what you read if you make an outline of it. Think about what the general topic is. The general topic includes all the subtopics. When there are headings, use them to help you find the general topic and subtopics.

The sidenotes point out things to consider when outlining information. Refer to them as you read the selections. Try to answer the questions in them.

Outlining Information from Science

What is the general topic of this selection?

Mosses

Have you ever noticed tiny green plants growing in the shade near buildings or on trees? If so, you may have been looking at small plants called *mosses*.

If you were previewing this selection, would you expect to find information under this heading about where mosses grow?

What are mosses like? If you ever pulled mosses from the ground, you know they have roots that are not like those of other plants. Little hairs at the base of the stem hold the plant upright. These hairs take in water and minerals.

Mosses do not have stems or leaves that are like those of other plants, either. The tubes found in the roots, stems, and leaves of bigger green

220

Outlining Information from Science

1. Have students scan the headings and answer the question in the first sidenote. (mosses) Then have them read the first paragraph of the selection.

2. Before they read the second paragraph, have students try to answer the question in the second sidenote. (No, you would expect to find out what mosses are like under this heading.) Ask students to identify the heading under which they'd expect to find information about where mosses grow. (under the heading "Where are mosses found?")

plants are missing in mosses. These tubes carry water, minerals, and food through the bigger plants. In mosses, these things pass from cell to cell.

Where are mosses found? You could look for mosses in almost any cool, wet, shady place. They can be found in the woods. They can be found on the banks of streams and ponds. Even if a stream or pond dries up, mosses can live through long, dry spells. They start growing again when water returns.

On your outline, you might turn this heading into a statement: Where mosses are found. How would you turn the other two headings into statements of the topic?

Why are mosses important? People at flower shops often pack flowerpots with mosses. They do this because mosses hold water for a long time. Gardeners also mix mosses with their soil. They make the soil good for plants to grow in. Some mosses are dried and burned as fuel.

Mosses are also good soil builders. Their rootlike parts grow into the cracks of rocks. This helps break up the rocks to form soil. What other ways do you know of that plants help form soil?

— Exploring Science: Green Book
Laidlaw Brothers

221

Building Skills

Make an outline of the selection you just read. Use Roman numerals and capital letters. Remember to give your outline a title.

Outlining Information from Social Studies

Along the western coast of a map of South America you will find the country of Peru. Now look at the map below. You can see that Peru is divided into three regions. They are so

222

---

3. Have students read the rest of the selection and answer the question in the third sidenote. (What mosses are like; Why mosses are important) Then have students complete *Building Skills*.

Answers to *Building Skills*
Science Selection

Sample answer:

Mosses
  I. What mosses are like
     A. Hairlike roots
     B. No stems or leaves
 II. Where mosses are found
     A. Cool, shady places
     B. Woods
     C. On the banks of streams and ponds
III. Why mosses are important
     A. Hold water for a long time
     B. Make the soil good for plants
     C. Are soil builders

different from one another that some people speak of the three Perus. The first Peru is the narrow strip of desert that runs the whole length of the country along the coast. Almost no rain falls here, but there are about forty small rivers that flow through the desert. Near these rivers are Peru's large cities and towns. Among them is the capital city of Lima. Look at the map again. What other cities can you find in the first Peru?

Do you expect that the author will organize this section into three topics? What three topics do you think the author will now talk about?

To the east of the desert rises the second Peru. It is the Andes, the highest mountains in the Western Hemisphere. In this second Peru, several miles above the sea, the air is chilly most of the year. Few things grow here.

This is the second major topic. What Roman number will you give it on your outline?

The third Peru is on the other side of the Andes. There the land drops down sharply. That region is mostly rain forest. Very few people live in the third Peru.

—People in the Americas
Silver Burdett

Building Skills

Make an outline of the selection you just read. Remember to use Roman numerals and capital letters. Give your outline a title.

223

Outlining Information from Social Studies

1. Have students read the first paragraph and answer the questions in the first sidenote. (yes; the three regions of Peru) Ask them "which Peru" is discussed in the first paragraph. (the first Peru)

2. Have students read the rest of the selection and answer the question in the second sidenote. (Roman numeral II) Remind them to use Roman numerals for major topics and capital letters for subtopics.

3. Have students complete *Building Skills*.

Answers to *Building Skills*
Social Studies Selection

Sample answer:

      The Three Regions of Peru

  I. The first Peru
    A. Desert area
    B. Runs length of country
    C. Forty small rivers in desert
    D. Large cities, including Lima, the capital
 II. The second Peru
    A. Andes Mountains
    B. Chilly weather
    C. Few things grow
III. The third Peru
    A. The other side of the Andes
    B. Rain forest
    C. Few people

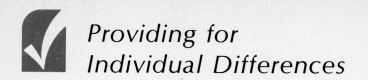 *Providing for Individual Differences*

Skills Lesson

Additional Practice

Worksheet 7, Teacher's Edition, page T486

Vocabulary Study

Additional Practice

■ **Identifying context clues** Write the words *mango, avocado,* and *rates* on the board. Explain that there are context clues to these words' meanings in the *Vocabulary Study* students read. Have students identify each context clue. (*avocado* and *mango:* fruits that can be squeezed to make drinks; *rates:* prices charged to customers)

■ **Using context clues to determine meaning**
Write the following list of words on the board and read aloud each sentence. Tell students to listen for context clues to help them figure out the meaning of each word. Then ask students to use each word in a sentence.

> nuisance: My uncle's pet monkey made such a *nuisance* of itself that everybody started calling it "pest." (pest)
> enrage: His actions often *enrage* her so that she cannot help showing her anger. (anger)
> disregard: If you know how to play, ignore this booklet and *disregard* these instructions. (ignore)
> perturb: the symptoms of the sick child were so alarming that they seemed to *perturb* even the doctor. (alarm)
> intellect: Her work showed the power of her *intellect* and that her mind was capable of meeting great challenges. (mind)

Reading Selection: Start Your Own Theater

Additional Practice

■ **Ordering topics** Write on the board the three major topics below. Tell students to write them on their papers in the order they would happen, leaving space for a few subtopics under each one.

> Things I do in the evening
> Things I do in the morning
> Things I do in the afternoon

List on the board the following things that someone might do during the day. Have students put these things in the right order under each of the major topics on their papers. Remind them to include in their outlines Roman numerals, capital letters, and a title.

> Eat breakfast   Eat lunch
> Go to bed   Eat supper
> Go home   Get up
> Go go school

Sample answer:
> Things I Do Each Day
> I. Things I do in the morning
>   A. Get up
>   B. Eat breakfast
>   C. Go to school
> II. Things I do in the afternoon
>   A. Eat lunch
>   B. Go home
> III. Things I do in the evening
>   A. Eat supper
>   B. Go to bed

(Answers may vary somewhat because of different living patterns and personal choice. Accept any outline students can justify.)

Challenge Activity

Refer students to the lists of things to take on a camping trip on page 205 and have them make an outline based on the lists. Remind them to use Roman numerals to show major topics and capital letters for subtopics and to give their outline a title.

Answer:
> Things to Take Camping
> I. Equipment
>   A. Camping gear
>   B. Cooking utensils
>   C. Photography equipment
> II. Clothing
>   A. Outer clothing
>   B. Inner clothing
> III. Supplies and other things
>   A. Food
>   B. Personal supplies
>   C. First-aid supplies

Evaluation

Periodic Test 2, Part III, Form A or *Form B,* may be administered after this unit to test skills marked **T**. If you have pretested using *Form A,* administer *Form B.*

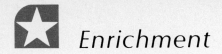

Enrichment

Start Your Own Theater

Bibliography

The following books are about the theater.

Average

Brunn-Rasmussen, Ole, and Grete Peterson. *Make-up, Costumes, and Masks for the Stage.* The basics of make-up, theories of light and shadow, specific character make-up, and a few costume ideas.

Kelly, Elizabeth Y. *The Magic If: Stanislavski for Children.* Dramatic exercises, ranging from easy to hard, to develop imagination in young actors.

Nuttall, Kenneth. *Your Book of Acting.* How to express yourself, use lighting, produce a play, use make-up, stage manage, etc.

Olfson, Lewy. *You Can Put On a Show.* Low- or no-budget variety shows, revues, puppet shows, and one-act plays.

Wehrum, Victoria. *The American Theatre.* A brief history of the American theater, from the time of colonial Williamsburg to the present.

Films and Filmstrips

NOTE: For more information, see *Resource Center.*

Skills

Harcourt Brace Jovanovich. *Bookmark Reading Filmstrips.* "Outlines That Work."

Selection content

Harcourt Brace Jovanovich. *Self-Expression and Conduct: The Humanities Sound Filmstrips.* "The Dramatic Experience": use of personal experiences by children in a rehearsal.

Scholastic. "Creative Dramatics." The production and creation of mini-dramas and plays.

Curriculum Coordination

Language Arts

1. Some or all of the students may wish to put on a play using the suggestions in this selection and information from books about the theater. The school librarian can help students locate books of plays. Some groups may prefer to write their own plays for staging.

2. Have students improvise a scene. Suggestions: taking a little brother or sister to the first day of kindergarten; getting a surprise visit from a friend. You might make a tape recording of each improvisation performed so that students can transcribe it into play form and revise it for future use.

Physical Education

For enjoyable work on concentration and nonverbal communication, have pairs of students play the "Mirror Game." Partners should face each other, with plenty of room between them. One partner should start a movement, such as raising a hand, in slow motion. The other partner should try to follow his or her movements accurately. Partners should not try to fool each other, but should coordinate their movements.

Art

Students can design posters and/or sets for their favorite play or an original production. They can research the various types of posters and set designs at the library, looking at the work of Henri Toulouse-Lautrec, Pablo Picasso, Jean Cocteau, Gordon Craig, Aline Bernstein, Ming Cho Lee, Santo Loquasto, and others.

Career Education

Invite an actor or director to class to discuss training for and work opportunities in the theater, films, and television. (A college with a theater or TV department might help you.)

TEACHING UNIT 9

Contents

Additional Materials

Reading Skills Workbook: Lessons 17–19, pages 55–66; Word Play, page 67
Duplicating Masters 11: pages 25–28
Worksheet 8: Teacher's Edition, page T487
Bookmark Reading Filmstrips: Purple: "What's What in the Library"
Periodic Test 2, Part IV

Key to Symbols

Skills Objectives
I* — Introduced in this unit
I — Introduced earlier in this level
M — Maintained from previous levels
T — Tested in periodic and cumulative tests for this level

Reduced Student Pages
underscore — words that appear in the glossary
wavy line — words pretaught in the Teacher's Edition
(these words also appear in the glossary)

Skills Lesson:
Using the Library
Pages 224–231

Objectives

		SKILLS CODE NUMBER
M, T	To locate and use library catalogue cards	*5.11.2*
M, T	To identify and use reference materials in which specific information may be found	*5.11*

If you wish to pretest the skills listed above, you may administer *Periodic Test 2, Part IV, Form A. Periodic Test 2, Part IV, Form B,* may be administered to posttest.

Introducing the Lesson

1. Have students name the three most common items that contain printed words. (books, magazines, and newspapers) Ask where one might expect to find more of these items than anywhere else. (in a library)

2. Point out that modern libraries contain many sources of information besides printed items, including tapes, records, photographs, films, and filmstrips. Discuss the use of *microfilm* to conserve space in libraries. Point out that printed items are photographed and the photographs are reduced in size for easy storage in a small space. Show students a microfilm or microfiche if possible.

Using the Library

PHILADELPHIA PUBLIC LIBRARY

ESTABLISHED 1731

"Nice building. But what are we going to put in it?"

As you know, Ben Franklin put *books* into his library. But in today's libraries (often called "media centers"), you'll find a lot more than books. You can find films, picture and pamphlet files, magazines, and newspapers. You can find records, tapes, and "talking books." In some libraries you can use a *microfilm* room. Large books or long articles are put on film. When you want to see what a book or article says, you run the film through a microfilm machine. Some of today's libraries even move around on wheels.

224

Of course, today's libraries have mostly books, books, and more books. How do you go about finding the book you want among the thousands that line the shelves? Usually the best place to start is the **card catalogue.**

The card catalogue is simply a set of small drawers. In them are cards that give information about the books in the library. There are three kinds of cards: *author cards, title cards,* and *subject cards.* Suppose you don't have a special book or author in mind. You're just looking for books on a certain subject. Then the subject cards are for you. If you already know the name of the book you want or the author's name, use the title or author cards.

Look at the three cards that follow. Pay attention to the notes under each card. They will help you understand how to read a catalogue card.

AUTHOR CARD

> J
> 413
> Kra
>
> **Kraske, Robert.**
> The story of the dictionary/by Robert Kraske.—
> 1st ed., illustrated with photos.—New York: Harcourt Brace Jovanovich [1975]
> 67 p.: ill.
> Bibliography
> Includes Index.
> SUMMARY: Traces the history of the dictionary and describes what goes into the making of this second most popular book in the English language.

Each nonfiction book in the library has a *call number.* The call number is on the top left-hand part of the card. The *J* means this book can be found in the juvenile or children's

225

3. Explain that libraries often hold "book chats," puppet shows, and demonstrations of how to make things that are described in books. Perhaps some of your students have attended a library presentation. Have students tell about their experiences in a library.

4. Have students look at the cartoon on page 224. Ask them what Ben Franklin put in the building. (books) Explain that Ben Franklin started the first circulating library in America. Then have students read the first paragraph.

Developing the Skill

The card catalogue helps you find the book you need.

1. Have students read the first three paragraphs on page 225 and look at the catalogue cards on pages 225–227. Point out that each card can be found in the card catalogue. Ask why the card on page 225 is called an author card. (The author's name, Robert Kraske, is the first piece of information given.) Ask why the card on page 226 is called a subject card and the card on page 227 is called a title card. (The subject and the title are the first pieces of information on these cards.)

2. Have students read the three paragraphs following the author card. Ask them to identify the call number of the book whose author card is shown on page 225. (J 413 Kra) Ask students what the letters *Kra* might mean. (They are the first three letters of the author's name.) Ask what the title of the book is. *(The Story of the Dictionary)*

area of the library. To find this book on the shelves, you'd only have to find the section of the library with books that have call numbers in the 400's.

Both fiction and nonfiction books have title cards. If you were looking for the title card for *The Story of the Dictionary*, you'd look in the drawer marked *S*. The words *A*, *An*, and *The* are not considered when title cards are filed.

Suppose you did not know the title or author of this book, but wanted a book about dictionaries. You might look under the subjects *English Language*, *Words*, or *Dictionaries* in the card catalogue.

Now suppose you wanted to know about the Braille system. You can see that the subject is listed at the top of the following card. Information about a book that is on the *Braille System* follows the subject listing.

SUBJECT CARD

```
J      Braille System.
371.9
Nei    Neimark, Anne E.
           Touch of light; the story of Louis Braille [by]
       Anne E. Neimark. Illustrated by Robert Parker. [1st
       ed.] New York: Harcourt Brace Jovanovich [1970]
           186 p. illus.
           SUMMARY: The life of the nineteenth-century Frenchman
       who invented a system of reading for the blind.
           Bibliography.
```

Not all catalogue cards have a summary like the one above. Why is such a summary useful?

226

TITLE CARD

```
J      Touchmark.
F
Law    Lawrence, Mildred.
           Touchmark/by Mildred Lawrence; illustrated by
       Deanne Hollinger. — 1st ed. — New York: Harcourt
       Brace Jovanovich [1975]
           184 p.: ill.
           SUMMARY: An orphaned girl living in pre-Revolutionary
       Boston longs to be apprenticed to a pewterer.
```

The letter *F* means you should look for this book on the fiction *shelves*. Fiction books do not usually have call numbers. These books are arranged in alphabetical order by the author's last name. The *Law* under the letter *F* on the card shows the first three letters of the author's last name.

Fiction books also have author cards. If you were looking for another fiction book by Mildred Lawrence, you'd look in the drawer marked *L* and find Lawrence by using alphabetical order.

Try This

Answer the following questions about the book on the subject card on page 226.

1. Is this book fiction or nonfiction?
2. Who is the author of this book?
3. What is the title of this book?
4. What is the call number of this book?

227

---

3. Have students read the last two paragraphs on page 226. Ask why the summary on the card is useful. (It can help the reader determine if the book has the information he or she wants.)

4. Have students read the two paragraphs below the title card. Ask in which drawer this title card would be found. (the drawer labeled *T*) Ask students if the title *Touchmark* helps them know what the book is about. (no) Then have students read the summary on the card. Ask how many students think they'd like to read the book.

Try This

Have students complete *Try This*.

Answers to *Try This*

1. nonfiction; 2. Anne E. Neimark; 3. *Touch of Light: The Story of Louis Braille*; 4. J 371.9 Nei

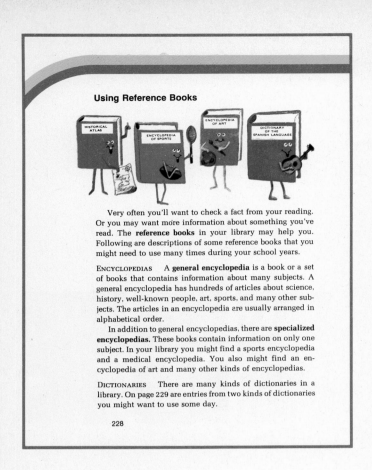

Using Reference Books

Very often you'll want to check a fact from your reading. Or you may want more information about something you've read. The **reference books** in your library may help you. Following are descriptions of some reference books that you might need to use many times during your school years.

ENCYCLOPEDIAS   A **general encyclopedia** is a book or a set of books that contains information about many subjects. A general encyclopedia has hundreds of articles about science, history, well-known people, art, sports, and many other subjects. The articles in an encyclopedia are usually arranged in alphabetical order.

In addition to general encyclopedias, there are **specialized encyclopedias**. These books contain information on only one subject. In your library you might find a sports encyclopedia and a medical encyclopedia. You also might find an encyclopedia of art and many other kinds of encyclopedias.

DICTIONARIES   There are many kinds of dictionaries in a library. On page 229 are entries from two kinds of dictionaries you might want to use some day.

228

sixty, *a.* and *n.* Soixante. *About sixty,* une soixantaine (de).
sizable ['saizəbl], *a.* D'une bonne grosseur; de la grosseur voulue (par les règlements).

— *The New Cassell's French Dictionary* Funk & Wagnalls

Foreign language dictionaries give English words and foreign words. You can find such dictionaries for almost every language. When might you want to use a foreign dictionary?

Anderson,   Marian.   1902– American concert contralto, b. Philadelphia. Began singing career (1924); appeared on concert stage in Europe; recital in New York (Dec. 30, 1935), subsequently appearing successfully throughout U.S. Awarded Spingarn medal (1939).

A biographical dictionary gives facts about well-known people from the past or present.

— By permission.
From *Webster's Biographical Dictionary* © 1980 by G. & C. Merriam Co., Publishers of the Merriam-Webster Dictionaries.

229

Using Reference Books

A. *General encyclopedias contain information about many subjects, and specialized encyclopedias contain information about one subject.*

1. Have students read the first three paragraphs on page 228. Ask students if any of them has used an encyclopedia recently. Ask if they know whether or not the encyclopedia they used was a general or a specialized encyclopedia. Have students describe the encyclopedia. Did it have many volumes, or just one? Were many subjects covered, or just one?

2. If students are not aware of any specialized encyclopedias in the school library, you might establish a committee to visit the library and identify the specialized encyclopedias available.

B. *There are many types of dictionaries in the library.*

1. Have students read the last paragraph on page 228 and the entries from the French-English dictionary on page 229. Have them answer the question in the sidenote at the top of page 229. (when you come across a foreign word in your reading; if you are studying a foreign language; etc.)

2. Have students read the entry from the biographical dictionary and its sidenote on page 229. Ask when Marian Anderson began her singing career. (1924) Point out that such a short biographical summary is often all that is needed for a brief report.

3. Explain that in addition to foreign language dictionaries and biographical dictionaries, there are other specialized dictionaries. One kind is a *thesaurus,* which lists synonyms and antonyms. There are also dictionaries that list rhyming words, dictionaries that list special terms used in a certain field, and other kinds of dictionaries.

ATLASES   An **atlas** is a book of maps. There are many different kinds of maps in an atlas. There are also, at the back of an atlas, tables listing important geographical facts, such as the highest mountains in the world. If you want to know what the longest river in the world is or what the major products of a certain country are, an atlas is a useful tool.

ALMANACS   How much rain fell in your state last year? What is the birthday of your favorite TV star? What is the population of Hawaii? What is the most popular book in the English language? An **almanac** may give you answers to these and many, many other questions. Almanacs are books of information. They come out every year. So they are useful sources of up-to-date information. Next time you're in the library, look at this year's almanac. You'll be surprised at how many different kinds of facts can be listed in one book.

230

Try This

1. What reference book would you use to answer each of the following questions? You may find that more than one book would give an answer to some of the questions.

   a. Who was Marie Curie?
   b. How high is Mount Everest?
   c. What does the Spanish word *caballo* mean?
   d. How is glass made?
   e. What are the major products of Chile?
   f. What states border New Jersey?

2. In which reference book would you probably find the following information?

   a. a map of Europe
   b. the year Babe Ruth was born
   c. the yearly rainfall in South Africa
   d. the pronunciation of *platitude*
   e. the origin of the Olympic Games

C. *Atlases contain maps and information about geographical locations.*

Obtain an atlas and show students the many different types of maps and tables in it. Have students read the first paragraph on page 230. Ask how an atlas might be useful to them. (It is a quick form of reference for certain information and may be more detailed than a book containing other kinds of information. Accept other answers.)

D. *Almanacs are books that provide up-to-date information on a variety of special topics.*

1. Have students read the last paragraph on page 230. If possible, provide an almanac for students to look through. Review an almanac by describing its features or by reading aloud portions of its table of contents or index.

2. Have students ask questions that might be answered in the almanac. For instance, they might ask for birth dates of famous people, names of people in baseball and basketball halls of fame, dates of various national holidays, names and altitudes of mountain peaks, and the population of a given state in a given year.

Try This

Have students complete *Try This.*

Answers to *Try This*

1. **a.** biographical dictionary, encyclopedia, almanac, dictionary; **b.** atlas, encyclopedia, almanac, dictionary; **c.** Spanish-English dictionary; **d.** encyclopedia; **e.** atlas, encyclopedia, almanac; **f.** atlas, encyclopedia 2. **a.** encyclopedia, atlas; **b.** encyclopedia, biographical dictionary; **c.** almanac, atlas, encyclopedia; **d.** dictionary; **e.** encyclopedia. Accept reasonable answers.

 Use *Reading Skills Workbook,* Lesson 17, pages 55–62. See *Providing for Individual Differences,* page T204, for additional practice.

Vocabulary Study:
Multiple Meanings
Pages 232–233

Objective

		SKILLS CODE NUMBER
M	To use context clues to determine meanings of multiple-meaning words	3.5.5; 3.0.2

Developing the Skill

1. Tell students that the *Vocabulary Study* they are about to read is about Zigmore's Before-and-After Cream. Explain that in it they'll find words with multiple meanings. Write the words *mint, mine,* and *seal* on the board. Ask students if they can think of at least two meanings for each of these words.

2. Have students read the *Vocabulary Study* and do the *Word Play* activities.

Answers to *Word Play*

1. Sentences will vary. 2. Sentences will vary.

 Use *Reading Skills Workbook,* Lesson 18, page 63. See *Providing for Individual Differences,* page T204, for additional practice.

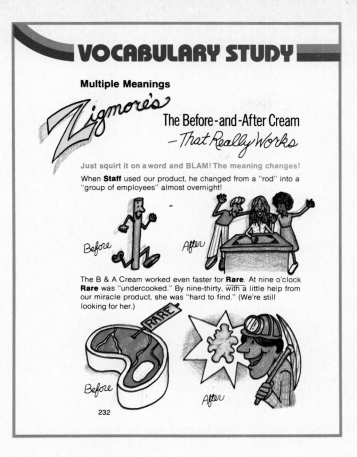

VOCABULARY STUDY

Multiple Meanings

Zigmore's The Before-and-After Cream — *That Really Works*

Just squirt it on a word and BLAM! The meaning changes!

When **Staff** used our product, he changed from a "rod" into a "group of employees" almost overnight!

Before   After

The B & A Cream worked even faster for **Rare**. At nine o'clock **Rare** was "undercooked." By nine-thirty, with a little help from our miracle product, she was "hard to find." (We're still looking for her.)

Before   After

232

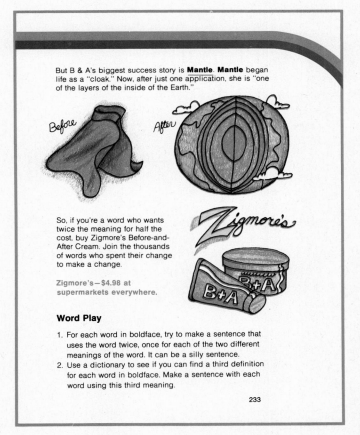

But B & A's biggest success story is **Mantle**. **Mantle** began life as a "cloak." Now, after just one application, she is "one of the layers of the inside of the Earth."

Before   After

So, if you're a word who wants twice the meaning for half the cost, buy Zigmore's Before-and-After Cream. Join the thousands of words who spent their change to make a change.

Zigmore's—$4.98 at supermarkets everywhere.

Word Play

1. For each word in boldface, try to make a sentence that uses the word twice, once for each of the two different meanings of the word. It can be a silly sentence.
2. Use a dictionary to see if you can find a third definition for each word in boldface. Make a sentence with each word using this third meaning.

233

Reading Selection:
Life with the Li'l Folks

Pages 234–242

Objectives

		SKILLS CODE NUMBER
M, T	To locate and use library catalogue cards	5.11.2
M, T	To identify and use reference materials in which specific information may be found	5.11
M	To identify clues to time-order relationships	3.1.2
M	To determine the correct sequence for a set of events	3.3.7.4
M	To draw conclusions based on given information and personal knowledge	3.4.1

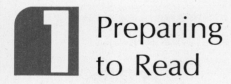

1 Preparing to Read

Summary

Charles Schulz, the creator of the comic strip "Peanuts," describes the way in which his childhood interest in cartooning led to his successful career as a cartoonist. He describes how the cartoon "Peanuts" has changed since it first began and how he has taken the names and personalities of real people and pets he has known for the characters in his comic strips.

Background

Cartoons did not gain wide popularity until the 1800's. By 1900, editorial cartoons and comic strips had become firmly established in American newspapers. A comic strip consists of a series of pictures with the characters' words printed near their heads in areas called balloons.

Charles Schulz was born in Minnesota in 1924. From the age of six on, he planned to become a cartoonist. His famous comic strip "Peanuts" began as "Li'l Folks." As time passed, the personalities of his characters changed and deepened, and the comic strip became immensely popular. Today the comic strip "Peanuts" appears in approximately 1,700 newspapers and magazines around the world, including approximately 1,500 in North America.

The following books will provide you with additional background information.

Breger, Dave. *How to Draw and Sell Cartoons.* Comprehensive coverage, from ideas to selling.
Hoff, Syd. *The Art of Cartooning.* Wide coverage, from techniques to surviving rejection slips.

Developing Vocabulary and Concepts

breed: a particular kind of animal; for example, *beagle* is a breed of dog
markings: the color pattern of an animal's fur
crushing: putting down; overwhelming; defeating
frustration: the feeling of discouragement or anger that comes from not being able to do or achieve something
rejection: the act of refusing to accept something
feature: a special article, story, or column, as in a newspaper

1. **a.** Read aloud the following sentences or write them on the board. If you read them aloud, write the underlined vocabulary on the board.

   After thinking about different breeds of dogs, Charles Schulz decided that Snoopy would be a beagle.
   The markings of the two dogs were different. Snoopy had black ears and a black spot on his back and tail; the other dog had black paws and a black spot around one eye.
   It was another crushing defeat for Charlie Brown's baseball team. They lost 15 to 1.
   Charlie Brown feels a lot of frustration because his baseball team never wins a game.
   Tamara was discouraged by the magazine's rejection of her cartoons. But she sent some more drawings and hoped the magazine would accept them this time.
   My favorite feature in the newspaper is a comic strip that appears every day. My mother's favorite feature is a column on books that appears three times a week.

   b. Ask students to give the meaning of each vocabulary word. Remind them to use the context clues in the sentences to help them.

The top of the page shows two facsimile textbook pages (234 and 235).

Page 234:

Newspapers and TV aren't the only places you'll see Charlie Brown and Snoopy. Most libraries have books about them. In the selection below, look for clues to help you know how to find such books in your library.

How did Charles Schulz get his ideas for Lucy and Linus? What parts of Snoopy's personality are based on a real dog's? Charles Schulz is here to tell you about his . . .

Life with the Li'l Folks
by Charles M. Schulz

234

Page 235:

I have been asked many times if I ever dreamed that Peanuts would become as successful as it is. My answer often surprises people. I say, "Well, I guess I did expect it. After all, it was something I had planned since I was six years old."

When I was in grade school, I was a great fan of all the Disney characters. I also enjoyed Popeye and

235

---

2. Ask students what comic strips they like to read in the Sunday or weekday newspapers and why they like to read them. Students may name "Peanuts" among their favorites. If not, ask them if they are familiar with "Peanuts." Ask them to describe Charlie Brown, Snoopy, and Lucy and to name other characters from the strip. Explain to students that Charles Schulz writes and draws "Peanuts" and that he is the author of the selection they are about to read.

 Use *Duplicating Masters 11,* page 25.

Setting Purposes

Skills

Have students read the skills note at the top of page 234. Remind them that there are three kinds of cards in the library card catalogue. Ask students what they are. (author cards, title cards, and subject cards) Tell them that the name of the author of the selection is one means of locating books about Charlie Brown and Snoopy. Topics mentioned in the selection are other clues.

Content

Have students read the lead-in to the title. Discuss answers to the questions. Have students read the selection to find out Charles Schulz's answers.

2 Reading and Discussing

Have students read the selection. Most students will be able to complete it in one sitting. If you prefer, the selection may be read in two parts, breaking before the last paragraph on page 238.

NOTE: The questions that appear in the student's text at the end of the selection focus on comprehension of selection content and on application of the *Skills Lesson* to the selection. Answers to these questions begin on page T194.

Wimpy very much. I used to decorate my loose-leaf binders with drawings of Mickey Mouse, the Three Little Pigs, and Popeye. Whenever friends in class saw these drawings, I would be asked to draw them on their notebooks as well. I used to buy every comic magazine that came out and study the different ways of drawing.

My dad loved to read the comic strips. We talked about them together and worried about what was going to happen next to some of the characters. On Saturday evening, I would run up to the drugstore at nine o'clock. I'd buy the two Sunday Minneapolis papers. The next morning, I got the two St. Paul papers. So we had four comic sections to read.

Several years later, I became a delivery boy for one of our town's printing firms. I used to pass the windows of the St. Paul *Pioneer Press* and look in. There I saw

the huge presses and the Sunday funnies tumbling down across the rollers. I wondered if I would ever see my own comics on these presses.

My mother also encouraged me in my drawing but, sadly, never lived to see any of my work in print.

When I was thirteen, we were given a black-and-white dog. Spike was a mixed breed and a little larger than the beagle Snoopy is supposed to be. On Saturday evenings, just before nine, he always put his paws on my dad's chair to let him know it was time to get in the car and drive up to the store to buy those newspapers. When I decided to put a dog in Peanuts, I used the general appearance of Spike, with similar markings.

I had decided that the dog in the strip was to be named Sniffy. Then one day, when I was walking past a newsstand, I glanced down at the rows of comic magazines. There I saw one about a dog named Sniffy. So I had to go back to my room and think of another name. Before I even got home, I remembered my mother once saying that if we ever had another dog, we should name it Snoopy.

I never wanted to have Snoopy talk. But it became important that he do some kind of thinking. When Snoopy began to think, he took on a personality that was very different from any other cartoon dog's. He was a little smarter than the kids in the strip. But he did suffer a few defeats—you might say, at his own paws. However, most of the time he won out over the kids.

In my childhood, sports were pretty important to my friends and me. I have always tried to use my own knowledge of games in my sports comic strips. Anytime I had crushing defeats in sports, I transferred my frustrations to poor Charlie Brown.

During my senior year in high school, my mother

showed me an ad that read: ''Do you like to draw? Send in for our free talent test.'' This was how I first knew about Art Instruction Schools, Inc. It was and still is in Minneapolis. Even though I could have taken my drawings there in person, I did all the lessons by mail because I was not that proud of my work.

When I was just out of high school, I started to send cartoons to most of the major magazines. But I received only rejection slips. Several years later, I again tried to sell my work. I visited several places in the Twin Cities to try to get a job in an art department. One day, with my sample comic strips in hand, I visited the offices of Timeless Topix comic magazines. The art director seemed to like my lettering. He gave me several comic-book pages that had already been drawn by others but with the balloons left blank. He told me that I should fill in the words. This was my first job.

Soon after I took the job at Timeless Topix, I was also hired by Art Instruction Schools. My job at the school was to correct some of the lessons. There I met many people who did much to help me in my later work. I learned how important it is to draw properly—whether it be a shoe, a doghouse, or a child's hand. Cartooning,

PEANUTS

Copr. 1950 by United Feature Syndicate, Inc.

after all, is simply good design. A good cartoon comes from learning how to design a human hand *after* knowing how to draw it properly.

Some of the people who worked at Art Instruction Schools with me have remained friends all of these years. I have used the names of several people in Peanuts. Charlie Brown was named after my very good friend, Charlie Brown, whose desk was across the room. I remember the day he came over and first looked at the little cartoon face that had been named after him. ''Is that what he looks like?'' he asked sadly. The characters of Linus and Frieda were also named after friends of mine who were teachers.

I used my spare time, after correcting lessons, to work on my own cartoons. I sold fifteen of them to the *Saturday Evening Post.*

It was an exciting time for me because I was doing just what I wished to do. One day I sold a page of little cartoons that I had drawn and titled ''Just Keep Laughing.'' In one of them was a small boy who looked like Schroeder sitting on the curb with a baseball bat in his hands. He was talking to a little girl who looked like Patty. I made more drawings of little kids. Then I sold

By Schulz

Copr. 1950 by United Feature Syndicate, Inc.

them as a weekly feature called "Li'l Folks" to the St. Paul *Pioneer Press*. Later, the name Li'l Folks was changed to Peanuts.

When Peanuts began in 1950, there were only four characters: Patty, Charlie Brown, Shermy, and Snoopy. I was not sure which one would become the lead. But the personalities soon took care of that. The good lines were given to Charlie Brown or to one of the new characters. After the year 1950, Charlie Brown turned into the loser he is known as today.

240

When Lucy came into the strip she was a very tiny girl with round eyes. Later I cut the circles in half. She and her brother, Linus, now are the only ones to have tiny half-circles on each side of their eyes.

Lucy's personality was based on that of our oldest daughter, Meredith. We called Meredith a "fussbudget" when she was very small. Linus came from a drawing that I made one day of a face almost like the one he now has. I showed it to a friend of mine whose name was Linus Maurer. He thought it was kind of funny, and we both agreed it might make someone new for the strip. It also seemed that Linus would fit very well as Lucy's younger brother.

I have always believed that you can make the characters do things you want them to. But the characters themselves should give you ideas. The more you can tell one character from another, the better the comic strip will be. Readers can then believe that the characters are real.

241

To create something out of nothing is a wonderful experience. To take a blank piece of paper and draw characters that people love and worry about is very satisfying. I hope very much that I will be allowed to do it for many years to come.

Understanding What You've Read

1. When did Charles Schulz become interested in comics?
2. How did Schulz's parents help him?
3. From what sources did Schulz get some of his ideas for his comic characters?

Applying the Skills Lesson

1. The selection you just read came from the book *Peanuts Jubilee* by Charles Schulz. How would you find the title card for this book in the card catalogue? How would you find the author card? Under what subjects might you look for other books about comic characters?

2. In which reference books would you find the information asked for in the lettered items below? Choose your answers from the following list of reference sources.

biographical dictionary   atlas
dictionary   general encyclopedia

a. where St. Paul, Minnesota, is
b. Charles Schulz's date of birth
c. the meaning of the word *frustration*
d. general information on comics and cartoons

242

Questions preceded by a bullet are additional questions and appear in the Teacher's Edition only. The other questions appear in the student's text after the selection.

Understanding What You've Read

1. *When did Charles Schulz become interested in comics?* (when he was in grade school or when he was six years old   page 235) LITERAL   Recalling specific details

● *Why did Charles Schulz buy every comic magazine that came out?* (to study the different ways of drawing   page 236) INFERENTIAL   Drawing conclusions

2. *How did Schulz's parents help him?* (His father used to read the comics and talk with him about them. His mother encouraged him in his drawing.   pages 236 and 237) LITERAL   Recalling specific details

● *Why do you think Charles Schulz took the job at Timeless Topix when all he did was fill in the words on comic strips drawn by others?* (Answers will vary. Students should recognize that Schulz might have been glad for the chance to work in the comic-strip business. Even though he wasn't drawing cartoons, he felt he would gain valuable experience.) INFERENTIAL   Drawing conclusions

3. *From what sources did Schulz get some of his ideas for his comic characters?* (from people and pets in his own life) INFERENTIAL   Making generalizations

● *Why was the real Charlie Brown sad when he saw the comic-strip character named after him?* (Answers will vary, but may include the following: The character didn't really look like him; he didn't like the drawing.) INFERENTIAL   Drawing conclusions

● *How is Lucy like Schulz's daughter?* (They have similar personalities—both are "fussbudgets."   page 241) INFERENTIAL   Making comparisons

● *Does Charles Schulz enjoy his work? How do you know?* (Yes. He says that creating something out of nothing is a wonderful experience and that he hopes to be allowed to do it for many years to come. page 242) INFERENTIAL   Drawing conclusions

Applying the Skills Lesson

1. *The selection you just read came from the book* Peanuts Jubilee, *by Charles Schulz. How would you find the title card for this book in the card catalogue? How would you find the author card? Under what subjects might you look for other books about comic characters?* (Title card: Look under the letter *P.* Author card: Look under the letter *S.* Other books: Look under the subjects "Comics" and "Cartoons.")   Using library catalogue cards

2. *In which reference books would you find the information asked for in the lettered items below? Choose your answers from the following list of reference sources.*
biographical dictionary   atlas
dictionary   general encyclopedia
a. *where St. Paul, Minnesota, is*
b. *Charles Schulz's date of birth*
c. *the meaning of the word* frustration
d. *general information on comics and cartoons*
(a. atlas, general encyclopedia, dictionary; b. biographical dictionary, general encyclopedia; c. dictionary; d. general encyclopedia)   Identifying reference materials

- *Read the following list of books by Charles Schulz. Under what letters would you look in the card catalogue to find the title cards for these books?*
  1. *Snoopy on Stage*
  2. *Win a Few, Lose a Few, Charlie Brown*
  3. *The Charlie Brown Dictionary*
  4. *You're on Your Own, Snoopy*
  5. *Be My Valentine, Charlie Brown*
  6. *A Charlie Brown Thanksgiving*
  7. *It's the Great Pumpkin, Charlie Brown*
  (1. S; 2. W; 3. C; 4. Y; 5. B; 6. C; 7. I)

Using library catalogue cards

✔ Use *Duplicating Masters 11*, page 26. See *Providing for Individual Differences*, page T204, for additional practice.

3 Maintaining Skills

Comprehension Skills

Identifying time-order relationships   Write the following sentences from the selection on the board or dictate them. Remind students that authors frequently provide clues to when events happen. Have volunteers identify the time clues in each sentence. Then have students arrange the sentences in the correct time order.

1. When I was thirteen, we were given a black-and-white dog. (When I was thirteen)
2. Several years later, I again tried to sell my work. (Several years later; again)
3. During my senior year in high school, my mother showed me an ad that read: "Do you like to draw? Send in for our free talent test." (During my senior year in high school)
4. When I was in grade school, I was a great fan of all the Disney characters. (When I was in grade school)
5. When I was just out of high school, I started to send cartoons to most of the major magazines. (When I was just out of high school)
(Correct order: 4, 1, 3, 5, 2)

✔ Use *Reading Skills Workbook*, Lesson 19, pages 64–66.

Drawing conclusions   Ask students the following questions. Answers for each question will vary, but they should include the information in parentheses.

Why did Charles Schulz's classmates ask him to draw on their notebooks? (because they liked the characters, or because his drawings were so good)

Why does Charles Schulz say that he was sad that his mother never lived to see his drawings in print? (Remind students that she had encouraged him in his work. If she had lived, she would have been proud of him and would have been happy to see that he had succeeded.)

Why didn't Charles Schulz use the name "Sniffy" for the dog in his strip? (There was already a dog named Sniffy in a comic magazine. He wanted his dog to have a different name so people wouldn't confuse the two characters. He wanted his character to be unique; otherwise people might think he was copying.)

★ For additional resources and curriculum-related activities, see *Enrichment*, page T205.

Reading Selection:
Truly a Ballerina

Pages 243–247

Objectives

		SKILLS CODE NUMBER
M, T	To locate and use library catalogue cards	5.11.2
M, T	To identify and use reference materials in which specific information may be found	5.11
M	To identify clues to time-order relationships	3.1.2
M	To determine the correct sequence for a set of events	3.3.7.4
M	To identify cause-and-effect relationships	3.3.3

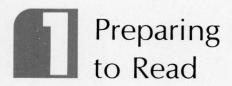

Preparing to Read

Summary

At twelve, Betty Marie Tallchief felt torn between the two things she loved most—music and dance. By the time she was seventeen, she knew that she wanted to be a dancer. She joined the Ballet Russe in New York City and trained under the famous choreographer George Balanchine, whom she later married. Tallchief became the leading dancer in the company Balanchine formed and was considered one of the best dancers in the world.

Background

Ballet: Ballet originated in France in the 1500's. It is considered the ultimate dance expression since it combines the arts of dance, music, drama, and painting. With the use of five basic positions, dancers can tell the whole story of a ballet. Classical ballet generally tells a specific and often popular story. Modern ballet, however, tends to be more abstract and introduces elements from other forms of dance.

Ballet dancers usually begin their training between the ages of eight and ten, at first concentrating mostly on muscle (athletic) development. Students are usually not allowed to dance on their toes until they've had a few years' training, because a child's bone structure is soft and may be permanently harmed if pushed too far before the age of about eleven.

Your students may want to know the term for the male equivalent of *ballerina*. It is *danseur*.

Maria Tallchief: Maria Tallchief (b. 1925), a member of the Osage tribe, was born in Fairfax, Oklahoma. Balanchine was born in Russia and began studying dance there when he was nine. Fondly known by his students and the ballet world as "Mr. B," he was the ballet master of the New York City Ballet until his death in 1983. Maria Tallchief is the ballet director of the Lyric Opera Ballet of Chicago.

The following books and magazine article will provide you with additional background information.

Brinson, Peter. *International Book of the Ballet.* History, synopses, commentary, and choreography of 115 major ballets.

Terry, Walter. *The Ballet Guide.* Backgrounds, listings, credits, and descriptions of more than 500 of the world's major ballets.

Time Magazine. "U.S. Ballet Soars." May 1, 1978.

Developing Vocabulary and Concepts

stage name: the name a professional performer uses instead of the name given at birth

choreographer: a person who makes up the steps for a dance

company: a group of actors, dancers, or musicians who regularly perform together

slashed: cut through quickly, as with a knife

leading: most important; having a starring role in a stage or film performance

1. **a.** Read aloud the following sentences or write them on the board. If you read them aloud, write the underlined vocabulary on the board.

    When the famous ballerina performs, she uses her stage name rather than the name her parents gave her.

    That choreographer makes up dances with very difficult steps.

    A group of fifty dancers worked in the ballet company.

    The dancer slashed, or cut through, the air with razorlike leaps.

    The leading dancer played the most important part in the dance.

b. Ask students to give the meaning of each vocabulary word. Remind them to use the context clues in the sentences to help them.

2. a. Introduce the topic of ballet by showing magazine pictures of ballet dancers and asking students what they know about the type of dancing in the pictures. (If no pictures are available, write the word *ballet* on the board.)

Ask students where they might see this kind of dance (on TV or in a theater), what the dancers wear (costumes, leotards, tutus), and how this kind of dance is different from other dance forms. (It uses formal steps, it conveys a story, theme, or atmosphere, and the women often dance on their toes.)

b. If any students study ballet, they may wish to explain or demonstrate the five basic positions or discuss the training they are receiving.

 Use *Duplicating Masters 11,* page 27.

Setting Purposes

Skills

Have students read the skills note at the top of page 243. Students should recall that possible sources of information about Maria Tallchief include a biographical dictionary and an encyclopedia.

Content

Have students read the lead-in to the title. If possible, play a lively portion of Stravinsky's *Firebird Suite.* Tell students to imagine a ballerina dancing to this music in a costume of brightly colored feathers.

What reference books would quickly give you information about Maria Tallchief? As you read, think of other ways the library can help you.

Betty Marie Tallchief spent many years of hard work developing her talent. One day the whole world would see her as . . .

Truly a Ballerina
by Tobi Tobias

243

2 Reading and Discussing

Have students read the selection. Most students will be able to complete it in one sitting. If you prefer, the selection may be read in two parts, breaking before the last paragraph on page 244.

NOTE: The questions that appear in the student's text at the end of the selection focus on comprehension of selection content and on application of the *Skills Lesson* to the selection. Answers to these questions begin on page T199.

To celebrate her twelfth birthday, Betty Marie Tallchief gave a concert. For the first half she played the piano, and for the second half she danced. That concert, she said, showed how she felt inside. She was split in half between the two things she loved most. One day she would have to choose between them.

By the time she was seventeen, Betty Marie realized what she wanted more than anything else. It was to be a dancer. Her mother understood how much she wanted to dance. She allowed her to go to New York City. Many important dance groups work in New York. There, Betty Marie hoped to find a job in a ballet company.

Betty Marie found a place with the Ballet Russe [roōs] de Monte Carlo. The company traveled from city to city, giving performances. Betty Marie danced so well that people began to notice her. Soon she was given some solo parts.

Ballet life was often hard, though, and Betty Marie was sometimes unhappy. She kept to herself at first, and many people in the company thought she was unfriendly. Some of them were jealous because she was doing so well. Betty Marie missed her family, too. She wrote long letters home.

Still she went on trying, working hard, and learning. Finally, the director of the Ballet Russe, Sergei Denham [ser·gā′ den′əm], asked her to stay on in the company. Of course, she said yes.

Then Mr. Denham decided that she should have a beautiful stage name. So Betty Marie became "Maria." But she refused to change Tallchief. She was proud of her American Indian name.

Maria Tallchief soon had an exciting chance. George Balanchine joined the Ballet Russe. Mr. Balanchine was

244

a well-known choreographer. He also taught dancers. If he picked out a young woman and trained her, she might become a great ballerina.

Maria caught Mr. Balanchine's eye at once. Her dancing was fast and brilliant. She could jump up and beat her long, shapely legs together eight times in the air. She could turn in the air and land on the points of her strong toes. Her balance was sure. Her leaps were sharp and high. Her turns were quick and powerful!

Day after day, Mr. Balanchine worked with Maria. He was a gentle, patient teacher. But he often asked her to perform steps that seemed impossible. She tried over and over again, until she could do what he wanted. Soon she was dancing better than ever before.

Maria Tallchief in the Nutcracker ballet.

After some time, Mr. Balanchine asked Maria to be his wife. She was twenty-one when they were married.

After a short stay in Paris, Mr. Balanchine went back to work at his own studio in New York, the School of American Ballet. He formed a company called Ballet Society with dancers he had trained there. In time, this group would grow into the New York City

245

Maria Tallchief and George Balanchine rehearse.

Ballet and become one of the best ballet companies in the world. Maria joined this company as its leading dancer when she was twenty-two.

246

Mr. Balanchine created many wonderful ballets for his company, especially for Maria. One of them was *Firebird*. Maria danced the part of a beautiful, wild bird with magic powers.

Mr. Balanchine set very difficult steps for her. They made the audience gasp with wonder and surprise. Maria flashed across the stage. She flew, she whirled, she slashed through space like a flaming arrow. *Firebird* proved that Maria was truly a ballerina. She was not just a fine dancer, but one of the best in the world.

Understanding What You've Read

1. Why did Maria's mother let her go to New York City?
2. What was ballet life like for Maria when she was dancing with the Ballet Russe?
3. How did George Balanchine help Maria to become a better dancer?

Applying the Skills Lesson

In which reference books would you find the numbered items below? Choose your answers from the following list of reference sources.

atlas   dictionary
biographical dictionary   specialized encyclopedia
general encyclopedia   of dancing

1. how far Fairfax, Oklahoma, is from New York
2. George Balanchine's date of birth
3. information about the history of ballet
4. information about well-known dancers

247

Questions preceded by a bullet are additional questions and appear in the Teacher's Edition only. The other questions appear in the student's text after the selection.

Understanding What You've Read

1. *Why did Maria's mother let her go to New York City?* (She knew how much she wanted to dance and knew there were many important dance companies in New York City.   page 244) LITERAL   Identifying stated information

- *Why did Betty Marie feel as if she were "split in half"?* (She knew that one day she would have to choose between the two things she loved—becoming a dancer or a musician.   page 244) INFERENTIAL Drawing conclusions

2. *What was ballet life like for Maria when she was dancing with the Ballet Russe?* (It was hard and, at first, lonely. However, she was able to learn a great deal and was given many opportunities, which she took.   pages 244–245) LITERAL   Recalling specific details

- *What was the reason Betty Marie refused to change her last name?* (She was proud of her American Indian name and wanted it to be part of her stage name.   page 244) LITERAL   Identifying cause-and-effect relationships

- *Who was George Balanchine?* (a famous choreographer and dance teacher who worked at the Ballet Russe and who founded the New York City Ballet   pages 244 and 245) LITERAL   Recalling specific details

3. *How did George Balanchine help Maria to become a better dancer?* (He worked with Maria day after day. He was a gentle and patient teacher, but he often asked Maria to perform steps that seemed impossible.   page 245) LITERAL   Recalling stated information

- *How did Balanchine help Maria Tallchief to become famous?* (She became the leading dancer in his company. He created many wonderful ballets for her, including *Firebird*.   pages 246 and 247) INFERENTIAL Drawing conclusions

Applying the Skills Lesson

In which reference books would you find the numbered items below? Choose your answers from the following list of reference sources.
atlas   dictionary
general encyclopedia   biographical dictionary
specialized encyclopedia of dancing
1. *how far Fairfax, Oklahoma, is from New York*
2. *George Balanchine's date of birth*
3. *information about the history of ballet*
4. *information about well-known dancers*
(1. atlas, general encyclopedia; 2. biographical dictionary, general encyclopedia, specialized encyclopedia; 3. general encyclopedia, specialized encyclopedia; 4. biographical dictionary, general encyclopedia, specialized encyclopedia)   Identifying reference materials in which specific information may be found

- *The call number of the book from which this selection was taken is J 920.*
1. Is the book fiction or nonfiction? How do you know?
2. What does the letter J in the call number mean?
(1. Nonfiction; you can tell by the fact that it has a call number. 2. The letter J means that the book can be found in the juvenile, or children's, section.) Using library catalogue cards

- *In which reference books would you find the following numbered items? Choose your answers from the list of reference sources below.*

  almanac   dictionary
  biographical dictionary   general encyclopedia
  encyclopedia of music and musicians
  1. the composer of the music for the Firebird ballet
  2. information about the Osage tribe
  3. information about Sergei Denham
  (1. encyclopedia of music and musicians; 2. general encyclopedia, dictionary, almanac; 3. biographical dictionary, encyclopedia of music and musicians)
  <u>Identifying reference materials in which specific information may be found</u>

 Use *Duplicating Masters 11*, page 28. See *Providing for Individual Differences*, page T204, for additional practice.

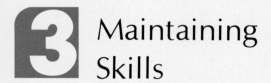 ## 3 Maintaining Skills

Comprehension Skills

Identifying time-order relationships   Read the following list of events and have students identify each event according to the period of Maria's life—*childhood, teen-age years, early twenties*—in which it occurred. Then have students list the events in the order in which they occurred. Allow them to check back to the selection if they need to.

> 1. Maria danced the *Firebird.* (early twenties)
> 2. Maria went to New York City and joined the Ballet Russe. (teen-age years)
> 3. Maria began to learn ballet. (childhood)
> 4. Maria joined the New York company called Ballet Society. (early twenties)
> 5. Maria married George Balanchine. (early twenties)
> (Correct order: 3, 2, 5, 4, 1)

 Use *Reading Skills Workbook*, Lesson 19, pages 64–66.

Identifying cause-and-effect relationships   Remind students that to find an effect, they should answer the question "What happened?" To find a cause, they should ask "Why did this happen?" Then refer students to the following paragraphs in the selection. Have them find the answers to the questions.

page 244, third paragraph: What made people begin to notice Maria? (she danced so well)

page 244, fourth paragraph: What caused Betty Marie to be so unhappy sometimes? (Many people in the company thought she was unfriendly, and some were jealous because she was doing so well. Betty Marie also missed her family.)

page 244, next-to-last paragraph: What word signals a cause-and-effect relationship in this paragraph? (so) What was the effect of Maria's being proud of her American Indian name? (She refused to change it.)

 Use *Reading Skills Workbook*, Word Play, page 67, for vocabulary review.

 For additional resources and curriculum-related activities, see *Enrichment*, page T205.

Textbook Study:
Learning to Use Sources of Information
Pages 248–251

Objectives

		SKILLS CODE NUMBER
M, T	To locate and use library catalogue cards	5.11.2
M, T	To identify and use reference materials in which specific information may be found	5.11

Applying the Skill

1. Before students read the textbook selections, you may wish to list the vocabulary words on the board and discuss them or have students look them up in the glossary.

   Language Arts Selection
   puffin: a sea bird of the North Atlantic Ocean

   Social Studies Selection
   equator: an imaginary line that circles the earth halfway between the North Pole and the South Pole

2. Have students read the introduction and the two selections. You may wish to have them read the selections on their own and then do *Building Skills*. Or you may wish to direct students, using the following procedure.

Using the Library to Learn More in Language Arts

1. Have students answer the question in the first sidenote. (You can find this book by looking in the card catalogue under the subject *Stamps*, the author *DePree, Mildred*, or the title *A Child's World of Stamps*. You would look under the letter *C* for the title.)

TEXTBOOK STUDY

Learning to Use Sources of Information

Sometimes you may need to learn more about something you have read in one of your textbooks. If your library skills are sharp, they can save you a lot of time as you gather information. While reading the first selection, think about what sources you could look in to find out more about the information in them. Use the sidenotes to help you.

Using the Library to Learn More in Language Arts

A Book to Read

How would you find this book in the library? Under what letter in the card catalogue would you look for the title?

TITLE: *A Child's World of Stamps*
AUTHOR: *Mildred DePree*
PUBLISHER: Parents' Magazine Press

Whether you are a stamp collector or not (yet), you can have fun on a "tour of the world" by way of the postage stamp. Along with bright, enlarged pictures of stamps, this book presents poems, stories, and interesting facts from all parts of the globe that make stamps come to life.

For example, with a stamp showing an African elephant, you will learn that one of these beasts eats over fifty kilograms of leaves and grass each day. You will see and learn about parrots from South America, pandas from China, and puffins from Scotland.

248

Some countries have issued stamps to honor certain folk heroes. A stamp from the Middle East shows Sinbad the Sailor being carried away by an enormous bird. What folk hero do you think the United States has placed on a stamp? Johnny Appleseed.

How can you find out what folk heroes are? What reference source would help you?

– Language for Daily Use: Purple
Harcourt Brace Jovanovich

Building Skills

1. What reference source might help you find out who Johnny Appleseed and Sinbad the Sailor are? Under what topic would you look to find the information on these folk heroes?
2. Which of the following three reference sources might you use to learn about the hobby of stamp collecting?

   a. a specialized encyclopedia of stamps
   b. an atlas
   c. a biographical dictionary

Using the Library to Learn More in Social Studies

There are no sidenotes for this selection. Read it and then answer the questions that follow.

The Air Above Us

Air is an ever-present resource in our natural **environment**. But people usually take it for granted.

249

What does air do? For one thing, it moves. When it moves, we call it wind, and we can feel it on our skin.

The sun's heat warms air and causes it to rise. Then cooler air rushes in to take its place. This happens at the equator. It also happens over large land areas. When the sun strikes dry

250

2. Have students read the selection and answer the questions in the second sidenote. (You can find out what a folk hero is by looking in a dictionary or encyclopedia.) Ask students under what subjects they might find information on *folk heroes*. (Folklore; Folktales; Literature)

3. Have students complete *Building Skills.*

Answers to *Building Skills* Language Arts Selection

1. An encyclopedia would help students find out who Johnny Appleseed and Sinbad are. You might look for Johnny Appleseed under the name *Appleseed, Johnny* or under the subjects *Folklore, United States; Folktales;* or *Literature, United States.* You might look for Sinbad under *Sinbad* or under *Folklore, Middle East.* **2.** a

Using the Library to Learn More in Social Studies

1. Before students read the selection, point out that there are no sidenotes.

land, the land becomes hotter than the surrounding water. Here, too, air rises. The movement of air, up and down and from place to place, brings changes in the weather.

Why does air move? Air has weight just like anything else. Warm air is lighter than cold air. It has low weight, or low air pressure. Cold air is heavier; it has high weight or high air pressure. Differences in temperature cause differences in the pressure or weight of air. These pressure differences make the wind blow and the weather change.

– The United States
Houghton Mifflin

Building Skills

1. What reference book would tell you what the word *environment* means and how to pronounce it?
2. Below is a list of topics you might find in a general encyclopedia. Which would give you a great deal of information about air? Which would give you some information about air? Which would give you very little or no information about air?

Air
Environment
Weather
United States History

251

Books About Expressions

Backyard Vacation: Outdoor Fun in Your Own Neighborhood by Ann Cole, Carolyn Haas, and Barbara Naftzger. Illustrated by Roland Rodegast. Little, 1980. Ideas for summer vacation activities are listed in this book.

Chinese and Japanese Crafts and Their Cultural Background by Jeremy Comins. Lothrop, 1978. Many photographs and drawings help tell the story of the beautiful crafts of two rich cultures.

American Indian Music and Musical Instruments by George S. Fitcher. McKay, 1978. You'll find out about the songs and instruments of many different Native American cultures.

What Can She Be? A Newscaster by Gloria Goldreich and Esther Goldreich. Lothrop, 1973. Barbara Lamont is a television newscaster. You'll find out how she and other television newspeople do their jobs.

The Story of Stevie Wonder by James Haskins. Lothrop, 1976. This is about Stevie Wonder's life and how he writes and performs his music.

I Can Cook Cookbook by Sophie Kay. Illustrated by Bill Sanders. Ideals, 1980. This collection of recipes is an easy introduction to cooking.

How to Be a Clown by Charles R. Meyer. McKay, 1977. Here is information about the history of clowning. You'll also find out how to do some of the things that today's circus clowns do to make people laugh.

252

2. Have students complete *Building Skills*.

Answers to *Building Skills*
Social Studies Selection

1. dictionary; **2.** great deal of information: *Air;* some information: *Environment* and *Weather;* little or no information: *United States History*

If students have not already read these books, you may wish to recommend them at this time. Bibliographic information about these and other books for students is given in the *Resource Center.*

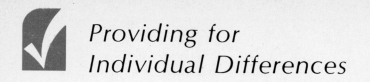

Providing for Individual Differences

Skills Lesson

Additional Practice

Worksheet 8, Teacher's Edition, page T487

Vocabulary Study

Additional Practice

■ **Determining meaning from context**   Write the words *meal* and *frame* on the board. Then read aloud each of the following sentences. Have students give the meaning of each word as it is used in the sentence.

> My favorite *meal* is lunch. (an eating time)
> The farmer gave the animals *meal* and water. (ground grain)
>
> I am in a pleasant *frame* of mind. (state)
> The legislators decided to *frame* a law to lower taxes. (make)
> One *frame* on the film was blurred. (one picture on a movie film)

Challenge Activity

■ **Determining meaning from context**   Write the words *flip, crown,* and *harbor* on the board. Then read each of the following sentences. Have students give the meaning of each word as it is used in the sentence.

> My mother didn't appreciate my *flip* answers. (impertinent; fresh)
> I love to drink hot apple *flip.* (a kind of drink)
>
> If I had half a *crown* a day, I'd surely spend it on you. (British money)
> The dentist put a *crown* on my broken tooth. (a cap for a tooth)
> At the *crown* of the mountain, it was hard to breathe. (mountaintop)
>
> The colonists had to *harbor* British soldiers in their homes. (house)
> I still *harbor* good feelings for the people who cared for me. (hold in mind)

Reading Selection: Life with the Li'l Folks

Additional Practice

■ **Using the library catalogue**   Write the following three lists of authors, titles, and subjects on the board. Have students identify the letter they would look under to find each in the card catalogue.

Authors	Titles
Maurice Sendak (S)	The First Book of Rocks and Minerals (F)
Robert Lawson (L)	A Time for Singing (T)
Sterling North (N)	Ben and Me (B)

Subjects
Explorers' Trips to the Antarctic (*E* for Explorers or *A* for Antarctic)
The Presidents of the United States (*P* for Presidents or *U* for United States Presidents)
How to Knit (*K* for Knitting)

Challenge Activity

Using the library catalogue (creating cards for classroom books)   Have students make author, subject, and title cards for books that are normally kept in your classroom. Have them use the sample cards on pages 225–227 as examples.

Reading Selection: Truly a Ballerina

Additional Practice

Using the library catalogue   Refer students to the lists of books to read on pages 94, 252, 372, and 500. Have them use the library card catalogue to identify which of the books their library has. Have them obtain any book of their choosing (not necessarily from these lists) to read on their own.

Evaluation

Periodic Test 2, Part IV, Form A or *Form B,* may be administered after this unit to test skills marked **T.** If you have pretested using *Form A,* administer *Form B.*

To posttest all the skills marked **T** in the four teaching units in "Expressions," Part 3, use *Periodic Test 2, Parts I–IV.*

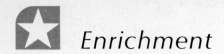

Enrichment

Life with the Li'l Folks

Bibliography

The following books are about comics and cartooning.

Average

Zaidenberg, Arthur. *How to Draw Cartoons: A Book for Beginners.* How to draw faces, bodies, clothes, and other things necessary for good cartoons.

Challenging

Cummings, Richard. *Make Your Own Comics for Fun and Profit.* Useful information on techniques, and examples of comic strips by young people.

Glubok, Shirley. *The Art of the Comic Strip.* A lively exploration of the development of this distinctively American art form from its beginnings to the present.

Horn, George F. *Cartooning.* A how-to book: facial features, shadings, shapes, and action poses.

Films and Filmstrips

NOTE: For more information, see *Resource Center.*

Skills

Harcourt Brace Jovanovich. *Bookmark Reading Filmstrips.* "What's What in the Library."

Guidance Assocs. "The Library: What's in It for You?" Use of the card catalogue, general and special dictionaries, indexes, and audiovisual resources.

Selection Content

Prentice-Hall Media. *Famous Artists at Work.* "Hank Ketcham": inside the studio of a cartoonist.

Curriculum Coordination

Language Arts

1. Arrange a trip to your local public library. Remind students to take their library cards with them. If students do not have library cards, arrange with the librarian to have them issued. Suggest to students that they get a book by Charles Schulz or Walt Disney or any of the books in the bibliography related to comics or cartoons.

2. Have students create a new character for the comic strip "Peanuts." They might write a composition describing the new character, the character's name, and his or her relationships with other characters in the comic strip.

3. Play "Descriptions." Write the names of about ten comic strip characters on the board. Have each student choose one character and list ten descriptive words (adjectives only) for the character. Allow volunteers to read aloud their lists. Other students should try to guess who the character is. Remind students not to use general or overworked descriptive words, but to try to use more lively words.

Social Studies

Editorial cartoons call attention to important current events or problems and encourage the reader to develop an opinion about a person or event in the news. Have students follow the editorial cartoons in a newspaper over a period of time. Can they identify the issues? What opinion does the newspaper have? Do they agree or disagree?

Art

Students can create their own comic strips. They might work in pairs, one student doing the drawings and the other, the lettering. Before drawing, students should discuss with each other the plot, the sequence of events to be shown, and what the characters will look like and say.

Truly a Ballerina

Bibliography

The following books are about either Maria Tallchief or the ballet.

Easy

Hamilton, David. *La Danse.* Pictures of young boy and girl dancers in class and at rest, and photo essays and portraits of some famous dancers.

Krementz, Jill. *A Very Young Dancer.* The training of a young girl who has a part in *The Nutcracker.*

Swope, Martha. *The Nutcracker: The Story of the New York City Ballet's Production.* An account of the story and how the production is presented.

Average

De Leeuw, Adele. *Maria Tallchief: American Ballerina.* The life story of Maria Tallchief, from her first ballet lessons to her life as a professional dancer.

Challenging

Gridley, Marion E. *Maria Tallchief*. A biography of Tall-chief and the history of the Osage tribe.

Jessel, Camilla. *Life at the Royal Ballet School*. Brief text and over 300 photographs explore the training and life of boys and girls at the Royal Ballet School (England).

Films and Filmstrips

NOTE: For more information, see *Resource Center*.

Skills

Harcourt Brace Jovanovich. *Bookmark Reading Filmstrips*. "What's What in the Library."

Guidance Assocs. "The Library: What's in It for You?" Use of the card catalogue, general and special dictionaries, indexes, and audiovisual resources.

Selection content

International Arts, Inc. *Don Quixote*. Excerpted from feature-length version and danced by Rudolf Nureyev and Lucette Aldous of the Royal Ballet.

Prentice-Hall Media. *Music Stories*. Appropriate: "The Firebird."

Prentice-Hall Media. *The Ballet*. History, training, and final performance.

Curriculum Coordination

Language Arts

1. Many ballets are based on folktales or fairy tales or children's stories, such as "Sleeping Beauty" and "Peter and the Wolf." Students may enjoy reading the original stories and suggesting others that they think would make good ballets.

2. Students might write a story about a dancer in one of Degas' paintings.

Social Studies

Students who wish to learn about American Indians and their contributions to our nation's heritage should explore library books and reference sources.

Art

Students might enjoy designing a set and costumes for a ballet.

Music

You might play the music from a famous ballet for the class after or while you tell the story behind it. Suggested ballets: *Firebird*, *West Side Story*, *Coppelia*, and *Rodeo*. (See *Resource Center*.)

Career Education

Invite a dancer or a dance teacher to talk about the dancing profession.

Part 4
The Poet's Way

RESOURCE CENTER

Enrichment Materials and Activities

The Whales Off Wales
Autumn Leaves
Glory, Glory . . .
Check
Comma in the Sky
I Go Forth to Move About the Earth
Pages 258–264

Enrichment Materials:
Records or tapes providing a variety of music
A tape recorder
Drawing paper and crayons or paint

On Our Bikes
Open Range
Skiing
Foul Shot
Pages 265–270

Enrichment Materials:
A tape recorder
A camera

The Snopp on the Sidewalk
The Dream Woman
Nancy Hanks
Pages 271–277

Enrichment Materials:
Drawing paper
Crayons or paints

Activity Needing Advance Planning:
A class Poetry Day

Guest Speaker:
A poet

Bibliography

For Students

NOTE: For more information about these books, see the *Enrichment* section at the end of the Teaching Unit.

Abercrombie, Barbara, ed. *The Other Side of a Poem.* Harper & Row, 1977.

Adoff, Arnold. *Eats.* Lothrop, 1979.

Baron, Virginia Olsen, ed. *Sunset in a Spider Web: Sijo Poetry of Ancient Korea.* Holt, Rinehart & Winston, 1974.

Benét, Stephen Vincent, and Rosemary Benét. *A Book of Americans.* Holt, Rinehart & Winston, 1933.

Caudill, Rebecca. *Wind, Sand, and Sky.* Dutton, 1976.

Cole, William, ed. *The Sea, Ships and Sailors.* Viking Press, 1967.

Fisher, Aileen. *Cricket in a Thicket.* Scribner, 1963.

_____. *In the Woods, In the Meadow, In the Sky.* Scribner, 1965.

Frost, Robert. *You Come Too: Favorite Poems for Young Readers.* Holt, Rinehart & Winston, 1959.

Hubbell, Patricia. *Catch Me a Wind.* Atheneum, 1968.

Jones, Hettie, ed. *The Trees Stand Shining: Poetry of the North American Indians.* Dial, 1971.

Kennedy, X. J. *The Phantom Ice Cream Man.* Atheneum, 1979.

Kherdian, David, ed. *If Dragon Flies Made Honey.* Morrow, 1977.

_____. *The Dog Writes on the Window with His Nose and Other Poems.* Four Winds, Schol. Bk. Service, 1977.

_____. *Poems Here and Now.* Viking Press, 1976.

Lewis, Richard, ed. *The Moment of Wonder: A Collection of Chinese and Japanese Poetry.* Dial, 1964.

Merriam, Eve. *Catch a Little Rhyme.* Atheneum, 1966.

_____. *Finding a Poem.* Atheneum, 1970.

Moore, Lilian, ed. *Go with the Poem.* McGraw, 1979.

_____. *See My Lovely Poison Ivy, and Other Verses About Witches, Ghosts, and Things.* Atheneum, 1976.

Morrison, Lillian. *The Sidewalk Racer and Other Poems of Sport and Motion.* Lothrop, 1977.

O'Neil, Mary. *Winds.* Doubleday, 1971.

_____. *Words, Words, Words.* Doubleday, 1966.

Plotz, Helen, ed. *As I Walked Out One Evening.* Morrow, 1976.

Prelutsky, Jack. *Nightmares: Poems to Trouble Your Sleep.* Morrow, 1976.

_____. *The Queen of Eene.* Morrow, 1978.

_____. *The Snopp on the Sidewalk and Other Poems.* Morrow, 1977.

Rasmussen, Knud, ed. *Beyond the High Hills: A Book of Eskimo Poems.* Collins-World, 1961.

For Teachers

NOTE: For more information about these books, see the *Background* section that precedes each group of poems.

Huck, Charlotte S. *Children's Literature in the Elementary School.* Holt, Rinehart & Winston, 1976.

Koch, Kenneth. *Rose, Where Did You Get That Red? Teaching Great Poetry to Children.* Random, 1973.

_____. *Wishes, Lies, and Dreams: Teaching Children to Write Poetry.* Chelsea House, 1970.

Larrick, Nancy, ed. *Somebody Turned On a Tap in These Kids: Poetry and Young People Today.* Delta, 1972.

Sebesta, Sam L., and William J. Iverson. *Literature for Thursday's Child.* Science Research, 1975.

Sutherland, Zena, and May Hill Arbuthnot. *Children and Books,* 6th ed. Scott, Foresman, 1981.

Films and Filmstrips

Caedmon Records. *What Is Poetry?* Ten filmstrips, ten records, teacher's guide, duplicating masters (#CFS 501).

Eye-Gate House. *Enjoying Poetry.* Four filmstrips with record (#DF 179) or cassette (#TF 179).

Miller-Brody Productions. *Learning About Poetry—Imagery and Figurative Language.* Filmstrip (#D1329).

NBC-TV. *Hailstones and Halibut Bones I.* A six-minute 16mm film; *Hailstones and Halibut Bones II.* A six-minute 16mm film. Order by title.

Pied Piper. *Descriptive Words.* Filmstrip. Order by title.

Records and/or Tapes

NOTE: Recordings may also be available on other labels.

"An Anthology of Negro Poetry for Young People" (Folkways Records FC 7114)

"Catch a Little Rhyme: Poems for Activity Time" (Caedmon Records TC 1339; cassette CDL 51339)

"Classics of American Poetry for the Elementary Curriculum" (Caedmon Records TC 2041; cassette CDL 52041)

"Poems and Songs of Middle Earth" (Caedmon Records TC 1231; cassette CDL 51231)

OVERVIEW

Part 4
The Poet's Way

The skills focus of "The Poet's Way" is on understanding imagery and comparison in poetry. The first group of poems highlights sensory imagery. Students are asked to identify the sense to which a specific image appeals. The second group contains poems about activities people enjoy, such as biking, camping, and watching a basketball game. Students are asked to recognize specific types of comparison: similes, metaphors, and personification. The third group contains narrative poems about three imaginary characters: a "snopp," a dream woman, and a spirit. Students are asked to identify sensory images and forms of poetic comparison.

Previewing "The Poet's Way"

Have students examine the title and the photograph on page 253. Ask students to describe the photograph and tell how it relates to the title. (The title and the photograph suggest journeys, traveling, or ways of getting from place to place.)

Ask students to imagine that they are walking in the scene pictured in the photograph. Ask them to use sensory words to describe what they see, hear, feel, smell, and taste along the way.

Have students look at the illustrations in the rest of Part 4, from page 254 to page 276. As they do so, ask them to think about what the illustrations remind them of and to what they might compare the various pictures. Then explain that in Part 4 they will learn several ways in which poets make comparisons that help readers see, hear, feel, smell, and taste.

Objectives

The following list of objectives is provided to help you plan your teaching of "The Poet's Way." All the objectives listed under *Introduced* are for skills presented in the student's text in *Understanding and Appreciating Literature.* Objectives listed under *Maintained* are for skills previously taught in the HBJ BOOKMARK READING PROGRAM, EAGLE EDITION and reinforced either in the *Understanding and Appreciating Literature* section in the

student's text or in the *Reading and Discussing* sections in this Teacher's Edition. Since the emphasis in these lessons is on appreciating literature, the literature skills introduced and maintained in Teaching Unit 10 are not tested.

The symbols I*, I, and M are used throughout this Teacher's Edition. The symbol I* indicates skills introduced for the first time in the program. The I indicates skills introduced earlier in Level 11. The M indicates skills taught at earlier levels and maintained in Level 11. The italicized numbers following the objectives are part of a code developed by the HBJ School Department to facilitate the correlation of skills within and between programs. See page T499 for more information.

Introduced

These skills are introduced for the first time at Level 11 in the HBJ BOOKMARK READING PROGRAM, EAGLE EDITION.

	SKILLS CODE NUMBER
To identify simile	6.6.6.4
To identify metaphor	6.6.6.5
To identify personification	6.6.6.8

Maintained

These skills were previously taught at earlier levels in the HBJ BOOKMARK READING PROGRAM, EAGLE EDITION.

	SKILLS CODE NUMBER
To recognize sensory imagery in poetry	6.6.6.3
To recognize lyric poetry	6.2.2
To recognize narrative poetry	6.2.3
To recognize rhyme as an element of poetry	6.6.1
To recognize stanzas in poetry	6.6.2

Contents

Additional Materials

Reading Skills Workbook: Lesson 20, pages 68–70; Word Play, page 71
Duplicating Masters 11: pages 29–31

Key to Symbols

Skills Objectives
I* — Introduced in this unit
I   — Introduced earlier in this level
M   — Maintained from previous levels

Reduced Student Pages
<u>underscore</u> — words that appear in the glossary
wavy line   — words pretaught in the Teacher's Edition
~~~~~~   (these words also appear in the glossary)

Understanding and Appreciating Literature:
Imagery and Comparisons in Poetry
Pages 254–257

Objectives

		SKILLS CODE NUMBER
M	To recognize sensory imagery in poetry	6.6.6.3
I*	To identify simile	6.6.6.4
I*	To identify metaphor	6.6.6.5
I*	To identify personification	6.6.6.8

Introducing the Lesson

1. Ask students to name their five senses. (sight, hearing, touch, smell, and taste) Explain to students that we use each of our five senses to take in information about our world.

2. Ask students to be aware of their surroundings in the classroom and to take an inventory of what each of their five senses is telling them. Then ask students to tell what they see, hear, feel, and smell. Explain that poets often use words and images that appeal to the senses; that is, poets write words and phrases to help their readers imagine that they see, hear, feel, smell, and taste the things the poet is writing about.

3. Write the following short rhyme on the board:

Shiny new roller skates
Flash in the sun,
Buzz-click down the sidewalk.
Spring has begun.

Tell students that this poem contains words and phrases that appeal to two senses. Ask students to identify the two senses and the words in the poem that appeal to each sense. (The two senses are sight and hearing. The words *shiny, new,* and *flash* are visual—they appeal to the sense of sight; the words *buzz* and *click* appeal to the sense of hearing.)

4. Have students look at the poem and cartoon at the top of page 254. Tell them to look at the illustration and listen as you read aloud "Oliphaunt."

5. Ask students what they think Oliphaunt looks like. (an elephant) Ask them to describe an elephant. (Students might describe it as a big, gray animal with a long trunk.) Ask students which sense the poet appeals to in the first three lines. (the sense of sight)

6. Provide time for students to read "Oliphaunt" silently, and then ask for volunteers to read the poem aloud.

Developing the Skill

A. *Poets often use sensory imagery to help readers imagine what they are describing.*

1. Have students read the first two paragraphs beginning on page 254 and ending on page 255. Ask students which word in the poem appeals to their sense of touch. (shake) Ask which word appeals to their sense of hearing. (crack)

UNDERSTANDING AND APPRECIATING LITERATURE

Imagery and Comparisons in Poetry

from
OLIPHAUNT

by J. R. R. TOLKIEN

Grey as a mouse,
Big as a house,
Nose like a snake,
I make the earth shake,
As I tramp through the grass;
Trees crack as I pass.

Authors often use **imagery**—words that appeal to one or more of your senses—to help you imagine and understand more clearly the things they are describing.

Understanding Imagery and Comparisons in Poetry

Read the poem in the cartoon. How does the poet describe Oliphaunt? How does imagery help in the poet's description? The poet uses imagery that helps you *see, hear,* and *feel* an elephant-like animal walking through the jungle. Which word appeals to your sense of touch? Which word appeals

254

to your sense of hearing? You would feel the earth *shake* beneath your feet and hear the trees *cracking* if you were in the jungle with Oliphaunt. How does J. R. R. Tolkien describe Oliphaunt? He tells you that it is "grey as a mouse," and "big as a house," and that it has a "nose like a snake."

The imagery that describes Oliphaunt is based on **comparisons**. How is Oliphaunt like a mouse? They are the same color, gray. How is Oliphaunt like a house? They are both about the same size—big. How is Oliphaunt's nose like a snake? They are shaped the same.

Similes and **metaphors** are two kinds of comparisons. Similes use the word *like* or *as* in their comparisons. Metaphors use just the word *is* or another form of the verb *to be* to link the two things that are being compared.

Read the following sentences. Which ones contain similes? Which contain metaphors?

1. The fresh carrot tasted as sweet as honey.
2. The moon was a silver balloon.
3. The wind is a galloping pony.

Sentence 1 uses a simile. Sentences 2 and 3 use metaphors.

What two things are compared in each sentence? Sentence 1 compares a carrot and honey. Which of your senses does this comparison appeal to? Carrots and honey both *taste* sweet. Sentence 2 compares the moon to a silver balloon. What does this comparison appeal to? This comparison appeals to your *sight*. A full moon may have the same color and shape that a silver balloon does. Sentence 3 compares the wind to a galloping pony. What sense does this comparison appeal to? This comparison appeals to two of your senses. The wind can move so quickly that it *feels* like a pony rushing by. The wind can also *sound* like a pony galloping by. Sometimes comparisons, as well as other kinds of imagery, can appeal to more than one of your senses at the same time.

255

Personification is another kind of comparison. When authors use personification, they describe an object or animal by giving it human characteristics or qualities. Look for personification in this poem about the seasons.

Pencil and Paint

by ELEANOR FARJEON

Winter has a pencil
For pictures clear and neat,
She traces the black tree-tops
Upon a snowy sheet,

But autumn has a palette
And a painting-brush instead,
And daubs the leaves for pleasure
With yellow, brown, and red.

What two things are given human qualities in "Pencil and Paint"? The poet describes winter and autumn as if they were two artists at work. Which of your senses does the imagery in this poem appeal to? This poem uses color words to appeal to your sense of sight. What colors do you see in winter? What colors do you see in autumn? The colors of winter are described as the *black* of the trees and the *white* of the snowy ground and sky. The colors of autumn are described as *yellow*, *brown*, and *red*.

Authors use imagery, or special comparisons, to create descriptions that appeal to your senses. Three kinds of imagery are *simile*, *metaphor*, and *personification*. Remember, a *simile* compares one thing to another by using the word *as* or *like* to link the two things being compared. A *metaphor* compares one thing to another by using the verb *is* or another form of the verb *to be*. A metaphor does not use *as* or *like* in stating a comparison. *Personification* helps you see something in a new way by giving it human characteristics.

You can use similes, metaphors, and personification as tools to help you more fully understand and enjoy literature and the world around you.

256

---

2. Have students read the first full paragraph on page 255. Ask them what Oliphaunt is compared to. (a mouse, a house, and a snake) Ask how Oliphaunt is similar to those things. (It is gray, like a mouse; it is big, like a house; its nose is shaped like a snake.)

B. *Similes and metaphors are forms of comparison.*

1. Ask students to read the second paragraph on page 255. Then have them identify the three similes in "Oliphaunt." (Grey as a mouse; Big as a house; Nose like a snake) Be sure to point out that the words *as* and *like* signal a simile.

2. Ask students to read the third paragraph on page 255 and the example sentences. Ask them whether the examples are similes or metaphors and how they know. (1. simile, uses the word *as*; 2. metaphor, uses a form of the verb *to be*; 3. metaphor, uses a form of the verb *to be*)

3. Have students read the last paragraph on page 255. Explain that if they wish to identify what is being compared in a simile or metaphor, they should look for two things that are alike in some way. For example, ask students: "How is the moon like a silver balloon?" When they think of how the two things are alike, they will understand the comparison the poet is making.

C. *Personification is a form of comparison.*

1. Write the word *personification* on the board. Tell students that in this word there is a shorter word that is a clue to the word's meaning. Ask students if they can find this shorter, familiar word in *personification*. (person)

2. Explain that when poets use personification, they compare an object, an animal, or a force of nature to a person by giving it human qualities or actions.

3. Have students read the first paragraph on page 256.

4. Ask students to listen as you read aloud "Pencil and Paint" (page 256). Then have students silently read the poem and the paragraph that follows it.

5. Ask students to tell what two things in the poem have a human ability. (winter and autumn) Ask what this human ability is. (Winter and autumn are described as if they were able to create, like artists.)

6. Ask students which words and phrases personify winter and autumn. (Winter has a pencil and is referred to as *she*; the poet says this season *traces* the black tree-tops. Autumn has a palette and painting-brush and *daubs* leaves with color. Using a pencil and paintbrush are human activities. Similarly, tracing and daubing paint are also done by people.)

D. *Authors use similes, metaphors, and personification to make comparisons.*

1. Ask students to read the final two paragraphs on page 256. At this time, you may wish to review what the five senses are and how to identify simile, metaphor, and personification.

2. Explain to students that discovering examples of imagery and comparison in poems adds to the fun and excitement of reading them. You might compare the ability to find examples of simile, metaphor, and personification to the ability to break a code: the more of a code one knows, the easier it is to read and understand a coded message. Similarly, the more imagery one understands, the easier it is to read and appreciate a poem.

Try This

Have students complete *Try This*.

Answers to *Try This*

1. a dragon; a metaphor; 2. *roars;* 3. sight; 4. touch; *trembles*

Writing

(Optional) Have students complete one or both of the *Writing* activities.

1. Tell students to list or outline their ideas before they begin writing. For *Writing* activity 1, tell students to select an object to personify. Have students answer the following questions: How might the object (a) look like a person? (b) sound like a person? (c) act like a person? You may wish to write the following titles on the board to help students get started.

The Wind's Temper
The Happy Dinosaur
The Car That Had a Cold

For *Writing* activity 2, tell students to imagine that they are riding in one of the vehicles mentioned. Tell them to think about how they'd be using their senses by asking themselves, "What do I see? hear? smell? taste? touch?" You may wish to write the following incomplete sentences on the chalkboard to help students get started.

The bus ride felt as bumpy as _____.
The plane looked like a _____.

2. Encourage students to share their finished work with the class.

 Use *Reading Skills Workbook,* Lesson 20, pages 68–70.

Reading Selections:

The Whales Off Wales
Autumn Leaves
Glory, Glory . . .
Check
Comma in the Sky
I Go Forth to Move
About the Earth

Pages 258–264

Objectives

		SKILLS CODE NUMBER
M	To recognize sensory imagery in poetry	6.6.6.3
I*	To identify metaphor	6.6.6.5
I*	To identify simile	6.6.6.4
I*	To identify personification	6.6.6.8

Preparing to Read

Summary

In this group, X. J. Kennedy's "The Whales Off Wales" is nonsensical; Eve Merriam's "Autumn Leaves" is a lyric poem; and Ray Patterson's "Glory, Glory . . ." is a three-line metaphor. Night is personified in "Check" by James Stephens; Aileen Fisher's "Comma in the Sky" compares the moon in different phases to punctuation marks; and "I Go Forth to Move About the Earth" by Alonzo Lopez may remind readers of an ancient chant.

Background

Eve Merriam writes many types of poems. In *Finding a Poem*, she takes the reader step by step through the process of composing a poem. X. J. Kennedy is known for his nonsense verse, which includes the collection titled *The Phantom Ice Cream Man*. Aileen Fisher is a particularly keen observer of nature and has many poetry collections to her credit, including *In the Woods*, *In the Meadow*, *In the Sky*, and *Cricket in a Thicket*.

The following books will provide you with additional background information on teaching poetry to children.

Huck, Charlotte S. *Children's Literature in the Elementary School*. An invaluable source book with many teaching suggestions.

Koch, Kenneth. *Rose, Where Did You Get That Red? Teaching Great Poetry to Children*. Starting with classic poetry, Kenneth Koch demonstrates how he teaches children to appreciate and write poetry.

_____. *Wishes, Lies, and Dreams: Teaching Children to Write Poetry*. A creative approach to poetry writing.

Developing Vocabulary and Concepts

walloping: hitting or beating; large, impressive

1. Read the following sentence aloud or write it on the board. If you read it aloud, write the underlined vocabulary on the board.

    The girl hit the ball with a <u>walloping</u> sound.

2. Ask students to give the meaning of *walloping*. Remind them to use context clues in the sentence to help them.

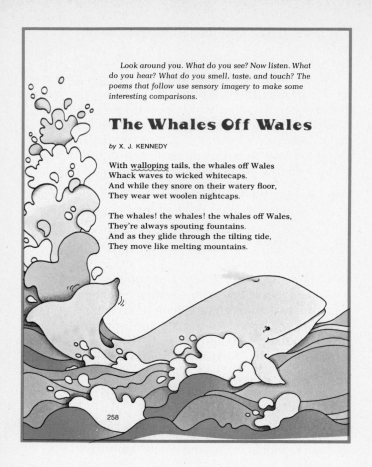

Look around you. What do you see? Now listen. What do you hear? What do you smell, taste, and touch? The poems that follow use sensory imagery to make some interesting comparisons.

The Whales Off Wales

by X. J. KENNEDY

With walloping tails, the whales off Wales
Whack waves to wicked whitecaps.
And while they snore on their watery floor,
They wear wet woolen nightcaps.

The whales! the whales! the whales off Wales,
They're always spouting fountains.
And as they glide through the tilting tide,
They move like melting mountains.

258

Autumn Leaves

by EVE MERRIAM

Down
   down
      down
Red
   yellow
      brown
Autumn leaves tumble down
Autumn leaves crumble down
Autumn leaves bumble down
Flaking and shaking,
Tumbledown leaves.

Skittery
Flittery
Rustle by
Hustle by
Crackle and crunch
In a snappety bunch.

Run and catch
Run and snatch
Butterfly leaves
Sailboat leaves
Windstorm leaves.
Can you catch them?

Swoop,
Scoop,
Pile them up
In a stompy pile and
Jump
  Jump
    JUMP!

Setting Purposes

Skills

Have students read the note at the top of page 258. As students read the poems in this section, ask them to be aware of sensory images that the various poets have used in their poems. If possible, complete the silent reading of these poems in two sessions, breaking before "Check" on page 261.

Content

Ask students to look for comparisons in the poems they are going to read. Remind them that sometimes either *like* or *as* is used to compare two things, while at other times the poet simply states that one thing is another. Still another kind of comparison gives human characteristics to animals or objects.

 Reading and Discussing

Use the following procedure to read aloud and discuss briefly some of the poems with students. It would be best to read half the poems and save half for another class period so that students can more easily absorb the new poems.

NOTE: The questions that appear in the student's text at the end of the selections focus on comprehension of poetry content and on sensory imagery in poetry. Answers to these questions begin on page T218.

1. **a.** Ask students to listen as you read aloud "The Whales Off Wales" (page 258).

   b. Then ask students to describe what they imagined as they listened. (Answers may include: whales whipping waves to whitecaps with their tails; whales in woolen nightcaps snoring away; whales spouting water like fountains; whales gliding like mountains.)

   c. Read the poem again, and ask students to listen for words that begin with the same sound. Have them identify the initial consonant sounds that are repeated over and over in the poem. (Example: /w/ as in *Wales* and /hw/ as in *whales*) Tell students that this repetition of sounds is called alliteration.

2. **a.** Ask students to think about autumn. Then ask them to name some things that they see, hear, feel, taste, and smell in autumn. (Accept all reasonable answers.)

   b. Now read aloud "Autumn Leaves" on page 259.

Glory, Glory . . .

by RAY PATTERSON

Across Grandmother's knees
A kindly sun
Laid a yellow quilt.

Check

by JAMES STEPHENS

The Night was creeping on the ground!
She crept and did not make a sound,

Until she reached the tree: And then
She covered it, and stole again

Along the grass beside the wall!
—I heard the rustling of her shawl

As she threw blackness everywhere
Along the sky, the ground, the air,

And in the room where I was hid!
But, no matter what she did

To everything that was without,
She could not put my candle out!

So I stared at the Night! And she
Stared back solemnly at me!

261

Comma
in the Sky

by AILEEN FISHER

A comma hung above the park,
a shiny punctuation mark;
we saw it curving in the dark
the night the moon was new.

A period hung above the bay,
immense though it was far away;
we saw it at the end of day
the night the moon was full.

262

3. Ask students to listen as you read aloud "Glory,
   Glory . . ." (page 260).

4. **a.** Write the following sentences on the board:

   I was about to lose my temper, but I was able to
   check myself in time.
   My chess opponent called "Check!" when she
   moved her queen across from my king.

   Ask students to use the context of the first sentence
   to discover the meaning of the word *check*. (to
   bring to a stop; to halt; to hold back) Ask a student
   who plays chess to explain the meaning of *check* in
   the second sentence.

   b. Now ask students to listen as you read the poem
   "Check" (page 261). Ask them to suggest why it has
   this title. (Students may suggest that with the light of
   the candle, the person holds back, or checks, the
   night; or that the poem represents a chess match in
   which one of the players is held in check by the
   other.)

5. **a.** Tell students that the title of the next poem they
   are going to hear is "Comma in the Sky" (page 262).
   Ask them what this title brings to mind. (Students
   may suggest the moon at crescent phase; others
   may suggest the pattern of a constellation; still
   others may say a shooting star.)

   b. Ask students to listen as you read "Comma in the
   Sky." Then ask them what the comma is. (a new
   moon)

I Go Forth to Move About the Earth

by ALONZO LOPEZ

I go forth to move about the earth.
I go forth as the owl, wise and knowing.
I go forth as the eagle, powerful and bold.
I go forth as the dove, peaceful and gentle.
I go forth to move about the earth
　　in wisdom, courage, and peace.

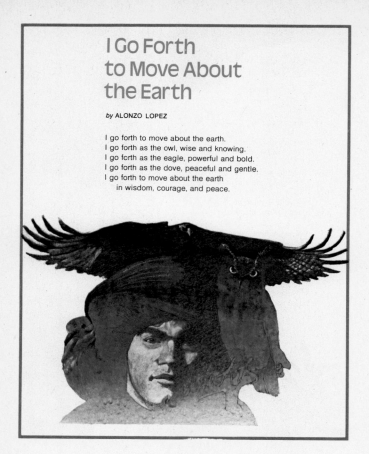

Understanding What You've Read

1. Find at least one example of personification in the first stanza of "The Whales Off Wales" (page 258). What simile is used in the second stanza?
2. Which stanza of "Autumn Leaves" (page 259) uses imagery that appeals mostly to your sense of hearing? Find at least three words in this stanza that tell you how autumn leaves sound.
3. In "Comma in the Sky" (page 262), what two things does the poet compare the moon to? What do these comparisons tell you about the moon?

Writing

1. "Glory, Glory . . ." (page 260) compares sunlight to a yellow quilt. Write a sentence that uses another metaphor for sunlight.
2. "The Whales Off Wales" (page 258) is a funny poem because of the imagery and because of the poet's use of personification. The poet gives the whales human characteristics: they snore and they wear woolen nightcaps. Write your own paragraph or poem about an animal. Use at least one simile and one example of personification. You may wish to write about one of the following animals:

A seal giving itself a bubble bath
A monkey chatting with a friend

264

6. Ask students to listen as you read "I Go Forth to Move About the Earth" (page 263). After they have heard the poem, ask who they think the narrator is and what he or she is saying. (It is not made clear in the poem who the narrator actually is. It could be the sun, the poet or another human being, a good spirit, or the spirit of nature.)

7. Have students read the poems silently and discuss them in small groups. Encourage students to read these poems aloud after discussing them.

Questions preceded by a bullet are additional questions and appear in the Teacher's Edition only. The other questions appear in the student's text after this group of poems.

Understanding What You've Read

1. *Find at least one example of personification in the first stanza of "The Whales Off Wales" (page 258). What simile is used in the second stanza?* (There are two examples of personification in the first stanza: whales snoring and whales in woolen nightcaps. In the second stanza, the line "They move like melting mountains" is a simile.) CRITICAL　Identifying personification and simile

- *In the first stanza of "The Whales Off Wales," what word rhymes with whitecaps? In the second stanza, what word rhymes with fountains?* (Nightcaps rhymes with whitecaps in the first stanza, and mountains rhymes with fountains in the second.　page 258) LITERAL　Recognizing rhyme in poetry

2. *Which stanza of "Autumn Leaves" (page 259) uses imagery that appeals mostly to your sense of hearing? Find at least three words in this stanza that tell you how autumn leaves sound.* (Accept all reasonable answers. The second stanza has words that appeal to the sense of hearing. Some words are *rustle, crackle, crunch,* and *snappety.*) CRITICAL　Recognizing sensory imagery in poetry

- *In the third stanza of "Autumn Leaves," the poet compares leaves to two other things. What are they?* (a butterfly and a sailboat　page 259) CRITICAL　Identifying metaphor

- *In what ways are falling leaves like the butterfly and a sailboat mentioned in stanza three?* (Accept all reasonable answers. A leaf might look like a butterfly as it flutters to the ground; a falling leaf might be caught by the wind as a sail on a sailboat is.　page 259) CRITICAL　Making judgments

- *How do you think Eve Merriam feels about autumn?* (Accept all reasonable answers. Students should recognize the happy, playful attitude expressed in the poem and should be able to point out words like *tumble, bumble, skittery,* and *flittery* that speak of that enjoyment.   page 259) CRITICAL   Interpreting a poet's feelings

- *In "Glory, Glory . . ." (page 260), what is personified? What action does the poet say this object performs that might be a human action?* (The sun is personified. It lays a quilt across Grandmother's knees.) CRITICAL   Identifying personification

- *In the poem "Check" (page 261), what is personified? What actions does it perform that a human might perform?* (Night. The poem says Night "was creeping on the ground," "stole again along the grass," wore a shawl, and stared at the person.) CRITICAL   Identifying personification

3. *In "Comma in the Sky" (page 262), what two things does the poet compare the moon to? What do these comparisons tell you about the moon?* (The poet compares the moon to a comma and a period. They tell about two shapes of the moon—the new moon is like a comma, and the full moon like a period.) CRITICAL   Identifying metaphor

- *In the poem "I Go Forth to Move About the Earth" (page 263), what does the I in the poem say that it goes forth as? What kind of comparison is this? How can you tell?* (The I in the poem says that it goes forth as the owl, as the eagle, and as the dove. These comparisons are similes. A student should be able to recognize these as similes by the use of the word as.) CRITICAL   Identifying simile

Writing

(Optional) Have students complete one or both of the *Writing* activities on page 264. Or ask students to do one or more of the writing activities under *Additional Writing Activity.*

1. *"Glory, Glory . . ." (page 260) compares sunlight to a yellow quilt. Write a sentence that uses another metaphor for sunlight.*   Writing a metaphor

Tell students to think of metaphors for sunlight. Have them think of individual words that answer these questions: How does sunlight look? How does it feel? Have them think of situations where they might encounter sunlight. For example, explain that the quality of sunlight on a beach is different from the quality of sunlight in a forest, where sunlight is dappled on the ground because the leaves and branches are casting shadows.

2. *"The Whales Off Wales" (page 258) is a funny poem because of the imagery and because of the poet's use of personification. The poet gives the whales human characteristics: they snore and they wear woolen nightcaps. Write your own paragraph or poem about an animal. Use at least one simile and one example of personification. You may wish to write about one of the following animals: A seal giving itself a bubble bath A monkey chatting with a friend* Writing a poem using personification

You may wish to help students start a poem using personification by writing the following opening lines on the chalkboard:

The happy parrots of Paris
Marched in a parrot parade . . .

You may wish to help students think of words that rhyme with *parade (lemonade, paid, trade).* You may wish to help students think of other human characteristics they might give the parrots. Write their suggestions on the board and form them into a short poem.

Additional Writing Activity (Optional)

- *Think of your favorite season. Write a short lyric poem showing your feelings about this season.* Writing a poem using sensory imagery

You might want to write a lyric poem with the entire class. If students need additional help with the *Writing* activity, you may wish to write the name of a season on the chalkboard. Have students suggest things they see, hear, feel, smell, and taste during that particular season. Form these sensory images into a short poem.

- *Choose one of the following items to personify in a short poem: a pair of roller skates   spring   a tree stars in the sky   porpoises* Writing a poem using personification

Tell students to think of ways in which each item could be compared to a person. For example, stars in the sky could be said to wink and blink, which is an action people do with their eyes.

- *Night suggests many things to many people. Write a poem about night. You may wish to use sensory images, similes, metaphors, or personification to help readers understand just how you feel about night.* Writing a poem using sensory imagery

Tell students to reread "Check" (page 261). Ask them how the narrator feels about night. Have students compare these feelings to their own.

⭐ For additional resources and curriculum-related activities, see *Enrichment,* page T231.

Reading Selections:

On Our Bikes
Open Range
Skiing
Foul Shot

Pages 265–270

Objectives

		SKILLS CODE NUMBER
M	To recognize lyric poetry	6.2.2
I*	To identify personification	6.6.6.8
I*	To identify simile	6.6.6.4
M	To recognize rhyme and stanzas in poetry	6.6.1; 6.6.2

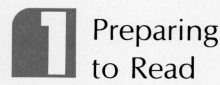 # Preparing to Read

Summary

This group presents four poems about exciting, enjoyable activities. "On Our Bikes" by Lillian Morrison explores the exuberance of a bike ride to the beach. "Open Range" by Kathryn and Byron Jackson describes the freshness and wonder of camping by an open fire. Rose Burgunder's "Skiing" tells of an early-morning run down a slope. "Foul Shot" by Edwin A. Hoey dramatizes the suspense and excitement of a basketball game.

Background

Lillian Morrison writes poems about sports and other fast-paced activities that people don't usually think of as topics for poems. In a collection of her poems, *The Sidewalk Racer and Other Poems of Sport and Motion,* she shows how erroneous this attitude can be.

The following book provides additional background information on teaching poetry to children.

Larrick, Nancy, ed. *Somebody Turned On a Tap in These Kids: Poetry and Young People Today.* A collection of essays on teaching children to appreciate and write poetry.

Developing Vocabulary and Concepts

soothes: calms; softens or relieves
exasperates: annoys almost to the point of anger
coy: shy; pretending to be shy in order to flirt

1. Read the following sentences aloud or write them on the board. If you read them aloud, write the underlined vocabulary on the board.

   Breathing deeply often calms and <u>soothes</u> me when I am excited or nervous.
   His constant talking in class <u>exasperates</u> other students who are trying to listen to the teacher.
   Since she was an outgoing person, she was never <u>coy</u>, or shy, when she met a new person.

2. Ask students to give the meaning of each vocabulary word. Remind them to use context clues in the sentences to help them.

 Use *Duplicating Masters 11,* page 29.

Setting Purposes

Skills

Have students read the note at the top of page 265. Remind students that similes, metaphors, and personification are comparisons used by poets. You may wish to review the way to identify each type of comparison at this time. Ask students to look for examples of each kind of comparison as they read the poems in the following section.

Content

Remind students that poets use sensory imagery and comparison to say something special about their topics. Ask students to be aware of the unique way in which each poet uses imagery and comparison in each poem.

 # Reading and Discussing

Use the following procedure to read aloud and discuss briefly some of the poems with students.

NOTE: The questions that appear in the student's text at the end of the selections focus on comprehension of poetry content and on sensory imagery in poetry. Answers to these questions begin on page T223.

The following poems are all about things people like to do. You will see how poets use similes, metaphors, and personification to help you feel what it is like to take a bike ride, camp out under the stars, ski down a hill, and watch an exciting basketball game.

On Our Bikes

by LILLIAN MORRISON

The roads to the beach
                  are winding
we glide down
                  breeze-whipped
curving
                past hills of sand
pedal and coast
          through wide smell of the sea
             old familiar sunfeel
windwallop.

Race you to the water's edge!

265

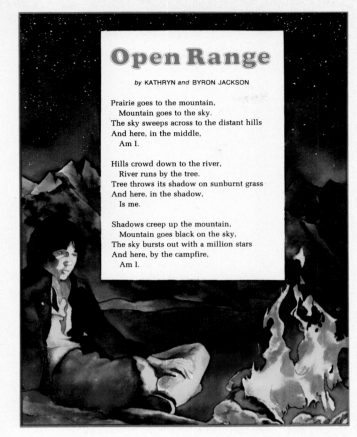

Open Range

by KATHRYN *and* BYRON JACKSON

Prairie goes to the mountain,
  Mountain goes to the sky.
The sky sweeps across to the distant hills
And here, in the middle,
  Am I.

Hills crowd down to the river,
  River runs by the tree.
Tree throws its shadow on sunburnt grass
And here, in the shadow,
  Is me.

Shadows creep up the mountain,
  Mountain goes black on the sky,
The sky bursts out with a million stars
And here, by the campfire,
  Am I.

Skiing

by ROSE BURGUNDER

Fast as foxes,
buzzy as bees,
down the slope
on our silver-tipped skis—

early in the morning
Roseanna and I
far from our house
on the hilltop fly.

A snowbird's yawning,
the sky's all pink,
somewhere in the valley
the lights still blink.

No one's awake
but us, and a bird.
The day's too beautiful
to speak a word.

267

1. Tell students that each poem deals with an activity that they may find enjoyable. Although the poems have this in common, each is unique in the attitude expressed by the poet toward the particular activity. Ask students to be aware of the different ways in which the poets express their feelings.

2. **a.** Ask students to tell how they feel when they are riding their bikes fast. Write their responses on the board. You might wish to arrange these responses to form a free-verse poem if the responses lend themselves to this activity. Remind students that poems do not have to rhyme but that word choice and the arrangement of words give free-verse poems their own sense of rhythm.

   b. Ask students to listen for words in "On Our Bikes" to help them experience what a ride to the beach feels like. Ask them to describe how the poet helps them see, smell, and feel.

3. Tell students to imagine they are camping out. Ask them to describe what they are seeing, hearing, smelling, touching, and tasting. Then have them listen to the way two poets describe camping and the outdoors in "Open Range."

4. Ask students who have skied to describe their experiences, or ask students to imagine what skiing might be like. Then ask them to listen to the description of a morning run in "Skiing" on page 267.

Foul Shot

by EDWIN A. HOEY

With two 60's stuck on the scoreboard
And two seconds hanging on the clock,
The solemn boy in the center of eyes,
Squeezed by silence,
Seeks out the line with his feet,
<u>Soothes</u> his hands along his uniform,
Gently drums the ball against the floor,
Then measures the waiting net,
Raises the ball on his right hand,
Balances it with his left,
Calms it with fingertips,
Breathes,
<u>Crouches,</u>
<u>Waits,</u>
And then through a stretching of stillness,
<u>Nudges</u> it upward.

The ball
Slides up and out,
Lands,
Leans,
Wobbles,
Wavers,
Hesitates,
<u>Exasperates,</u>
Plays it coy
Until every face begs with unsounding screams—

And then

   And then

     And then,

Right before ROAR-UP,
Dives down and through.

269

5. **a.** Ask students familiar with the game of basketball to explain what a foul shot is and how it differs from other shots during a game. (The clock stops for a foul shot. One player stands before a foul line in front of the basket. The spectators and other players are very still while the player shoots. During the rest of the game, all of the players are in action, running around the court.) Tell students to imagine a basketball game that's tied with just two seconds left and a player on the foul line ready to shoot. Ask them to describe what the feeling in the stands would be. (Students should describe a very tense situation, since so much depends on the foul shot.)

b. Ask students to listen to the way one poet describes this moment as you read aloud "Foul Shot" (pages 268–269).

6. Encourage students to read these poems aloud after discussing them.

Questions preceded by a bullet are additional questions and appear in the Teacher's Edition only. The other questions appear in the student's text after this group of poems.

Understanding What You've Read

1. *Find at least one example of imagery in "On Our Bikes" (page 265) that appeals to your sense of touch. Find an example of imagery in the same poem that appeals to your sense of smell.* (Accept all reasonable answers. Images that appeal to the sense of touch are: "glide down," "breeze-whipped," "old familiar sunfeel," and "windwallop." An image that appeals to the sense of smell is "wide smell of the sea.") CRITICAL <u>Recognizing sensory imagery in poetry</u>

● *How do you think the poet who wrote "On Our Bikes" feels about riding a bike down to the ocean? What words in the poem tell you how the poet feels?* (Accept all reasonable answers. Encourage students to recognize the good feelings that come across in the poem. The poet has taken great care to select words that describe how pleasurable the ride to the beach is. The words *glide, coast, breeze-whipped, sunfeel,* and *windwallop* all help the reader to experience what the poet is describing. The final line conveys a sense of fun.   page 265) CRITICAL <u>Recognizing a lyric poem</u>

● *Look at the way "On Our Bikes" is written. Does it have stanzas? How would you describe the way it is placed on the page? What is the poet suggesting by arranging the lines of the poem in this way?* (The poem does not have traditional stanzas. It is written zigzag down the page. Encourage students to recognize that this poem's shape suggests the way the roads curve to the beach.   page 265) CRITICAL <u>Comparing a poem's shape to its content</u>

● *How many stanzas are there in "Open Range" (page 266)? How are the stanzas all alike?* (The poem is written in three stanzas. Encourage students to respond that the stanzas are alike in their structure: Each presents three elements of nature and ends with a similar last line about the narrator's being in the midst of all this. Accept all other reasonable answers.) CRITICAL <u>Recognizing stanzas in poetry</u>

2. *In "Skiing" (page 267), what does the poet compare the skiers to? Are these comparisons similes, metaphors, or personification?* (The poet compares skiers to foxes and bees. The comparisons are similes because of the use of the word *as* in each comparison.) CRITICAL <u>Identifying similes</u>

● *What words in "Skiing" rhyme? Do you think this poem would be as effective if it did not rhyme?* (The rhyming words are *bees* and *skis; I* and *fly; pink* and *blink; bird* and *word.* Students may have different opinions about the effectiveness of rhyme in the poem "Skiing." Accept all reasonable answers.   page 267) CRITICAL <u>Recognizing rhyme in poetry</u>

● *The poems "On Our Bikes" and "Skiing" both describe enjoyment of a sport. Yet even though these poems are about similar topics, they are very different. What are some of the ways in which they are different?* (Accept all reasonable answers. The poem "On Our Bikes" is written in an unconventional shape, does not rhyme, and contains words that appeal mainly to the sense of touch. The poem "Skiing" is written in traditional stanzas, does rhyme, and contains similes that appeal mainly to the sense of sight.   pages 265 and 267) CRITICAL <u>Contrasting poems</u>

3. *What are some of the words in "Foul Shot" (pages 268–269) that compare a basketball to a person?* (Accept all reasonable answers. Encourage students to recognize that the words and phrases *hesitates, exasperates, plays it coy,* and *dives down and through* personify the basketball.   page 269) CRITICAL <u>Identifying personification</u>

- *The poet who wrote "Foul Shot" uses many action words to help readers experience what the foul shooter is going through. What are these words? To what senses do they appeal? Which ones do you think are the most effective?* (The action words appeal to the sense of touch. The poet wants readers to experience the anticipation and anxiety of shooting a foul shot with the game tied and only two seconds left to play. Some of the words the poet uses are *seeks, soothes, drums, measures, raises, balances, calms, breathes, crouches, waits,* and *nudges.* Give students an opportunity to tell which words help them experience what the player is feeling.   page 268) CRITICAL   Recognizing sensory imagery

Writing

(Optional) Have students complete one or both of the *Writing* activities on page 270, or ask students to do one or both of the writing activities under *Additional Writing Activity.*

1. *Use comparisons to write three sentences or a short poem about one of the following sports. Use imagery that appeals to your senses of smell, touch, and sight.*
   swimming   baseball   running
   Writing sentences using imagery

2. The imagery in "Open Range" appeals mostly to your sense of sight. Think about what it would be like to go camping. Then write your own paragraph or poem. Use imagery that tells what you would hear, taste, or smell.   Writing a paragraph or poem using sensory imagery

   Before students begin writing, you might wish to have them suggest some of the things they would observe through their senses on a camping trip. Write their observations on the board. If students need additional help with the *Writing* activity, have them consider the following: (1) the smell of food cooking over a campfire; (2) the sound of logs snapping and crackling as they burn; (3) the sound of an animal in the night; (4) the sound of stepping on dried leaves; and (5) the taste of food cooked over an open fire.

Additional Writing Activity (Optional)

- *Pick a stanza from "Skiing" (page 267) or "Open Range" (page 266) and rewrite it in paragraph form. Substitute words of your own for some of the poet's words. How does your paragraph sound? Which do you like better, the stanza or your paragraph?*
  Writing a stanza in paragraph form

Before students begin writing, you might ask the class to convert the first stanza of "Skiing" to a paragraph. For example, *With the great speed of a fox and the loud noise of a bee, we go down the slope wearing skis that have silver tips.*

- *The poem "Skiing" uses two similes: fast as foxes and buzzy as bees. Because foxes are fast and bees do buzz, these similes work. Think of some similes for the following words.*
  smart as   slow as   happy as
  quick as   tired as   hungry as
  Writing similes

Encourage students to think of new similes. You might ask them questions to help them get started. For example: *What kinds of people or things do we consider smart?* Possible answers might be: a scholar, a genius, a computer.

⭐ For additional resources and curriculum-related activities, see *Enrichment,* page T232.

Reading Selections:

The Snopp on the Sidewalk
The Dream Woman
Nancy Hanks

Pages 271–277

Objectives

		SKILLS CODE NUMBER
I*	To identify simile	6.6.6.4
M	To recognize rhyme and stanzas in poetry	6.6.1; 6.6.2
I*	To identify metaphor	6.6.6.5
M	To recognize narrative poetry	6.2.3

 # Preparing to Read

Summary

This group contains three narrative poems. Jack Prelutsky's "The Snopp on the Sidewalk" tells of meeting a snopp, which resembles "a gray old ragged mop," and how difficult it is to leave a snopp once you have found one. "The Dream Woman" by Patricia Hubbell has an eerie quality in its description of a woman who collects dreams during the night. The final poem in this section is "Nancy Hanks" by Rosemary Benét and Stephen Vincent Benét. It explores the feelings that Abe Lincoln's mother might have had about her son when she returns as a ghost.

Background

Jack Prelutsky is widely known for his nonsense poems, which readers of all ages enjoy. The poem in this section is from a collection titled *The Snopp on the Sidewalk and Other Poems.* Rosemary Benét and Stephen Vincent Benét collaborated on *A Book of Americans,* from which "Nancy Hanks" was taken. Stephen Vincent Benét is a famous American poet and recipient of the Pulitzer prize for poetry.

The following books will provide you with additional background information on teaching poetry to children.

Sebesta, Sam L., and William J. Iverson. *Literature for Thursday's Child.* In Chapter 10, discussions of various types of poems and suggestions for teaching poetry.

Sutherland, Zena, and May Hill Arbuthnot. *Children and Books,* 6th ed. In Chapter 10, a discussion of poetry for children.

Developing Vocabulary and Concepts

wrings: squeezes or twists, usually to get water out of; gets by force, violence, or threat

clasp: a fastening or hook to hold two parts together

darning: mending cloth by stitching the hole with thread

embellishment: something added for attractiveness; decoration

1. Read the following sentences aloud or write them on the board. If you read them aloud, write the underlined vocabulary on the board.

   When he twists, squeezes, and <u>wrings</u> out the wet clothes before hanging them on the line, they dry more quickly.

   The <u>clasp</u> on this belt is broken, and the belt will not stay closed.

   I was <u>darning</u> a hole in one of my socks when I dropped my needle.

   Her dress was plain except for the <u>embellishment</u> of lace around the collar.

2. Ask students to give the meaning of each vocabulary word. Remind them to use context clues in the sentences to help them.

 Use *Duplicating Masters 11,* page 30.

Setting Purposes

Skills

Have students read the note at the top of page 271. Remind students that poets use figurative language to appeal to their readers' senses so that they will experience the poems as fully as possible. Ask students to watch for examples of figurative language and sensory images as they read these poems.

Content

Ask students to imagine as they read these poems what each poet was thinking as he or she wrote these narrative poems about imaginary characters. Ask students to look for clues to whether or not the poets' imaginary characters could have been based on real people or things.

Get ready to meet a snopp, a dream woman, and a ghost. Look for the imagery and comparisons the poets use to help describe the imaginary characters and create the mood in each of the narrative poems that follow.

The Snopp on the Sidewalk

by JACK PRELUTSKY

It was lying on the sidewalk
like a gray old ragged mop,
but the second that I saw it,
I was sure I'd found the snopp.

It did not move a fiber
of its long and shaggy hair,
as if seeming not to notice
that I stood and watched it there.

At first I thought, "I'll touch it,"
and then I thought, "I won't,"
but when again I thought, "I will,"
the snopp said softly, "Don't."

271

This startled me so greatly
that I turned to run away,
but as I started down the street,
the snopp called after, "Stay."

I asked, "What do you want of me,
for snopp, I cannot guess?"
The snopp, still never stirring,
only answered me with, "Yes."

I did not understand this
so I tried once more to go,
but I'd <u>barely</u> started homeward
when the snopp said sweetly, "No."

And so I stayed that day and night,
and yes, I stayed a week,
and nevermore in all that time
did either of us speak.

At last I said, "Oh snopp, dear snopp,
I really have to go."
The snopp showed no emotion
as it whispered only, "Oh."

I headed home, not looking back,
afraid to ever stop.
I knew that if I paused but once
I'd never leave the snopp.

But the snopp remains within my mind,
I'm sure it always will—
that strange thing on the sidewalk
that I'm certain lies there still.

272

Reading and Discussing

Use the following procedure to read aloud and discuss briefly some of the poems with students.

NOTE: The questions that appear in the student's text at the end of the selections focus on comprehension of poetry content and on sensory imagery in poetry. Answers to these questions begin on page T228.

1. Write the word *snopp* on the board, and ask a volunteer to pronounce it. Ask students to imagine what a creature called a "snopp" might look like. Ask students to listen for the description of the snopp as you read aloud "The Snopp on the Sidewalk" (pages 271–272).

2. After you finish reading "The Snopp on the Sidewalk," ask students to retell the story told in the poem. Ask them what name is given to a poem that tells a story. (a narrative poem) Students may wish to speculate on why the snopp has such an attraction for the poem's narrator. (No answer is given in the poem.)

The Dream Woman

by PATRICIA HUBBELL

Early in the morning
Before the lights are on,
The dream woman scurries
Uptown and down.
Leaping in my window
She rushes to my bed,
Grasps at my dream
And wrings it from my head.
Quickly, quietly, she stuffs it in her bag,
Snaps shut the clasp
And runs from my side.
Out at the window,
Down a film of air,
The dream woman hurries
Lest the dawn appear.

When her bag is piled high
With dreams sad and gay,
She hurries to her home
To spin them all away.
She sits beside her spinning wheel,
She sits beside her loom,
And spins without ceasing
From morning until noon.

She gathers up the dreams
From her small black bag,
Shuffles them and sorts them
By color and by size,
Piles up the pink dreams,
Irons out the black,
Dyes a little white one
To match another scrap;
Gets out the darning needle,
Mends one that's torn,
And adds a slight embellishment
To one that's worn.

275

3. Tell students that they are going to meet a very different type of imaginary character in the next narrative poem you will read. Ask them if they have ever thought about what happens to their dreams when they have finished dreaming. After they have had an opportunity to respond, explain that this thought may have been the starting point for Patricia Hubbell as she began to write "The Dream Woman." Ask students to listen as you read "The Dream Woman" (pages 273–275).

4. After they have heard "The Dream Woman," ask students to describe what they think the dream woman is like. (She seems like a quick-moving creature. The verbs used to describe her actions—*scurries, leaping, rushes, runs,* and so on—all connote hurried movements. From the last half of the poem, students may describe her as a seamstress, working with the fabric of dreams.)

Nancy Hanks

by ROSEMARY BENÉT *and* STEPHEN VINCENT BENÉT

If Nancy Hanks
Came back as a ghost,
Seeking news
Of what she loved most,
She'd ask first
"Where's my son?
What's happened to Abe?
What's he done?"

"Poor little Abe,
Left all alone
Except for Tom,
Who's a rolling stone;
He was only nine
The year I died.
I remember still
How hard he cried.

"Scraping along
In a little shack,
With hardly a shirt
To cover his back,
And a prairie wind
To blow him down,
Or pinching times
If he went to town.

"You wouldn't know
About my son?
Did he grow tall?
Did he have fun?
Did he learn to read?
Did he get to town?
Did you know his name?
Did he get on?"

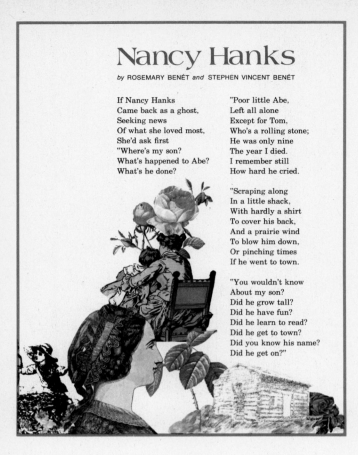

Understanding What You've Read

1. In the first stanza of "The Snopp on the Sidewalk" (page 271), what does the poet compare the snopp to? What does this tell you about the snopp?
2. What does the dream woman do with the dreams she gathers? What does the poet compare dreams to? Which of your senses does the imagery in the poem appeal to most?
3. Look at the third stanza of "Nancy Hanks" (page 276). What words show that Nancy was worried about Abe's being poor and feeling cold?

Writing

1. Write at least three sentences about an imaginary animal. Use similes to help you describe it. You may wish to use one of the following imaginary animals:

    a babbit   a flouse   a prump

2. Write a paragraph or a narrative poem about an imaginary person. Use similes, metaphors, and personification in your descriptions. You may wish to use one of the following people:

    The Star Hanger   The Mountain Builder
             The Ocean Mover

277

5. If students do not know who Nancy Hanks was, explain that she was the mother of Abraham Lincoln. Ask students to recall any facts they know about Abe Lincoln. Rather than saying anything further about Abe Lincoln or Nancy Hanks, simply ask students to listen as you read "Nancy Hanks" (page 276).

6. Ask students to tell what they learned about Nancy Hanks and Abe Lincoln from the poem. (Abe's mother died when he was only nine years old. He was left with his father, Tom, who is referred to as a "rolling stone." They had few personal belongings and lived in a shack.)

7. Encourage students to read these poems aloud after discussing them.

Questions preceded by a bullet are additional questions and appear in the Teacher's Edition only. The other questions appear in the student's text after this group of poems.

Understanding What You've Read

1. *In the first stanza of "The Snopp on the Sidewalk" (page 271), what does the poet compare the snopp to? What does this tell you about the snopp?* (The poet compares the snopp to "a gray old ragged mop." Students should realize that the moplike snopp is gray, old, ragged, and not very attractive.)
CRITICAL   Identifying simile

● *What kind of comparison is the poet using when he compares the snopp to a mop? How can you tell?* (The comparison is a simile. Students should be able to tell this by the use of the word *like*.   page 271)
CRITICAL   Identifying simile

● *A narrative poem tells a story, whereas a lyric poem expresses a poet's feelings. Which kind of poem is "The Snopp on the Sidewalk"?* (It is a narrative poem; it tells a story.   page 271) CRITICAL   Recognizing narrative poetry

2. *What does the dream woman do with the dreams she gathers? What does the poet compare dreams to? Which of your senses does the imagery in the poem appeal to most?* (The dream woman stuffs the dreams in her bag and hurries home, where she unpacks the bag, sorts the dreams by color and size, and fixes them up—by ironing them, dyeing them, mending them, or adding embellishments. The poet is comparing dreams to pieces of fabric. The imagery in the poem appeals mostly to the sense of sight. pages 273–275) CRITICAL   Recognizing sensory imagery and metaphor

- *The rhyme pattern of "The Dream Woman" is irregular. What words at the ends of lines actually rhyme? What words at the ends of lines are close to being rhyming words? What words within the lines rhyme with other words?* (Accept reasonable answers. End-of-line rhymes are: bed, head; gay, away; torn, worn. End-of-line words close to rhyming are: on, down; air, appear; loom, noon; high, size; black, scrap. Other words that rhyme in the poem are grasps, clasp; hurries, scurries.   pages 273–275) CRITICAL Recognizing rhyme in poetry

- *The dream woman is an imaginary character. What real thing do you think the poet may be talking about in her description of the dream woman?* (Accept any answer that students can justify. The dream woman may represent the time between sleep and waking, or she may represent dreams.) CRITICAL Drawing conclusions

3. *Look at the third stanza of "Nancy Hanks" (page 276). What words show that Nancy was worried about Abe's being poor and feeling cold?* ("Scraping along/In a little shack,/With hardly a shirt/To cover his back" Also, the image of the prairie wind blowing him down and the poverty described as "pinching times" show Nancy's concern.)   INFERENTIAL Recognizing word meaning

- *How many stanzas are there in "Nancy Hanks"? Why do you think there are this many?* ("Nancy Hanks" is written in four stanzas. Each stanza acts as a paragraph to tell part of the story.   page 276) CRITICAL   Recognizing stanzas in poetry

Writing

(Optional) Have students complete one or both of the *Writing* activities on page 277. Or ask students to do one or more of the writing activities under *Additional Writing Activity.*

1. *Write at least three sentences about an imaginary animal. Use similes to help you describe it. You may wish to use one of the following imaginary animals:*
   a babbit   a flouse   a prump
   Writing sentences using similes

Students may wish to write about one of the imaginary animals suggested in their text. Write the following opening lines on the board to help students get started.

The babbit is as soft as _____.
The flouse is as small as _____.
A prump is just like a _____.

2. *Write a paragraph or a narrative poem about an imaginary person. Use similes, metaphors, and personification in your descriptions. You may wish to use one of the following people:*
   The Star Hanger
   The Mountain Builder
   The Ocean Mover
   Writing a paragraph or narrative poem

Before students begin writing, have them list similes, metaphors, and personification appropriate to the person they are describing. Write the following lines on the board to help students get started.

quiet as the dawn
He was a flame, a fire.
The wind spoke to us.

Additional Writing Activity (Optional)

- *Write a narrative poem that tells about a meeting with an imaginary creature.*   Writing a narrative poem

Tell students that a good way to pick a name for such a creature is to think of a name that rhymes with many words. If students need additional help with the *Writing* activity, you may wish to write a narrative poem on the board about something called a Caloo. (Words that rhyme with *Caloo* are *blue, do, goo, who, moo, new, through, knew,* and so on.) Involve the entire class in this activity.

- *Imagine that Nancy Hanks came back as a ghost and you saw her. Write a short poem or paragraph telling what you would say to her about her son, Abe Lincoln. Use similes and metaphors in your poem or paragraph.*   Writing a poem/Writing a paragraph

Before students begin writing, you might ask them for examples of similes and metaphors that they could use to describe Abe Lincoln. Write their responses on the board. Some examples that might get them started are: Abe was as honest as _____. Abe worked as hard as _____. When he grew up, Abe was a _____.

 Use *Duplicating Masters 11,* page 31.
Use *Reading Skills Workbook,* Word Play, page 71, for vocabulary review.

 For additional resources and curriculum-related activities, see *Enrichment,* page T232.

More Poems to Read

Four Corners of the Sky selected by Theodore Clymer. Little, 1975. Native American poems, chants, and oratory from many cultures are beautifully illustrated.

Straight On till Morning: Poems of the Imaginary World selected by Helen Hill, Agnes Perkins, and Althea Helag. T. Y. Crowell, 1977. This book includes poems of magic and mystery.

On Our Way: Poems of Pride and Love selected by Lee Bennett Hopkins. Knopf, 1974. Here are poems by twenty-two black poets, including Gwendolyn Brooks, Nikki Giovanni, and Langston Hughes.

Piping Down the Valleys Wild edited and introduced by Nancy Larrick. Delacorte, 1968. This book includes popular poems of many moods.

The Moment of Wonder: A Collection of Chinese and Japanese Poetry collected by Richard Lewis. Dial, 1974. Here is a book of beautiful, imaginative poems.

As I Walked Out One Evening: A Book of Ballads selected by Helen Plotz. Greenwillow Bks., 1976. Here are 130 ballads of the English-speaking world.

Laughing Time compiled by William Jay Smith. Delacorte, 1980. This collection of poems is bound to make you laugh.

How Beastly! A Menagerie of Nonsense Poems by Jane Yolen. Collins, 1980. These poems are all about imaginary animals.

278

If students have not already read these books, you may wish to recommend them at this time. Bibliographic information about other books for students is given in the *Resource Center.*

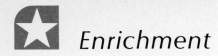 *Enrichment*

"The Whales Off Wales"; "Autumn Leaves"; "Glory, Glory . . ."; "Check"; "Comma in the Sky"; "I Go Forth to Move About the Earth"

Bibliography

The following books include poems that contain sensory imagery.

Easy

Merriam, Eve. *Catch a Little Rhyme*. A general collection that offers a variety of poetic forms and images.
O'Neill, Mary. *Winds*. A lyric look at wind and its effects on people.

Average

Caudill, Rebecca. *Wind, Sand, and Sky*. The beauty and mystery of the desert, described through short, haiku-like poems.
Jones, Hettie, ed. *The Trees Stand Shining: Poetry of the North American Indians*. A collection of traditional chants, proverbs, and songs from American Indian cultures.
Kennedy, X. J. *The Phantom Ice Cream Man*. Nonsense poems, including a wolf that eats health food, and other funny characters.
Kherdian, David, ed. *The Dog Writes on the Window with His Nose and Other Poems*. Twenty-two brief poems by some of America's leading poets.

Challenging

Abercrombie, Barbara, ed. *The Other Side of a Poem*. A collection of poems filled with surprises for people who aren't sure they like poetry.
Baron, Virginia Olsen, ed. *Sunset in a Spider Web: Sijo Poetry of Ancient Korea*. A collection of Sijo poetry, a type of verse used by Korean poets to celebrate nature and everyday life.
Rasmussen, Knud, ed. *Beyond the High Hills: A Book of Eskimo Poems*. Thoughts and images of the Eskimo world.

Films and Filmstrips

NOTE: For more information, see *Resource Center*.

Caedmon Records. *What Is Poetry?* Each of the ten filmstrips introduces one basic element essential to understanding poetry. Narration by Claire Bloom.

Miller-Brody Productions. *Learning About Poetry—Imagery and Figurative Language*. Explores the use of figurative language and the creation of imagery in poems.

Records and/or Tapes

NOTE: Recordings may also be available on other labels.

Caedmon Records. "Classics of American Poetry for the Elementary Curriculum." The classic poems, old and new, ranging from the easy-to-understand to the more complex.

Curriculum Coordination

Language Arts

1. As an extension of reading the poem "Comma in the Sky," have students consider the shapes of these punctuation marks: period, exclamation point, question mark, comma, quotation marks, apostrophe, and parentheses. Write the marks on the board as they are suggested. Ask students to think of objects in school, at home, or in nature that each mark reminds them of. Have students use these ideas as the basis of a poem.

2. Have a group of students give a choral presentation of "I Go Forth to Move About the Earth." One possibility for a choral reading is to have choral speaking of the twice-repeated title line, with individual students or small groups speaking, in turn, the lines in between. The last line could be a continuation of the choral reading.

Music

Background music adds to the enjoyment of listening to poems. Encourage students to listen to different types of music until they find something that seems to match the mood of some of the poems in this section. For example, eerie music might match "Check," and playful music might match "Autumn Leaves." Have students use music to accompany presentations of these poems. You may wish to record the presentations for your listening center.

Art

Have interested students choose a poem to illustrate. Their illustrations should capture the mood of the poem. Students may wish to illustrate some of the imagery in the poem in a special way to transform it into a visual image.

"On Our Bikes"; "Open Range"; "Skiing"; "Foul Shot"

Bibliography

The following books contain poems about things people like to do.

Average

Adoff, Arnold. *Eats.* Poems about enjoying food and eating.

Moore, Lilian, ed. *See My Lovely Poison Ivy, and Other Verses About Witches, Ghosts, and Things.* Gently ghoulish poems that are fun for young readers and listeners, especially at Halloween.

Challenging

Frost, Robert. *You Come Too: Favorite Poems for Young Readers.* Fifty-one poems by Frost for children.

Moore, Lilian, ed. *Go with the Poem.* Covers a wide range of topics and includes poems by Lucille Clifton and Eve Merriam, as well as a poem from the Cherokee Indians.

Morrison, Lillian. *The Sidewalk Racer and Other Poems of Sport and Motion.* Poems about baseball, boxing, tennis, track, and other sports.

O'Neil, Mary. *Words, Words, Words.* A book of imaginative poems about language.

Plotz, Helen, ed. *As I Walked Out One Evening.* A collection of ballads from the English-speaking world.

Films and Filmstrips

NOTE: For more information, see *Resource Center.*

Eye-Gate House. *Enjoying Poetry.* Illustrates four narrative poems and discusses how they were composed.

NBC-TV. *Hailstones and Halibut Bones I* and *II.* Films are made from poems exploring color in many imaginative ways.

Records and/or Tapes

NOTE: Recordings may also be available on other labels.

Caedmon Records. "Catch a Little Rhyme: Poems for Activity Time." Eve Merriam reads some of her poems that ask students to respond verbally and bodily.

Folkways Records. "An Anthology of Negro Poetry for Young People." Classic poetry from modern and past poets.

Curriculum Coordination

Language Arts

1. Action words are very important in poetry about sport and motion. Have students write "action poems"—simply a list of verbs—to describe an event such as a dog chasing a ball, a cat stalking a bird, a girl batting a ball, or a boy playing Frisbee. These action words may stand by themselves or be expanded by adding other words to make more traditional poems.

2. A group of students can effectively read the poem "Foul Shot." Rather than asking them to read the poem in chorus, ask them to take turns speaking the individual lines. Students will enjoy dividing the poem for a dramatic reading. They may wish to record their results.

Art/Language Arts

If a camera is available, arrange to take snapshots of your students during gym or athletic events. You may wish to take—or have volunteers take—some of these as candid shots and others posed. When the pictures have been developed, have students use them as take-off points for writing poems. Encourage them to use sensory imagery and comparisons in their poems.

"The Snopp on the Sidewalk"; "The Dream Woman"; "Nancy Hanks"

Bibliography

The following books contain poems, many of which are about imaginary beings.

Easy

Prelutsky, Jack. *Nightmares: Poems to Trouble Your Sleep.* A collection of twelve scary but enjoyable poems.

Average

Kherdian, David, ed. *If Dragon Flies Made Honey.* Twenty-five poems representing the lighter side of well-known modern poets.

Prelutsky, Jack. *The Snopp on the Sidewalk and Other Poems.* These poems are filled with imaginary beings.

———. *The Queen of Eene.* A book of verse about a kingdom filled with immortal zanies.

Challenging

Cole, William, ed. *The Sea, Ships and Sailors.* Narrative poems that capture the excitement of life at sea.

Hubbell, Patricia. *Catch Me a Wind.* A collection of poems that reflect children's varying moods.

Kherdian, David, ed. *Poems Here and Now.* A collection of modern poets' works dealing with happiness.

Lewis, Richard, ed. *The Moment of Wonder: A Collection of Chinese and Japanese Poetry.* Imaginative poems, both ancient and modern, from these two cultures.

Films and Filmstrips

NOTE: For more information, see *Resource Center.*

Pied Piper. *Descriptive Words.* Presents poems by noted authors and by children to encourage creation of free verse. Emphasizes descriptive words.

Records and/or Tapes

NOTE: Recordings may also be available on other labels.

Caedmon Records. "Poems and Songs of Middle Earth." Tolkien reads poems from his Hobbit series. Also includes songs based on his poems.

Curriculum Coordination

Language Arts

1. Have interested students plan a short production of "The Snopp on the Sidewalk." You might wish to have a narrator read the poem as if he or she is remembering the meeting with the snopp, while two students play the part of the person and the snopp. It might be fun to have the snopp say its few lines.

2. Plan a Poetry Day in your classroom. Ask interested students to prepare poems to present to the class. They may choose poems they have written or ones that they particularly like. You may wish to ask that the poems contain sensory images or poetic comparisons. Have each student present his or her poem to the class in whatever form seems best. For example, one student might read a poem with music in the background; another might wish to dress in costume to read a poem; another might wish to read a poem into a tape recorder ahead of time and then pantomime actions to match the poem.

3. Have interested students rewrite the story of "The Snopp on the Sidewalk" from the point of view of the snopp.

Art

Have interested students draw their own interpretations of the dream woman. You might wish to arrange a display on a bulletin board with the poem and pictures of "dream women" or "dream people."

Career Education

Invite someone who writes poetry to visit your class. If no known poets live in your area, you might check your local newspaper for other writers of fiction or poetry. Have the writer read some of his or her poems to the class and possibly compose some poems with your students.

RESOURCE CENTER

Enrichment Materials and Activities

Lady Moody's Dream
Pages 292-296

Enrichment Materials:
A map of Holland and a map of New York

Activity Needing Advance Planning:
A trip to a restored colonial village

Guest Speaker:
An architect or an urban planner

The Peddler's Pack
Pages 306-311

Guest Speaker:
A traveling salesperson

The Secret of the Sea
Pages 312-318

Enrichment Materials:
Recordings of sea chanteys

Activities Needing Advance Planning:
A trip to a whaling museum or naval museum
A tour of a U.S. Navy ship

Guest Speaker:
A representative of the Navy or Coast Guard

Golden Ghosts
Pages 330-335

Guest Speaker:
A jeweler, jewelry maker, or goldsmith

Whatever Happened to Main Street?
Pages 362-367

Activity Needing Advance Planning:
A trip to a local historical site

Guest Speaker:
A local historian

Bibliography

For Students

NOTE: For more information about these books, see the *Enrichment* section at the end of each Teaching Unit.

Atkin, Mary Gage. *Paul Cuffe and the African Promised Land.* Nelson, 1977.

Banner, Lois W. *Elizabeth Cady Stanton: A Radical for Women's Rights.* Little, 1980.

Beatty, Patricia. *Blue Stars Watching.* Morrow, 1969.

Clyne, Patricia Edwards. *Patriots in Petticoats.* Dodd, 1976.

Coatsworth, Elizabeth. *American Adventures.* Macmillan, 1968.

Comins, Jeremy. *Totems, Decoys and Covered Wagons: Cardboard Constructions from Early American Life.* Lothrop, 1976.

Constant, Alberta. *Motoring Millers.* T. Y. Crowell, 1969.

Earle, Alice Morse. *Home and Child Life in Colonial Days.* Macmillan, 1969.

Emrich, Duncan, comp. *The Nonsense Book of Riddles, Rhymes, Tongue Twisters, Puzzles, and Jokes from American Folklore.* Four Winds, Schol. Bk. Serv., 1970.

Fox, Mary V. *Lady for the Defense: A Biography of Belva Lockwood.* Harcourt Brace Jovanovich, 1975.

Franchere, Ruth. *Westward by Canal.* Macmillan, 1972.

Freedman, Russell. *Immigrant Kids.* Dutton, 1980.

Fritz, Jean. *Why Don't You Get a Horse, Sam Adams?* Coward, 1974.

Glubok, Shirley. *The Art of America in the Gilded Age.* Macmillan, 1974.

_____. *The Art of the Old West.* Macmillan, 1971.

Goodnough, David. *The Colony of New York.* Watts, 1973.

Grant, Matthew G. *De Soto: Explorer of the Southeast.* Childrens, 1974.

Habenstreit, Barbara. *Cities in the March of Civilization.* Watts, 1974.

Hults, Dorothy Niebrugge. *New Amsterdam Days and Ways: The Dutch Settlers of New York.* Harcourt Brace Jovanovich, 1963.

Johnston, Johanna. *Women Themselves.* Dodd, 1973.

Jupo, Frank. *Walls, Gates, and Avenues: The Story of the Town.* Prentice-Hall, 1964.

Laycock, George. *How the Settlers Lived.* McKay, 1980.

Le Sueur, Meridel. *Conquistadores.* Watts, 1973.

Levenson, Dorothy. *Homesteaders and Indians.* Watts, 1971.

————. *Women of the West.* Watts, 1973.

Levitin, Sonia. *The No-Return Trail.* Harcourt Brace Jovanovich, 1978.

Loeb, Robert H., Jr. *New England Village: Everyday Life in 1810.* Doubleday, 1976.

Place, Marian T. *The First Book of the Santa Fe Trail.* Watts, 1966.

Ross, Pat. *Whatever Happened to the Baxter Place?* Pantheon, 1976.

Rounds, Glen. *The Cowboy Trade.* Holiday, 1972.

————. *The Treeless Plains.* Holiday, 1967.

Rutland, Jonathan. *Ships.* Watts, 1976.

Sackett, S. J. *Cowboys and the Songs They Sang.* Addison-Wesley, 1967.

Schnacke, Dick. *American Folk Toys: How to Make Them.* Penguin, 1974.

Schwartz, Alvin, ed. *When I Grew Up Long Ago.* Lippincott, 1978.

Speare, Elizabeth George. *Life in Colonial America.* Random, 1963.

Tunis, Edwin. *Colonial Craftsmen: The Beginnings of American Industry.* T. Y. Crowell, 1976.

Wilder, Laura Ingalls. *By the Shores of Silver Lake.* Harper & Row, 1953.

————. *Farmer Boy.* Harper & Row, 1953.

————. *First Four Years.* Harper & Row, 1971.

————. *Little House in the Big Woods.* Harper & Row, 1953.

————. *Little House on the Prairie.* Harper & Row, 1953.

————. *Little Town on the Prairie.* Harper & Row, 1953.

————. *The Long Winter.* Harper & Row, 1953.

————. *On the Banks of Plum Creek.* Harper & Row, 1953.

————. *These Happy Golden Years.* Harper & Row, 1953.

Yep, Laurence. *Dragonwings.* Harper & Row, 1975.

For Teachers

NOTE: For more information about these books, see the *Background* section that precedes the reading selections.

Bridenbaugh, Carl. *Cities in the Wilderness: The First Century of Urban Life in America.* Oxford U. Press, 1971.

Cooke, Alistair. *Alistair Cooke's America.* Knopf, 1973.

Hall-Quest, Olga. *Conquistadors and Pueblos: The Story of the American Southwest, 1540–1848.* Dutton, 1969.

Harris, Sheldon H. *Paul Cuffe.* Simon & Schuster, 1972.

Jeffrey, Julie Roy. *Frontier Women: The Trans-Mississippi West, 1840–1880.* Hill & Wang, 1979.

Jenkinson, Michael. *Ghost Towns of New Mexico: Playthings of the Wind.* U. of New Mexico Press, 1967.

Langdon, William Chauncy. *Everyday Things in American Life,* Vol. 1 and Vol. 2. Scribner, 1937–1941.

Riegel, Robert. *America Moves West.* Holt, Rinehart & Winston, 1964.

Weisberger, Bernard A. *The Age of Steel and Steam: The Life History of the United States, 1877–1890.* Time-Life, 1974.

Weymouth, Lally, and Milton Glaser. *America in 1876: The Way We Were.* Vintage, 1976.

Films and Filmstrips

Sources related to skills

Harcourt Brace Jovanovich. *Bookmark Reading Filmstrips: Purple.* "Topics, Main Ideas, and Details," "Out West with Maps and Graphs."

Guidance Assocs. *Geography: Concepts and Skills Series.* Titles: "Maps," "Shelter," "Land Use," "Climate." Teacher's guide for each title. Four filmstrip programs with records (#9A–304 848) or cassettes (#9A–304 855).

Guidance Assocs. *Using Your Reading Skills Series.* Titles: "Getting the Main Idea," "Charts, Tables, Maps, and Graphs," "Finding Word Clues," "Skim, Scan, or Study?" Discussion guide and spirit duplicating masters for each title. Four filmstrip programs with records (#9A–305 068) or cassettes (#9A–305 076).

Sources related to reading selections

Coronet Instructional Media. "Gold Rush Days." One 16mm film (#1154). Available for rental.

Coronet Instructional Media. "Inventions in America's Growth—II (1850–1910)." One 16mm film (#915). Available for rental.

Coronet Instructional Media. "Our Small Town Heritage: Memories of Main Street." One 16mm film (#3310). Available for rental.

Coronet Instructional Media. "Spanish Influences in the United States." One 16mm film (#3599). Available for rental.

Encyclopaedia Britannica Educational Corp. *The Age of Exploration.* Titles: "Prince Henry the Navigator," "Sir Francis Drake: Rise of English Sea Power," "Spain: Setting the Stage for Empire," "Spain in the New World," "The Invention of Printing," "Magellan: West to the Orient." Six filmstrips (#11340).

Encyclopaedia Britannica Educational Corp. *Life in Early America.* Titles: "Life in New Amsterdam," "Life in Plymouth Colony," "Life in Early Philadelphia," "Life in Old Santa Fe," "Life in the Early Midwest," "Life in Early Carolina." Six filmstrips (#8340).

National Geographic. *Transportation in America.* Titles: "Yesterday's Travel," "People on the Move," "Supplying the Market," "Traffic in the City," "Tomorrow's Travel." Five filmstrips with records (#03762) or cassettes (#03763).

OVERVIEW

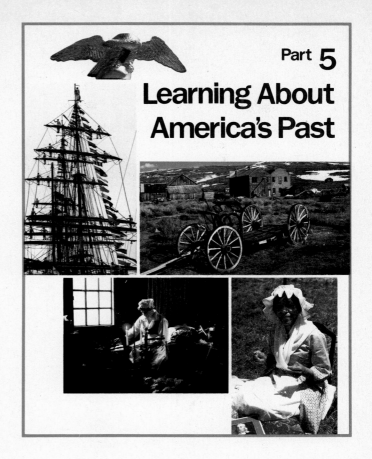

Part 5

Learning About America's Past

The skills focus of "Learning About America's Past" is on identifying topics, main ideas, and details in paragraphs and on using graphic aids. The selections highlight interesting events and people in American history from the 1500's to "modern" life in the 1880's. For example, they explain the contributions and life-styles of a pioneer family, a peddler, the country's first woman landowner-architect, and a seafarer. The final selection explains how students can have fun researching the history of their own town or city.

Using the Management System

Periodic Test 3, Forms A and *B,* covers the tested skills in "Learning About America's Past." The test may be administered in parts preceding and/or following instruction in each Teaching Unit. Or, Parts I through IV may be administered together for pretesting and/or post-testing all the tested skills in "Learning About America's Past." For full information on administering tests, see the Teacher's Edition of *Periodic Tests, Level 11.* In addition, the following activities within the student's text may be used as part of your ongoing assessment of students' progress:

> *Try This* sections of the *Skills Lessons*
> *Applying the Skills Lesson* activities following each selection
> *Building Skills* sections of *Textbook Studies*

Previewing "Learning About America's Past"

Have students examine the photographs on page 279. Ask them to identify the settings. Ask if anyone has ever been to any of the places pictured, and, if so, have students describe what they saw and what they learned there. Discuss the differences between the clothing shown in the pictures and the clothing of modern America. Explain that the selections in this part of the book will give them a chance to look at the way people lived in America a long time ago. Also explain that most of the people they "meet" in the selections, although they are not well known, had a part in America's growth. Tell them to examine the pictures and titles of the selections for a few minutes and to look at the illustrations in the *Skills Lessons* as well.

Objectives

The following list of objectives is provided to help you plan your teaching of "Learning About America's Past." All the objectives listed under *Maintained and Tested* are for skills presented in the four *Skills Lessons* of "Learning About America's Past" in the student's text. *Applying the Skills Lesson* sections following each selection in the student's text, as well as the *Try This* activities within the *Skills Lessons,* informally assess students' progress with these skills. *Periodic Test 3* may be used for more formal evaluation.

The objectives listed under *Maintained* are for skills presented in the *Maintaining Skills* sections in this Teacher's Edition.

The symbols I*, I, M, and T are used throughout the Teacher's Edition. The symbol I* indicates skills introduced for the first time in the program. The I indicates skills introduced earlier in Level 11. The M indicates skills taught at earlier levels and maintained in Level 11. The T indicates a skill that is taught for mastery and tested. The italicized numbers following the objectives are part of a code developed by the HBJ School Department to facilitate the correlation of skills within and between programs. See page T499 for more information.

Maintained and Tested

These skills were introduced earlier in the HBJ BOOK-MARK READING PROGRAM, EAGLE EDITION. They are developed in Level 11 and tested in *Periodic Test 3*.

	SKILLS CODE NUMBER
To identify the topic and stated main idea of a paragraph	3.3.8
To identify details that support the stated main idea of a paragraph	3.3.1; 3.3.8.3
To use details to determine the unstated main idea of a paragraph	3.3.1; 3.4.7
To compare information obtained from graphic aids to textual information	5.4.7
To interpret information from a picture	5.4.5
To interpret information from a diagram	5.4.4
To identify types of graphic aids	5.4
To interpret information from a map	5.4.3
To interpret information from a bar graph or pictograph	5.4.1
To interpret information from a line graph	5.4.1
To interpret information from a circle graph	5.4.1
To interpret information from a time line	5.4.1

Maintained

Each of these skills was previously taught in the HBJ BOOKMARK READING PROGRAM, EAGLE EDITION. None of them are tested in *Periodic Test 3*. In planning your teaching, select those exercises from the *Maintaining Skills* sections that best meet your students' specific needs for maintaining skills presented earlier in the program.

	SKILLS CODE NUMBER
To distinguish between fact and opinion	3.6.3
To locate and use library catalogue cards	5.11.2
To use an encyclopedia	5.11.1
To identify cause-and-effect relationships	3.3.3
To use a table of contents	5.5.3
To identify base words in compound words	4.2.1
To write a topical outline	7.1.5.1
To identify topical organization	5.10.1
To use a dictionary to find word meaning	5.6.4

To identify and use reference materials in which specific information may be found	5.11
To use a dictionary to find meanings of multiple-meaning words	5.6.4
To classify stated details by identifying groups to which they belong	3.2.1
To use an index	5.5.8
To predict outcomes based on given information and personal knowledge	3.4.2

Vocabulary

The following skills are practiced on the *Vocabulary Study* pages in the student's text for "Learning About America's Past." These skills are not tested in *Periodic Test 3*.

	SKILLS CODE NUMBER
To identify and use synonyms as context clues	3.5.4; 3.0
To identify word parts: root words and suffixes	4.1
To identify word parts: root words and prefixes	4.1
To identify base words in compound words	4.2.1

Contents

Additional Materials

Reading Skills Workbook: Lessons 21–23, pages 72–77
Duplicating Masters 11: pages 32–35
Worksheet 9: Teacher's Edition, page T488
Bookmark Reading Filmstrips: Purple: "Topics, Main
  Ideas, and Details"
Periodic Test 3, Part I

Key to Symbols

Skills Objectives
I* — Introduced in this unit
I   — Introduced earlier in this level
M   — Maintained from previous levels
T   — Tested in periodic and cumulative tests for this level

Reduced Student Pages
underscore — words that appear in the glossary
wavy line — words pretaught in the Teacher's Edition
              (these words also appear in the glossary)

Skills Lesson:
Finding the Topic and Main Idea of a Paragraph
Pages 280–284

Objective

SKILLS CODE
NUMBER

M, T   To identify the topic and stated   3.3.8
        main idea of a paragraph

If you wish to pretest the skill listed above, you may
administer *Periodic Test 3, Part I, Form A. Periodic Test
3, Part I, Form B,* may be administered to posttest.

Introducing
the Lesson

1. **a.** Write the following two lists of words on the
   board. Ask students what each group of words has
   in common.

   apple   baseball
   pear   hockey
   banana   tennis
   peach   swimming

   Elicit that the first group of words is *names of fruit*
   and the second group is *names of sports activities.*

   b. Write the word *topic* on the board, and explain
   that students have just found the topic, or subject,
   of each list.

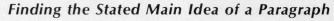
2. Direct students to the pictures at the top of page 280, and ask what the pictures have in common. (The animals are all members of the cat family.)

3. Explain that, just as the *topic* of a group of words or a group of pictures tells what they have in common, the *topic of a paragraph* tells what all or most of the sentences have in common.

Developing the Skill

The topic of a paragraph is what all or most of the sentences are about.

Have students read the first three paragraphs of the *Skills Lesson*. Call on students to read aloud the sentences in the sample paragraph about authors' pen names. Point out that each sentence in the paragraph says something about the topic.

Finding the Stated Main Idea of a Paragraph

A. *The main idea of a paragraph is the most important thing the paragraph says about the topic.*

1. Have students read the first two paragraphs under the heading on page 281. Then have them go back to the sample paragraph about pen names and find the sentence that states the main idea. (First sentence: "Many famous authors are better known by their pen names than by their real names.")

2. Have students read the paragraph about wind-chill and identify the topic (wind-chill) and stated main idea. (Wind-chill gives a truer measure of cold weather than temperature alone does.) Then have them read the explanatory paragraph.

A main idea may also be stated in the last sentence of a paragraph. Find the topic and main idea in the following paragraph.

● The first kind of energy used for transportation most likely was water. Perhaps someone fell into a rushing river and held on to a floating log. This might have given the person the idea of making a raft. Sometime after that, someone had the idea of "catching" the wind—in sails. Perhaps a few hundred years later someone decided to hitch an ox to a cart. Animal power was born. Until about four hundred years ago, water, wind, and animal power were the only kinds of energy that people used for transportation.

282

What is the topic of the paragraph?

1. energy for transportation
2. the first raft
3. animal power

Is every sentence about the first raft? No. Does every sentence tell you about animal power? No. But every sentence says something about *energy for transportation*. Which sentence in the paragraph states the most important idea about the topic?

You have seen that a main idea can be stated in the first or the last sentence of a paragraph. But remember, a main idea can also be stated somewhere in the middle of a paragraph.

283

B. *A main idea may be stated anywhere in a paragraph.*

1. Have students read the two paragraphs on page 282 and identify the topic from the choices on page 283. (energy for transportation) Have them find and read aloud the main idea. (last sentence)

2. Have students read the two explanatory paragraphs on page 283.

C. *A topic is stated in a word or group of words. A main idea is stated in sentence form.*

Write the following topics and main ideas on the board, one at a time. Do not begin the sentences or phrases with capital letters or end them with periods. Have students tell whether each one is a topic or a main idea.

the Earth's changing climate (topic)
scientists believe that the Earth's climate is changing (main idea)
one of the strangest animals is the duck-billed platypus (main idea)
the duck-billed platypus (topic)

Try This

Have students complete *Try This*.

Answers to *Try This*

1. Topic: the almanac; Main idea: "You can find the answers to these and other questions in an almanac." **2.** Topic: zoos in America; Main idea: "As you can see, America has many wonderful zoos." **3.** Topic: Rebecca Boone; Main idea: "Rebecca Boone was as much a pioneer as her husband, Daniel Boone."

 Use *Reading Skills Workbook,* Lesson 21, pages 72–74. See *Providing for Individual Differences,* page T256, for additional practice.

Vocabulary Study:

Synonyms

Page 285

Objective

		SKILLS CODE NUMBER
M	To identify and use synonyms as context clues	3.5.4; 3.0

Developing the Skill

1. Tell students that the *Vocabulary Study* they are about to read is another entry from the diary of Professor Crum. Tell them to look for pairs of synonyms as they read.

2. Have students read the *Vocabulary Study* and do the *Word Play* activities.

Answers to *Word Play*

1. a. Chan is *judged* the best . . .; **b.** Miranda *said* that she . . .; **c.** They melted into one *huge* cookie; **2.** Sample answers: *disgusting, frightful, estimation.* Sentences will vary.

 Use *Reading Skills Workbook,* Lesson 22, page 75. See *Providing for Individual Differences,* page T256, for additional practice.

VOCABULARY STUDY

Synonyms

The not-so-evil Professor Crum sat in the flickering light of a candle and wrote in his diary.

Dear Diary,
I'm sure I **mentioned** that I work part-time in a health food store. I think I said it in my last entry. Well, things have gone from bad to worse. You know how I'm **considered** to be the foulest, most rotten person alive. People have judged me even more horrible than Billy the Kid. But that was yesterday. Today I am on shaky ground. The owner of the health food store says I'm the best juice squeezer this side of the Rockies. And that is a huge, **immense** blow to my evil reputation. What will the world think of me? I'd better do something nasty soon, or I'm finished for good. But don't worry, Diary, because I'm hatching a plan.

Word Play

1. Professor Crum used synonyms to explain the boldfaced words in the diary page above. Reword each sentence below using the *synonym* for each boldfaced word. Remember that synonyms are words that have nearly the same meanings.

   a. Chan is **considered** the best goalie on our soccer team.
   b. Miranda **mentioned** that she was planning to visit.
   c. When Jan baked cookies, she put them too close together on the tray. They melted into one **immense** cookie.

2. Look up *foul, horrible,* and *reputation* in a dictionary. Then find a synonym for each word and use the synonym in a sentence.

285

Reading Selection:
Journey of the Tejas Woman

Pages 286–291

Objectives

		SKILLS CODE NUMBER
M, T	To identify the topic and stated main idea of a paragraph	3.3.8
M	To distinguish between fact and opinion	3.6.3
M	To locate and use library catalogue cards	5.11.2
M	To use an encyclopedia	5.11.1

Preparing to Read

Summary

Between 1540 and 1543, two parties of Spanish adventurers came to the New World in search of treasure. Hernando De Soto led his party westward from Florida. Francisco de Coronado led his group northward from Mexico and then eastward. The Tejas Woman joined Coronado's party, but later left them and traveled alone across the Barrancas, a land of ravines and canyons, to her home. A year later, De Soto's group came through the Tejas Woman's village, and she told them of her journey. Because her nine-day journey across Texas formed a link between Coronado's group in western Texas and De Soto's group in eastern Texas, the continent was crossed for the first time in history.

Background

Hernando De Soto (1500?–1542) and Francisco de Coronado (1510–1554) both set out for the New World in search of gold and gems. De Soto's explorations took him through territory that now includes Florida, the Carolinas, Alabama, Mississippi, Arkansas, and Louisiana. Coronado explored parts of the Rio Grande, the Grand Canyon, and central Texas.

The Tejas, a tribe from eastern Texas, were an agricultural people. They were also skillful potters and basket makers who used intricate designs.

The following books will provide you with additional background information.

Hall-Quest, Olga. *Conquistadors and Pueblos: The Story of the American Southwest, 1540–1848*. The colonization and exploration of the Southwest.
Jeffrey, Julie Roy. *Frontier Women: The Trans-Mississippi West, 1840–1880*. Examines the part women played in the history of the West.

Developing Vocabulary and Concepts

vast: of a very great area or size
contact: a coming together; a meeting; being in touch
rivals: people who try to equal, outdo, or compete with others
link: something that joins or connects
spanned: stretched or extended across
tribal: of or having to do with a tribe or tribes
rolling: hilly

1. **a.** Read the following sentences aloud, or write them on the board. If you read them aloud, write the underlined vocabulary on the board.

   The <u>vast</u> grasslands stretched on for miles and miles.
   Talking about home among themselves gave the explorers a feeling of <u>contact</u>, or a sense of being in touch, with their own people.
   The two groups of explorers were <u>rivals</u> because each group wanted to find the treasure first.
   The Tejas Woman's journey was a <u>link</u> that joined the western and eastern parts of Texas.
   The journeys of the Tejas Woman and the two groups of explorers <u>spanned</u>, or stretched across, the continent.
   Although the Pueblos and the Tejas are both Western tribes, they have different <u>tribal</u> customs.
   The Tejas Woman reached the <u>rolling</u> prairie land. Once she crossed over that hilly area, she knew she was almost home.

   b. Ask students to give the meaning of each vocabulary word. Remind them to use the context clues in the sentences to help them.

2. Ask students to tell you what they know about Texas. During the discussion, explain that the name Texas comes from a Native American word—*Tejas* [tä'hos]—and pronounce this word for students.

A brave <u>Native</u> American woman wanted to get back to her home. Little did she know that history books would later record her trip and explain the importance of the . . .

Journey of the Tejas Woman

by Kathryn Hitte

In the years from 1540 to 1543, two huge parties of adventurers explored much of the land that is now the United States. They were Spanish men who had come to the New World in search of treasure. They had heard tales of great riches to be found north of Mexico—unbelievable riches! Some said there were golden cities there!

Hernando De Soto led one party westward from what is now Florida. Almost at the same time, Francisco de Coronado led *his* men first northward from Mexico and then eastward. Each group was eager to be first to find the treasure. They never met on their journeys. But a Native American woman became a <u>link</u> that joined them.

As far as we know, she was a Tejas woman. The Tejas tribe made their home in what is today eastern Texas. It is from their <u>tribal</u> name—which means "Hello, friend"—that the state's name comes.

We know very little about the Tejas Woman. Her story is found in a history of Coronado's journey. It was recorded by Castañeda, who was with Coronado. Castañeda did not tell us the woman's name.

Her part in history begins in the land of the <u>Pueblo</u> people of

286   287

3. Ask students to pretend they are taking a cross-country trip. Ask them how they would travel and what preparations they would make. Then tell them to imagine what it would have been like to make the same trip 400 years ago. What problems would they have had to face? Explain that the selection they will read tells about the first known crossing of the North American continent in the early 1540's.

 Use *Duplicating Masters 11,* page 32.

Setting Purposes

Skills

Have students read the skills note at the top of page 286. Remind them that the *topic* is whatever all or most of the sentences in a paragraph are about and that the *main idea* is the most important thing the paragraph says about the topic.

Content

Have students read the lead-in to the title. Ask them to think of other people—like Columbus or Magellan—whose journeys or explorations later became important in history. Explain that most of these people knew, at the time of their journeys, that they were doing something of historical importance. But in the selection they are about to read, no one knew that history was being made.

2 Reading and Discussing

Have students read the selection. Most students will be able to complete it in one sitting. If you prefer, the selection may be read in two parts, breaking before the paragraph beginning "We know what the land was . . ." on page 289.

NOTE: The questions that appear in the student's text at the end of the selection focus on comprehension of selection content and on application of the *Skills Lesson* to the selection. Answers to these questions begin on page T247.

the area now called New Mexico. She was living there, far from her home, when Coronado's party reached this area. How she got there we can only guess.

When Coronado headed east again, several Native Americans went along. The Tejas Woman was one of them.

It was the spring of 1541. Coronado's group of explorers came to vast, treeless grasslands that went on mile after mile. Thousands of buffalo grazed here. The land was so flat, Castañeda wrote, that he could "see the sky under a horse's body."

Did the woman know how close they were coming to her home? We wonder.

The plains ended. A world of rocky cliffs and canyons lay before the explorers. They had reached what the Spanish called the *Barrancas*. Here were steep cliffs of colored rock carved by the winds. Here were many ravines and canyons, deep hollows in the earth. They blocked the way east for many miles.

To Coronado and his men,

the Barrancas brought only problems and discouragement. But they brought joy to the heart of the Tejas Woman.

"She recognized the country," Castañeda wrote. He was a good reporter. As you read his report, you feel that he was not making anything up. The woman had been here before! She must have shown some kind of excitement that Castañeda noticed.

Coronado decided not to try to cross the Barrancas. Instead, he would take a small

group of horsemen northward and search for the golden cities there. The rest of his party must camp here, near the Barrancas, until he sent them word.

The Tejas Woman may not have understood the talk among the Spanish. But she knew what she saw. She knew what was happening.

According to Castañeda's report, "She fled down the Barrancas." She went eastward through the ravines and canyons—alone.

We know what the land was like there. We can easily imagine that the Tejas Woman must have known how to make her own way in the wild. She would get water from the rushing streams and shelter from the trees. Fruits and nuts and fish would be her food.

She would come out of the canyons into rolling prairie land—little hills and fields. Then would come forests and the best farmland around. She would be home. Home among the farms and villages of her own people, the Tejas, at last!

We have no facts of her homecoming. We know only what came later. It happened almost exactly one year after the woman left Coronado's party. It concerns those rival gold seekers, De Soto's men.

They had traveled westward, remember. By this time, De Soto himself was dead. His men had journeyed on under a new leader. They were weary and discouraged. They had come a long, long way. But they had found no treasure.

In the summer of 1542, they reached a Tejas village. There

they learned of a woman who had traveled with others like themselves, other Spaniards. De Soto's men found the woman and somehow talked with her. They were excited by her story. They told it in Mexico afterward.

Think back a minute. What a strange, wild chance that meeting was! Think of the size of the North American continent! How many other ways De Soto's men might have gone! Yet they came *this* way. They reached *this* village, where *this* woman lived. And she remembered names.

Those Spanish names told De Soto's men that she spoke the truth. She gave them a sense of contact with their own people that must have cheered them. And they could guess from her story that their rivals had found no riches, either.

Of what importance, really, is the Tejas Woman's story? She did not play a great part in an explorer's journey, as the Shoshone woman Sacajawea later did. (From 1804 to 1806, Sacajawea led Lewis and Clark on their famous journey.) The Tejas Woman meant little to the Coronado party.

Questions preceded by a bullet are additional questions and appear in the Teacher's Edition only. The other questions appear in the student's text after the selection.

Understanding What You've Read

1. *Why was the Tejas Woman's journey an important event in United States history?* (Answers should include: The Tejas Woman's journey formed a link between Coronado's group and De Soto's group; the continent was crossed for the first time. The size of North America could be properly judged, so that eventually more accurate maps could be made. page 291) LITERAL   Identifying an author's conclusions

- *In what year did the Tejas Woman's journey take place?* (1541   page 288) LITERAL   Recalling specific details

2. *What was the difference between the journey of the Tejas Woman and that of Sacajawea?* (Answers should include: Sacajawea led Lewis and Clark on their famous journey, whereas the Tejas Woman did not lead a group of explorers. The journeys were in different parts of North America. There were 263 years between the journeys.   page 290) CRITICAL   Contrasting ideas

- *How does the author think the Tejas Woman got along in the wild?* (The author imagines that she ate fruits, nuts, and fish and obtained water from the streams and shelter from the trees.   page 289) LITERAL   Identifying an author's conclusions

3. *How do we know about the Tejas Woman's journey?* (Castañeda, a man from Coronado's party, wrote about her in his history of Coronado's journey.   page 287) INFERENTIAL   Identifying cause-and-effect relationships

- *Why was the meeting between the Tejas Woman and De Soto's party a chance event?* (Answers should include the facts that the North American continent is very large and that there were many other routes that De Soto's men could have taken.   page 290) INFERENTIAL   Identifying an author's conclusions

- *Why did the Tejas Woman's journey have a happy ending?* (She was able to find her home.   page 291) INFERENTIAL   Identifying the author's conclusions

Applying the Skills Lesson

1. *Read the first paragraph of the selection on pages 286–287. What is the topic of that paragraph? What is the main idea?* (Topic: exploration of the United States, 1540–1543; Main idea: "In the years from 1540 to 1543, two large parties of adventurers explored much of the land that is now the United States.")   Identifying the topic and stated main idea of a paragraph

- *What is the topic of the last paragraph on page 288? What is the main idea?* (Topic: Coronado's decision; Main idea: "Coronado decided not to try to cross the Barrancas.")   Identifying the topic and stated main idea of a paragraph

2. *What is the topic of the first full paragraph on this page (page 291)? Which sentence states the main idea of that paragraph?* (Topic: the Tejas Woman's journey; Main idea: "Because of her, the continent was crossed for the first time.")   Identifying the topic and stated main idea of a paragraph

 Use *Duplicating Masters 11*, page 33. See *Providing for Individual Differences*, page T256, for additional practice.

3 Maintaining Skills

Comprehension Skills

Distinguishing between fact and opinion   Have students identify each of the following sentences from the selection as a fact or as the author's opinion. Have them explain their reasoning.

> In the years from 1540 to 1543, two huge parties of adventurers explored much of the land that is now the United States. (fact)
> The Tejas Woman may not have understood the talk among the Spanish. (opinion)
> We can easily imagine that the Tejas Woman must have known how to make her own way in the wild. (opinion)
> After the 1500's, maps of America slowly began to improve, to look more as they should. (fact)
> She gave them (De Soto's men) a sense of contact with their own people that must have cheered them. (opinion)

 Use *Reading Skills Workbook,* Lesson 23, pages 76–77.

Study Skills

Using the library   Assign small groups of students to gather information on one of the following topics: Pueblo tribes, the Tejas tribe, Hernando De Soto, Francisco de Coronado. Half the groups can use the card catalogue to locate books on these subjects; the other half can use different sets of encyclopedias. Students who use nonfiction books can then compare their information with that gathered by students who use encyclopedias. Point out that information on these topics may be listed under various headings. For example, information on the Tejas tribe might be found under *Texas; Indians, American;* or *Native Americans.* Materials on De Soto and Coronado may be found under *Explorers.*

 For additional resources and curriculum-related activities, see *Enrichment,* page T258.

Reading Selection:
Lady Moody's Dream

Pages 292–296

Objectives

		SKILLS CODE NUMBER
M, T	To identify the topic and stated main idea of a paragraph	3.3.8
M	To identify cause-and-effect relationships	3.3.3
M	To use a table of contents	5.5.3

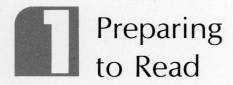

Preparing to Read

Summary

Lady Deborah Moody left England to come to America in 1640. She dreamed of finding a place where people could worship and think as they pleased. She did not find this freedom in Boston or in Salem, Massachusetts, so she finally traveled to New Amsterdam (now New York City). There she went about making her dream come true on her own. She bought a large piece of land in the southern part of Brooklyn, drew up a plan for her town, and started the settlement she named Gravesend. Lady Moody became the first woman to buy land in America, the first woman to start an American settlement, and one of America's first architects.

Background

Dutch pioneers founded the first settlement in Brooklyn in 1636, naming it "Breuckelen" after a town in Holland. This was soon followed by other settlements—Flatlands, Wallabout, the Ferry, and Gravesend.

The English title "Lady" is used with the last name of a woman married to a baron, count, duke, or other nobleman, but it is used with the first name for the daughter of a baron, count, etc. The title character in this selection married a nobleman. She is therefore referred to as "Lady Moody" rather than "Lady Deborah."

The following book will provide you with additional background information.

Banner, Lois W. *Elizabeth Cady Stanton: A Radical for Women's Rights.* A biography of one of the founders of the women's movement who became a political figure by the late nineteenth century.

Developing Vocabulary and Concepts

mansion: a large and impressive house
tutor: a person who teaches another, usually privately
architect: a person who designs and draws up plans for buildings or other structures and sees that the plans are carried through by the builders
triangular: of, having to do with, or shaped like a triangle
lack: be without or have too little
reality: an actual thing or fact
tap: release liquid from something by drilling a hole
faith: religion or belief

1. **a.** Read the following sentences aloud, or write them on the board. If you read them aloud, write the underlined vocabulary on the board.

   The beautiful mansion Lady Moody had lived in had fifteen rooms.
   As a child, Lady Moody did not attend school. She had tutors come to her home to teach her privately.
   Although Lady Moody had no training as an architect, the plan she designed for the town was a good one.
   According to Lady Moody's plan, each lot was triangular. These three-sided lots surrounded the town square.
   The lack of freedom in Boston made Lady Moody unhappy. She decided she could not live without freedom any longer.
   Lady Moody worked hard to make her dream become a reality.
   In order to tap a maple tree, the colonists first drilled a hole in the tree. Then they put a bucket underneath the hole to collect the maple sap as it slowly dripped out.
   Lady Moody's plan included a church where people of all faiths and beliefs could worship.

   b. Ask students to give the meaning of each vocabulary word. Remind them to use the context clues in the sentences to help them.

2. Ask students to imagine what their area might have been like before their city or town was built. Encourage them to imagine a time when their area was without buildings or streets. Then ask students to think about the sort of place they would like to live in if they could plan their own city or town. What

In this selection, some paragraphs deal with the topic of Lady Moody's life in Boston. Other paragraphs deal with the topic of her plans for a settlement. As you read, think about the topic of each paragraph. Look for sentences that state the main idea of the paragraph.

A place where all people could find freedom. In the early 1600's, this was . . .

Lady Moody's Dream

by Dina Brown Anastasio

292

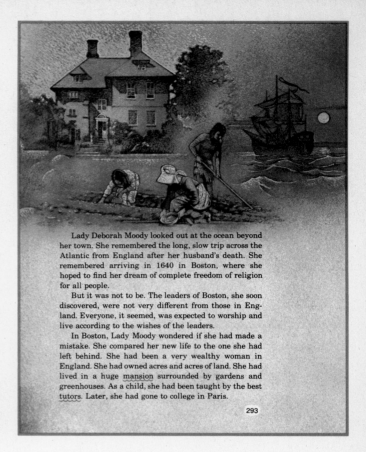

Lady Deborah Moody looked out at the ocean beyond her town. She remembered the long, slow trip across the Atlantic from England after her husband's death. She remembered arriving in 1640 in Boston, where she hoped to find her dream of complete freedom of religion for all people.

But it was not to be. The leaders of Boston, she soon discovered, were not very different from those in England. Everyone, it seemed, was expected to worship and live according to the wishes of the leaders.

In Boston, Lady Moody wondered if she had made a mistake. She compared her new life to the one she had left behind. She had been a very wealthy woman in England. She had owned acres and acres of land. She had lived in a huge mansion surrounded by gardens and greenhouses. As a child, she had been taught by the best tutors. Later, she had gone to college in Paris.

293

would they include? Allow time for discussion. Explain that the selection they will read tells about a woman who drew up plans to start her own town.

 Use *Duplicating Masters 11,* page 34.

Setting Purposes

Skills

Have students read the skills note at the top of page 292. Remind them that the main idea of a paragraph is the most important thing stated about the topic.

Content

Have students read the lead-in to the title. Ask what happens when a person's freedom is limited. How does this affect someone's life?

2 Reading and Discussing

Have students read the selection. All students should be able to complete it in one sitting.

NOTE: The questions that appear in the student's text at the end of the selection focus on comprehension of selection content and on application of the *Skills Lesson* to the selection. Answers to these questions begin on page T252.

Nevertheless, during the two years that she lived in Boston, she found things that she had never known in England. She found the joy of sharing hardship and laughter with her neighbors. She lived in a fine stone house near the village green. Every night, her neighbors left their small log homes and joined her in front of the fire in her kitchen. During the day their children gathered in her home, and she taught them to read and write.

Her life was a hard one, and there was a great deal of work to be done. But the work soon proved to be fun. The colonists had learned from the American Indians how to tap the maple sugar trees. Every year, sugar-making time brought with it a party. Corn planting—also learned from the American Indians—was another chance for a party.

But the lack of freedom in Boston finally became too much for Lady Moody. She realized that she must move on.

From Boston, Lady Moody, her son Sir Harry, and several of their friends sailed to Salem, Massachusetts. But again they failed to find the freedom they were seeking.

Once more they set out in search of their dream. They sailed down the New England coast in 1642 and reached the mouth of the Hudson River at what is now New York City. At that time it was a Dutch settlement called New Amsterdam.

One day shortly after their arrival, Lady Moody stood on the tip of New Amsterdam and looked across the river to Brooklyn. At that moment she knew that her search was over at last. She knew that if she could not find the freedom she was searching for, she would make it herself. So she bought a large piece of land in the southern part of Brooklyn, which was then wilderness. She was

294

the first woman ever to buy land in America. She became the first woman to start an American settlement.

Lady Moody chose a name for her settlement—Gravesend. It was the name of the small town in England where, before her husband's death, Lady Moody and her family had spent many happy moments.

Lady Moody did not think of herself as an architect. She had no such training. But she drew up a plan for her town. Three hundred years later, her plan would be put in a museum. She would be known as one of America's first architects.

In Lady Moody's plan, forty triangular lots surrounded a town square. In the square, the settlers and the American Indians could gather to make plans and talk with their neighbors. Near the square there would be a meeting house. There would also be a church where people of all faiths could worship.

295

Questions preceded by a bullet are additional questions and appear in the Teacher's Edition only. The other questions appear in the student's text after the selection.

Understanding What You've Read

1. *Why did Lady Moody move to Boston?* (She hoped people in Boston would be free to worship and think as they pleased.   page 293) LITERAL   Identifying cause-and-effect relationships

2. *How were Boston's leaders like England's leaders?* (The leaders of Boston and the leaders in England expected everyone to worship and live the way they did.   page 293) LITERAL   Making comparisons

3. *What was Lady Moody's life like in Boston?* (Her life was hard, and there was a great deal of work to be done. However, she and her neighbors shared good times together and learned useful things from the American Indians.   page 294) INFERENTIAL   Making generalizations

● *In what places did Lady Moody live?* (Lady Moody lived first in England and then sailed to Boston.   page 293   From Boston, she went to Salem, Massachusetts.   page 294   Then she sailed to New Amsterdam.   page 294   Finally, she moved to Brooklyn.   page 294) LITERAL   Determining the correct sequence for a set of events

4. *How did Lady Moody make her dream come true?* (She bought a large piece of land in Brooklyn, drew up a plan for the sort of town in which she would like to live, and started her own settlement.)
INFERENTIAL   Identifying the main idea of a selection

● *Describe the town that Lady Moody designed.* (The town that Lady Moody designed had forty triangular lots surrounding a town square. Near the square there were a meeting house and a church.   page 295) LITERAL   Recalling specific details

Applying the Skills Lesson

1. *The list below states the topics of some of the paragraphs in the selection you just read. Look back at the selection. Find the paragraphs whose topics are listed below.*
  a. the paragraph on page 293 about Lady Moody's life in England
  b. the paragraph on page 295 about the topic the name Gravesend
  c. the paragraph on page 295 about the topic how Gravesend would look
  (a. paragraph that begins "In Boston, Lady Moody wondered . . ."; b. paragraph that begins "Lady Moody chose a name . . ."; c. paragraph that begins "In Lady Moody's plan . . .")   Identifying the topic of a paragraph

● *What is the topic of the second paragraph on page 293?* (Lady Moody's life in Boston *or* the leaders of Boston and England)   Identifying the topic of a paragraph

2. *The main idea of the first paragraph on page 294 is stated. What is the main idea of that paragraph?* ("Nevertheless, during the two years that she lived in Boston, she found things that she had never known in England.")   Identifying the stated main idea of a paragraph

● *The main idea of the first paragraph on page 296 is stated. What is the main idea of that paragraph?* ("Within a few years, the town grew.")   Identifying the stated main idea of a paragraph

 Use *Duplicating Masters 11*, page 35. See *Providing for Individual Differences*, page T256, for additional practice.

3 Maintaining Skills

Comprehension Skills

Identifying cause-and-effect relationships Write the following incomplete sentences on the board, or read them aloud. Have students complete each sentence by supplying an appropriate cause or effect. (Accept all reasonable answers.) Have students identify their answers as either causes or effects.

> Because of the lack of freedom in Boston, . . . (Lady Moody moved on to Salem, Massachusetts; effect)
>
> When Lady Moody did not find freedom in Salem, Massachusetts, . . . (she sailed to New Amsterdam; effect)
>
> . . ., therefore she chose the name Gravesend for her settlement. (Gravesend was the town in England where Lady Moody had lived happily with her family; cause)
>
> . . ., so Lady Moody became known as one of America's first architects. (She drew up a plan for her town; cause)

Study Skills

Using a table of contents Write the following table of contents on the board. Ask students the questions that follow the table of contents.

Table of Contents

Unit 1 American Indians in New Amsterdam
1. The Canarsies
2. The Mohicans
3. The Iroquoians

Unit 2 Early Explorers in New York
4. Hudson, Verrazano, and Champlain
5. Other early explorers

Unit 3 Settlements
6. Fort Nassau (Albany)
7. New Amsterdam (New York City)

Which unit probably gives information about the American Indians who lived in Brooklyn in the 1600's? (Unit 1)

In which chapter might there be information about Lady Moody's settlement? (Chapter 7)

What is this book generally about? Choose from the following.
1. early settlements in America
2. the early history of New York
3. American Indians in New York
(Answer: 2)

Can you tell from this table of contents the exact pages on which you might find information about Lady Moody? (no)

What part of the book would help you find information about Lady Moody? (the index)

★ For additional resources and curriculum-related activities, see *Enrichment*, page T258.

Textbook Study:
Recognizing Topics and Main Ideas

Pages 297–299

Objective

		SKILLS CODE NUMBER
M, T	To identify the topic and stated main idea of a paragraph	3.3.8

Applying the Skill

Have students read the introduction and the two selections. You may wish to have students read the selections on their own and then do *Building Skills*. Or you may wish to direct students, using the following procedure.

Recognizing Topics and Main Ideas in Science

1. Have students read the first paragraph and the sidenote. Help them understand that each sentence tells about where plants will grow.

2. Have students read the second paragraph and answer the question in the sidenote. (The first paragraph tells about places where plants will grow. The second paragraph tells about objects that plants will grow on.)

TEXTBOOK STUDY

Recognizing Topics and Main Ideas

Since textbooks are written to give information, they are generally arranged to help the reader easily find the main ideas of paragraphs. Often, the main idea of a paragraph is stated.

Think about each paragraph's topic. Then look for the main idea. Use the sidenotes to help you.

Recognizing Topics and Main Ideas in Science

Some kind of plant will grow almost anywhere on the earth. Plants grow in the spaces between the parts of the sidewalks. They grow in window boxes in cities. You would have a hard time finding a place where plants do not grow. Some plants grow in damp soil; some in deserts. Some grow in ponds and streams, while others grow in the ocean. Plants can grow on mountaintops and in the cold of the Arctic.

Ask yourself what all of the sentences in the first paragraph are about. Your answer is the topic of the paragraph.

Plants can grow on many kinds of objects. Perhaps you have seen plants growing on rocks and trees. Plants even grow on old shoes and on animals. Where else have you seen plants growing?

Notice that the topic of this paragraph is very much like the topic of the paragraph above. What is the difference between the two topics?

—Understanding Your Environment
Silver Burdett

297

---

3. Have students complete *Building Skills*.

Answers to *Building Skills* Science Selection

1. first paragraph: b; second paragraph: a; not a topic: c; **2.** first paragraph: "Some kind of plant will grow almost anywhere on the earth"; second paragraph: "Plants can grow on many kinds of objects."

Recognizing Topics and Main Ideas in Language Arts

1. Have students read the two headings and the first sidenote. Then have them read the first paragraph of the selection and answer the question in the second sidenote. (the first sentence)

2. Have students read the second, third, and fourth paragraphs and answer the question in the last sidenote. (eight)

3. Have students complete *Building Skills*.

Answers to *Building Skills* Language Arts Selection

1. second paragraph: where the names of settlements on the East Coast came from; third paragraph: where the names of Western settlements came from; fourth paragraph: where the names of other cities in America came from; **2.** "As settlers moved westward across America, the same names went right along with them."

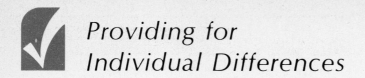

Providing for Individual Differences

Additional Practice

Worksheet 9, Teacher's Edition, page T488

Vocabulary Study

Additional Practice

■ **Identifying synonyms**   Write the following italicized words on the board, and read each sentence aloud. Have students identify the synonym in each sentence.

> *humanely:* You should treat animals humanely if you want them to respond kindly to you. (kindly)
>
> *falsehood:* No matter what the reason for Jerry's falsehood, it was still wrong for him to tell a lie. (lie)
>
> *saturated:* I was soaked by the rain, and the clothes on the line were saturated, too. (soaked)

Challenge Activity

■ **Identifying synonyms**   Read each of the following sentences aloud, or write them on the board. Have students identify the synonyms in each sentence.

> Although Andrea's attire is beautiful, her clothes are not appropriate for a barbecue. (attire, clothes)
>
> The art in this book is enchanting, and the story is captivating. (enchanting, captivating)
>
> Superstition can't prevent calamity, but common sense often prevents catastrophe. (calamity, catastrophe)
>
> I have no real reason to feel peevish today; nevertheless, I'm cranky. (peevish, cranky)
>
> Don't fret, Dad. There's nothing to worry about. (fret, worry)

Reading Selection: Journey of the Tejas Woman

Additional Practice

■ **Identifying topic and main idea**   Read the following paragraphs aloud. Have students select the topic from the choices given and then identify the sentence that states the main idea.

> One of the most interesting animals in the world is the great gray kangaroo. Large numbers of these animals are found in Australia. The gray kangaroo may reach a height of 1.5 meters (five feet) and can weigh 75 kilograms (200 pounds). This animal is also a very fast runner. It runs on its hind legs only and can clear as much as 6 meters (twenty feet) in one leap.
>
> 1. animals in Australia
> 2. the height and weight of the gray kangaroo
> 3. the gray kangaroo
> (Topic: 3. the gray kangaroo; Main idea: "One of the most interesting animals in the world is the great gray kangaroo.")

> Cats are clean, easy to care for, and don't have to be walked. Their curiosity and playfulness are fascinating to watch. They never seem to tire of exploring. Cats are well known for their independence. But they can also be quite friendly. Cats can be wonderful house pets.
>
> 1. house pets
> 2. cats
> 3. the curiosity of cats
> (Topic: 2. cats; Main idea: "Cats can be wonderful house pets.")

Challenge Activity

■ **Identifying topic and main idea**   Refer students to the selection "Start Your Own Theater." Have them find the topic and main idea of the fourth paragraph on page 215. (Topic: the producer; Main idea: "In other words, the producer is the boss.") Also have them find the topic and main idea of the second paragraph on page 217. (Topic: sound; Main idea: "The sound can be handled in a number of ways.")

Reading Selection: Lady Moody's Dream

Additional Practice

■ **Identifying topic and main idea**   Read the following paragraph aloud. Have students identify the topic and the sentence that states the main idea of the paragraph.

> Did you know that there were great paved highways thousands of years ago? More than 100,000 people worked on one road in Egypt. Over this road came the carts that carried stones used to build the pyramids. In 200 B.C., there was a saying, "All roads lead to Rome." The Romans built hundreds of long roads throughout Europe, Asia, and northern Africa. In the West, the Incas of Peru made many roads. One of them stretched for more than 2,000 kilometers. (Topic: ancient roads; Main idea: ". . . there were great paved highways thousands of years ago.")

Challenge Activity

Identifying topic and main idea　Assign specific paragraphs in a science or social studies textbook that your class uses. Ask students to identify the topic and main idea of each paragraph.

Evaluation

Periodic Test 3, Part I, Form A or *Form B,* may be administered after this unit to test skills marked **T.** If you have pretested using *Form A,* administer *Form B.*

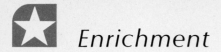

Enrichment

Journey of the Tejas Woman

Bibliography

The following books are about the exploration of America and about women who played important roles in American history.

Easy

Grant, Matthew G. *De Soto: Explorer of the Southeast.* A biography of Hernando De Soto, the first European to reach the Mississippi.

Average

Comins, Jeremy. *Totems, Decoys and Covered Wagons: Cardboard Constructions from Early American Life.* How to make copies of American Indian and colonial toys and furniture.

Levitin, Sonia. *The No-Return Trail.* A fictionalized account of the 1841 Bidwell-Bartleson expedition, which included seventeen-year-old Nancy Kelsey, the first American woman to journey from Missouri to California.

Challenging

Clyne, Patricia Edwards. *Patriots in Petticoats.* Biographies of twenty-eight women who played important parts in American history—Anne Bailey, Sybil Luddington, Deborah Sampson, and others.

Le Sueur, Meridel. *Conquistadores.* The explorations of Cortes, Pizarro, Coronado, and other Spanish explorers.

Films and Filmstrips

NOTE: For more information, see *Resource Center.*

Skills

Harcourt Brace Jovanovich. *Bookmark Reading Filmstrips: Purple:* "Topics, Main Ideas, and Details."

Guidance Assocs. *Using Your Reading Skills Series.* "Getting the Main Idea": solution of a mystery through analysis of main-idea sentences in newspapers and other sources.

Selection content

Coronet Instructional Media. "Spanish Influences in the United States." Present-day traces of Spanish exploration.

Encyclopaedia Britannica Educational Corp. *The Age of Exploration.* "Spain: Setting the Stage for Empire" and "Spain in the New World" are appropriate.

Curriculum Coordination

Language Arts

Have students write a diary as the Tejas Woman might have written one, describing her travels and adventures during her nine-day journey. You might suggest that students write about each day, or ask them just to cover the highlights of the journey.

Alternate composition: If Castañeda had been present at the Tejas Woman's homecoming, what would he have written in his report?

Social Studies

1. Have students investigate other famous Native Americans, such as Sacajawea, Chief Joseph, and Pocahontas. Have students share their findings with the class.

2. Have students investigate and make a map showing the locations of different Native American tribes and nations.

Art

Have students locate books that contain illustrations of Pueblo homes and villages. They may then construct models or dioramas depicting Pueblo homes and ways of life.

Lady Moody's Dream

Bibliography

The following books are about the history of New York or about women who played important roles in American history.

Average

Johnston, Johanna. *Women Themselves.* Women in American history, including Anne Hutchinson, Phillis Wheatley, Lady Deborah Moody, Elizabeth Blackwell, and others.

Challenging

Clyne, Patricia Edwards. *Patriots in Petticoats.* Biographies of twenty-eight women who played important parts in American history.

Goodnough, David. *The Colony of New York.* The history of New York from the Indian Wars to the end of the American Revolution.

Hults, Dorothy Niebrugge. *New Amsterdam Days and Ways: The Dutch Settlers of New York.* New York in the 1600's—the way people lived and their history.

Films and Filmstrips

NOTE: For more information, see *Resource Center*.

Skills

Harcourt Brace Jovanovich. *Bookmark Reading Film-strips: Purple.* "Topics, Main Ideas, and Details."
Guidance Assocs. *Using Your Reading Skills Series.* "Getting the Main Idea": solution of a mystery through analysis of main-idea sentences in newspapers and other sources.

Selection content

Encyclopaedia Britannica Educational Corp. *Life in Early America.* "Life in New Amsterdam" and "Life in Plymouth Colony" are appropriate.

Curriculum Coordination

Language Arts

1. Have students write compositions about the kind of place they would like to live in if they could plan their own city or town. How would it be similar to or different from the city or town they live in now?

2. Have students pretend they are Lady Moody or her son and they are writing a letter to a relative in England describing life in Boston.

Social Studies

1. Integrate a lesson on colonial life with this selection.

2. Some students may want to research the American Indian tribes that lived in New Amsterdam.

3. Make a map of Holland and a map of New York available to students. Have students find the names of towns and cities from which New York names might have been taken. Have students note spelling changes.

4. If there is a restored colonial village near your area, arrange to take students to see it.

Art/Language Arts

Ask students to draw up Lady Moody's plan for the town of Gravesend by following the description given in the last paragraph on page 295. Be sure they include the forty triangular lots, the town square, the meeting house, the church, the library, and the beaches on the Atlantic Ocean.

Career Education

Invite an architect or urban planner to talk to the class about his or her profession.

Contents

Additional Materials

Reading Skills Workbook: Lessons 24–25, pages 78–80
Duplicating Masters 11: pages 36–39
Worksheet 10: Teacher's Edition, page T489
Bookmark Reading Filmstrips: Purple: "Topics, Main Ideas, and Details"
Periodic Test 3, Part II

Key to Symbols

Skills Objectives
I* — Introduced in this unit
I   — Introduced earlier in this level
M   — Maintained from previous levels
T   — Tested in periodic and cumulative tests for this level

Reduced Student Pages
underscore — words that appear in the glossary
wavy line   — words pretaught in the Teacher's Edition
            (these words also appear in the glossary)

Skills Lesson:
Understanding Unstated Main Ideas and the Details in a Paragraph
Pages 300–304

Objectives

		SKILLS CODE NUMBER
M, T	To identify details that support the stated main idea of a paragraph	3.3.1; 3.3.8.3
M, T	To identify the topic and stated main idea of a paragraph	3.3.8
M, T	To use details to determine the unstated main idea of a paragraph	3.3.1; 3.4.7

If you wish to pretest the skills listed above, you may administer *Periodic Test 3, Part II, Form A. Periodic Test 3, Part II, Form B,* may be administered to posttest.

Introducing the Lesson

1. Play a simplified version of "Twenty Questions." Explain to students that you are thinking of a specific animal and that they may ask up to twenty questions about the animal to guess what it is. Questions can only be answered yes or no. Write the correct details on the board. Students should try to guess the animal you are thinking of from the details.

Understanding Unstated Main Ideas and the Details in a Paragraph

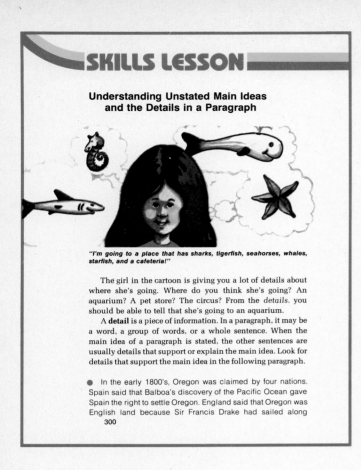

"I'm going to a place that has sharks, tigerfish, seahorses, whales, starfish, and a cafeteria!"

The girl in the cartoon is giving you a lot of details about where she's going. Where do you think she's going? An aquarium? A pet store? The circus? From the *details*, you should be able to tell that she's going to an aquarium.

A **detail** is a piece of information. In a paragraph, it may be a word, a group of words, or a whole sentence. When the main idea of a paragraph is stated, the other sentences are usually details that support or explain the main idea. Look for details that support the main idea in the following paragraph.

● In the early 1800's, Oregon was claimed by four nations. Spain said that Balboa's discovery of the Pacific Ocean gave Spain the right to settle Oregon. England said that Oregon was English land because Sir Francis Drake had sailed along

300

Oregon's coast in 1579. A Russian sailor named Bering had explored the northern Pacific Ocean in the 1700's. Russia therefore claimed rights to both Alaska and Oregon. The United States based its claim to Oregon on the explorations made by Sacajawea and Lewis and Clark from 1804 to 1806.

The main idea of the paragraph is stated in the first sentence: "In the early 1800's, Oregon was claimed by four nations." How do the other sentences support this idea?

When the Main Idea Is Not Stated

In many paragraphs, the main idea is not stated in one sentence. But you can state the main idea yourself if you understand what all the details add up to. You can find an unstated main idea in the same way you found the main idea of the cartoon on page 300. You added up the details and were able to figure out that the little girl is going to an aquarium.

The main idea of the following paragraph is not stated.

301

2. Write the word *detail* on the board. Ask students to explain how they arrived at the answer by using each detail about the animal.

3. Ask students to look at the cartoon at the top of page 300 and read the paragraph below it. Explain that, just as they added up the details to guess where the girl in the cartoon was going, they can add up the details in a paragraph to determine its main idea.

Developing the Skill

When the main idea of a paragraph is stated, the other sentences are usually details that support or explain the main idea.

Remind students that a stated main idea often, but not always, appears in the first sentence of a paragraph. Have students read the second paragraph on page 300 and the sample paragraph about Oregon.

Ask them to identify the stated main idea. ("In the early 1800's, Oregon was claimed by four nations.") Then have students read the other sentences in the paragraph and tell how they support or explain the main idea. (Each tells about one of the four nations that claimed Oregon.)

When the Main Idea Is Not Stated

The unstated main idea of a paragraph can be determined by identifying the topic of the paragraph and then adding up the given details.

1. Have students read the first two paragraphs under the heading. Then have students read the sample

Use the details in order to figure out the paragraph's main idea. Remember, the main idea is the most important idea about the topic of a paragraph.

● For many years, most Americans lived in small towns or on farms. As late as 1880, only two people out of every ten lived in a city. By 1920, however, half the people in the United States lived in cities. Today more than seven out of ten Americans are city-dwellers.

Each sentence tells where Americans lived at a special time in our history—in 1880, 1920, and today. Each sentence gives a detail that contributes to the main idea. Which of the following sentences states that main idea best?

1. For many years, most Americans lived in small towns or on farms.
2. Since 1880, the United States has changed from a nation of country-dwellers to a nation of city-dwellers.
3. Today many people live in cities.

302

Read sentence 1 again. Does this sentence tell you anything about where Americans live today? No. It tells you only about the way things were in the past. It is a detail. Why is sentence 3 only a detail? The paragraph tells you that Americans have moved from the country to cities over the years. Therefore, sentence 2 best states the main idea.

Try This

In each of the following paragraphs, the main idea is not stated in one sentence. First find the topic of each paragraph. Then think of what the paragraph *says* about that topic. Notice the details that support the main idea.

1.   In 1608, France sent many families to settle in "New France" in America. Holland also sent settlers to America. The Dutch settlement of New Amsterdam was started in 1624. From 1580 until the early 1600's, many English people also tried to start colonies in America.

What is the topic of the paragraph?

a. English settlements in America
b. European settlements in America
c. French settlements in America

What is the main idea of the paragraph?

a. France, Holland, and England tried to build American colonies in the late 1500's and early 1600's.
b. Early settlements in America were successful.
c. From 1580 until the early 1600's, many English people tried to start colonies in America.

303

2.   Lara tries to get enough sleep each night. She makes sure that she gets the right kinds of food. She avoids eating sweets or too much of any one kind of food. Lara also makes a point of getting lots of fresh air and exercise.

What is the topic of the paragraph?
a. what Lara likes to eat
b. what Lara does every day
c. how Lara takes care of her body's needs

What is the main idea of the paragraph?
a. Lara is an interesting person.
b. Lara does things to keep healthy.
c. Lara tries to get enough sleep at night.

3.   Cities are interesting places to many people. For example, New York has many museums, art galleries, theaters, and restaurants for people to enjoy. It also has great landmarks like the Empire State Building, the Statue of Liberty, the United Nations headquarters, and Rockefeller Center. Some people even find riding New York's subways interesting.

What is the main idea of the paragraph?
a. New York is an interesting place.
b. Cities are interesting places to many people.
c. New York's subways are interesting.

304

paragraph on page 302. Ask them to identify the topic. (where Americans lived in 1880, 1920, and today) Have them check their responses by noting that all the sentences in the paragraph are about this topic.

2. **a.** Have students read the three suggested main ideas and select the appropriate one. (2. Since 1880, the United States has changed from a nation of country-dwellers to a nation of city-dwellers.)

b. Ask them why sentence 1 is not the main idea. (It tells only about the past, not about today.) Ask why sentence 3 is not the main idea. (It tells only about today, not about the past.)

Try This

Have students complete *Try This*.

Answers to *Try This*

1. b, a; 2. c, b; 3. a

✔ Use *Reading Skills Workbook*, Lesson 24, pages 78–79. See *Providing for Individual Differences*, page T276, for additional practice.

Vocabulary Study:
Suffixes
Page 305

Objective

M   To identify word parts: root words and suffixes

SKILLS CODE NUMBER

4.1

Developing the Skill

1. Tell students that the *Vocabulary Study* they are about to read, or sing, has "The Suffix Song" in it. Ask them what a suffix is. (a word part added to the end of a root word to change the word's meaning)

2. Have students read the *Vocabulary Study.* If you wish, they may sing "The Suffix Song" to the tune of "MacNamara's Band" or the "Brownie Song." Then have students do the *Word Play* activities.

Answers to *Word Play*

1. nameless, treeless, endless; 2. Sentences will vary.

 Use *Reading Skills Workbook,* Lesson 25, page 80. See *Providing for Individual Differences,* page T276, for additional practice.

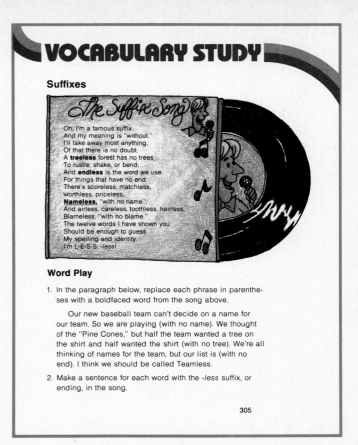

VOCABULARY STUDY

Suffixes

The Suffix Song

Oh, I'm a famous suffix
And my meaning is "without."
I'll take away most anything,
Of that there is no doubt.
A **treeless** forest has no trees
To rustle, shake, or bend;
And **endless** is the word we use
For things that have no end.
There's scoreless, matchless,
Worthless, priceless,
Nameless, "with no name";
And airless, careless, toothless, hairless,
Blameless, "with no blame."
The twelve words I have shown you
Should be enough to guess
My spelling and identity.
I'm L-E-S-S, -*less*!

Word Play

1. In the paragraph below, replace each phrase in parentheses with a boldfaced word from the song above.

   Our new baseball team can't decide on a name for our team. So we are playing (with no name). We thought of the "Pine Cones," but half the team wanted a tree on the shirt and half wanted the shirt (with no tree). We're all thinking of names for the team, but our list is (with no end). I think we should be called Teamless.

2. Make a sentence for each word with the -*less* suffix, or ending, in the song.

305

Reading Selection:
The Peddler's Pack
Pages 306–311

Objectives

		SKILLS CODE NUMBER
M, T	To use details to determine the unstated main idea of a paragraph	3.3.1; 3.4.7
M, T	To identify the topic and stated main idea of a paragraph	3.3.8
M	To identify base words in compound words	4.2.1
I	To write a topical outline	7.1.5.1

Preparing to Read

Summary

Peddlers played an important role in colonial America. During colonial times, almost all manufactured goods were imported from England. The peddlers came to the ships when they docked, bought cloth, tea, tools, and utensils, and then went into the wilderness to barter with settlers. Until roads were built, peddlers often traveled by river.

After the United States won its independence from England, Americans began to manufacture their own goods. Many peddlers began to carry only one kind of product, such as cloth or tin. As American factories grew, so did the peddlers' wagons. The Conestoga wagon, the largest wagon of all, could carry up to six tons of merchandise. The era of the peddler came to a close at the end of the nineteenth century with the establishment of railroads.

Background

Mercantilism was a European economic policy from the 1500's to the 1700's. Mercantilism was based on the premise that a strong country must have more exports than imports. Great Britain therefore imported only raw materials from its colonies; the raw materials were made into goods in England. The manufactured goods were exported back to the colonies. The colonial rulers effectively restricted manufacturing in the American colonies until the Revolution, so colonists were forced to buy goods from England.

The following book will provide you with additional background information.

Langdon, William Chauncy. *Everyday Things in American Life.* Discussion of home, family, peddlers, trading, etc. Two volumes. Illustrated, with bibliography and index.

Developing Vocabulary and Concepts

barter: trade by exchanging goods or services without using money
raft: a floating platform made of logs
thicket: a thick, dense growth, as of trees and bushes
merchandise: goods for sale
restriction: the act of holding or keeping within limits or bounds
pike: a road or highway
schooner: a sailing ship having two or more masts

1. **a.** Read the following sentences aloud, or write them on the board. If you read them aloud, write the underlined vocabulary on the board.

   The peddlers cut down small trees, tied the trunks together, and traveled on the river on these rafts.
   The peddlers had to chop down many tree branches and bushes just to make a small path through the thicket.
   The merchandise that the peddlers sold included almost anything farmers needed in their homes or fields.
   When the American colonies became independent, there were no more restrictions on manufacturing. Americans were not limited in any way in starting their own factories.
   The wagon called the prairie schooner got its name because its high, rounded top looked like a ship's sail.

   b. Ask students to give the meaning of each vocabulary word. Remind them to use the context clues in the sentences to help them.

2. Ask students what they use to pay for something. (money) Explain to students that in the 1600's and 1700's, Americans weren't allowed to coin their own money, so if they wanted to buy something, they might *barter* for it.

   Write the word *barter* on the baord, and explain to students that it means to trade something, like eggs for milk, or to agree to do something, such as cook dinner, in order to get something else.

In many of the paragraphs in this selection, the main idea is not stated. You can state the main idea yourself. First find the topic. Then use the details to figure out the main idea.

If you lived two hundred years ago, you might wonder what you'd find in . . .

The Peddler's Pack

by Charlotte MacLeod

306

Have you ever heard someone say, "I'm waiting for my ship to come in"? Before the American Revolution, colonists were always waiting for their ships to come in because they were not supposed to manufacture anything for sale. Their British rulers wanted them to buy goods made in England. The only way to buy a piece of cloth or a pan or a printing press or even a pin was to order it from the "old country." When a ship docked, everybody would run to the waterfront and <u>barter</u> with the sailors for whatever had been brought on the voyage.

As time went on and more colonists came, towns around the waterfront got too crowded. People began moving away from the seaports. In the <u>vast</u> wilderness, they found plenty of places to settle.

Now, however, they were too far away to trade with the ships for the many things they needed. They had no stores in which to shop. They had no neighbors to lend them a tool or a dish or a pinch of salt.

Still, the settlers didn't have to go <u>entirely</u> without the manufactured articles that made life a little bit easier. Some brave and clever young people decided to become peddlers. They went to the ships and bought everything they could from the sailors. Then, with big packs on their backs, they walked into the wilderness looking for customers.

Peddlers could make a great deal of money if they weren't afraid of danger and hard work. Most of the time there were no roads to follow. A peddler had to rely on the sun and stars to guide the way. He had to hope he would be lucky enough to find a settlement. When a peddler did find one, the people gathered around him. He told them news of the

---

3. Ask students if they know what a turnpike is. (highway) Explain that in colonial times people called some roads "pikes." Sometimes a road that went through a person's land would have a turnstile on it. In order to be allowed to pass through the turnstile and continue along the road, a traveler would have to pay a toll. Explain that the word *pike* is rarely used today as a synonym for *road*.

4. Ask students if traveling salespeople have ever come to their homes to sell things. Ask what kinds of products these people were selling. Explain that when the United States was first settled, there were no stores, and people who lived in the wilderness depended on the traveling salespeople, or peddlers, to come to their homes with things to buy.

 Use *Duplicating Masters 11,* page 36.

Setting Purposes

Skills

Have students read the skills note at the top of page 306. Then ask them what steps they should follow to identify the unstated main idea of a paragraph.

Content

Have students read the lead-in to the title. Ask them if they've ever taken part in a "grab bag." Explain that the colonists often thought of a peddler's pack as rather like a grab bag. They never knew what new "treasures" they'd find in it.

2 Reading and Discussing

Have students read the selection. Most students will be able to complete it in one sitting. If you prefer, the selection may be read in two parts, breaking before the sentence "As more and more settlers moved into the wilderness . . ." on page 309.

NOTE: The questions that appear in the student's text at the end of the selection focus on comprehension of selection content and on application of the *Skills Lesson* to the selection. Answers to these questions begin on page T267.

outside world. Perhaps he carried a message from a friend or relative. For a while, he joked and told stories. Then he opened his pack and began to trade.

In early times, it didn't much matter what the peddler showed the settlers. They needed so many things that there was always a customer for every _item_ in his pack. Even a needle or thread was a treasure.

Everyone wanted to buy, but few had money—partly because the colonists were forbidden to make their own _coinage_. So instead of nickels and dimes and dollar bills, the settlers might offer the peddler food grown on their farms, yarn _spun_ from their sheep, or skins of animals.

Sometimes, a peddler might use a river as his "expressway." Poling a _raft_ was often better than cutting a path through swamps and _thickets_. Still, travel by water could be hard and dangerous. The peddler might be caught in a

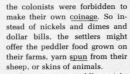

storm and swept overboard with his precious cargo.

Picture a tired peddler poling a heavy raftload of goods he hoped to trade along the riverbank. How happy he must have been to find a farmhouse. Perhaps he would say, "If you help me, I will stay and keep a store. Settlers will come to trade and be your neighbors. You can build a school."

Soon, news of the store would spread up and down the riverbank. People would ask, "Does the storekeeper have much to sell?" Others would reply, "Yes, he has a whole raft of things."

The next time you hear someone talk about having a whole raft of stuff, remember that this was the way peddlers helped to start new cities and towns.

As more and more settlers moved into the wilderness, more and more peddlers shouldered packs to trade with the growing population. In time, the townspeople built roads. Peddlers could use pack horses, mules, or wagons to bring in more _merchandise_ than they could carry on their backs.

When the United States won independence from Great Britain and there were no more _restrictions_ on manufacturing, factories _sprang_ up everywhere. Peddlers no longer had to rely on the ships for goods. Many peddlers worked for single factories, carrying only one kind of merchandise.

When the tin peddler came down the _pike_, the metal pots and pans in his wagon rattled and banged together loudly. People heard him coming long before they caught sight of his horse. Cloth peddlers had special wagons built to carry bolts of material on long rollers. Customers could climb up and look at all the different patterns before choosing the one they liked best.

By this time, America had its own coinage. Customers could pay in money instead of animal skins or _homespun_ yarn. But many purchases were still made by barter. A peddler didn't mind if someone chose to pay for a new skillet with a dozen fresh eggs and a loaf or two of home-baked bread. The peddler just ate the food along the way, saving the cost of dining at an inn.

As the factories grew, so did the peddlers' wagons. Largest of

them all was the Conestoga wagon, made in Conestoga, Pennsylvania. It could carry up to six tons of merchandise. Its high, rounded top looked like a ship's sail in the distance. The wagons were soon nicknamed "prairie _schooners_." When you picture covered wagons, you probably think of the westward journeys of the pioneers. But it was the demand for bigger and better freight carriers that caused the first Conestogas to be built.

By the end of the nineteenth century, _prairie schooners_ sailed the plains no more. Railroad trains had changed the peddler's way of life.

Today, salesmen and saleswomen may travel thousands of miles in a week by airplane and automobile. Many sell more in one day than an old-time peddler sold in a lifetime. But they are still carrying on one of our country's earliest and most colorful _professions_.

Understanding What You've Read

1. Why was the arrival of a ship from England an exciting event for the colonists?
2. How did the settlers pay for the peddler's goods?
3. Name the different ways in which peddlers traveled with their goods.
4. Why were the Conestoga wagons built?
5. Why were Conestogas called "prairie schooners"?
6. What does a peddler's pack remind you of?

Applying the Skills Lesson

1. Read the first full paragraph in the right-hand column on page 309. Which of the three sentences below best states its main idea?
   a. Some peddlers sold only things made of metal.
   b. Some peddlers sold only cloth.
   c. Some peddlers carried only one kind of merchandise.
2. State the topic of the second paragraph in the right-hand column on page 309. Then state the main idea of that paragraph.

311

Questions preceded by a bullet are additional questions and appear in the Teacher's Edition only. The other questions appear in the student's text after the selection.

Understanding What You've Read

1. *Why was the arrival of a ship from England an exciting event for the colonists?* (Answers should include: Since the colonists were not allowed to manufacture their own goods, the only way to buy things was to order them from England and wait until the ship came in. Also, it was exciting to see what else besides ordered goods the sailors would bring.   page 307) INFERENTIAL   Drawing conclusions

● *How were peddlers an important part of early colonial life?* (They brought the settlers needed goods. They also brought news about the outside world and messages from friends and relatives.   pages 307–308) INFERENTIAL   Identifying the main idea of a selection

2. *How did the settlers pay for the peddler's goods?* (Before colonists were able to coin their own money, they traded home-grown food, yarn spun from the wool of their sheep, or skins of animals.   page 308) LITERAL   Recalling stated information

3. *Name the different ways in which peddlers traveled with their goods.* (They traveled by foot, by raft, and on horses, mules, and wagons.   pages 307–309) LITERAL   Making comparisons

● *Why did the peddlers' trade undergo change after the American colonies won their independence?* (Peddlers no longer had to rely on the ships for goods. Many peddlers worked for single factories, carrying only one kind of merchandise. Customers could now pay in money, although many purchases were still made by barter.   page 309) INFERENTIAL   Identifying cause-and-effect relationships

4. *Why were the Conestoga wagons built?* (to carry the peddlers' growing loads of merchandise   page 309) LITERAL   Identifying cause-and-effect relationships

● *Why did the railroads change the peddlers' way of life?* (Peddlers were no longer needed to bring goods to the people—the railroads brought goods to the people.   page 310) INFERENTIAL   Drawing conclusions

5. *Why were Conestogas called "prairie schooners"?* (because the high, rounded top looked like a ship's sail in the distance   page 310) LITERAL   Identifying cause-and-effect relationships

6. *What does a peddler's pack remind you of?* (Accept all reasonable answers.) CRITICAL   Making judgments

Applying the Skills Lesson

1. *Read the first full paragraph in the right-hand column on page 309. Which of the three sentences below best states its main idea?*
   a. *Some peddlers sold only things made of metal.*
   b. *Some peddlers sold only cloth.*
   c. *Some peddlers carried only one kind of merchandise.*
   (Answer: c)   Determining the unstated main idea of a paragraph

● *Why are sentences a and b poor choices for stating the main idea?* (Both a and b refer only to details in the paragraph. They do not give the general idea of the paragraph.)   Determining the unstated main idea of a paragraph

2. *State the topic of the second paragraph in the right-hand column on page 309. Then state the main idea of that paragraph.* (Topic: how the settlers paid the peddler; Sample main idea: Some settlers now paid in money and some continued to barter.) <u>Identifying the topic/Determining the unstated main idea of a paragraph</u>

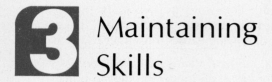 Use *Duplicating Masters 11*, page 37. See *Providing for Individual Differences*, page T276, for additional practice.

3 Maintaining Skills

Language Skills

Identifying base words in compound words   Read the following definitions aloud, or write them on the board. Tell students to find a compound word in "The Peddler's Pack" to match each definition. In most cases, the meaning of the compound word is determined by the combined meanings of the base words.

> an area next to a body of water, especially a part of a city that contains docks (waterfront)
> a port or town accessible to seagoing ships (seaport)
> a highway designed for rapid travel (expressway)
> the land bordering a river (riverbank)
> a person who keeps a store or shop (storekeeper)
> quantity that can be carried on a raft at one time (raftload)
> people who live in towns (townspeople)
> spun at home (homespun)
> system of tracks and stations used in transportation (railroad)

Study Skills

Writing a topical outline   Write the following incomplete outline on the board. Have students fill in the missing information, using the items at the right as subtopics. Allow them to look back at the selection. Remind students to use Roman numerals and capital letters and to give their outline a title.

____ In early colonial times	Conestoga wagons
____ _____	Rafts
____ _____	Horses or mules
____ As more settlers moved west	Wagons with many kinds of merchandise
____ _____	Wagons with one kind of merchandise
____ _____	Walking
____ As American factories were built	
____ _____	

Sample answer:

      The Peddlers' Means of Transportation

  I. In early colonial times
    A. Walking
    B. Rafts
 II. As more settlers moved west
    A. Horses or mules
    B. Wagons with many kinds of merchandise
III. As American factories were built
    A. Conestoga wagons
    B. Wagons with one kind of merchandise

⊠ For additional resources and curriculum-related activities, see *Enrichment*, page T278.

Reading Selection:
The Secret of the Sea
Pages 312–318

Objectives

		SKILLS CODE NUMBER
M, T	To use details to determine the unstated main idea of a paragraph	3.3.1; 3.4.7
M, T	To identify the topic and stated main idea of a paragraph	3.3.8
I	To identify topical organization	5.10.1
M	To use a dictionary to find word meaning	5.6.4

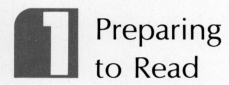

Preparing to Read

Summary

Paul Cuffe was born on Cuttyhunk Island, Massachusetts, in 1759. As a young boy, Paul was fascinated by ships and the sea. He studied and saved during his youth to achieve his dream of someday sailing and owning his own ship. Cuffe encountered many difficulties and misfortunes before his dream was finally realized. However, because of his intense love for the sea and his determination, he succeeded in establishing himself as a prosperous sea trader who owned six ships, a wharf, and a storehouse in Westport, Massachusetts.

Background

Paul Cuffe (1759–1817) was the son of an African-born Massachusetts slave who purchased his freedom. Cuffe's mother was a Nantucket Indian. Cuffe was actively involved in securing legal rights for black people in Massachusetts. His efforts led to a law, passed in 1783, that gave black people in Massachusetts the right to vote. He was also an advocate of the resettlement of black Americans in Africa. In 1811, his diplomatic contact with both white and black citizens of Sierra Leone led to the founding of an agency that helped to arrange immigration. In 1815, Cuffe sailed to Sierra Leone with thirty-eight free black Americans who settled there. Cuffe's health failed, however, before he could promote the venture further.

The following book will provide you with additional background information.

Harris, Sheldon H. *Paul Cuffe*. A biography.

Developing Vocabulary and Concepts

spellbound: fascinated, as if under a spell
sacrifice: give up something important, usually for the sake of something else
navigation: the art of charting the position or course of a ship or aircraft
patrols: people or groups guarding an area
menace: threaten with evil or harm
intense: very strong, great, or deep
fascination: great interest or attraction
profits: the amount of money gained in a business deal after deducting all expenses
philanthropist: a person who gives time and money to help others

1. **a.** Read the following sentences aloud, or write them on the board. If you read them aloud, write the underlined vocabulary on the board.

    Paul was spellbound by the sea. He felt as if he were under a spell.
    Paul had to work to help support his family when he was young. So he had to give up, or sacrifice, his wish to get an education.
    He learned about navigation so that when he had his own boat, he would know how to sail from one place to another.
    In the 1700's there were no patrols to guard the waters. Today the Coast Guard protects the shores of the United States.
    Pirates were able to menace and threaten any ships that came by.
    Because Paul had a strong, intense love for the sea, he would not give up his dream of owning a ship.
    His fascination for the ocean started as a young boy, and this strong attraction grew as he got older.
    Paul made large profits from his trading. He used the money to buy more ships.
    Paul became known as a philanthropist because he used his money to help others.

    b. Ask students to give the meaning of each vocabulary word. Remind them to use the context clues in the sentences to help them.

There are many details in this selection. By noting how they are related, you can find the main ideas.

In Massachusetts in the 1760's, young Paul Cuffe was finding out everything possible about ships. He had one dream—to learn . . .

THE SECRET OF THE SEA

by Lavinia Dobler and Edgar A. Toppin

312

A boy stood on a windy shore in southern Massachusetts. He was spellbound by the restless ocean.

The sea seemed to give Paul Cuffe strength and courage. When the waves rose high in the air with a roar, Paul was sure the ocean was trying to tell him something he should know. Other times, when the sea was as calm as glass, he looked far away to the horizon. What was beyond?

Paul Cuffe lived on Cuttyhunk Island, about seven miles from the Massachusetts coast. Paul was the seventh child of the ten children.

In 1766, when Paul was almost eight years old, his parents bought land in Dartmouth, Connecticut. Six years later, when Paul was thirteen, his father died. Paul and his brother John took on much of the responsibility for the farm.

Caring for his family and managing the farm made Paul older than his years. It also meant a great sacrifice—his dream of getting an education. But more than ever, he was determined to find out about ships. Whenever he had a free moment, he hurried to the shore to study them.

Paul never forgot the day he had his first lesson in navigation. He had looked forward to it eagerly. But when the teacher started explaining the use of mathematics to figure position and direction, Paul was lost. As soon as the lesson was over, Paul walked out of the room, his head down, his feet dragging. He went back to the farm. His sister was waiting at the door.

"Paul, tell me about the lesson," she asked.

Her brother looked at her, pain written on his face. "It was all as dark as midnight," he said.

313

2. Ask students if they have ever been on boats. What kinds? Ask them if they have ever seen pictures of tall ships with huge sails, the kind that captains used to sail in the 1700's. Have students describe them. Explain that the selection they will be reading is about a boy who wanted to own and sail such a ship.

 Use *Duplicating Masters 11,* page 38.

Setting Purposes

Skills

Have students read the skills note on page 312. Remind them that if they are having difficulty figuring out the unstated main idea, they should first try to identify the topic of the paragraph.

Content

Have students read the lead-in to the title. Display a classroom map of the United States, and have students locate Massachusetts. Tell them that Paul Cuffe grew up on the island of Cuttyhunk (south of New Bedford). Ask students to think about how growing up on an island might have helped shape Paul's dream of owning his own ship.

 # Reading and Discussing

Have students read the selection. Most students will be able to complete it in one sitting. If you prefer, the selection may be read in two parts, breaking before the sentence "One day in 1780 . . ." on page 315.

NOTE: The questions that appear in the student's text at the end of the selection focus on comprehension of selection content and on application of the *Skills Lesson* to the selection. Answers to these questions begin on page T272.

"After a while you will understand it," his sister said to comfort him.

"I hope so," he said, "because someday I am going to sea!"

At the age of sixteen, part of Paul's dream came true. This was in 1775, the first year of the American Revolution.

Paul worked on a ship bound for the Gulf of Mexico. On his second trip, he sailed to the West Indies. On his third voyage, in 1776, when he was seventeen years old, Paul was captured by the British. He was in prison in New York City for three months.

While behind bars, Paul made up his mind that when he was set free he would study harder than ever. He was determined that someday he would own a ship. He couldn't afford to buy a ship, but one day he might build one.

When the British released him from prison, Paul went to Westport, a village in Massachusetts. He farmed and studied, never forgetting his dream.

Three years later, in 1779, while the British and the American colonists were still at war, Paul built a boat. His brother David helped him.

Paul was certain he could make money by having his own boat. He planned to trade with the people of Connecticut.

But there were many difficulties. The sea was often rough with storms. There was constant trouble with pirates. During the American Revolution, there were no patrols protecting the coast, so pirates were able to menace all the ships on the Atlantic seaboard.

314

If Paul had not had his dream and his intense love for the sea, he would not have made it. His drive kept him going while others without such a goal would have given up.

One day in 1780, Paul set out to sea in the boat that he and David had built. But, loaded with valuable cargo, it was lost in a bad storm that raged along the Connecticut coast. Paul somehow made it back to shore.

Paul built a second boat. The day he launched it, Paul's heart beat fast. He wasted no time sailing it out into the bay.

Unfortunately, luck was not with him on this journey. Pirates seized his boat.

315

There are no records telling how Paul Cuffe finally reached land. He escaped from the pirates and probably swam to shore.

When Paul finally got back to his home town, he considered giving up the plan to trade along the seacoast. Whenever he glanced at the water and the rolling waves, though, they held the same fascination for him as they had when he was a boy. He began to build another boat. He was able to borrow money to buy a cargo.

Even though the route was still dangerous, Paul dared to take the risk. He started bravely for Nantucket, some sixty miles southeast of Westport.

Pirates chased him.

As he tried desperately to get away, his boat hit a rock. This time, however, the pirates did not capture him or his boat. Even though the boat was

badly damaged, Paul finally got back to Westport. He wasted no time, working night and day to repair the boat. Later he sailed to Nantucket with his cargo.

Some months later, Paul bought a boat. He also found a good sailor who was willing to be his crew. By the time the Revolutionary War ended in 1783, the pirates were forced to seek other waters. Paul soon started to make large profits.

The year 1783 was important to Paul for another reason. He married Alice Pequit [pek'it], a woman who belonged to the same Native American tribe that Paul's mother belonged to.

The Cuffes had six daughters and two sons. By 1797, Paul was very successful. With profits from his trading, he bought a large farm on the Westport river.

In 1797, when he and his family settled in Westport, they found no schoolhouse or teacher in the neighborhood. Paul was troubled, for he wanted his children to have a good education. He could now afford to educate them, for his trading business was very successful.

Paul used his own money to pay for a schoolhouse to be built on his farm. Then he offered the school to the people of Westport. He also paid the teacher's salary and all the expenses of operating the school.

Paul Cuffe's first years of shipbuilding and sailing the seas were hard. He worked, and he succeeded. A less determined young person would have given up many times. But Paul Cuffe did not! Between the years 1793 and 1806, Paul's fleet grew to include six ships.

317

In 1817, Paul's health began to fail. He died at his home in Westport on September 9 of that year. Almost a hundred years later, in 1913, Cuffe's great-grandson put up a monument at the grave. Cut into the stone are these words:

〜〜〜〜〜

In the memory of Captain Cuffe,
Patriot, Navigator, Educator, Philanthropist,
Friend.

〜〜〜〜〜

Understanding What You've Read

1. Why did Paul have to sacrifice his dream of getting an education?
2. How did Paul plan to make money with the first boat he built?
3. Why did Paul decide to risk building a third boat?
4. What things happened in 1783 that began to change Paul's fortune for the better?

Applying the Skills Lesson

1. Read the sixth paragraph on page 313. Use the details from that paragraph to state its main idea in one sentence.
2. Read the fifth paragraph on page 317. Which of the following sentences best states the main idea of that paragraph?

   a. Paul had a schoolhouse built on his farm.
   b. Paul paid a teacher to work in a schoolhouse.
   c. Paul gave Westport a schoolhouse and paid the operating costs and the teacher's salary.

318

Questions preceded by a bullet are additional questions and appear in the Teacher's Edition only. The other questions appear in the student's text after the selection.

Understanding What You've Read

1. *Why did Paul have to sacrifice his dream of getting an education?* (When his father died, Paul had to help care for his family and manage the farm. page 313) INFERENTIAL   Identifying cause-and-effect relationships

● *What subject that you study in school would be most important if you wanted to learn about navigation?* (Mathematics   page 313) INFERENTIAL   Drawing conclusions

2. *How did Paul plan to make money with the first boat he built?* (He planned to trade with the people of Connecticut. page 314) LITERAL   Recalling specific details

● *What happened to Paul's first and second boats?* (His first boat was lost in a storm. His second boat was seized by pirates. page 315) LITERAL   Recalling specific details

3. *Why did Paul decide to risk building a third boat?* (He decided to take a risk because of his love for the sea and his desire to sail his own boat. page 316) INFERENTIAL   Drawing conclusions

● *What happened to Paul's third boat?* (Paul's third boat was chased by pirates. It was badly damaged when it hit a rock, but Paul managed to sail it back to Westport. He repaired the boat and set sail again for Nantucket with his cargo. page 316) LITERAL   Recalling stated information

4. *What things happened in 1783 that began to change Paul's fortune for the better?* (In 1783, the Revolutionary War ended and the danger of pirates no longer existed. It was also the year in which Paul married Alice Pequit, but the selection does not say whether or not she had an effect on Paul's business. page 317) INFERENTIAL   Identifying cause-and-effect relationships

● *Why might Paul Cuffe be called a philanthropist?* (Answers should include: He used his own money to pay for a schoolhouse that was built on his farm and that he offered to the people of Westport. He also paid the teacher's salary and the operating expenses of the school. page 317) INFERENTIAL   Drawing conclusions

Applying the Skills Lesson

1. *Read the sixth paragraph on page 313. Use the details from that paragraph to state its main idea in one sentence.* (Sample answer: Paul felt discouraged after his first lesson in navigation.)   Determining the unstated main idea of a paragraph

● *Read the second paragraph on page 316. Use the details from that paragraph to state its main idea in one sentence.* (Sample answer: Paul's fascination with the sea was too great for him to give up his dream.)   Determining the unstated main idea of a paragraph

2. *Read the fifth paragraph on page 317. Which of the following sentences best states the main idea of that paragraph?*
   a. Paul had a schoolhouse built on his farm.
   b. Paul paid a teacher to work in a schoolhouse.
   c. Paul gave Westport a schoolhouse and paid the operating costs and the teacher's salary.
   (Answer: c)   Determining the unstated main idea of a paragraph

- *Why are sentences* a *and* b *poor choices?* (Sentences *a* and *b* take into account only a few details mentioned in the paragraph. They do not sum up the main idea.) Determining the unstated main idea of a paragraph

 Use *Duplicating Masters 11,* page 39. See *Providing for Individual Differences,* page T276, for additional practice.

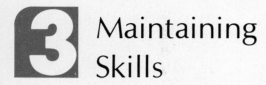
Maintaining Skills

Study Skills

Identifying topical organization Write the following headings on the board. Explain to students that these headings might be inserted into the selection "The Secret of the Sea." Ask students to find an appropriate place in the selection for each topical heading.

> Lessons in Navigation (page 313, above paragraph 6)
> Captured by the British (page 314, above paragraph 3 or 4)
> Paul's First Boat (page 314, above paragraph 7)
> Paul Builds a Second Boat (page 315, above paragraph 3)
> Paul Tries Again (page 316, above paragraph 2)
> 1783—An Important Year (page 317, above paragraph 1 or 2)
> Life in Westport (page 317, above paragraph 3 or 4)

Using a dictionary Read aloud the following sentences from the selection, and write the underlined words on the board. Have students use a dictionary to find at least two appropriate synonyms for each word. Remind students to choose a definition that fits the context in which the word is used.

> He was spellbound by the restless ocean. (fascinated, awed)
> Other times, when the sea was as calm as glass, he looked far away to the horizon. (quiet, peaceful, still)
> He was determined that someday he would own a ship. (resolved, earnest)
> If Paul had not had his dream and his intense love for the sea, he would not have made it. (strong, great, deep)
> His drive kept him going, when others without such a goal might have given up. (aim, objective)

 For additional resources and curriculum-related activities, see *Enrichment,* page T278.

Textbook Study:
Using the Details to State a Main Idea

Pages 319–321

Objectives

		SKILLS CODE NUMBER
M, T	To identify the topic and stated main idea of a paragraph	3.3.8
M, T	To use details to determine the unstated main idea of a paragraph	3.3.1; 3.4.7

Applying the Skill

1. Before students read the textbook selections, you may wish to list the vocabulary words on the board and discuss them or have students look them up in the glossary.

   Social Studies Selection
   droplet: a tiny drop
   visible: capable of being seen

2. Have students read the introduction and the two selections. You may wish to have students read the selections on their own and then do *Building Skills.* Or you may wish to direct students, using the following procedure.

TEXTBOOK STUDY

Using the Details to State a Main Idea

In some paragraphs in textbooks, the main idea is stated. In other paragraphs, you have to examine the details and then discover the main idea yourself. Sometimes you'll find the most important details in only two sentences. Other times, you'll have to use details from many sentences in order to state the main idea. As you read the following selections, refer to the sidenotes. They will help you find the important ideas.

Finding the Main Idea in Social Studies

All air contains some water, usually in droplets too small to be seen. When air is warm, it can hold a lot of invisible moisture. If the air grows cooler, the water in it becomes visible. Above us, we see the moisture as clouds. Around us, it appears as fog or mist. (Have you ever ridden an airplane into a white, fleecy cloud? Instant dirty, gray fog!)

The details in this paragraph help explain what a cloud is. What is a cloud?

Suppose the cloudy air becomes still cooler. Then it will let go its moisture as rain, snow, or sleet. We call this **precipitation.** What could cause air suddenly to grow cooler? For one thing, being pushed upward, away from the warm earth. This happens when winds move against a range of high mountains.

The details in this paragraph tell you why it rains or snows. What causes precipitation?

—*The United States*
Houghton Mifflin

319

Finding the Main Idea in Social Studies

1. Have students read the first paragraph and answer the question in the sidenote. (A cloud is visible moisture in cool air.)

2. Have students read the second paragraph. Ask them what precipitation is. (moisture in the form of rain, snow, or sleet) Then have students answer the question in the sidenote. (A cloud's becoming cooler causes precipitation.)

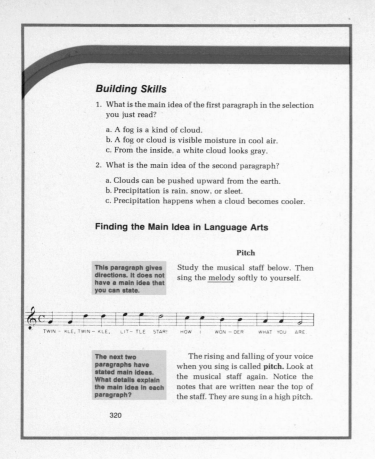

Building Skills

1. What is the main idea of the first paragraph in the selection you just read?

   a. A fog is a kind of cloud.
   b. A fog or cloud is visible moisture in cool air.
   c. From the inside, a white cloud looks gray.

2. What is the main idea of the second paragraph?

   a. Clouds can be pushed upward from the earth.
   b. Precipitation is rain, snow, or sleet.
   c. Precipitation happens when a cloud becomes cooler.

Finding the Main Idea in Language Arts

Pitch

This paragraph gives directions. It does not have a main idea that you can state.

Study the musical staff below. Then sing the melody softly to yourself.

TWIN – KLE, TWIN – KLE, LIT – TLE STAR! HOW I WON – DER WHAT YOU ARE

The next two paragraphs have stated main ideas. What details explain the main idea in each paragraph?

The rising and falling of your voice when you sing is called **pitch.** Look at the musical staff again. Notice the notes that are written near the top of the staff. They are sung in a high pitch.

320

Notice the notes that are written near the bottom of the staff. They are sung in a low pitch.

The rising and falling of your voice when you speak is also called pitch. The words in the sentences below are printed like the notes on a musical staff. Say each sentence softly to yourself. Listen to the pitch of your voice rise and fall.

1. I watched $t^{ele}vis_{io_n}$.

2. Did you bring the $p_o{}^{p}{}^{corn}$?

— *Discovery in English*
Laidlaw Brothers

Building Skills

State the topic of the second and third paragraphs. Then state the main idea of each of those paragraphs.

321

---

3. Have students complete *Building Skills*.

Answers to *Building Skills*
Social Studies Selection

1. b; **2.** c

Finding the Main Idea in Language Arts

1. Have students read the title of the selection, the first paragraph, and the sidenote.

2. Have students read the second and third paragraphs. Ask for responses to the second sidenote.

3. Have students complete *Building Skills*.

Answers to *Building Skills*
Language Arts Selection

Paragraph 2: Topic: pitch in singing; Main idea: "The rising and falling of your voice when you sing is called pitch." **Paragraph 3:** Topic: pitch in speaking; Main idea: "The rising and falling of your voice when you speak is also called pitch."

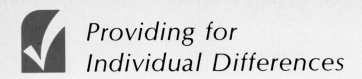

Providing for Individual Differences

Skills Lesson

Additional Practice

Worksheet 10, Teacher's Edition, page T489

Vocabulary Study

Additional Practice

■ **Identifying word parts: root words and suffixes**
Write the following words on the board. Explain that the spelling of each root word was changed when the suffix was added. Have students write the root word and explain the meaning of each word containing a suffix.

> identification (identify; something used to identify a person or thing)
> famous (fame; quality of having fame)
> inflatable (inflate; able to be inflated)
> multipliable (multiply; able to be multiplied)
> sitter (sit; one who sits)
> pianist (piano; one who plays the piano)
> remembrance (remember; something remembered)
> remittance (remit; something remitted)

Reading Selection: The Peddler's Pack

Additional Practice

■ **Identifying topic and unstated main idea**   Read the following paragraph aloud. Have students select the topic and the unstated main idea from the choices that follow the paragraph.

> Have you ever bartered for something? Suppose your friend owns three comic books that you like, and you have a football that you hardly ever use. You might trade. Another way of buying through barter is to trade services for goods. Some people have jobs as superintendents of apartment buildings. They help take care of the building. In return for their service, they live in an apartment rent-free. Of course, the most common way to buy things is with money. Today, money is generally accepted as a measure of value and a means of payment.

Topic:	Unstated Main Idea:
1. bartering	1. Money is the best way to buy something.
2. money	2. You can live without money.
3. becoming a superintendent	3. One way of getting goods and services is through barter.
(Answer: 1)	(Answer: 3)

Challenge Activity

■ **Identifying topic and unstated main idea**   Read the following paragraph aloud. Tell students to think carefully about the details in the paragraph and then identify the topic and the unstated main idea.

> Next time you walk down the street, notice what the trucks are carrying. You may see a load of new cars being trucked from the factory to the dealers. You may see bread being delivered from the bakery to the stores. Freight trains also help transport our nation's merchandise. Next time you are stopped at a railroad crossing, count the number of freight cars. Can you guess what they are carrying? If you live near a big harbor or a large river, you may have seen barges carrying wood, coal, or large machinery. Barges are another link in the national transportation system.

> (Topic: the transportation of goods; Sample main idea: Goods in this country are transported by trucks, trains, and barges.)

Reading Selection: The Secret of the Sea

Additional Practice

■ **Recognizing the unstated main idea**   Read the following paragraphs aloud. Have students select the unstated main idea of each paragraph from the choices given.

> Tony opened the box and dumped the cake mix into a bowl. He read the directions on the side of the box. It said, "Preheat oven to 350°." Tony did this. "Add one cup water, four eggs, and one-half cup oil. Beat well." "That sounds easy enough," said Tony.

1. Tony read the directions.
2. Tony was making a cake.
3. Tony thought it was easy.
(Answer: 2)

Every day after school Abby did chores to earn money. She washed her neighbors' cars and windows, mowed lawns, or helped out at the grocery store. Then every evening before going home, she ran to the pet shop to make sure the little poodle she wanted to buy was still there.

1. Abby worked hard.
2. Abby visited the pet shop.
3. Abby was working to earn money to buy a puppy.

(Answer: 3)

Challenge Activity

■ Identifying topic and unstated main idea   Read the following paragraph aloud. Ask students to think carefully about the details in the paragraph and then identify the topic and the unstated main idea.

Very few people have ever caught a live wild rabbit. Only the fastest, most skilled dogs are able to catch one. The wild rabbit is able to run swiftly and to leap, twist, and turn. Its sensitive ears and keen eyesight also help it defend itself against enemies.

(Topic: how a wild rabbit defends itself; Sample main idea: A wild rabbit's speed, hearing, and eyesight help it protect itself.)

Evaluation

Periodic Test 3, Part II, Form A or *Form B,* may be administered after this unit to test skills marked **T.** If you have pretested using *Form A,* administer *Form B.*

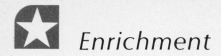

Enrichment

The Peddler's Pack

Bibliography

The following books are about colonial life in America.

Average

Comins, Jeremy. *Totems, Decoys and Covered Wagons: Cardboard Constructions from Early American Life.* How to make copies of toys, houses, furniture, and objects from early Indian and colonial life.

Earle, Alice Morse. *Home and Child Life in Colonial Days.* A fascinating picture of how people lived in 1776. Originally published in 1892.

Challenging

Speare, Elizabeth George. *Life in Colonial America.* How Americans lived, from early settlements at Jamestown to the Revolution.

Tunis, Edwin. *Colonial Craftsmen: The Beginnings of American Industry.* All types of industry and crafts.

Films and Filmstrips

NOTE: For more information, see *Resource Center.*

Skills

Harcourt Brace Jovanovich. *Bookmark Reading Filmstrips: Purple.* "Topics, Main Ideas, and Details."

Selection content

Encyclopaedia Britannica Educational Corp. *Life in Early America.* All filmstrips are appropriate.

National Geographic. *Transportation in America.* Appropriate: "Yesterday's Travel."

Curriculum Coordination

Language Arts

1. Traveling salespeople have taken over the role of the peddler. Have students work in pairs to write or improvise a dramatic sketch about such a salesperson who is trying to sell a product or service to a customer.

2. Have half the class pretend they are living in eastern America during colonial times. Have them write letters that a peddler will deliver to their relatives in the wilderness. Have the other half of the class pretend they are the western settlers as they write to the "eastern colonists."

Social Studies

1. Have students investigate the history of the Conestoga wagon. Several students may also want to design and build a model.

2. Have students research the first American factories that were built. When were they built? Where were they located? What did they produce? Who owned them? How were the working conditions?

Mathematics

Have students gather data on how merchandise is transported within the United States. Help them construct a circle graph showing what percentage of this merchandise travels by truck, by rail, by air, and by boat.

Career Education

Invite a salesperson to talk about his or her profession and to explain the terms *wholesale, retail,* and *commission.* Encourage the speaker to share his or her opinions about what constitutes a "good sales personality." Before the salesperson visits the class, it might be a good idea to ask him or her to read "The Peddler's Pack" to know the background for some of the students' questions.

The Secret of the Sea

Bibliography

The following books are about Paul Cuffe or the history of ships.

Average

Rutland, Jonathan. *Ships.* The history of ships and how they work, with good illustrations.

Challenging

Atkin, Mary Gage. *Paul Cuffe and the African Promised Land.* Paul Cuffe's interest in Sierra Leone. Taken from his journal.

Films and Filmstrips

NOTE: For more information, see *Resource Center.*

Skills

Harcourt Brace Jovanovich. *Bookmark Reading Filmstrips: Purple.* "Topics, Main Ideas, and Details."

Selection content

National Geographic. *Transportation in America.* Appropriate: "Yesterday's Travel."

Curriculum Coordination

Language Arts

1. Explain to students that a ship's log is a daily record of a ship's voyage. Have them write a log for one of Paul Cuffe's first three boat trips. Have them give a time and date for each entry and describe daily events, weather conditions, navigational position, and so on.

2. Have students write poems expressing fascination about the sea. Before beginning this assignment they might obtain examples of poems about the sea and share their findings with the class. Tell them to try to focus on an image of the sea at a particular time of day and during certain weather conditions.

Social Studies

1. Students might enjoy researching pirates in the eighteenth century and in other times.

2. Have students look further into the life and work of Paul Cuffe. Some students might look into Cuffe's work in securing legal rights for black people in Massachusetts and in resettling black Americans in Africa.

3. Students might investigate and illustrate different kinds of ships used in history, such as Viking ships, ancient Egyptian and Greek barges, frigates of the Spanish Armada and of early colonial times, and primitive canoes and boats carved out of trees.

Art

Interested students can draw pictures or construct models of ships.

Music

Play examples of sea chanteys and have students learn one of them.

Career Education

1. In some port cities, the U.S. Navy allows people to visit their ships. Also, in coastal areas, there are whaling or naval museums. Arrange for such class trips, if possible.

2. Invite a representative of the Coast Guard or U.S. Navy to talk to students about careers. The representative might explain some nautical terms and show pictures or slides of modern ships.

Contents

Additional Materials

Key to Symbols

Skills Objectives
I* — Introduced in this unit
I — Introduced earlier in this level
M — Maintained from previous levels
T — Tested in periodic and cumulative tests for this level

Reduced Student Pages
underscore — words that appear in the glossary
wavy line — words pretaught in the Teacher's Edition
 (these words also appear in the glossary)

Skills Lesson:
Getting Information from Pictures and Diagrams
Pages 322–327

Objectives

		SKILLS CODE NUMBER
M, T	To compare information obtained from graphic aids to textual information	5.4.7
M, T	To interpret information from a picture	5.4.5
M, T	To interpret information from a diagram	5.4.4

If you wish to pretest the skills listed above, you may administer *Periodic Test 3, Part III, Form A. Periodic Test 3, Part III, Form B,* may be administered to posttest.

Introducing the Lesson

1. Have students look at the pictures on page 469. Then ask them the following questions.

   What are the people in the pictures doing? (making paper)
   What kinds of materials are used to make paper? (Accept reasonable answers, such as natural fibers, bark, trees, and reeds.)
   Why do you think the pictures show Chinese people making paper? (Paper was invented in China.)

**Getting Information from
Pictures and Diagrams**

A country schoolhouse, 1880.

What can you learn from this picture? Look again! You can learn more than you think.

Books, magazines, and newspapers are made up of more than words (called the **text**). The text works together with different kinds of **graphic aids** to help you learn.

Pictures are one kind of graphic aid. Pictures include photographs, drawings, paintings, and cartoons. Pictures give you details that explain the text. Or they give you information that you will not find in the text. Read the following paragraph. Look for details that are given both in the paragraph and in the picture above.

322

● In the 1800's, most country schoolhouses had only one room and one teacher. The schoolhouse was not comfortable at all. Children sat on long, hard, wooden benches. Some children walked more than sixteen kilometers each day—from home to school and back—even in the worst weather.

Below is a list of details. Which details came only from the text? Which came only from the picture? Which appeared in both the text and the picture?

1. In the 1800's, most country schoolhouses had only one room and one teacher.
2. The schoolhouse was not comfortable.
3. Children sat on long, hard, wooden benches.
4. Some children walked more than sixteen kilometers each day—from home to school and back—even in the worst weather.
5. In cold weather, the schoolroom was warmed by a small stove.
6. To keep warm, some children wore their outer clothing indoors.

You can get the information in sentences 2 and 3 from either the text or the picture. You can get the information from sentences 1 and 4 only from the text. Notice that the information in sentences 5 and 6 is not in the text. You could learn these details only from the picture.

Above or below many pictures, you will see a **caption**. A caption, like a title, tells about the picture. Look at the photograph of the blacksmith on page 324. What details does the caption give?

323

Point out that the pictures alone told them two things: that paper is made from plant fiber and that long ago, paper was made in the Orient without using machines.

2. Refer students to the pictures on pages 81, 86, 187, and 196. Have them tell why each picture is important or why they don't think it is important.

3. Have students turn to page 322 and examine the picture carefully. Ask them to tell you as much as they can about the picture.

Developing the Skill

A. *Pictures give details that explain the text or give information that you will not find in the text.*

1. Have students read the three paragraphs on page 322 and the sample paragraph on page 323. Then have them look at the list of details. Ask them which details are given only in the text (1 and 4); which details are given only in the picture (5 and 6); and which details are given in both the text and the picture. (2 and 3)

2. Now have students read the paragraph below the list of details.

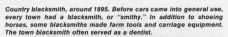

Country blacksmith, around 1895. Before cars came into general use, every town had a blacksmith, or "smithy." In addition to shoeing horses, some blacksmiths made farm tools and carriage equipment. The town blacksmith often served as a dentist.

When you turn to a page that has a picture, don't just look at the picture—*study* it! Use details from the picture (and the caption, if there is one) to help you understand the text.

Diagrams

A **diagram** is a special kind of graphic aid. It is always a drawing and often has a caption above or below it. Look at the three diagrams that follow. Read the captions and the notes. Use both to help you understand the diagrams.

324

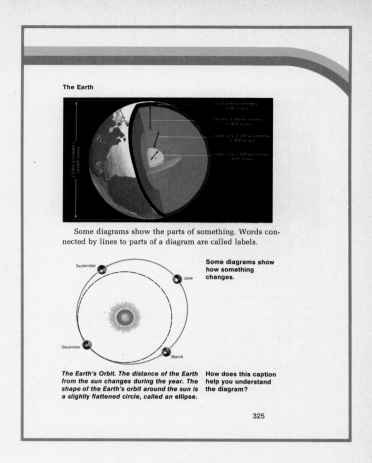

The Earth

Some diagrams show the parts of something. Words connected by lines to parts of a diagram are called labels.

Some diagrams show how something changes.

The Earth's Orbit. The distance of the Earth from the sun changes during the year. The shape of the Earth's orbit around the sun is a slightly flattened circle, called an ellipse.

How does this caption help you understand the diagram?

325

B. *The caption tells about the picture.*

1. Have students read the last paragraph on page 323 and look at the photograph of the blacksmith and the caption on page 324. Explain that a caption may be only one word, or it may be a group of words, a whole sentence, or even a long explanation such as the one given above the picture of the blacksmith.

2. Have students identify the caption for the drawing on page 322. (A country schoolhouse, 1880.)

Diagrams

A diagram is a labeled drawing that shows the parts of something, how something changes or works, or how to do or make something.

1. Have students read the paragraph at the bottom of page 324 and look at the first diagram on page 325. Ask them to identify the caption. (The Earth) Have a volunteer read the paragraph below the first diagram aloud and identify labels on the diagram. (Labels on the diagram: crust, mantle, outer core, inner core)

2. Have students examine the second diagram. Ask a student to read the labels aloud (June, September, December, March) and identify the caption. ("The Earth's Orbit" and text following) Have students read the sidenotes at the right of the diagram and answer the question in the second sidenote. (The diagram shows that Earth is closer to the sun in December than it is in June. The caption explains that the distance of Earth from the sun changes during the year and tells you that the shape of this pathway is called an ellipse.)

Another kind of diagram shows you how to do something or how to make something.

Model of the Sun, Moon, and Earth. You can use three people to make a "living" model of the sun, the moon, and the Earth. Which movement takes less time—the movement of the Earth around the sun or the movement of the moon around the Earth?

Try This

1. Read the paragraph below.

The Earth is made up of layers. The outside, or *crust*, is from 5 to 65 kilometers thick. Under the crust is the *mantle*, which is 3,000 kilometers thick. The *outer core*, which comes between the mantle and the *inner core*, is 2,100 kilometers thick. The inner core is extremely hot. Scientists believe it is made up of iron and nickel.

Which of the following details is only in the diagram *The Earth* on page 325? Which detail is in the paragraph above but not in the diagram?

326

a. The diameter of the Earth from the North Pole to the South Pole is 13,000 kilometers.
b. The Earth's inner core is made up of iron and nickel.

2. Read the following paragraph. Study the picture. What details can you find only in the picture? What can you find only in the paragraph? What can you find in *both* the picture and the paragraph?

The country store was a popular place in a nineteenth-century town. The store provided a meeting place where people shared the local news. Townspeople could buy almost anything they needed at the country store. There was clothing for men, women, and children. There were tools and seeds for farmers. And there were books, toys, and candy for children.

327

3. Have students examine the diagram on page 326 and identify the caption. (Model of the Sun, Moon, and Earth and text following) Have a volunteer read the caption and answer the question in the caption. (The movement of the moon around the Earth takes less time than the movement of the Earth around the sun.)

Try This

Have students complete *Try This*.

Answers to *Try This*

1. **a.** only in the diagram; **b.** only in the paragraph;
2. Details only in the picture: Accept any not given in text; Details only in the paragraph: The country store was a popular place in a nineteenth-century town; the store provided a meeting place where people shared local news; there were clothing, seeds, toys, and candy; Details in both the picture and the paragraph: There were tools and books. Also accept "anything they needed."

 Use *Reading Skills Workbook,* Lesson 26, pages 81–84. See *Providing for Individual Differences,* page T298, for additional practice.

Vocabulary Study:
Prefixes Meaning "Not"

Pages 328–329

Objective

M	To identify word parts: root words and prefixes	SKILLS CODE NUMBER *4.1*

Developing the Skill

1. Tell students that in the *Vocabulary Study* they will learn more about prefixes. Ask students what a prefix is. (a word part added to the beginning of a word to make a different word)

2. Have students read the *Vocabulary Study* and do the *Word Play* activity.

Answers to *Word Play*

unfortunately: not fortunately; *uncertain:* not certain; *undamaged:* not damaged; Sentences will vary.

 Use *Reading Skills Workbook*, Lesson 27, page 85. See *Providing for Individual Differences*, page T298, for additional practice.

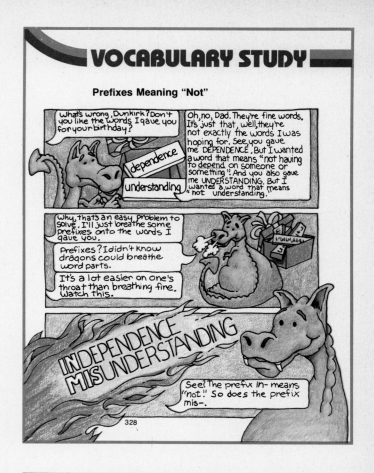

Reading Selection:
Golden Ghosts

Pages 330–335

Preparing to Read

Summary

No western state is without its ghost towns. They were the cities of dreams—mining towns that sprang up during the great gold rushes of the last half of the 1800's. Not every mining town met the same fate. In some towns, the mines are still going strong. In others, different industries have taken their place. The true ghost towns are almost completely deserted. These towns grew rapidly while the mining was good, and often they died just as quickly. The dream of gold drew thousands of people to the West. In 1849, the "forty-niners" began to stream into California. This was the start of the great American gold rush, which brought great wealth to some but little or nothing to most. The ghost towns are a reminder of that era.

Background

Until the 1840's, territories in the West were sparsely populated and virtually wilderness. The gold rush made possible the expansion and development of the West. Most of the gold finds were small and quickly exhausted. The three big finds were the Comstock silver lode in Nevada (1859) and the gold deposits in the Black Hills of South Dakota (1874) and in Cripple Creek, Colorado (1891). This period was soon followed by the discovery of gold in Alaska. By making the westward expansion possible, the gold rush led inevitably to America's industrial revolution.

The following books will provide you with additional background information.

Cooke, Alistair. *Alistair Cooke's America.* Chapters 5 and 7 give many interesting facts about the westward movement in America. Illustrated.

Jenkinson, Michael. *Ghost Towns of New Mexico: Playthings of the Wind.* A history of the ghost towns of New Mexico. Illustrated, with maps.

Developing Vocabulary and Concepts

sagebrush: a small shrub with white or yellow flowers, found on the dry plains of the western United States

surveyor: a person whose profession is measuring and mapping land

strode: (past tense of *stride*) walked with long, sweeping steps

boom: a sudden increase, as in growth or wealth

1. **a.** Read the following sentences aloud, or write them on the board. If you read them aloud, write the underlined vocabulary on the board.

   The sagebrush, small shrubs with white or yellow flowers, had grown so thick that it almost covered the old road.

   Surveyors mapped out the land around the mines.

   The miners strode down the streets, their long, sweeping steps showing their excitement at the discovery of gold.

   The discovery of gold brought a population boom to the West. The number of people increased by the thousands.

   b. Ask students to give the meaning of each vocabulary word. Remind them to use the context clues in the sentences to help them.

2. Ask students if they've ever seen a house that looked haunted. Why did the house look haunted? How could they tell that the house was empty? (tall grass, broken windows, boarded windows, etc.) Ask students if they know what a ghost town is. (a deserted town, especially an abandoned mining town in the West) Tell students that the selection they are about to read is about ghost towns.

 Use *Duplicating Masters 11,* page 40.

330

What details do you get from the picture of the ghost town that you cannot get from the text? What details does the text give that the pictures do not? A good reader *reads* both the text and the graphic aids.

They were born when gold was discovered in the West. But after a few years, most of them had become . . .

GOLDEN GHOSTS

Based on a story by Robert Silverberg

A few crumbling buildings stand beside an unpaved road overgrown with sagebrush. One building was once a bank. There, weary miners stood in line to deposit their new wealth. Another building was a grand hotel. Some dimly seen lines in the ground mark the foundations of houses never built. A narrow path winding into the mountains leads to the mines whose gold made this town sprout overnight.

331

Setting Purposes

Skills

Have students read the skills note at the top of page 331. Point out the bell on the sign in the picture. Ask if they know what it means. (There was a public telephone in the building.) Ask what that sign tells them about the age of this town. (People lived here until sometime during the 1900's, when public telephones were widely used.) Ask students to suggest other things that can be learned from the pictures in the selection.

Content

Have students read the lead-in to the title. Ask them what they picture in their minds when they hear the expression "ghost town."

2 Reading and Discussing

Have students read the selection. Most students will be able to complete it in one sitting. If you prefer, the selection may be read in two parts, breaking before the heading "Westward, Ho!" on page 334.

NOTE: The questions that appear in the student's text at the end of the selection focus on comprehension of selection content and on application of the *Skills Lesson* to the selection. Answers to these questions begin on page T288.

No one has ever counted the ghost towns of the American West. Many have been completely destroyed by time and the weather.

No western state is without its ghost towns. They were places of dreams which grew from mining camps that sprang up during the great gold rushes of the 1800's. They grew with sudden, furious energy. They lived for ten or twenty years and then faded and died.

Not every mining town met the same sort of death. Some did not die at all. In some places, the mines are still going

Panning for gold.

332

strong: places like Butte [byōōt], Montana, and Globe, Arizona. These have become modern cities, very much alive.

In some of the other early mining towns, the mines have played out. But other industries have taken their place.

In Virginia City, Nevada, and Tombstone, Arizona, many buildings of the gold-rush days are well protected for visitors.

The true ghost towns are wholly deserted or perhaps lived in by one or two families. Bodie, California, and Bullfrog, Nevada, belong in this class.

There are also places where nothing at all remains, except perhaps the stump of a building or the shadowy outlines of what were once streets. Some ghosts of this sort are Silver Reef, Utah, and Charleston, Arizona.

These ghost towns remind us of the mining booms that began in 1849 in California. People from all over the world set out toward the Sierra Nevada in search of quick wealth. Some of those who went west in '49 made great fortunes. Most did not.

An 1850's gold-rush town—San Francisco.

Towns sprang up and grew like mushrooms while the mining was good. But they often died as easily as they had been founded. Again and again, when there was a strike of gold somewhere, miners arrived and a busy camp was born.

Then came those who hoped to grow rich serving the miners. There were bankers and storekeepers, surveyors and engineers. Presto! A mining camp became a town. Within three or four years, twenty tents turned into a city with an opera house, a hotel, and a row of busy shops.

Then the flow of treasure from the earth slowed down. Or someone came into town with tales of even easier wealth somewhere else. Off the miners went. Perhaps later on, other miners would come and find new treasures there—silver or copper instead of gold. The town would grow again. Some of the mining camps went through perhaps three or four lifetimes this way before becoming ghosts.

333

Westward, Ho!

The real westward movement began in 1840. Times were hard east of the Mississippi. An endless frontier beckoned to many Easterners. "Oregon fever" and "California fever" sent trains of covered wagons crawling through the immense western lands.

These pioneers were not generally seeking gold. They wanted a place to settle and raise cattle or crops. They thought that beyond the treeless prairie and the great, dry deserts there were rich

farmlands free for the taking.

By the mid-1840's, there were about five thousand people in Oregon and about one thousand in California. Most of those in California lived near the lower Sacramento River. There, a Swiss adventurer named John Sutter had built a fort and mill.

In the spring of 1848, a man named Sam Brannan appeared in the little port of San Francisco. He strode down San Francisco's streets, shouting, "Gold! Gold from the American River near Sutter's fort!"

Gold! The word spread, and

Sutter's Mill. In 1848, gold was found nearby.

334

by 1849 the gold rush was on.

Seeking pay dirt, the "forty-niners" streamed into California to start the great American gold rush. The rush brought great wealth to some but little or nothing to most. It left behind the ghost towns whose ruins stir our imaginations today.

John A. Sutter.

Understanding What You've Read

1. What happened to the old mining camps that sprang up during the gold rushes of the 1800's?
2. What were "Oregon fever" and "California fever"?
3. Why were miners of the late 1840's often referred to as "forty-niners"?
4. What sequence of events created mining towns in the 1800's?

Applying the Skills Lesson

Here are some details from the selection you just read. Which details come only from the pictures or their captions? Which come only from the text? Which come from both the text and the pictures?

1. In the 1850's, gold-rush towns were busy places.
2. Hundreds of gold-mining camps sprang up during the 1800's.
3. In the gold rush, some people panned for gold.
4. Gold was found near Sutter's fort in 1848.

335

Questions preceded by a bullet are additional questions and appear in the Teacher's Edition only. The other questions appear in the student's text after the selection.

Understanding What You've Read

1. *What happened to the old mining camps that sprang up during the gold rushes of the 1800's?* (Some of them have become ghost towns. In others, either the mines are still going strong or other industries have moved in to take the place of the mines. page 332) LITERAL   Identifying the main idea of a selection

• *Why did the miners leave the mining towns?* (because the gold ran out or because miners heard of even greater wealth to be had somewhere else page 333) INFERENTIAL   Identifying cause-and-effect relationships

2. *What were "Oregon fever" and "California fever"?* (These were terms used to describe the desire of pioneers to settle and raise cattle or crops in the West. page 334) INFERENTIAL   Drawing conclusions

• *What happened in 1848 near San Francisco to cause the gold rush?* (Sam Brannan announced that gold had been discovered in the American River near Sutter's fort. page 334) INFERENTIAL   Identifying cause-and-effect relationships

3. *Why were miners of the late 1840's often referred to as "forty-niners"?* (It was in 1849 that the gold rush began; miners streamed into California in search of gold. pages 332 and 334) INFERENTIAL   Drawing conclusions

• *Would you have wanted to be a "forty-niner"?* (Accept all reasonable answers.) CRITICAL   Making judgments

4. *What sequence of events created mining towns in the 1800's?* (When there was a strike of gold, miners arrived and a busy camp was born. Then came bankers, storekeepers, surveyors, and engineers who hoped to grow rich. page 333) INFERENTIAL   Determining the correct sequence for a set of events

Applying the Skills Lesson

Here are some details from the selection you just read. Which details come only from the pictures or their captions? Which come only from the text? Which come from both the text and the pictures?
1. In the 1850's, gold-rush towns were busy places.
2. Hundreds of gold-mining camps sprang up during the 1800's.
3. In the gold rush, some people panned for gold.
4. Gold was found near Sutter's fort in 1848.
(1. both text and picture; 2. text only; 3. picture only; 4. both text and picture)
Comparing information obtained from graphic aids to textual information

 Use *Duplicating Masters 11,* page 41. See *Providing for Individual Differences,* page T298, for additional practice.

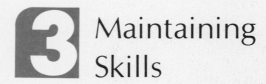 Maintaining Skills

Study Skills

Identifying and using reference materials   Have students tell which reference source or sources—encyclopedias, almanacs, or atlases—they would use to find the answer to each of the following questions. Then have students use the reference sources to find the answers.

What is the largest gold-producing country? (almanac; encyclopedia)

How much gold did the United States produce last year? (almanac)

In what country did the Incas live? (encyclopedia)

How far is it from Virginia City, Nevada, to the capital of Nevada? (atlas)

What was the price of an ounce of gold last year? (almanac)

Is Tombstone, Arizona, in the northwestern or southeastern part of Arizona? (atlas; encyclopedia)

What are the Mayans famous for? (encyclopedia)

Using a dictionary Read the following sentences from the selection aloud, and write the italicized words on the board. Explain that these words have multiple meanings. Ask students to find each word in a dictionary and to choose the definition that best fits the context of each sentence. (If you prefer, you may give students the numbered definitions following each sentence and have them select the appropriate one.)

There (at a bank), weary miners stood in line to *deposit* their new wealth.
1. to set down; put
2. material laid down by natural forces
3. to give over or entrust for safekeeping
(Answer: 3)

There are also places where nothing at all *remains,* except perhaps the stump of a building or the shadowy outlines of what were once streets.
1. a dead body
2. is left behind after others have left
3. objects from the past
(Answer: 2)

These ghost towns remind us of the mining *booms* that began in 1849 in California.
1. sudden increases in growth and wealth
2. deep, loud sounds
3. long poles or beams
(Answer: 1)

Again and again, when there was a *strike* of gold somewhere, miners arrived and a busy camp was born.
1. to come into forceful contact; hit
2. in baseball, a pitch that the batter misses
3. a new or unexpected discovery
(Answer: 3)

 For additional resources and curriculum-related activities, see *Enrichment,* page T300.

Reading Selection:
"Modern" America in the 1880's
Pages 336–341

Objectives

		SKILLS CODE NUMBER
M, T	To interpret information from a picture	5.4.5
M, T	To compare information obtained from graphic aids to textual information	5.4.7
M	To identify topical organization	5.10.1
M	To classify stated details by identifying groups to which they belong	3.2.1
M	To use an index	5.5.8

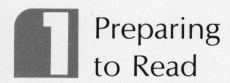 **Preparing to Read**

Summary

This selection surveys "modern" life in the late 1880's. The general store was the center of country social life. There people exchanged the latest news and played cards, chess, and checkers. Montgomery Ward's "Wish Book" revolutionized the clothing industry by selling ready-made clothing by mail. Almanacs predicted the weather. People took time each summer to enjoy something called a "vacation." Trains moved at the amazing speed of forty miles an hour. There was no such thing as standard time—there was clock time and sun time. Cities began growing upward instead of outward when elevators were invented, and telephones began to link one place with another. Department stores were a brand-new idea. Many of the things we take for granted today were very modern 100 years ago.

Background

The "modern" America of the late 1800's was a period of prosperity. It was the dawn of the "Industrial Age" in the United States—an age made possible by the expansion of the West. The Industrial Revolution had begun in England years before and was just beginning to be felt in the United States. The expansion of the West gave America new resources—ore and lumber, among others—and created a demand for interstate commerce and industry. Immigration brought millions of new workers to the eastern seaboard. The railroad, which linked the East and the West, brought natural resources to the factories in the East and returned the products of these factories to the West. New inventions filled the needs created by this Industrial Age: the telephone, typewriter, linotype, phonograph, electric lights, cash register, air brakes, the refrigerator car, and, finally, the automobile.

The following books will provide you with additional background information.

Cooke, Alistair. *Alistair Cooke's America*. Chapter 8 gives an account of the growth of American technology. Illustrated.

Weisberger, Bernard A. *The Age of Steel and Steam: The Life History of the United States, 1877–1890*. Political, industrial, social, and economic history. Illustrated, with index and bibliography.

Weymouth, Lally, and Milton Glaser. *America in 1876: The Way We Were*. A good guide to America in the late 1800's. Illustrated, with diagrams, maps, and bibliography.

Developing Vocabulary and Concepts

standard: serving as a model or system for measuring
hazy: misty; unclear
policy: a plan or method of action or conduct
clogged: blocked up or stopped
pilgrim: any wanderer or traveler

1. **a.** Read the following sentences aloud, or write them on the board. If you read them aloud, write the underlined vocabulary on the board.

   Once a system of measuring, or underline{standard} sizes, was established, people could buy clothing by mail and know it would fit.
   When the moon was pale with underline{hazy}, or fuzzy, edges, people thought it would rain.
   The department stores' pricing underline{policy} was different from the smaller stores' methods. In the smaller stores different people paid different prices, but in the department stores everyone paid the same price.

The road was so <u>clogged</u> with horse-drawn carriages that no one was able to get through the blocked-up road.

The <u>pilgrim</u> stopped at the inn to rest before continuing with her travels.

b. Ask students to give the meaning of each vocabulary word. Remind them to use the context clues in the sentences to help them.

2. Discuss the word *modern* with students. Point out that *modern* means "new and up-to-date." Ask students for examples of things that would be considered modern today. Then ask students if they consider summer vacations a modern idea. Tell students that the selection they will read tells about what was "modern" in the 1880's—such as a summer vacation.

 Use *Duplicating Masters 11,* page 42.

Setting Purposes

Skills

Have students read the skills note at the top of page 336. Tell students to look at the pictures in the selection carefully to help them understand the text.

Content

Have students read the lead-in to the title. Ask them to think of other ways in which life might have been different in the 1880's from how it is today.

2 Reading and Discussing

Have students read the selection. Most students will be able to complete it in one sitting. If you prefer, the selection may be read in two parts, breaking before the heading "Travel" on page 338.

NOTE: The questions that appear in the student's text at the end of the selection focus on comprehension of selection content and on application of the *Skills Lesson* to the selection. Answers to these questions begin on page T293.

The graphic aids in this selection will help you understand more about life in America in the 1880's. Look for details in the pictures to help you understand the text.

Eat penny candies in the general store. Look at the pictures in your parents' "Wish Book." These are some things you might have done if you were a child in . . .

"Modern" America in the 1880's
by Suzanne Hilton

Painting of a general store and post office.

336

In the 1880's young people were happy that they were growing up in a "modern" world. Let's take a look at what "modern" meant when your great-great-grandparents were your age.

The General Store

For probably the last time in history, there was plenty of space in the United States. Cities were not too large yet. Most people lived in the country.

The general store was the center of country social life. Children always found something new at the store. There were toys and books, trading cards, and colorful posters. At the end of the year there was a new almanac that had new jokes and stories. Then there were the smells—of sour pickles, ground coffee, freshly made soup, and salted fish. Crackers were sold from barrels. Jars of candy made the shelves sing with color. Children with a penny to spend could buy a whole bag of candy. They could buy corn kisses, hearts, gibraltars, cinnamon red-hots, fortune candies, and other candies you may never have heard of. Very few things in the store came already wrapped in small packages. Almost everything had to be measured and put in a paper bag or wrapped in paper.

During the winter, the store was heated by a little stove. A few people were always in the store, just relaxing or playing cards, checkers, or chess. The store was the best place to find out the latest news.

The Wish Book

The general store had almost everything a person needed for country living. But when people wanted something that the store didn't carry, they might turn to what they called the "Wish Book." This was a catalogue that started a whole industry—the mail order business. The idea for it came from a man named Montgomery Ward. The "Wish Book" listed more than four thousand items, including "ready-made" clothing.

Before the War Between the States, tailors thought that everyone was a different size and shape. But uniform makers soon noticed that certain leg and waist

337

measurements generally went together. The "Wish Book" said that the "ready-mades nine times out of ten give you a fit." And they did fit! That's why clothing comes in standard sizes today.

The Weather

In the 1880's people didn't have TV or radio news to tell them what the weather would be like. They did have almanacs which gave the weather forecasts for a whole year. However, they were wrong as often as they were right.

Country-dwellers had their own ways to tell the weather. Fish swimming near the surface of a pond meant rain. People also thought it would rain if frogs croaked more than usual and if the moon was pale with hazy edges. Enough blue sky showing "to make a pair of pants" meant that the clouds would soon disappear. A glowing red moon meant a windy day coming. Everyone knew: "An evening red and a morning gray will set the traveler on his way. But evening gray and morning red will pour down rain on the pilgrim's head."

Travel

In the 1880's, for the first time, people had a little extra time for something called a "vacation." They wanted to see a little of the world beyond the small area they lived in.

"Summer tramps" was the name for people who took a vacation in the summer. It was a brand-new idea, but nothing like a vacation today. There were country inns. But no one could be sure of having a private room. Innkeepers never refused a traveler just because there was no room. They simply woke up people who were happily sleeping and told them to move over for another traveler.

Also, the traveler could not

338

just point to a spot on the map and say, "I'm going there tomorrow." Sometimes there was no way to get from place to place.

People called railroad travel "going in the cars." Some trains had sleeping cars in which the seats used by day could be turned into beds at night. People could eat in dining cars in some trains. And best of all, trains moved at the amazing speed of forty miles an hour!

Standard Time

The hardest part of going from one place to another was finding out what time the train arrived and what time it left. Standard Time had not been invented yet. There was clock time and there was sun time. Sun time changed every day as the days grew longer or shorter. So clock time was the "right" time, meaning that when it was noon in New York City, it was five minutes before noon in Philadelphia and two minutes before noon in Washington, D. C. That made it exactly 11:30 A.M. in Cleveland, Ohio. And in Albany, New York, it was already one minute and six seconds past noon! The train people became famous for being able to tell passengers exactly what time it was at the very spot in the country where they asked the time.

City Life

Although there was still plenty of open space in the West in the 1880's, the major Eastern cities were becoming very crowded. One look at a large city's streets would show this.

The streets were clogged with horse-drawn carriages. Carriage drivers were allowed to move at only six miles an hour. They were fined $5.00 for driving on the sidewalk.

Cities had public transportation called horsecars, or street

339

railroads. They charged 25 cents for four rides. Horse-drawn hacks, like our taxicabs, cost 75 cents a mile for one passenger and $1.25 for two.

Inventions

A little more than a hundred years ago in the United States was a great time for inventions. One invention that changed the shape and height of the city was the elevator. In 1876, a man named Otis showed this invention at the Philadelphia Centennial Exposition. Within a few years, cities were growing up instead of out.

Department stores were a new idea. Instead of shopping in dozens of small stores, people could find almost everything they needed under one roof. Department stores had a one-price policy. The smaller stores generally charged different prices to different customers for the same item.

In 1876, a new invention—the telephone—was shown in Philadelphia by Alexander Graham Bell. In a year there would be 800

340

- *Why do you suppose vacations came into being for the first time 100 years ago?* (Accept answers which reflect an understanding that the growth of technology gave people extra time and money to take vacations. That is, machines helped people do more work in less time and at a lower cost than in the past.) CRITICAL   Drawing conclusions

3. *Why were railroad cars considered "modern"?* (People could sleep and eat on the railroad cars, which moved at forty miles an hour.   page 339) INFERENTIAL   Identifying cause-and-effect relationships

- *What were some of the modern inventions of 100 years ago?* (sleeping cars and dining cars, the elevator, department stores, and the telephone   pages 339 and 340) LITERAL   Recalling specific details

4. *What was meant by a one-price policy in department stores?* (All customers paid the same price for an item.   page 340) LITERAL   Recalling specific details

- *What do you think our "modern" world of today will seem like to people 100 years from now?* (Encourage free discussion. Students should explain that things that seem modern to us today may not seem that way to people 100 years from now.) CRITICAL   Predicting outcomes

Questions preceded by a bullet are additional questions and appear in the Teacher's Edition only. The other questions appear in the student's text after the selection.

Understanding What You've Read

1. *What was a general store like in the 1880's?* (It was the center of social life. People shared the latest news and played cards, checkers, and chess. The general store sold toys, books, candy, and food.   page 337) LITERAL   Recalling stated information

- *Why was Montgomery Ward's catalogue called the "Wish Book"?* (It listed over 4,000 items that people ordered or merely wished they had.   page 337) INFERENTIAL   Drawing conclusions

2. *What were some of the ways people forecast the weather?* (People forecast the weather by looking around them or consulting almanacs. Fish swimming near the surface of the pond, frogs croaking more than usual, or a pale moon with hazy edges meant it was going to rain. Enough blue sky showing "to make a pair of pants" meant that the clouds would soon disappear. A glowing red moon meant a windy day was coming.   page 338) LITERAL   Recalling stated information

Applying the Skills Lesson

1. *Look at the picture (page 339) of people on a train in the 1880's. Which of the following details can you learn from the picture only?*
   a. Passenger trains were generally comfortable in the 1880's.
   b. In the 1880's, trains moved at forty miles per hour.
   c. Travel by railroad in the 1880's was called "going in the cars."
   (Answer: a)   Interpreting information from a picture

- *Look at the cover of the catalogue at the top of page 336. Which of the following things did you learn from that picture? Which did you learn from the text on page 337?*
   a. Montgomery Ward ran a wholesale store in Chicago.
   b. People often called this catalogue the "Wish Book."
   c. This catalogue started the mail order industry.
   (Item a comes only from the picture. Items b and c come only from the text.)   Comparing information obtained from graphic aids to textual information

2. *What can you learn about the Philadelphia Exposition from the pictures on page 340 that you cannot learn from the text?* (Accept reasonable answers, including that the Exposition was held in a large, domed building and that the first elevator was an open platform rather than a boxlike structure.) <u>Comparing information obtained from graphic aids to textual information</u>

● *Who are the people pictured on page 338? How do you know?* (They are a traveler and an innkeeper. You can tell because this picture appears directly over an explanation of traveling and country inns.) <u>Interpreting information from a picture</u>

3. *What can you learn from the third paragraph on page 337 that you cannot learn from the picture on page 336?* (Accept any specific examples of wares mentioned in that paragraph.)   <u>Comparing information obtained from graphic aids to textual information</u>

☑ Use *Duplicating Masters 11,* page 43. See *Providing for Individual Differences,* page T298, for additional practice.

3 Maintaining Skills

Comprehension Skills

Classifying details   On the board, write the topical headings from the selection as shown in the first *Study Skills* exercise. Then read the following sentences from the selection. Have students identify the appropriate topical heading under which each sentence belongs.

Before the War Between the States, tailors thought that everyone was a different size and shape. (The Wish Book)

Fish swimming near the surface of a pond meant rain. (The Weather)

Children with a penny to spend could buy a whole bag of candy. (The General Store)

People called railroad travel "going in the cars." (Travel)

Department stores were a new idea. (Inventions)

There were country inns. (Travel)

There was clock time and there was sun time. (Standard Time)

Cities had public transportation called horsecars, or street railroads. (City Life)

The store was the best place to find out the latest news. (The General Store)

They did have almanacs which gave the weather forecasts for a whole year. (The Weather)

This was a catalogue that started a whole industry—the mail order business. (The Wish Book)

So clock time was the "right" time, meaning that when it was noon in New York, it was five minutes before noon in Philadelphia and two minutes before noon in Washington, D.C. (Standard Time)

The streets were clogged with horse-drawn carriages. (City Life)

Study Skills

Identifying topical organization   Explain that the following topics are covered in the selection. Have students arrange the topics in the order in which they appear in the selection. Allow students to use their books to complete this activity.

1. Standard Time
2. The Weather
3. The General Store
4. Inventions
5. City Life
6. Travel
7. The Wish Book

(Correct order: 3, 7, 2, 6, 1, 5, 4)

Using an index   Supply students with the following index for a book on the 1880's. Then ask the questions that follow it.

Almanac, 32, 39
City life, 3–15, 29–60
  transportation, 32–33, 59
Clothing, 62, 102
Elevator. See *Inventions.*
General store, 24
Inventions, 35–40, 79–89
  department store, 40
  elevator, 42
  ketchup, 79
  telephone, 36, 39
Mail-order catalogues, 19
Standard time, 17
Telephone. See *Inventions.*
Transportation. See *City life.*
Travel, 61–77
  railroad, 61–65
  vacation, 70
Weather, 37–39

On what pages should you look for information about transportation? (32–33 and 59)

Which entries above contain cross-references? (Elevator; Telephone; Transportation)

On what pages might you find information about standard sizes in clothing? (62, 102)

Suppose you want to find out who invented the telephone. You look on page 36, but the information isn't there. On what other page should you look? (39)

✪ For additional resources and curriculum-related activities, see *Enrichment,* page T300.

Textbook Study:
Pictures and Diagrams
Pages 342–345

Objectives

		SKILLS CODE NUMBER
M, T	To interpret information from a picture	5.4.5
M, T	To interpret information from a diagram	5.4.4

Applying the Skill

1. Before students read the selection, you may wish to list the vocabulary words on the board and discuss them or have students look them up in the glossary.

   Health Selection
   respiratory: of or having to do with breathing
   oxygen: a colorless, tasteless, odorless gaseous element, making up about a fifth of the Earth's atmosphere
   circulatory: of or having to do with circulation, as of the blood

2. Have students read the introduction and the two selections. You may wish to have students read the selections on their own and then do *Building Skills.* Or you may wish to direct students, using the following procedure.

TEXTBOOK STUDY

Pictures and Diagrams

What's the first thing you do when you get a new textbook? Most people leaf through and look at the pictures, diagrams, and other graphic aids. Pictures and diagrams not only make the text more interesting, they also give you the important details to help you understand the text. You'll find many graphic aids in your textbooks, because at times, they explain things better than words alone.

As you read the following selections, look at the pictures or diagrams. They will help you understand the text.

Pictures in Mathematics

The following selection is from a math textbook. The pictures show familiar objects. They help the reader to see the difference between a liter and a milliliter.

Study the text and pictures. Then answer the questions that follow.

Capacity: Liter and Milliliter

A.

One **liter** is a little more than a quart. You can write "1 l" to mean one liter.

342

Pictures in Mathematics

1. Have students read the two paragraphs above the mathematics textbook selection and then study the text and the pictures.

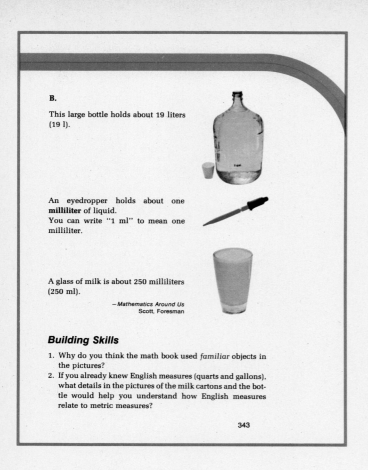

B.

This large bottle holds about 19 liters (19 l).

An eyedropper holds about one **milliliter** of liquid.
You can write "1 ml" to mean one milliliter.

A glass of milk is about 250 milliliters (250 ml).

—Mathematics Around Us
Scott, Foresman

Building Skills

1. Why do you think the math book used *familiar* objects in the pictures?
2. If you already knew English measures (quarts and gallons), what details in the pictures of the milk cartons and the bottle would help you understand how English measures relate to metric measures?

343

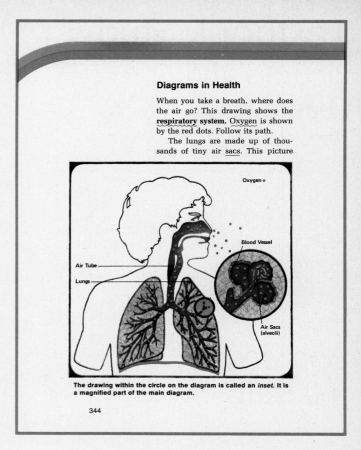

Diagrams in Health

When you take a breath, where does the air go? This drawing shows the **respiratory system.** Oxygen is shown by the red dots. Follow its path.

The lungs are made up of thousands of tiny air sacs. This picture

The drawing within the circle on the diagram is called an *inset*. It is a magnified part of the main diagram.

344

---

2. Have students complete *Building Skills.*

Answers to *Building Skills*
Mathematics Selection

1. The mathematics book used familiar objects so that you could get a good idea of the relative volume of a liter and a milliliter; **2.** The milk cartons are labeled *1 liter* and *1 quart* and the bottle is labeled *5 gallons* to help you see the relationship between English measure and metric measure.

Diagrams in Health

1. Have students read the first paragraph. Have them answer the question "When you take a breath, where does the air go?" (down the air tube to the lungs)

2. Have students read the second paragraph and the two sentences below the diagram. Ask them what the inset shows. (a magnified air sac containing blood vessels) Now ask them what other word is given in the label for air sacs. (alveoli)

shows some of these air sacs. After the oxygen reaches these air sacs, where does it go? How is it carried all over your body? Your heart and **blood vessels** are your **circulatory** system. Is there any part of your body that does not get oxygen from your blood?

—Balance in Your Life: Purple
Harcourt Brace Jovanovich

Notice how the text explains the diagram on page 344.

Building Skills

1. Which of the following titles would best fit the diagram? The text will help you find the answer.

   a. The Circulatory System
   b. The Respiratory System
   c. Oxygen

2. Below are three questions asked in the text. Where would you find the answer to each one: in the diagram, in the text, or in both?

   a. When you take a breath, where does the air go?
   b. After the oxygen reaches these air sacs, where does it go?
   c. How is it carried all over your body?

345

3. Have students complete *Building Skills*.

Answers to *Building Skills*
Health Selection

1. b. The Respiratory System; **2. a.** diagram; **b.** both; **c.** text

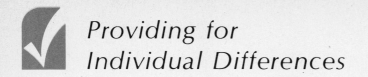

Providing for Individual Differences

Skills Lesson

Additional Practice

Worksheet 11, Teacher's Edition, page T490

Vocabulary Study

Additional Practice

■ **Identifying word parts: root words and prefixes**
List the following prefixes meaning "not" on the board:

> non-   in-   mis-   un-   im-   dis-

Now write the following words on the board. Have students identify which prefixes can be used with each word. Allow them to check their answers in a dictionary.

proper (im-)	fiction (non-)
agree (dis-)	adequate (in-)
satisfied (un-, dis-)	flying (non-)
realistic (un-, non-)	comfort (dis-)
correct (in-)	loyal (dis-)
perfect (im-, un-)	trust (dis-, mis-)
pure (im-, un-)	behave (mis-)

Reading Selection: Golden Ghosts

Additional Practice

■ **Interpreting information from a picture**   Tell students to look at page 172. Ask where the children pictured come from. Have them read the last paragraph on page 171 to check their answers. (boy, left—cave boy; boy, right—Amazon River; girl—Kansas City)

Have students look at page 168. Ask where the children pictured come from, based on paragraph 3 on page 169. (from left to right—United States; England; top middle—United States; lower middle—Rome; United States; China)

Challenge Activity

■ **Interpreting information from a picture**   Have students look at the picture on page 38 and answer these questions.

> Was this picture taken in Burma, Thailand, the United States, or New Zealand? (New Zealand page 41, paragraphs 1–3)

What is making the lights: fireflies, shrimp, or glow-worms? (glowworms)

Have students write one-word captions for the pictures on the following pages:

> page 45 (Wetlands)
> page 47, top (Flea *or* Parasite)
> page 47, bottom (Microorganisms *or* Microbes)

Reading Selection: "Modern" America in the 1880's

Additional Practice

■ **Comparing information obtained from graphic aids to textual information**   Have students read the third paragraph on page 192. Then ask them whether they could find each of the following six details in the text only, in the picture only, or in both the text and the picture.

> You can find several shell-identification books at most bookstores or in your library. (text only)
> The family name of the baby's foot shell is *Anomia*. (both text and picture)
> All shells have family names which almost always come from Latin. (text only)
> A kitten's paw shell looks like its name. (picture only)
> In the center of the baby's foot shell there is a tiny print that looks like a baby's foot. (both text and picture)
> Most guidebooks list a shell under both its common name and its family name. (text only)

Challenge Activity

■ **Interpreting information from a diagram**   Draw the following diagram on the board, and ask students the questions that follow.

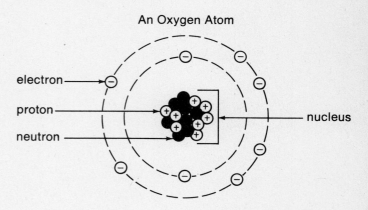

What is the title of the diagram? (An Oxygen Atom)
How many labels does the diagram have? (four)
What are the labels? (nucleus, electron, proton, neutron)

Can you tell from the diagram that there is one atom of oxygen in a water molecule? (no)

Can you tell from the diagram that the electrons are outside the nucleus? (yes)

How many electrons does an atom of oxygen have? (8)

How many protons does an atom of oxygen have? (8)

Evaluation

Periodic Test 3, Part III, Form A or *Form B,* may be administered after this unit to test skills marked **T**. If you have pretested using *Form A,* administer *Form B.*

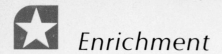

Enrichment

Golden Ghosts

Bibliography

The following books are about the Old West.

Easy

Rounds, Glen. *The Cowboy Trade.* A good picture of the cowhand in the Old West.

Sackett, S. J. *Cowboys and the Songs They Sang.* Songs of the range, the trail, and what it was like to be a cowhand.

Average

Glubok, Shirley. *The Art of the Old West.* The American West of the 1800's and examples of all types of its art.

Films and Filmstrips

NOTE: For more information, see *Resource Center.*

Selection content

Coronet Instructional Media. "Gold Rush Days." Life in a gold-mining settlement and effects of the gold rush.

Curriculum Coordination

Language Arts

The West is full of towns and cities with interesting and unusual names. Ask students to select a town or city and try to find out the origin of its name. Students may refer to this list to start them off:

Cripple Creek, Colorado
Leadville, Colorado
Pike's Peak, Colorado
Sutter's Mill, California
Hungry Horse, Montana
Surprise, Nebraska
Peculiar, Missouri
Broken Arrow, Oklahoma
Dime Box, Texas
Riddle, Oregon
Sweet Home, Oregon
Talent, Oregon
Gold Run, California
Death Valley, California
Dutch John, Utah
Mexican Hat, Utah

Alternate suggestion: Students can pick one of these towns and make up a story about how it got its name.

Science

Have students do research on how miners panned for gold and how geologists and archaeologists use this technique to locate precious ores and objects in riverbeds today.

Music

American music is rich with songs from this period of history, such as "My Darling Clementine," "Shenandoah," and the songs of Stephen Foster. Interested students can locate these and other songs in an anthology of American folk songs and give a concert for the class.

Career Education

Invite a jeweler, jewelry maker, or goldsmith to talk about jewelry making, working with precious metals, and the relative values of precious stones and metals. The jeweler might explain the process that gold undergoes from its extraction from a mine to its transformation into a piece of jewelry.

"Modern" America in the 1880's

Bibliography

The following books are about American history.

Easy

Emrich, Duncan, comp. *The Nonsense Book of Riddles, Rhymes, Tongue Twisters, Puzzles, and Jokes from American Folklore.* A collection of riddles, etc., taken from American folklore and history.

Glubok, Shirley. *The Art of America in the Gilded Age.* Historical events and artistic developments from the end of the Civil War to the end of the nineteenth century.

Average

Loeb, Robert H. *New England Village: Everyday Life in 1810.* A New England village and what life was like.

Schwartz, Alvin, ed. *When I Grew Up Long Ago.* Brief statements from people whose childhoods were in the period 1890–1914, on such areas of their past lives as food, social life, music, holidays, and health, provide glimpses of life in the United States at that time.

Challenging

Schnacke, Dick. *American Folk Toys: How to Make Them.* How toys from the frontier era of America were used, where they were made, and how to make them.

Films and Filmstrips

NOTE: For more information, see *Resource Center.*

Selection content

Coronet Instructional Media. "Inventions in America's Growth—II (1850–1910)." The telephone, phonograph, electric lamp, streetcar, etc.

National Geographic. *Transportation in America.* Appropriate: "Yesterday's Travel."

Curriculum Coordination

Language Arts/Social Studies

1. Students might wish to write an article titled "Modern America in the 1980's" with future readers in mind. You may wish to suggest that students organize the article around topics that might be of interest to future readers.

2. Have students interview their parents, grandparents, or other adults to find out what "modern" life was like when they were children. Students may ask which of the following things did not yet exist: frozen orange juice, jet planes, TV, cassettes, transistor radios, satellite weather forecasts, solar heating, pocket calculators, push-button phones, electric typewriters, overhead projectors, felt-tipped pens. What other things were considered modern when they were children? Students might record survey results on a time line.

Music

Have students do research on the popular music of the 1880's and share their findings with the class.

Art

Students may investigate the art of the Old West in the work of artists such as Frederic Remington, Charles Russell, George Bingham, and Howard Pyle.

Science

Have students do research on how a telephone works. Perhaps some students can find a diagram that illustrates this and make an enlarged copy or model for the class. If possible, have a representative from the telephone company talk about modern advances in telephone communication.

TEACHING UNIT 14

Pages 346–372

Contents

Additional Materials

Reading Skills Workbook: Lessons 28–30, pages 86–99; Word Play, page 100
Duplicating Masters 11: pages 44–47
Worksheet 12: Teacher's Edition, pages T491–T492
Bookmark Reading Filmstrips: Purple: "Out West with Maps and Graphs"
Periodic Test 3, Part IV

Key to Symbols

Skills Objectives
I* — Introduced in this unit
I   — Introduced earlier in this level
M   — Maintained from previous levels
T   — Tested in periodic and cumulative tests for this level

Reduced Student Pages
underscore — words that appear in the glossary
wavy line   — words pretaught in the Teacher's Edition
            (these words also appear in the glossary)

Skills Lesson:
Getting Information from Maps and Graphs
Pages 346–352

Objectives

		SKILLS CODE NUMBER
M, T	To identify types of graphic aids	5.4
M, T	To interpret information from a map	5.4.3
M, T	To interpret information from a bar graph or pictograph	5.4.1
M, T	To compare information obtained from graphic aids to textual information	5.4.7
M, T	To interpret information from a line graph	5.4.1
M, T	To interpret information from a circle graph	5.4.1
M, T	To interpret information from a time line	5.4.1

If you wish to pretest the skills listed above, you may administer *Periodic Test 3, Part IV, Form A. Periodic Test 3, Part IV, Form B,* may be administered to post-test.

Getting Information from Maps and Graphs

·WELCOME TO NEW YORK·

TOLL

Map reading is an important skill that drivers use. It's an important skill for students in school, too. You'll find many maps in your reading. Maps, like pictures and diagrams, are graphic aids. If you can read the maps in your books, you'll be able to understand the text better.

On pages 347 and 348 are three different kinds of maps. As you study them, read the notes above and below the maps. They will help you understand the parts of a map.

346

Area Map

An *area map* shows cities, bodies of water, mountains, and rivers.

California

OREGON
Mt. Shasta
PACIFIC OCEAN
Sacramento River
★ Sacramento
San Francisco
San Joaquin River
NEVADA
Mt. Whitney
Death Valley
Los Angeles
Colorado River
San Diego
ARIZONA
SCALE
0   100   200
kilometers
MEXICO

Sacramento is the capital of California. It is marked with a star. How are cities like Los Angeles marked?

A *compass rose* shows direction. When you read a map, north is usually to the top; west is usually to the left of the page.

Topographical Map

A *topographical map* shows what the land is like. What places in California are mountainous? Which places are very low? Refer to the *key*, or *legend*. It shows what the colors mean.

California

OREGON
COAST RANGES
CASCADE RANGE
PACIFIC OCEAN
SIERRA NEVADA
NEVADA
MOJAVE DESERT
IMPERIAL VALLEY
ARIZONA
KEY
MEXICO
METERS
1525
610
305
152.5
SEA LEVEL
BELOW SEA LEVEL

347

Introducing
the Lesson

1. Display a map of the United States. Call on three students to locate the states of Ohio, New York, and California. Ask the class in which direction a driver should go to get from Ohio to California. (west)

2. Ask students to name occasions when they have used maps outside school. What kind of maps? (road maps; bus or train maps; amusement park maps; etc.) What information were they looking for?

3. Have students look at the cartoon at the top of page 346. Ask them what the driver should have done to get from California to Ohio. Then explain that they will be learning about maps and graphs in this *Skills Lesson:* Maps give information about a certain land area; graphs show numerical information in a way that can easily be compared.

4. Have students read the two paragraphs on page 346.

Developing
the Skill

A. *An* area map *shows cities, bodies of water, mountains, and rivers.*

1. Have students identify the title of the area map. (California) Have them read the boldfaced notes and find the compass rose on the map. Ask why a compass rose is useful. (It shows direction.) Ask where south and east are on the map. (South is on the bottom, and east is on the right side.)

2. Ask them to name some of the cities, mountains, and rivers on the map.

3. Have students locate the capital, Sacramento, on the map.

B. *A* topographical map *shows what the land is like.*

Have students read the boldfaced note above the topographical map and then refer to the key to answer the questions. (Examples: Cascade Range, Sierra Nevada, and Coastal Ranges are mountainous. Death Valley and Imperial Valley in the southeast are low.) Make sure students understand that the colors in the key correspond to the colors used on the map.

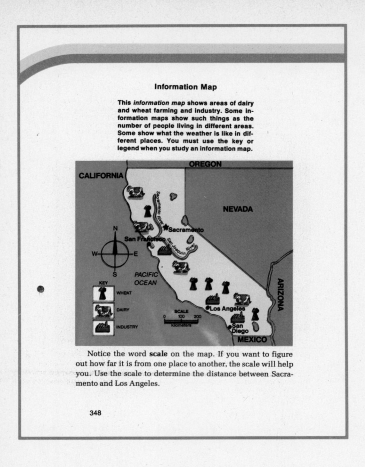

Information Map

This *information map* shows areas of dairy and wheat farming and industry. Some information maps show such things as the number of people living in different areas. Some show what the weather is like in different places. You must use the key or legend when you study an information map.

KEY

WHEAT

DAIRY

INDUSTRY

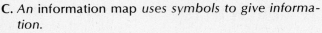

Notice the word **scale** on the map. If you want to figure out how far it is from one place to another, the scale will help you. Use the scale to determine the distance between Sacramento and Los Angeles.

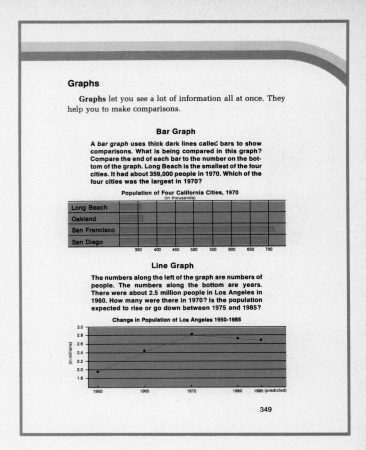

Graphs

Graphs let you see a lot of information all at once. They help you to make comparisons.

Bar Graph

A *bar graph* uses thick dark lines called bars to show comparisons. What is being compared in this graph? Compare the end of each bar to the number on the bottom of the graph. Long Beach is the smallest of the four cities. It had about 359,000 people in 1970. Which of the four cities was the largest in 1970?

Population of Four California Cities, 1970
(in thousands)

Line Graph

The numbers along the left of the graph are numbers of people. The numbers along the bottom are years. There were about 2.5 million people in Los Angeles in 1960. How many were there in 1970? Is the population expected to rise or go down between 1975 and 1985?

Change in Population of Los Angeles 1950-1985

C. *An* information map *uses symbols to give information.*

1. Have students read the boldfaced note and study the map on page 348. Ask what three symbols are given on the information map. (cow, wheatstalk, and factory) Ask where most manufacturing takes place in California. (near the cities)

2. Have students read the paragraph at the bottom of page 348. Then have them find the distance between San Francisco and Los Angeles. (approx. 480 km or 300 miles)

Graphs

A. *A bar graph* uses thick lines called bars to show comparisons.

1. Have students read the boldfaced note above the bar graph and answer the first question. (The populations of Long Beach, Oakland, San Francisco, and San Diego are being compared.)

2. Make sure students understand that the end of each bar corresponds to the number on the bottom of the graph and that the number refers to thousands. Then have students find the answer to the last question in the boldfaced note. (San Francisco was the largest.)

B. *A line graph* uses lines and dots to show comparisons.

Have students read the boldfaced note above the line graph and answer the questions. (In 1970, there were about 2.8 million people in Los Angeles. The population is expected to go down between 1975 and 1985.)

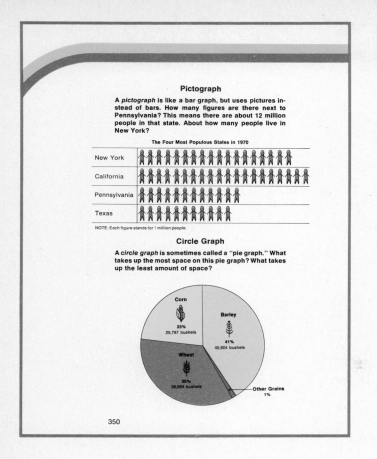

Pictograph

A *pictograph* is like a bar graph, but uses pictures instead of bars. How many figures are there next to Pennsylvania? This means there are about 12 million people in that state. About how many people live in New York?

The Four Most Populous States in 1970

New York	𝍖𝍖𝍖𝍖𝍖𝍖𝍖𝍖𝍖𝍖𝍖𝍖𝍖𝍖𝍖𝍖𝍖𝍖
California	𝍖𝍖𝍖𝍖𝍖𝍖𝍖𝍖𝍖𝍖𝍖𝍖𝍖𝍖𝍖𝍖𝍖
Pennsylvania	𝍖𝍖𝍖𝍖𝍖𝍖𝍖𝍖𝍖𝍖𝍖𝍖
Texas	𝍖𝍖𝍖𝍖𝍖𝍖𝍖𝍖𝍖𝍖𝍖

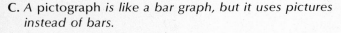
NOTE: Each figure stands for 1 million people.

Circle Graph

A *circle graph* is sometimes called a "pie graph." What takes up the most space on this pie graph? What takes up the least amount of space?

Corn
23%
25,787 bushels

Barley
41%
45,604 bushels

Wheat
35%
38,994 bushels

Other Grains
1%

350

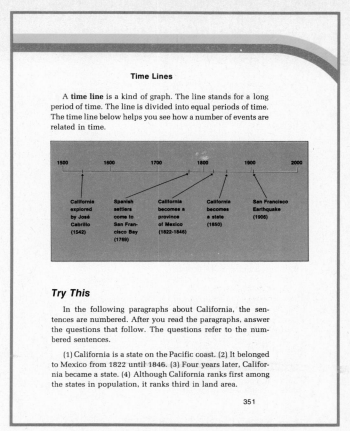

Time Lines

A **time line** is a kind of graph. The line stands for a long period of time. The line is divided into equal periods of time. The time line below helps you see how a number of events are related in time.

| 1500 | 1600 | 1700 | 1800 | 1900 | 2000 |

California explored by José Cabrillo (1542)

Spanish settlers come to San Francisco Bay (1769)

California becomes a province of Mexico (1822-1846)

California becomes a state (1850)

San Francisco Earthquake (1906)

Try This

In the following paragraphs about California, the sentences are numbered. After you read the paragraphs, answer the questions that follow. The questions refer to the numbered sentences.

(1) California is a state on the Pacific coast. (2) It belonged to Mexico from 1822 until 1846. (3) Four years later, California became a state. (4) Although California ranks first among the states in population, it ranks third in land area.

351

C. *A pictograph is like a bar graph, but it uses pictures instead of bars.*

Have students read the boldfaced note above the pictograph on page 350. Call their attention to the line at the bottom of the pictograph that explains that each figure stands for one million people. Have students answer the questions in the boldfaced note. (There are twelve figures next to Pennsylvania. About 18 million people live in New York.)

D. *A circle graph or "pie graph" shows parts of a whole.*

1. Have students examine the circle graph. Point out that each portion of this graph gives percentages as well as the amount in numbers. Explain that some circle graphs give only percentages and some give only numbers.

2. Have students read the boldfaced note above the circle graph and answer the questions. (Barley takes up the most space. "Other grains" takes up the least space.)

E. *A time line shows events over a period of time.*

Have students read the paragraph and examine the time line. Ask them how many years the time line covers. (500 years) Into what equal periods of time is this line divided? (100-year periods) Why is a time line a useful kind of graph? (At a glance, it tells you when different events happened and shows how these events are related across time.)

Try This

Have students complete *Try This*.

Answers to *Try This*

1. all three maps; 2. time line; 3. pictograph; Land area rank is not given in any graphic aid used in the *Skills Lesson*; 4. information map; 5. No graphic aid gives this information; 6. No graphic aid gives this information; 7. circle or pie graph; 8. bar graph; 9. It explains that the estimated population of Los Angeles is expected to remain the same or fall in the next few years.

 Use *Reading Skills Workbook*, Lesson 28, pages 86-96. See *Providing for Individual Differences*, page T322, for additional practice.

(5) California has both farming and machine industry. (6) The state produces one third of all of America's vegetables. (7) California is well-known for its fruit and nut crops. (8) The state also produces much of the grain used in America, including wheat, barley, and corn.

(9) The largest cities in California are Los Angeles, San Diego, San Francisco, San José, Long Beach, and Oakland. (10) Although the population of large cities like Los Angeles rose in the past, it is expected to remain the same or fall in the next few years. (11) More people are coming to live in California, and the population of one city, San Diego, is increasing.

1. Which graphic aids in this lesson show the information given in sentence 1?
2. Which graph gives the information in sentences 2 and 3?
3. Two facts are given in sentence 4. Which graphic aid shows you that California has the largest population among the states? Does any graphic aid show you that California is the third largest state?
4. Read sentence 5. Which of the three maps shows some of California's industries?
5. Do any of the graphic aids show the information given in sentence 6?
6. Do any of the graphic aids show the information given in sentence 7?
7. Which graph shows the information explained in sentence 8?
8. Do any of the graphic aids give you any of the information that is stated in sentence 9?
9. Sentence 10 explains something shown on the line graph. What does this sentence explain?

352

Vocabulary Study:
Compound Words
Page 353

Objective

M   To identify base words in compound words

SKILLS CODE NUMBER

4.2.1

Developing the Skill

1. Tell students that the *Vocabulary Study* they are about to read is about an amazing "wordmaker." Tell them to look for compound words as they read.

2. Have students read the *Vocabulary Study* and do the *Word Play* activities.

Answers to *Word Play*

1. *upriver:* up the river; *windstorm:* a storm of strong winds with no rain; *farmland:* land covered by farms; *horsecars:* cars pulled by horses; *innkeeper:* person who keeps the inn; *townspeople:* people who live in town; **2.** Other compound words: Bullfrog, grandparents, everywhere, carfare, typewriters, airplane, Wordmaker, ballpoint, watermelon, blueberries, grapefruit; Sentences will vary.

 Use *Reading Skills Workbook,* Lesson 29, page 97. See *Providing for Individual Differences,* page T322, for additional practice.

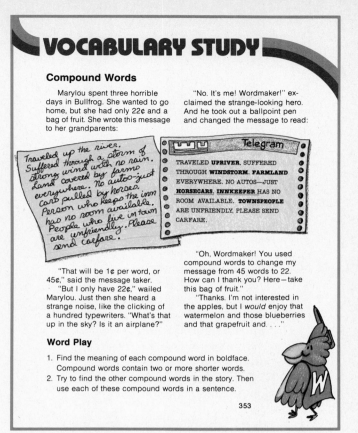

Reading Selection:
Sod-Shanty Pioneers

Pages 354–361

Objectives

		SKILLS CODE NUMBER
M, T	To identify types of graphic aids	5.4
M, T	To interpret information from a line graph	5.4.1
M, T	To interpret information from a map	5.4.3
M, T	To compare information obtained from graphic aids to textual information	5.4.7
M	To predict outcomes based on given information and personal knowledge	3.4.2
M	To classify stated details by identifying groups to which they belong	3.2.1

 # Preparing to Read

Summary

When the Homestead Act of 1862 made large stretches of land available to settlers at $1.25 per acre, Grace McCance's family moved to the Nebraska prairie. Like most other homesteaders on the Great Plains, they lived in a small sod house, worked long and hard, and learned to cope with blizzards, floods, and fires. After the McCances had worked their homestead for five years, the land legally became theirs. They then sold it and started all over again on a new site. Life slowly improved. The family got a kitchen stove with a water heater and then a washing machine run by "child power." In 1895 the family moved again. Their new home was a tall house made of lumber. Eventually Grace became a teacher, married, raised a family of her own, and, when she was in her eighties, wrote a book about her family's life as sod-shanty pioneers.

Background

The Homestead Act of 1862 was passed by Abraham Lincoln and a pro-Union Congress as the result of a long political struggle. Questions of land policy became involved with the slavery issue. Southern sympathizers did not want to allow more "free" territories, and Northern sympathizers did not want to allow further areas to be opened to slavery.

In the frontier areas, laws and customs were favorable to women's owning and managing their own lands and businesses. The only stipulations of the act were that applicants had to be citizens or aliens who intended to become citizens, had to be at least twenty-one years of age, and must never have fought against the United States. Between 1863 and 1890, there were 956,922 homestead applications filed in this country.

The following book will provide you with additional background information.

Riegel, Robert. *America Moves West*. The expansion and development of the United States from 1600 to 1900. Illustrated, with maps and index.

Developing Vocabulary and Concepts

sod: the top layer of earth held together by twisted roots of grass and weeds
shanty: a roughly made, hastily built shack or cabin
homestead: a house and its land, etc., used as a home
established: set up on a firm or lasting basis
peril: danger, risk
prosperity: a successful condition; material wealth or success
drought: a lack of rain for a long period
sloshing: moving or being thrown about in water

1. a. Read the following sentences aloud, or write them on the board. If you read them aloud, write the underlined vocabulary on the board.

The family lived and worked on their 160-acre homestead for five years.
Schools weren't permanently established. If the teacher moved away, there was no longer a school.
Floods were one peril. Blizzards were another danger.
A period of prosperity and wealth followed the years of poverty.
During the drought, the crops died because they couldn't survive without rain.
After the clothes had been sloshing around in the water for fifteen minutes, Grace took them out of the washing machine.

b. Ask students to give the meaning of each vocabulary word. Remind them to use the context clues in the sentences to help them.

2. a. Ask students what materials houses or apartment buildings are made of. (concrete, bricks, wood, etc.) Ask students what else could be used to build a house. (Accept reasonable answers.) Ask students if houses can be made of earth. Write the word *sod* on the board. Explain to students that *sod* is the top layer of earth held together by twisted roots of grass and weeds and that at one time people did build houses out of it.

b. Tell students that a house made out of sod was called a sod shanty. Write the word *shanty* on the board, and explain that a shanty is a roughly made shack or cabin. Explain to students that the selection they will read is about a family who lived in a sod shanty.

 Use *Duplicating Masters 11,* page 44.

Setting Purposes

Skills

Have students read the skills note on page 354. Remind them to refer to the map and time line as they read in order to learn more.

Content

Have students read the lead-in to the title. Ask them to think about how the weather would make life hard for the pioneers.

2 Reading and Discussing

Have students read the selection. Most students will be able to complete it in one sitting. If you prefer, the selection may be read in two parts, breaking before the heading "Toward a Better Life" on page 359.

NOTE: The questions that appear in the student's text at the end of the selection focus on comprehension of selection content and on application of the *Skills Lesson* to the selection. Answers to these questions begin on page T312.

How far did Grace McCance and her family travel in 1885? Where were the railroads at that time? The map in the selection will add information to the text.

Winter blizzards and summer droughts made life hard for the brave . . .

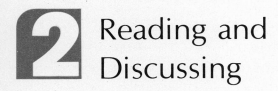

SOD-SHANTY PIONEERS

by Dorothy M. Johnson

After the covered-wagon pioneers went west to seek their fortunes, another frontier opened up. To the <u>prairies</u> of the Dakotas and Nebraska, with their uncertain rainfall and wild windstorms, came the sod-shanty pioneers.

One of them was Grace McCance. She was only three years old at the time her family moved from Missouri to Nebraska, in 1885.

One reason for the great westward movement during the nineteenth century was that people wanted land for farming. There was land in plenty—thousands of square miles of it. Farmers and their families moved westward to <u>claim</u> it.

In 1862, President Abraham Lincoln signed the first <u>Homestead Act.</u> It threw vast stretches open to settlement at a very low cost. Any citizen twenty-one years old or older could <u>file</u> a claim on 160 acres. After five years of working the land, the man or woman could buy it for only $1.25 an acre. This was known as "proving up."

By 1885, pioneers moving to Nebraska traveled by railroad. Grace's father, Charles, sold his only milk-giving cow to pay for moving everything the family owned—household goods, farm tools, three horses, and a mule.

A Tough Beginning

Like most homesteaders on the Great Plains, the McCances lived in a house made of earth. The *soddy* was the <u>typical</u> first home of most people who filed for free land on the prairie. Trees were too scarce to be cut for building log cabins. So the tough prairie sod itself was used for building material. It was cut into neat blocks which were piled up solidly to make thick walls. The roof, supported by planks, was made of sod, too.

The McCances' first soddy was one room only twelve by fourteen feet in size. Compared to many others, however, it was a lovely home. It had a wooden floor, and the side walls were whitewashed. Grace's mother bleached flour sacks to make curtains for the three little windows.

355

Every drop of water for the family and the animals had to be carried in barrels by wagon from another <u>homestead</u> two miles away, where there was a well with a windmill to run the pump. Another hardship was that, with no cow or chickens at first, the family had no milk, butter, or eggs.

For a field crop, Mr. McCance raised corn. A kitchen garden provided much of the family's food—onions, beans, watermelons, and sweet corn.

Even very small children had their own work to do. Grace was not yet six years old when her father gave her the job of herding the cows he had bought. It was lonesome work, and she wanted something to keep her mind and hands busy. She begged her mother for some tiny scraps of cloth and learned how to piece quilts. In later years, her beautiful quilts took many prizes and made her famous.

When Grace was six, she had a chance to go to school for three months, walking three miles each way. Schools weren't <u>permanently established</u>. When a teacher and

356

a room could be found, children went to school. If the teacher moved away, there was no longer a school.

Living with the Weather

Farmers always live by the weather. You can't do anything about weather except enjoy it or put up with it, <u>depending</u> on what kind of weather you're having. For Nebraska homesteaders, weather seemed especially bad because there was no shelter or forest in that wide, flat land.

The McCance family adjusted to the weather as well as anybody could. Blizzards—blinding snow whirled by screaming winds—were a <u>peril</u> in the winter. During a blizzard it wasn't safe to go out of the soddy. But it was necessary because the <u>stock</u> had to be fed and fuel had to be brought in for the stove. To get from the house to the barn, it was necessary to have a rope tied between the two buildings. You can hold on to a rope and feel your way along it even when you can't see a thing.

Another kind of prairie wind

is the welcome chinook. It melts snow unbelievably fast so that there is rushing water everywhere. Then there is another peril—floods.

Sometimes children could not get home from school for a day or two because of snow or wind or a flood. There was no way of getting word back to their parents. Everybody simply had to be patient.

Another <u>menace</u> on the prairie was fire, roaring through the wild grass with a howling wind whipping it on. Sometimes buildings, animals,

and even human lives were lost. Grace's father, like other homesteaders, plowed fire <u>guards</u>. These strips of <u>raw</u> earth with no grass on them to burn saved the family more than once.

There was no end to the sudden dangers that weather produced. One warm night in July, a lightning storm struck. Fierce winds blew the roof off the kitchen that had been added to the sod house. Mrs. McCance had a hard time finding enough undamaged food in the mass of mud to prepare

357

breakfast. Many things, blown out across the prairie, never were found at all.

Daily Life

Grace went barefoot except in winter. Once she stepped on a nail, injuring her foot. Even when she couldn't walk, Grace kept busy. She pounded bits of broken dishes and old buffalo bones into a <u>grit</u> that the chickens needed.

Grace's father finally found time to dig a well. Water was brought up by mule power.

That is, one of the children would lead an old mule that pulled the heavy bucket up from the well. Mr. McCance no longer had to haul water from two miles away. But the family still had to be careful not to waste any water, because somebody had to carry it up a steep hill to the house.

In five years, the McCances had "proved up" on their homestead. They had lived on it long enough and put enough work into it so that the land was legally theirs. They then sold it, bought a quarter <u>section</u> (160

acres), and started all over on a new farm. The new farm's soddy had a bedroom, a sitting room, and a big kitchen.

Toward a Better Life

When Grace was nine, she attended school again, but only part of each day. She was needed to herd cattle mornings and afternoons.

That year, the McCance family got something wonderful. They bought a new kitchen stove with an attached tank for heating water. Later they got something else that delighted them—a washing machine. It wasn't electric. That kind of washing machine was yet to be invented. But it certainly beat the old washboard. A three-legged "dolly" under the lid was attached to a handle on top and was turned back and forth by means of "child power." Fifteen minutes of sloshing could clean a whole tubful of laundry.

At the same time that the McCances got their "child-powered" washing machine, another fine improvement was then added. Grace's mother had always done her canning in tin cans. She sealed the lids on with hot sealing wax. Now she had glass jars for the first time, with lids that screwed on. They were easier to use, they looked very pretty lined up on the shelves, and they didn't have to be labeled.

Bad Times, Good Times

Prosperity wasn't always with the McCances, however. In 1894, there was a drought. The cattle became thin. There was no corn for the pigs. Two younger sisters now herded the cattle, while Grace kept moving the pigs to fields where they could find enough shoots and stems to keep them alive.

One day a terrible windstorm sent the family flying to the cellar for safety. The barn was ruined, and the corn crib was damaged. Most of the chickens were killed. When harvest time came, there was nothing to harvest. Mr. McCance tried to sell his cattle because there was no feed for them. But he couldn't even give them away, because nobody else had feed either.

In 1895, things were better. The family moved again. Their new house was a tall house made of real lumber. It was big enough so that, for the first time, they didn't have to keep a bed in the parlor.

Within the next few years, Grace's younger sisters took over much of the farm work. Grace was now able to study to become a teacher. After the turn of the century, Grace married and started to raise her own family. More than sixty years later, when Grace was in her eighties, she wrote a book about her family's life as sod-shanty pioneers.

359

360

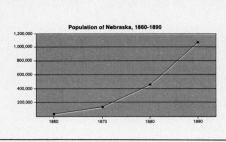

Population of Nebraska, 1860-1890

Understanding What You've Read

1. How could a person get land under the Homestead Act?
2. What was a soddy and how was it made?
3. Describe the weather of the Nebraska prairie.
4. Why do you think Grace McCance wrote a book about her family's life as sod-shanty pioneers?

Applying the Skills Lesson

1. Look at the graph above. Is this a bar graph, a line graph, or a pictograph?
2. During which ten-year period did the population of Nebraska increase most?
3. When did the McCance family move to Nebraska? Did they move during the ten-year period of the greatest or least growth of Nebraska?
4. Estimate the number of kilometers distance the McCance family traveled when they moved from Missouri to Nebraska. Use the center of each state as end points to figure the distance.

361

Questions preceded by a bullet are additional questions and appear in the Teacher's Edition only. The other questions appear in the student's text after the selection.

Understanding What You've Read

1. *How could a person get land under the Homestead Act?* (Under the Homestead Act, any citizen at least twenty-one years old could file a claim on 160 acres. After five years of working the land, the person could buy it for $1.25 an acre. page 355) LITERAL Recalling stated information

● *Do you think the Homestead Act made the West grow faster? Explain your answer.* (Yes. Explanations should reflect the fact that many people came to get the land at low cost. Once these pioneers had settled the land, schools, banks, railroads, and stores began to move in to serve the needs of established farm communities.) CRITICAL Drawing conclusions

2. *What was a soddy and how was it made?* (A soddy was a house made of earth. It was made by cutting sod into neat blocks and then piling them up solidly to make thick walls. The roof, supported by planks, was made of sod, too. page 355) LITERAL Recalling stated information

● *What was life like for Grace as a child?* (Life was hard for Grace. Elicit details that would support this statement—for example: Before Grace was six years old, she had the job of herding cows. When she was six, she had the chance to go to school for three months, and she walked three miles each way to get there and back. page 356) INFERENTIAL Identifying the main idea of a selection

3. *Describe the weather of the Nebraska prairie.* (Blizzards were a peril in the winter, with blinding snow and screaming winds. The chinook was a kind of prairie wind that melted snow so quickly that there was rushing water everywhere, and this sometimes caused floods. There were also fierce winds that caused fires to spread or could blow the roof off a house. pages 356 and 357) LITERAL Recalling stated information

● *Why did the McCances sell their land after five years and start all over?* (They probably were able to make a profit by selling the land for more than $1.25 per acre. The new land might have been better or larger. The new soddy was better than the old soddy. page 359) INFERENTIAL Drawing conclusions

● *How did life slowly improve for the McCances?* (They were able to get a new kitchen stove, a washing machine, and glass jars for preserving food. page 359) LITERAL Recalling specific details

4. *Why do you think Grace McCance wrote a book about her family's life as sod-shanty pioneers?* (Answers should include: She wanted to share her experiences with others; she thought she could give others a look at part of the country's past; she liked writing about and remembering the past.) INFERENTIAL Making judgments

Applying the Skills Lesson

1. *Look at the graph above. Is this a bar graph, a line graph, or a pictograph?* (line graph) Identifying types of graphic aids

2. *During which ten-year period did the population of Nebraska increase most?* (during the period between 1880 and 1890) Interpreting information from a line graph

● *During which ten-year period did the population of Nebraska increase the least?* (during the period between 1860 and 1870) Interpreting information from a line graph

3. *When did the McCance family move to Nebraska? Did they move during the ten-year period of the greatest or least growth of Nebraska?* (in 1885, during the ten-year period of the greatest growth) Comparing information obtained from graphic aids to textual information

- *Use the graph to estimate the population of Nebraska in 1885.* (Students can find the median, or mid-point, between the dates, which would indicate the 1885 population was about 800,000.)   <u>Interpreting information from a line graph</u>

4. *Estimate the number of kilometers distance the McCance family traveled when they moved from Missouri to Nebraska. Use the center of each state as end points to figure the distance.* (Accept answers in the range of 700–850 kilometers.)   <u>Interpreting information from a map</u>

- *Estimate the number of kilometers from the easternmost border of Nebraska to the westernmost border of Nebraska.* (Accept answers in the range of 650–750 kilometers.)   <u>Interpreting information from a map</u>

 Use *Duplicating Masters 11*, page 45. See *Providing for Individual Differences*, page T322, for additional practice.

3 Maintaining Skills

Comprehension Skills

Predicting outcomes   Have students reread the first two paragraphs under "Bad Times, Good Times" on pages 359 and 360. Tell them to suppose that the drought will last one more year. Ask them which of the following statements tell what is likely to happen. Point out that each statement tells something that is possible but that not every prediction is likely.

> The farmers in the area will get rich. (not likely)
> Many cattle will starve. (likely)
> There will not be much food for the people, and some people might leave their farms and move elsewhere. (likely)
> The McCances will buy more cattle. (not likely)

Have students reread the third paragraph under the heading "Daily Life" on pages 358 and 359. Ask them to predict what is likely to happen to the family that bought the McCances' farm in 1890. Give them the following choices:

> They will build a new sod house. (not likely)
> They will plow the land and plant crops. (likely)
> They will have the same kinds of problems with weather as the McCances did. (likely)
> They will use the well that Mr. McCance dug. (likely)
> They will grow tomatoes instead of corn. (not likely)

 Use *Reading Skills Workbook*, Lesson 30, pages 98–99.

Classifying details   On the board, write the following three headings from the selection:

> A Tough Beginning
> Living with the Weather
> Toward a Better Life

Now read the following sentences from the selection. Have students identify the appropriate heading under which each sentence belongs.

> They bought a new kitchen stove with an attached tank for heating water. (Toward a Better Life)
> During a blizzard it wasn't safe to go out of the soddy. (Living with the Weather)
> The *soddy* was the typical first home of most people who filed for free land on the prairie. (A Tough Beginning)
> Later they got something else that delighted them—a washing machine. (Toward a Better Life)
> Fierce winds blew the roof off the kitchen that had been added to the sod house. (Living with the Weather)
> The McCances' first soddy was one room only twelve by fourteen feet in size. (A Tough Beginning)
> One warm night in July, a lightning storm struck. (Living with the Weather)

 For additional resources and curriculum-related activities, see *Enrichment*, page T323.

Reading Selection:
Whatever Happened to Main Street?

Pages 362–367

Objectives

		SKILLS CODE NUMBER
M, T	To interpret information from a map	5.4.3
M, T	To interpret information from a time line	5.4.1
I	To write a topical outline	7.1.5.1
M	To identify base words in compound words	4.2.1

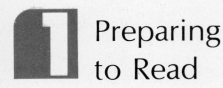

Preparing to Read

Summary

The selection describes how to discover a town's history by exploring older sections of the town. It suggests starting on such streets as Main Street, Center Street, or First Avenue in order to uncover clues to the past. There may be cornerstones, sidewalks, railings, or fences with dates on them. There may be old signs on the sides of buildings that reveal some of the original industries of the town. Perhaps there is an old railroad station with grain silos or sawmills nearby that were established early in the town's history. The selection explains that the more carefully a person looks, the more information he or she will be able to gather. It also suggests gathering more information by doing research at the city or county clerk's office and the library.

Background

The following book will provide you with background information.

Bridenbaugh, Carl. *Cities in the Wilderness: The First Century of Urban Life in America.* The importance of urban society in contrast with rural and frontier society. With index and bibliography.

Developing Vocabulary and Concepts

county seat: the center of local government
cornerstone: a stone at the corner of a building, especially one laid during a ceremony to mark the start of construction
trough: a long, narrow, open container for holding food or water for animals
investigating: looking into thoroughly in order to find out facts or details
plaque: a flat piece of metal, wood, etc., having designs or lettering on one side
silo: a tower in which green fodder, grain, or other feed is stored
arches: curved structures over openings such as windows and doors

1. **a.** Read the following sentences aloud, or write them on the board. If you read them aloud, write the underlined vocabulary on the board.

   You can find out how old a building is by looking for a date on its <u>cornerstone</u>, a stone at the corner of the building.
   The horse drank water from a long, narrow, open container called a <u>trough</u>.
   <u>Investigating</u> your town's history will help you find out more facts about your town.
   The name of the building and the date it was built were written on a metal <u>plaque</u>.
   The old grain <u>silo</u> in which the feed was stored was near the railroad.
   You can look for dates on the <u>arches</u> of buildings— curved structures over doors or windows.

   b. Ask students to give the meaning of each vocabulary word. Remind them to use the context clues in the sentences to help them. Also have them check the glossary for the pronunciation of *trough*.

2. Write the word *county* on the board, and explain to students that a county is one of the sections into which a state is divided. Ask students if they know the name of the county in which they live. Write the words *county seat* on the board, and ask students what they think it means. Explain to them that a county seat is the place where the county government's offices are located.

3. **a.** Ask students to imagine entering a time machine that can take them back 300 years. Do they think they could recognize their own town or city? Why or why not? Then ask them to imagine that the time machine took them back 100 years. Would some of the same buildings and street signs still be there?

   b. Tell students to imagine what the "life story" of their town is. When was their town "born"? Explain that the selection they are about to read will give them ideas on how to find out about the history of their town.

Use *Duplicating Masters 11,* page 46.

Setting Purposes

Skills

Have students read the skills note at the top of page 362. Tell them to use all the graphic aids as they read the text.

Content

Have students read the lead-in to the title. Tell them to keep in mind the "main" street of their town as they read this selection.

2 Reading and Discussing

Have students read the selection. Most students will be able to complete it in one sitting. If you prefer, the selection may be read in two parts, breaking before the paragraph beginning "One way is to spend . . ." on page 364.

NOTE: The questions that appear in the student's text at the end of the selection focus on comprehension of selection content and on application of the *Skills Lesson* to the selection. Answers to these questions begin on page T317.

In this selection, you'll find many details in the graphic aids. The graphic aids and the text may help you to learn how to learn about the history of your town or city.

Does your town or city have a Main Street? If it does, you can learn a lot about your local history if you find the answer to the question . . .

Whatever Happened to Main Street?

by David Weitzman

Does your town or city have a Main Street, a Center Street, a First Avenue, or an A Street? If it does, it may be the oldest-looking street around. If you were to look closely for dates on the cornerstones and arches along that street, you'd probably find that it has some of the first buildings built in your town or city.

Chances are this street is not the main street, center street, or first avenue anymore. But it once was. So let's take a walk down Main Street, into the past.

Here on Main Street you can close your eyes and imagine the sounds of the past: old cars, horses, trolley cars, and carts.

Here you can begin to understand something of your town's or city's history if you watch carefully for the small bits of the past. Sometimes there are cobblestones showing through the pavement. Sometimes there are old trolley tracks. There may be an iron drinking trough for horses.

Lots of cities began as railroad stations. Today they may still have railroad tracks running right through them. Let your imagination carry you back into the past. Imagine that just off Main Street of Anywhere, U.S.A., is the old yellow and brown station. Take a look inside its

363

windows. Seventy or a hundred years ago that station may have stood alone. Perhaps there was nothing for miles around until the cattle drive began. Thousands of head of cattle arrived for shipment by train to the big city. Then, over the years, things changed. Bigger cattle pens were built. Hotels sprang up, as did general stores. There were banks and firms that bought and sold cattle. Of course, there had to be houses for all the people running these businesses.

Soon manufacturers arrived so that they could be near railroads. The town then became a large transportation and manufacturing center. It had more houses and stores. Soon the town became a city, which grew out and away from its reason for being—the railroad tracks.

Other cities began as transportation towns, too. They were for ships and shipping. These towns grew around the docks along rivers or around natural harbors on the seacoast. Even today, you can see the pattern of growth of river and seaport towns as you walk away from the docks. You may notice how the

city becomes newer the farther out you get.

Still another kind of city started at a crossroad. It began with a gas station, then a restaurant and bus stop, then a general store. Then there were some houses, schools, and other buildings.

There are still other kinds of beginnings for cities. Some begin as university towns, county seats, state capitals, and mining towns. Whole cities have grown around recreation areas.

Now, does that give you any ideas on how your town or city began and why? It may be a little hard to tell just what the first purpose of your town or city was— things have changed so much. For example, many railroad towns may have become manufacturing towns. If you don't come up with an answer right away, there are some ways that you can find out more about the history of your community.

One way is to spend some time in the old part of your community. There you can "collect" some bits and pieces of the past that interest you.

The first thing you can do is to

364

make an Old Town map. It doesn't have to be a fancy map. It should be one you can write all over and keep notes on. Before you leave home, make sure you've got a pencil and either a note pad or a clipboard with some paper. If you have a camera, take it with you.

If you've made a guess about how your town or city began, start investigating. Begin at the railroad tracks or at the dock. Or you can begin at a large meat-packing plant. Don't worry if your guess turns out to be wrong. You'll have fun anyway.

When you get to what you think is the oldest part of your community, try to make a rough map as you go along. Your first notes might look like this.

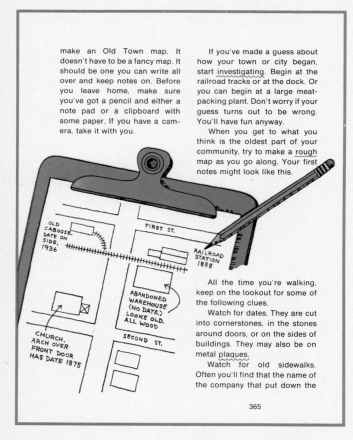

All the time you're walking, keep on the lookout for some of the following clues.

Watch for dates. They are cut into cornerstones, in the stones around doors, or on the sides of buildings. They may also be on metal plaques.

Watch for old sidewalks. Often you'll find that the name of the company that put down the

365

sidewalk is stamped into the wet cement. The stamps are often dated. Metal plates are sometimes set into the sidewalk.

Watch for cast-iron building fronts. Watch for lampposts and fire hydrants. Watch for railings and fences with dates on them.

Watch for old signs on the sides of buildings. What kinds of businesses are here? Is there more of one kind of business than another? Write down some of the names you see on the old

signs. Were the townspeople once mostly of one nationality?

Watch for clues at the railroad station. Are there maps painted on the sides of the old freight cars or the station's walls that show the old routes? Is there something around that shows what the trains carried in and out of your community? For example, do you see grain silos or sawmills?

Do you suppose you've really found the oldest part of your community all by yourself? Most likely you have. If you want to check up on how you're doing, there are several ways of finding out how well you have guessed.

Go to the town, city, or county clerk's office. Ask to see the oldest map of your community that they have. Ask how you can get a copy of the map.

Visit your main library. Ask the librarian where the local history section is. Ask if there are any histories of the community in a special collection.

Tell people what you're doing. They'll get interested, too. They may be able to give you information and ideas for many history projects.

366

Find groups of people who, like you, are interested in the history of their community and are trying to save it.

History of Anytown, U.S.A.

| 1830 | 1850 | 1870 | 1890 | 1910 | 1930 | 1950 |

Founding of town 1838

Railroad station built 1883

Main St. Church 1895

Fourth Street paved 1918

Abandoned caboose made in 1936

Town library built 1949

Understanding What You've Read

1. What are some clues to the past that the author suggests you might find in your community?
2. Name at least three ways in which cities have begun.
3. How does the author suggest you find out about the history of your community?
4. The author tells you to look for dates as you walk the older streets of your community. Where does he suggest these dates might be found?

Applying the Skills Lesson

1. Look at the rough map on page 365. Which of the following details does the map show?
   a. location of railroad station and date
   b. the first building in the town
   c. information about the location of some buildings that are still standing
2. Look at the time line above. Which is older, the railroad station or the church? Which is older, the church or the library?

367

Questions preceded by a bullet are additional questions and appear in the Teacher's Edition only. The other questions appear in the student's text after the selection.

Understanding What You've Read

1. *What are some clues to the past that the author suggests you might find in your community?* (There are many examples throughout the selection, including cobblestones, trolley tracks, an iron drinking trough, cast-iron building fronts, lampposts, and fire hydrants. pages 363, 366, etc.) LITERAL Recalling specific details

2. *Name at least three ways in which cities have begun.* (Some cities began as railroad stations or grew around the docks as shipping centers. Another kind of city started at a crossroad. Still others began as university towns, county seats, state capitals, mining towns, or recreation areas. pages 363 and 364) LITERAL Recalling stated information

● *Why would you find the oldest buildings near docks, rivers, or harbors in cities that began as shipping centers?* (The towns grew around the dock, along rivers, or around natural harbors on the seacoast. page 364) LITERAL Identifying cause-and-effect relationships

3. *How does the author suggest you find out about the history of your community?* (The author suggests the following: Spend some time in the old part of your community; make a map. page 364 Obtain an old map of your community; visit the library; tell others what you're doing. pages 366 and 367) LITERAL Recalling specific details

● *Why does the author suggest that you bring a camera?* (The author suggests that you bring a camera so you can take pictures of any interesting clues to your town's history. Accept other reasonable answers. page 365) LITERAL Drawing conclusions

4. *The author tells you to look for dates as you walk the older streets of your community. Where does he suggest these dates might be found?* (on cornerstones and arches; near doors; on the sides of buildings; on metal plaques, sidewalks, railings, and fences pages 363, 365, and 366) LITERAL Recalling specific details

● *How would a sawmill or a grain silo near a railroad station show what the trains carried in and out of town?* (A sawmill would show that wood was brought in by railroad, sawed, then carried out again. A silo would show that green fodder or grain was carried in, stored, then carried out again.) INFERENTIAL Drawing conclusions

Applying the Skills Lesson

1. *Look at the rough map on page 365. Which of the following details does the map show?*
   a. *location of railroad station and date*
   b. *the first building in the town*
   c. *information about the location of some buildings that are still standing*
   (Answers: a and c) Interpreting information from a map

● *Look at the map on page 365. Is First Street north, south, east, or west of the church?* (north) Interpreting information from a map

● *In which direction would you walk to get from the railroad station to the caboose?* (west) Interpreting information from a map

2. *Look at the time line above. Which is older, the railroad station or the church? Which is older, the church or the library?* (The railroad station is older than the church. The church is older than the library.) Interpreting information from a time line

- *Look at the time line on page 367. When was the town founded? How many years after its founding was the railroad station built?* (The town was founded in 1838. The railroad was built forty-five years later.) <u>Interpreting information from a time line</u>

✔ Use *Duplicating Masters 11*, page 47. See *Providing for Individual Differences*, page T322, for additional practice.

3 Maintaining Skills

Language Skills

Identifying base words in compound words Read the following sentences aloud, and write the underlined compound words on the board. Have students identify the shorter words in each compound word and give the meaning of the compound word.

> The date on the <u>cornerstone</u> was 1799. (corner, stone; a stone at the corner of a building)
> The old street was made of <u>cobblestones</u>. (cobble, stones; rounded stones that were once used to pave streets)
> The boy was dizzy, so he leaned against the <u>lamp-post</u>. (lamp, post; a post supporting a lamp in a street, park, etc.)
> Meet me at the <u>crossroad</u>. (cross, road; the place where two main roads cross each other)
> I kept all my notes on a <u>clipboard</u>. (clip, board; a board with a clip at the top, used to hold papers for writing)

Writing Skills

Writing a topical outline Write the following incomplete outline on the board. Have students fill in the missing information, using the items at the right as subtopics. Allow them to refer to the selection if they need to. Have students use Roman numerals and capital letters.

Investigating Your Town's History

I. How cities began
   A. _____
   _____ _____
   _____ _____
   _____ _____
   _____ _____
   _____ Where to look for dates
   _____ _____
   _____ _____
   _____ _____
   _____ _____
   _____ _____
   _____ _____
   _____ Where to find town records
   _____ _____
   _____ _____

Arches
University towns
City or county
   clerk's office
Library
Mining towns
Sidewalks
Recreation areas
Metal plaques
Shipping centers
Railroad stations
Railings
Crossroads
Cornerstones

Sample answer:

Investigating Your Town's History
   I. How cities began
      A. University towns
      B. Mining towns
      C. Recreation areas
      D. Shipping centers
      E. Railroad stations
      F. Crossroads
  II. Where to look for dates
      A. Arches
      B. Sidewalks
      C. Metal plaques
      D. Railings
      E. Cornerstones
 III. Where to find town records
      A. City or county clerk's office
      B. Library

✔ Use *Reading Skills Workbook*, Word Play, page 100, for vocabulary review.

★ For additional resources and curriculum-related activities, see *Enrichment*, page T323.

Textbook Study:
Maps and Graphs

Pages 368–371

Objectives

		SKILLS CODE NUMBER
M, T	To identify types of graphic aids	5.4
M, T	To interpret information from a map	5.4.3
M	To interpret information from a pictograph	5.4.1
M, T	To compare information obtained from graphic aids to textual information	5.4.7

Applying the Skill

Have students read the introduction and the two selections. You may wish to have them read the selections on their own and then do *Building Skills.* Or you may wish to direct students, using the following procedure.

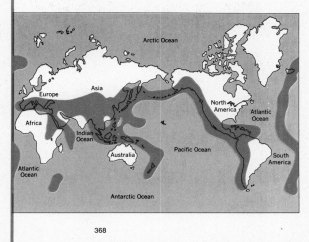

TEXTBOOK STUDY

Maps and Graphs

In many of your textbooks you'll find maps and graphs. These special kinds of graphic aids give important information. They give details that explain the text or details that you will not find in the text. As you read each selection and study the graphic aid that goes with it, refer to the sidenotes. They will help you understand some of the information.

Maps in Science

368

You might well think that there is nothing people can do about earthquakes. It turns out, however, as scientists <u>investigate</u>, that something can be done. Scientists have made maps showing where earthquakes happen. The areas colored orange on the map are called earthquake belts. Notice that earthquake belts are along some seacoasts. Some belts are along chains of islands. These belts show where earthquakes are likely to happen. A building put up in an earthquake belt can be built to <u>resist</u> earthquake shocks.

> *Refer to the map as you read the text. Then study the map to see what else it shows that the text does not mention.*

—*Concepts in Science:* Purple
Harcourt Brace Jovanovich

Building Skills

Below are some details from the science textbook. Which ones are in the text only? Which are in the map only? Which are in both the text and the map?

1. Earthquake belts are along some seacoasts.
2. A building put up in an earthquake belt can be built to resist earthquake shocks.
3. Some belts are along chains of islands.
4. All along the west coast of North and South America there is an earthquake belt.
5. Part of the Indian Ocean is an earthquake belt.

369

Graphs in Mathematics

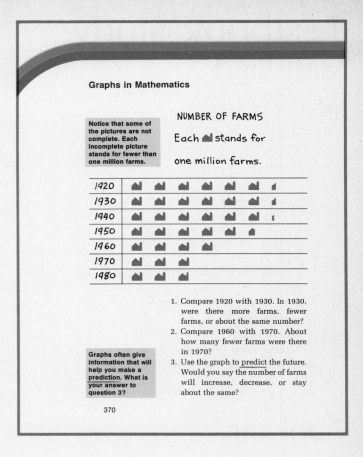

> *Notice that some of the pictures are not complete. Each incomplete picture stands for fewer than one million farms.*

1. Compare 1920 with 1930. In 1930, were there more farms, fewer farms, or about the same number?
2. Compare 1960 with 1970. About how many fewer farms were there in 1970?
3. Use the graph to <u>predict</u> the future. Would you say the number of farms will increase, decrease, or stay about the same?

> *Graphs often give information that will help you make a prediction. What is your answer to question 3?*

370

Maps in Science

1. Have students read the sidenote and the paragraph about earthquakes. Then ask them what the map shows that the text does not mention. (The map clearly shows the regions in which earthquakes occur.)

2. Have students try to name one area in which earthquakes occur. (Accept any region shown in orange on the map on page 368.)

3. Have students complete *Building Skills.*

Answers to *Building Skills*
Science Selection

1. both text and map; **2.** text only; **3.** both text and map; **4.** map only; **5.** map only

Graphs in Mathematics

1. Have students examine the graph on page 370 and read the first sidenote. Ask what years the graph covers. (1920–1980)

2. Have students read questions 1 and 2 and use the graph to find the answers. (1. about the same number; 2. one million fewer)

3. Have students answer the question in the sidenote at the bottom of page 370. (decrease or stay the same)

AVERAGE SIZE OF FARMS

Each ▪ stands for 10 hectares.

1920	▪ ▪ ▪ ▪ ▪
1930	▪ ▪ ▪ ▪ ▪
1940	▪ ▪ ▪ ▪ ▪ ▪
1950	▪ ▪ ▪ ▪ ▪ ▪ ▪
1960	▪ ▪ ▪ ▪ ▪ ▪ ▪ ▪ ▪ ▪
1970	▪ ▪ ▪ ▪ ▪ ▪ ▪ ▪ ▪ ▪ ▪ ▪
1980	▪ ▪ ▪ ▪ ▪ ▪ ▪ ▪ ▪ ▪ ▪ ▪ ▪ ▪

4. Is the <u>average</u> size of a farm increasing or decreasing?

5. The average size of a farm in the 1920's was about 60 hectares. By what year did the average size double?

6. The number of farms is decreasing. The average size of a farm is increasing. Do you think farms today are producing more food, less food, or about the same amount as in 1920?

—Growth in Mathematics: Purple Harcourt Brace, Jovanovich

Building Skills

Answer questions 4, 5, and 6 above.

371

Books About America's Past

Totems, Decoys and Covered Wagons: Cardboard Constructions from Early American Life by Jeremy Comins. Lothrop, 1976. The author tells how to make copies of toys, houses, furniture, and other important objects from early Native American and colonial life.

Lady for the Defense by Mary V. Fox. Harcourt Brace Jovanovich, 1975. You'll learn about Belva Lockwood, a lawyer who took many interesting cases and ran for President of the United States in 1884.

Immigrant Kids by Russell Freedman. Photos by Jacob Riis and others. Dutton, 1980. The lives of children who arrived in America during the late 1800's and early 1900's are illustrated in this book.

Why Don't You Get a Horse, Sam Adams? by Jean Fritz. Coward, 1974. Take a funny but fact-filled look at one of the founders of the United States.

How the Settlers Lived by George Laycock, Illustrated by Alexander Farquharson. McKay, 1980. This book shows how the pioneers carved their lives out of the American wilderness.

New England Village: Everyday Life in 1810 by Robert H. Loeb, Jr. Doubleday, 1976. This lively book recreates life in New England nearly 200 years ago.

What Ever Happened to the Baxter Place? by Pat Ross. Pantheon, 1976. You'll find out how a quiet farm gradually changed as a nearby town grew.

372

---

4. Have students examine the graph on page 371 and complete *Building Skills.*

Answers to *Building Skills*
Mathematics Selection

4. increasing; **5.** 1960; **6.** more food

If students have not already read these books, you may wish to recommend them at this time. Bibliographic information about these and other books for students is given in the *Resource Center.*

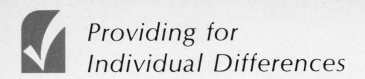

Providing for Individual Differences

Skills Lesson

Additional Practice

Worksheet 12, Teacher's Edition, pages T491–T492

Vocabulary Study

Additional Practice

■ **Identifying base words in compound words**
Write the following words on the board. Challenge students to make as many compound words as they can. Have students check their answers in a dictionary.

> ache   back   board   half   head   rest
> track   way

> (headache, backache, headboard, backboard, headway, halfway, halftrack, headrest, backrest; Accept other compound words listed in the dictionary your class uses.)

Reading Selection: Sod-Shanty Pioneers

Additional Practice

■ **Interpreting information from a map**   Refer students to an area map of the United States, and have them answer questions such as the following:

> What is the capital of Indiana? (Indianapolis)
> Name two cities in Maine other than the capital. (Answers will vary.)
> Which states border Kansas? (Nebraska, Colorado, Missouri, and Oklahoma)
> What is the capital of Wisconsin? (Madison)
> Which states border Wyoming? (Idaho, Montana, South Dakota, Nebraska, Colorado, and Utah)

Challenge Activity

Interpreting information from maps and graphs
Refer students to their social studies textbook or another book they use. Make up questions referring to either a map or graph, and have students answer them.

Reading Selection: Whatever Happened to Main Street?

Additional Practice

■ **Interpreting information from a bar graph**
Draw the following bar graph on the board or repro-

duce it for students. Then ask students the questions that follow the graph.

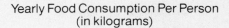

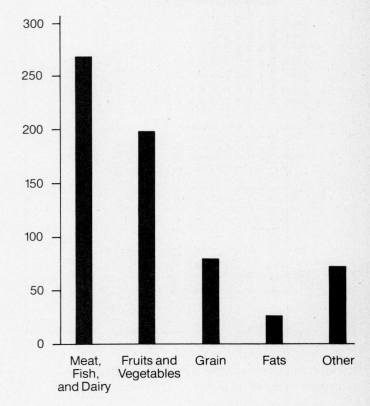

Which category of food do people eat the most of? (Meat, Fish, and Dairy)
Which category of food do people eat the least of? (Fats)
In which category do you think sugar is accounted for? (Other)
Can you tell from the graph what the most popular meat is? (no)
Can you tell from the graph how many kilograms of fats people eat each year? (yes—about 25 kilograms per person)
How many kilograms of fruits and vegetables do people eat each year? (almost 200 kilograms per person)

Evaluation

Periodic Test 3, Part IV, Form A or *Form B,* may be administered after this unit to test skills marked **T.** If you have pretested using *Form A,* administer *Form B.*

To posttest all the skills marked **T** in the four Teaching Units in "Learning About America's Past," Part 5, use *Periodic Test 3, Parts I–IV.*

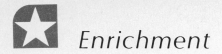 *Enrichment*

Sod-Shanty Pioneers

Bibliography

The following books are about the settlement of the western United States.

Average

Levenson, Dorothy. *Women of the West.* The roles of women during the western settlement.
Place, Marian T. *The First Book of the Santa Fe Trail.* Life on the trail in the 1820's and how and why the trail was started.

Challenging

Levenson, Dorothy. *Homesteaders and Indians.* Native Americans in the Midwest and their relationship with the settlers on the prairie.
Rounds, Glen. *The Treeless Plains.* Life in Kansas, Nebraska, and the Dakotas in the 1800's.

Films and Filmstrips

NOTE: For more information, see *Resource Center.*

Skills

Harcourt Brace Jovanovich. *Bookmark Reading Filmstrips: Purple.* "Out West with Maps and Graphs."
Guidance Assocs. *Geography: Concepts and Skills Series.* Appropriate: "Maps."
Guidance Assocs. *Using Your Reading Skills Series.* Appropriate: "Charts, Tables, Maps, and Graphs."

Curriculum Coordination

Language Arts

Ask students to identify the kind of work "Sod-Shanty Pioneers" is from the following choices:

historical fiction   autobiography
nonfictional biography   fictional biography
(Answer: nonfictional biography)

Explain if necessary what each kind of work on the list is. Then supply students with the list of books for students beginning on page T234 in the *Resource Center.* Have them read and report on the book of their choice.

NOTE: The books by the following authors listed on pages T234–T235 are classified as historical fiction: Laura Ingalls Wilder, Elizabeth Coatsworth, Laurence Yep, Patricia Beatty, Alberta Constant.

Social Studies

1. Explain that mapmakers know that *only four* different colors are needed in order to color a map of *any* land area—countries of the world, states, regions, etc.—so that no two bordering regions are the same color. Allow students to test this principle by coloring a duplicated black-and-white map of the United States with four different colors. Remind them not to use the same color for any two states bordering each other.

2. Have students do research on the Homestead Act of 1862 and how it affected the growth of the United States.

Mathematics

Have students research the population growth (or decline) of their own state, city, or community. They can make a line graph or a bar graph to show population comparisons across a number of years.

Art

Some students may want to gather more information about how sod houses were built and then draw or construct a model of what Grace McCance's home might have looked like.

Whatever Happened to Main Street?

Bibliography

The following books are about the development of towns and cities.

Easy

Jupo, Frank. *Walls, Gates, and Avenues: The Story of the Town.* The development of towns and how they became the centers of people's lives.

Average

Ross, Pat. *Whatever Happened to the Baxter Place?* How a quiet farm changed because of the growth of a nearby town.

Challenging

Franchere, Ruth. *Westward by Canal.* The importance of the canal in early America and the growth of cities and towns that followed the canals.
Habenstreit, Barbara. *Cities in the March of Civilization.* Cities from ancient times to the future.

Films and Filmstrips

NOTE: For more information, see *Resource Center*.

Skills

Harcourt Brace Jovanovich. *Bookmark Reading Film-strips: Purple.* "Out West with Maps and Graphs."
Guidance Assocs. *Geography: Concepts and Skills Series.* Appropriate: "Maps."
Guidance Assocs. *Using Your Reading Skills Series.* Appropriate: "Charts, Tables, Maps, and Graphs."

Selection content

Coronet Instructional Media. "Our Small Town Heritage: Memories of Main Street." Settlement life west of the Alleghenies.

Curriculum Coordination

Language Arts

Have students follow the suggestions in the selection to investigate the age and growth of their town or city. Let them share the results of their investigations. For a project with more guidance, you might assign teams to answer the following questions about your town or city.

When did it get its present name?
Was it ever known by another name?
What is the oldest section?
Where and how old is the oldest building still standing?
What are the backgrounds of some of the people for whom streets have been named?
What Native American tribes lived in this area?

Social Studies

1. Have students research the lives and careers of people who were important to the history of their town or city.

2. Invite a local historian to talk to the class about local historical sites and important changes the town or city has undergone. If possible, plan a class visit to a historical site in your area.

3. Have students watch the local newspaper for articles on various events related to your town's or city's history. They might clip such articles and keep a file or scrapbook on the town or city.

Art

If possible, under supervision, students can make rubbings of dates engraved in cornerstones, sidewalks, or metal plaques.

Part 6
How They Told It

RESOURCE CENTER

Enrichment Materials and Activities

The Oba Asks for a Mountain:
A Nigerian Tale
Pages 378-383

Enrichment Materials:
Long rolls of paper, crayons, dowels, tape, cardboard
  boxes
An atlas

Activity Needing Advance Planning:
Dramatization of folktale

Guest Speaker:
A storyteller

The Seeing Stick
Pages 384-392

Enrichment Materials:
A group of commonplace objects
A blindfold
A tape recorder

Guest Speaker:
A representative from an institute for the blind

Petronella
Pages 393-405

Enrichment Materials:
Large sheets of paper and paint

Activity Needing Advance Planning:
Dramatization of folktale

Bibliography

For Students

NOTE: For more information about these books, see the
  Enrichment section that follows each Teaching Unit.

Andersen, Hans Christian. *Hans Andersen's Fairy Tales.*
  Schocken, 1980.

Courlander, Harold. *The King's Drum and Other African
  Stories.* Harcourt Brace Jovanovich, 1962.
_____. *People of the Short Blue Corn: Tales and Leg-
  ends of the Hopi Indians.* Harcourt Brace Jovanovich,
  1970.
_____. *Piece of Fire and Other Haitian Tales.* Harcourt
  Brace Jovanovich, 1964.
_____. *Son of the Leopard.* Crown, 1974.
Dayrell, Elphinstone. *Why the Sun and the Moon Live
  in the Sky: An African Folktale.* Houghton Mifflin,
  1968.
Degering, Etta. *Seeing Fingers: The Story of Louis
  Braille.* McKay, 1962.
Espenshade, Edward B., Jr., and Joel Morrison, eds.
  Goode's World Atlas, 15th ed. Rand McNally, 1977.
Grimm, Jacob. *Snow White.* Little, 1974.
Hammond, C. S., & Co. *First Book Atlas,* 2nd ed. Watts,
  1973.
Manning-Sanders, Ruth. *A Book of Kings and Queens.*
  Dutton, 1978.
Minard, Rosemary. *Womenfolk and Fairy Tales.*
  Houghton Mifflin, 1975.
Murphy, Shirley Rousseau. *Silver Woven in My Hair.*
  Atheneum, 1977.
Neimark, Anne E. *Touch of Light: The Story of Louis
  Braille.* Harcourt Brace Jovanovich, 1970.
Riordan, James. *Tales from Central Russia,* Vol. I. Pen-
  guin, 1976.
Roberts, Moss. *Chinese Fairytales and Fantasies.* Pan-
  theon, 1979.
Todd, Loreto. *Tortoise the Trickster and Other Folk-
  tales.* Schocken, 1979.
Ungerer, Tomi, comp. *A Storybook: A Collection of
  Stories Old and New.* Watts, 1974.
Williams, Jay. *Bag Full of Nothing.* Parents Magazine
  Press, 1974.
_____. *Hawkstone.* Walck, 1971.
_____. *The Practical Princess and Other Liberating
  Fairy Tales.* Parents Magazine Press, 1969.
Wolkstein, Diane, coll. *The Magic Orange Tree and
  Other Haitian Folktales.* Knopf, 1978.
Yellow Robe, Rose. *Tonweya and the Eagles and Other
  Lakota Indian Tales.* Dial, 1979.

Yolen, Jane. *The Boy Who Had Wings.* T. Y. Crowell, 1974.

_____. *Dream Weaver.* Collins, 1979.

_____. *The Girl Who Cried Flowers and Other Tales.* T. Y. Crowell, 1974.

_____. *Greyling: A Picture Story from the Islands of Shetland.* World, 1968.

_____. *The Moon Ribbon and Other Tales.* T. Y. Crowell, 1976.

_____. *Transfigured Hart.* T. Y. Crowell, 1975.

_____. *Wizard Islands.* T. Y. Crowell, 1973.

For Teachers

NOTE: For more information about these books, see the *Background* section that precedes the reading selections.

Bettelheim, Bruno. *The Uses of Enchantment: The Meaning and Importance of Fairy Tales.* Knopf, 1976.

Cook, Elizabeth. *The Ordinary and the Fabulous: An Introduction to Myths, Legends, and Fairytales.* Cambridge U. Press, 1976.

Egoff, Sheila, comp. *Only Connect: Readings on Children's Literature.* Oxford U. Press, 1969.

Huck, Charlotte S. *Children's Literature in the Elementary School.* Holt, Rinehart & Winston, 1976.

Opie, Iona, and Peter Opie, eds. *The Classic Fairy Tales.* Oxford U. Press, 1974.

Rudman, Masha K. *Children's Literature: An Issues Approach.* Heath, 1976.

Sawyer, Ruth. *The Way of the Storyteller.* Viking Press, 1962.

Sutherland, Zena, and May Hill Arbuthnot. *Children and Books,* 6th ed. Scott, Foresman, 1981.

Films and Filmstrips

Coronet Instructional Media. "Chinese Folktales: The Magic Brocade." Filmstrip and tape (#M0267).

Encyclopaedia Britannica. "The Frog Prince." Film (#2833).

Film Fair Communications. "Petronella." A 16mm, 12-minute film. Color (#C348).

Filmstrip House. *African Trickster Tales.* Four filmstrips. Titles: "The Birds, the Turtle, and the Lion" (#40FRS), "The Rabbit and the Turtle" (#51FRS), "The Rabbit, the Rhinoceros, and the Elephant" (#53FRS), "The Tiger and the Rabbit" (#49FRS).

Holt, Rinehart & Winston. "Latin American Folktales." Four filmstrips with two records or cassettes (#3AY000).

Learning Corp. of America. "The Seven Ravens." Film. Order by title.

Macmillan. "African Legends and Folk Tales." Six filmstrips with two records or three cassettes. Order by title.

McGraw-Hill. "Jack and the Beanstalk." Film (#402472-8).

Miller-Brody Productions. "Shen of the Sea," Vols. I and II. Sound filmstrip with record (#3022) or cassette (#3022C).

Over the Rainbow. "The Forest Princess." Filmstrip and cassette, with book and teacher's guide.

Popular Science. "Louis Braille—He Taught Fingers to Read." Filmstrip. Order by title.

Sterling Educational Films. "The Practical Princess." Film. Order by title.

Weston Woods. "Anansi the Spider," filmstrip with cassette (#SF151C); "The Musicians of Bremen," filmstrip with cassette (#SF238C); "Strega Nonna," animated film (#SF198C); "A Story! A Story!" filmstrip with cassette (#SF123C); "Why Mosquitos Buzz in People's Ears," filmstrip with cassette (#SF199C).

Records and/or Tapes

NOTE: Recordings may also be available on other labels.

"African Folk Tales: Umusha Mwaice" (CMS Records CMS-547)

"American Folk Songs and Other Stories" (Spoken Arts cassettes MK 35, MK 36)

"Chinese Fairy Tales" (Caedmon Records TC-1328; cassette CDL5-1328)

"The Emperor and the Nightingale" (Miller-Brody Productions cassette 903-C)

"The Emperor's New Clothes and Other Tales" (Caedmon Records TC-1073; cassette CDL5-1073)

"The Fisherman and His Wife" (Miller-Brody Productions cassette 901-F)

"Folk Tales of the Tribes of Africa" (Caedmon Records TC-1267; cassette CDL5-1267)

"Indian Fairy Tales," Part II (Spoken Arts cassette SAC 6134)

"Richard Chase Tells Three 'Jack' Tales from the Southern Appalachians" (Folk-Legacy FTA-6)

"The Seventh Princess and Other Fairy Tales" (CMS Records CMS-502)

"Uncle Bouqui of Haiti" (Folkways Records 7107)

"The Ugly Duckling" (Miller-Brody Productions cassette 901-G)

OVERVIEW

Part 6
How They Told It

The skills focus of "How They Told It" is on theme. Students are asked to identify themes in folk literature and to recognize details that relate to specific themes.

The tales in Part 6 are representative of a variety of cultures. The first selection is a Nigerian folktale; the second is a tale set in ancient China; and the third is a humorous tale that embodies present-day thoughts in a traditional fairy-tale form.

Previewing "How They Told It"

Have students turn to page 373. Ask students to look at the photograph and describe what is happening. (A storyteller is telling a story to eager listeners.) Ask students how the title "How They Told It" might relate to the photograph. (Help students make the connection between the teller of tales pictured in the photograph and the storytelling tradition that underlies folk literature.)

Have students read the titles of the reading selections and examine the characters and settings in the illustrations on pages 378–404. Explain that each of these selections is a folktale, either a traditional one or a modern version in traditional folktale form. Explain to students that in Part 6 they will learn ways to find out the important idea behind a story. This will enable them to understand what the author wishes to communicate through the story.

Objectives

The following list of objectives is provided to help you plan your teaching of "How They Told It." All the objectives listed under *Introduced* are for skills presented in the student's text in *Understanding and Appreciating Literature.* Objectives listed under *Maintained* are for skills previously taught in the HBJ BOOKMARK READING PROGRAM, EAGLE EDITION and reinforced either in *Understanding and Appreciating Literature* in the student's text or in the *Reading and Discussing* sections in this Teacher's Edition. Since the emphasis in these lessons is on appreciating literature, the literature skills introduced and maintained in Teaching Unit 15 are not tested.

The symbols I*, I, and M are used throughout the Teacher's Edition. The symbol I* indicates skills introduced for the first time in the program. The I indicates skills introduced earlier in Level 11. The M indicates skills taught at earlier levels and maintained in Level 11. The italicized numbers following the objectives are part of a code developed by the HBJ School Department to facilitate the correlation of skills within and between programs. See page T499 for more information.

Introduced

These skills are introduced for the first time at Level 11 in the HBJ BOOKMARK READING PROGRAM, EAGLE EDITION.

	SKILLS CODE NUMBER
To identify theme in a story	6.12
To identify story details that relate to theme	6.12.1

Maintained

These skills have been introduced in earlier levels of the HBJ BOOKMARK READING PROGRAM, EAGLE EDITION and are further developed or refined in Level 11.

	SKILLS CODE NUMBER
To identify characters in a story or selection	6.9.1
To compare and contrast story characters	6.9.2
To interpret characters' feelings and traits	6.9.4
To recognize elements of plot	6.11.1
To recall specific details	3.3.1
To recognize author's techniques of characterization	6.9.3
To recognize elements of humor	6.6.5

Contents

Additional Materials

Reading Skills Workbook: Lesson 31, pages 101–103;
Word Play, page 104
Duplicating Masters 11: pages 48–51

Key to Symbols

Skills Objectives
I* — Introduced in this unit
I — Introduced earlier in this level
M — Maintained from previous levels

Reduced Student Pages
underscore — words that appear in the glossary
wavy line — words pretaught in the Teacher's Edition
(these words also appear in the glossary)

Understanding and Appreciating Literature:
Theme
Pages 374–377

Objectives

		SKILLS CODE NUMBER
I*	To identify theme in a story	6.12
I*	To identify story details that relate to theme	6.12.1

Introducing the Lesson

1. **a.** Read the following tale aloud to students. Ask them to listen for the important idea or message in the story.

Many years ago, a king, queen, and prince lived in a beautiful castle. The king and queen rose early every morning to greet the people of their kingdom. But the prince slept well into the afternoon and insisted that the servants bring him breakfast in bed.

b. Ask students what this story is about. (a lazy prince) Tell students that this story is similar to other folk or fairy tales that they may have read. Many folk or fairy tales are based on three characters. Two of these characters behave the way they should. The third character behaves differently. Ask students to speculate what might happen in the story. (The king and queen might worry about the prince, and then

UNDERSTANDING AND APPRECIATING LITERATURE

Theme

Prince Royal in the cartoon above seems to have ignored some good advice. Read the cartoon. Does Prince Royal turn back when the people warn him? Does he pay attention when he sees the warning signs? No, he doesn't. What is the important idea in this cartoon story? The author has a dragon tell you—"Listen to good advice if you want to keep out of trouble." This is the theme of the cartoon story.

374

Understanding Theme

The **theme** of a story is an important idea that the author wishes to share with you. The events in the story and the things the characters do and say work together to illustrate the theme.

Most authors do not state the theme of a story in one sentence. You must think about what happens in the story and what the characters do and say. Then you must decide for yourself what important idea the author wants to share with you. This is the theme.

Read the following story. What is the theme?

Once there were three poor sisters. Their names were Tam, Cam, and Maria. One day the sisters came to a wide river. They met a little boy carrying a dog.

"Please," he said. "My home is across the river. Will you help me build a raft and take my poor dog home?"

Tam and Cam shook their heads. "It would take too much time and trouble. We will swim across."

Maria's answer was different. She immediately began to bind tree branches together to make a raft.

When Tam and Cam tried to swim across the river, the waves forced them back to shore. They became frightened and ran home.

Maria was not afraid. When the raft was ready, Maria, the boy, and his dog got aboard. The waves carried the raft across the river.

When the travelers reached the other shore, the boy and his dog suddenly turned into a king and his brother. The king explained that Maria had broken an evil spell.

375

something might happen to teach the prince that being lazy will do him no good. Accept any answers students can justify.)

c. Ask students to tell what important idea the author of this story might be trying to communicate. (Possible answers are: Laziness will get you nowhere; nothing is achieved without work.)

2. Have students turn to page 374 and look at the cartoon. Ask students what important idea is being expressed. (Listen to good advice if you want to keep out of trouble.)

Developing the Skill

A. *The theme of a story is an important idea that the author wishes to share with the reader.*

1. Tell students to read the first paragraph on page 374. Then ask them to look back at the cartoon and tell what warning signs Prince Royal ignored. (The woman with the child who says, "Be careful!"; the man and woman who tell him, "Turn back!" and

"Watch out!"; the signs saying "Forbidden Forest," "Keep Out," and "This Means You.")

2. Ask students how the cartoonist communicates the important message or theme to the reader. (The cartoonist has the dragon state the theme.)

B. *The events in the story and what the characters do and say work together to illustrate the theme of a story.*

1. Tell students to read the two paragraphs at the top of page 375.

2. Ask students to name the two ways an author communicates the important idea to the readers. (through events in the story and through what the characters do and say)

3. Ask students whether the author will always come right out and state the theme of the story. (Sometimes the author will state the theme, but more often the theme is something that readers must decide for themselves after reading a story and thinking about it.)

4. Tell students to read the third paragraph on page 375 and then to read the story about the three sisters that ends on page 376.

5. Once students finish reading, ask them to tell in their own words the theme of the story. (Accept reasonable answers on the theme "Kindness pays.")

6. Tell students to read the first paragraph following the story on page 376. Then ask them what happens to Cam and Tam when they don't take the time or trouble to help the little boy and his dog. (Waves prevent them from crossing the river, and they run home; they never do much of anything.) Ask what happened to Maria because she was kind. (She became a great and famous woman.) Ask students to state the theme of this story based on what they learned about the characters. (If you are kind, you will do well.)

7. Tell students to read the next paragraph on page 376. Ask them how the theme of the story might apply to life today. (Students should conclude that kindness is important in real life as well as in stories.)

Try This

Have students complete *Try This*.

Answers to *Try This*

1. He was unhappy because he felt he needed gold to be a great ruler. 2. Midas expected to have a palace full of golden objects. Midas had no control over his golden touch and turned his daughter to gold. Then he was very unhappy and realized that his daughter was a true treasure, while gold was less important. 3. c

Writing

(Optional) Have students complete one or both of the *Writing* activities on page 377, using the following procedures:

1. Tell students to list or outline their ideas before they begin writing. For *Writing* activity 1, tell students to think about an ending to the story that fits the theme "If you are kind, you will be rewarded." Have students talk about possible rewards, such as a new puppy or feeling good. Some possible endings for the story are:

The dog's owners saw the posters and came to Nancy's house.
The dog's owners didn't see the posters, but the dog led Nancy back to its owner's house.

For *Writing* activity 2, have students turn back and look at the cartoon on page 374. Review the theme of the story (listen to good advice if you want to keep out of trouble) and the different characters in it. (prince, woman and child, man, woman, dragon) Remind students that what characters say and do tells readers the theme of the cartoon.

2. Encourage students to share their finished work with the class.

 Use *Reading Skills Workbook,* Lesson 31, pages 101–103.

Reading Selection:
The Oba Asks for a Mountain: A Nigerian Tale

Pages 378–383

Objectives

		SKILLS CODE NUMBER
I*	To identify theme in a story	6.12
M	To identify characters in a story or selection	6.9.1
M	To compare and contrast story characters	6.9.2
M	To interpret characters' feelings and traits	6.9.4
M	To recognize elements of plot	6.11.1

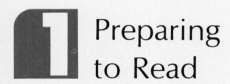# Preparing to Read

Summary

An Oba, a powerful chief, is eager to loot the prosperous kingdom of Ilesha. He sends messengers to tell the people of Ilesha that, unless they do exactly what he asks, he will declare war. The people do not want war, but the Oba's demands seem impossible to meet, until a wise man, Agiri-Asasa, thinks of ways to outwit the Oba. Twice the people of Ilesha follow the wise man's advice and, to the Oba's astonishment, give the Oba what he demands. On the third occasion, the Oba asks for a mountain to be brought to him. Agiri-Asasa has 10,000 men from Ilesha surround the mountain, each with a carrying pad on his head. They pull at the trees and rocks, but they cannot lift the mountain. So messengers are sent back to tell the Oba that the people of Ilesha are ready to carry the mountain if he can send strong men to lift it onto their carrying pads. From then on, the Oba never bothers the people of Ilesha.

Background

This story, from the Yoruba people of western Nigeria, is retold by Harold Courlander, a specialist in African folktales and Afro-American culture. Assisted by Ezekiel Aderogba Eshugbayi, a Nigerian from Ilesha, Courlander has retained much of the spirit of the oral tradition from which this tale is derived.

The following books will provide you with additional background information on folktales, fairy tales, and storytelling.

Bettelheim, Bruno. *The Uses of Enchantment: The Meaning and Importance of Fairy Tales.* An examination of folklore and its relationship to children's needs and feelings.
Cook, Elizabeth. *The Ordinary and the Fabulous: An Introduction to Myths, Legends, and Fairytales.* A discussion of the appeal of different themes and types of folklore for children aged eight through thirteen.
Egoff, Sheila, comp. *Only Connect: Readings on Children's Literature.* Articles (in Part 2) by folklorist Martin Gardner and others on folklore and fantasy.

Developing Vocabulary and Concepts

virtues: good qualities; moral excellence
prosperous: successful; thriving; wealthy and comfortable
tribute: money or other payment given by one group of people to another on demand, often as the price of peace and protection
perplexed: puzzled; bewildered
yam: a kind of sweet potato
carrion: dead and rotting flesh
compelled: forced

1. **a.** Read the following sentences aloud, or write them on the board. If you read them aloud, write the underlined vocabulary on the board.

   One prince was as evil as could be, but the other was good, with many <u>virtues.</u>
   You could see at a glance that the kingdom was <u>prosperous</u> and that all the citizens were wealthy and comfortable.
   The townspeople had to pay <u>tribute</u> to the giant so that he would allow them to cross his bridge.
   The princess was <u>perplexed</u> by the king's actions, so she sat down to think and to try to figure them out.
   The shepherd had a piece of dry bread and a <u>yam</u>, a kind of sweet potato, for supper.
   When the vultures spotted the dead animals below, they circled above the <u>carrion.</u>
   Each night the princesses are <u>compelled</u> by a spell to go dancing.

b. Ask students to give the meaning of each vocabulary word. Remind them to use the context clues in the sentences to help them.

2. Read aloud the following "riddle." Ask students how they would solve it.

   If you lived a fifteen-day walk from a chieftain and he told you that you had to bring him vegetables from your garden, and that the vegetables had to be as fresh as the day they were picked, what would you do?

   Allow students to suggest a variety of possible solutions, and even if someone comes up with the solution presented in the story (digging up the vegetables and transporting them in huge pots), do not confirm it.

3. Explain to students that the riddle they have just been asked could be called a "task" in a folktale. Tell them that in old stories, tasks are very often given by powerful people to less powerful people. Remind them of the task in "Rumpelstiltskin" of spinning straw into gold or of tasks given to princes by kings to prove themselves worthy of marrying princesses. Students may be able to suggest other "task" situations with which they are familiar. Tell students that in two stories they will read in "How They Told It," they will encounter characters who are able to carry out seemingly impossible tasks.

 Use *Duplicating Masters 11*, page 48.

Setting Purposes

Skills

Tell students to pay attention to what happens and what the characters do and say in the next story. This will enable them to understand the theme, or important idea, that the author wants to communicate.

Content

Ask students to think of their own solutions as they read the story. Have them compare their solutions with those of the wise man in the story.

The Oba Asks for a Mountain

a Nigerian tale

by HAROLD COURLANDER
and EZEKIEL ADEROGBA ESHUGBAYI

It was long ago. There was an Oba, or powerful chief, in the land of the Yoruba. He was not known for any virtues but for his love of war. It came to his ears that the kingdom of Ilesha was rich and prosperous. He decided he would loot Ilesha of its wealth, but he had no excuse to make war. So he sent messengers to Ilesha with a demand for tribute. The messengers arrived. They said, "The great Oba has sent us. He demands that a certain thing be done. If it is not done, his soldiers will come. They will make war. That is all. What is your answer?"

The people said, "What is the thing that is to be done? We will do it. We do not want war."

The messengers said, "The Oba has heard of the fine vegetables that are grown here. He wants a great quantity of these vegetables brought to him by the next festival day. But there is one thing. They must not be wrinkled and dried. They must be as fresh as when they are just taken from the earth."

The people said, "We shall bring them." But when the messengers had departed, the people said, "How can the vegetables be fresh when it takes a person fifteen days to go from here to there? They will be wrinkled and dried, and the Oba will make war upon us."

378

2 Reading and Discussing

Have students read the selection. Most students will be able to complete it in one sitting. If you prefer, the selection may be read in two parts, breaking after the last sentence on page 380.

NOTE: The questions that appear in the student's text at the end of the selection focus on comprehension of selection content and on theme. Answers to these questions begin on page T335.

There was a man among them named <u>Agiri-Asasa</u>. He listened thoughtfully to what they said. "There is a way this thing can be done," Agiri-Asasa said. "Bring many pots and bowls. Dig up the vegetables with the earth around them and transplant them into these vessels. In this fashion they can be carried to the Oba."

As he described it, so it was done. They dug up the vegetables, earth and all, and carried them in pots and bowls to the distant town where the Oba lived. There they took the vegetables from the earth and brought them to the Oba's house. He was <u>perplexed</u>, for the vegetables were fresh and sweet. He said nothing. He wondered what task he could give to the people of Ilesha

379

that they could not perform, so that he would have an excuse for war.

The next morning as the people of Ilesha were preparing to leave, the Oba sent for them. He presented them with a thigh of beef, saying, "One thing more must be done if there is to be no war. This thigh of beef I entrust to you to keep for me. Return it to me on the third day before the <u>yam</u> harvest festival. But take care that it is returned to me as fresh as it is now. Do not allow it to become spoiled and moldy. Otherwise I shall send my soldiers to make war against Ilesha."

The people took the thigh of beef. They went out of the town. They talked. One said, "How can we do it? This meat will be spoiled before we reach home. It will soon be nothing but <u>carrion</u>." Another said, "Yes, it is so. The Oba means to destroy us."

Then Agiri-Asasa spoke, saying, "No, there is a way to deal with this matter. Let us take it with us a little way." So they took the thigh of beef and continued their journey. Even before the sun went down, they came to a place where a man was preparing to slaughter a bull. Agiri-Asasa said to him, "Do not hurry to slaughter the bull. Take this thigh of beef instead. We entrust it to your keeping. Three days before the yam festival we will come again. Slaughter your bull on that day and give us the thigh. Thus nothing will be lost, and it will save us from carrying this meat on the road." It was arranged.

On the third day before the festival, the people of Ilesha returned and received the thigh of the newly slaughtered bull. They carried it to the Oba, saying, "See, as you have directed, we return the beef thigh to you. It is as fresh as the day it was given to us." The Oba examined the meat. He was puzzled. He sent the people away.

380

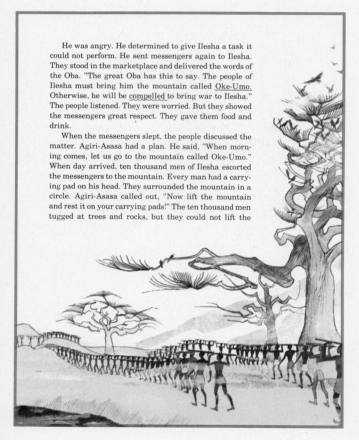

He was angry. He determined to give Ilesha a task it could not perform. He sent messengers again to Ilesha. They stood in the marketplace and delivered the words of the Oba. "The great Oba has this to say. The people of Ilesha must bring him the mountain called <u>Oke-Umo</u>. Otherwise, he will be <u>compelled</u> to bring war to Ilesha." The people listened. They were worried. But they showed the messengers great respect. They gave them food and drink.

When the messengers slept, the people discussed the matter. Agiri-Asasa had a plan. He said, "When morning comes, let us go to the mountain called Oke-Umo." When day arrived, ten thousand men of Ilesha escorted the messengers to the mountain. Every man had a carrying pad on his head. They surrounded the mountain in a circle. Agiri-Asasa called out, "Now lift the mountain and rest it on your carrying pads!" The ten thousand men tugged at trees and rocks, but they could not lift the

mountain. At last Agiri-Asasa addressed the messengers this way: "Messengers of the great Oba, you see that we are willing to bring the mountain as the Oba has demanded. You see that we have ten thousand men ready to carry it. However, we cannot lift it. If the Oba will send his strongest men here to lift it onto our carrying pads, we will bring it to him without delay."

The messengers went home. They told the Oba. He listened. He said no more about the matter. He put Ilesha out of his mind.

Since that day, there has been a saying in Ilesha:

"There are people to carry the mountain,
But there is nobody to lift it."

Questions preceded by a bullet are additional questions and appear in the Teacher's Edition only. The other questions appear in the student's text after the selection.

Understanding What You've Read

1. *Why did the Oba ask the people of Ilesha to do things that seemed impossible?* (He wanted an excuse for starting a war.   page 378) CRITICAL   Interpreting characters' thoughts and feelings

2. *What was the first thing the Oba asked the people of Ilesha to do? How did they do it?* (He asked them to bring fresh vegetables on the next festival day. They did it by bringing the vegetables in pots so that the vegetables stayed fresh.   pages 378–379) LITERAL   Recalling specific details

● *How did the people of Ilesha feel when they heard what the Oba wanted? What did they think would happen?* (They felt terrible. They did not see how they could accomplish the task that the Oba had set, and they thought that the Oba would declare war on them.   page 378) CRITICAL   Interpreting characters' feelings

● *What do you learn about Agiri-Asasa on page 379 that helps you understand what kind of person he is?* (The story says that Agiri-Asasa listened "thoughtfully" and came up with a plan. Students should realize that he is a thoughtful, resourceful, and wise person.) CRITICAL   Interpreting characters' traits

● *What did the Oba say and think when he saw that the people of Ilesha had completed his impossible task? What do you learn about him?* ("He said nothing. He wondered what task he could give to the people of Ilesha that they could not perform, so that he would have an excuse for war." Students should realize that the Oba is not easily swayed from pursuing what he wants.   pages 379–380) LITERAL, CRITICAL   Interpreting characters' traits

3. *What was the last thing the Oba asked the people to do? What was their reason for not doing it?* (He asked them to bring him a mountain. They said they couldn't bring the mountain because they couldn't lift it.   pages 381–382) LITERAL   Recalling specific details

4. *Which of the following sentences best explains the theme of this story?*
   a. *It takes many people to lift a mountain.*
   b. *Fresh vegetables taste better than dried ones.*
   c. *Don't ask someone to do the impossible unless you are ready to do it yourself.*
   (Answer: c)
   CRITICAL   Identifying theme in a story

● *Why do you think that Agiri-Asasa and the people of Ilesha decided that they would take the Oba's messengers with them to the mountain Oke-Umo?* (Students should understand that the 10,000 men with carrying pads on their heads were for the benefit of the messengers so that they would go back and tell the Oba what they had seen.) CRITICAL   Recognizing elements of plot

Writing

(Optional) Have students complete one or both of the *Writing* activities on page 383. Or ask students to do the writing activity under *Additional Writing Activity*.

1. *Write one or more sentences to complete the story below. The theme of this story is: "Cleverness can be more valuable than power." Make sure that the story ending you write fits the theme.*   Writing a story ending

One day a hungry lion trapped the Oba, ten of his men, and Agiri-Asasa in a hut. Although the Oba and his men had weapons, none of them wanted to go out the door and face the lion. Agiri-Asasa knew that they would all be safe if they could somehow get out. Quickly, he snatched the Oba's sword and cut an opening in the back of the hut.

Tell students to think about possible endings that fit the theme of the story. You may wish to list the following lines on the board to help students get started.

The lion remained guarding the door and _____.
The men escaped and the lion _____.

2. *Write a sentence in which you explain in your own words the theme of "The Oba Asks for a Mountain."* <u>Writing a sentence that identifies theme</u>

Tell students to think about how cleverness could come in handy in everyday life. You may wish to list students' responses on the board.

Additional Writing Activity (Optional)

● *Write a sentence that tells the theme of the following short story.* <u>Writing a sentence that identifies theme</u>

Once there was a bird that wished to fly to the moon. The other birds thought she was foolish, but she did not give up. Each night she flew just a little bit higher into the sky. But dawn always came before she could reach the moon. The bird decided she had to begin from the highest place on Earth; so she flew off to the highest mountain. The other birds never saw her again, but one night, as they were looking at the pale face of the moon, they saw the shadow of a bird, and they knew that the bird had reached the moon.

Tell students to think about what important idea the author wants to share with the reader. Tell students to think about what the characters do that helps to illustrate the theme of this story.

 For additional resources and curriculum-related activities, see *Enrichment*, page T350.

Reading Selection:
The Seeing Stick

Pages 384–392

Objectives

		SKILLS CODE NUMBER
M	To recall specific details	3.3.1
I*	To identify theme in a story	6.12
M	To interpret characters' feelings	6.9.4
I*	To identify story details that relate to theme	6.12.1

Preparing to Read

Summary

Hwei Ming, the only daughter of a Chinese emperor, was blind. Her father resolved that anyone who could help her see would be given a fortune. Many tried, but no one could help.

An old man in tattered clothing arrived at the gates of the city. He said he had a stick that could see. The guards scoffed, but when the old man whittled his story into the stick and included the guards' faces, the guards were captivated. They took him to see the emperor, who also scoffed, but Hwei Ming was curious. The old man touched her face and carved her likeness on his stick. She felt the tiny image on the stick. It was like having eyes on her fingertips.

The old man stayed in the city and was rewarded with jewels, which he gave away. Every day he told the princess a story. She in turn taught other blind children to "see" the stories that the old blind man carved on his seeing stick.

Background

Jane Yolen has written many folktales for young readers. Using traditional folk material and her own insight and vision, she has created new tales that make her one of today's prime preservers of the art of storytelling. Many of her works are listed in the *Enrichment* section at the end of this Teaching Unit.

The following books will provide you with additional background information on folk and fairy tales and storytelling.

Huck, Charlotte S. *Children's Literature in the Elementary School.* A good overview of folk literature for children in Chapter 4. Activities and procedures for extending literature studies through art, media, music, movement, drama, writing, and games in Chapter 11.

Rudman, Masha K. *Children's Literature: An Issues Approach.* Chapter 9, "The Female," includes an interesting discussion of sex-role stereotypes found frequently in folktales and fairy tales.

Developing Vocabulary and Concepts

citadel: a building that overlooks a city in order to protect it

jade: a type of stone, usually green but sometimes white, used in jewelry or carving

ascended: succeeded to; took over (when one becomes king or queen, one "ascends" the throne)

incantations: the speaking of words or syllables supposed to have magical results

1. **a.** Read the following sentences aloud, or write them on the board. If you read them aloud, write the underlined vocabulary on the board.

   The guards protected the city by watching for invaders from the top of the <u>citadel</u>.
   She wore lovely <u>jade</u> jewelry in several shades of green.
   The princess <u>ascended</u> the throne to become queen when her parents died.
   When the old man muttered a strange <u>incantation</u>, he put a magical spell on the princess.

   b. Ask students to give the meaning of each vocabulary word. Remind them to use the context clues in the sentences to help them.

2. **a.** Tell students that we use the word *see* to mean many different things. Ask students to suggest sentences that contain *see* used in various ways.

   b. Write the following sentences and definitions on the board. Have students match them.

1. He can't <u>see</u> far without glasses.	a. to find out; determine
2. I <u>see</u> what you mean.	b. to notice by means of the eyes
3. Let me <u>see</u> how that works.	c. to understand
4. The king will <u>see</u> you now.	d. to receive as a visitor

   (Answers: 1. b; 2. c; 3. a; 4. d)

The Seeing Stick

by JANE YOLEN

Once, in the ancient walled citadel of Peking, there lived an emperor who had only one daughter, and her name was Hwei Ming.

Hwei Ming had long black hair smoothed back with ivory combs. She had tiny feet encased in embroidered slippers. And she had small slim fingers covered with jade rings.

But rather than making her happy, such possessions made her sad. For Hwei Ming was blind, and all the beautiful handcrafted things in the kingdom brought her no pleasure at all.

Her father was also sad that his only daughter was blind, but he could not cry for her. He had given up weeping when he ascended the throne. Yet still he had hope that one day Hwei Ming might see. So he resolved that anyone who could help her would be rewarded with a fortune in jewels, and he sent word of his offer to the Inner and Outer Cities of Peking and to all the towns and villages for hundreds of miles around.

Monks came with their prayers and prayer wheels, for they thought in this way to help Hwei Ming see. Magician-priests came with their incantations and spells, for they thought in this way to help Hwei Ming see. Physicians came with their potions and pins, for they thought in this way to help Hwei Ming see.

But nothing helped. Hwei Ming had been blind from the day of her birth, and no one could cure her.

Now one day an old man, his clothes tattered from his travel, stopped by the gates of the Outer City. Far away in the south country where he lived, he had heard tales of the blind princess and of the emperor's offer. And so he had taken his few possessions—a long walking stick, made from a single shoot of golden wood, and his whittling knife—and started down the road.

The sun rose hot on his right side, and the sun set cool on his left as he made his way north to Peking to help the princess see.

385

c. Tell students that just as we use the word *see* to mean many things, there are many kinds of seeing. Tell them that they will read about a different way of seeing in the next literature selection.

3. Have students locate the city of Peking (also called Beijing) on a wall map of China or in an atlas. Explain that the name *Peking* means "northern capital" and that it is China's capital. Tell them that the ancient city was divided into two parts, the Inner City and the Outer City. The royalty lived in the Inner City, which was square and about four miles long on each side. Walls fifty feet tall surrounded the Inner City. The Outer City was for the common people.

 Use *Duplicating Masters 11*, page 49.

Setting Purposes

Skills

Remind students that the theme of a story is an important idea that the author wants to communicate to readers. Ask students to notice the details in the story and what the characters do and say. This will help them state the theme of "The Seeing Stick" when they have finished reading.

Content

Ask students to find out why Hwei Ming and her father are so unhappy and what happens to change the way they feel. Ask them to think about what the title of the story may mean.

 Reading and Discussing

Have students read the selection. Most students will be able to complete it in one sitting. If you prefer, the selection may be read in two parts, breaking before the first paragraph on page 388.

NOTE: The questions that appear in the student's text at the end of the selection focus on comprehension of selection content and on theme. Answers to these questions begin on page T341.

The guards at the gate of the Outer City did not want to let in such a ragged old man. "Grandfather, go home. There is nothing here for such as you," they said.

The old man touched each of their faces in turn with his rough fingers. "So young," he said, "and already so old." He turned as if to go.

Ashamed that they had been unkind to an old man, the guards stared at the ground and shifted their feet uneasily.

The old man smiled to himself at their distress and turned back. Then he propped his walking stick against his side and reached into his shirt for his whittling knife.

"What are you doing, Grandfather?" called out one of the guards.

"I am going to show you my stick," said the old man. "For it is a stick that sees."

"Grandfather, that is nonsense," said the second guard. "That stick can see no more than the emperor's daughter. And she, poor child, has been blind from birth."

"Just so, just so," said the old man, nodding his head. "Still, it is a stick that sees."

"Indeed, Grandfather," said the second guard, "to repeat nonsense does not turn it into sense. You might as well say that the princess has eyes in her fingers."

"Just so, just so," said the old man. "But stranger things have happened." And so saying, he picked up the stick and told the guards how he had walked the many miles through villages and towns till he came with his seeing stick to the walls of Peking. As he told his tale, he carved pictures into the stick: an old man, the two guards, the walls of Peking.

The two guards watched in amazement. They were flattered by their likenesses in the golden wood of the old

386

man's stick. Indeed, they had never witnessed such skill. "Surely this is something the guards at the wall of the Inner City should see," they said. So, taking the old man by the arm, they guided him through the streets of the Outer City, past flower peddlers and rice sellers, past silk weavers and jewel merchants, up to the great stone walls.

When the guards of the Inner City saw the story stick, they were surprised and delighted. "Carve our faces, too," they begged like children. Laughing and touching their faces as any fond grandfather would, the old man did as they bid.

In no time at all, the guards of the Inner City took the old man by the arm and led him to the wall of the Imperial City and through the gate to the great wooden doors of the emperor's palace.

Now when the guards and the old man entered the throne room of the palace, it happened that the emperor's blind daughter, Hwei Ming, was sitting by his side — silent, sightless, and still. She listened as the guards told of the wonderful pictures carved on the golden shoot. When they finished, the princess clapped her hands. "Oh, I wish I could see that wondrous shoot," she said.

"Just so, just so," said the old man. "I will show it to you. For it is no ordinary stick, but a stick that sees."

"What nonsense," said her father in a voice so low it was almost a growl.

But the princess did not hear him. She had already bent toward the sound of the old man's voice. "A seeing stick?"

The old man did not say anything for a moment. Then he leaned forward and touched Hwei Ming's head and cheek. For though she was a princess, she was still a child. The old man smiled, reached into his shirt, and pulled out his knife.

388

Then, with the stick in one hand and his knife in the other, he began again to tell the story of his long journey to Peking. As he introduced each character and object, he carved a face and figure into the shoot. And as he finished each one, the old man took Hwei Ming's small fingers in his and placed them on the shoot. Finger on finger he helped her trace the likenesses.

"Feel the long flowing hair of the princess," the old man said. "Grown as she herself has grown, straight and true."

And Hwei Ming touched the carved shoot.

"Now feel your own long hair," he said.

And she did.

"Feel the lines in the old man's face," he said. "Years of worry and years of joy." He put the stick into her hands again.

And Hwei Ming's slim fingers felt the carved shoot.

Then he put her fingers onto his face and traced the same lines there. It was the first time the princess had touched another person's face since she was a very small girl.

The princess jumped up from her throne and thrust her hands before her. "Guards, guards," she cried out. "Come here to me."

And the guards lifted their faces to the princess Hwei Ming's hands. Her fingers, like little breezes, brushed their eyes and noses and mouths, and then found each face on the seeing stick.

Hwei Ming turned to her father, the emperor, who sat straight and tall and unmoving on his great throne. She reached out, and her fingers ran eagerly through his hair, down his nose and cheek, and rested curiously on a tear they found there. And that was strange, indeed, for had not the emperor given up crying when he ascended the throne?

They brought her through the streets of the city, then, the emperor himself leading the procession. And Princess Hwei Ming touched men and women and children as they passed. Till at last she stood before the walls of Peking and felt the great stones themselves.

390

Then she turned to the old man, her voice bright and full of laughter. "Tell me another tale," she said.

"Tomorrow, if you wish," he replied,

For each tomorrow as long as he lived, the old man dwelt in the Innermost City. The emperor rewarded him with a fortune in jewels, but the old man gave them all away. Every day he told the princess a story. Some were as ancient as the city itself. Some were as new as the events of the day. And each time he carved wonderful images onto a shoot of golden wood.

As the princess listened, she grew eyes on the tips of her fingers—at least that is what she told the other blind children whom she taught to see as she saw, with her hands. Certainly it was as true as saying she had a seeing stick.

But the blind princess Hwei Ming believed that both things were true.

And so did all the blind children in her city of Peking. And so did the blind old man.

Questions preceded by a bullet are additional questions and appear in the Teacher's Edition only. The other questions appear in the student's text after the selection.

Understanding What You've Read

1. *Why was Hwei Ming unhappy?* (She was unhappy because she could not see the beautiful things around her.   page 385) CRITICAL   Interpreting characters' feelings

• *Although the emperor was saddened by his daughter's blindness, why didn't he cry for her?* (He had given up weeping because it wasn't appropriate for an emperor.   page 385) INFERENTIAL   Making inferences

2. *What did the emperor do to help his daughter?* (The emperor offered a reward of a fortune in jewels to anyone who could help Hwei Ming see.   page 385) LITERAL   Recalling specific details

• *Before the old man arrived, who came to help Hwei Ming see? How did they try to help? Did they succeed?* (Monks came with their prayers and prayer wheels, magician-priests came with their incantations and spells, physicians came with their potions and pins, but nothing helped.   page 385) LITERAL   Recalling specific details

• *What do you think the old man meant when he said to the guards on page 386, "So young and already so old"?* (The old man may have meant that the guards were young in years but that they were old and set in their ways if they would judge him so harshly because his clothes were tattered. Accept any answer the students can justify.) CRITICAL   Making inferences

• *On page 386, the guards thought the old man was talking nonsense. What did the guards think was nonsense? What two things did the guards say that seemed like nonsense but that the old man said were true?* (The guards thought the old man was talking nonsense when he said he had a stick that could see. The guards thought that they were talking nonsense when they said, "That stick can see no more than the emperor's daughter" and "The princess has eyes in her fingers." Yet the old man said, "Just so, just so.") CRITICAL   Identifying story details that relate to theme

• *As the old man carved and told his tale, what impressed the guards the most?* ("They were flattered by their likenesses."   page 386) INFERENTIAL   Interpreting characters' feelings

• *Why do you think the emperor said "What nonsense" when he heard the old man say that he had a stick that sees?* (Accept all reasonable answers. Encourage students to realize that the emperor probably said this because having a stick that sees does sound like nonsense. The emperor may have been disappointed so many times before when people tried to help his daughter see that he had become skeptical.   page 388) CRITICAL   Interpreting characters' feelings

• *Why did Hwei Ming call to the guards and feel their faces with her hands?* (so that she could compare the guards' faces to the tiny images of their faces that the old man had carved on the seeing stick   page 390) INFERENTIAL   Making inferences

• *What did Princess Hwei Ming find when she touched her father's face? How did the emperor feel?* (Hwei Ming felt a tear on her father's cheek. Students should realize that the emperor was crying for joy because his daughter was "seeing" for the first time.   page 390) CRITICAL   Interpreting characters' feelings

• *What did Hwei Ming mean when she said she "grew eyes on the tips of her fingers"?* (Students should realize that her fingers were her instruments for seeing, just as for a sighted person the eyes are used for seeing.) INFERENTIAL   Drawing conclusions

3. Which of the following sentences best fits the theme of this story?
   a. Sticks and stones may break your bones, but names will never hurt you.
   b. You see and understand the world around you not with your eyes but with your heart.
   c. Princesses and emperors lived in Peking.
   (Answer: b) CRITICAL   Identifying the theme of a story

4. Why do you think the old man succeeded in helping the princess when so many others had failed? (Accept all reasonable answers. Students should realize that he understood what it was like to be blind, and he knew that "seeing" is more than just taking in information with one's eyes.) CRITICAL   Drawing conclusions

Writing

(Optional) Have students complete one or more of the *Writing* activities on page 392. Or ask students to do the writing activity under *Additional Writing Activity*.

1. Pretend that you are the princess or the old man. Write a sentence or two that explains how the seeing stick helps you see.   Writing a sentence

Tell students to list or outline their ideas before they begin writing. If students need additional help with the *Writing* activity, tell them to pretend that they are actually the princess or the old man and to imagine what it would be like to "see" through their fingertips.

2. Write a paragraph or two that explains this theme: "You see and understand the world around you, not with your eyes, but with your heart." Use one of the following real people as a character in your paragraphs:
   a. Louis Braille, a blind man who invented an alphabet people read with their fingertips
   b. Helen Keller, a blind and deaf young woman who learned how to read using the braille alphabet and became a famous author
   c. José Feliciano, a blind musician discussed earlier on pages 175–178 in this book   Writing a paragraph

Have students list or outline their ideas before they begin writing. Have students talk about each of the three people they are asked to write about. If students need help with the *Writing* activity, suggest that they consider the following: (a) the hardships these people encountered; (b) how these hardships were overcome; (c) the contributions these people made to society. You may wish to have students do some reading about these people before they do the *Writing* assignment.

Additional Writing Activity (Optional)

● Write a paragraph with the following for a theme: "There is more than one way to see." You may use the emperor, Princess Hwei Ming, and the old man as characters in your paragraph, or make up characters of your own.   Writing a paragraph

Tell students to list or outline their ideas before they begin writing. If students need additional help with this activity, you may wish to list and discuss the following different ways of "seeing" to help students get started.

eyes—the physical act of seeing
hands—feeling in the dark
mind—understanding a new idea

★ For additional resources and curriculum-related activities, see *Enrichment*, page T351.

Reading Selection:
Petronella
Pages 393–405

Objectives

		SKILLS CODE NUMBER
I*	To identify theme in a story	6.12
I*	To identify story details that relate to theme	6.12.1
M	To interpret characters' feelings and traits	6.9.4
M	To recognize author's techniques of characterization	6.9.3
M	To recognize elements of humor	6.6.5

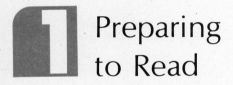

Preparing to Read

Summary

Petronella had to find a prince with whom she could one day rule the kingdom of Skyclear Mountain. So she traveled to the house of Albion the enchanter, where she was told she would find a captive prince. To rescue him, Petronella had to pass three tests.

When she had passed her tests, Petronella was free to rescue the prince. Unfortunately, the prince was very self-centered and hardly seemed worth rescuing. But being dutiful, Petronella stole him away from the enchanter. When the enchanter realized that Petronella and the prince had gone, he chased after them. At last, Petronella trapped the enchanter, but she could not stand the thought of his starving to death, so she stopped to rescue him.

It was then that the enchanter told her that he had been chasing them to try to keep *her* from leaving. In fact, the prince had been an unwelcome guest who had refused to leave. Petronella realized that she liked the enchanter more than the prince, so she decided to take him home instead.

Background

Jay Williams has written a variety of stories and poems for children. Many of his stories, such as "The Practical Princess," are based on traditional tales.

The following books will provide you with additional background information on folktales, fairy tales, and storytelling.

Sawyer, Ruth. *The Way of the Storyteller.* A classic work that emphasizes the philosophy and describes the art of storytelling and encourages each new storyteller to develop a personal style.

Sutherland, Zena, and May Hill Arbuthnot. *Children and Books,* 6th ed. Chapters 7, 8, and 16 cover folklore, fables, and the art of storytelling. A comprehensive reference source.

Developing Vocabulary and Concepts

haughtily: proudly and scornfully
enchanter: magician; sorcerer
sinister: threatening evil, trouble, or bad luck

1. **a.** Read the following sentences aloud, or write them on the board. If you read them aloud, write the underlined vocabulary on the board.

    The prince shook his head <u>haughtily</u> and walked off with his nose in the air.
    The <u>enchanter</u> cast a spell over the forest so that no one could pass through it.
    The thick vines on the trees and the dark shadows on the ground gave the forest a <u>sinister</u> appearance.

    b. Ask students to give the meaning of each vocabulary word. Remind them to use the context clues in the sentences to help them.

2. **a.** Explain to students that our folktales and fairy tales come from the "oral tradition." That is, they were passed down from generation to generation by storytellers long before they were written down. They often contain devices to help storytellers' memories. Explain that one such device is the use of the number *three*. Ask students to think of some examples from tales they know in which the number *three* is used. (Accept all reasonable answers. Some possible answers are: kings and queens often have three children; things often happen three times; people are granted three wishes.)

    b. Tell students that they will encounter the number *three* more than once in the story they are about to read.

Petronella

by JAY WILLIAMS

In the kingdom of Skyclear Mountain, three princes were always born to the king and queen. The oldest prince was always called Michael, the middle prince was always called George, and the youngest was always called Peter. When they were grown up, they always went to seek their fortunes. What happened to the oldest prince and the middle prince no one ever knew. But the youngest prince always rescued a princess, brought her home and, in time, ruled over the kingdom. That was the way it had always been. And so far as anyone knew, that was the way it would always be.

Until now.

"Now" was the time of King Peter the Twenty-ninth and Queen Blossom. An oldest prince was born and a middle prince. But the youngest prince turned out to be a girl.

"Well," said the king gloomily, "we can't call her Peter. We'll have to call her Petronella. And what's to be done about it, I'm sure I don't know."

There was nothing to be done. The years passed, and the time came for the princes to go out and seek their fortunes. Michael and George said good-by to the king and queen and mounted their horses. Then out came Petronella. She was dressed in traveling clothes, with a sword by her side and her bag packed.

"If you think," she said, "that I'm going to sit at home, you are mistaken. I'm going to seek my fortune, too."

"Impossible!" said the king.

393

"What will people say?" cried the queen.

"Look here," said Prince Michael, "be reasonable, Pet. Stay home and wait. Sooner or later a prince will turn up."

Petronella smiled. She was a tall, handsome girl with flaming red hair, and when she smiled in that particular way, it meant she was trying to keep her temper.

"I'm going with you," she said. "I'll find a prince if I have to rescue one from something myself. And that's that."

The grooms brought out her horse, and she said good-by to her parents. Up she sprang to the saddle, and away she went behind her two brothers.

They traveled into the flat lands below Skyclear Mountain. After many days, they entered a great, dark forest. They came to a place where the road divided into three, and there at the fork sat a little, wrinkled old man covered with dust and spider webs.

Prince Michael said, <u>haughtily</u>, "Where do these roads go, old man?"

"The road on the right goes to the city of Gratz," said the old man. "The road in the center goes to the castle of Blitz. The road on the left goes to the house of Albion the enchanter. And that's one."

"What do you mean by 'And that's one'?" asked Prince George.

"I mean," said the old man, "that I am forced to sit on this spot without stirring, and that I must answer one question from each person who passes by. And that's two."

Petronella's kind heart was touched. "Is there anything I can do to help you?" she asked.

The old man sprang to his feet. The dust fell from him in clouds.

394

---

3. **a.** The number *three* is not the only thing that folktales and fairy tales have in common. Ask students to recall other typical situations that they have observed in such tales. (Accept all reasonable answers. Some possible answers are: A youngest son will go off on a quest and will succeed where his two older brothers have failed; a magician or fairy godmother is often called on to help a good person; goodness is rewarded. Naming specific tales, such as "Cinderella," "Sleeping Beauty," "Rumpelstiltskin," "Rapunzel," "Snow White and the Seven Dwarfs," and "The Elves and the Shoemaker" can help students name elements these tales have in common.)

b. Tell students that the story they are going to read is not a traditional tale but one by a modern writer who is having fun with some of the situations found in old tales. Ask them to be aware of the various elements of old tales that this story uses.

✓ Use *Duplicating Masters 11,* page 50.

Setting Purposes

Skills

Tell students that although this story is poking gentle fun at traditional tales, it has the theme of a fairy tale. Ask students to be aware of story details and of things that characters do and say that reveal the story's theme.

Content

Ask students to look for elements of humor as they read "Petronella."

2 Reading and Discussing

Have students read the selection. Most students will be able to complete it in one sitting. If you prefer, the selection may be read in two parts, breaking at the end of page 397.

NOTE: The questions that appear in the student's text at the end of the selection focus on comprehension of selection content and on theme. Answers to these questions begin on page T348.

"You have already done so," he said. "For that question is the one which releases me. I have sat here for sixty-two years waiting for someone to ask me that." He snapped his fingers with joy. "In return, I will tell you anything you wish to know."

"Where can I find a prince?" Petronella said promptly.

"There is one in the house of Albion the enchanter," the old man answered.

"Ah," said Petronella, "then that is where I am going."

"In that case I will leave you," said her oldest brother, Michael. "For I am going to the castle of Blitz to see if I can find my fortune there."

"Good luck," said Prince George. "For I am going to the city of Gratz. I have a feeling my fortune is there."

They embraced her and rode away.

Petronella looked thoughtfully at the old man, who was combing spider webs and dust out of his beard. "May I ask you something else?" she said.

"Of course. Anything."

"Suppose I wanted to rescue that prince from the enchanter. How would I go about it? I haven't any experience in such things, you see."

The old man chewed a piece of his beard. "I do not know everything," he said, after a moment. "I know that there are three magical secrets that, if you can get them from Albion, will help you."

"How can I get them?" asked Petronella.

"You must offer to work for him. He will set you three tasks, and if you do them you may ask for a reward. You must ask him for a comb for your hair, a mirror to look into, and a ring for your finger."

"And then?"

"I do not know. I only know that when you rescue the prince, you can use these things to escape from the enchanter."

"It doesn't sound easy," Petronella sighed.

"Nothing we really want is easy," said the old man. "Look at me—I have wanted my freedom, and I've had to wait sixty-two years for it."

Petronella said good-by to him. She mounted her horse and galloped along the third road.

It ended at a low, rambling house with a red roof. It was a comfortable-looking house, surrounded by gardens and stables and trees heavy with fruit. On the lawn, in an armchair, sat a handsome young man with his face turned to the sky and his eyes closed.

Petronella tied her horse to the gate and walked across the lawn.

"Is this the house of Albion the enchanter?" she said.

396

The young man blinked up at her in surprise.

"I think so," he said. "Yes, I'm sure it is."

"And who are you?"

The young man yawned and stretched. "I am Prince Ferdinand of Firebright," he replied. "Would you mind stepping aside? I'm trying to get a sunburn, and you're standing in the way."

Petronella snorted. "You don't sound like much of a prince."

"That's funny," said the young man, closing his eyes. "That's what my father always says."

At that moment, the door of the house opened and out came a man dressed all in black and silver. He was tall and thin and as sinister as a cloud full of thunder. His face was stern but full of wisdom. Petronella knew at once that he must be the enchanter.

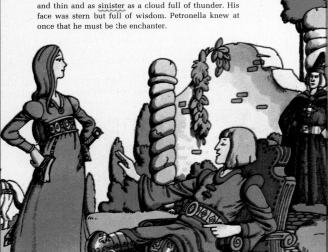

He bowed to her, politely. "What can I do for you?"

"I wish to work for you," said Petronella.

Albion nodded. "I cannot refuse you," he said. "But I must warn you it will be dangerous. Tonight I will give you a task. If you do it, I will reward you. But if you fail, you must die."

Petronella glanced at the prince and sighed. "If I must, I must," she said. "Very well."

That evening, they all had dinner together in the enchanter's cozy kitchen. Then Albion took Petronella out to a stone building and unbolted its door. Inside were seven huge black dogs.

"You must watch my hounds all night," said he.

Petronella went inside, and Albion closed and locked the door.

At once, the hounds began to snarl and bark. They showed their teeth at her. But Petronella was a real princess. She plucked up her courage. Instead of backing away, she went toward the dogs. She began to speak to them in a quiet voice. The dogs stopped snarling and sniffed at her. She patted their heads.

"I see what it is," she said. "You are lonely here. I will keep you company."

And so all night long she sat on the floor and talked to the hounds and stroked them. They lay close to her, panting.

In the morning, Albion came to let her out. "Ah," said he, "I see that you are brave. If you had run from the dogs, they would have torn you to pieces. Now you may ask for what you want."

"I want a comb for my hair," said Petronella.

The enchanter gave her a comb carved from a piece of black wood.

398

Prince Ferdinand was sunning himself and working at a crossword puzzle. Petronella said, in a low voice, "I am doing this for you."

"That's nice," said the prince. "What's 'selfish' in nine letters?"

"You are," snapped Petronella. She went to the enchanter. "I will work for you once more," she said.

That night, Albion led her to a stable. Inside were seven huge white horses.

"Tonight," he said, "you must watch my steeds."

He went out and locked the door. At once, the horses began to rear and neigh. They pawed at her with their iron hooves.

399

But Petronella was a real princess. She looked closely at them and saw that their ribs stuck out. Their coats were rough and their manes and tails full of burrs.

"I see what it is," she said. "You are hungry and dirty."

She brought them as much hay as they could eat and began to brush them. All night long, she fed them and groomed them, and they stood quietly in their stalls.

In the morning, Albion let her out. "You are as kind as you are brave," said he. "If you had run from them, they would have trampled you under their hooves. What will you have as a reward?"

"I want a mirror to look into," answered Petronella. The enchanter gave her a mirror made of gray silver.

400

She looked across the lawn at Prince Ferdinand, who was doing sitting-up exercises. He was certainly very handsome. She said to the enchanter, "I will work for you once more."

That night, Albion led her to a loft above the stables. There, on perches, were seven great red hawks.

"Tonight," said he, "you must watch my falcons."

As soon as Petronella was locked in, the hawks began to beat their wings and scream at her.

Petronella laughed. "That is not how birds sing," she said. "Listen."

She began to sing in a sweet voice. The hawks fell silent. All night long she sang to them, and they sat like feathered statues on their perches, listening.

In the morning, Albion said, "You are as talented as you are kind and brave. If you had run from them, they would have pecked and clawed you without mercy. What do you want now?"

"I want a ring for my finger," said Petronella.

The enchanter gave her a ring made from a single diamond.

All that day and all that night, Petronella slept, for she was very tired. But early the next morning she crept into Prince Ferdinand's room. He was sound asleep, wearing purple pajamas.

"Wake up," whispered Petronella. "I am going to rescue you."

Ferdinand awoke and stared sleepily at her. "What time is it?"

"Never mind that," said Petronella. "Come on!"

"But I'm still sleepy," Ferdinand objected. "And it's so pleasant here."

Petronella shook her head. "You're not much of a prince," she said, grimly. "But you're the best I can do. Come along."

401

She grabbed him by the wrist and dragged him out of bed. She hauled him down the stairs. His horse and hers were in another stable, and she saddled them quickly. She gave the prince a shove, and he mounted. She jumped on her own horse, seized the prince's reins, and away they went like the wind.

They had not gone far when they heard a tremendous thumping. Petronella looked back. A dark cloud rose behind them, and beneath it she saw the enchanter. He was running with great strides, faster than her horse could go.

"What shall we do?" she cried.

"Don't ask me," said Prince Ferdinand, grumpily. "I'm all shaken to bits by this fast riding."

Petronella desperately pulled out the comb. "The old man said that this would help me," she said. And because she didn't know what else to do with it, she threw it on the ground. At once, a forest rose up between her and the enchanter. The trees were so thick that no one could get between them.

Away went Petronella and the prince. But the enchanter turned himself into an ax and began to chop. Right and left he chopped, flashing, and the trees fell

before him. Soon he was through the wood, and once again Petronella heard his footsteps thumping behind.

She reined in her horse. She took out the mirror and threw it on the ground. At once, a wide lake spread out behind her, gray and glittering.

Off they went again. But the enchanter sprang into the water, turning himself into a salmon as he did so. He swam across the lake and leaped out of the water onto the other bank. Petronella heard him coming thump! thump! behind them again.

This time, she threw down the ring. It didn't turn into anything, but lay shining on the ground.

The enchanter came running up. He jumped over the ring. And as he jumped, the ring opened wide and then snapped up around him, holding his arms tight to his body in a magical grip from which he could not escape.

"Well," said Prince Ferdinand, "that's the end of him."

Petronella looked at him in annoyance. Then she looked at the enchanter, held fast in the ring.

"Brother!" she said. "I can't just leave him here. He'll starve to death."

She got off her horse and went up to him. "If I release you," she said, "will you promise to let the prince go free?"

Albion stared at her in astonishment. "Let him go free?" he said. "What are you talking about? I'm glad to get rid of him."

It was Petronella's turn to look surprised. "I don't understand," she said. "Weren't you holding him prisoner?"

"Certainly not," said Albion. "He came to visit me for a weekend. At the end of it, he said, 'It's so pleasant here, do you mind if I stay on for another day or two?' I'm very

403

polite, and I said, 'Of course.' He stayed on and on and on. I didn't like to be rude to a guest, and I couldn't just kick him out. I don't know what I'd have done if you hadn't dragged him away."

"But then—" said Petronella. "But then—why did you come running after him this way?"

"I wasn't chasing him," said the enchanter. "I was chasing you. You are just the woman I've been looking for. You are brave and kind and talented—and beautiful as well."

"Oh," said Petronella.

"I see," she said.

"Hm," said she. "How do I get this ring off you?"

"Give me a kiss."

She did so. The ring vanished from around Albion and reappeared on Petronella's finger.

"I don't know what my parents will say when I come home with you instead of a prince," she said.

"Let's go and find out, shall we?" said the enchanter, cheerfully.

He mounted one horse and Petronella the other. And off they trotted, side by side, leaving Ferdinand of Firebright to walk home as best he could.

Questions preceded by a bullet are additional questions and appear in the Teacher's Edition only. The other questions appear in the student's text after the selection.

Understanding What You've Read

1. *Why did Petronella go to the house of Albion the enchanter?* (She went there to rescue Prince Ferdinand.   page 395) LITERAL   Recalling specific details

- *What was unusual about Petronella's birth? How did she get her name?* (The kingdom of Skyclear Mountain always had queens who gave birth to three sons. Petronella was the first daughter born to the royal family. Usually, the youngest son was named Peter, but since that was a boy's name, her parents named her Petronella.   page 393) LITERAL   Recalling specific details

- *What does the reader learn about Petronella from what she says in the conversation with her family on pages 393–394? What does the reader learn about her from the author's description?* (The reader learns that she is determined and has a mind of her own when she says, "If you think that I'm going to sit at home, you are mistaken. I'm going to seek my for-

tune, too" and "I'll find a prince if I have to rescue one from something myself." We learn that she is handsome and strong-willed and has a temper when the author tells us, "She was a tall, handsome girl with flaming red hair, and when she smiled in that particular way, it meant she was trying to keep her temper.") CRITICAL   Recognizing author's techniques of characterization

- *What does the reader learn about Petronella from her encounter with the old man at the fork in the road?* (Students should recognize that she is kind. page 394) CRITICAL   Interpreting characters' traits

- *What did Petronella gain by asking the old man if she could help him? How does this help show the theme of the story?* (The old man said that in return for her help, he would tell Petronella anything she wished to know. Students should recognize that this incident helps point out the theme "kindness is rewarded."   page 395) CRITICAL   Identifying details that relate to theme

- *What did the old man tell Petronella to ask the enchanter for after she completed her tasks?* ("You must ask him for a comb for your hair, a mirror to look into, and a ring for your finger."   page 396) LITERAL   Recalling specific details

- *What advice does the old man give Petronella on page 396? Why do you think this advice is as true for a real person as it is for a story character?* (He says, "Nothing we really want is easy." Students should recognize that this advice is applicable to their everyday lives as well as to Petronella's situation.) CRITICAL   Identifying details that relate to theme

- *How is Prince Ferdinand different from the usual prince in folktales? Do you find him humorous? Why or why not?* (Typical princes are active characters, but Prince Ferdinand is discovered sunbathing. He yawns and stretches and asks Petronella not to block his sun. Some students may find that he is humorous. pages 396–397) CRITICAL   Recognizing elements of humor

2. *Which of the following themes best fits this story? a. Horses need to be brushed and combed every night. b. All princes are selfish. c. If you are kind and brave, you will do well.* (Answer: C) CRITICAL   Identifying theme in a story

3. *Find at least three details on pages 398–401 that illustrate the story's theme.* (Petronella showed she was kind and brave in the three tasks she performed—taming the wild dogs, the wild horses, and the hawks.) CRITICAL   Identifying story details that relate to theme

- *What is Prince Ferdinand doing while Petronella is completing her tasks so that she can rescue him? What does this tell you about him?* (He is sunning himself, working a crossword puzzle, doing sitting-up exercises. This tells the reader he is selfish.) LITERAL, CRITICAL   Interpreting characters' traits

4. *Before Petronella got to know Albion and Ferdinand, what did she think of them? What details on pages 397–398 tell you this? What did she think of them at the end of the story? What details on pages 403–404 tell you this?* (In the beginning of the story, Petronella thought Ferdinand was a nice prince. She thought Albion was evil. At the end of the story, she knew Ferdinand was selfish, vain, and lazy. She thought Albion was generous and very nice.) CRITICAL Interpreting characters' thoughts and feelings

Writing

(Optional) Have students complete one or both of the *Writing* activities on page 405. Or ask students to choose one of the writing activities under *Additional Writing Activity.*

1. *Pretend that you are the old man who met Petronella. (See pages 394–396.) Write two or more sentences about the meeting. Explain how she was kind to you, and tell what you did in return to help her do well.*   Writing sentences

Before students begin writing, have them discuss the old man and how he must have felt when he at last gained his freedom.

2. *Write a paragraph that tells what happens after Petronella returns home. The theme for your paragraph is: "A kind heart can be better than a royal name." Include in your paragraph, along with Petronella and Albion, the characters Prince Ferdinand and the king and queen.*   Writing a paragraph

Tell students to think about what might have happened when Petronella and Albion arrived at her parents' home. Have students list or outline their ideas before they begin writing.

Additional Writing Activity (Optional)

- *Write one or two sentences telling about Petronella and her activities from the viewpoint of Prince Ferdinand. Go back to the story and read some of his conversation. Try to write your sentences in the selfish tone in which Ferdinand might have said them.* Writing sentences

Tell students to list or outline their ideas before they begin writing. If students need additional help with

---

> ### More Folktales to Read
>
> **The Golden Lynx and Other Tales** selected by Augusta Baker. Lippincott, 1960. A well-known storyteller retells tales of spells and enchantment from sixteen countries.
>
> **And It Is Still That Way** edited by Byrd Baylor. Scribner, 1976. In this book, Papago, Navajo, Hopi, Pima, Apache, Quechei, and Cocepah legends of how and why are retold by today's children of these cultures.
>
> **The Enchanted Orchard and Other Folktales of Central America** edited by Dorothy Sharp Carter. Harcourt Brace Jovanovich, 1973. These tales of magic and adventure reflect the many cultures that make up Central America.
>
> **The Piece of Fire and Other Haitian Tales** by Harold Courlander. Harcourt Brace Jovanovich, 1964. Here are twenty-six tales that reflect Haiti's European and African heritages.
>
> **Clever Gretchen and Other Forgotten Folktales** retold by Alison Lurie. T. Y. Crowell, 1980. These folktales tell of clever and brave women from all over the world.
>
> **The Toad Is the Emperor's Uncle and Other Stories** by Vo-Dinh. Doubleday, 1970. These folktales from Vietnam are full of animals, surprises, and humor.
>
> **The Moon Ribbon and Other Tales** by Jane Yolen. T. Y. Crowell, 1976. These six stories are traditional in feeling, yet all are new and original.
>
> 406

---

this activity, suggest that they pretend that the prince is speaking with a friend.

- *Write several paragraphs to tell how a character has to perform three tasks. You may use one of the story characters you have been reading about in this part or make up one of your own.*   Writing paragraphs

You may wish to list the following opening lines on the board to help students get started.

Hwei-Ming's three good deeds were appreciated by the entire kingdom.
The prince had to perform three tests of courage.
The enchanter made Petronella do three mysterious tasks.

 Use *Duplicating Masters 11*, page 51.
Use *Reading Skills Workbook*, Word Play, page 104, for vocabulary review.

 For additional resources and curriculum-related activities, see *Enrichment*, page T352.

If students have not already read the books listed on page 406, you may wish to recommend them at this time. Bibliographic information about other books for students is given in the *Resource Center.*

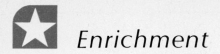

Enrichment

The Oba Asks for a Mountain: A Nigerian Tale

Bibliography

The following books contain folktales from around the world.

Easy

Courlander, Harold. *Piece of Fire and Other Haitian Tales.* Twenty-six Haitian folktales including funny stories and supernatural tales.

Dayrell, Elphinstone. *Why the Sun and the Moon Live in the Sky: An African Folktale.* A Nigerian tale of how the sun and the moon came to live in the sky.

Average

Courlander, Harold. *The King's Drum and Other African Stories.* Folktales from many African countries south of the Sahara.

Riordan, James. *Tales from Central Russia,* Vol. I. Russian fairy tales and animal tales with universal themes.

Todd, Loreto. *Tortoise the Trickster and Other Folktales.* Twenty-seven short trickster tales, each with a clear theme.

Wolkstein, Diane, coll. *The Magic Orange Tree and Other Haitian Folktales.* Wolkstein, a well-known storyteller, traveled throughout Haiti in search of these tales that blend African and European folk traditions.

Challenging

Courlander, Harold. *People of the Short Blue Corn: Tales and Legends of the Hopi Indians.* Seventeen legends based on the Hopi belief that the short ear of blue corn indicates a long life filled with struggle.

———. *Son of the Leopard.* A boy of the Adi Keriteba regains the acceptance of his people.

Related nonfiction—atlases of the world

Espenshade, Edward B., Jr., and Joel Morrison, eds. *Goode's World Atlas.* A standard reference atlas.

Hammond, C. S., & Co. *First Book Atlas,* 2nd ed. A compilation of maps covering all countries of the world.

Films and Filmstrips

NOTE: For more information, see *Resource Center.*

Filmstrip House. "African Trickster Tales." Four animal tales in which cleverness wins out over size.

Holt, Rinehart & Winston. "Latin American Folktales." Magical and humorous tales from Puerto Rico.

Macmillan. "African Legends and Folk Tales." Humorous African animal tales in which cleverness and justice prevail.

McGraw-Hill. "Jack and the Beanstalk." Jack must recover the goose that lays the golden eggs from a nasty giant.

Weston Woods. "Anansi the Spider." Award-winning art by Gerald McDermott illustrates this African tale.

———. "A Story! A Story!" Anansi the Spider successfully completes three tasks demanded of him.

———. "Why Mosquitos Buzz in People's Ears." A West African tale retold by Verna Aardema.

———. "The Musicians of Bremen." A humorous animal tale told with the help of a musical quartet.

Records and/or Tapes

NOTE: For more information, see *Resource Center.*

Caedmon Records. "Folk Tales of the Tribes of Africa." Seven tales from African folk literature, told by Eartha Kitt.

CMS Records. "African Folk Tales: Umusha Mwaice." An African variation of the Cinderella theme, told by Bertha Parker.

Folkways Records. "Uncle Bouqui of Haiti." Haitian tales told by Harold Courlander about the clown, Uncle Bouqui.

Folk-Legacy. "Richard Chase Tells Three 'Jack' Tales from the Southern Appalachians." North American versions of European tales, featuring Jack and his animal friends.

Spoken Arts. "Indian Fairy Tales," Part II. Stories from India in which cleverness outwits evil.

Curriculum Coordination

Language Arts

1. Have students write a few paragraphs or a short story in which a character uses cleverness to solve a problem.

2. Have students write a story about further adventures of the wise man Agiri-Asasa and how he outsmarts another powerful person. If they wish, students can write the story using the folktale style.

3. Work with students to divide "The Oba Asks for a Mountain" into scenes that could be dramatized. Have students change the folktale into play form and put on the play for other students.

Art

Have interested students retell "The Oba Asks for a Mountain" by making a filmstrip of the story. On a roll of paper, or on strips of drawing paper taped together, have students draw scenes from the story. They may wish to add speech balloons for the dialogue or to narrate the story themselves. Then have students attach the filmstrip in a scroll-like manner to dowel rods or rolls from paper towels. Have students cut a TV-screen-shaped hole in the front of a cardboard box to use as a viewing machine. Students may wish to make filmstrips of other stories and compile a filmstrip library.

Social Studies

Have interested students check an atlas containing a map of Africa. Have them locate Nigeria and other West African countries. Encourage students to make a bulletin-board display or to write a report using new facts they have learned.

Career Education

If possible, invite a storyteller to visit your classroom and tell the students a story. The local library might help you locate a storyteller.

The Seeing Stick

Bibliography

The following are traditional folktales or modern tales based on the folk tradition.

Easy

Yolen, Jane. *The Boy Who Had Wings*. A boy named Aetos is rejected by his family because he is born with wings. But when his father is trapped in a snowstorm, it is the golden-white wings that enable Aetos to save his father.

_____. *Greyling: A Picture Story from the Islands of Shetland*. One day a fisherman brings home a gray baby seal that turns into a boy child.

Average

Yellow Robe, Rose. *Tonweya and the Eagles and Other Lakota Indian Tales*. The author has recalled and written down the tales she was told as a child by her father.

Yolen, Jane. *Dream Weaver*. A blind old man weaves dreams for passers-by.

_____. *The Girl Who Cried Flowers and Other Tales*. Five mysterious and haunting stories follow the themes of old fairy tales. Good for reading aloud.

_____. *The Moon Ribbon and Other Tales*. Six new and original stories that are traditional in feeling and tone.

_____. *Transfigured Hart*. Richard and Heather see a white hart in Five Mile Wood, and Richard is convinced that it is a unicorn. Together the children try to save the animal from hunters.

Challenging

Roberts, Moss. *Chinese Fairytales and Fantasies*. Universal themes in heroic sagas, pithy fables, and romantic tales.

Yolen, Jane. *Wizard Islands*. Nonfiction about islands, including such mysterious places as Easter Island, the Galápagos, and Atlantis.

Related nonfiction—books about Louis Braille

Average

Degering, Etta. *Seeing Fingers: The Story of Louis Braille*. The story of the blind French boy who developed the braille system.

Neimark, Anne E. *Touch of Light: The Story of Louis Braille*. Blinded in an accident when he was three years old, Louis Braille developed a way to make books available to the blind.

Films and Filmstrips

NOTE: For more information, see *Resource Center*.

Coronet Instructional Media. "Chinese Folktales: The Magic Brocade." Three sons, their mother, and a fairy princess are the main ingredients in this imaginative and witty tale.

Popular Science. "Louis Braille—He Taught Fingers to Read." Louis Braille proved that communication can be achieved in many ways.

Records and/or Tapes

NOTE: For more information, see *Resource Center*.

Caedmon Records. "Chinese Fairy Tales." A collection of classic tales based on Isabelle Chang's book of the same title. Read by Siobhan McKenna.

Miller-Brody Productions. "The Emperor and the Nightingale." Andersen's classic tale.

_____. "The Fisherman and His Wife." The Grimm tale of the fisherman and his wife who wasted away their wishes.

_____. "The Ugly Duckling." Another Andersen tale with a memorable theme.

Curriculum Coordination

Language Arts

1. Have interested students rewrite "The Seeing Stick" as it might be told by Hwei Ming.

2. Collect a group of common objects found in a home or at school. Have several blindfolded students try to identify what the items are just by touching them. Afterward, ask them to write a paragraph describing how it felt to rely only on the sense of touch without being able to see.

3. Have interested students practice reading aloud "The Seeing Stick," as well as other tales by Jane Yolen. Students may want to make a tape for their listening center of some of Ms. Yolen's stories.

Career Education

Invite a speaker from a local Braille Institute or other institution for the blind to speak to your class. Ask the speaker to bring examples of braille so that students will have an opportunity to "see" with their fingertips.

Petronella

Bibliography

The following books contain modern and traditional fairy tales.

Easy

Grimm, Jacob. *Snow White.* This new translation by Paul Heins of this classic tale presents the characters with depth and sensitivity.

Williams, Jay. *Bag Full of Nothing.* While taking a walk one day, a boy and his father find a brown paper bag that is full of magic.

————. *The Practical Princess and Other Liberating Fairy Tales.* Princess Bedelia experiences many of the problems that princesses face, but, through common sense, solves her problems practically.

Average

Andersen, Hans Christian. *Hans Andersen's Fairy Tales.* Favorites in this collection include "The Little Mermaid," "The Ugly Duckling," and "The Emperor's New Clothes."

Manning-Sanders, Ruth. *A Book of Kings and Queens.* A wide variety of kings and queens in ten traditional tales from different countries. Good for reading aloud.

Minard, Rosemary. *Womenfolk and Fairy Tales.* Tales from many lands, with a variety of strong, masterful women.

Ungerer, Tomi, comp. *A Storybook: A Collection of Stories Old and New.* Zany retellings of many traditional favorites illustrated by Ungerer. This collection includes "The Tinder Box," "Little Red Riding Hood," and Jay Williams's "Petronella."

Williams, Jay. *Hawkstone.* A twelve-year-old boy finds an ancient, magical Indian stone with which he can recreate history 200 years past.

Challenging

Murphy, Shirley Rousseau. *Silver Woven in My Hair.* A sensitive, believable story based on the Cinderella theme.

Films and Filmstrips

NOTE: For more information, see *Resource Center.*

Encyclopaedia Britannica. "The Frog Prince." Trapped in the form of a frog, a prince must wait to be freed from the spell by a loving princess.

Film Fair Communications. "Petronella." A twelve-minute animated version of this lively tale.

Learning Corp. of America. "The Seven Ravens." Seven brothers are transformed into ravens under an evil spell that only their sister can break.

Miller-Brody Productions. "Shen of the Sea," Vols. I and II. Humorous tales from the book by Arthur Bowie Chrisman.

Over the Rainbow. "The Forest Princess." The wry and delightful tale of a princess who is true to herself.

Sterling Educational Films. "The Practical Princess." This modern princess wins her prince by being what she really is—active, intelligent, and witty.

Weston Woods. "Strega Nonna." Tomie de Paola's enchanting tale of the magic pasta pot.

Records and/or Tapes

NOTE: Recordings may also be available on other labels.

Caedmon Records. "The Emperor's New Clothes and Other Tales." The tale of the foolish emperor who is proud of all his new fine clothing when in fact he is wearing nothing at all.

CMS Records. "The Seventh Princess and Other Fairy Tales." A modern fairy tale in which six princesses are concerned only with themselves, while the seventh princess is concerned with helping her mother.

Spoken Arts. "American Folk Songs and Other Stories." Tales and songs from all over the United States, including American Indian tales and mountain songs.

Curriculum Coordination

Language Arts

1. Have students pick a classic fairy tale, such as "Cinderella" or "Little Red Riding Hood," and write a modern version of it. Have them use dialogue like that in "Petronella." For example, in a traditional tale, no princess would say, "If you think I'm going to sit at home, you're mistaken."

2. Have interested students transform "Petronella" into a play that they could put on for other classes. The entire class could participate by having several students play the parts of the hounds, steeds, and ravens.

Art

Have interested students make an illustrated storybook of "Petronella." They might do this on large paper that could be propped on an easel and flipped as the story progresses.

Part 7
Discoveries, Ideas, and Inventions

RESOURCE CENTER

Enrichment Materials and Activities

The Wind Watchers
Pages 416–423

Enrichment Materials:
A shallow box, soil, gravel, small rocks, a white cloth, a small electric fan

Guest Speaker:
A meteorologist

Curiosities from the Cliffs
Pages 436–443

Activities Needing Advance Planning:
A field trip to an archaeological site
A trip to a natural history museum

Guest Speaker:
An archaeologist or a science teacher

Ben Franklin Changes the World
Pages 444–449

Guest Speaker:
A civil engineer or an electrician

Gifts from China
Pages 467–471

Activity Needing Advance Planning:
A tour of a paper recycling or newspaper plant

Daniel Villanueva: The Idea Is to Care
Pages 489–493

Activity Needing Advance Planning:
A trip to a TV station or a college TV department

Bibliography

For Students

NOTE: For more information about these books, see the *Enrichment* section at the end of each Teaching Unit.

Asimov, Isaac. *How Did We Find Out About Electricity?* Walker, 1973.

———. *The Kite That Won the Revolution.* Houghton Mifflin, 1973.

Blow, Michael. *Men of Science and Inventions.* American Heritage, 1960.

Brondfield, Jerry. *Roberto Clemente: Pride of the Pirates.* Garrard, 1976.

Clark, Margaret Goff. *Benjamin Banneker: Astronomer and Scientist.* Garrard, 1971.

Coerr, Eleanor, and Dr. William Evans. *Gigi: A Baby Whale Borrowed for Science and Returned to the Sea.* Putnam, 1980.

Cooke, David C. *Inventions That Made History.* Putnam, 1969.

Corbett, Scott. *What Makes a Light Go On?* Atlantic Monthly Press-Little, 1966.

Cross, Jeanne. *Simple Printing Methods.* S. G. Phillips, 1972.

Curtis, Richard. *Ralph Nader's Crusade.* Macrae, 1972.

Daniel, Anita. *The Story of Albert Schweitzer.* Random, 1957.

Daugherty, Charles M. *Benjamin Franklin.* Macmillan, 1965.

De Bono, Edward. *Eureka! An Illustrated History of Inventions from the Wheel to the Computer.* Holt, Rinehart & Winston, 1974.

Dwiggins, Don. *Why Kites Fly: The Story of the Wind at Work.* Golden Gate, 1976.

Englebart, Stanley L. *Miracle Chip: The Microelectronic Revolution.* Lothrop, 1979.

Epstein, Sam, and Beryl Epstein. *The First Book of Electricity.* Watts, 1977.

Felder, Eleanor. *Careers in Publishing and Printing.* Raintree, 1976.

Fisher, Leonard Everett. *The Printers.* Viking Press, 1972.

Gallant, Roy A. *Exploring the Weather.* T. Y. Crowell, 1971.

Garrison, Webb. *Why Didn't I Think of That? From Alarm Clocks to Zippers.* Prentice-Hall, 1977.

Goodsell, Jane. *The Mayo Brothers.* T. Y. Crowell, 1975.

Gruber, Ruth. *Felisa Rincón de Gautier: The Mayor of San Juan.* Dell, 1975.

Haber, Louis. *Black Pioneers of Science and Invention.* Prentice-Hall, 1970.

Hayden, Robert C. *Eight Black American Inventors.* Simon & Schuster, 1969.

Hirsch, S. Carl. *Printing from a Stone: The Story of Lithography.* Viking Press, 1972.

———. *Stilts.* Watts, 1965.

Hussey, Lois J. *Collecting Small Fossils.* T. Y. Crowell, 1971.

Jupo, Frank. *The Story of Things.* Harcourt Brace Jovanovich, 1970.

Kalina, Sigmund. *How to Make a Dinosaur.* Lothrop, 1976.

Kerman, Stephen D. *Color Television and How It Works.* Viking, 1967.

Kirk, Ruth. *The Oldest Man in America: An Adventure in Archaeology.* Harcourt Brace Jovanovich, 1970.

McKown, Robin. *Marie Curie.* Putnam, 1971.

Martin, Alice Fitch. *Dinosaurs.* Golden Press, Western Pub., 1973.

Milgrom, Harry. *Understanding Weather.* Macmillan, 1970.

Papallo, George. *What Makes It Work?* Arco, 1977.

Pine, Tillie S., and Joseph Levine. *The Polynesians Knew.* McGraw, 1974.

Sattler, Helen. *Nature's Weather Forecasters.* Nelson, 1978.

Seidelman, James E., and Grace Mintonye. *Creating with Paper.* Macmillan, 1967.

Shuttlesworth, Dorothy E. *To Find a Dinosaur.* Doubleday, 1973.

Smith, Don, and Dr. Anne Marie Muesser. *How Sports Began.* Watts, 1977.

Smith, Howard E. *Play with the Wind.* McGraw, 1972.

Soong, Maying. *The Art of Chinese Paper Folding for Young and Old.* Harcourt Brace Jovanovich, 1948.

For Teachers

NOTE: For more information about these books, see the *Background* section that precedes the reading selections.

Calder, Nigel. *The Weather Machine: How Our Weather Works and Why It Is Changing.* Viking Press, 1975.

Chappell, Warren. *A Short History of the Printed Word.* Knopf, 1970.

Cole, Jonathan R. *Fair Science: Women in the Scientific Community.* Macmillan, 1979.

Fenton, Carroll Lane, and Mildred Adams Fenton. *The Fossil Book: A Record of Prehistoric Life.* Doubleday, 1959.

Franklin, Benjamin. *The Autobiography of Benjamin Franklin.* Yale U. Press, 1964.

Jennette, Sean. *Pioneers in Printing.* Routledge and Paul, 1958.

Klein, Aaron E. *The Hidden Contributors: Black Scientists and Inventors in America.* Doubleday, 1971.

Meyer, Jerome S. *World Book of Great Inventions.* World, 1956.

Films and Filmstrips

Sources related to skills

Harcourt Brace Jovanovich. *Bookmark Reading Filmstrips: Purple.* "Looking for Comparison and Contrast."

Sources related to reading selections

Educational Activities. *Man Studies Space.* Titles: "Story of Astronomy," "Space Age Astronomy." Two filmstrips with records or cassettes (#72-732739).

Guidance Assocs. *Career Discoveries Series.* Titles: "People Who Create Art," "People Who Make Things," "People Who Work in Science," "People Who Influence Others," "People Who Help Others," "People Who Organize Facts." Discussion guide for each title. Six programs, twenty-four parts with records (#9A-302 909) or cassettes (#9A-302 917).

Harcourt Brace Jovanovich. *Concepts in Science Sound Filmstrips.* Level 5. Titles: "A Push Is a Push," "Vanishing Act," "The Wandering Fossils," "Fitness," "Seeing the Unseen," "Making Change." Teacher's notes for each title. Six filmstrips with records (#2317-3661915) or cassettes (#2317-3661907).

Miller-Brody Productions. *Know Your Weather.* Titles: "Exploring Weather," "Forecasting Weather." Two filmstrips with records or cassettes.

Troll Assocs. *How Things Work.* Titles: "Simple Machines: The Pendulum," "Simple Machines: The Lever," "Simple Machines: Wheel and Axle and Pulley," "The Magic World of Light," "Shadows," "Discovering Simple Power and Energy," "True or False: Optical Illusions," "What Is a Magnet?" Eight film loops, Super-8, silent. Order by title.

Troll Assocs. "Wonders of Science: Flash, Crash, and Glow, Electricity in a Bulb." One filmstrip.

Visual Education Consultants. "A Modern Mastodon Hunt." One filmstrip (#3901).

Visual Education Consultants. "A Telephone Story." One filmstrip (#1687).

Vocational and Industrial Films. "Mideast: Pioneers of Science." Color, with teacher's guide (#11788).

Weston Woods. "How a Picture Book Is Made." One filmstrip with cassette (#SF 451C).

Records and/or Tapes

NOTE: Recordings may also be available on other labels.

"Daphnis et Chloë" by Maurice Ravel (Columbia Records M 33523)

"Dialogue of Wind and the Sea (Part III of *La Mer*)" by Claude Debussy (Columbia Records MY 37261)

"The Flying Dutchman (Overture and Act I)" by Richard Wagner (Columbia Records MS 6884)

"Valley Wind" by Hale Smith (Composers Recordings, Inc.)

OVERVIEW

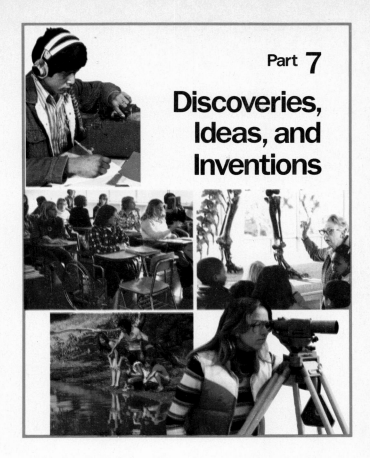

Discoveries, Ideas, and Inventions

The skills focus of "Discoveries, Ideas, and Inventions" is on inferential and other comprehension skills. The selections include examples of the ingenuity of famous people and of little-known people. Among the inventions described are the safety pin, the alarm clock, the zipper, the paper drinking straw, and other small common objects, as well as the ancient Chinese inventions of paper and movable type. In one selection, the main characters are children who have fun using scientific ideas in practical ways.

Using the Management System

Periodic Test 4, Forms A and *B,* covers the tested skills in "Discoveries, Ideas, and Inventions." The test may be administered in parts preceding and/or following the instruction in each Teaching Unit. Or, Parts I through IV may be administered together for pretesting and/or posttesting all the tested skills in "Discoveries, Ideas, and Inventions." For full information on administering tests, see the Teacher's Edition of *Periodic Tests, Level 11.* In addition, the following activities within the student's text may be used as part of your ongoing assessment of students' progress.

Try This sections of the *Skills Lessons*

Applying the Skills Lesson activities following each selection

Building Skills sections of *Textbook Studies*

Following instruction in Part 7, you may administer *Cumulative Test, Level 11* to test all the skills marked T in this Teacher's Edition.

Previewing "Discoveries, Ideas, and Inventions"

Have students open their books to page 407. Ask them what the difference is between a discovery and an invention. (A discovery is finding out for the first time about something that exists. An invention is a person's creation—something made for the first time by a human.) Then have students examine the photographs on page 407. Ask them if a fossil is an invention or a discovery. (discovery) Then tell students to examine the titles and illustrations on pages 408–497 to find other discoveries or inventions.

Objectives

The following list of objectives is provided to help you plan your teaching of "Discoveries, Ideas, and Inventions." All the objectives listed under *Introduced and Tested* and *Maintained and Tested* are for skills presented in the four *Skills Lessons* in the student's text. *Applying the Skills Lesson* sections following the selections in the student's text, as well as the *Try This* activities within *Skills Lessons,* informally assess students' progress with these skills. *Periodic Test 4* may be used for more formal evaluation.

The objectives listed under *Maintained* are for skills presented in the *Maintaining Skills* sections that accompany each selection in this Teacher's Edition.

The symbols I*, I, M, and T are used throughout the Teacher's Edition. The symbol I* indicates skills introduced for the first time in the program. The I indicates skills introduced earlier in Level 11. The M indicates skills taught at earlier levels and maintained in Level 11. The T indicates a skill that is taught for mastery and tested. The italicized numbers following the objectives are part of a code developed by the HBJ School Department to facilitate the correlation of skills within and between programs. See page T499 for more information about this code.

Introduced and Tested

These skills are introduced for the first time in Level 11 of the HBJ BOOKMARK READING PROGRAM, EAGLE EDITION. They are tested in *Periodic Test 4.*

	SKILLS CODE NUMBER
To distinguish between facts and fictional details	3.6.7
To identify facts on which fictional accounts may be based	3.6.9
To identify information on which stated conclusions are based	3.6.8
To identify faulty conclusions	3.6.1
To distinguish valid from faulty generalizations	3.6.1
To make generalizations based on given information	3.4.3
To identify qualifying words in generalizations	3.6.1

Introduced

The following skill is formally introduced at Level 11.

	SKILLS CODE NUMBER
To identify information on which stated conclusions are based	3.6.8

Maintained and Tested

The following skills were introduced earlier in the HBJ BOOKMARK READING PROGRAM, EAGLE EDITION. They are developed in Level 11 and tested in *Periodic Test 4.*

	SKILLS CODE NUMBER
To draw conclusions based on given information and personal knowledge	3.4.1
To identify words that signal comparisons and contrasts	3.3.8.5
To identify comparisons and contrasts	3.3.8.5

Maintained

Each of these skills was previously taught in the HBJ BOOKMARK READING PROGRAM, EAGLE EDITION. None of them are tested in *Periodic Test 4.* In planning your teaching, select those exercises from the *Maintaining Skills* sections that best meet your students' specific needs for maintaining skills presented earlier in the program.

	SKILLS CODE NUMBER
To interpret information from a map	5.4.3
To interpret information from a bar graph	5.4.1
To interpret information from a line graph	5.4.1
To identify the topic and stated main idea of a paragraph	3.3.8
To determine the correct sequence for a set of events	3.3.7.4
To use guide words in a dictionary	5.6.3
To identify cause-and-effect relationships	3.3.3
To identify antecedents of pronouns	4.6.2
To compare information obtained from graphic aids to textual information	5.4.7
To identify the number of syllables in a word	2.6
To use details to determine the unstated main idea of a paragraph	3.3.1; 3.4.7
To identify clues to time-order relationships	3.1.2
To scan a selection for specific information	5.9
To identify an author's purpose	3.6.4
To identify word parts: root words and suffixes	4.1

Vocabulary

The following skills are practiced on the *Vocabulary Study* pages in the student's text for "Discoveries, Ideas, and Inventions." These skills are not tested in *Periodic Test 4.*

	SKILLS CODE NUMBER
To identify and use antonyms as context clues	3.5.3; 3.0
To distinguish between homophones	3.5.1
To identify word parts: root words and suffixes	4.1
To use context clues to determine word meaning	3.0.2

TEACHING UNIT 16

Pages 408–429

Contents

Additional Materials

Reading Skills Workbook: Lessons 32–33, pages 105–109
Duplicating Masters 11: pages 52–53
Worksheet 13: Teacher's Edition, page T493
Periodic Test 4, Part I

Key to Symbols

Skills Objectives
I*   —   Introduced in this unit
I   —   Introduced earlier in this level
M   —   Maintained from previous levels
T   —   Tested in periodic and cumulative tests for this level

Reduced Student Pages
underscore — words that appear in the glossary
wavy line   — words pretaught in the Teacher's Edition
            (these words also appear in the glossary)

Skills Lesson:
Separating Facts from Fictional Details

Pages 408–413

Objectives

			SKILLS CODE NUMBER
I*, T	To distinguish between facts and fictional details		3.6.7
I*, T	To identify facts on which fictional accounts may be based		3.6.9

If you wish to pretest the skills listed above, you may administer *Periodic Test 4, Part I, Form A. Periodic Test 4, Part I, Form B,* may be administered to posttest.

Introducing the Lesson

1. **a.** Show students a photograph in a book or a newspaper of a famous person. Ask them the name of the person and what he or she is wearing. Then ask the class to make up a story about what the person is thinking.

   b. Point out that everyone can agree about who the person in the photograph is and what he or she is wearing. These are *facts.* However, there may be different ideas regarding the person's thoughts. Explain that when students made up the person's thoughts, they were supplying *fictional details.*

SKILLS LESSON

Separating Facts from Fictional Details

KNOBBY

1   2

What is the main difference between the two pictures above? Picture 1 is a photograph of a real computer. Picture 2 also shows a computer. Like a real computer, "Knobby" has dials and buttons and gives answers. But the big difference between the two pictures is that the computer in picture 1 is real. Knobby, however, is made up. An artist **imagined** what a computer with a personality would be like.

Is It a Fact?

We say that stories that are made up or imagined are **fiction**. Many books are a mixture of fact and fiction. Some details are facts. A **fact** is something that can be proved. Some details are fiction — that is, the author made up these details.

408

Which of the sentences below state facts?

● 1. Marie and Pierre Curie discovered radium in 1898.
2. Benjamin Franklin invented the lightning rod.
3. Covered in bearskin blankets, the Stone Age family shivered in their cave.

In an article about Marie and Pierre Curie in an encyclopedia, you would find that statement 1 is a fact. Marie and Pierre Curie did discover radium in 1898. You could also find the fact in sentence 2 in an encyclopedia.

Is sentence 3 a statement of fact or of fiction? Since no one living today was alive during the Stone Age, and since Stone Age people left no written records, the writer must have imagined this scene.

Imagination is an important tool for authors who want to tell about the past. In order to make books about the past seem real and interesting, authors often imagine conversations and actions that may have happened. They do this after learning everything they can about the person or time they are writing about.

409

---

2. Have students look at the pictures at the top of page 408 and read the introductory paragraph. Ask how the computers differ. (Picture 1 is a photograph of a real computer; picture 2 shows an imaginary computer.)

3. Explain that some selections in *Blazing Trails* are based on facts and that some selections are fictional. Also point out that some selections in the book combine facts and fictional details. Have students look at the illustrations in one of the selections in *Blazing Trails* and explain how the illustrations help them determine whether the selection is made up of facts, fictional details, or both.

which sentences are statements of fact and which statements are fiction based on fact. (Sentences 1 and 2 are facts; sentence 3 is a fictional statement.)

2. Have students explain why sentence 3 is not a fact. (Stone Age people left no written records.) Now have students read the three paragraphs on page 409.

Developing the Skill

Is It a Fact?

A fact is something that can be proved. Fiction is something made up.

1. Have students read the last paragraph on page 408 and the sentences at the top of page 409. Ask

Fictional Details Based on Facts

When you read about something that happened in the past, do you ever wonder where the author got his or her information? As you read the following paragraphs about Betty Zane, think about which details might be facts. Which details do you think the author may have made up?

1. In September 1782, the settlement of Fort Henry, in what is now Wheeling, West Virginia, was attacked. Thirteen-year-old Betty, her uncle Ebenezer Zane, and the other settlers were in the fort when the fighting began. When the settlers' supply of gunpowder was almost gone, Betty's uncle realized that their only hope was a keg of gunpowder that had been forgotten in the Zane cabin. The cabin was outside the fort. But who would make that dangerous run? Many were wounded and too weak to make the run. Colonel Shepard finally agreed to allow Betty to go.

2. "Please let me run for the gunpowder, Colonel Shepard," Betty pleaded. "You can't spare a sharpshooter. Many are too weak from wounds to go. I am young and I am a fast runner."

There are no records to prove that Betty said these words to Colonel Shepard. However, the facts in paragraph 1 show that Betty *might* have said such words.

Here are some other facts about Betty Zane and this event:

a. Betty brought the gunpowder back to the fort.
b. The settlers were able to fight off the attackers and save Fort Henry.
c. It was the last frontier battle of the American Revolution.

410

411

Fictional Details Based on Facts

Sometimes fictional details are based on facts.

1. Have students read the introductory paragraph and the two numbered paragraphs that follow it on page 410. Explain that Betty Zane was a real person.

2. Ask students which details in the numbered paragraphs might be facts and which the author probably made up. (The details in paragraph 1 are facts; the details in paragraph 2 were probably made up.) Point out that although there are no records to prove that Betty Zane spoke the words in paragraph 2, the facts in paragraph 1 show that she *might* have said something like that.

3. Have students read the rest of page 410 and all of page 412. Ask if it is possible that Betty Zane and Colonel Shepard spoke the dialogue in paragraphs 3 and 4. (Given facts *a*, *b*, and *c*, it is possible.)

Now read paragraphs 3 and 4. Notice how the author presents some of the facts through Betty's and Colonel Shepard's words.

● 3. "You are a brave young woman, Betty," Colonel Shepard said. "You made it possible for us to withstand the fight and save Fort Henry."
4. "Thank you, Colonel Shepard," Betty answered. "I'm glad I was able to make the run. I can tell you now that no trip of one hundred miles could have seemed longer than the hundred yards back to the fort."

There are no records that show that Betty and Colonel Shepard said these words. But is it *possible* that they said these words?

412

How to Recognize the Difference Between Facts and Fictional Details

It is not always easy—or even possible—to recognize the difference between facts and fictional details. Authors generally try to make imagined events seem like facts. Nevertheless, as a critical reader, you should be aware that an author may be using fictional details along with facts. You should try to understand where the author got the facts on which to base his or her writing. Was a conversation written down at the time it was held? Did the famous person in history keep a diary or write a book about his or her experiences? Did an event take place long before anyone kept records? Is an event taking place in the future? If you ask yourself such questions, you will understand how the writer has made fact and fiction work together to make a more interesting story.

Try This

Read the paragraphs below. Which one states only facts? Which one seems to mix facts and fictional details? What are the fictional details?

1. Sacajawea saw Clark's compass fall from his hand into the rushing waters. Sacajawea knew how much the red-haired man needed the compass. She dived. Immediately she felt the shock of the cold and the current's force.
2. Sacajawea, a Shoshone woman, led the Lewis and Clark expedition over the Rocky Mountains in 1804. Sacajawea knew how to get food in the wilderness. She was able to judge the best ways over the mountains and across the rivers. Lewis and Clark's journals make it clear that she was the most important member of the expedition.

413

How to Recognize the Difference Between Facts and Fictional Details

Sometimes is it difficult to recognize the difference between facts and fictional details.

1. Have students read the paragraph on page 413. Write the following two terms on the board, and explain (or have students try to guess) what each kind of work is.

    nonfictional history (all facts or mostly facts)
    historical fiction (a fictional story using real events or real people with made-up details)

2. **a.** Explain that historical fiction books are usually put in the fiction section of the library. Have students examine the summary for *Touchmark* on the catalogue card on page 227. Ask if this book is fiction or nonfiction. (fiction) Ask what details in the summary help the reader to know that it is based on fact. (It is set in pre-Revolutionary Boston.)

    b. Now have students examine the card for *Touch of Light* on page 226. Ask what kind of book it is. (nonfictional biography) Explain that although the book is nonfiction, it may have some made-up or fictional details, just as the paragraphs about Betty Zane were nonfiction but had made-up conversations.

Try This

Have students complete *Try This.*

Answers to *Try This*

Paragraph 1 mixes fact and fictional details (sample fictional detail: Immediately she felt the shock of the cold and the current's force); paragraph 2 states only facts.

 Use *Reading Skills Workbook*, Lesson 32, pages 105–108. See *Providing for Individual Differences*, page T374, for additional practice.

Vocabulary Study:
Antonyms
Pages 414–415

Objective

		SKILLS CODE NUMBER
M	To identify and use antonyms as context clues	3.5.3; 3.0

Developing the Skill

1. Tell students that the *Vocabulary Study* they are about to read is another entry from Professor Crum's diary. In it, Professor Crum uses antonyms as context clues.

2. Have students read the *Vocabulary Study* and do the *Word Play* activities.

Answers to *Word Play*

1. c. dislike; 2. b. defeat; 3. c. dull; 4. a. good. Sentences will vary.

 Use *Reading Skills Workbook*, Lesson 33, page 109. See *Providing for Individual Differences*, page T374, for additional practice.

VOCABULARY STUDY

Antonyms

The almost kind Professor Crum sat in the flickering light of a candle and wrote in his diary.

Dear Diary,

Oh horror of horrors! My **evil** plan has failed! Instead of a **victory**, I'm afraid I must record my defeat. You see, I had the nasty idea of not removing the grapefruit seeds from the freshly squeezed grapefruit juice (hee, hee, hee). I expected everybody to develop a great dislike toward me. You know how much I love to be hated. But guess what happened? They showered me with **affection**! They thought the grapefruit seeds were a good gift! How was I supposed to know they grow into nice plants?

Gosh! Being rotten used to be **fascinating**. Now it's dull. I'm afraid the evil Professor Crum is all washed up.

414

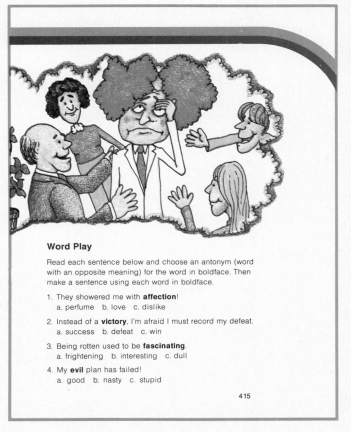

Word Play

Read each sentence below and choose an antonym (word with an opposite meaning) for the word in boldface. Then make a sentence using each word in boldface.

1. They showered me with **affection**!
   a. perfume   b. love   c. dislike

2. Instead of a **victory**, I'm afraid I must record my defeat.
   a. success   b. defeat   c. win

3. Being rotten used to be **fascinating**.
   a. frightening   b. interesting   c. dull

4. My **evil** plan has failed!
   a. good   b. nasty   c. stupid

415

Reading Selection:
The Wind Watchers
Pages 416–423

Objectives

		SKILLS CODE NUMBER
I*, T	To distinguish between facts and fictional details	3.6.7
I*, T	To identify facts on which fictional accounts may be based	3.6.9
M	To interpret information from a map	5.4.3
M	To interpret information from a bar graph	5.4.1
M	To interpret information from a line graph	5.4.1

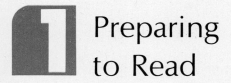

Preparing to Read

Summary

A fifth-grade class at a California public school conducted an experiment designed to prove that the wind blows from west to east. Class members spent much time planning the experiment. Finally, each student in the school—and the school's principal—launched a balloon. There were over 500 in all. To find out where the balloons landed, the students and the principal attached a post card to each one. One balloon traveled 1,000 miles.

Background

Wind is moving air. The prevailing westerlies are winds that circulate from west to east and occur in the belts between 30° and 60° latitude north and south of the equator.

The speed and direction of wind affect temperature and atmospheric changes. They also affect the way we perceive temperature through our bodies. The faster the wind blows, the faster the body loses heat and,

consequently, the cooler the temperature seems. The speed of wind close to the Earth is measured by means of an *anemometer*. Helium-filled weather balloons are used to measure the speed and direction of high-altitude winds.

The following book will provide you with additional background information.

Calder, Nigel. *The Weather Machine: How Our Weather Works and Why It Is Changing.* Meteorological discoveries around the world; how weather works. Illustrated, with bibliography and index.

Developing Vocabulary and Concepts

jet stream: a very strong wind that blows from the west at a high altitude
helium: a gas that is lighter than air and does not burn
hydrogen: the lightest of all gases
straggled: lagged behind
admitted: confessed or acknowledged
graze: feed on growing grass

1. **a.** Read the following sentences aloud, or write them on the board. If you read them aloud, write the underlined vocabulary on the board.

   Helium and hydrogen are gases that are lighter than air.
   The last balloon straggled across the telephone lines behind all the other balloons.
   The principal admitted that the students had a good idea. She said they were very clever.
   The farmers allowed the cows to graze in the meadow. While the cows were eating the grass, three balloons landed in the meadow.

   b. Ask students to give the meaning of each vocabulary word. Remind them to use the context clues in the sentences to help them.

2. Have students look for the term *jet stream* in their glossaries. Ask them to imagine a plane flying eastward in the jet stream. Would the wind help the plane move forward faster, or would the plane be flying against the wind? (The wind would be helping the plane, since in the jet stream the wind comes from the west.) Tell students to suppose another plane were flying westward in the jet stream. Would that plane be flying against the wind? (yes)

3. Discuss wind with students. What is it? What can it do? How does it cause weather changes? Explain to students that the selection they will read is about a class in California that decided to find out the direction in which the wind blows. Ask students to spec-

ulate on how they could find out the wind's direction. Accept reasonable answers, but don't give away the selection's plot.

 Use *Duplicating Masters 11,* page 52.

Setting Purposes

Skills

Have students read the skills note at the top of page 416. Remind them that a fact is a statement that can be proved and that facts and fictional details are often skillfully combined.

Content

Have students read the lead-in to the title. Ask them to think about what they would do with more than 500 balloons. How do they think a class in California used 501 balloons to become "The Wind Watchers"? (Accept reasonable answers.)

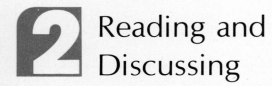 Reading and Discussing

Have students read the selection. Most students will be able to complete it in one sitting. If you prefer, the selection may be read in two parts, breaking before the heading "Up, Up, and Away" on page 420.

NOTE: The questions that appear in the student's text at the end of the selection focus on comprehension of selection content and on application of the *Skills Lesson* to the selection. Answers to these questions begin on page T368.

The events in the following selection took place a few years ago. The author made up some of the conversation. Look for facts on which the conversations were based.

Why did a school in California need 501 balloons? It was so that the students could be . . .

THE WIND WATCHERS
by Edith Battles

Mr. Boone, the principal, looked surprised. "Five hundred balloons! Whatever would you do with five hundred balloons?"

"Oh, not just for us," said Scott. "For the whole school. Everybody."

"We need balloons," Lori said, "to let them float away. Then we will know in which direction the wind blows."

"Wouldn't one balloon do?" asked Mr. Boone.

Scott frowned. "One might get lost and we'd never know where it went. Besides, there are 500 kids at 230th Street School. All the kids will want to launch their own balloons. And, out of 500, some of them have got to be found."

"Well," said the principal slowly, "I really don't see how we can do it with 500 balloons. I'm sure that is the wrong number." The children's hopes fell.

"So I'll order 501," said Mr. Boone. "You see," he went on, "each child will want to launch a balloon. They add up to 500. I want to launch one, too! That's one more."

Making Plans

Scott and Lori's class began to make plans right away. They knew that for a balloon to stay up, it must be filled with a gas that is lighter than air. Hydrogen or helium will keep a balloon up. But the class decided to use only helium. It is a safe gas because it will not burn or explode.

Ms. Green, Lori and Scott's teacher, sent for books and movies about wind and weather. The children searched through the books and the encyclopedia. They made instruments to measure the wind's speed. They made wind vanes to show the direction of the wind. Each morning and afternoon for a week, they checked how fast the wind blew and where

417

it blew from. They wrote down what they learned.

"What did you find out?" asked Ms. Green a week later.

"The wind has more speed in the afternoon," said Lori. "And it usually blows from the west."

Joan waved her hand wildly. "They call our California winds the 'prevailing westerlies.' I read it in the encyclopedia."

Jerry raised his hand. "Well, we *think* the balloons will all blow to the east. But how can we know for sure? We won't see any of them land."

"Why will the balloons land at all? Why don't they just stay up?" asked Mary.

"They lose some of the gas," said John. "Then they are too heavy to float in air."

"Jerry's question wasn't answered," said Ms. Green. "How can we check to find where the balloons land?"

The children all had ideas, but Scott had the best one. He suggested that they tie a post card to each balloon. The school's address would be on one side. A message on the other side would ask the finders to write to the school about when and where they found the balloons.

Then Scott had a question. "We are near an airport. Will our balloons bother the pilots?"

418

To find out, one of the children called the airport. "Your balloons are not large enough to cause us any problem," said the man at Airport Tower Control. "But we must be told the time you plan to release them so that our pilots will not be surprised."

Scott and Lori made a note on their long list of things to do.

Getting Started

Scott and Lori thought that only a few people would want to send messages, but nearly every child in the school brought nickels and pennies to buy a post card. Then Scott and Lori went to the post office and bought enough post cards for everyone. The children all signed their names on the cards.

Scott and Lori decided to sign the same card. Each of them made a secret wish about whom they wanted to find their balloon.

One morning Mr. Boone came to the classroom. "The Weather Service says that no storm will come until the end of the week. So let's set the day for Wednesday. I ordered balloons to be here by then."

As Wednesday drew near, Ms. Green's class was very busy. Scott checked off the things that needed to be done. When each job was finished, he drew a line through it on the list.

"The balloons are here," Mr. Boone told them. There were more than 500 of them, just in case some balloons burst. Scott drew a line through the words ORDER BALLOONS.

"The helium is here," said the science teacher. Scott drew a line through the words ORDER HELIUM.

"Your cards are finally stamped with the school's address," said the school secretary. Scott drew a line through ADDRESS POST CARDS.

419

The children brought large plastic bags. Scott drew a line through the words GET BAGS TO HOLD FILLED BALLOONS.

On the last day, the younger children tied the post cards on strings. In the science room, the teacher and older children took turns filling the many balloons with helium.

Sometimes a balloon burst. Sometimes a balloon got away and went straight to the ceiling.

Up, Up, and Away

A few minutes before two o'clock, the teachers led their classes to the playground. When everyone was gathered—all 500 children and many, many balloons—Mr. Boone gave the go signal.

The children released their balloons. Everyone began to shout. The big balloon clusters lifted smoothly. In a few seconds they were colorful shapes in the sky. Post cards fluttered in the sunlight.

"They're going east! They're going east!" Ms. Green's children called out.

"I see mine!" "There it goes!" "I lost it!" "It's gone."

Mr. Boone let his own balloon go free. It rose in the sunlight. It, too, went east with the others. The balloons were like marbles now, and then stars, and then—nothing.

"We may never know where most of them go," said Ms. Green. "Away from the cities, America has much empty land. Many balloons will be lost. But some will be found and their cards returned. We'll mark each place on our map."

The Answers Come

Two days later, two post cards arrived in the mail. On the same day as the launching, three small boys had found a balloon near the freeway. A workman had found some balloons in a half-built building twenty miles east.

Each day during the next two weeks, cards arrived from farther away. Every balloon had gone eastward. A few had fallen fifty miles east of the city.

Joan's card was signed by a motel owner in Arizona, over 400 air miles away. "It *did* go over the mountains!" she said.

Each time a post card arrived, a colored pin was placed on the

420

map showing where it came from. Most of the pins were clustered near the city. But more and more began to scatter farther east.

As the days followed, fifty-four children learned where their balloons had gone.

"But not me," said Lori. "I wished on my balloon, but I never got an answer."

Scott was very quiet. He had wished on the same balloon as Lori.

Some Surprises

One day, nearly a week after the last post card had straggled back, Mr. Boone came to the classroom.

"Boys and girls, my card came in the mail today."

"From where?" asked the children.

"Guess," said the principal.

All the children raised their hands and made guesses. No one was right. "We give up."

"Hawaii!" said Mr. Boone.

They all laughed and hooted. "It couldn't go to Hawaii," John said. "That is west. The winds carried your balloon east. I saw it go. Even if it rose as high as the jet stream, it just couldn't get all the way around the world and back to Hawaii."

"Well," admitted Mr. Boone, "it needed a little help. It landed on an ocean liner in Long Beach

harbor, and the finder mailed the card to me from Hawaii.

"But that isn't the main reason I came. I have a letter for Scott and Lori. It's postmarked Colorado. Do you know anybody in Colorado?"

Scott and Lori raced to the front of the room. They read the letter together:

Dear Lori and Scott,

I was feeling very lonely today when our dog, Alfred, found your balloon in my yard. It was like having a visit with grandchildren to have your message drop in that way. I live a thousand miles from California on an old-fashioned sheep ranch in Colorado. My husband and I take care of the ranch ourselves. When we take the sheep to the high mountains to graze each summer, Alfred helps us watch the sheep.

My husband and I think it would be very nice to have a letter from California telling us all about your school. If you know any children out there who would like to write to two faraway grandparents, tell them about us.

> *Your balloon friends,*
> *Jennie and George Johnson*
> *and Alfred*

Lori read each word with delight.
"The wish did it! Wishes really *can* be made on balloons!"

Scott said, "Well, I wished that our balloon would be found by someone who has lots of room to run and play and a dog and other pets to play with. I want to visit them someday."

"I wished my balloon would find me a grandmother," Lori told Scott. "And it did."

"We both got our wish then!"

Understanding What You've Read

1. What did the children wish to show through their balloon launching?
2. What materials did the children need in order to do their study?
3. In which direction did the children *expect* the balloons to go? In which direction did the balloons go? What did this show about the winds in California?

Applying the Skills Lesson

1. Find at least three examples of quotations the author might have made up. Explain why you think these words are made up.
2. Read again the sixth and seventh paragraphs on page 420. Who is saying the words in quotation marks? Do you think the speakers actually said these exact words—or did they say something *like* this?

423

Questions preceded by a bullet are additional questions and appear in the Teacher's Edition only. The other questions appear in the student's text after the selection.

Understanding What You've Read

1. *What did the children wish to show through their balloon launching?* (the direction in which the wind blows   page 417) LITERAL   <u>Identifying the main idea of a selection</u>

• *Why were Scott and the other children disappointed when they asked Mr. Boone about the balloons?* (They thought Mr. Boone was not going to provide a balloon for everyone in the school.) INFERENTIAL <u>Drawing conclusions</u>

• *What kind of person do you think Mr. Boone was?* (Friendly, kind, etc. Have students explain their answers by citing things he said or did.) CRITICAL <u>Making judgments</u>

2. *What materials did the children need in order to do their study?* (balloons; helium, books and movies about wind and weather, and instruments to measure speed and direction of wind; post cards and string; large plastic bags   pages 417, 418, and 420) LITERAL   <u>Recalling specific details</u>

• *Was the study well planned? Explain your answer.* (Yes; plans were made about what to do and why, a list was written, and as tasks were done they were crossed off.) CRITICAL   <u>Making judgments</u>

• *As the balloons were being filled, some of them got away and floated to the ceiling. Why?* (They were filled with helium, which is lighter than air. When the balloons got loose, they went to the highest point. page 420) INFERENTIAL   <u>Drawing conclusions</u>

3. *In which direction did the children expect the balloons to go? In which direction did the balloons go? What did this show about the winds in California?* (The children expected the balloons to move eastward and they did. This shows that the winds in California come from the west and blow east.   pages 418 and 420) LITERAL, INFERENTIAL   <u>Drawing conclusions</u>

• *How do you think Ms. Green's class felt when the study was completed?* (Accept all reasonable answers. The class probably felt proud about proving the direction of the wind; they were happy that some of their wishes about the balloons came true; they were disappointed that the study was over.) CRITICAL   <u>Drawing conclusions</u>

Applying the Skills Lesson

1. *Find at least three examples of quotations the author might have made up. Explain why you think these words are made up.* (Throughout the selection there are examples of imagined quotations, such as on page 417, paragraphs 1–8. Although the events in the story actually took place, it is unlikely that someone kept a record of the words spoken while the events were taking place.)   <u>Distinguishing between facts and fictional details</u>

• *Reread the conversation Scott and Lori had with Mr. Boone on page 417. On what facts might this conversation be based?* (The principal was asked for balloons; the balloons would be used to determine the direction of the wind; there were 500 students at the 230th Street School; the principal wanted to launch a balloon, so 501 balloons would be needed; the principal ordered the balloons.)   <u>Identifying facts on which fictionalized accounts may be based</u>

2. *Read again the sixth and seventh paragraphs on page 420. Who is saying the words in quotation marks? Do you think the speakers actually said these exact words—or did they say something like this?* (Some members of Ms. Green's class are speaking. They might have said something like this.)   <u>Distinguishing between facts and fictional details</u>

- *Reread the first through the eighth paragraphs on page 422. On what facts might this conversation be based?* (Mr. Boone got a post card; his balloon landed on a ship bound for Hawaii; the finder of the post card mailed it from Hawaii; Scott and Lori got a post card from Colorado.)   Identifying facts on which fictional accounts may be based

 Use *Duplicating Masters 11*, page 53. See *Providing for Individual Differences*, page T374, for additional practice.

3 Maintaining Skills

Study Skills

Interpreting information from a map   Use a map of the United States. Review directionality. If there is a compass on the map, point it out. Otherwise, have students note that north is toward the top of the map and west is toward the left of the map. Then ask students to locate California. Once this is done, ask students to use the map to answer the following questions.

In what direction must one travel from California to reach Arizona? (east or southeast)
Through what other state might some of the balloons have traveled? (Nevada)
Whose balloon landed farthest from California? (Lori and Scott's)
Through which two states might Lori and Scott's balloon have traveled in order to land in Colorado? (Nevada and Utah, or Arizona and Utah, or Arizona and New Mexico)
Is Hawaii east or west of California? (west)
The winds in New York state also blow from west to east. Where would balloons launched from this state probably land? (Accept reasonable answers. Answers might include the Atlantic Ocean or any of the New England states.)

Interpreting information from a bar graph   On the board, copy the following bar graph, which is based partially on some facts taken from the selection. (NOTE: Do not copy the numbers shown in brackets to the right of each bar on the graph. They are for your information only.) Review the features of a bar graph, noting the use of *bars* (thick horizontal lines) to

show comparisons, the use of *labels* down the left side, and the use of a *scale* of numbers along the bottom of the graph. Then ask students the questions following the graph.

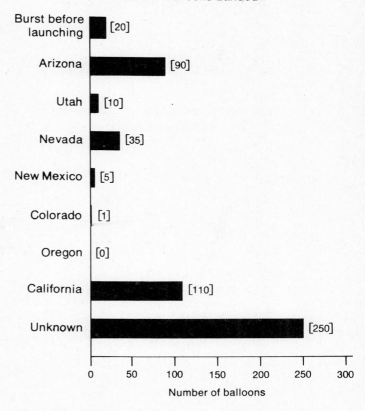

Where the Balloons Landed

(Write the numbers below in a column on the board.) Here are numbers that show how many balloons landed in the states named on the graph. Match each number with a state.

35 (Nevada)
10 (Utah)
110 (California)
0 (Oregon)
5 (New Mexico)
90 (Arizona)
1 (Colorado)
250 (Unknown)

What happened to balloons that did not land in one of the states named? (Either they burst before the launching, or it is not known where they landed.)
How many post cards were sent back to the school? (251)
How many balloons were not accounted for? (250)
About how many burst before the launching? (20)
In which of the seven states listed did the most balloons land? (California)

Interpreting information from a line graph   Copy on the board the line graph below. Then ask students the following questions.

What is the title of the graph? (Average Windspeed in Anytown, California [in kilometers per hour])

Which two months have the lowest windspeed? (July and August)

Which month has the highest windspeed? (March)

What is the average windspeed in October? (16 kph)

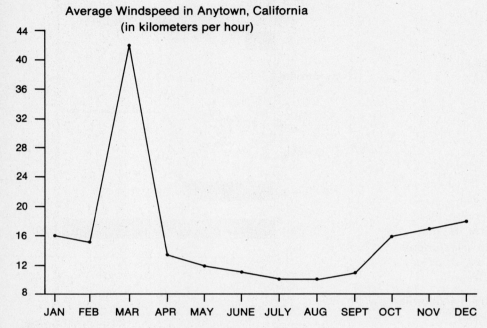

 For additional resources and curriculum-related activities, see *Enrichment,* page T375.

Textbook Study:

Separating Facts from Fictional Details

Pages 424–429

Objectives

		SKILLS CODE NUMBER
I*, T	To distinguish between facts and fictional details	3.6.7
I*, T	To identify facts on which fictional accounts may be based	3.6.9

Applying the Skill

Have students read the introduction and the two selections. You may wish to have students read the selections on their own and then do *Building Skills.* Or you may wish to direct students, using the following procedure.

TEXTBOOK STUDY

Separating Facts from Fictional Details

Textbooks are mostly factual. Sometimes, however, the facts are not known for certain. When you read about people and events from the past, be aware that only some statements may be based on facts. The author may also have used fictional details.

As you read the following selections, think about which statements may be based on facts. Try to answer the questions in the sidenotes that go with the first selection.

Separating Facts from Fictional Details in Social Studies

The Canoe

Black Moon stepped out of his wigwam with a tingle of excitement. It flowed through him as he stood there in his moccasins and leather trousers. Today, after long weeks of labor, his canoe would be finished.

This story is set about 500 years ago. Black Moon is a *fictional character*. That is, the author made him up. What facts might the author have based this story on?

Long ago he had found a birch tree of the size and type he needed. Carefully, using his stone knife, he cut great sheets of bark from the birch. He had then chopped down a giant cedar tree. It gave him strong, clean wood for the ribs and framework of his boat. Finally, he dug up long tough roots from a black spruce tree. With these he sewed together the sheets of bark.

424

Separating Facts from Fictional Details in Social Studies

1. Have students read the two paragraphs on page 424 and answer the question in the sidenote. (Some Native Americans lived in wigwams; some wore moccasins and leather trousers; some built canoes from birch and cedar.)

2. Have students identify the fictional details in the first paragraph. (Black Moon was excited. He was building a canoe.)

Now all around him lay his tools. There were his axe, hammer, wedge, scraper, and his knife with its leather handle. All of these he had made himself from stone. There were also pointed sticks of hard wood, and the bow of bone with which he drilled holes for the framework of his canoe. Finally there was his measuring stick with its carefully placed notches. With it he made sure that the sides of his boat were even and the ribs properly placed.

How would the author know that Black Moon's tools were made of stone? How would the author know what kinds of tools Black Moon made?

— *The United States*
Houghton Mifflin

Building Skills

Below are some facts that the author might have used when writing about Black Moon. In the selection above, find sentences based on the following facts:

1. Archaeologists have found 500-year-old stone tools in North America.
2. Scientists have been able to make a canoe using stone tools like those described in the selection.
3. Some Native Americans today make canoes from cedar, birch, and spruce trees.
4. For hundreds of years, some Native Americans have worn leather moccasins and trousers.
5. Archaeologists have found 500-year-old "drills," fashioned out of animal bone, that could be used to bore holes.

425

Separating Facts from Fictional Details in Language Arts

There are no sidenotes for this selection. Read it and then answer the questions that follow it.

Study the following notes. They are based on an encyclopedia article about Christopher Columbus.

Oct. 10, 1492
Unhappy crew agreed to sail three more days before going back home
Oct. 12, 1492
Island of San Salvador sighted
Columbus thought he was near Japan or an island of the Indies
Oct. 28, 1492
Reached Cuba, thinking he was in China
Saw people smoking cigars
Jan. 16, 1493
Began return trip to Spain
Mar. 15, 1493
Reached Palos, Spain. Went to Barcelona and received grand reception
Named *Admiral of the Ocean Sea* and *Viceroy of the Indies*
Began getting ready for second voyage

426

3. Have students read the paragraph on page 425 and answer the questions in the sidenote. (The author probably had knowledge of archaeological findings of tools Native Americans used. Probably the author had learned of ancient stone axes, hammers, wedges, scrapers, knives with leather handles, bone drills, and measuring sticks.)

4. Have students complete *Building Skills*.

Answers to *Building Skills*
Social Studies Selection

1. "Carefully, using his stone knife, he cut great sheets of bark from the birch"; all of last paragraph; 2. all of second and third paragraphs; 3. all of second paragraph; 4. "It flowed through him as he stood there in his moccasins and leather trousers"; 5. "There were also pointed sticks of hard wood, and the bow of bone with which he drilled holes for the framework of his canoe."

Separating Facts from Fictional Details in Language Arts

1. Have students read the dated notes about Columbus on page 426. Ask them how the author knew that some of these events really happened. (Students should recognize that written records exist from Columbus's time.)

Now pretend for a moment that you are a Spanish newspaper reporter in 1493. Read this example of a news story you might have written for your newspaper.

Explorer Returns Safely

Barcelona. March 30, 1493. Christopher Columbus was the guest of honor at a large party given by the King and Queen last week. Columbus was given the title of *Admiral of the Ocean Sea* for his great courage in sailing west to China. Besides the

427

weather, he had to worry about a possible mutiny among his crew members.

Columbus was named *Viceroy of the Indies* for discovering a new route to that part of the world. He reached an island of the Indies on October 12, 1492, and he named the island San Salvador. He was very interested in meeting the Chinese emperor, but he couldn't find anyone who knew where the emperor lived.

Columbus has many stories to tell about the people of the islands he visited. One such story has to do with their custom of smoking a leaf that they grow. Columbus said it smells awful.

He is now preparing for his second voyage to the Indies. This time he hopes to meet the emperor of China and the rulers of Japan.

—Discovery in English
Laidlaw Brothers

Building Skills

Read the following sentences from the newspaper story. On which facts from the encyclopedia article is each sentence based?

428

1. Christopher Columbus was the guest of honor at a large party given by the King and Queen last week.
2. Besides the weather, he had to worry about a possible mutiny among his crew members.
3. One such story has to do with their custom of smoking a leaf that they grow.
4. Columbus said it smells awful.
5. He is now preparing for his second voyage to the Indies.

429

2. Have students read the rest of the selection and complete *Building Skills.*

Answers to *Building Skills*
Language Arts Selection

1. "Mar. 15, 1493 . . . Went to Barcelona and received grand reception"; **2.** "Oct. 10, 1492 Unhappy crew agreed to sail three more days. . . ."; **3.** "Oct. 28, 1492 . . . Saw people smoking cigars"; **4.** "Oct. 28, 1492 . . . Saw people smoking cigars"; **5.** "Mar. 15, 1493 . . . Began getting ready for second voyage."

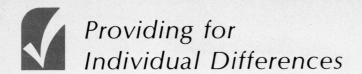

Providing for Individual Differences

Skills Lesson

Additional Practice

Worksheet 13, Teacher's Edition, page T493

Vocabulary Study

Additional Practice

■ **Using antonyms as context clues**   On the board, draw a grid seven boxes across and seven boxes down as shown below. Write the word ANTONYM in the top row across. Have students fill in the grid downward with seven-letter antonyms for the following words.

Clues:

A = unskillfulness (ability)
N = artificial (natural)
T = unknotted (tangled)
O = youngness (oldness)
N = everything (nothing)
Y = older (younger)
M = shrink (magnify)

A	N	T	O	N	Y	M

Reading Selection: The Wind Watchers

Additional Practice

■ **Distinguishing between facts and fictional details**
Explain to students that you are going to read a paragraph that mixes facts and fictional details about George Washington. Then read the following paragraph aloud and ask the questions that follow it.

George heard the sound of hoofbeats coming from far down the road to Fredericksburg. He climbed onto the fence for a look. He was tall and strong for a nine-year-old boy. His straight nose was sprinkled with freckles. He brushed a lock of sand-colored hair from his forehead and squinted his gray-blue eyes.

How can it be proved that Washington lived near a road that led to Fredericksburg? (Records of Washington's homes still exist.)

Can it be proved that Washington heard hoofbeats and climbed onto a fence? (Probably not. It is not likely that Washington recorded such an event or told anyone about it.)

Is it likely that Washington was tall and strong as a boy? Why or why not? (Yes. He was so as an adult, as shown in pictures and as described by historians.)

What kinds of things might prove that Washington had gray-blue eyes and sandy hair? (pictures and written descriptions of Washington made in his lifetime)

Evaluation

Periodic Test 4, Part I, Form A or *Form B*, may be administered after this unit to test skills marked **T**. If you have pretested using *Form A*, administer *Form B*.

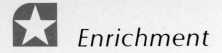 *Enrichment*

The Wind Watchers

Bibliography

The following books are about the wind and the weather.

Easy

Smith, Howard E. *Play with the Wind.* Experiments to determine wind velocity and direction.

Average

Dwiggins, Don. *Why Kites Fly: The Story of the Wind at Work.* Aerodynamics of kites as well as supersonic airplanes, plus a history of kites.

Gallant, Roy A. *Exploring the Weather.* Includes air, hurricanes, tornadoes, and thunderstorms.

Milgrom, Harry. *Understanding Weather.* Information about weather satellites and experiments.

Films and Filmstrips

NOTE: For more information, see *Resource Center.*

Selection content

Guidance Assocs. *Career Discoveries Series.* "People Who Work in Science." Demonstrations of chemical analysis.

Miller-Brody Productions. *Know Your Weather.* "Exploring Weather," "Forecasting Weather." Explanations of weather and instruments used to forecast it.

Curriculum Coordination

Language Arts

1. Have students pretend they took part in an experiment. Have them write a paragraph or composition describing it.

2. Students may write or find a poem about the wind and share it with the class.

Science

1. Integrate a science lesson on wind with this selection.

2. Let students demonstrate the erosion effect of wind on soil by performing the following experiment. Have students draw conclusions about the effects of wind on large areas of land. (It would be best to do this experiment outdoors.)

Fill a shallow box with soil, gravel, and small rocks. Put the box in front of a wall. Put a white cloth on the wall behind the box. Direct a small fan at the box. Notice that the wind blows the soil onto the white cloth.

Mathematics

Have students find the numbers of balloons needed if each student had sent up 3 balloons, 17 balloons, and 200 balloons. Extend this lesson to percentages or fractions by asking questions such as "What percentage (or fraction) of answers would you have if you sent 500 balloons and 240 post cards came back?"

Art

Have students make drawings in which they show the effects of the wind.

Music

Have students listen to music that gives the impression of wind.

Career Education

Invite a meteorologist to speak to students about his or her profession.

Contents

Additional Materials

Reading Skills Workbook: Lessons 34–35, pages 110–116
Duplicating Masters 11: pages 54–57
Worksheet 14: Teacher's Edition, page T494
Periodic Test 4, Part II

Key to Symbols

Skills Objectives
I* – Introduced in this unit
I   – Introduced earlier in this level
M – Maintained from previous levels
T   – Tested in periodic and cumulative tests for this level

Reduced Student Pages
<u>underscore</u> – words that appear in the glossary
wavy line – words pretaught in the Teacher's Edition
           (these words also appear in the glossary)

Skills Lesson:
Drawing Conclusions

Pages 430–433

Objectives

		SKILLS CODE NUMBER
M, T	To draw conclusions based on given information and personal knowledge	3.4.1
I*	To identify information on which stated conclusions are based	3.6.8
I*, T	To identify faulty conclusions	3.6.1

If you wish to pretest the skills listed above, you may administer *Periodic Test 4, Part II, Form A. Periodic Test 4, Part II, Form B,* may be administered to posttest.

Introducing the Lesson

1. **a.** Borrow a student's copy of *Blazing Trails,* open it to page 281, and hold it up for the class to see. Ask students if they think the mercury line on the cartoon thermometer will be low or high.

b. Write the word *conclusion* on the board, and tell students that they have just drawn a conclusion about what the thermometer will read. Ask them why they drew the conclusion that the thermometer would show a low temperature. (The thermometer is caricatured as shivering and is dressed in a winter scarf, hat, mittens, and boots.)

Drawing Conclusions

What's happening in the picture? What are the children doing? How are they feeling?

If you said that the children are watching a funny movie, you **drew a conclusion.** How did you draw this conclusion? If you've ever been to a movie theater, you know it is dark and has rows of seats like those in the picture. What made you draw the conclusion that the movie is *funny?*

You have been drawing conclusions most of your life. For instance, suppose you see smoke. You draw a conclusion that there's a fire. Suppose you hear a horn honking outside your window. You draw the conclusion that the driver of a car or truck is trying to get someone's attention.

430

Using the Facts

When you read, you draw conclusions, too. You think about the facts that the author presents. You use these facts to draw a conclusion. Read the paragraph below. What conclusions can you draw from the facts given?

● Supposedly, around the year 2,000 B.C., some Phoenician sailors moored their ship off a beach in the Mediterranean Sea. The ship had been carrying blocks of soda. The sailors built a fire on the beach to cook their dinner. They needed something to hold their cooking pot over the fire. So they used a block of soda. The soda and the sand, heated by the fire, turned into a bubbly liquid. How surprised the sailors must have been when the liquid cooled and turned into a smooth sheet of glass!

431

c. Allow students to open their books to page 281. Point out that their conclusion was correct: The red mercury line is at about –15°C.

2. Have students turn to page 430, look at the picture, and read the three questions below it. Have them tell what's happening in the picture. (The children are watching a funny movie.)

3. Have students read the last two paragraphs on page 430.

Developing the Skill

Using the Facts

You can draw conclusions based on facts that the author presents.

1. Have students read the two paragraphs on page 431. (NOTE: Soda is a chemical compound containing sodium plus other elements.)

Which of the following conclusions can you draw from the facts given in the paragraph?

1. Glass can be made by heating sand and soda.
2. Glass can *only* be made by heating sand and soda.
3. The Phoenician sailors discovered glass by accident.

Sentence 1 is a good conclusion. The paragraph tells you that the soda and sand, heated by the fire, turned into a liquid. The end result was a smooth sheet of glass.

The paragraph does not give you enough information to draw the conclusion in sentence 2.

Why is sentence 3 a good conclusion? Did the Phoenician sailors set out to make glass? What words in the paragraph help you to know that their discovery was an accident?

Using Facts Plus Your Own Experience

Sometimes, to draw a conclusion, you need more than the facts that the author gives. You may also need to use your own experience or knowledge. What conclusion can you draw from the following sentence?

 When the woman heard the news, her face turned pale, her eyes filled with tears, and her smile turned to a frown.

The author did not actually say that the news was bad. But you can draw the conclusion that it was. In the sentence, there are three clues to help you: (1) the woman's face turned pale; (2) her eyes filled with tears; and (3) her smile turned to a frown. You know that people who behave in this way are usually upset. So you can *conclude* that the woman was upset because the news was bad.

432

Authors depend on the reader to draw conclusions. They expect the reader to use knowledge and reasoning to understand ideas that are not actually stated. In this way, authors expect the reader to "read between the lines."

Try This

Read the following paragraphs. Study the conclusions that follow each. Choose the one conclusion that can be drawn from each paragraph.

1. The farther a planet is from the sun, the colder it is. Pluto is the ninth planet from the sun. Neptune is the eighth planet from the sun.

   a. Neptune is colder than Pluto.
   b. Pluto is colder than Neptune.
   c. Neptune and Pluto are the same temperature.

2. An island is a body of land surrounded by water. Hawaii is made up of 8 major islands and 124 small islands. The largest of the 8 islands is called Hawaii.

   a. Hawaii is a state.
   b. Each of the Hawaiian Islands is surrounded by water.
   c. There is no map large enough to show all 132 of Hawaii's islands.

3. Jane sat between Rob and Carl. Carl sat between Jane and Leslie. Rob was on the end of the row, but Leslie was the next-to-the-last person in the row.

   a. Leslie sat between Carl and Rob.
   b. Only four people are in the row.
   c. Jane and Carl sat between Rob and Leslie.

433

Next, ask students to read the three conclusions on page 432. Have them identify the ones that could be drawn from the facts given in the paragraph. (sentences 1 and 3)

2. Ask students why conclusion 2 cannot be drawn. (The paragraph does not say that it is the only way to make glass.) Then have students read the three paragraphs that explain the answer.

Using Facts Plus Your Own Experience

Sometimes you need facts plus your own experience in order to draw a conclusion.

1. Have students read the paragraph below the heading on page 432. Ask students what conclusions they can draw from the sample sentence. (The news was bad.) Then have students read the paragraph at the bottom of the page.

2. Point out the expression "read between the lines" in the paragraph on page 433. Ask students if they've heard this expression before and what it means. (understand ideas that are not specifically stated)

Try This

Have students complete *Try This*.

Answers to *Try This*

1. b; 2. b; 3. c

Use *Reading Skills Workbook*, Lesson 34, pages 110–115. See *Providing for Individual Differences*, page T393, for additional practice.

Vocabulary Study:
Homophones
Pages 434–435

Objective

		SKILLS CODE NUMBER
M	To distinguish between homo-phones	3.5.1

Developing the Skill

1. Tell students that the *Vocabulary Study* they are about to read is about a woman called Doc Mirth. Write *dock* and *doc* on the board. Ask students which is a slang abbreviation for *doctor*. (*doc*) Ask if students remember what two words that sound alike but have different meanings and spellings are called. (*homophones*)

2. Have students read the *Vocabulary Study* and do the *Word Play* activity.

Answers to *Word Play*

skull: the skeleton of the head; *scull:* a long oar
principals: people who are heads of schools; *principles:* good moral standards
piers: landing places jutting out into the water; *peers:* persons of equal standing
Sentences will vary.

✔ Use *Reading Skills Workbook,* Lesson 35, page 116. See *Providing for Individual Differences,* page T393, for additional practice.

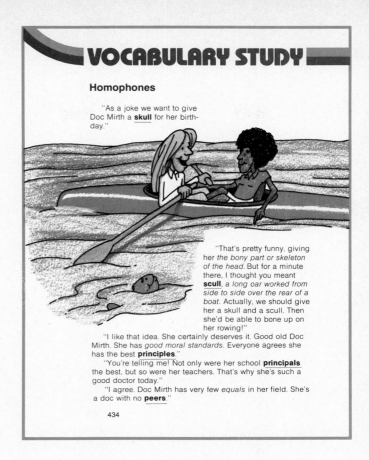

VOCABULARY STUDY

Homophones

"As a joke we want to give Doc Mirth a **skull** for her birth-day."

"That's pretty funny, giving her *the bony part or skeleton of the head.* But for a minute there, I thought you meant **scull**, *a long oar worked from side to side over the rear of a boat.* Actually, we should give her a skull and a scull. Then she'd be able to bone up on her rowing!"

"I like that idea. She certainly deserves it. Good old Doc Mirth. She has *good moral standards.* Everyone agrees she has the best **principles**."

"You're telling me! Not only were her school **principals** the best, but so were her teachers. That's why she's such a good doctor today."

"I agree. Doc Mirth has very few *equals* in her field. She's a doc with no **peers**."

434

"Hmmm. No **piers**, eh? No *landing places jutting out into the water*? Maybe we shouldn't get her that scull after all. She won't have any place to keep it."

"Sure she will! Why do you think we call her *Doc*?"

Word Play

Homophones are two words that sound the same but have dif-ferent meanings. Match the homophone in the column on the left with its definition in the column on the right. Then make a sentence using each homophone.

skull	good moral standards
scull	persons of equal standing
principals	the skeleton of the head
principles	landing places jutting out into the water
piers	a long oar
peers	people who are heads of schools

435

Reading Selection:
Curiosities from the Cliffs

Pages 436–443

Objectives

		SKILLS CODE NUMBER
I*	To identify information on which stated conclusions are based	3.6.8
M, T	To draw conclusions based on given information and personal knowledge	3.4.1
M	To identify the topic and stated main idea of a paragraph	3.3.8
M	To determine the correct sequence for a set of events	3.3.7.4
M	To use guide words in a dictionary	5.6.3

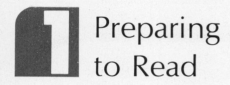 Preparing to Read

Summary

In the early 1800's, Mary Ann Anning and her father collected and sold "curiosities"—that is, fossils. In 1811, twelve-year-old Mary unearthed the bones of a huge ancient creature. Later it was named *icthyosaurus* ("fish-lizard") because it was thought to have been a seagoing reptile. Mary continued to make remarkable discoveries and made the study of fossils her life's work.

Background

This selection deals with two sciences: paleontology (the study of ancient animals by means of their remains) and geology (the study of the earth's history). Scientific study of the earth's history didn't begin until 1750, when Georges Le Clerc tried—but failed—to find a way to determine the earth's age. In the nineteenth century, James Hutton thought he would find clues by studying the earth's surface layers—an approach that

the scientists Charles Darwin and Lord Kelvin supported and that modern science still employs. Later, radioactive dating provided evidence that the earth is about 4.6 billion years old.

The following books will provide you with additional background information.

Cole, Jonathan R. *Fair Science: Women in the Scientific Community*. A systematic and extensive study of the position of women scientists in the American scientific community.

Fenton, Carroll Lane, and Mildred Adams Fenton. *The Fossil Book: A Record of Prehistoric Life*. A comprehensive survey—what fossils are, where they are found, and their relation to plants and animals. Illustrated, with bibliography, glossary, and index.

Developing Vocabulary and Concepts

fossil: the hardened, preserved remains of a plant or animal
assembled: put parts together into one piece
geology: the study of the history and structure of the earth's crust
exposing: uncovering
quarry: an open place from which stone is removed
fearsome: causing fear or alarm

1. **a.** Read the following sentences aloud, or write them on the board. If you read them aloud, write the underlined vocabulary on the board.

   When the workers finished putting together the separate bones, they had <u>assembled</u> an enormous skeleton.
   In her <u>geology</u> book, Mary found the names of the layers of the earth.
   Mary dug away the top layers of earth. In a while she was <u>exposing</u> the lower layers.
   Marble comes from a <u>quarry</u>, a large hole dug in the earth.
   Almost everyone thinks the tyrannosaurus was a <u>fearsome</u> dinosaur. The brontosaurus doesn't seem quite as frightening.

   b. Ask students to give the meaning of each vocabulary word. Remind them to use the context clues in the sentences to help them.

2. Explain that what is known today about dinosaurs and other prehistoric creatures comes from studying their remains. Ask students if they know what scientists call the preserved remains of prehistoric plants or animals. If students cannot supply the word *fossil*, write this word on the board.

Within the bordered facsimile of the student's page:

Think about the details in Mary Ann Anning's life. What conclusions can you draw from these details?

In the 1800's, Mary Ann Anning became famous for her . . .

Curiosities from the Cliffs

by Ruth Van Ness Blair

The cliffs near Lyme Regis in England were once part of the sea bottom. Millions of years ago, the ancestors of mollusks—soft creatures without backbones—died and drifted down to the ocean floor. Many of the ancient mollusks were much like the snails and clams of today. They had outer shells. Others, with inner shells, looked like squid.

After a long time, the mollusks were covered with mud that slowly hardened. In most cases, the minerals in their shells slowly became petrified—that is, they turned to stone.

436

These shells were the "curiosities" Mary Ann Anning and her father collected. Scientists called them *fossils*. Mr. Anning sold them in his carpentry shop in Lyme Regis.

A Good Hunting Day

One day in the early 1800's when Mary was about nine years old, she and her father set out for the cliffs to look for more curiosities. A storm the day before had broken great chunks of earth from the cliffs, exposing the rock underneath. The Annings began their search in this rock and in the mud at the cliffs' base.

Almost at once, Mary found a curiosity that pleased her. She began to tap at it.

"Be patient, lass," her father said. "Use your hammer and chisel with great care. Curiosities are easily broken."

As the Annings worked their way along the cliffs, Mary asked, "What are curiosities, Father? Where did they come from?"

"About three hundred years ago," Mary's father explained, "there was an artist named Leonardo da Vinci. He thought curiosities might be the remains of living creatures."

"Was he right, Father?"

---

3. Ask students if they have ever seen the skeleton of a dinosaur in a museum or a picture of one in a book. Point out that photos of dinosaurs do not exist. Ask students to explain why. (There were no people— and certainly no cameras—around during the age of the dinosaurs.)

 Use *Duplicating Masters 11,* page 54.

Setting Purposes

Skills

Have students read the skills note at the top of page 436. Tell them to look at the drawings in the selection. Ask them to draw a conclusion about what the "curiosities" were.

Content

Have students read the lead-in to the title. Ask them if they've ever discovered "curiosities," such as old bottles, parts of toys, shells, or tools.

2 Reading and Discussing

Have students read the selection. Most students will be able to complete it in one sitting.

NOTE: The questions that appear in the student's text at the end of the selection focus on comprehension of selection content and on application of the *Skills Lesson* to the selection. Answers to these questions begin on page T383.

"I do not know, lass. But it does seem it might be true."

"If this were a living creature," said Mary, "it must have died a long time ago."

Mr. Anning turned the shell over and over in his hand. This one, like most of the other curiosities they found, was a curled shell. The Annings called such shells "horns of ammon." They looked like rams with curled horns.

Mary smiled at her father. "Today was a good hunting day!"

Mary's Monster

Within a few years of that day, Mary's father died. Mary took over his business of selling curiosities. Her collection grew larger and more interesting. In it was a strange skull over two feet long. It had a long mouth, full of sharp teeth. Mary's brother, Joseph, found it, quite by accident, and gave it to her.

"I think the rest of it is somewhere in the cliff near Charmouth," he said.

Mary thought the skull was that of a crocodile. She put it away on a shelf with some other strange bones she had found.

One night after Mary went to bed, there was a terrible storm. The next morning, Mary got up early and, with her dog, Tray, set out for the cliffs.

It was a beautiful day in the year 1811. Mary was almost twelve years old. The sun shone as if there had been no storm. But the beach was littered with overturned fishing boats.

Mary noticed that the cliffs had lost great chunks of soil and rock which now lay in piles at their base. Very carefully, she began to search for curiosities.

As Mary peered at the cliffs, something unusual caught her eye. She saw what seemed to be bones lying in the rock in front of her.

She tapped the crumbling rock with her hammer. Chunks of it fell away. Mary tapped again. More bones appeared. She backed away for a better look. "What is it?" she thought.

With her chisel, Mary carefully lifted away pieces of the splintered rock. Underneath lay

438

other bones. Finally, a huge backbone, with large curving ribs, stood out as the rock fell away.

She walked along the cliff face a few feet, tapping as she went. At every tap, more bones appeared. Soon the skeleton of a strange, large animal began to take shape.

"But what can it be?" cried Mary. "Where is its head?" Then she remembered. The skull that

Joseph gave her—could that be it? She would find out as soon as she could remove this huge curiosity from the cliff.

As Mary stood there wondering how she could get it safely out of the cliff, her friend Henry ran down the beach toward her.

"What is that?" he yelled.

"I don't know."

"What are you going to do with it?"

Mary thought a bit. "I'll hire

439

the quarry workers," she said. "They can cut it out of the cliff."

"I'll fetch them," Henry cried as he darted away.

"Wait," said Mary. "Tell Joseph to bring the head."

"The head! What head?"

"Just tell him to bring it. He'll know."

It was almost an hour before Henry and Joseph came running back with the quarrymen. As soon as Joseph saw the bones in the cliff, he shouted, "You found it, Mary. You found the rest of it!" He ran to the skeleton and held the skull where the head should have been.

What a fearsome thing the creature became when its head was added. Now it was a monster! It was twice as long as Joseph was tall. It had short flippers or feet. Its sharp teeth looked ready to bite. And its enormous eye socket seemed to glare at those who looked at it.

It took most of the afternoon for the quarrymen, with the help of Joseph and Henry, to remove the monster from its resting place. Tray stood guard. Mary gave directions as the skeleton was carefully cut into pieces small enough to lift.

Mary would rather have kept her monster. It was the biggest

curiosity she had ever seen. But where could she put it? No shelf in her house would hold such a large skeleton. So when someone in the town offered her twenty-three pounds (then about $50.00) for it, she accepted.

A Very Old Monster, Indeed!

As soon as scientists heard of Mary's fantastic discovery, they flocked to Lyme Regis. Some had seen petrified bones of such a creature before, but no one had seen such bones assembled in an almost perfect skeleton.

One of the scientists who came to Lyme Regis was William Buckland.

440

"Miss Anning," he said, "would you care to show me where you found your mysterious creature?"

Mary was delighted to have such an important person interested in her discovery. So the two of them, with Tray in the lead, went tramping off to the Charmouth cliffs.

As they neared the cliffs, Tray raced ahead with excited yelps. He stopped suddenly at a pile of rocks.

"That's the place," said Mary. "Tray remembers it. I found the skeleton there—in the blue Lias [lī′əs] layer of the cliff."

Mary and her scientist friends could tell that the earth was in

layers. But at that time no one knew that the Lias layer was about 180 million years old. It was formed in an age when great dinosaurs roamed the earth. Flying reptiles and birdlike creatures had just begun to appear.

Other strange bones had been found in England. But no one knew for certain that they were dinosaur bones. Many people still thought they were the remains of dragons, elephants, or giants. So Mary and her friends had no way of knowing that her monster was a dinosaur.

Naming the Curiosities

When Mary was fourteen years old, a friend gave her a geology book. This book was a great help. Now Mary could study the layers of the earth with greater knowledge. She learned to call horns of ammon "ammonites." She began to recognize other forms of fossils, such as footprints in rocks.

Seven years passed and Mary's monster still had no name.

Finally, in 1818, George Koenig, of the British Museum, said: "Everyone agrees the creature is a seagoing reptile. It has a fishlike shape. So why not call it ichthyosaurus? The Greek word

441

ichthyo means 'fish.' Sauros means 'lizard.'

It must have been a good name, for it hasn't changed to this day.

More Monsters

In 1821, Mary discovered another monster. It, too, was a sea reptile. It had a short, wide body with four large paddles and a long, long neck. It looked like a turtle shell with a snake threaded through it. This monster was later called plesiosaurus—meaning "nearly like a lizard."

In 1828 Mary discovered the bones of a very different creature. It was a flying reptile. Because of the long finger that edged the wing, it was called pterodactyl—meaning "winged finger."

Mary kept on hunting for monsters. The creatures she discovered were <u>remarkable</u>. And so was Mary. No other woman of her day made the study and selling of fossils her full-time <u>profession</u>.

Many of Mary's monsters can now be seen at the British Museum of Natural History in London. There is also a picture of Mary with her old dog, Tray.

Today, scientists remember Mary with <u>affection</u> and great pride. For they knew that, in 1811, Mary and her monster had helped open the door to the far-distant and <u>fascinating</u> past of all living things.

442

Understanding What You've Read

1. What "curiosities" did Mary and her father collect? What is the scientific name for these "curiosities"?
2. Why were scientists so interested in Mary's discovery of the monster skeleton?
3. How old was the ichthyosaurus that Mary found?
4. Why is the discovery of fossils important?

Applying the Skills Lesson

Answer the following questions *yes* or *no*. Explain how you drew your conclusions.

1. Did Mary and the scientists of her time know that the ichthyosaurus was 180 million years old?
2. Could the scientists tell what color skin "Mary's Monster" had?
3. Have all the fossil bones from 180 million years ago been found by scientists?
4. In 1811, did scientists know everything there is about the distant past of living things?

443

Questions preceded by a bullet are additional questions and appear in the Teacher's Edition only. The other questions appear in the student's text after the selection.

Understanding What You've Read

1. *What "curiosities" did Mary and her father collect? What is the scientific name for these "curiosities"?* (petrified mollusk shells; fossils page 436) LITERAL <u>Recalling specific details</u>

● *What made Mary believe that the "curiosities" must have lived many years ago?* (They were buried deep in the cliffs and were like stone but easily broken. page 436) INFERENTIAL <u>Drawing conclusions</u>

2. *Why were scientists so interested in Mary's discovery of the monster skeleton?* (They had never before seen petrified bones preserved as a whole skeleton. page 440) INFERENTIAL <u>Identifying cause-and-effect relationships</u>

● *What made Mary and Joseph think that the skeleton they found was that of a "monster"?* (It was huge; it had short flippers or feet, sharp teeth, and a huge eye socket. page 440 Accept other details from the text that describe the ichthyosaurus.) LITERAL <u>Recalling stated information</u>

3. *How old was the ichthyosaurus that Mary found?* (about 180 million years old, an estimate based on the fact that it was found in the layer of the earth dating from that period page 441) INFERENTIAL <u>Drawing conclusions</u>

● *What other "monsters" did Mary discover?* (a plesiosaurus, a pterodactyl, and many other "monsters" page 442) LITERAL <u>Recalling specific details</u>

4. *Why is the discovery of fossils important?* (Accept answers that students can justify.) CRITICAL <u>Making judgments</u>

Applying the Skills Lesson

Answer the following questions yes or no. Explain how you drew your conclusions.
1. Did Mary and the scientists of her time know that the ichthyosaurus was 180 million years old?
2. Could the scientists tell what color skin "Mary's Monster" had?
3. Have all the fossil bones from 180 million years ago been found by scientists?
4. In 1811, did scientists know everything there is about the distant past of living things?
(1. No. They did not know that the blue Lias in which the ichthyosaurus was found was about 180 million years old.

2. No. Only the bones were preserved and found.
3. No. Students should reason that not every part of the earth has been explored and dug up. They may know that modern scientists are still discovering fossils.
4. No. Students should base their conclusions on the following facts in the selection: "Other strange bones had been found in England. But no one knew for certain that they were dinosaur bones." Scientists had not seen a fossilized plesiosaurus or a pterodactyl. The selection also states that "in 1811, Mary and her monster had helped open the door to the far-distant and fascinating past of all living things." In addition to facts from the selection, students might use personal knowledge about the present-day lack of knowledge about prehistory.   pages 441–42)
Drawing conclusions

- *Open your books to page 441. Find facts in the selection that support this conclusion: Scientists often give names from Greek words to different kinds of dinosaurs.* (The selection explains that the name *ichthyosaurus* comes from Greek words. The selection also explains that the name *plesiosaurus* comes from Greek words. You might point out that *pterodactyl* also comes from Greek words meaning "winged finger," although the selection does not mention this.   pages 441–442)   Identifying information on which stated conclusions may be based

- *Read again the third paragraph on page 438. Ammon is the name of an Egyptian god. Which sentence do you think describes Ammon's statues?*
1. Ammon's statues picture him as a man with a lion's mane around his head.
2. Ammon's statues picture him as having the body of a horse and the head of a man.
3. Ammon's statues picture him as a man with ram's horns.
4. Ammon's statues picture him as having the body of a bull and the head of a hunter.
(Answer: 3)   Drawing conclusions

 Use *Duplicating Masters 11*, page 55. See *Providing for Individual Differences*, page T393, for additional practice.

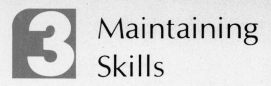
Comprehension Skills

Identifying the topic and stated main idea of a paragraph   Have students read paragraphs 5 and 6 on page 441. Ask them to state the topic and main idea of each paragraph. (In paragraph 5, the topic is *the Lias layer*; stated main idea is "But at that time no one knew that the Lias layer was about 180 million years old." In paragraph 6, the topic is *strange bones*; stated main idea is "But no one knew for certain that they were dinosaur bones.")

Determining the correct sequence for a set of events   Write the following statements on the board. Ask students to arrange the statements in the order in which they occurred in the selection. Some students may be able to complete the task without looking back at the selection. However, allow those who need help to look at the selection before completing the task.

1. Mary discovered the remains of an ichthyosaurus.
2. Joseph found a skull.
3. The dinosaur was named ichthyosaurus.
4. Mr. Anning died.
5. Mary discovered the remains of a plesiosaurus.

(Correct order: 4, 2, 1, 3, 5)

Study Skills

Using guide words in a dictionary   List on the board the following entry words and guide words. Have students tell whether each entry appears before, after, or on the page with the given guide words.

Entry Word	*Guide Words*	
fossil	forthwith–foundry	(on)
pterodactyl	provocation–psychoanalyze	(after)
ammonite	ammunition–amplifier	(before)
geology	geometry–get	(before)

 For additional resources and curriculum-related activities, see *Enrichment*, page T394.

Reading Selection:
Ben Franklin Changes the World
Pages 444–449

Objectives

		SKILLS CODE NUMBER
M, T	To draw conclusions based on given information and personal knowledge	3.4.1
I*	To identify information on which stated conclusions are based	3.6.8
I*, T	To identify faulty conclusions	3.6.1
M	To identify cause-and-effect relationships	3.3.3
M	To identify antecedents of pronouns	4.6.2

 **Preparing to Read**

Summary

In 1752, Ben Franklin made a scientific discovery that affected everyday life: He discovered that lightning was a huge discharge of electricity. This discovery, together with the knowledge he gained through his experiments with static electricity and Leyden jars, enabled him to make a device designed to protect buildings from lightning. He called this device a lightning rod. Because of the lightning rod, for the first time many people relied on the powers of science rather than on superstition to control the forces of nature.

Background

Benjamin Franklin (1706–1790) was a scientist, inventor, philosopher, statesman, legislator, publisher, and diplomat. He was the only person to sign all four of the major documents that marked the founding of the United States: the Declaration of Independence, the Treaty of Alliance with France, the Treaty of Peace with England, and the United States Constitution.

The following book will provide you with additional background information.

Franklin, Benjamin. *The Autobiography of Benjamin Franklin.* Covers the earlier parts of Franklin's life.

Developing Vocabulary and Concepts

superstition: the belief, without reason, that certain actions will cause good or bad luck
disaster: an event causing great distress or ruin
punctured: pierced
expands: becomes larger
inoculate: inject substances into the body in order to prevent disease
affected: had an effect on; acted on
device: something built for a special purpose
hurled: threw with great force
twine: a heavy string made of two or more thin strands twisted together
edition: a copy of a book, magazine, or newspaper printed at a particular time

1. a. Read the following sentences aloud, or write them on the board. If you read them aloud, write the underlined vocabulary on the board.

Lightning can cause <u>disaster</u>. It can kill people and damage homes.
The <u>punctured</u> balloon lost all its air through the hole.
A balloon <u>expands</u> when it is blown up.
The doctors began to <u>inoculate</u> people so that they would be protected from the disease.
The invention of the lightning rod <u>affected</u> everyday life. It helped people to feel they had some control over nature.
The lightning rod is a <u>device</u> that was built to allow an electrical charge to be released slowly.
Long ago, most people believed that a god <u>hurled</u>, or threw, lightning bolts down to earth.
Instead of plain string, Franklin used heavy string called <u>twine</u> to fly his kite.
A new copy, or <u>edition</u>, of the almanac appeared every year for several years.

b. Ask students to give the meaning of each vocabulary word. Remind them to use the context clues in the sentences to help them.

2. a. Ask students which of the following statements they believe:

Lightning is caused by evil imps as a punishment to humans.
Lightning is caused by a discharge of electricity in the air.

*It's 1753. Through his simple
idea for "catching" lightning
bolts . . .*

Ben Franklin Changes the World

by Isaac Asimov

444

Modern science began about the year 1600, but for nearly one hundred fifty years, it didn't have much effect on the lives of ordinary people. Scientists, for example, found out that the earth went around the sun instead of the sun circling the earth, but that didn't make the crops grow better or keep people healthy.

Then, in 1752, for the first time, a scientific discovery was made that affected everyday life. It saved people from a natural disaster. And it changed the world. From then on, many people turned to science rather than superstition to keep harm away.

You might have thought this would have happened in Europe, where, in those days, science was most advanced. It didn't. It happened in Philadelphia, in the American colonies.

In the early 1700's, many scientists in Europe were interested in electricity. They had found that if they rubbed rods of glass or sealing wax, the rods attracted lightweight objects such as feathers and small bits of wood. The rubbed objects were said to be "charged" with electricity.

Some devices could be charged with a great deal of electricity. One such device was studied at the University of Leyden in the Netherlands. It was called a "Leyden jar." If a Leyden jar is filled with a particularly large charge of electricity, that electricity might suddenly pour out the way air pours out of a punctured balloon. When electricity pours out, or "discharges," it heats the air, causing a little spark. The air expands with the heat. Then the air cools and contracts, all in a split second, making a crackling sound.

In the American colonies, a scientist named Benjamin Franklin was interested in electricity and experimented with Leyden jars, too. He discovered that if he attached a small metal rod to the Leyden jar, the discharge came off the end of the rod. If the Leyden jar was charged highly enough, and if something was brought near the rod, a spark would shoot off the rod. There would be a crackle.

The thinner the rod, the quicker the discharge would come. If a very thin rod with a sharp end was used, a charge couldn't be built up in the Leyden

445

---

b. Explain that a few hundred years ago, people knew very little about electricity. There was no electric power of any kind until the 1800's. People didn't know much about why things happened, so they used *superstitions* as explanations. Have students give examples of superstitions.

 Use *Duplicating Masters 11,*
page 56.

Setting Purposes

Skills

Have students read the skills note at the top of page 444. Remind them that good conclusions are based upon facts.

Content

Have students read the lead-in to the title. Ask them to name important things Benjamin Franklin did. (Answers might include: signed the Declaration of Independence; invented a stove, a printing press, bifocals; wrote almanacs; was ambassador to France.) Explain that it would be hard to choose which of Franklin's accomplishments had the greatest effect on the world. Tell them to read to find out why Isaac Asimov concludes that Franklin's invention of the lightning rod was so important.

2 Reading and Discussing

Have students read the selection. Most students will be able to complete it in one sitting. If you prefer, the selection may be read in two parts, breaking before the paragraph beginning "In June, 1752 . . ." on page 446.

NOTE: The questions that appear in the student's text at the end of the selection focus on comprehension of selection content and on application of the *Skills Lesson* to the selection. Answers to these questions begin on page T388.

jar at all. As fast as an electric charge was transferred into the jar, it leaked out of the sharp end of the rod. And it leaked out so quietly that there was no spark or crackle.

Some people said the spark and crackle were like tiny lightning and thunder. Franklin thought of it the other way. Could real lightning and thunder be a huge electric discharge from a cloud or from the ground?

This was an important new thought. Everyone was afraid of lightning. It struck without warning. It could set a house or a barn on fire. It could kill an animal or a human being. The ancients believed that lightning was a weapon used by the gods. The Greeks thought that Zeus hurled lightning bolts. And the Norse thought that Thor threw his fiery hammer. Now, if Franklin could find out that lightning was an electric discharge, it might be possible to understand lightning better—and fear it less.

In June, 1752, Franklin made a kite and tied a metal rod to it. He ran a large twine from the kite and placed a metal key at the bottom end. Then, during a thunderstorm, he went out to fly the

446

kite. He hoped to see if electricity would flow from the clouds down to the key. He didn't hold the twine with his hand for fear the electricity would flow into him and kill him. Instead, he tied a silk thread to the twine and held that, because electricity doesn't travel through silk.

When the kite vanished into a storm cloud, he carefully brought one knuckle near the key. The key discharged, producing a spark and a crackle, just as a Leyden jar would. And the spark felt the same on his knuckle as a spark from a Leyden jar.

Franklin had an uncharged Leyden jar with him. He brought it near the key. Electricity flowed from the clouds into the key and from the key into the Leyden jar. The Leyden jar was charged with electricity from the sky, but it behaved just as though the charge had been produced on Earth. Franklin thought this meant that lightning in the sky would follow the same rules that electricity on Earth would.

During a thunderstorm, the ground could become filled with a charge of electricity. If it did, there might eventually be a huge discharge—a lightning bolt. If the

discharge worked its way through a building, the heat could set the building on fire.

But Franklin had found that if a thin rod was attached to a Leyden jar, it wouldn't build up a charge. The electrical charge would leak out of the sharp end of the rod as quickly as it was built up. There would be no spark. Suppose the same thing was done to a building? Suppose a thin metal rod was placed on top of a building and connected to the ground? In a thunderstorm, the ground under the building would not build up a charge because the charge would leak quietly away through the thin rod. The building would therefore not be hit by lightning.

Franklin called such a device a "lightning rod." Every year, he published an almanac in which he printed information about all

447

sorts of things. In the 1753 edition, he described how to put a lightning rod on a house or a barn to keep it from being hit by lightning.

It was such a simple thing to do, and people were so afraid of lightning, that soon after the almanac came out, lightning rods began to be placed on houses all over the colonies. They were used in Europe, too.

And it wasn't a superstition. It worked! For the first time in history, one of the terrors of the world could be controlled—and it was science that did it. Never

mind spells and magic. Simply by understanding what lightning was and how electricity worked, people could take advantage of that knowledge and protect themselves.

Gradually people began to understand that science worked and superstition didn't. In 1767, for instance, the citizens of the Italian city of Brescia [bre'shä] stored a great deal of gunpowder in the cellar of a tall building that did not have a lightning rod. They thought the gunpowder was safe there because the building was a church. But the church was

struck by lightning during a storm and all the gunpowder exploded, destroying much of the city and killing three thousand people. This great tragedy ended any doubts about lightning rods.

From that time on, in many, many ways, science helped people where superstition had just fooled and confused them. In 1798, an English doctor learned how to inoculate against smallpox. That was the beginning of the victory of science over sickness. In the 1840's, doctors learned how to use certain chemicals to put patients to sleep during operations. That was the beginning of the victory of science over pain.

And these beginnings, which enabled science to help ordinary people in a practical way, owed much to a remarkable American colonial named Benjamin Franklin, who flew a kite in a thunderstorm and changed the world.

Understanding What You've Read

1. Why does Isaac Asimov say that the discovery of the lightning rod "changed the world"?
2. Why was it more likely in the 1700's that great scientific discoveries would be made in Europe rather than in America?
3. What is the difference between superstition and science?

Applying the Skills Lesson

Below are two conclusions you can draw using facts from the selection, plus your own knowledge. What facts from the selection support each conclusion?
1. In the early 1700's there were many more universities in Europe than there were in America.
2. Benjamin Franklin was interested in a great many things.

449

Questions preceded by a bullet are additional questions and appear in the Teacher's Edition only. The other questions appear in the student's text after the selection.

Understanding What You've Read

1. *Why does Isaac Asimov say that the discovery of the lightning rod "changed the world"?* (Isaac Asimov says that the lightning rod "changed the world" because, after its discovery, many people turned to science rather than to superstition to keep harm away.   page 445) INFERENTIAL   Identifying cause-and-effect relationships

• *In what year does the author say that modern science began to affect everyday life?* (1752   page 445) LITERAL   Identifying the author's conclusions

2. *Why was it more likely in the 1700's that great scientific discoveries would be made in Europe rather than in America?* (Science was more advanced there.   page 445) LITERAL   Identifying the author's conclusions

• *How did the ancients, people who lived thousands of years ago, explain lightning?* (They believed that lightning was a weapon used by the gods Zeus and Thor.   page 446) LITERAL   Recalling specific details

• *Why is lightning called a natural disaster?* (It is an event produced by nature that can cause great harm or ruin.) INFERENTIAL   Drawing conclusions

3. *What is the difference between superstition and science?* (Superstition involves the use of spells and magic in the belief that they will protect a person from danger. Science involves learning how something works through experiments, tests, and proof.) INFERENTIAL   Contrasting ideas

• *What event does the author say marked the beginning of the victory of science over sickness?* (inoculation against smallpox   page 449) LITERAL   Identifying the author's conclusions

Applying the Skills Lesson

Below are two conclusions you can draw using facts from the selection, plus your own knowledge. What facts from the selection support each conclusion?
1. In the early 1700's there were many more universities in Europe than there were in America.
2. Benjamin Franklin was interested in a great many things.
(Conclusion 1: The selection states that science was more advanced in Europe and that scientists at the University of Leyden in the Netherlands were experimenting with electricity. Students should use their own knowledge to infer that if science was advanced in Europe, institutions of higher learning were more numerous there than in the United States. Also, the building of America was just under way in the early 1700's. European countries had been in existence for some time. Conclusion 2: The author points out that Franklin was interested in electricity and wrote an almanac with "information about all sorts of things." Students should add to these facts their knowledge of Franklin as a statesman, city planner, and educator to support their conclusions. Page 224 shows Franklin setting up the first circulating library in the U.S.   pages 445 and 447)   Identifying information on which stated conclusions are based

• *What conclusions can you draw about the kind of man Ben Franklin was, based on the following facts and your own knowledge?*
Almost everyone was afraid of lightning in the 1700's. Lightning could kill an animal or a human being. Benjamin Franklin went out to fly his kite in a thunderstorm.
(Students will probably conclude that Franklin was an unusual and courageous man because he conducted the experiment despite the danger. Accept other reasonable conclusions.)   Drawing conclusions

- Which conclusions can you draw about science, based on the following facts?
  After Franklin's discovery in 1752, lightning rods began to be placed on houses all over the colonies.
  After smallpox vaccine was invented in 1798, people were protected from this disease.
  In the 1840's, doctors learned how to put people to sleep during operations.
  Conclusions:
  1. Modern science did not begin until the 1900's.
  2. Science began to affect everyday life in the 1700's.
  3. After 1752, no one was afraid of lightning.
  4. Before 1798, there was no way to prevent smallpox.
  (Conclusions 2 and 4 may be drawn.)   Drawing conclusions

- Explain why the following conclusions are not good ones.
  1. Through science we can learn the answers to everything.
  2. Today, nobody is superstitious.
  3. If Franklin had not invented the lightning rod, Thomas Edison could never have invented the electric light.
  (1. There are many things for which science does not have an answer or for which there are conflicting answers.
  2. Students probably know people who are superstitious.
  3. Natural lightning does not have much to do with the ability to produce electricity artificially. Also, Edison or someone else might have invented the electric light even if no one had invented the lightning rod.)   Identifying faulty conclusions

- Which of the following conclusions can be drawn about the people who stored gunpowder in Brescia, Italy?
  1. They believed in science.
  2. They believed in superstition more than they believed in science.
  3. They did not know about lightning rods.
  (Conclusion 2 may be drawn.)   Drawing conclusions

 Use *Duplicating Masters 11,* page 57. See *Providing for Individual Differences,* page T393, for additional practice.

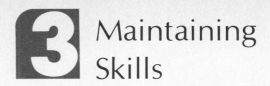

3 Maintaining Skills

Comprehension Skills

Identifying cause-and-effect relationships   Refer students to the following sentences in the fifth paragraph on page 445. For each sentence, ask the question or questions in italics.

If a Leyden jar is filled with a particularly large charge of electricity, that electricity might suddenly pour out the way air pours out of a punctured balloon.
What is the effect of filling a Leyden jar with a particularly large charge of electricity? (The electricity might suddenly pour out of the jar.)

When electricity pours out, or "discharges," it heats the air, causing a little spark.
What causes the air to be heated? (the electricity pouring out from the Leyden jar)
What is the effect of the air's being heated? (There is a little spark.)

The air expands with the heat. Then the air cools and contracts, all in a split second, making a crackling sound.
Which of the following events causes the sound?
1. The air expands with the heat.
2. The air cools and contracts.
3. Both 1 and 2 happen in a split second.
(Answer: 3)

Language Skills

Identifying antecedents of pronouns   Write the following sentences from the selection on the board, or read them aloud to students. If you read them aloud, write the underlined pronoun on the board. Ask students to identify what the pronoun refers to.

Modern science began about the year 1600, but for nearly one hundred fifty years, it didn't have much effect on the lives of ordinary people. (modern science)

Then, in 1752, for the first time, a scientific discovery was made that affected everyday life. It saved people from a natural disaster. (the scientific discovery)

In the 1840's, doctors learned how to use certain chemicals to put patients to sleep during operations. That was the beginning of the victory of science over pain. (using certain chemicals to put patients to sleep during operations)

★ For additional resources and curriculum-related activities, see *Enrichment,* page T394.

Textbook Study:
Drawing Conclusions
Pages 450–453

Objectives

		SKILLS CODE NUMBER
M, T	To draw conclusions based on given information and personal knowledge	3.4.1
I*, T	To identify faulty conclusions	3.6.1
I*	To identify information on which stated conclusions are based	3.6.8

Applying the Skill

Have students read the introduction and the two selections. You may wish to have them read the selections on their own and then do *Building Skills*. Or you may wish to direct students, using the following procedure.

TEXTBOOK STUDY

Drawing Conclusions

Textbook authors often give you information and then draw a conclusion from it. You have to ask: Is the conclusion supported by the information given? Sometimes an author gives information and allows the reader to draw a conclusion from it. You have to think about the evidence and weigh the ideas carefully in your mind.

As you read the following selections, refer to the side-notes. They point out information that will help you draw conclusions.

Drawing Conclusions in Science

450

Protecting the Young

In early spring, robins build their nests. A male robin and female robin collect twigs and mud and build a nest shaped like a bowl. (Other birds build other kinds of nests. The robin always builds a robin's nest, not an oriole's or an eagle's nest.) In the nest, the female robin lays from 4 to 6 blue eggs.

> **Can you draw the conclusion that some scientists can tell what kinds of birds live in an area from the kinds of empty nests the scientists find?**

While a robin's egg is developing, it is kept warm and protected by the parents. How different this is from what happens to a frog's eggs! Frogs do not protect their eggs. Their egg cells divide and develop in the water. Most of the eggs, and most of the young, are eaten by other animals.

> **Which egg has a better chance of hatching—a robin's egg or a frog's egg? Which facts support your conclusion?**

—*Concepts in Science:* Purple
Harcourt Brace Jovanovich

Building Skills

Which of the following conclusions is a good one? Which are *not* supported by the facts from the selection?

1. Robins' eggs are white.
2. It is not unusual for a robin to lay five eggs during one spring.
3. It takes longer for a robin's egg to hatch than it does for a frog's egg to hatch.

451

Drawing Conclusions in Health

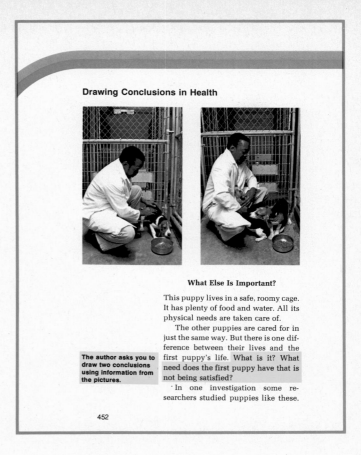

What Else Is Important?

This puppy lives in a safe, roomy cage. It has plenty of food and water. All its physical needs are taken care of.

The other puppies are cared for in just the same way. But there is one difference between their lives and the first puppy's life. What is it? What need does the first puppy have that is not being satisfied?

> **The author asks you to draw two conclusions using information from the pictures.**

In one investigation some researchers studied puppies like these.

452

Drawing Conclusions in Science

1. Have students read the first paragraph on page 451 and answer the question in the first sidenote. (yes)

2. Have students read the second paragraph and answer the questions in the second sidenote. (A robin's egg. "While a robin's egg is developing, it is kept warm and protected by the parents." "Frogs do not protect their eggs." "Most of the eggs, and most of the young, are eaten by other animals.")

3. Have students complete *Building Skills*.

Answers to *Building Skills*
Science Selection

1. Not a good conclusion. Selection says ". . . robin lays from 4 to 6 blue eggs." 2. Good conclusion. "In the nest, the female robin lays from 4 to 6 blue eggs." 3. Not a good conclusion. Selection does not say how long either kind of egg takes to hatch.

Drawing Conclusions in Health

1. Have students read the first two paragraphs and the sidenote on page 452. Ask a student to read aloud the sentences that ask for conclusions. ("What is it?" "What need does the first puppy have that is not being satisfied?")

They found that puppies that were kept by themselves grew up differently from others. The lonely puppies stayed away from other puppies. They didn't seem able to get along with them. And they didn't get along with people. What might be the reason for this?

— Balance in Your Life: Purple
Harcourt Brace Jovanovich

First the author gives facts. Then the author asks you to draw a conclusion from the facts.

Building Skills

Find the three sentences that ask you to draw conclusions. State the three conclusions you can draw.

453

2. Have students read the rest of the selection and the sidenote on page 453.

3. Have students complete *Building Skills.*

Answers to *Building Skills* Health Selection

Three sentences asking reader to draw conclusions are: "What is it?" "What need does the first puppy have that is not being satisfied?" and "What might be the reason for this?" Also accept the title "What Else Is Important?"

The three conclusions are: (1) The difference is that one puppy lives alone while the others live together; (2) The first puppy needs the companionship of other puppies, and that need is not being satisfied; (3) The reason might be that the puppies who were kept by themselves never learned to get along with other puppies or with people.

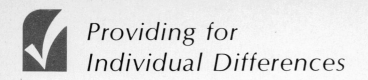# Providing for Individual Differences

Skills Lesson

Additional Practice

Worksheet 14, Teacher's Edition, page T494

Vocabulary Study

Additional Practice

Distinguishing between homophones   List the following words on the board. Have students find a homophone on page 434 or page 435 for each word listed.

butt (but)	sew (so)
ewe (you)	wee (we)
sighed (side)	fore (for)
eye (I)	or (oar)
two (to)	bee (be)
inn (in)	knot (not)
their (there)	know (no)

Reading Selection: Curiosities from the Cliffs

Additional Practice

Drawing conclusions   Read the following sentences to students, and ask them to conclude how each person is feeling.

When Janice heard she had won, nothing could remove the smile from her face. (happy)

The loud thunder caused the young child to hide and cry. (frightened)

Tony stared out the window, wishing his friends were around. (lonely)

Jackie's best friend was moving away. It was hard for her to say good-by. (sad)

Anne's friends all had permission to go to a movie. Anne's mother told her she could go, too. (happy)

Challenge Activity

Drawing conclusions   Have students turn to the selection on pages 175–178 in their books and answer the following questions.

From the facts in paragraph 2 on page 176, what can you conclude about how José Feliciano felt as a child? (Students may conclude that José felt lonely, since he was "cut off from much of the fun" that other children had.)

From the facts in the whole selection, what conclusions can you make about how easy it is to become a music star? (Students may conclude—from such incidents as José's making the rounds of coffee houses and the time it took him to develop a distinctive singing style—that it is not easy to become a star.)

Reading Selection: Ben Franklin Changes the World

Additional Practice

Drawing conclusions   Read aloud the pairs of sentences below, or write them on the board. Have students draw conclusions about the condition of the person based on the facts in the sentences and on their own experience.

The swimmer shivered and her teeth chattered. She hugged her body and jumped up and down to make her blood circulate faster. (cold)

Jason yawned and his eyes grew heavy. He leaned heavily on his desk and could hardly keep his head up. (sleepy)

Karen's stomach rumbled, and she couldn't stop thinking of food. When she saw the sandwich, she grabbed it and gulped it down. (hungry)

Challenge Activity

Drawing conclusions   Read the following description of an experiment. Then ask students to choose the one conclusion that can be drawn from those given.

Ethylene is a gas that makes fruits ripen quickly. Bananas that are green at the tip give off ethylene. Susannah put one small green tomato into a jar and covered it. Then she put another small green tomato and an unripe banana into another jar and covered it. She put both jars in a dark, warm place. The next day, the tomato in the jar *without* the banana was still green and hard. But the tomato in the jar *with* the banana was red and soft.

1. The tomato that didn't ripen was bad.
2. The ethylene from the ripening banana helped the tomato to ripen.
3. Ethylene ripens only some tomatoes but not others.

(Answer: 2)

Evaluation

Periodic Test 4, Part II, Form A or *Form B,* may be administered after this unit to test skills marked **T.** If you have pretested using *Form A,* administer *Form B.*

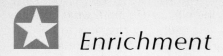

Enrichment

Curiosities from the Cliffs

Bibliography

The following books are about fossils and prehistoric animals.

Easy

Hussey, Lois J. *Collecting Small Fossils*. How to collect fossils, where to find them, the equipment needed, and what they look like.

Average

Martin, Alice Fitch. *Dinosaurs*. Dinosaurs—their evolution, why they disappeared, and the methods used to discover their remains.

Shuttlesworth, Dorothy E. *To Find a Dinosaur*. Important dinosaur discoveries, early expeditions, and information on amateur fossil hunting.

Challenging

Kalina, Sigmund. *How to Make a Dinosaur*. Three dinosaurs to make from papier-mâché—stegosaurus, brontosaurus, and tyrannosaurus rex.

Kirk, Ruth. *The Oldest Man in America: An Adventure in Archaeology*. The story of a dig in southwest Washington that turned up a skull fragment of a man 10,000 years old.

Films and Filmstrips

NOTE: For more information, see *Resource Center*.

Selection content

Harcourt Brace Jovanovich. *Concepts in Science Sound Filmstrips*. "The Wandering Fossils." A probe into the geologic cycle.

Visual Education Consultants. "A Modern Mastodon Hunt." The methods used by scientists in discovering and classifying bones and fossils.

Curriculum Coordination

Language Arts

1. Have students begin a "diary of curiosities" based on items they see or discover in their neighborhoods or en route to and from school. Their descriptions should include the objects' dimensions, shapes, and ages and information on when and where they were observed or found.

2. Remind students that *saurus* comes from the Greek, meaning "lizard." Have students use a dictionary that identifies the meanings of Greek prefixes in order to determine the meanings of the names of dinosaurs.

Science

1. With the help of an archaeologist or a science teacher, have students explore what prehistoric life might have existed in your area. If there have been archaeological finds in your community, arrange a field trip to one of the sites.

2. Arrange to take your class to a natural history museum.

3. Encourage students to make their own natural history museum in the classroom.

4. Coordinate a science lesson on the layers of the earth with this selection.

Career Education

1. Students might investigate the life and work of famous anthropologists or archaeologists, such as Margaret Mead, Richard Leakey, Mary and Louis Leakey, Ruth Benedict, and Kamoya Kimeu, the African fossil hunter.

2. Invite an amateur or professional archaeologist to discuss his or her training and work.

Ben Franklin Changes the World

Bibliography

The following books are about Benjamin Franklin or electricity.

Average

Asimov, Isaac. *How Did We Find Out About Electricity?* The discovery and development of electricity.

Corbett, Scott. *What Makes a Light Go On?* The nature of electricity and how different types of electricity work.

Daugherty, Charles M. *Benjamin Franklin*. Franklin's scientific research and practical inventions.

Epstein, Sam, and Beryl Epstein. *The First Book of Electricity*. The everyday uses of electricity in toasters, television, etc.

Challenging

Asimov, Isaac. *The Kite That Won the Revolution*. Benjamin Franklin's electrical research and his achievements.

NOTE: For more information, see *Resource Center.*

Selection Content

Troll Assocs. "Wonders of Science: Flash, Crash, and Glow, Electricity in a Bulb." Concepts of electricity.

Visual Education Consultants. "A Telephone Story." A history of the invention of the telephone.

Curriculum Coordination

Language Arts

1. Have students use an encyclopedia or a nonfiction library book to obtain information about superstitions. Then have them write a story about a day in the life of a fictional superstitious person.

2. Have students write a poem in which they describe the sounds and sights of a thunderstorm. They should include descriptions of wind, clouds, temperature, thunder, and lightning.

Science

1. Follow up "Ben Franklin Changes the World" with a science lesson on electricity and static electricity.

2. Have a class discussion about the importance of electricity in our modern world. Discuss what it would be like in a world without electricity.

Social Studies

1. Interested students might prepare a report on other aspects of Ben Franklin's life and share it with the class.

2. Students might investigate scientific explorations and discoveries in Europe during the 1700's (the "Age of Enlightenment") and share what they learn with the class.

Health Education

Have a discussion about the safety procedures to follow during an electrical storm. You may wish to invite a science teacher to talk about the procedures.

Art

Have students prepare a poster illustrating how Ben Franklin changed the world through his inventions, writing, and statesmanship.

Career Education

Invite a civil engineer or an electrician to describe his or her occupation.

Contents

Additional Materials

Reading Skills Workbook: Lessons 36–37, pages 117–122
Duplicating Masters 11: pages 58–61
Worksheet 15: Teacher's Edition, page T495
Periodic Test 4, Part III

Key to Symbols

Skills Objectives
I* — Introduced in this unit
I — Introduced earlier in this level
M — Maintained from previous levels
T — Tested in periodic and cumulative tests for this level

Reduced Student Pages
underscore — words that appear in the glossary
wavy line — words pretaught in the Teacher's Edition
                 (these words also appear in the glossary)

Skills Lesson:
Generalizing
Pages 454–457

Objectives

		SKILLS CODE NUMBER
I*, T	To distinguish valid from faulty generalizations	3.6.1
I*, T	To make generalizations based on given information	3.4.3
I*, T	To identify qualifying words in generalizations	3.6.1

If you wish to pretest the skills listed above, you may administer *Periodic Test 4, Part III, Form A. Periodic Test 4, Part III, Form B,* may be administered to post-test.

Introducing the Lesson

1. **a.** Read the following sentences aloud, or write them on the board.

Carol likes baseball.
Carol likes to swim.
Carol likes to jog every day.
Carol plays tennis at least once a week.

b. Ask students to give you a general statement about Carol that sums up the four sentences. (Sample answer: Carol likes sports.) Explain that another term for a general statement is *generalization* and that a generalization is a broad statement based on several facts.

Generalizing

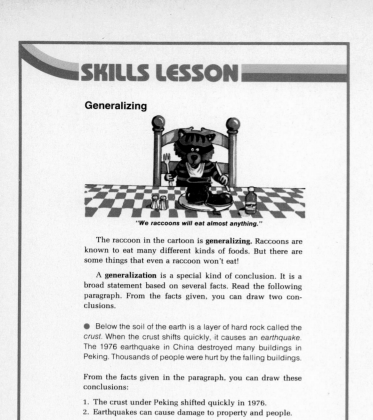

"We raccoons will eat almost anything."

The raccoon in the cartoon is **generalizing**. Raccoons are known to eat many different kinds of foods. But there are some things that even a raccoon won't eat!

A **generalization** is a special kind of conclusion. It is a broad statement based on several facts. Read the following paragraph. From the facts given, you can draw two conclusions.

● Below the soil of the earth is a layer of hard rock called the *crust*. When the crust shifts quickly, it causes an *earthquake*. The 1976 earthquake in China destroyed many buildings in Peking. Thousands of people were hurt by the falling buildings.

From the facts given in the paragraph, you can draw these conclusions:

1. The crust under Peking shifted quickly in 1976.
2. Earthquakes can cause damage to property and people.

454

Notice that sentence 2 is more than a conclusion. It is a generalization. It is a broad, or general, statement about earthquakes.

Using the Facts

Generalizing is "making a broad statement *based on several facts.*" A valid generalization should cover more than one or two specific cases.

Read the following paragraph. What's wrong with the generalization in the last sentence?

● My first grade teacher, Mrs. Zimmerman, had gray hair. My cousin's first grade teacher, Mrs. Carr, also had gray hair. All first grade teachers have gray hair.

The generalization in the last sentence is not valid. It is based on only two cases. Is it possible that some first grade teachers do not have gray hair?

455

---

2. **a.** You may want to give students a second example to reinforce the concept.

Mark listens to classical music on the radio.
Mark owns many record albums.
Mark plays the piano and the guitar.
Mark reads books about famous composers.

b. Ask students to give you a broad statement or generalization based on the facts about Mark. (Sample answers: Mark is very interested in music; Mark enjoys music a great deal.)

Developing the Skill

A generalization is a special kind of conclusion. It is a broad statement based on several facts.

1. Have students read page 454. Ask why sentence 2 is a generalization. (It makes a broad statement about earthquakes.)

2. Write the word *exception* on the board. Explain that there are usually one or more exceptions to any generalization. Ask if all earthquakes cause damage.

Explain that those that do not cause any damage are exceptions to the generalization.

Using the Facts

A valid generalization should cover more than one or two specific cases.

1. Have students read the three paragraphs above the illustration on page 455. Ask students what *valid* means. (true or correct)

2. **a.** Ask whether the generalization about first grade teachers is valid and why it is or is not. (It is not valid because it is based on only two cases.)

b. Now have students read the last paragraph on page 455 and answer the question "Is it possible that some first grade teachers do not have gray hair?" Allow them to give specific examples to support their answers.

Using Qualifying Words

Read the following paragraph.

● Three First Ladies of the United States—Elizabeth Kartwright Monroe, Eleanor Roosevelt, and Jacqueline Kennedy Onassis—were born in New York State. The famous opera singers Beverly Sills and Roberta Peters were also born in New York State. Some famous actors born in New York State are Kirk Douglas, Lauren Bacall, Peter Falk, and Lucille Ball.

Which of the following generalizations can you make based on the facts from the paragraph?

1. All famous people are born in New York State.
2. Some famous people are born in New York State.
3. Most famous people are born in New York State.

456

Sentences 1 and 3 are not valid generalizations based on facts from the paragraph. The paragraph does not tell you about *all* famous people. It doesn't even tell you about *most* famous people. It tells you about only *some* famous people. So only sentence 2 in the list on page 456 is a *valid* generalization based on facts from the paragraph.

Words like *all, some, many, most, several, none,* and *a few* are **qualifying words** that are often used in generalizations. When you make a generalization, be careful to think about the qualifying words you use. If the facts deal with *all* cases, you may use words such as *all, every, none,* or *always.* If the facts do *not* deal with all cases, use *most, many, some, several,* or another qualifying word.

Try This

Read the following paragraph and the generalizations that follow it. Choose the one generalization that can be made based on the facts from the paragraph.

Albert Einstein was a poor student when he was young. He grew up to be an important scientist. Wilma Rudolph was crippled as a child. She exercised and later became a champion athlete. Helen Keller became blind, deaf, and mute when she was about nineteen months old. She grew up to be an author and educator.

1. Everyone who has a problem as a child grows up to be successful.
2. Some people who have problems in their childhoods can grow up to be successful.
3. No one who has problems as a child can grow up to be successful.

457

Using Qualifying Words

When you make a generalization, be careful to choose the appropriate qualifying word.

1. Have students read page 456. Ask them to explain which generalization is valid (2) and which are not valid (1 and 3). Then have students read the two explanatory paragraphs on page 457.

2. Remind students of the invalid generalization "All first grade teachers have gray hair." Then ask them to change the sentence to a valid statement by substituting another qualifying word for the word *all.* (Accept changed sentences with the qualifying word *some.*) Ask students to explain why substituting *most* or *a few* would not make the statement valid. (*Most* probably implies too many, while *a few* perhaps implies too few. *Some* is nonspecific enough to make the generalization valid.)

Try This

Have students complete *Try This.*

Answer to *Try This*

2. Some people who have problems in their childhoods can grow up to be successful.

 Use *Reading Skills Workbook,* Lesson 36, pages 117–121. See *Providing for Individual Differences,* page T413, for additional practice.

Vocabulary Study:
Suffixes
Pages 458–459

Objective

M   To identify word parts: root words and suffixes

SKILLS CODE NUMBER

4.1

Developing the Skill

1. Tell students that the *Vocabulary Study* they are about to read is about a chef named Luigi Macaroni. Tell them to look for words that contain suffixes as they read.

2. Have students read the *Vocabulary Study* and do the *Word Play* activities.

Answers to *Word Play*

1. **a.** like a balloon; **b.** the result of being developed; **c.** like a living thing; **d.** the result of being measured.
2. Sentences will vary.

 Use *Reading Skills Workbook*, Lesson 37, page 122. See *Providing for Individual Differences*, page T413, for additional practice.

VOCABULARY STUDY

Suffixes

"Stop the cooking contest!"

"Who are you?"

"I am the famous Luigi Macaroni, author of the book, *How to Cook Spaghetti and Play Tennis at the Same Time.*"

"Are you a tennis pro?"

"No! I'm a chef. I also wrote the screenplay for the movie, *2001 Tricks with Spaghetti.* Tell me, what is that awful **pastelike** mess you're making?"

"You mean this white stuff that 'looks like paste'? It's a spaghetti patty."

"Leaping linguini! Spaghetti is **threadlike**. It's supposed to 'look like threads,' not a big round blob. How do you expect to wind that around a fork?"

"I don't, and that's the beauty of it. You see, the tomato sauce is inside. It's an all-in-one dish. It's a real **improvement** on the original design, don't you think?"

"You call that the 'result of being improved'? Bah! It's the dumbest thing I've ever seen! You never got that stupid recipe from my book!"

"No. That's true. I didn't. I saw the movie."

458

Word Play

1. Give the meaning of each word in boldface below.

    a. The spaghetti patty looked very **balloonlike**.
    b. This land is a good spot for a housing **development**.
    c. My goodness! Those plastic figures look so **lifelike**.
    d. Sal took a **measurement** of the room.

2. In the story, find other words with suffixes. Make up sentences using the words you find.

459

Reading Selection:
Little Things You Use Every Day
Pages 460–466

Objectives

		SKILLS CODE NUMBER
I*, T	To distinguish valid from faulty generalizations	3.6.1
I*, T	To identify qualifying words in generalizations	3.6.1
M	To identify the number of syllables in a word	2.6
M	To compare information obtained from graphic aids to textual information	5.4.7

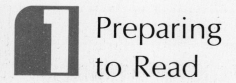

Preparing to Read

Summary

This selection presents the stories behind several small inventions: the safety pin, the ice-cream cone, the alarm clock, the zipper, and pencils with erasers. The reader is encouraged to speculate on the stories behind other inventions—were they invented by accident, to fill a personal need, or as a way to make money?

Background

A patent is granted by the U.S. Patent and Trademark Office to any inventor of a process, machine, or other invention that is useful, usable, and original. A patent protects a new item for seventeen years against its manufacture, use, or sale by anyone other than the inventor. A fee is charged for a patent of any new invention. In addition, inventors usually hire patent attorneys to conduct a search of Patent Office files to be sure the invention is not already patented. A detailed description of the invention must accompany any application for a patent. Applications can be obtained from the U.S. Government Printing Office, Washington, DC 20402.

The following book will provide you with additional background information on inventions.

Meyer, Jerome S. *World Book of Great Inventions.* The history of great inventions, from the earliest versions of the wheel and lever to the most sophisticated of modern inventions. Illustrated, with many diagrams and an index.

Developing Vocabulary and Concepts

patent: a government document giving an inventor the sole right to make and sell a new invention or to use a new process for a certain number of years
amusing: causing enjoyment, fun, and laughter
praised: gave a high opinion of something or showed approval

1. **a.** Read the following sentences aloud, or write them on the board. If you read them aloud, write the underlined vocabulary on the board.

   It's amusing to read about how some things were invented. It's even more fun to try to invent something yourself.
   The teacher praised the students for their invention. She said that it was a brilliant idea to make an automatic chalkboard eraser.

   b. Ask students to give the meaning of each vocabulary word. Remind them to use the context clues in the sentences to help them.

2. Ask students to imagine that they had invented something that they wanted to make and sell. Have them imagine that someone found out about their invention and decided to make and sell the very same thing. What might they do? Explain that inventors are able to protect their ideas by getting a patent from the government. Write the word *patent* on the board. Point out that a patent protects the inventor from having anyone else make or sell the invention or process for a certain number of years.

3. Have students conduct a "small inventions" hunt. For a few minutes, have students explore their desks, pockets, notebooks, or book bags for small items such as a wrist watch, pencil with an eraser, zipper, key chain, bobby pin, or ballpoint pen. Point out that these items are *inventions*—someone created them.

 Use *Duplicating Masters 11,* page 58.

Setting Purposes

Skills

Have students read the skills note at the top of page 460. Remind students that generalizations are broad statements based on facts. Ask them to name some exceptions to the generalization "There's a simple idea behind each of the 'Little Things You Use Every Day.' "

Content

Tell students to consider how items from their "hunt" might have been invented. What needs do these items serve? What might have been used before the invention of these items? Tell students that the selection they are going to read will give them the story behind a few of the everyday things they use. Have students read the lead-in to the title.

2 Reading and Discussing

Have students read the selection. Most students will be able to complete it in one sitting. If you prefer, the selection may be read in two parts, breaking before the first paragraph on page 464.

NOTE: The questions that appear in the student's text at the end of the selection focus on comprehension of selection content and on application of the *Skills Lesson* to the selection. Answers to these questions begin on page T403.

The sentence that leads into the title states a generalization. What other generalizations can you make, based on the facts given in the selection?

There's a simple idea behind each of the . . .

460

Little Things You Use Every Day

by Kathryn Hitte

One day more than a hundred years ago, Mr. Walter Hunt sat down to think. He needed fifteen dollars badly. If he could come up with a good idea for a new invention, he was sure he could sell it. He often did. Well, then! What kind of invention would people find useful, really useful, and want to buy? How about— how about a pin with a guard to cover the point?

Hunt made a drawing and then a sample. It worked. It was safer to use than the common straight pin. Users would not be so likely to pin *themselves!* So the safety pin was born, and Hunt sold his idea for $400.

Walter Hunt got a bright idea when he needed one. Once another man had a bright idea when a neighbor needed one. And as a result he gave us the ice-cream cone.

461

It happened in 1904, at The World's Fair in St. Louis, Missouri. An ice-cream salesman was doing a big business—so big that he kept running out of dishes. A neighboring dealer had a helpful thought. Why not make a dish that could be eaten? Why not roll a waffle into a cone shape? We've had ice-cream cones ever since.

They're "little" inventions, the cone and the safety pin. They haven't really changed the world, as the greatest inventions have. But we're used to them and we like them. We wouldn't want to do without them—or without a lot of other "little things," either.

We don't know much, as a rule, about the invention of everyday things. Often we have only a jumble of facts about their history. Some of these are odd facts, and rather useless. But they can be fun. Like these:

The first alarm clock in America would ring only at four o'clock. It couldn't be set for any other time. The inventor, Levi Hutchins, made it that way because he needed to wake up each morning at four. He wasn't inventing a clock for the world— just for himself. It took many improvements by other inventors to give us the alarm clocks we have today.

The first zippers were called "hookless fastenings." They were used only for shoes. Whitcomb L. Judson had invented the zipper in 1893 when people wore high shoes with many buttons. The new fastener saved a lot of time and trouble. Later the zipper was used on many things.

Imagine going into a field of grain to get a hollow stem to use as a drinking straw: For hundreds of years, the only straws people had were grain straws. Paper straws were invented about 1885. Cleaner and stronger than grain straws, they were a big success. Today, of course, most drinking straws are made of plastic.

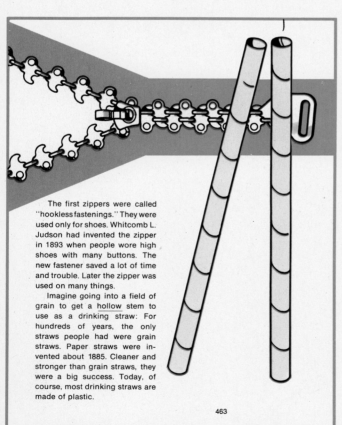

463

The history of many other "little things" can only be guessed at. What brought the inventions about? Accidents? Bright ideas at the right time? Certain needs? Take the first pencil with its own eraser, for instance. It was invented in 1858 by Hyman L. Lipman. What pushed him to do it? Was he always losing erasers?

It's fun to imagine the stories behind many of these little inventions. But it would take a lot of hunting to find out all the facts. And even a lifetime of hunting might not give us facts about who invented many common things we use each day.

We do know one amazing fact, though. More than three million inventions have been created in the United States alone. Probably at least half of these are everyday things. Surely thousands more must have been invented elsewhere.

Figures like these are hard for some people to believe. An amusing story is told about a man in the United States Patent Office. That's a place that deals every day with new inventions. A long time ago, the Director of the Patent Office wanted to give up his job. "Everything seems to have been done," he said. He knew of about 10,000 inventions. What would he think of the millions we know of today?

"If you can build a better mousetrap," a wise person once said, "the world will make a beaten path to your door." It's

464

generally true. People do want new things, better things, more useful things. But somehow the maker of the "mousetrap" is often forgotten. The work doesn't get praised in the history books. And that seems a shame.

So how about a little praise right now? Three cheers for the paper clip! Three cheers for thumbtacks, and zippers, and snaps! And for easy-open bottle caps! Shoelaces, and the helpful little tips on the ends. Those tiny gummed circles for mending notebook-paper holes. Potato peelers. Bobby pins. Safety matches, envelopes, pocket knives . . . and more, more, more! For all the "better mousetraps" of the world—hurrah! Three cheers for our *wonderful* little ordinary, everyday things!

465

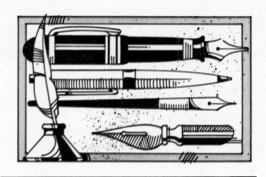

Understanding What You've Read

1. Why did Walter Hunt invent the safety pin?
2. The selection gives examples of two reasons why things are invented. Find these reasons.
3. What is the Patent Office?
4. What was the author's purpose in writing this selection—to inform, entertain, or both?

Applying the Skills Lesson

Which of the following generalizations are valid?

1. Some inventions are the results of "lucky accidents."
2. Inventions always need improvements.
3. All inventors become rich.
4. Many inventions are born from need.

466

Questions preceded by a bullet are additional questions and appear in the Teacher's Edition only. The other questions appear in the student's text after the selection.

Understanding What You've Read

1. *Why did Walter Hunt invent the safety pin?* (He needed money.   page 461) LITERAL   Identifying cause-and-effect relationships

• *What steps did Hunt take in producing his new invention?* (First he had the idea, then he made a drawing, then he made a sample. Finally, he sold the idea for $400.   page 461) LITERAL   Determining the correct sequence for a set of events

2. *The selection gives examples of two reasons why things are invented. Find these reasons.* (The inventor is filling a need—ice-cream cone, alarm clock. The inventor sets out to make money—safety pin.) INFERENTIAL   Drawing conclusions

• *How are the alarm clocks we use today different from the one invented by Levi Hutchins?* (Hutchins's alarm clock could ring only at four o'clock. Today's alarm clocks can be set for any time.   page 462) INFERENTIAL   Identifying contrasts

• *Which of the following inventions mentioned in the selection existed in 1900?*
1. *plastic drinking straws*
2. *zippers on shoes*
3. *pencils with built-in erasers*
(Answers: 2 and 3) INFERENTIAL   Drawing conclusions

3. *What is the Patent Office?* (the place that deals with new inventions   page 464) LITERAL   Recalling specific details

• *What do you think of the opinion of the Director of the Patent Office who wanted to give up his job because "everything seems to have been done"? Was his opinion correct? Give your reasons.* (Students will probably judge that his opinion was not sound. People will always want newer and better things. To meet this need, inventors will always come up with new ideas.) CRITICAL   Drawing conclusions

• *About how many inventions have been created in the United States, according to the author?* (over three million   page 464) LITERAL   Recalling specific details

4. *What was the author's purpose in writing this selection—to inform, entertain, or both?* (both) CRITICAL   Identifying an author's purpose

Applying the Skills Lesson

Which of the following generalizations are valid?
1. Some inventions are the results of "lucky accidents."
2. Inventions always need improvements.
3. All inventors become rich.
4. Many inventions are born from need.
(Generalizations 1 and 4 are valid.)   Distinguishing valid from faulty generalizations

- *Identify the qualifying words in the four generalizations in Applying the Skills Lesson.* (1. Some; 2. always; 3. All; 4. Many)   Identifying qualifying words in generalizations

- *Reword generalizations 2 and 3 on page 466 so that they state valid generalizations.* (2. Inventions sometimes need improvements, or Some inventions need improvements. 3. Some inventors become rich.)   Making generalizations

- *Which word in each sentence qualifies the generalization?*
  1. Many inventions are "little" inventions.
  2. The history of most inventions is interesting.
  3. Every invention that helps us should be appreciated.
  (1. Many; 2. most; 3. Every, that helps us)   Identifying qualifying words in generalizations

- *Which of the following generalizations are faulty?*
  1. New inventions always sell.
  2. Many inventions help to make our life easier.
  3. We do not know the history of some inventions.
  4. All inventions are useful.
  (Generalizations 1 and 4 are faulty.)   Distinguishing valid from faulty generalizations

 Use *Duplicating Masters 11*, page 59. See *Providing for Individual Differences*, page T413, for additional practice.

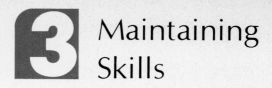

3 Maintaining Skills

Word Service/Decoding

Identifying the number of syllables in a word
Write the following words from the selection on the board. Have students complete the chart by identifying the number of vowel letters in each word, the number of vowel sounds in each word, and the number of syllables in each word. You may wish to have students check their work in a dictionary.

	Vowel Letters	Vowel Sounds	Syllables
invention	4 (i, e, i, o)	3	3
improvements	4 (i, o, e, e)	3	3
fastenings	3 (a, e, i)	3	3
eraser	3 (e, a, e)	3	3
ordinary	4 (o, i, a, y)	4	4

Study Skills

Comparing information from graphic aids to textual information   Review the usefulness of pictures as graphic aids that add information to the text. Have students turn to the picture of Walter Hunt on page 460. Read the following sentences aloud, and ask students to tell whether the information is given in the picture only, the text only, or in both the text and the picture.

The first safety pin and the safety pin we use today are similar to each other in appearance. (picture only)
Walter Hunt sold his idea for the safety pin for $400. (text only)
Hunt made a drawing and a sample of the safety pin. (text and picture)
The safety pin was safer to use than the common straight pin. (Accept either text only or text and picture.)

Follow the same procedure for the picture of the alarm clock on page 462.

The clock Levi Hutchins made had a round face with a bell on top. (picture only)
The alarm clock would ring only at four o'clock. (Text only. Point out that although the picture shows the clock's hands at four, you can't tell from the picture that it can't ring at any other time.)
It took many improvements by other inventors to give us the alarm clocks we have today. (text only)

 For additional resources and curriculum-related activities, see *Enrichment*, page T415.

Reading Selection:
Gifts from China

Pages 467–471

Objectives

		SKILLS CODE NUMBER
I*, T	To make generalizations based on given information	3.4.3
I*, T	To distinguish valid from faulty generalizations	3.6.1
M	To determine the correct sequence for a set of events	3.3.7.4
M	To identify the topic and stated main idea of a paragraph	3.3.8
M	To use details to determine the unstated main idea of a paragraph	3.3.1; 3.4.7

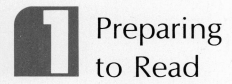

Preparing to Read

Summary

The papermaking process was developed in China in the year A.D. 105. It gave people in China something to write on that was cheaper than silk and lighter than wood. The Chinese also developed a way to print on paper by using movable clay type. Papermaking and printing remained Chinese secrets for many years before the processes were smuggled to other countries.

Background

The demand for paper increased with Johann Gutenberg's invention of the printing press about 1450. Gutenberg's press used movable type that was set in place by hand. This process continued for several centuries until a mechanical means of setting type was invented in the late nineteenth century. Today, type is set very rapidly by various processes. You might wish to point out to students that the text in *Blazing Trails* was set with typesetting machines that employ computers and cameras.

NOTE: The selection mentions that the Chinese alphabet is made up of more than 40,000 different symbols. From this students might correctly conclude that it is harder to learn to write Chinese than it is to write our language that is based on a 26-character alphabet. For this reason, in the late 1970's, in hopes of increasing literacy among its people, the People's Republic of China instituted in its schools a writing system in which symbols stand for sounds, as in the Roman alphabet that English uses.

The following books will provide you with additional background information.

Chappell, Warren. *A Short History of the Printed Word.* The art and process of printing, from the earliest times to twentieth-century technology. Illustrated.

Jennette, Sean. *Pioneers in Printing.* Biographies of Gutenberg, Caxton, Baskerville, and others.

Developing Vocabulary and Concepts

West: the Western Hemisphere and Europe
scholar: a person who has learned a great deal through study
original: the first form of a piece of writing
smuggle: secretly bring something in or take something out of a place
tiresome: boring and time-consuming
process: a way of making or doing something
eventually: in time; after a while; in the end
clumsy: not smooth or easy; awkward
impression: a mark or stamp made by pressing

1. a. Read the following sentences aloud, or write them on the board. If you read them aloud, write the underlined vocabulary on the board.

   The lack of paper did not keep <u>scholars</u> from learning about the world.

   First a writer would write an <u>original</u> piece. Then artists would carefully copy the original so there would be more than one.

   Great works of art are sometimes taken from one country to another by thieves. It's possible to <u>smuggle</u> an idea, too.

   The first form of printing was a <u>tiresome</u> method. Later, this <u>process</u> was made easier and less boring.

   The Chinese wanted to keep the secret of papermaking in China. <u>Eventually</u>, however, the secret was passed to the rest of the world.

   The printer couldn't risk a <u>clumsy</u>, or awkward, mistake.

   Press your finger onto an inked pad. Then press your finger onto a piece of paper. The <u>impression</u> you make on the paper is called a fingerprint.

b. Ask students to give the meaning of each vocabulary word. Remind them to use the context clues in the sentences to help them.

2. a. Point out the vertical lines that run from the North to the South Pole on a world map or a globe. Then have a student locate Australia, New Zealand, and Iceland on the map or globe. Explain that the part of the world including the Americas between the line that runs between Australia and New Zealand and the line that runs through Iceland is the Western Hemisphere. The other part of the world, including Asia, Europe, and Africa, is the Eastern Hemisphere. Ask students which hemisphere they live in. (Western)

b. Ask students whether China is in the eastern or western half of the world. (eastern)

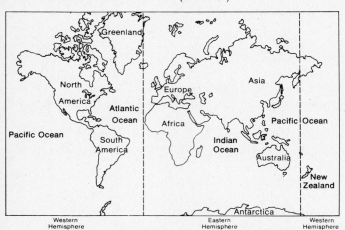

c. Point out that although most of Europe is in the eastern half of the world, when students see the word *West* capitalized in the selection they are about to read, they should understand that *West* means North America, South America, and Europe (but not Africa).

3. a. Have students enumerate some of the ways in which paper is used. You may want to list their answers on the board. The list should include common uses: for writing on, wall covering, towels, bags, cups, etc.

b. Next, ask students to imagine that paper does not exist. What might be used instead? Have students consider their answers in relation to the various uses they enumerated for paper.

 Use *Duplicating Masters 11,* page 60.

Setting Purposes

Skills

Have students read the skills note on page 467. Ask them what a generalization is. (a broad statement based on several facts)

As you read, look for generalizations that the author makes. Use the facts given to make your own generalizations.

How different our lives would be without our two precious . . .

GIFTS FROM CHINA

by Albert Barker

467

Content

Have students read the lead-in to the title. Ask them to recall some of the inventions they read about in previous selections, such as the lightning rod, the alarm clock, the zipper, the pencil with an eraser, and the safety pin. Point out that all of these are fairly recent inventions. Explain that students will now learn about something that was invented almost 2,000 years ago but that we still use every day in many forms.

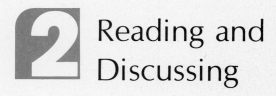 Reading and Discussing

Have students read the selection. Most students will be able to complete it in one sitting. If you prefer, the selection may be read in two parts, breaking before the first paragraph on page 470.

NOTE: The questions that appear in the student's text at the end of the selection focus on comprehension of selection content and on application of the *Skills Lesson* to the selection. Answers to these questions begin on page T408.

Suppose you woke up one morning and discovered that there were no newspapers and not a single book or magazine. Suppose there were no shopping bags, no tickets, no labels, no cardboard boxes, no paper money—nothing made of paper!

If you had lived two thousand years ago in China, the lack of paper wouldn't have bothered you. You would have written your lessons on strips of bamboo or on blocks of wood. Sometimes, you might write a letter on silk. But silk was expensive and wood was heavy.

One day in A.D. 105, a Chinese man named Ts'ai Lun got tired of carrying his master's heavy wooden blocks. He thought, "If I could make something that is light, strong and cheap, my master could write on it, and it would make my burden easier."

Ts'ai Lun noticed that old rags and fishnets were made out of tiny fibers—thousands of fine threadlike strings. Looking closely at the bark of mulberry trees and hemp plants, he

could see more fibers. These tiny fibers gave him an idea.

Taking the rags, nets, bark, and hemp, he dumped them into a kettle of boiling water. As they boiled, he pounded them to separate the fibers. When nothing remained but a thick soupy liquid, he poured it onto a flat screen. The thousands of fibers spread out across the top of the screen. When the fibers had dried, they formed a thick, rough sheet that could be written on.

At last, Ts'ai Lun had found a way to make his burden lighter! This was the first step in China's papermaking process. For many years, the Chinese were able to keep papermaking a secret.

468

The Chinese, however, were not satisfied just to write on their paper. They wanted to find a way to print on it.

The need for printing arose because hand-lettering was a slow, tiresome, and costly process. Printing would be faster and cheaper. Mainly, it would be a way to make many copies from one original piece of writing.

The Chinese carved designs on one side of small wooden blocks. In order for the blocks to print, only the raised surface of the designs were inked. The cut-away areas were not inked. A black pastelike ink was used.

Then the block was pressed down on the paper.

Printing with blocks was clumsy and slow, so the Chinese looked for a faster way to print. They took soft clay and carved a symbol on it. Then they baked the clay until it was hard. They made hundreds of these clay symbols, which could be arranged to form sentences.

After the clay symbols were inked, paper was pressed down on them. These symbols are called *type*, a word meaning "impression." Because this type could be rearranged and used over and over again, it is called *movable type*. However, the Chinese language is made up of over forty thousand different symbols. Even though the clay type could be moved, the work of printing a single book often took many months to complete.

Of course, these two secrets —papermaking and movable type—could not remain hidden forever. By the sixth century A.D., traders from the West were able to smuggle samples of paper and type into other

470

Questions preceded by a bullet are additional questions and appear in the Teacher's Edition only. The other questions appear in the student's text after the selection.

Understanding What You've Read

1. *What did people write on before the invention of paper?* (strips of bamboo, blocks of wood, and, sometimes, silk   page 468) LITERAL   Recalling specific details

• *Why did Ts'ai Lun want to invent something to replace earlier writing materials?* (because he was tired of carrying his master's heavy wooden blocks   page 468) INFERENTIAL   Identifying cause-and-effect relationships

• *If you had lived in ancient China before the discovery of paper, would you have written less or more than you do now? Why?* (Students will probably conclude that they would have written less because of the scarcity of materials and because of the expense and awkwardness of obtaining materials on which to write.) CRITICAL   Drawing conclusions

2. *How were copies of books made before the invention of wooden printing blocks?* (Students should conclude that copies were made by hand-lettering, because of the statement that the need for printing developed because hand-lettering was slow and tedious.   page 470) INFERENTIAL   Drawing conclusions

• *What one thing did Ts'ai Lun notice about old rags, fishnets, tree bark, and hemp plants?* (They all contain fibers.   page 468) LITERAL   Recalling specific details

• *What caused the rags, fishnets, bark, and hemp to turn into thick soupy liquid?* (Ts'ai Lun added them to boiling water and pounded them.   page 468) INFERENTIAL   Identifying cause-and-effect relationships

3. *Why was movable type an improvement over printing with wooden blocks?* (The letters in movable type could be rearranged and used over and over again. It was also faster.   page 470) INFERENTIAL   Drawing conclusions

• *What was the first movable type made of? What was later used?* (wood; then clay   page 470) LITERAL   Recalling specific details

4. *How many years passed between the time that Ts'ai Lun invented paper and the time that Europeans learned how to make paper?* (1,045 years   pages 468 and 471) INFERENTIAL   Determining the time between events

• *What was the effect of the secrets of papermaking and printing reaching Europe?* (Books could be printed that would teach many people to read.   page 471) LITERAL   Identifying cause-and-effect relationships

Applying the Skills Lesson

Which of the following generalizations are valid? Which of the valid generalizations are supported by facts from the selection? Which are supported only by something you already know?
1. *The world's most important inventions came from China.*
2. *Most writing today is done on paper.*
3. *All writing today is done on paper.*
4. *All people today know how paper is made.*
5. *The secrets of papermaking and movable type could not remain hidden forever.*
6. *It is harder to learn the Chinese writing symbols than it is to learn the alphabet.*
(1. invalid; 2. valid: based only on something students already know; 3. invalid; 4. invalid; 5. valid:

This is the author's conclusion, and students' own knowledge supports this generalization. 6. valid: supported by facts in the selection—there are 40,000 characters in the Chinese pictograph system. See NOTE in *Background,* page T405.)   Distinguishing valid from faulty generalizations

- *Choose the best generalization, based on these facts.*
  Facts:
  One third of all lumber cut in the United States is turned into pulp for paper. Paper is used to make every book, newspaper, and magazine. Paper is also used for most record-keeping.
  Generalizations:
  1. Paper makes the world go around.
  2. Paper is very important to modern life.
  (Answer: 2)   Making generalizations

 Use *Duplicating Masters 11,* page 61. See *Providing for Individual Differences,* page T413, for additional practice.

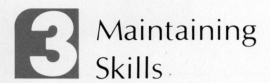

Maintaining Skills

Comprehension Skills

Determining the correct sequence for a set of events   Following are the steps that Ts'ai Lun followed in making paper. Have students put them in the correct order. Students may refer to the selection to check their answers.

1. Ts'ai Lun boiled rags, nets, bark, and hemp.
2. When nothing remained but a thick liquid, he poured it onto a screen.
3. When the fibers dried, they formed a sheet that could be written on.
4. The boiled rags, nets, bark, and hemp were pounded into fibers.
(Correct order: 1, 4, 2, 3)

Identifying the topic and stated main idea of a paragraph   Remind students that a topic is what the paragraph is about; the main idea is the most important thing said about the topic. Then have students identify the topic and stated main idea of the second paragraph in the selection. (Topic: the lack of paper in China two thousand years ago; Main idea: "If you had lived two thousand years ago in China, the lack of paper wouldn't have bothered you.")

Determining the unstated main idea of a paragraph
Have students choose from the following sentences the one that best expresses the main idea of the first paragraph in the selection.

1. Someday we will have no paper.
2. We didn't always have paper.
3. We use paper for many things in our lives.
(Answer: 3)

Now have students read the last paragraph on page 470. Then ask students to select from the following sentences the one that best expresses the main idea of that paragraph.

1. The secrets of papermaking and movable type were smuggled out of China and eventually reached Europe in 1150.
2. Traders in the West smuggled samples of paper and type into other Asian countries.
3. The Chinese tried to keep papermaking and movable type secrets.
(Answer: 1)

 For additional resources and curriculum-related activities, see *Enrichment,* page T415.

Textbook Study:

Recognizing Generalizations

Pages 472–475

Objectives

		SKILLS CODE NUMBER
I*, T	To distinguish valid from faulty generalizations	3.6.1
I*, T	To identify qualifying words in generalizations	3.6.1

Applying the Skill

Have students read the introduction and the two selections. You may wish to have them read the selections on their own and then do *Building Skills*. Or you may wish to direct students, using the following procedure.

Recognizing Generalizations in Science

1. **a.** Have students read the first paragraph and answer the question in the sidenote on page 472. (most) Point out that this is a broad statement about living things.

   b. Ask students to find the qualifying word in the first, unhighlighted part of the sentence. (many)

TEXTBOOK STUDY

Recognizing Generalizations

Remember that a generalization is different from a conclusion in that it is a broad statement. When you read textbooks, look for generalizations and the facts that support them. Often you will be asked to make a generalization based on facts that are given in the textbook. The sidenotes in the first selection will help you see some generalizations.

Recognizing Generalizations in Science

Cells

This part of the sentence is a generalization. What word *qualifies* the generalization?

Though living things are different in many ways, most living things are alike in one special way. That is, most living things are made up of *cells*.

472

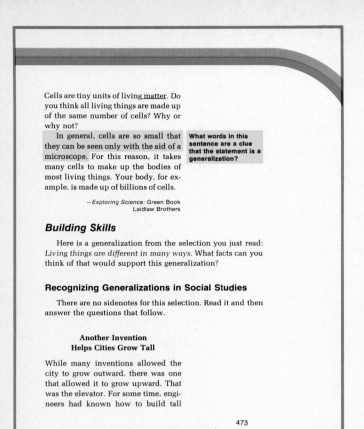

Cells are tiny units of living matter. Do you think all living things are made up of the same number of cells? Why or why not?

In general, cells are so small that they can be seen only with the aid of a microscope. For this reason, it takes many cells to make up the bodies of most living things. Your body, for example, is made up of billions of cells.

— Exploring Science: Green Book
Laidlaw Brothers

What words in this sentence are a clue that the statement is a generalization?

Building Skills

Here is a generalization from the selection you just read: *Living things are different in many ways.* What facts can you think of that would support this generalization?

Recognizing Generalizations in Social Studies

There are no sidenotes for this selection. Read it and then answer the questions that follow.

Another Invention
Helps Cities Grow Tall

While many inventions allowed the city to grow outward, there was one that allowed it to grow upward. That was the elevator. For some time, engineers had known how to build tall

473

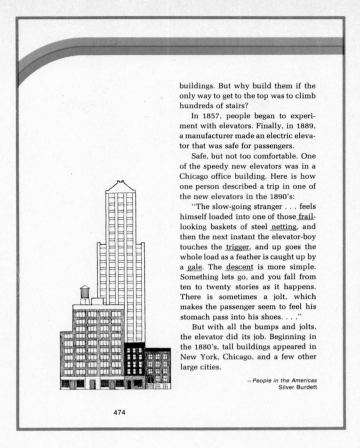

buildings. But why build them if the only way to get to the top was to climb hundreds of stairs?

In 1857, people began to experiment with elevators. Finally, in 1889, a manufacturer made an electric elevator that was safe for passengers.

Safe, but not too comfortable. One of the speedy new elevators was in a Chicago office building. Here is how one person described a trip in one of the new elevators in the 1890's:

"The slow-going stranger . . . feels himself loaded into one of those frail-looking baskets of steel netting, and then the next instant the elevator-boy touches the trigger, and up goes the whole load as a feather is caught up by a gale. The descent is more simple. Something lets go, and you fall from ten to twenty stories as it happens. There is sometimes a jolt, which makes the passenger seem to feel his stomach pass into his shoes. . . ."

But with all the bumps and jolts, the elevator did its job. Beginning in the 1880's, tall buildings appeared in New York, Chicago, and a few other large cities.

—People in the Americas
Silver Burdett

474

c. If you wish, have students try to answer the questions at the top of page 473.

2. Have students read the second paragraph and answer the question in the sidenote next to it on page 473. (In general) Point out that eggs are single cells but that they are easily seen without a microscope.

3. Have students complete *Building Skills.*

Answers to *Building Skills*
Science Selection

Accept all reasonable answers, such as: Some living things are able to move and others aren't; some living things are able to see and some aren't; and some living things can fly and some can't.

Recognizing Generalizations in Social Studies

1. Point out that there are no sidenotes for this selection. Remind students to look for generalizations and qualifying words as they read the selection.

2. Have students complete *Building Skills.*

1. Which of the following generalizations can you make based on the facts in the selection?

   a. All tall buildings built in the 1880's had elevators.
   b. Some tall buildings built in the 1880's had elevators.
   c. All passengers thought that the first elevators were uncomfortable.
   d. Most passengers thought that the first elevators were uncomfortable.

2. What is the qualifying word in each of the sentences above?

475

Answers to *Building Skills*
Social Studies Selection

1. b and d—valid generalizations based on the selection; **2.** a. All; b. Some; c. All; d. Most

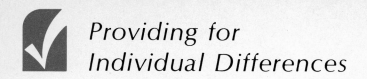

Providing for Individual Differences

Skills Lesson

Additional Practice

Worksheet 15, Teacher's Edition, page T495

Vocabulary Study

Additional Practice

Identifying suffixes with multiple meanings   Explain that many suffixes have more than one meaning. Write the following suffixes and meanings on the board.

-ful	1. as much as something can hold
	2. having a tendency
	3. full of
-able, -ible	1. worthy of being
	2. able to be
	3. having qualities of
-less	1. without
	2. that does not
-ize	1. to cause or make
	2. to act in a certain way

Now read the following sentences aloud, and have students tell what each italicized word means.

The illness made the baby *fretful.* (having a tendency to fret)
The rose is a *beautiful* flower. (full of beauty)
We bought a *tankful* of gas. (as much as a tank can hold)

That's a *lovable* puppy. (worthy of being loved)
This is a *comfortable* classroom. (having qualities of comfort)
The mathematics problem isn't *solvable.* (able to be solved)
It's not *permissible* to run in the hall. (able to be permitted)

Stephen is a *tireless* worker. (one who does not tire)
The car has no bumpers, and it's also *tireless.* (without tires)
Norman is a *thankless* person. (ungrateful, one who does not thank)
This job is *thankless.* (without thanks)

The architect wanted to *modernize* the building. (make modern)
I often *patronize* that store. (act as a patron, or customer)

Reading Selection: Little Things You Use Every Day

Additional Practice

■ **Distinguishing valid from faulty generalizations**
Read aloud the following paragraph. Then ask students to choose the two valid generalizations from the choices that follow.

The African tsetse fly causes sleeping sickness in people and cattle. The anopheles mosquito's bite can cause a disease called malaria. The sting of a wasp or a bee can cause an allergic reaction that may lead to death in some people. A flea carried on the bodies of European brown rats carries a deadly disease called bubonic plague.

All insects cause disease. (not valid)
Some insects cause disease. (valid)
All mosquitoes cause disease. (not valid)
Some kinds of mosquitoes cause disease. (valid)

Challenge Activity

■ **Distinguishing between valid and faulty generalizations**   Read the following paragraph aloud. Then have students identify as valid or not valid each of the generalizations that follow.

Two groups of Americans took part in a study about learning French. The people in the first group were twenty years old or older. Everyone in the second group was under the age of thirteen. No one in either group knew any French before the study began. Both groups were taught French by the same teacher for six months. Two years later, both groups took some tests. The adults didn't remember as much French as the children did. People who came from France could understand the children's French better than they could understand the adults' French.

Children are smarter than adults. (not valid)
People from France are more accustomed to talking to children than to adults. (not valid)
It's better to learn how to speak French as a child than as an adult. (valid)
French is easy to learn. (not valid)

Reading Selection: Gifts from China

Additional Practice

Distinguishing between valid and faulty generalizations
Read aloud the following statements, and ask students which are valid generalizations and which are not.

All dogs are playful. (not valid)

Most dogs have four legs. (valid)

Dogs are not able to see as well as most humans.
(valid)

Most dogs can be trained to do tricks or jobs.
(valid)

Challenge Activity

■ Identifying facts to support generalizations

Have students identify facts or examples in "A Street of
Games," pages 168–174, to support the following
generalizations.

Many people have different ways of playing hopscotch. (Students should cite examples from pages
169–170.)

Some people have different reasons for playing
some games than other people do. (The Koreans
and Japanese and the Alaskan Eskimos have different reasons from ours for playing tug of war.
page 171, paragraphs 2–3)

Many kinds of objects are useful in playing games.
(various examples given throughout selection: marbles, balls, stones, etc.)

Evaluation

Periodic Test 4, Part III, Form A or *Form B,* may be administered after this unit to test skills marked **T**. If you
have pretested using *Form A,* administer *Form B.*

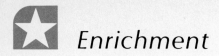

Enrichment

Little Things You Use Every Day

Bibliography

The following books are about inventions.

Average

Cooke, David C. *Inventions That Made History.* Paper, telegraphy, photography, TV, and many other inventions.

Garrison, Webb. *Why Didn't I Think of That? From Alarm Clocks to Zippers.* Well-known and little-known inventors of such things as blue jeans and windshield wipers.

Hirsch, S. Carl. *Stilts.* A history of stilts, their practical uses, and instructions for making a pair.

Jupo, Frank. *The Story of Things.* The origins and uses of mirrors, stoves, ovens, bells, pots, pans, needles, and pins.

Challenging

Englebart, Stanley L. *Miracle Chip: The Microelectronic Revolution.* An explanation of the microelectronic chips that have replaced transistors and now form the basis of a whole new technology in minicomputers, calculators, digital timepieces, and countless other devices.

Papallo, George. *What Makes It Work?* The workings of refrigerators, submarines, and other inventions.

Films and Filmstrips

NOTE: For more information, see *Resource Center.*

Selection content

Troll Assocs. *How Things Work.* Observations of some important inventions in "Simple Machines: The Pendulum," "Simple Machines: The Lever," "Simple Machines: Wheel and Axle and Pulley," and "What Is a Magnet?"

Curriculum Coordination

Language Arts

1. Have students make up and write a story telling about the invention of some small, real object by a fictional inventor.

2. Challenge students to think up a new invention and describe it. Written descriptions can be posted on the bulletin board with illustrations.

3. Have students write a letter to the U.S. Government Printing Office requesting information and applications for a patent. (Address is given on page T400.)

Art

Students can illustrate their inventions by making drawings, paintings, or collages, or they can build models of the inventions.

Social Studies

1. Students might look for inventors listed in the index of their social studies book. They might then scan to find out what the person invented and when he or she invented it.

2. People often confuse the concepts of patent, trademark, and copyright. Explain what each is, or have students find this out through research in a dictionary or an encyclopedia. (Patent: a legal right to profits on an invention; trademark: a legal right to the use of a name or a symbol for a product; copyright: a legal right to music, art, a computer program, or anything in printed form.) Show students examples of a trademark notice (®), a copyright notice (©), and a patent notice (the word *patent* or *pat.* or *pat. pend.*, plus a number). Then have them bring in examples of items marked with these notices. You might also refer them to the copyright page in *Blazing Trails.*

Gifts from China

Bibliography

The following books are about paper and printing.

Easy

Felder, Eleanor. *Careers in Publishing and Printing.* A description of different careers in these fields. Illustrated.

Soong, Maying. *The Art of Chinese Paper Folding for Young and Old.* Explicit, easy-to-follow directions for party novelties and miniatures.

Average

Cross, Jeanne. *Simple Printing Methods.* Methods of printing: relief printing, rubbings, and blockprinting.

Fisher, Leonard Everett. *The Printers.* The history and techniques of printing in colonial America.

Hirsch, S. Carl. *Printing from a Stone: The Story of Lithography.* The history of printing and biographies of some of the pioneers in printing.

Seidelman, James E., and Grace Mintonye. *Creating with Paper.* Various paper projects, from simple rings to dioramas.

Films and Filmstrips

NOTE: For more information, see *Resource Center*.

Selection content

Vocational and Industrial Films. "Mideast: Pioneers of Science." Presents the contributions made by the Middle East in the realm of science.

Weston Woods. "How a Picture Book Is Made." A description of the creation of a book from idea through printing.

Curriculum Coordination

Language Arts

1. Students may write their own fictionalized accounts of how the Chinese secrets of papermaking arrived in the West.

2. Students may wish to write poems on the subject of paper.

Social Studies

1. Have students investigate how the Chinese secrets of papermaking and printing reached other parts of Asia and eventually Europe. In particular, students may research the wars between the Arabs and the Chinese in Russian Turkestan; the establishment of the paper industry in Baghdad in A.D. 795; the Crusades; and the conquests in Spain by the Moors.

2. Have students research what commodities were exchanged between the Orient and Europe between the thirteenth and sixteenth centuries.

3. Arrange a tour of a paper-recycling plant, newspaper plant, or other location where some processing or major use of paper takes place.

4. Have students identify ways they might conserve paper at school and at home.

5. Have students research and report on other inventions that came from China, including gunpowder, and the use of coal as fuel.

Science

1. Under the teacher's supervision, students might make paper. There are directions for making paper in several of the books listed in the *Bibliography*, pages T354–T355.

2. Have students make charts of the yearly consumption of paper products, the number of acres of yearly reforestation, and the number of years it takes for a tree to mature. Have them make comparisons and predictions about the use of paper and the importance of conservation.

Art

1. Have students make small printing blocks from clay or linoleum with letters or designs that they can then ink and use in producing block prints.

2. Have students do an origami project.

Contents

Additional Materials

Reading Skills Workbook: Lessons 38–40, pages 123–130; Word Play, page 131

Duplicating Masters 11: pages 62–65

Bookmark Reading Filmstrips: Purple: "Looking for Comparison and Contrast"

Worksheet 16: Teacher's Edition, page T496

Periodic Test 4, Part IV

Cumulative Test for Blazing Trails

Key to Symbols

Skills Objectives
I* — Introduced in this unit
I — Introduced earlier in this level
M — Maintained from previous levels
T — Tested in periodic and cumulative tests for this level

Reduced Student Pages
underscore — words that appear in the glossary
wavy line — words pretaught in the Teacher's Edition (these words also appear in the glossary)

Skills Lesson:
Understanding Comparison and Contrast
Pages 476–479

Objectives

		SKILLS CODE NUMBER
M, T	To identify words that signal comparisons and contrasts	3.3.8.5
M, T	To identify comparisons and contrasts	3.3.8.5

If you wish to pretest the skills listed above, you may administer Periodic Test 4, Part IV, Form A. Periodic Test 4, Part IV, Form B, may be administered to post-test.

Introducing the Lesson

1. Display a basketball and a golf ball or any other two objects that can be compared and contrasted. Ask students to tell how the two objects are similar. (Both objects are round; both objects are used in games, etc.) Explain to students that they have just compared the two objects, and write the word compare on the board. Ask them to define the word compare. (to tell how things are alike)

Understanding Comparison and Contrast

"I'm a bird, too. I have feathers, I have wings—sort of!"

What is the little penguin doing? It is thinking about how it is like the eagle. The penguin is **comparing** itself to the eagle.

Authors often make comparisons, too. What is being compared in each of the following sentences?

●　1. The plesiosaurus looked like a turtle shell with a snake threaded through it.
　　2. Many ancient mollusks were like the snails and clams of today.

476

Authors make comparisons in order to help readers understand a new idea. You may not know what a plesiosaurus looked like. But you can imagine a turtle shell with a snake threaded through it. Do you know what snails and clams look like? If so, then you know what ancient mollusks were like. Sometimes an author uses words such as *like, as, too, also,* or *in comparison* to signal a comparison.

Study the cartoon below. The penguin is *not* thinking about how it is like the eagle. What is the penguin thinking?

"I can't fly like an eagle. However, I'm kind of cute. Eagles are not cute!"

Now the penguin is thinking about how it is *different* from the eagle. It is **contrasting** itself with the eagle.

Authors sometimes use contrasts to help you understand a new idea. Words such as *but, however, nevertheless,* and *although* are often clues that two things are being contrasted. What two things are being contrasted in each of the following pairs of sentences?

●　1. In the northern half of the world, July is a summer month. But in the southern half of the world, July is a winter month.
　　2. The "covered wagon pioneers" crossed America by foot or in wagons. However, the "sod-shanty pioneers" traveled west by railroad.

477

2. Next, ask students to tell how the two objects are different. (The objects differ in size, color, weight, and texture.) Explain to students that they have now *contrasted* the basketball and golf ball. Write the word *contrast* on the board and ask them to define the word *contrast*. (to tell how things are different)

3. Have students turn to page 476 and look at the cartoon at the top of the page. Ask what the penguin is doing. (It is comparing itself to the eagle.) Explain to the class that they will be learning more about the use of comparison and contrast in this lesson.

4. Have students read the first paragraph on page 476.

Developing the Skill

A. *Authors make comparisons to help readers understand a new idea.*

Have students read the second paragraph and the example sentences on page 476. Ask how, in sentence 1, the author helps the reader to understand what the plesiosaurus looked like. (The author compares the plesiosaurus to familiar things—a turtle and a snake.) Follow the same procedure for sample sentence 2.

B. *Words such as* like, also, as, in comparison, *and* too *often signal comparisons.*

Have students read the first paragraph on page 477.

C. *Authors sometimes use contrasts to help readers understand a new idea.*

Have students read the second paragraph on page 477 and examine the cartoon. Ask what the penguin is doing. (contrasting itself with the eagle)

D. *Words such as* but, nevertheless, although *or* however *often signal contrasts.*

1. Have students read the last paragraph on page 477, noting the words that signal contrasts. Have them read the pairs of sample sentences.

2. Ask students to tell what is being contrasted in the first pair of sentences and to identify the clue word. (the seasons in the northern and southern halves of the world; But) Follow the same procedure for the second pair of sentences. (Clue in sentence pair 2: However)

In the first pair of sentences the word *but* is a clue to a contrast. July in the northern half of the world is contrasted with July in the southern half of the world. In the second sentence pair, "covered wagon pioneers'" and "sod-shanty pioneers'" choices of travel are contrasted. What word is a clue to this contrast?

Time words can also be clues to contrasts. In the following paragraph, two different times are contrasted.

● Long ago, most sports equipment was made from natural materials like wood and leather. Today fiberglass or plastic is often used instead of wood or leather.

In the paragraph above, the materials used long ago to make sports equipment are being contrasted with what is often used today. Time words, such as *today, now,* and *used to,* are often clues that two different times are being contrasted.

478

Try This

1. What is being compared in the following sentences?

   a. The modern Olympics are very much like the ancient Greek Olympics.
   b. Then, as now, contestants had to train for a long time.

2. What is being contrasted in the following sentences?

   a. People came from all over Greece to take part in the ancient contests. Today's Olympic contestants come from most of the countries throughout the world.
   b. The first Olympics were held to honor the Greek gods and goddesses. However, the reason for today's Olympics is to build a spirit of world friendship.

3. Give the clue words that signal a comparison or contrast in the following sentences. Then make up a sentence using a clue word that signals a comparison or contrast.

   a. Maria's dress is like mine, but it's a different color.
   b. Although my car is smaller than yours, it uses more gas.

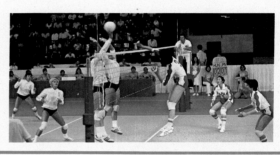

E. *Time words can be clues to a contrast.*

Have students read the first paragraph on page 478 and the sample paragraph. Then ask students what was contrasted. (Materials used long ago to make sports equipment are contrasted with materials used today.) Ask students to name the time words that are clues to the contrast. (Long ago, today) Then have students read the final paragraph of the lesson.

Try This

Have students complete *Try This.*

Answers to *Try This*

1. a. modern Olympics and ancient Greek Olympics; **b.** training for ancient Greek Olympics and training for modern Olympics; **2. a.** where contestants in the ancient contests came from and where today's contestants come from; **b.** the reason for ancient Greek Olympics and the reason for modern Olympics; **3. a.** like, but; **b.** although. Sentences will vary.

 Use *Reading Skills Workbook,* Lesson 38, pages 123–126. See *Providing for Individual Differences,* page T435, for additional practice.

Vocabulary Study:
Getting Meaning from Context Clues

Pages 480–481

Objective

M   To use context clues to determine word meaning

SKILLS CODE NUMBER
3.0.2

Developing the Skill

1. Tell students that the *Vocabulary Study* they are about to read is another entry from Professor Crum's diary.

2. Have students read the *Vocabulary Study* and do the *Word Play* activities.

Answers to *Word Play*

1. *loyal:* faithful to; *insisted:* felt so strongly; *competent:* capable; *career:* life's work; *eventually:* not right away; *considerable:* rather large; *worth:* valuable quality; *extra:* additional; *recommend:* praise; 2. Sentences will vary. 3. Diary entries will vary.

 Use *Reading Skills Workbook*, Lesson 39, page 127. See *Providing for Individual Differences*, page T435, for additional practice.

Getting Meaning from Context Clues

The kind Professor Crum excused himself from the party in his honor to scribble something quickly in his diary.

Dear Diary,
    I have to make this fast because my **loyal** friends are waiting for me in the next room. The people who have been faithful to me while I worked in the health food store are giving me a party. They **insisted** we celebrate my new job. They felt so strongly about it that I had to give in.
    You see, I'm a full-time juice squeezer! Everyone says I'm **competent**. And I guess I am capable of making good juice. They think I should make squeezing juice my **career**. I can't imagine selling cherry juice as my life's work, but it's a start.
    Eventually—not right away, of course—I'd like to buy an orchard. That would take a **considerable** amount of work, but that's OK. The rather large effort would be **worth** it. To me, the value of the orchard would be that my beautiful peaches and apples would make people happy.
    By the way, I told Leo the Rat about how I earned **extra** money in the health food store. He wants me to set him up with a part-time job so he can also earn additional money. I think I'll **recommend** him for the sandwich bar (hee, hee, hee). After all, if I can't praise him, who can? Besides, he makes a mean omelette. And who knows? Maybe we can turn him into a good egg!

480

Word Play

1. Look back over the diary page. The meaning of each word in boldface is suggested by other nearby words or phrases. These words or phrases are called context clues. Find the context clues to the meaning of each word in boldface.
2. Look up *orchard, effort,* and *omelette* in a dictionary. Use each word in a sentence. Try to include context clues for the word.
3. Write a short page to go into a make-believe diary. Use as many of the words in boldface as you can.

481

Reading Selection:
He Reached for the Stars
Pages 482–488

Objectives

		SKILLS CODE NUMBER
M, T	To identify comparisons and contrasts	3.3.8.5
M, T	To identify words that signal comparisons and contrasts	3.3.8.5
M	To identify clues to time-order relationships	3.1.2
M	To determine the correct sequence for a set of events	3.3.7.4
M	To scan a selection for specific information	5.9

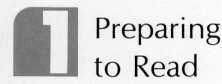

Preparing to Read

Summary

Benjamin Banneker was born in Maryland in 1731. His grandmother taught him to read and to appreciate nature. During his nine years of schooling, he developed a love of mathematics. At fifteen, he left school but continued to study on his own. He invented a wooden clock, predicted a solar eclipse, discovered the seventeen-year cycle of the locust, and was one of the first Americans to write and publish an almanac. Banneker also surveyed the site that became the city of Washington, D.C.

Background

Benjamin Banneker's grandfather had been a slave, but was freed. Young Benjamin attended a small elementary school open to both blacks and whites. After his formal schooling ended, Banneker continued to educate himself.

Banneker worked on a farm for most of his life, and he inherited a 100-acre tobacco farm from his father. In 1791, George Washington appointed Banneker to the committee that planned Washington, D.C. As a skilled surveyor and a brilliant mathematician, Banneker played a vital role in building one of the most beautiful capital cities of the world.

The following book will provide you with additional background information.

Klein, Aaron E. *The Hidden Contributors: Black Scientists and Inventors in America.* Notable black scientists, doctors, and inventors. Illustrated.

Developing Vocabulary and Concepts

obsession: a feeling or idea that fills the mind and cannot be driven out
eclipse: a complete or partial hiding of the sun or moon
tribute: an act that shows someone is worthy of admiration or respect
cycle: a regular period of time
considerable: a large, noticeable amount
farsighted: able to look ahead and make good judgments or decisions
commissioner: a person chosen or elected to be in charge of a government department or assignment
colleague: a person who works in the same job or field as another
ably: skillfully

1. **a.** Read the following sentences aloud or write them on the board. If you read them aloud, write the underlined vocabulary on the board.

   Benjamin's <u>obsession</u> with nature sometimes caused him to forget his chores.
   Banneker's invention was a <u>tribute</u> to his scientific mind. It showed he deserved admiration for the way he thought and worked.
   Banneker noticed events in nature that happened over and over again in regular <u>cycles</u>.
   Everyone knew of Benjamin's <u>considerable</u> talent in mathematics because he had solved so many hard problems.
   Benjamin's predictions about nature showed that he was <u>farsighted</u>.
   The city <u>commissioners</u> were named to plan and build the city.
   Banneker's discoveries and inventions made him a <u>colleague</u> of other inventors and engineers.
   Banneker proved his talents by <u>ably</u> handling any job that he was given.

   b. Ask students to give the meaning of each vocabulary word. Remind them to use the context clues in the sentences to help them.

2. Write *solar* and *eclipse* on the board. Have students look these words up in the glossary. Copy the following diagrams on the board. Point out that the selection explains that Banneker predicted a solar eclipse.

Solar eclipse (The sun is hidden by the moon.)

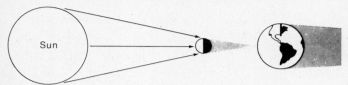

Lunar eclipse (The moon is hidden by the Earth.)

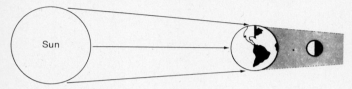

3. Have students identify subjects that they became interested in through their parents, other relatives, or other adults. Have them try to recall specific things they learned from an older person. Point out that the person they are going to read about had an interest in science and nature that was influenced by his family, especially his grandmother.

 Use *Duplicating Masters 11,* page 62.

Setting Purposes

Skills

Have students read the skills note at the top of page 482. Remind them that *comparisons* tell how things are alike; *contrasts* tell how they are different.

Content

Have students read the lead-in to the title. Ask students to interpret the title "He Reached for the Stars." Students should recognize that the expression means Banneker attempted great things. Ask students to identify other people who "reached for the stars." They may consider people who did things far ahead of their time or took great risks or made important contributions to the world. Have students discuss what they themselves would want to accomplish if they were to "reach for the stars."

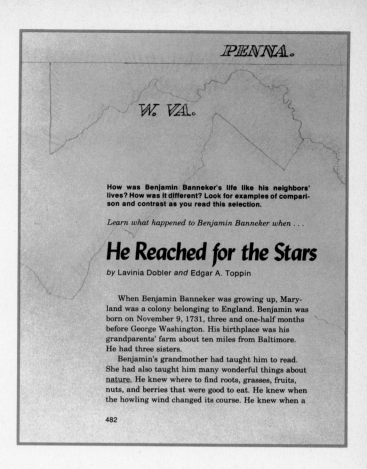

How was Benjamin Banneker's life like his neighbors' lives? How was it different? Look for examples of comparison and contrast as you read this selection.

Learn what happened to Benjamin Banneker when . . .

He Reached for the Stars

by Lavinia Dobler *and* Edgar A. Toppin

When Benjamin Banneker was growing up, Maryland was a colony belonging to England. Benjamin was born on November 9, 1731, three and one-half months before George Washington. His birthplace was his grandparents' farm about ten miles from Baltimore. He had three sisters.

Benjamin's grandmother had taught him to read. She had also taught him many wonderful things about nature. He knew where to find roots, grasses, fruits, nuts, and berries that were good to eat. He knew when the howling wind changed its course. He knew when a

482

2 Reading and Discussing

Have students read the selection. Most students will be able to complete it in one sitting. If you prefer, the selection may be read in two parts, breaking before the first paragraph on page 486.

NOTE: The questions that appear in the student's text at the end of the selection focus on comprehension of selection content and on application of the *Skills Lesson* to the selection. Answers to these questions begin on page T424.

THE FARM

BALTIMORE

MARYLAND

N.J.

DEL.

WASHINGTON D.C.

VA.

CHESAPEAKE BAY

deer or fox had been in the fields or orchards. He knew how to tell the age of a tree.

One spring morning in 1737, five-year-old Benjamin woke up and quickly dressed. All he could think of was "This is the day!" Today his parents and his grandparents were going to buy land.

Buying the land proved to be a good _investment._ People often talked about the fine crops that the Banneker family produced, even when there was no rain and other farmers had poor crops.

Benjamin's father had grown crops in Africa. So he knew a lot about the soil. He dug ditches. Then when the soil was dry, the water from the deep springs on the hill _irrigated_ the land. He and his wife Mary also built gates and _locks_ to control the flow of the spring water.

Benjamin started school in 1737. Every school day was a new adventure for him. He listened carefully to every word the teacher said. But it was arithmetic that he liked best of all. He quickly learned how to add and subtract. And he liked multiplication and division.

In 1746, when he was fifteen, his nine years of schooling were over. Benjamin missed going to school, especially because there were so few books at home. He continued to be a careful observer of nature. He listened to anyone who could give him information.

Benjamin was twenty-eight when his father died. Benjamin continued to live on the farm. He plowed and hoed the fields, planted crops and cared for the bees. He also found time to study mathematics.

People who knew Benjamin Banneker were _impressed_ with his ability. When, in 1761, he built a wooden clock, his fame spread far beyond Baltimore County.

484

Banneker had never seen a clock before. But he had seen a pocket watch which served as his model. The clock he made was many times larger than the watch.

A century later, an article in _The Atlantic Monthly_ described the wooden clock: ". . . this was the first clock of which every part was made in America. It is certain that it was purely his own invention. It was as if none had ever been made before."

When word got around that he had made a clock with wooden parts that worked, visitors came from miles around to the Banneker farm.

As time went by, people became more aware of Banneker's _remarkable_ abilities. He was now known as one of the best mathematicians in the Baltimore area. _Scholars_ from other _sections_ of the thirteen colonies sent him puzzles to test him. As soon as he received them, he would sit down at his table and start figuring them out. With his quick mind, he would have the correct answers in no time at all.

485

Even though Banneker was becoming well known, he was really very lonely. There was no one in his neighborhood who could talk about mathematical and scientific problems with him.

Then, in 1772, something wonderful happened. That year the three Ellicott brothers—George, Joseph, and Andrew—moved nearby. They were millers. Joseph, like Banneker, had made a clock that had received _considerable_ attention.

The Ellicotts became lifelong friends of Banneker and helped him in many ways. Indeed, their arrival marked the turning point in Banneker's career.

One day, in 1787, George Ellicott offered to lend Banneker some books on astronomy. From that time on, astronomy became almost an _obsession_ with Benjamin Banneker. As a boy, he had been fascinated with the stars that shone so brightly. But up to now he had never had the good fortune to see books on the subject.

Every night as soon as it was dark, Banneker would leave his log cabin so that he could watch the stars. In the early dawn, he was still outside, his eyes fixed on the heavens.

Banneker's scientific _observations_ brought results. Through his study of astronomy, Banneker predicted a _solar eclipse_ in 1789. Through watching nature he was able to _observe_ that _locusts_ seem to come in seventeen-year _cycles._ He was able to explain how they lay eggs. Banneker also observed that a strong hive of bees often takes the honey of a weaker hive.

Until the 1790's, Banneker was still known only locally. Then in the next ten years he became known around the world in two ways. In July 1790, Congress passed a law to make a United States capital on the Potomac River. President George Washington was to

486

Map of the city of Washington by Andrew Ellicott, 1792.

name three <u>commissioners</u> to <u>survey</u> and plan the <u>location</u> of the buildings.

In February 1791, President Washington sent Andrew Ellicott to survey the general site, under the direction of the three commissioners.

At the request of Mr. Ellicott and Thomas Jefferson, then Secretary of State, Benjamin Banneker was given the job of helping Ellicott survey the land. This was the first <u>national recognition</u> of Banneker's abilities.

Banneker worked <u>ably</u> on the survey, impressing his <u>colleagues.</u> He served from 1791 to 1793.

During that time, Banneker put some of his mathematical and astronomical findings into an <u>almanac.</u> This was to be his second well-known <u>accomplishment.</u> Almanacs then were one of the highest examples of scientific <u>achievement.</u> They served as a needed <u>source</u> of weather and tide news and of entertainment.

487

Banneker was sixty years old when his first *Almanac* was published in 1791. He continued to publish almanacs regularly until 1802.

In his *Almanac* for 1793, Banneker <u>proposed</u> a remarkable Plan for Peace. He suggested that a Secretary of Peace be appointed to the President's cabinet. This plan contained <u>farsighted</u> ideas about making the world better. The plan, too, was a great <u>tribute</u> to Banneker's <u>independent</u> thinking.

Understanding What You've Read

1. What kinds of things did Banneker learn from his grandmother?
2. Why did Banneker miss going to school?
3. Several things that Banneker did brought him fame. Name three of these things.

Applying the Skills Lesson

Read each of the following sentences. Which states comparison? Which show contrast? What is being compared or contrasted in each sentence?

1. Joseph, like Banneker, had made a clock that had received considerable attention.
2. Even though Banneker was becoming well known, he was really very lonely.
3. The clock he made was many times larger than the watch.

488

Questions preceded by a bullet are additional questions and appear in the Teacher's Edition only. The other questions appear in the student's text after the selection.

Understanding What You've Read

1. *What kinds of things did Banneker learn from his grandmother?* (His grandmother taught him to read; to find wild roots, grasses, fruits, and nuts that were good to eat; and to observe and understand the wind. She taught him how to notice if a fox or deer had been in a field or orchard and how to tell the age of a tree.   pages 482 and 484) LITERAL   <u>Recalling stated information</u>

- *Why was the Banneker family able to grow good crops even when there was no rain?* (Benjamin's parents dug ditches, built water gates and locks and irrigated their land with spring water when the soil was dry.   page 484) LITERAL   <u>Identifying cause-and-effect relationships</u>

- *Why was buying land a good investment for the Banneker family?* (Students should conclude from the family's success in raising crops that the Bannekers were able to make a good living from their farm. Some students may also recognize that the value of farmland usually increases over time.) INFERENTIAL   <u>Drawing conclusions</u>

2. *Why did Banneker miss going to school?* (Because there were so few books in his home. Also accept reasonable inferences that show an understanding that Banneker enjoyed learning and regretted not being able to continue his formal education.   page 484) INFERENTIAL   <u>Drawing conclusions</u>

- *How did Banneker continue to learn after his nine years of schooling were over?* (He continued to be a careful observer of nature; he listened to anyone who would give him information. He studied mathematics on his own. He studied astronomy.   pages 484 and 486) LITERAL   <u>Recalling specific details</u>

3. *Several things that Banneker did brought him fame. Name three of these things.* (He solved difficult mathematical problems. He built a wooden clock. He predicted a solar eclipse and identified the seventeen-year cycle of the locust. He helped survey the site for the United States capital.   pages 484, 485, 486, and 487) LITERAL   <u>Recalling specific details</u>

Applying the Skills Lesson

Read each of the following sentences. Which states comparison? Which show contrast? What is being compared or contrasted in each sentence?
1. Joseph, like Banneker, had made a clock that had received considerable attention.
2. Even though Banneker was becoming well known, he was really very lonely.
3. The clock he made was many times larger than the watch.
(1. comparison of Joseph and Banneker
2. contrast of Banneker's success or fame with his loneliness
3. contrast of the clock Banneker made with the watch that served as a model)
Identifying comparisons and contrasts

- *For each of the following sentences: Which state comparisons? Which states contrasts? What is being compared or contrasted in each sentence? What word in each sentence signals the comparison or contrast?*
1. The Banneker family, like their neighbors, were farmers.
2. Benjamin's parents knew how to irrigate their land, but their neighbors did not.
3. Benjamin Franklin, like Benjamin Banneker, wrote an almanac.
(1. comparison of the Bannekers' and their neighbors' occupations; Signal: like
2. contrast of the Bannekers' and their neighbors' knowledge of irrigation; Signal: but
3. comparison of Benjamin Banneker and Benjamin Franklin; Signal: like)
Identifying comparisons and contrasts

- *Read each of the following sentences. Which state comparisons? Which state contrasts? What word or words in each sentence signal the comparison or contrast?*
1. Like many other boys of his time, Benjamin had only nine years of schooling.
2. In contrast to George Washington, Banneker was not well known.
3. The United States' capital is now Washington, D.C., but it was once New York City.
4. Banneker's almanac was as well known as his clock.
(1. comparison; Signal: like
2. contrast; Signal: In contrast
3. contrast; Signal: but
4. comparison; Signal: as)
Identifying comparisons and contrasts

 Use *Duplicating Masters 11*, page 63. See *Providing for Individual Differences*, page T435, for additional practice.

3 Maintaining Skills

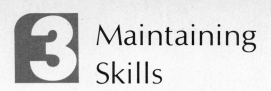

Comprehension Skills

Identifying clues to time-order relationships   Remind students that a time clue may be a date, a word, a group of words, or even a whole sentence. Have students find the time clues in the last three paragraphs on page 484. (In 1746, when he was fifteen; his nine years of schooling were over; Benjamin was twenty-eight when his father died; When, in 1761, he built a wooden clock)

Determining the correct sequence for a set of events   Have students arrange the following events from Banneker's life in the order in which they happened. You may wish to allow students to look back at the selection if they need to.

1. He finished his schooling.
2. He met the Ellicotts.
3. He predicted a solar eclipse.
4. He published an almanac.
5. He began to study astronomy.
6. He built a wooden clock.
7. His father and grandfather bought land.
(Correct order: 7, 1, 6, 2, 5, 3, 4)

Study Skills

Scanning a selection for specific information   Have students scan the selection to find answers to the following questions.

In what year and in which month was Benjamin Banneker born? (November, 1731—page 482)
Where was Banneker born? (ten miles from Baltimore—page 482)
In what year did Banneker predict a solar eclipse? (1789—page 486)
In what year did Congress pass a law to make the United States capital on the Potomac River? (1790—page 486)
Who sent Andrew Ellicott to survey the site for the capital? (George Washington—page 487)
In what magazine was Banneker's wooden clock described? (*The Atlantic Monthly*—page 485)
Who was Secretary of State in 1791? (Thomas Jefferson—page 487)

 For additional resources and curriculum-related activities, see *Enrichment*, page T436.

Reading Selection:
Daniel Villanueva: The Idea Is to Care

Pages 489–493

Objectives

		SKILLS CODE NUMBER
M, T	To identify comparisons and contrasts	3.3.8.5
M, T	To identify words that signal comparisons and contrasts	3.3.8.5
M	To identify an author's purpose	3.6.4
M	To identify word parts: root words and suffixes	4.1

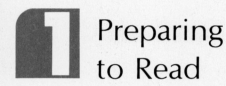

Preparing to Read

Summary

Daniel Villanueva played professional football for the Los Angeles Rams and the Dallas Cowboys. He left football in order to help serve the needs of Spanish-speaking Americans. In 1968 he began working for KMEX-TV, a Los Angeles Spanish-language station. Within two years he became vice-president and general manager. He also helped create SIN-West, part of the first Spanish TV network in the United States. He is a respected business leader who has received many honors for his efforts to help Spanish-speaking people.

Background

Spanish International Network (SIN) estimates that there are more than twelve million Spanish-speaking people in the United States and that SIN reaches eight million of them. SIN also has stations in Mexico. The stations are all community-oriented and have long been reminding viewers to "register to vote." KMEX-TV has won the Peabody Award for broadcast journalism.

Daniel Villanueva is something of a local youth hero in Los Angeles because of his football career. He played for eight seasons and set a Rams field-goal record as well as an all-time professional record for scoring fifty-six consecutive points after touchdowns in 1966. In the 1971 Los Angeles earthquake, Villanueva organized workers at KMEX-TV to provide food, clothing, and other aid to earthquake victims. In 1979 Daniel Villanueva became president of KMEX-TV.

Developing Vocabulary and Concepts

questionnaire: a list of questions, usually printed, used to get information
executive: a person in charge of managing a business
memorable: worth remembering
community: the public in general
relations: connections between people and groups brought about by business or other contacts
influence: a person who has the power to affect another person
dedication: the act of devoting oneself to a special purpose
commitment: the state of being bound to a promise or pledge
mission: calling; one's chief purpose in life

1. **a.** Read the following sentences aloud or write them on the board. If you read them aloud, write the underlined vocabulary on the board.

   Daniel Villanueva is an <u>executive</u> at station KMEX-TV. He is president and general manager.
   Playing pro football is an experience Daniel Villanueva will always remember. And he has had other <u>memorable</u> experiences.
   He started as director of <u>community relations</u>. In that job, he was responsible for working with the public in Los Angeles.
   Daniel admired his father's <u>dedication</u> to helping others. Daniel, too, spends much of his time helping people.
   Daniel Villanueva has a <u>commitment</u> to others. He feels that it is very important to help other people.

   b. Ask students to give the meaning of each vocabulary word. Remind them to use the context clues in the sentences to help them.

2. **a.** Write the word *questionnaire* on the board and ask students if they have ever filled out a questionnaire. Ask them what the word means. Point out the doubled *n* in the word.

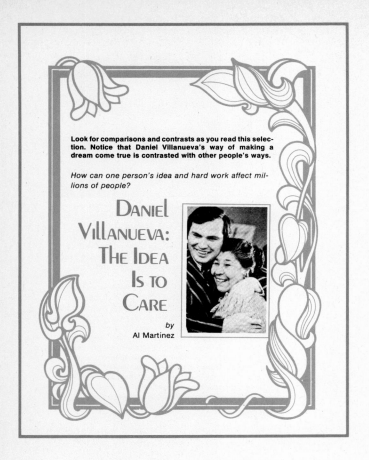

Look for comparisons and contrasts as you read this selection. Notice that Daniel Villanueva's way of making a dream come true is contrasted with other people's ways.

How can one person's idea and hard work affect millions of people?

DANIEL VILLANUEVA: THE IDEA IS TO CARE

by
Al Martinez

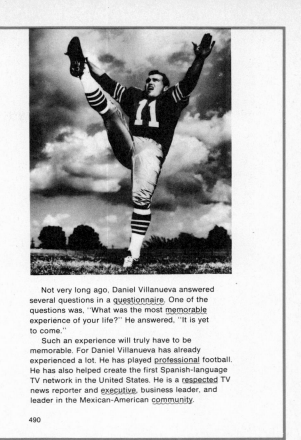

Not very long ago, Daniel Villanueva answered several questions in a questionnaire. One of the questions was, "What was the most memorable experience of your life?" He answered, "It is yet to come."

Such an experience will truly have to be memorable. For Daniel Villanueva has already experienced a lot. He has played professional football. He has also helped create the first Spanish-language TV network in the United States. He is a respected TV news reporter and executive, business leader, and leader in the Mexican-American community.

490

b. Write the word *influence* on the board. Then ask students to imagine they have read this question in a questionnaire: "Who has been the greatest influence in your life?" Tell students to ask this question in another way without using the word *influence*. (Sample answer: "Who has had the greatest effect on your life?")

3. Write the word *mission* on the board and read these sentences aloud:

Martin Luther King's mission was to help people.
Jonas Salk's mission was to find a way to prevent polio.
Susan B. Anthony's mission was to win for women the right to vote.

Ask students to define *mission* and to give examples of other people's missions in life.

 Use *Duplicating Masters 11,* page 64.

Setting Purposes

Skills

Have students read the skills note at the top of page 489. Ask them to explain how comparisons differ from contrasts. (Comparisons describe how things are alike. Contrasts tell how things are different.)

Content

Have students read the lead-in to the title. Tell them to read to find ways that Daniel Villanueva's work affects the lives of one very large group of people, as well as how he helps small groups of people.

2 Reading and Discussing

Have students read the selection. Most students will be able to complete it in one sitting.

NOTE: The questions that appear in the student's text at the end of the selection focus on comprehension of selection content and on application of the *Skills Lesson* to the selection. Answers to these questions begin on page T429.

Daniel Villanueva was born in Tucumcari [tōō´kəm·kä´rē], New Mexico, in 1937. He was one of eleven children. When he was a young child in school in New Mexico, some people thought Daniel was a "slow learner." However, he made it through school just fine.

After graduating from New Mexico State College, he played professional football. He began with the Los Angeles Rams and then played with the Dallas Cowboys. But while he loved sports, Villanueva felt that he could not serve the needs of his people by playing football. He left the sport in 1968 and joined KMEX-TV, a Spanish-language station in Los Angeles. He started as news <u>director</u> and director of <u>community relations</u>. In 1969 he became station manager. By 1971 he was vice-president and general manager. He is now president and general manager.

Some people sit back and just hope that their dreams will come true. But this wasn't the way for Daniel Villanueva. He worked hard to make his dream become real. For years he had wanted to see a Spanish-language TV network stretching beyond Los

491

Angeles. By 1972, he had helped create SIN-West, the first Spanish TV network in the United States. (SIN is for *Spanish International Network*.)

Daniel Villanueva is president and general manager of SIN-West. This network reaches millions of people in California and Mexico. The network also owns stations in cities such as Miami, New York, and San Antonio.

During his free time, Daniel Villanueva works hard helping people. He spends much of that time working for the Mexican-American community. He works with <u>scholarship</u> programs and youth programs. He is chairman of the board of a savings-and-loan <u>company</u>. He has also served as chairman of the California State Park and <u>Recreation</u> Commission.

For his work helping Spanish-speaking people, Daniel Villanueva has been given many honors. One of these was the Aztec Award. This award honored him for developing opportunities for Mexican-American workers. Villanueva received this award in

492

1971 from the Mexican-American Opportunity Foundation.

Remember the questionnaire that was mentioned earlier? Well, another question asked Daniel Villanueva who had been the most important influence in his life. He answered, "My father. Because of his total dedication to serving others, his total commitment to his mission."

Like father, like son.

Understanding What You've Read

1. What did Daniel Villanueva mean when he said his most memorable experience "is yet to come"?
2. Why did Daniel Villanueva leave professional football in 1968?
3. What is SIN-West? Why was its creation important?

Applying the Skills Lesson

The following sentences show comparisons and contrasts. What is being compared or contrasted in each group?

1. Some people sit back and just hope that their dreams will come true. But this wasn't the way for Daniel Villanueva. He worked hard to make his dream become real.
2. Another question asked Daniel Villanueva who had been the most important influence in his life. He answered, "My father. Because of his total dedication to serving others, his total commitment to his mission."

Like father, like son.

493

• In what ways has Daniel Villanueva helped people since leaving football? (He has worked with scholarship, youth, and community programs. Students should also recognize that he has been instrumental in bringing educational and other Spanish-language TV shows to the Spanish-speaking community. pages 491 and 492) INFERENTIAL Identifying facts to support the main idea

3. What is SIN-West? Why was its creation important? (SIN-West is a Spanish-language TV network. It is important because it reaches millions of people in California and Mexico. page 492) LITERAL Recalling specific details

Applying the Skills Lesson

The following sentences show comparisons and contrasts. What is being compared or contrasted in each group?
1. Some people sit back and just hope that their dreams will come true. But this wasn't the way for Daniel Villanueva. He worked hard to make his dream become real.
2. Another question asked Daniel Villanueva who had been the most important influence in his life. He answered, "My father. Because of his total dedication to serving others, his total commitment to his mission." Like father, like son.
(1. contrast of Daniel Villanueva's way of making his dream come true with other people's way of making their dreams come true
2. comparison of Daniel Villanueva to his father) Identifying comparisons and contrasts

• In group 1 in the preceding question, what word signals a contrast? In group 2, what word signals a comparison? (1. But; 2. Like) Identifying words that signal comparisons and contrasts

• What is being compared or contrasted in each of the following groups of sentences? What words signal the comparison or contrast?
1. When he was a young child in school in New Mexico, some people thought he was a "slow learner." However, he made it through school just fine.
2. But while he loved sports, Villanueva felt that he could not serve the needs of his people by playing football.
(1. contrast of label of "slow learner" with actual performance in school; Signal: However
2. contrast of love of sports with desire to serve needs of his people; Signal: But while)
Identifying comparisons and contrasts

 Use *Duplicating Masters 11*, page 65. See *Providing for Individual Differences*, page T435, for additional practice.

Questions preceded by a bullet are additional questions and appear in the Teacher's Edition only. The other questions appear in the student's text after the selection.

Understanding What You've Read

1. What did Daniel Villanueva mean when he said his most memorable experience "is yet to come"? (He meant he intends to keep on working hard and accomplishing things.) INFERENTIAL Drawing conclusions

• What facts in the selection support the author's opinion that Daniel Villanueva is a "business leader"? (He is president and general manager of KMEX-TV and of SIN-West. He is chairman of the board of a savings and loan company. pages 491 and 492) CRITICAL Identifying fact and opinion

2. Why did Daniel Villanueva leave professional football in 1968? (He felt he could not serve the needs of his people by playing football. page 491) LITERAL Identifying cause-and-effect relationships

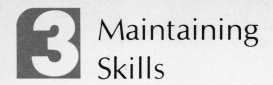

3 Maintaining Skills

Comprehension Skills

Identifying the author's purpose Refer students to each of the following paragraphs in the selection. Ask them to identify the author's purpose in writing each paragraph by choosing one statement from the choices given.

Page 491, first paragraph
1. The author is informing you about Villanueva's childhood.
2. The author is informing you about Villanueva's success as a business leader.
3. The author is informing you about Villanueva's work helping people.
(Answer: 1)

Page 491, second paragraph
1. The author is informing you about how well Villanueva played football.
2. The author is informing you about why Villanueva left football.
3. The author is informing you about the programs shown on KMEX-TV.
(Answer: 2)

Page 492, last paragraph
1. The author is informing you about things Villanueva did to help others.
2. The author is informing you about honors Villanueva was given.
3. The author is informing you about the Mexican-American Opportunity Foundation.
(Answer: 2)

 Use *Reading Skills Workbook,* Lesson 40, pages 128–130.

Language Skills

Identifying word parts: root words and suffixes
Read the following sentences from the selection and write the underlined words on the board. Have students identify the root word and suffix or suffixes in each word and give the meaning of each whole word.

He is a respected TV news reporter and executive, business leader, and leader in the Mexican-American community. (report, *-er,* one who reports; execute, *-ive,* one who carries out [executes] the business of a company; lead, *-er,* one who leads)

After graduating from New Mexico State College, he played professional football. (profess, *-ion, -al,* earning one's living from an activity not always thought of as an occupation)

He started as news director and director of community relations. (direct, *-or,* one who directs; relate, *-ion,* connection)

Two years later, he became vice-president and general manager. (manage, *-er,* one who manages)

 Use *Reading Skills Workbook,* Word Play, page 131, for vocabulary review.

 For additional resources and curriculum-related activities, see *Enrichment,* page T436.

Textbook Study:

Recognizing Comparison and Contrast

Pages 494–499

Objectives

		SKILLS CODE NUMBER
M, T	To identify comparisons and contrasts	3.3.8.5
M, T	To identify words that signal comparisons and contrasts	3.3.8.5

Applying the Skill

Have students read the introduction and the two selections. You may wish to have them read the selections on their own and then do *Building Skills*. Or you may wish to direct students, using the following procedure.

TEXTBOOK STUDY

Recognizing Comparison and Contrast

In order to help you understand something new, textbook authors may *compare* it to something you most likely already understand. Or they may *contrast* something new with something you already know about. When authors contrast ideas about different times, they often use words such as *today, now, then,* and *used to.* Look for these words as clues.

As you read the following selections, refer to the side-notes. Try to answer the questions in them.

Recognizing Comparison and Contrast in Language Arts

Read the following conversation. Then answer the questions that follow the conversation.

What is being contrasted in this selection? How is the American's language like the Englishman's? How is it different?

ENGLISHMAN: I'm going to the iron-monger's to buy a spanner.

AMERICAN: You're going where for what?

ENGLISHMAN: To the ironmonger's. That's a shop where they sell tools.

AMERICAN: Oh, you mean a hardware store. But what is a spanner?

ENGLISHMAN: That's a tool that you use for tightening nuts and bolts.

AMERICAN: A wrench? Well, I'll go with you. I need a flashlight.

ENGLISHMAN: What's a flashlight?

494

Recognizing Comparison and Contrast in Language Arts

1. Have students read the dialogue and answer the questions in the first sidenote. (Two kinds of English—British and American—are being contrasted. The two languages are alike in that they use most of the same words. The two languages are different in that they sometimes use different words to mean the same thing—for example, *torch* and *flashlight.*)

495

AMERICAN: It's a small light that
    operates on batteries.
ENGLISHMAN: That's what we call a
    torch.

- What country does each person
  come from?
- What language is each person
  speaking?
- Why are the two people having
  trouble understanding each other?

Notice that the
distances between the
countries are being
compared.

English is spoken in many countries around the world — countries as
far apart as America and England,
Canada and India, Scotland and Australia. In most ways the English spoken is the same in all countries where
it is used. But there are some differences.

— Discoveries in English
    Laidlaw Brothers

Building Skills

The selection beginning on page 494 showed you likenesses and differences by example. The sentences below state
the likenesses and differences. Which of the sentences is a
comparison? Which is a contrast?

1. The British, like the Americans, speak English.
2. The British and the Americans use different names for
   some things.

496

---

2. Have students read the rest of the selection and the
   second sidenote. Ask students to identify the words
   that signal the comparison of distances between
   countries. (as far away as)

3. Have students complete *Building Skills.*

Answers to *Building Skills*
Language Arts Selection

1. comparison; 2. contrast

Recognizing Comparison and Contrast in Health

This selection compares and contrasts the effects of transportation on people's lives. Notice that both the good effects and the harmful effects are described.

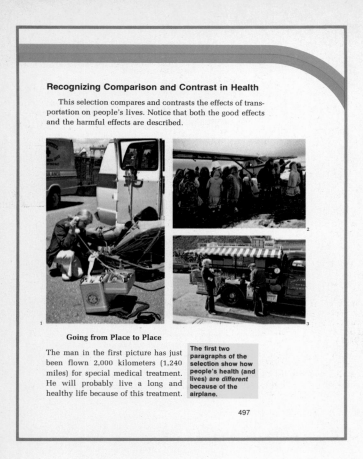

Going from Place to Place

The man in the first picture has just been flown 2,000 kilometers (1,240 miles) for special medical treatment. He will probably live a long and healthy life because of this treatment.

> The first two paragraphs of the selection show how people's health (and lives) are *different* because of the airplane.

497

Why couldn't this picture have been taken 100 years ago? What might have happened to the man if he had lived then?

This airplane is bringing a doctor to a village in Alaska. There are no roads into the village. It used to take a doctor two weeks to get here from the city. Today this doctor can visit five villages in one day. How has this airplane helped to keep the people in the villages healthy?

Other kinds of transportation also affect people's health. The truck in the third picture carries vegetables to people's houses. What else do trucks carry that is important to you? How do the clothes you wear get from factories to stores? How is meat carried long distances without spoiling?

> What things is the writer asking you to contrast here?

Suppose there were no trucks and cars. List five ways this would make a difference in your life.

For most of us, cars are necessary. Yet they can be dangerous, too. Car accidents kill thousands of people and injure millions every year.

Cars can be harmful in other ways, too. The smog in the air is partly caused by car waste products. A few years ago, a law was passed to help

498

Recognizing Comparison and Contrast in Health

1. Have students read the introductory paragraph, the first two paragraphs, and the first sidenote. Ask students to identify the two things that are being contrasted in the first paragraph. (a man being flown for medical treatment and the impossibility of his being flown 100 years ago)

2. Have students read the remaining paragraphs and answer the question in the last sidenote. (how your life would be different if there were no cars or trucks)

keep the air cleaner. Car owners must now make sure their cars are not adding to the pollution.

—*Balance in Your Life:* Purple
Harcourt Brace Jovanovich

Building Skills

1. Read again the second paragraph of the selection. What two things are being contrasted?
2. Both the good effects and the harmful effects of transportation are presented in the selection you just read.

   a. Which paragraphs describe the good effects? What are those effects?
   b. Which paragraphs describe the harmful effects? What are those effects?

499

Books About Discoveries, Ideas, and Inventions

Gigi: A Baby Whale Borrowed for Science and Returned to the Sea by Eleanor Coerr and Dr. William Evans. Putnam, 1980. A baby gray whale is captured so that scientists can study the behavior of a whale first-hand.

Why Didn't I Think of That: From Alarm Clocks to Zippers by Webb Garrison. Prentice-Hall, 1977. You'll meet the woman who invented windshield wipers, the man who invented blue jeans, and several other little-known inventors.

Eight Black American Inventors by Robert C. Hayden. Addison-Wesley, 1972. This is the story of eight inventors and their contributions to American life.

Marie Curie by Robin McKown. Putnam, 1971. You'll read about the life of a great scientist, her research with radium, and the uses of radium.

The Polynesians Knew by Tillie S. Pine and Joseph Levine. McGraw, 1974. The authors tell about the inventions and customs of the people of Polynesia, and how these inventions and customs compare with ours.

Nature's Weather Forecasters by Helen Sattler. Nelson, 1978. Here is information about some of the many ways people—and animals—use nature to predict the weather.

How Sports Began by Don Smith. Watts, 1977. This book is full of facts and legends about the beginnings of baseball, tennis, basketball, gymnastics, and so on.

500

---

3. Have students complete *Building Skills*.

Answers to *Building Skills* Health Selection

1. the time it takes a doctor to visit a village in Alaska now and the time it took before the airplane was used; **2. a.** The first three paragraphs describe the good effects. These are longer life and better health because of access to medical care and the availability of vegetables, clothes, and other products. **b.** The last two paragraphs describe the harmful effects. These are car accidents and smog.

If students have not already read these books, you may wish to recommend them at this time. Bibliographic information about these and other books for students is given in the *Resource Center*.

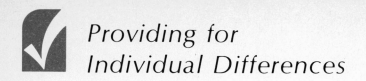

Providing for Individual Differences

Skills Lesson

Additional Practice

Worksheet 16, Teacher's Edition, page T496

Vocabulary Study

Additional Practice

Using context clues to determine word meaning Write the following categories on the board:

diseases   clothing   foods   living things

Now read each of the following sentences aloud and write each italicized word on the board. Tell students to use the context clues to help them determine which category each word belongs in.

Drosophilae are often used in biology experiments because of their short life cycles. (living things)

I don't like *shoofly* because it tastes too sweet. (foods)

I put sliced *mortadella* on my sandwich. (foods)

In pictures, the Spanish explorers are often shown with *morions* on their heads. (clothing)

A *hart's* antlers are fully formed by its fifth year. (living things)

A person needs vitamin D obtained from sunshine or from food to prevent *rickets*. (diseases)

All the girls in that private school wear green *weskits* over their blouses. (clothing)

Reading Selection: He Reached for the Stars

Additional Practice

Identifying comparisons and contrasts Write the following sentences on the board or read them aloud. Have students determine what or who is being compared or contrasted.

Unlike his father, the young man did not enjoy sports. (contrast of young man and his father)

Karen loves camping, but her brother does not. (contrast of Karen and her brother)

A zebra looks like a horse in striped pajamas. (comparison of a zebra and a horse in pajamas)

Reading Selection: Daniel Villanueva: The Idea Is to Care

Additional Practice

Identifying words that signal comparisons and contrasts Write the following sentences on the board or read them aloud. Have students tell whether a comparison or contrast is being made; what two things are being compared or contrasted; and what word gives them a clue to whether the sentence is a comparison or contrast.

The beach glistened in the sunlight like an endless silk sheet. (comparison; beach and silk sheet; like)

The child was as playful as a pup. (comparison; child and pup; as)

Although the sun was hot, the cool wind kept the temperature from soaring. (contrast; sun and wind; although)

Whales live in water but are not really fish. (contrast; Whales and fish; but)

December is a cold month; however, January is often colder. (contrast; December and January; however)

Challenge Activity

Recognizing comparisons in poetry Refer students to a poem or poems containing similes (comparisons using *as* or *like*) and/or metaphors (comparisons that do not contain the word *as* or *like*). Have students identify what is being compared.

Evaluation

Periodic Test 4, Part IV, Form A or *Form B,* may be administered after this unit to test skills marked **T.** If you have pretested using *Form A,* administer *Form B.*

To posttest all the skills marked **T** in the four teaching units in "Discoveries, Ideas, and Inventions," Part 7, use *Periodic Test 4, Parts I–IV.*

To test all the skills marked **T** in Level 11, you may use the *Cumulative Test, Level 11.*

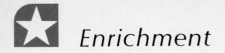

Enrichment

He Reached for the Stars

Bibliography

The following books have information about Benjamin Banneker.

Easy

Clark, Margaret Goff. *Benjamin Banneker: Astronomer and Scientist*. A simple biography.

Challenging

Haber, Louis. *Black Pioneers of Science and Invention*. The scientific contributions of fourteen men, including Charles Drew, Granville Woods, Elijah McCoy, and Benjamin Banneker.

Hayden, Robert C. *Eight Black American Inventors*. The story of eight inventors and their contributions to the development of America.

Films and Filmstrips

NOTE: For more information, see *Resource Center*.

Skills

Harcourt Brace Jovanovich. *Bookmark Reading Filmstrips*. "Looking for Comparison and Contrast."

Selection content

Educational Activities. *Man Studies Space*. The instruments and contributions of astronomers.

Curriculum Coordination

Language Arts

1. Have students write paragraphs or compositions comparing and contrasting life today with life in Banneker's time. The composition might include comparisons of the inventions, schooling, communication, dress, etc.

2. Have students make a class almanac for the rest of the school year. Students might form groups responsible for different parts of the almanac, such as weather forecasts, jokes, helpful hints, and illustrations. The class almanac might be copied for all students or posted where it is accessible to all.

Social Studies

1. Interested students can find out about the planning of the Capitol Building by referring to an encyclopedia or writing to the Architect of the Capitol, The Rayburn Building, Washington, DC 20515, for information. (See also activity 2 under *Art*, below.)

2. Have students investigate the lives and work of other inventors, such as Cyrus McCormick, Eli Whitney, George Washington Carver, Leonardo da Vinci, Guglielmo Marconi, Galileo, Louis Daguerre, Ferdinand von Zeppelin, Juan de la Cierva, and Ellen Butterick.

Science

1. Interested students can do research on locusts and why Banneker's discovery of the seventeen-year cycle was important.

2. Students can research solar and lunar eclipses and make drawings or models of what happens during one or both kinds of eclipses.

3. Students might investigate the mechanics of a clock, identifying basic parts and how they function. Students might examine or read about digital clocks as well as clocks with hands.

Art

1. Students might design clock faces or different styles of clocks. For example, students might explore making clock faces with new materials, with cartoon-character faces, with pencils or driftwood, combined with thermometers, and so on.

2. Have students make a simple map or model of Washington, D.C. They should include some of the important buildings, such as the White House and the Capitol. Some students may wish to make a scale model of one building.

Daniel Villanueva: The Idea Is to Care

Bibliography

The following books are about television and people who help others.

Easy

Brondfield, Jerry. *Roberto Clemente: Pride of the Pirates*. A biography of the professional baseball player who was known for his work helping other people.

Goodsell, Jane. *The Mayo Brothers*. A biography of the brothers who developed the Mayo Clinic.

Average

Daniel, Anita. *The Story of Albert Schweitzer.* A biography of the physician/humanitarian.

Challenging

Curtis, Richard. *Ralph Nader's Crusade.* A biography of the leader of the American consumer-protection movement.

Gruber, Ruth. *Felisa Rincón de Gautier: The Mayor of San Juan.* A biography of the woman who was mayor of the largest city in Puerto Rico for twenty-two years.

Kerman, Stephen D. *Color Television and How It Works.* How a control room is run; how a studio works; how color TV works.

Films and Filmstrips

NOTE: For more infomation, see *Resource Center.*

Skills

Harcourt Brace Jovanovich. *Bookmark Reading Filmstrips.* "Looking for Comparison and Contrast."

Selection content

Guidance Assocs. *Career Discoveries Series.* Most filmstrips in this series are appropriate.

Curriculum Coordination

Language Arts

1. Explain that similes and metaphors are poetic devices. Give students examples of these, then challenge them to write poems using these kinds of comparisons.

2. Have students explain the meaning of the following English words that come from the Spanish language. Allow them to look up any words that are unfamiliar to them.

canyon	cargo	rodeo
mosquito	cigar	cafeteria
vanilla	patio	fiesta

Science

Have interested students find out how a TV station works—how the picture and sound are transmitted to the TV. Let them share their findings with the class.

Career Education

Have students investigate and report on careers in the television industry. If possible, take them to see a TV taping or to a local station or to a college TV department.

RESOURCE CENTER

Enrichment Materials and Activities

Hamilton Hill: September 18, 1784
Pages 506–513

Enrichment Materials:
Letter-writing materials
Painting paper, paints, felt-tipped pens

Activity Needing Advance Planning:
A field trip to a historical site

Guest Speaker:
A historian, history teacher, or member of a local historical society with expertise in the history of the Revolutionary War era

The Temper of Tempe Wick
Pages 514–527

Enrichment Materials:
Pictures of the Revolutionary War era

Activity Needing Advance Planning:
A visit to a museum or historical site

The Little Riders
Pages 528–549

Enrichment Materials:
Clay or papier-mâché materials for making models

Guest Speaker:
An adult who was involved in World War II

Bibliography

For Students

NOTE: For more information about these books, see the *Enrichment* section at the end of the Teaching Unit.

Anderson, Margaret J. *Searching for Shona.* Knopf, 1978.
Baker, Betty. *Walk the World's Rim.* Harper & Row, 1965.

Benchley, Nathaniel. *Sam the Minuteman.* Harper & Row, 1969.
Blaine, Marge. *Dvora's Journey.* Holt, Rinehart & Winston, 1979.
Calhoun, Mary. *High Wind for Kansas.* Morrow, 1965.
Child Study Association of America. *Courage to Adventure: Stories of Boys and Girls Growing Up with America.* T. Y. Crowell, 1976.
Coatsworth, Elizabeth. *The Princess and the Lion.* Pantheon, 1963.
Colby, C. B. *Early American Crafts: Tools, Shops and Products.* Coward, 1967.
Color Crafts. *Papier-Mâché, Dyeing, and Leatherwork.* Watts, 1972.
Denzer, Ann Wiseman. *Making Things: The Hand Book of Creative Discovery.* Little, 1973 and 1975.
Dodge, Nanabah Chee. *Morning Arrow.* Lothrop, 1975.
Duncan, Jane. *Brave Janet Reachfar.* Seabury, 1975.
Finlayson, Ann. *The Silver Bullet.* Nelson, 1978.
Frank, Anne. *The Diary of a Young Girl.* Doubleday, 1967.
Fritz, Jean. *And Then What Happened, Paul Revere?* Coward, 1973.
———. *Brady.* Coward, 1960.
———. *Brendan the Navigator: A History Mystery About the Discovery of America.* Coward, 1979.
———. *The Cabin Faced West.* Coward, 1958.
———. *Can't You Make Them Behave, King George?* Coward, 1977.
———. *Early Thunder.* Coward, 1967.
———. *I, Adam.* Coward, 1963.
———. *Stonewall.* Putnam, 1979.
———. *What's the Big Idea, Ben Franklin?* Coward, 1976.
———. *Where Was Patrick Henry on the 29th of May?* Coward, 1975.
———. *Why Don't You Get a Horse, Sam Adams?* Coward, 1974.
———. *Will You Sign Here, John Hancock?* Coward, 1976.
Gorsline, Douglas. *What People Wore: A Visual History of Dress from Ancient Times to Twentieth-Century America.* Viking Press, 1952.

Haar, Jaap ter. *Boris*. Blackie & Son, 1969.

Higgenbotham, Don, and Kenneth Nebenzahl. *Atlas of the American Revolution*. Rand McNally, 1974.

Kerr, Judith. *A Small Person Far Away*. Coward, 1979.

Knudson, R. *Fox Running*. Harper & Row, 1975.

Krumgold, Joseph. *. . . And Now Miguel*. T. Y. Crowell, 1953.

Lasker, Joe. *The Strange Voyage of Neptune's Car*. Viking Press, 1977.

Lee, Susan, and John R. Lee. *Philadelphia*. Childrens, 1975.

Levy, Harry. *Not Over Ten Inches High*. McGraw, 1968.

Little, Jean. *Mine for Keeps*. Little, 1962.

Naden, Corinne J. *The Colony of New Jersey*. Watts, 1974.

Putnam, Alice. *The Spy Doll*. Elsevier/Nelson, 1979.

Smucker, Barbara. *Runaway to Freedom*. Harper & Row, 1978.

For Teachers

NOTE: For more information about these books, see the *Background* section that precedes the reading selections.

Egoff, Sheila A., comp. *Only Connect: Readings on Children's Literature*. Oxford U. Press, 1969.

Huck, Charlotte S. *Children's Literature in the Elementary School*. Holt, Rinehart & Winston, 1976.

Rudman, Masha K. *Children's Literature: An Issues Approach*. Heath, 1976.

Sebesta, Sam L., and William J. Iverson. *Literature for Thursday's Child*. Science Research, 1975.

Sutherland, Zena, and May Hill Arbuthnot. *Children and Books*, 6th ed. Scott, Foresman, 1981.

Films and Filmstrips

Coronet Instructional Media. "Famous Patriots of the American Revolution: Molly Pitcher." Filmstrip and cassette (#M0249).

Films, Inc. "My Side of the Mountain." Two filmstrips with cassettes. Order by title.

Miller-Brody Productions. "Call It Courage": filmstrip and record (#3002); "The Perilous Road": two filmstrips with record (#3068) or cassette (#3068C); "The Upstairs Room": two filmstrips with record (#3067) or cassette (#3067C).

National Geographic. "Not Worth a Continental." Film (#05914).

Norwood Films. "Defense of Antwerp Against the V-1." Film (FIE52-1614).

Pictura Films. "A Nation Is Born: Rugged Ragamuffins of the Continental Army." Film. Order by title.

Walt Disney Productions. "Treasure Island." Parts I and II. Two filmstrips with two records. Order by title.

Warren Schloat Productions. "Folk Songs of American History. Set I: Revolutionary War." Six filmstrips with record (#501).

Records and/or Tapes

NOTE: Recordings may also be available on other labels.

"And Then What Happened, Paul Revere?" (Weston Woods cassette WW 478C)

"Can't You Make Them Behave, King George?" (Weston Woods cassette WW 481C)

"Oscar Brand's Songs of '76: A Folksinger's History of the Revolution" (Miller-Brody Productions 78177-5; cassette 78178-3)

"Transport" (Viking Press 067072430-0; cassette 067072431-9)

"What's the Big Idea, Ben Franklin?" (Weston Woods cassette WW 476C)

"Where Was Patrick Henry on the 29th of May?" (Weston Woods cassette WW 744C)

"Why Don't You Get a Horse, Sam Adams?" (Weston Woods cassette WW 479C)

"Will You Sign Here, John Hancock?" (Weston Woods cassette WW 480C)

"Women in United States History: Women During the Revolutionary War Era" (Imperial cassette W3KL 5600)

OVERVIEW

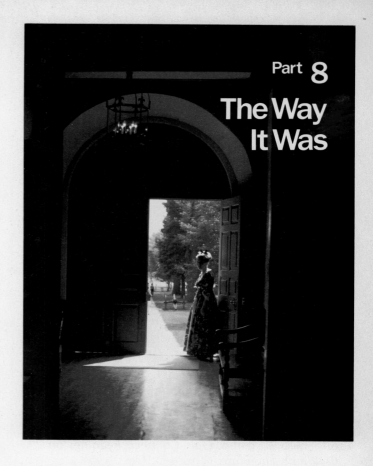

Part **8**

The Way It Was

The skills focus of "The Way It Was" is on understanding historical fiction, in which real people and actual events in history are recreated with fictional details. Students are asked to identify which characters and events in the selections are based on historical fact and which are fictional. The selections in "The Way It Was" include two stories set in colonial America and one story set in Holland during World War II.

Previewing "The Way It Was"

Have students examine the title and the photograph on page 501. Ask students to describe the photograph. (The photograph shows a woman in colonial costume, at the door of her house in a colonial town.) Ask students to tell what they think Part 8 might be about. (the past)

Have students read the title of each selection and examine the illustrations on pages 506–549. Ask students to think about which people and events might be real and which might be fictional. Explain to students that in Part 8 they will learn about historical fiction, in which authors combine historical facts with fictional details to make history come alive.

Objectives

The following list of objectives is provided to help you plan your teaching of "The Way It Was." All the objectives listed under *Introduced* are for skills presented in the student's text in *Understanding and Appreciating Literature*. All the objectives listed under *Maintained* are for skills previously taught in the HBJ BOOKMARK READING PROGRAM, EAGLE EDITION and reinforced either in the *Understanding and Appreciating Literature* section in the student's text or in the *Reading and Discussing* sections in this Teacher's Edition. Since the emphasis in these lessons is on appreciating literature, the literature skills introduced and maintained in Teaching Unit 20 are not tested.

The symbols I*, I, and M are used throughout this Teacher's Edition. The symbol I* indicates skills introduced for the first time in this program. The I indicates skills introduced earlier in Level 11. The M indicates skills taught at earlier levels and maintained in Level 11. The italicized numbers following the objectives are part of a code developed by the HBJ School Department to facilitate the correlation of skills within and between programs. See page T499 for more information.

Introduced

These skills are introduced for the first time at Level 11 in the HBJ BOOKMARK READING PROGRAM, EAGLE EDITION.

	SKILLS CODE NUMBER
To identify historical fiction	6.4.7
To identify historical events and real people in historical fiction	6.4.7.1
To identify fictional details in historical fiction	6.4.7.2

This skill is introduced earlier in Level 11 in the HBJ BOOKMARK READING PROGRAM, EAGLE EDITION.

	SKILLS CODE NUMBER
To distinguish between facts and fictional details	3.6.7

Maintained

These skills have been introduced in earlier levels of the
HBJ BOOKMARK READING PROGRAM, EAGLE EDITION and are
further developed or refined in Level 11.

	SKILLS CODE NUMBER
To interpret characters' feelings	6.9.4
To recognize author's techniques of characterization	6.9.3
To make inferences	3.4
To identify the setting of a story	6.10
To identify the plot of a story	6.11

TEACHING UNIT 20

Pages 502–550

Additional Materials

Reading Skills Workbook: Lesson 41, pages 132–134;
  Word Play, page 135
Duplicating Masters 11: pages 66–70

Key to Symbols

Skills Objectives
I* — Introduced in this unit
I   — Introduced earlier in this level
M   — Maintained from previous levels

Reduced Student Pages
underscore — words that appear in the glossary
wavy line   — words pretaught in the Teacher's Edition
              (these words also appear in the glossary)

Understanding and Appreciating Literature:

Historical Fiction

Pages 502–505

Objectives

		SKILLS CODE NUMBER
I*	To identify historical fiction	6.4.7
I*	To identify historical events and real people in historical fiction	6.4.7.1
I*	To identify fictional details in historical fiction	6.4.7.2

Introducing the Lesson

1. **a.** Ask students to think about the Pilgrims, who came here on the *Mayflower.* (Or, if students have recently studied or discussed some other historical event, you may wish to have them think about that event instead.) Review with students some facts about the voyage of the *Mayflower:* the year it took place (1620), who was aboard the ship (the Pilgrims from England), how long the voyage took (2 months), and where the Pilgrims landed (Plymouth Rock). You may wish to have students research this event briefly.

b. Have students imagine they are aboard ship. Ask them to think about how they might feel and what they might say as they first sight land.

c. Ask students to volunteer to say things they might have said if they were passengers on the *Mayflower*. (You may wish to help students begin by reading the following lines: "Look! I see land! I can hardly wait to put my feet down on some solid ground!")

d. When students have finished, ask them to tell which details in the story they have just recreated were based on facts. (There was a voyage of the *Mayflower*, which landed at Plymouth Rock with Pilgrims aboard.) Ask them to tell which parts did not really happen, or were fictionalized. (the dialogue they invented)

e. Explain to students that their story was part fact and part fiction, and that sometimes authors write stories that combine historical fact and fiction. Tell students that such stories are called *historical fiction*.

2. Direct students to the first picture at the top of page 502 and ask them to read the speech balloons. Ask students if they can identify the three men in the first picture. (Thomas Jefferson, John Adams, and Ben Franklin) Ask students if these men were real people. (yes) Ask students if they think this conversation between the men actually took place. (no)

3. Direct students to the second picture at the top of page 502. Ask students if any of the characters pictured here are important historical figures. (no) Ask them if they know whether the events described here actually took place. (Yes, there was a gold rush to California in 1849.)

UNDERSTANDING AND APPRECIATING LITERATURE

Historical Fiction

A realistic story that contains made-up characters and events is called realistic fiction. Realistic fiction that contains facts about important real people or events from history and fictional details is called **historical fiction**. Historical fiction combines historical facts with fiction.

Understanding Historical Fiction

Read box 1. Who are the important people from history in the cartoon? They are Thomas Jefferson, John Adams, and

502

Developing the Skill

A. *Historical fiction contains facts about important real people or events from history combined with fictional details.*

1. Ask students to read the first paragraph on page 502. Then ask them to tell how historical fiction differs from other kinds of realistic fiction. (It contains facts about important real people or events.)

2. Have students read the next two paragraphs. Then ask students to tell why they think historical fiction is written, and why people enjoy reading it. (Accept all reasonable answers.)

Benjamin Franklin. What is made-up, or fictional, in the cartoon? The meeting for a meal and the conversation of these important people are fictional.

Read box 2. The people in this cartoon are not important historically. What important historical event is shown? The California gold rush of 1849 is an actual historical event. The characters, conversation, and details such as the sign on the wagon are fictional.

Read the following paragraph. Look for real historical characters and events and fictional details.

Ben Franklin's Trip to France

My name is Benjamin Franklin Bache. I came to France with Benjamin Franklin, my grandfather, to get help for the United States. Grandfather wants to make a treaty saying that France and the United States are friends. But he can't do much about that treaty now, because he can't get to see the king of France. The king of France doesn't want to meet Grandfather yet. He's waiting to see how General Washington makes out with the war.

Which characters were real people? Benjamin Franklin, the king of France, and George Washington were important historically. Benjamin Franklin really had a grandson named Benjamin Franklin Bache. What events are important historically? The treaty between the United States and France during the Revolutionary War is a real historical event. What is fictional? Benjamin Franklin Bache's words and his grandfather's words are fictional. The combination of historical people and events with fictional details makes this paragraph historical fiction.

Read the following story. Look again for the historical facts and the fictional details.

503

The Big Race

Amanda had heard about a strange race in Baltimore between two horses, an "iron horse" and a real one. Amanda hurried to see the iron horse.

It didn't look like a horse. It was a wagon with a big round tank on top and four iron wheels. A fire was in a stove under the tank. Steam was spitting from the pipes. Amanda learned that a man named Peter Cooper had made it and named it the *Tom Thumb* because it was small. It ran on two iron strips called a track.

The race started and Amanda followed in her wagon. The *Tom Thumb* pulled ahead. Everybody clapped and whistled. Then there was a bang, and the *Tom Thumb* came to a stop. The real horse sailed by. Cooper and his "iron horse" lost the race.

Was there really a race? Yes, there was. Peter Cooper, an iron-maker, built the *Tom Thumb*, a train engine. In August 1830, the *Tom Thumb* lost a race to a horse in Baltimore. The race was important historically because the *Tom Thumb* was one of the first steam-powered train engines. Amanda and her words are fictional.

Historical fiction contains important historical people or events, and sometimes both. It also has fictional parts. In historical fiction, fact is combined with fiction to make history come alive.

Try This

Read the following story, then answer the questions.

In 1776, thirteen-year-old Phoebe Fraunces took an important job. Posing as a servant, she went to General George Washington's headquarters to try to

504

B. *Historical fiction usually contains a mixture of historical facts and fiction.*

1. Ask students to read the next paragraph on page 503 and the story that follows.

2. Ask students to tell which people in the story are historical figures. (Benjamin Franklin, the king of France, and General Washington) Tell students that Benjamin Franklin Bache actually was Franklin's grandson.

3. Ask students to identify a real historical event that is mentioned in the paragraph. (A treaty between the United States and France was made during the Revolutionary War. Guide students in their responses if they are unaware of this event.)

4. Ask students which details of the paragraph are fictional. (Students should recognize that the words of Benjamin Franklin Bache are probably fictional.) You may wish to point out that sometimes it is hard to tell what is historical fact and what is fiction if a reader is not familiar with a particular historical period or event. Explain that authors often add a note to a story explaining which events are based on fact and which details are fictional.

5. Ask students to read the paragraph on page 503 that follows Benjamin Franklin Bache's story.

C. *Authors combine historical facts with fictional details to make history come alive.*

1. Ask students to read the last paragraph on page 503 and to complete the story "The Big Race" on page 504.

2. Ask students to decide which people and events are real, and which are fictional. (Accept all reasonable answers.)

3. Have students check their answers by reading the paragraph on page 504 that follows the story.

4. Ask students to read the final paragraph before *Try This*. Have students discuss stories or books they have read that they think might have been historical fiction.

save his life. Phoebe knew that a person known as "T" was planning to harm Washington.

"But who is T?" Phoebe wondered.

Phoebe served dinner. Everyone looked friendly. Who wished to harm General Washington?

"Where is my bodyguard, Thomas Hickey?" Washington asked, as Phoebe gave him his dinner.

Could *T* be for "Thomas"? Phoebe remembered that Mr. Hickey was in the kitchen when she prepared dinner. Phoebe grabbed the plate of food.

General Washington was astonished. Phoebe had saved his life. Thomas Hickey had tried to poison the general.

1. Which characters were probably real people? Which events might really have taken place?
2. Which parts of the story are fictional, or made-up?

Writing

1. Choose one of the historical people and events below. Write a sentence telling something fictional about that person.

   a. telegraph invented by Samuel F. B. Morse
   b. Lewis and Clark Expedition, guided by Sacajawea
   c. phonograph invented by Thomas A. Edison

2. Choose some facts from a selection listed below and write a paragraph of historical fiction.

   a. "Lady Moody's Dream" (page 292)
   b. "The Peddler's Pack" (page 306)
   c. "The Journey of the Tejas Woman" (page 286)

   The stories in "The Way It Was" are historical fiction. As you read, look for the real people and events from history.

505

Try This

Have students complete *Try This*.

Answers to *Try This*

1. George Washington, Phoebe Fraunces, Thomas Hickey; the dinner at General Washington's headquarters, Hickey's presence in the kitchen, and Phoebe's grabbing General Washington's plate might really have taken place; 2. Phoebe's thoughts and perhaps Washington's question: "Where is my bodyguard, Thomas Hickey?"

Writing

(Optional) Have students complete one or both of the *Writing* activities on page 505, using the following procedures:

1. You may wish to write the following lines on the board to help students begin.

   Can you imagine what it was like before the telegraph was invented?
   Sacajawea led Lewis and Clark over the high mountains.
   Thomas A. Edison was a music lover.
   Lady Moody looked out at the blue ocean beyond her town.
   People from the little town gathered around the peddler who came down the street with the big pack on his back.
   The Tejas Woman's face lit up with excitement.

2. Tell students to list or outline their ideas before they begin writing. For *Writing* activity 1, remind students of the following: (a) historical fiction contains facts about people and events from history; (b) historical fiction contains fictional details that make a story more interesting. For *Writing* activity 2, have students reread the selection they wish to use before they begin writing. For both activities, suggest that students make short lists or an outline of the historical facts they will use and the fictional details they will invent.

3. Encourage students to share their finished work with the class.

 Use *Reading Skills Workbook,* Lesson 41, pages 132–134.

Reading Selection:
Hamilton Hill:
September 18, 1784
Pages 506–513

Objectives

		SKILLS CODE NUMBER
I*	To identify historical fiction	6.4.7
I*	To identify historical events and real people in historical fiction	6.4.7.1
I*	To identify fictional details in historical fiction	6.4.7.2
M	To interpret characters' feelings	6.9.4
M	To recognize author's techniques of characterization	6.9.3
I	To distinguish between fact and fictional details	3.6.7

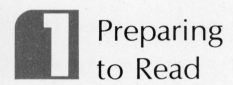 **Preparing to Read**

Summary

At midday on the hill near her home, young Ann Hamilton hears the hoofbeats of several horses. Fearful, she tries to hide from the riders, who she suspects are up to no good. But a deep voice rings out, "Little girl, . . . tell me what your family is having for dinner tonight." Ann looks up to see the strong, kind face of a man who looks strangely familiar. No longer afraid, she proudly tells him what's for dinner. The man asks her to tell her mother that General George Washington would like to eat with them.

That night the general speaks to the Hamiltons of his belief in the new country and its glorious future, a future that young people, such as Ann, will share. Later, Ann happily writes in her diary, "George Washington was here."

Background

Jean Fritz, author of "Hamilton Hill," explores her own heritage by studying American history and writing historical fiction. Ms. Fritz is the author of many lively works for young people, including *The Cabin Faced West,* the book from which "Hamilton Hill" was excerpted, and *Early Thunder,* set in Revolutionary War times in Salem, Massachusetts.

As Ms. Fritz explains in a postscript to "Hamilton Hill," Ann Hamilton was her great-great-grandmother, and she actually did spend a wonderful evening in the company of General George Washington.

The following books will provide you with additional background information on historical fiction.

Egoff, Sheila A., comp. *Only Connect: Readings on Children's Literature.* Several entertaining and informative articles on writing and appreciating historical fiction (see Part 3).

Huck, Charlotte S. *Children's Literature in the Elementary School.* Chapter 8 presents an excellent discussion of historical fiction.

Developing Vocabulary and Concepts

prickly: having small, sharp points; stinging
occasional: occurring now and then
curtsy: a bow made by bending the knees, used by women and girls as a sign of respect
linen: made of linen, which is thread or cloth made of flax fibers
gleaming: shining with reflected light
venison: the flesh of the deer, used as food
bated: a term used in the 1700's to mean "took supper"

1. **a.** Read the following sentences aloud or write them on the board. If you read them aloud, write the underlined vocabulary on the board.

    The cactus was very prickly; one of its tiny thorns stung my finger.
    Grandfather makes an occasional visit to our house, but we wish he would come more often.
    Doris made a deep curtsy by bowing when she was introduced to the First Lady.
    Her dress for special occasions was made of the finest linen cloth.
    I polished the silverware until it was gleaming brightly.
    After the deer hunt, we ate the venison for dinner.
    The general bated, or took supper, with the family.

    b. Ask students to give the meaning of each vocabulary word. Remind them to use the context clues in the sentences to help them.

Hamilton Hill

September 18, 1784

by JEAN FRITZ

All day long as Ann went about her chores, she felt out-of-sorts and out of courage. She didn't know what was bothering her, but everything she did went wrong. She cut her finger when she was chopping pumpkin for her mother to make a pumpkin pie. She spilled half a pail of milk. She caught her dress on a prickly bush and tore it. And every time she picked up the baby, he cried.

"This isn't your day," her mother said toward the middle of the afternoon. "Why don't you go on down the road and try to find some grapes? You'll like that. But mind you don't go too far."

It certainly wasn't her day, Ann thought crossly as she took the empty pail and went out the cabin door. But when she reached the road, she wondered. Maybe, after all, something might yet turn the day her way. The road seemed to have more magic to it than she had ever known. The sun's rays slanted down on it as though they were lighting up a stage where something important was going to happen. There was a difference in the mood of the road. It wasn't a happy, dancing mood, or a mysterious, moonlight mood. Today there was a grandness to the road, as though it were a carpet unfurling over the hill before some glorious secret. As Ann stood in the middle of the road, holding her pail in front of her, two golden leaves drifted down, turning slowly over

506

and over in the air, and settled in the bottom of her pail. A wild goose dipped low, honking, from the sky, like a herald sent ahead with news.

Ann walked down the hill, captured by the spell of the road. As she rounded each bend, she found herself half expecting something wonderful to be waiting on the other side. She didn't know what, but something. From time to time she stopped to pick grapes. On all the hill, the only sounds were the plopping of grapes in her pail and the occasional long honk of a passing goose. Ann followed the road as it wound its way down the hill, turning corner after corner, looking for grapes, but secretly hoping for something she couldn't even put into words.

Her pail was almost full when she suddenly noticed where she was. She was almost to the bottom of the hill. She had let the road lead her farther than she had ever gone alone.

And then Ann heard hoofbeats. They were coming from the east—not just one horse but three or four, and they were not far away.

Ann ducked down behind some tall grass by the side of the road and made herself into the smallest ball she could possibly squeeze into, wrapping her arms tightly around her knees. She held her breath as the first horse rounded the bend of the road. She must not move—not even a finger. She kept her eyes on the road, counting the legs of the horses as they came into sight. Now there were two horses . . . three

---

2. a. Write the story title "Hamilton Hill: September 18, 1784" on the board. Ask students what kind of writing might have the place and date written in this way. (Accept all reasonable answers, such as a letter or a diary entry.)

b. Ask students to give their impressions of what America was like in the year 1784. You may wish to remind them that the Declaration of Independence had been adopted on July 4, 1776, yet the Americans still had to fight to assert their independence from England. George Washington was not inaugurated as the first President until 1789.

Ask students to think about everyday life in the year 1784: what people wore, ate, did for fun, and so on. Their impressions can be confirmed or revised later when they read "Hamilton Hill."

 Use *Duplicating Masters 11,* page 66.

Setting Purposes

Skills

Tell students to look for the real characters and events in the following selection. Ask them also to be aware of the fictional elements in the story.

Content

Tell students that they are about to read a story about a girl named Ann Hamilton, who is not having a good day. Ask them to read to find out how Ann's day changes and what very important event takes place on this day.

2 Reading and Discussing

Have students read the selection. Most students will be able to complete it in one sitting. If you prefer, the selection may be read in two parts, breaking before the paragraph beginning "Afterward . . ." on page 509.

NOTE: The questions that appear in the student's text at the end of the selection focus on comprehension of selection content and on understanding of historical fiction. Answers to these questions begin on page T449.

. . . four. If four men were traveling together from the East to the West at this time of year, they were probably not settlers. They were likely up to no good. They must be the Doane gang that her brother David had warned her about.

All at once Ann began to tremble all over. The first horse had stopped on the road in front of her. Then the other horses came to a stop. As Ann peeped out between the tall grasses, all she could see was a forest of horse legs. From some place way up high above the legs of the first horse came a deep voice. "Little girl," it said, "I wonder if you could tell me what your family is having for dinner tonight."

The voice didn't sound like the voice of a horse thief. Slowly Ann lifted her eyes from the legs of the horse to the boots of the rider. Slowly she lifted them to the place where the voice had come from. Then she found herself looking into the most wonderful face she had ever seen.

It was a strong face, kind and good, and there was something strangely familiar about it. It was as if Ann ought to know this man, as if she almost knew him. No matter what David had said about strangers, somehow Ann knew deep inside that he hadn't been talking about this one. She stopped feeling afraid. She stood up.

"We are having peas and potatoes and corn bread for our evening meal," she said, "and my mother is baking pumpkin pie."

The man smiled. He leaned toward Ann. "Would you tell her," he said, "that General George Washington would like to take supper with her?"

For a moment Ann could not believe her ears. General Washington on Hamilton Hill! Then all at

508

once she knew it was true. This was the way she had pictured George Washington. This must have been just how Washington looked, riding among the men at Valley Forge.

Ann swallowed hard. She tried to drop a curtsy but it turned out to be just a stiff little bob. She tried to find her voice, but it didn't turn out any better than the curtsy. It was more like a squeak. "My mother will be pleased," she said. "I'll tell her."

Afterward Ann could never remember just how she introduced General Washington and his friends to her mother. When she caught her breath again, they had started on a tour of the farm with David. Ann and her mother were alone in the cabin with supper to prepare.

Mrs. Hamilton's eyes were shining as she stepped away from the door. "Now is the time to use the linen tablecloth, Ann," she said, "and the lavender flowered plates."

509

Ann spread out the white linen cloth on the table. She smoothed it gently over the rough boards. She pulled it to hang even on all sides. She unwrapped nine flowered plates and placed them around the table. She put knives, forks, and spoons at each place and set new tall candles in the center of the table.

Then Ann stepped back to look at what she'd done. Somehow the whole room seemed changed; it seemed larger and more dignified. The clothes hanging awkwardly on hooks along the wall drew back into the shadows. All the light from the fire and from the open doorway fell on the gleaming white party table, waiting for General Washington.

Later the table looked even more wonderful, piled high with steaming food—hot yellow corn bread, round bowls of green peas, roasted brown potatoes, a platter of cold venison, golden pumpkin pies. It was the same meal they had had nearly every evening all summer on Hamilton Hill, but tonight with the lavender flowered plates, it managed to look different.

"I hope I look different too," Ann thought as she fingered her two blue hair ribbons and hastily tied the sash of a fresh apron.

She felt different. General Washington and Mr. Hamilton led the others into the cabin, and suddenly Ann found herself feeling strangely shy. All the time they were taking their places at the table, she kept her eyes down. It was not until her father was asking the blessing that she stole her first look up from under half-closed eyelashes. When she saw George Washington's head bowed over the white tablecloth and lavender plate, the peas and potatoes, Ann thought she could hardly bear her happiness.

510

During the meal, Ann followed the conversation in a kind of daze. She didn't seem to hear anything that anyone said, except General Washington. Everything he said rang out clear, with a special meaning, it almost seemed, just for her.

"If I were a young man," General Washington said, "preparing to begin the world, I know of no country where I should rather live."

"I am determined to find a way," he said again, "that we can join the waters of the West with those of the East so that the two countries may be close together."

Ann held onto every word, turned them over in her mind, locked them away in her heart. It was after the evening meal, after all the thank-you's had been said and General Washington and his party were preparing to leave that he said what Ann was to treasure forever afterward. He stood at the doorway, looking toward the west, his eyes resting on Hamilton Hill, yet somehow going beyond.

General Washington turned to Ann. "Through the courage of young girls as much as anyone's, our country will grow. You will live to see this whole country a rolling farmland, bright with houses and barns. Some day. I envy you, Miss Hamilton."

Ann felt her heart turning over within her. Even after General Washington had gone, she went on standing in the doorway. She looked out on Hamilton Hill. It seemed to her she had never seen it so beautiful.

That night, in the home of a Colonel Cannon several miles west of Hamilton Hill, before he blew out his candle, General George Washington sat down at a table and wrote this in his diary:

511

"September 18, 1784. Set out with Doctr. Craik for my Land on Miller's Run, crossed the Monongahela at Devore's Ferry . . . bated at one Hamilton's about 4 miles from it, in Washington County, and lodged at Colo. Cannon's."

That night in the cabin on Hamilton Hill, Ann took down from her shelf her deerskin-covered diary. Her heart was too full to write all she wanted. Instead she wrote in big letters across a whole page:

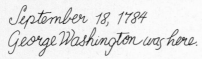

September 18, 1784
George Washington was here.

Tomorrow she would write more.

A Note from the Author

If you look in George Washington's diary, you will find that his words are written there exactly as they are in the diary in this story. On September 18, 1784, he "bated," or took supper, with the Hamiltons.

I don't know if Ann really kept a diary or not. Most of what happened to her in this story is just a story, but some of it is true. There really was an Ann Hamilton; she was my great-great-grandmother. As long as she lived, she told the story to her children and her children's children, about the wonderful evening when George Washington rode up Hamilton Hill.

512

Understanding What You've Read

1. Which characters and events in the story were probably real, not made up by the author?
2. Which parts of the story were probably made-up? Find five examples on pages 509–510.
3. Why was Ann excited when General Washington stopped at her house for dinner?
4. Why did Ann treasure Washington's words to her about her future as a young woman in the United States?
5. What do you learn in the Author's Note, page 512, about sources of the facts used in this story?

Writing

1. Suppose you wanted to write a historical fiction story about a boy or girl in the year 1930. Write some questions you could ask people to find out about that time in history. You might ask how they dressed, what they studied in school, and what games they played.
2. Pretend that you are George Washington writing in your diary on April 30, 1789, the day you became President of the United States. Tell what happened and how you felt. Use these historical facts to help you:

   a. George Washington rode to Federal Hall in his carriage as part of a big parade.
   b. He was sworn in on the steps of Federal Hall in New York City.
   c. The army gave him a thirteen-cannon salute at the conclusion of the ceremony.

513

Questions preceded by a bullet are additional questions and appear in the Teacher's Edition only. The other questions appear in the student's text after the selection.

Understanding What You've Read

1. *Which characters and events in the story were probably real, not made up by the author?* (Accept all reasonable answers. All the characters in the story were probably real people, but students should understand that George Washington and Ann Hamilton definitely were real people. It is historical fact that George Washington had dinner with the Hamilton family.) CRITICAL   Identifying historical fiction

● *What happened to Ann that made her think that "it wasn't her day"?* (She cut her finger when she was chopping pumpkin, spilled half a pail of milk, and tore her dress; and every time she picked up the baby, he cried.   page 506) LITERAL   Recalling specific details

● *How did Ann feel once she reached the road?* (She felt that the day might hold something in store for her after all. She felt a "grandness to the road" and was "captured" by its spell. She knew something was going to happen.   pages 506–507) CRITICAL Interpreting characters' feelings

● *What did Ann realize when she found herself almost at the bottom of the hill?* (She realized that she had gone farther than she had ever gone alone.   page 507) LITERAL   Recalling stated information

● *Why did Ann hide in the grass by the side of the road? Whom did she think the four men on horses were?* (Ann was frightened by the four men on horses. She thought they were the Doane Gang her brother had warned her about.   page 507) INFERENTIAL   Making inferences

● *What do you learn about General George Washington from Ann's thoughts about his voice and face?* ("The voice didn't sound like the voice of a horse thief." She "found herself looking into the most wonderful face she had ever seen." "It was a strong face, kind and good . . ." "No matter what David had said about strangers, somehow Ann knew deep inside that he hadn't been talking about this one."   page 508) CRITICAL   Recognizing author's techniques of characterization

● *What did General Washington request of Ann?* (He asked Ann to tell her mother that he would like to take supper with them.   page 508) CRITICAL   Identifying historical fiction

- *What did Ann and her mother do to get ready for dinner with General George Washington?* (They used the linen tablecloth and the lavender flowered plates; they used new tall candles.   pages 509–510) LITERAL   Recalling specific details

- *What did the Hamilton family have for dinner? How do you think they got the food they ate?* (hot yellow corn bread, green peas, roasted brown potatoes, cold venison, and pumpkin pie; students should realize that the Hamilton family probably grew their own corn, peas, potatoes, and pumpkins and hunted the deer that provided the cold venison.   page 510) LITERAL/CRITICAL   Recalling details/Drawing conclusions

2. *Which parts of the story were probably made-up? Find five examples on pages 509–510.* (The conversations between members of the Hamilton family and those between the Hamilton family and George Washington. Details of the setting—the description of the dinner table and the food that was served—are fictional details. Ann's thoughts and feelings while she was picking berries are probably fictional.) CRITICAL   Identifying fictional details

3. *Why was Ann excited when General Washington stopped at her house for dinner?* (Accept all reasonable answers. It must have been an unusual circumstance for the Hamiltons to have guests. The festive atmosphere and the importance of the guest made it exciting.) CRITICAL   Interpreting characters' feelings

- *What did George Washington say that seemed special to Ann? How did he express his dream for his country?* ("If I were a young man preparing to begin the world, I know of no country where I should rather live." "I am determined to find a way that we can join the waters of the West with those of the East so that the two countries may be close together." "Through the courage of young girls as much as anyone's, our country will grow. You will live to see this whole country a rolling farmland, bright with houses and barns. Some day. I envy you, Miss Hamilton." Washington dreamed of a united country with East and West close together.   page 511) CRITICAL   Interpreting characters' feelings

4. *Why did Ann treasure Washington's words to her about her future as a young woman in the United States?* (They were addressed specifically to Ann, and they suggested to her that she and other young women would play an important role in the development of the country.) CRITICAL   Interpreting characters' feelings

- *What did Ann write in her diary that night? Do you think this is a fitting way for this story to end? Why or why not?* (Ann wrote "George Washington was here." Accept all reasonable answers. Students may recognize this sentence, or the more familiar "George Washington slept here," as a common claim made for historical sites. This ending makes clever use of this claim since "Hamilton Hill: September 18, 1784" has told the story of Washington's actually being on Hamilton Hill.   page 512) LITERAL/CRITICAL   Recalling specific details/Making judgments

5. *What do you learn in the Author's Note, page 512, about sources of the facts used in this story?* (Students should be aware from reading this postscript that Jean Fritz used George Washington's diary as one of her sources.) CRITICAL   Identifying historical fiction

- *Name three or more elements in "Hamilton Hill" that you think were invented by the author to help make a more exciting story.* (Accept all reasonable answers. Students should cite examples of Ann's feelings, thoughts, and words; her diary entry; and the menu at the Hamilton house.) CRITICAL   Identifying fictional details

- *How do you think Jean Fritz found facts about Ann Hamilton?* (Accept all reasonable answers. Students should infer that Jean Fritz learned about Ann Hamilton from stories that were passed down through the generations in her family about the dinner with George Washington. Students may also speculate about letters or other documents that Ann Hamilton may have had that members of Jean Fritz's family owned.) CRITICAL   Making judgments

Writing

(Optional) Have students complete one or both of the *Writing* activities on page 513. Or ask students to do the writing activity under *Additional Writing Activity*.

1. *Suppose you wanted to write a historical fiction story about a boy or girl in the year 1930. Write some questions you could ask people to find out about that time in history. You might ask how they dressed, what they studied in school, and what games they played.*   Writing interview questions

Tell students to list or outline their ideas before they begin writing. If students need help with the *Writing* activity, suggest that they consider the following: (a) interview a person who grew up in a city in America in the 1930's; (b) interview a person who grew up in another country in the 1930's; (c) interview a person who grew up in a small town in America in the 1930's.

You may wish to write the following questions on the board to help students get started.

Did you have airports then?
What kinds of games did you play?
What subjects did you study in school?

Have students write their own questions or choose one from the board and begin writing.

2. *Pretend that you are George Washington writing in your diary on April 30, 1789, the day you became President of the United States. Tell what happened and how you felt. Use these historical facts to help you:*
a. George Washington rode to Federal Hall in his carriage as part of a big parade.
b. He was sworn in on the steps of Federal Hall in New York City.
c. The army gave him a thirteen-cannon salute at the conclusion of the ceremony.
Writing a diary entry

Tell students to list or outline their ideas before they begin writing. If students need help with the *Writing* activity, suggest that they consider the following: (a) describe George Washington's feelings as he saw the cheering crowd; (b) describe the presidential inauguration ceremony on the steps of Federal Hall in New York City; (c) describe George Washington's feelings as he heard the cannon salute.

You may wish to write the following opening lines on the board to help students get started.

It was the most memorable day of my life.
I will never forget the expressions of joy and pride on the faces of the cheering crowd.

Have students write their own opening lines or choose one from the board and begin writing.

Additional Writing Activity (Optional)

● *At the end of "Hamilton Hill" it is suggested that Ann would write more in her diary about what happened on the very special day George Washington came to visit. Imagine that you are Ann. Write a diary entry to tell about September 18, 1784.*
Writing a diary entry

Tell students to list or outline their ideas before they begin writing. If students need help with the *Writing* activity, suggest that they include all the following information: (a) describe Ann's first impression of George Washington; (b) describe the preparations she and her mother made for the special occasion; (c) describe the conversation at the dinner table.

You may wish to write the following opening lines on the board to help students get started.

I had not seen this man before, but there was something strangely familiar about him.
I held on to every single word he uttered.

Have students write their own opening lines or choose one from the board and begin writing.

 For additional resources and curriculum-related activities, see *Enrichment*, page T469.

Reading Selection:
The Temper of Tempe Wick

Pages 514–527

Objectives

		SKILLS CODE NUMBER
I*	To identify historical fiction	6.4.7
I*	To identify historical events and real people in historical fiction	6.4.7.1
I*	To identify fictional details in historical fiction	6.4.7.2
M	To make inferences	3.4
I	To distinguish between fact and fictional details	3.6.7

Preparing to Read

Summary

Tempe Wick had helped many soldiers during the American Revolution and when they turned on her, she was not going to let them take anything away. Tempe was determined to protect what was hers, and that meant her sick mother, her home, and her horse, Bon. One day, two soldiers followed Tempe home and demanded her horse. But Tempe cleverly hid Bon in her bedroom. The soldiers would not be put off so easily, however. One soldier entered the house, but Tempe grabbed his musket and kicked him out the door. The soldier and his friend finally went off, on foot, to Pennsylvania.

Background

"The Temper of Tempe Wick" is excerpted from a book by Patricia Lee Gauch called *This Time, Tempe Wick?* The author's research led her to discover the true and interesting story of Tempe Wick's revolutionary activities.

Patricia Lee Gauch has written many books for children, several of which are based on the lives of real people.

The following books will provide you with additional background information on historical fiction.

Rudman, Masha K. *Children's Literature: An Issues Approach.* Chapter 5 explores books for children and how they can be discussed.

Sebesta, Sam L., and William J. Iverson. *Literature for Thursday's Child.* Chapter 6 presents a general discussion of realistic and historical fiction.

Developing Vocabulary and Concepts

mutiny: a rebellion against authority, as by a group of soldiers or sailors against their commanders

fifed: played a fife, which is a small flute having a shrill tone used with drums in military music

smoke-shed: a small building or closed room where meat, fish, hides, etc., are hung and treated with smoke to preserve them

settee: a long bench or sofa with a back and arms, usually for two or three people

fiddleback chair: a straight-back chair with no arms and a center piece down the back that is shaped like a fiddle

scoffed: showed scorn or mocking disbelief

musket: an old type of firearm, now replaced by the rifle

1. **a.** Read the following sentences aloud or write them on the board. If you read them aloud, write the underlined vocabulary on the board.

   There was a <u>mutiny</u> aboard the ship, and the sailors refused to obey the captain.

   The soldiers marched as the fife players <u>fifed</u> a shrill tune.

   Henry hung the venison in the <u>smoke-shed</u> to preserve it so the family would have meat for the long winter.

   The <u>settee</u> in the parlor was crowded with four people sitting on it.

   The little boy sat back against the fiddle-shaped center-piece of the <u>fiddleback chair</u>.

   The onlookers <u>scoffed</u> at and mocked the horse that was trying to jump the high fence.

   In the firearms display at the museum, we saw a <u>musket</u> used by Revolutionary War soldiers.

   b. Ask students to give the meaning of each vocabulary word. Remind them to use the context clues in the sentences to help them.

2. Present the following information to the class:

   We know about the history of the American Revolution from books and newspapers preserved from that time. We know that Temperance Wick was a real person who lived in Jockey Hollow, New Jersey, and that 10,000 soldiers spent the winter of 1780–1781 there. Many soldiers mutinied, or rebelled, because there was little food or money. We know that they even robbed people who had once befriended them.

What we cannot know for sure is exactly what took place between Tempe Wick and the soldiers. What did they actually do or say? The author of this story used the historical information she found as the basis for her story. But because the story combines fictional details with true information from historical records, it is considered historical fiction.

3. Discuss with students the concept of mutiny. Explain that sometimes soldiers or sailors have had to exist under such terrible conditions that they have refused to fight for their leaders and have rebelled against them.

 Use *Duplicating Masters 11,* page 67.

Setting Purposes

Skills

Since students have heard a brief summary of the historical basis for the story they are about to read, ask them to look for the fictional details that help make the story exciting to read.

Content

Tell students they are going to read a story about a girl named Tempe Wick who really lived in the 1700's. In the story, Tempe is not much older than the students are.

Begin reading the introduction to the class. Remind students to be aware of time and place clues in the story. To help students appreciate the full flavor of the language, read aloud the opening scene, which consists mainly of conversation between Tempe and the blacksmith. Give full emphasis to "aye" and "agin"—words that reproduce the dialect of this place and period. Point out that one good way to get a feeling for the historical setting of the story is through the language used by the characters.

Tempe Wick was a real person who lived in Jockey Hollow, New Jersey. Ten thousand soldiers spent the winter of 1780–1781 at Jockey Hollow. Tempe Wick was glad to help feed and clothe these Revolutionary War soldiers, but when some soldiers mutinied, things changed.

The Temper of Tempe Wick

by PATRICIA LEE GAUCH

It was the camp blacksmith who ran by and told Tempe the news.

"It's a mutiny, ma'am. Take cover," said the blacksmith.

"From our own soldiers, sir?" said she.

"Aye. They're agin their own captains. They're agin their own general. They may be agin you! You've food to fill their stomachs and a horse to get them away. That's reason enough!"

And off he ran.

He didn't even see Tempe get mad. But she did.

"Agin me!" she said to herself, pushing up the sleeves of her nightgown. "Agin me, indeed! I've shared the

514

2 Reading and Discussing

Have students read the selection. Most students will be able to complete it in one sitting. If you prefer, the selection may be read in two parts, breaking at the end of page 519.

NOTE: The questions that appear in the student's text at the end of the selection focus on comprehension of selection content and on understanding of historical fiction. Answers to these questions begin on page T457.

wheat from my fields, sir, and the cows from my herd. And I do not see how it will serve their war to make a war on me. But if any soldier takes from my home or steals from my barn or tries to take my horse, he'll have to battle me first!''

Tempe loaded her rifle, then poked it through a small crack in the kitchen window. She vowed not to move from the spot until every soldier was off her farm.

And she kept her word. Until just after midnight. Then a thousand soldiers, followed by one general, marched off to Philadelphia. They wanted to tell the leaders of all America how they were hungry and cold and poor. As they passed, the men shouted. The fifers fifed. The drummers drummed. But when the cannoneer

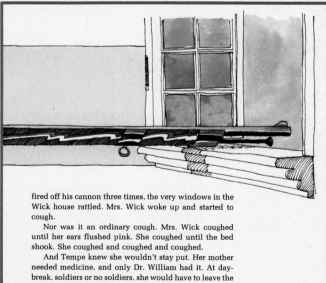

fired off his cannon three times, the very windows in the Wick house rattled. Mrs. Wick woke up and started to cough.

Nor was it an ordinary cough. Mrs. Wick coughed until her ears flushed pink. She coughed until the bed shook. She coughed and coughed and coughed.

And Tempe knew she wouldn't stay put. Her mother needed medicine, and only Dr. William had it. At daybreak, soldiers or no soldiers, she would have to leave the house. She would have to get to the barn. Then she would ride Bonny down the trail to the doctor's farm.

It was then she learned that all the soldiers had not gone to Philadelphia. Soldiers were everywhere. Some were still celebrating in the cornfield. Some were sleeping against the smoke-shed. Others were at the well.

But Tempe went anyway. She didn't go shouting, and she didn't go shooting. Not this time. After hiding her mother in the cellar, she bundled up in her Sunday coat and fine hat. She walked . . . slowly . . . to the barn, just as

if she were alone in the world. She pretended not to see the soldier peeking through the fence at her. She pretended not to see the soldier duck up into the loft.

She whistled a little tune and went right to Bonny's stall. Coolly and calmly and casually she put on her bridle and saddle and rode, coolly and calmly and casually, right past them all. It was as if she were the white-horse lead in a military parade.

The soldiers just watched.

Not until she got to the road did she hurry. Then she touched her Bon with a stick and raced down the road to Dr. William's. It had all been so easy. Probably, she thought, those soldiers didn't want anything from the Wicks at all. Probably the blacksmith had been just the smallest bit nervous.

But when she left Dr. William's with a full bottle of medicine, she learned differently. Out of the thicket, right in front of the doctor's house, jumped two soldiers.

Even Tempe's stomach took a flip.

"Pretty young lady," said the one, "that's a fine horse you have."

"Thank you, sir." She smiled and started by.

But the other, a thin man with sideburns that curled like an S around his ears, stopped her.

"I imagine a fine mare like that could carry me and my friend, say, all the way to Philadelphia," he said.

"I imagine," Tempe said. She tried to get by again.

"Then we'll try her now!" he said. Quickly, he grabbed the reins from Tempe. "Get down!"

Tempe didn't even blink. Not this time. She turned her head, coyly, so sweetly, so perfectly, and said, "But, sir, 'tis my best horse Bon."

"Then she'll do her best for us. Get down I say." He was terribly gruff.

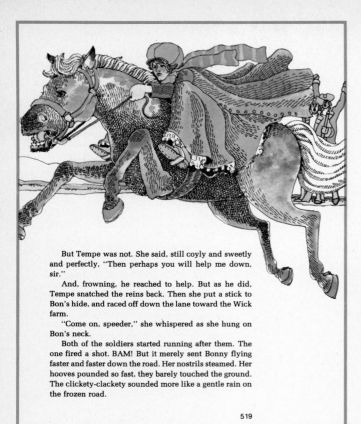

But Tempe was not. She said, still coyly and sweetly and perfectly, "Then perhaps you will help me down, sir."

And, frowning, he reached to help. But as he did, Tempe snatched the reins back. Then she put a stick to Bon's hide, and raced off down the lane toward the Wick farm.

"Come on, speeder," she whispered as she hung on Bon's neck.

Both of the soldiers started running after them. The one fired a shot. BAM! But it merely sent Bonny flying faster and faster down the road. Her nostrils steamed. Her hooves pounded so fast, they barely touched the ground. The clickety-clackety sounded more like a gentle rain on the frozen road.

519

All of the other soldiers were gone when Tempe rode up under the willow that guarded the back door. But she didn't try to squeeze Bonny in the smoke-shed. She'd quickly be found. Nor did Tempe even hide Bon in the woods. The soldiers knew the woods well.

No, Tempe did a most surprising thing. She led Bonny right in the back door and into the kitchen of the Wick house!

Of course, Tempe didn't tie her there. Everyone visited the kitchen first, particularly when the blizzards whipped around the Wick house in January. Tempe led Bon straight through the sitting room, too. Old Bon might not treat kindly her Grandmother Wick's fine desk from England or her mother's favorite fiddleback chair. And Tempe's mother's cough was not apt to improve with a horse sharing her bedroom!

So Tempe took the mare into her own room, the tiny dark room with the two tiny windows in the back of the house. She left her, happily nibbling at the flax-woven spread on Tempe's bed.

And just in time. Tempe had just brought her mother up from the cellar when there came a terrible thumping on the back door.

It was the man with the curled sideburns. He bellowed through the crack in the door, "I want that gray mare!"

But Tempe answered lazily, as if she had been spinning wool all afternoon, "A gray mare, sir? Have you lost one?"

Well, the man and his friend didn't even reply. They stalked off across the kitchen garden. Tempe scratched a peekhole in the frosted window. It was just big enough

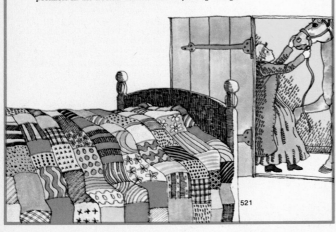

521

for her to see them stomp into the barn. They sent the cow out mooing. They sent chickens out flying. And hay tumbled out of the loft like a dust storm in January when they searched there. Nor had they any better luck in the smoke-shed or the woods.

The soldiers by now were terribly red in the face. They returned to the Wick house just long enough to promise, "We know she's here . . . somewhere, pretty lady. And we intend to wait until we find her!"

Wait?

Even Tempe was surprised at that! How long could she hide a horse in her bedroom?

But Tempe didn't worry long. Not this time. For now, her house was her fort. For later, perhaps the general and his men would come back from Philadelphia and capture the runaway soldiers. Perhaps Dr. William would drop by to see how her mother was faring and run the soldiers off. Perhaps with a healthy dose of medicine her mother could help. Two against two were happier odds. Or perhaps the two soldiers would just go away by themselves.

Satisfied with all the possibilities, Tempe stayed at her window post until dark. Then she curled up on the kitchen settee (having a guest in her bedroom) and went to sleep.

But the next morning the general and his men were not back from Philadelphia. There was no sight of Dr. William. The medicine had stopped Mrs. Wick's cough, but it had also made her sleep and sleep and sleep. And the two soldiers were still there. They were pacing the barnyard.

To make things worse, Bonny was hungry.

First she just walked angry circles around Tempe's bed. Then she started thumping her hoof at the door.

522

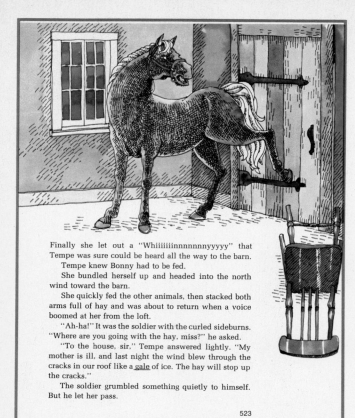

Finally she let out a "Whiiiiiiinnnnnnnyyyyy" that Tempe was sure could be heard all the way to the barn.

Tempe knew Bonny had to be fed.

She bundled herself up and headed into the north wind toward the barn.

She quickly fed the other animals, then stacked both arms full of hay and was about to return when a voice boomed at her from the loft.

"Ah-ha!" It was the soldier with the curled sideburns. "Where are you going with the hay, miss?" he asked.

"To the house, sir," Tempe answered lightly. "My mother is ill, and last night the wind blew through the cracks in our roof like a gale of ice. The hay will stop up the cracks."

The soldier grumbled something quietly to himself. But he let her pass.

523

All day the two soldiers hovered around the barnyard. There was nothing for Tempe to do but wait. Yet little happened. Her mother slept on and on. The general did not come, nor did Dr. William. And while the hay promised to last another day, Tempe saw the little water she had for Bonny was quickly disappearing.

In the morning it was gone. Bonny grew so thirsty she licked the frost off the window. She licked Tempe's washbowl dry. Finally she whinnied, this time so loudly Tempe was sure, had the soldiers been anywhere in Jockey Hollow, they would have heard her!

Bonny had to be watered.

When Tempe had drawn three buckets at the well, both soldiers stepped up behind her.

"May we help, pretty lady," said the one.

"No thank you, sir," said she. "I go only to the house, and I am quite able." She balanced one bucket under her arm and gripped the two in her hands.

"You must be very thirsty," said the other. "Why, there is enough water there for a horse!"

Tempe smiled. "Perhaps," she said, "but these bucketfuls are to wash my floors. It is said a fierce winter is followed by an early spring, and I am but preparing for that. But I thank you."

She curtsied slightly and started toward the door.

Again the soldiers grumbled, but let her pass.

On the third day, Tempe had stopped looking for anyone to come to help. The soldiers had moved closer to the house, and she worried about Bonny.

Bon didn't circle the bed or thump the door, and she let loose only the tiniest whinny. Tempe barely heard it in the kitchen. But that is what worried Tempe.

"Bonny's spirits are low," Tempe said to her mother, who was still half asleep. "She must need oats."

524

That morning Tempe fed the hog and the cows and the sheep as usual. Then she began to gather her oats. She put some in her pockets. She stuffed more in her bag. She filled her bucket to the brimful, then started back. The soldiers were waiting by the gate when she passed.

"Surely," said the one, looking in the bucket, "you don't eat unground oats, my dear."

"Oh yes," said Tempe, walking on. "Boiled, they make a fine porridge."

"But," said the one, following her, "so many oats for two ladies, and one so ill?"

"It is barely enough," said Tempe. "Some days, after chores, I eat three bowls at one sitting."

Still he followed.

"Some days," Tempe went on, "I eat four!"

He was at the door in front of her.

"Next to applesauce with brown sugar, I like oats most!" she said, looking directly into his eyes. "These will last only a day."

"Just the same," said the soldier, "I begin to think there is a third lady in the house. A gray mare that can race like the wind. And I wish to see for myself."

With that, the one soldier pushed right past Tempe into the house. He stomped into the kitchen, knocking the pots off the table and the wood across the floor. He stomped into the pantry, shaking the jars from the shelf.

Then he heard the slightest whinny—or was it a cough? He stomped through the sitting room toward the bedroom, brushing the ink from Grandmother's desk and finally tipping over Mrs. Wick's favorite fiddleback chair.

But that was one push too many. And this time Tempe didn't get mad, she got storming, had-quite-enough mad. She began to look a good bit like the Wicks' bull Joshua.

525

"That," she said—neither coyly, nor sweetly, nor perfectly—"was my mother coughing. But if it were a herd of gray horses feeding on my bed, I would not let you through that door, smashing and breaking."

The soldier scoffed. He went for the cellar door.

Tempe was there first. "Not into the cellar, sir."

He darted for the attic door.

Tempe beat him there, too. "Not into the attic."

He eyed the bedroom door again.

"Not anywhere," she said.

And before the soldier had time to doubt it, Tempe kicked open the door with one foot, kicked his musket out of his hand with the other—and pushed him right out the doorway.

For a moment—was it two?—the soldier lay sprawled on the path. He glared at Tempe, his face reddening around his curled sideburns. But Tempe stood firm in the doorway with *his* musket in *her* hand and glared back.

Finally, he picked up his hat and paced to his friend at the fence. They huddled, then started—on foot—down the road to Pennsylvania. At last they disappeared.

Questions preceded by a bullet are additional questions and appear in the Teacher's Edition only. The other questions appear in the student's text after the selection.

Understanding What You've Read

1. *What parts of this story are probably based on facts? What parts are probably made-up, or fictional?* (Accept all reasonable answers. Guide students through discussion to the following conclusions: Factual parts include Tempe Wick and her mother, the mutiny of the soldiers, food running out, no wages, and badly needed horses; fictional details include characters other than Tempe Wick and her mother, and all conversations.) CRITICAL   Identifying fact and fictional details in historical fiction

2. *What details tell you that this story takes place during the American Revolution?* (The speech of the characters—expressions such as "aye" and "agin"; the presence of the blacksmith; traveling by horse; the soldiers' muskets; and marching to a fife and drum.) CRITICAL   Identifying historical fiction

● *Why does Tempe Wick get angry at the beginning of the story? Is this event that angered her factual or fictional?* (Accept all reasonable answers. Students should recognize that Tempe was angry because the soldiers she had shared her wheat and her cows with were now mutinying and might try to steal from her house and barn or try to take her horse. This mutiny is a historical fact.   pages 514–516) INFERENTIAL/ CRITICAL   Identifying historical events

● *Why did Tempe have to ride to Dr. William's house?* ("Her mother needed medicine, and only Dr. William had it."   page 517) LITERAL   Recalling specific details

● *Why did the soldiers and the general march off to Philadelphia?* (They wanted to tell the leaders of all America how hungry, cold, and poor they were.   page 516) LITERAL   Recalling specific details

3. *What did Tempe do to be able to leave her farm without making the soldiers suspicious?* (Tempe put on "her Sunday coat and fine hat. She walked . . . slowly . . . to the barn, just as if she were alone in the world." She pretended not to notice the soldiers around her, saddled Bonny, and "rode, coolly and calmly and casually, right past them all."   pages 517–518) LITERAL   Recalling stated information

● *Why did the soldiers want to take Tempe's horse?* (Accept all reasonable answers. Encourage students to realize that the soldiers who mutinied chose not to walk to Philadelphia as their fellow soldiers did, but wanted to ride on horseback.   page 518) CRITICAL   Drawing conclusions

● *How did Tempe trick the soldier when he tried to take her horse?* (She cleverly asked the soldier to help her off her horse, and when he reached to help, Tempe snatched the reins. "Then she put a stick to Bon's hide, and raced off down the lane toward the Wick farm."   page 519) LITERAL   Recalling specific details

4. *Why did Tempe's room make a good hiding place for her horse?* (because the soldiers wouldn't think to look there) INFERENTIAL   Drawing conclusions

● *Which details on page 526 show how Tempe's actions helped get rid of the soldiers once and for all?* (Tempe's temper enabled her to speak angrily to the soldier and to beat him to his intended destinations; finally, she "kicked open the door with one foot, kicked his musket out of his hand with the other— and pushed him right out of the doorway.") INFERENTIAL   Making inferences

5. *How does the author's sense of humor increase your enjoyment of the story?* (Accept reasonable answers. Help students realize that the author's sense of humor enables the reader to enjoy Tempe's personality.) CRITICAL   Recognizing humor

6. *Why is "The Temper of Tempe Wick" a good title for this story? How did Tempe Wick's temper help her?* (At two important points in the story Tempe loses her temper. Tempe's temper helps her fool the soldiers and save the day.) INFERENTIAL   Making inferences

Writing

(Optional) Have students complete one or both of the *Writing* activities on page 527. Or ask students to do the writing activity under *Additional Writing Activity.*

1. *Think of a historical incident, such as the Boston Tea Party, the landing of the Pilgrims at Plymouth Rock, or the battle between the* Monitor *and the* Merrimack. *Write one or more sentences in which you tell what happened in the incident as though you were involved in what happened. Or, write one or more sentences in which you tell what happened from the point of view of an outsider. Use an encyclopedia to help you find important facts.*   Writing sentences

Tell students to list or outline their ideas before they begin writing. If students need help with the *Writing* activity, suggest that they use some of the folllowing information: (a) one of the Boston colonists describing what happened at Boston Harbor; (b) an American Indian sighting the *Mayflower* on the horizon; (c) a reporter describing the battle between the *Monitor* and the *Merrimack.*

You may wish to write the following lines on the board to help students get started.

We got so angry that we crept onto British ships and dumped their tea overboard.
That's the strangest boat I've ever seen! I wonder who is on it!

Have students write their own opening line or choose one from the board and begin writing.

2. *Pretend that General George Washington, leader of the American Army in the Revolution, visited Tempe Wick after the soldiers left her farm. Write a paragraph in which Tempe tells George Washington about the incidents that occurred on her farm. Tell what you think Washington might have said to Tempe about the incidents.*   Writing a paragraph

Tell students to list or outline their ideas before they begin writing. If students need help with the *Writing* activity, suggest that they include all the following information: (a) have Tempe tell about the soldiers who tried to take her horse, Bon, away; (b) have Tempe express anger at the unruly soldiers; (c) have General George Washington explain to Tempe the hardships that the soldiers were going through and what he would do to help them.

You may wish to write the following lines on the board to help students get started.

"I got so angry that I had to use my rifle, sir."
"I commend your courage, Miss Wick. Someday we shall all live in peace and harmony."

Have students write their own opening line or choose one from the board and begin writing.

Additional Writing Activity (Optional)

● *Rewrite a part of the story of Tempe Wick as a play.*   Writing a play

If students need help with the *Writing* activity, suggest that they consider the following information: (a) Who are the characters in your play? (b) What sentences in the story can you use as lines for the characters in the play? (c) What is the setting of your play? (d) What kind of costume will each of your characters wear?

You may wish to write the following lines from the story on the board (page 525, paragraphs 2–3) to help students get started.

Soldier 1 (looking in the bucket): Surely you don't eat unground oats, my dear.
Tempe (sweetly): Oh yes. Boiled, they make a fine porridge.
Soldier 1: But so many oats for two ladies, and one so ill?

★ For additional resources and curriculum-related activities, see *Enrichment,* page T470.

Reading Selection:
The Little Riders

Pages 528–549

Objectives

		SKILLS CODE NUMBER
I*	To identify historical fiction	6.4.7
I*	To identify historical events and real people in historical fiction	6.4.7.1
I	To distinguish between fact and fictional details	3.6.7
M	To interpret characters' feelings	6.9.4
M	To recognize author's techniques of characterization	6.9.3
M	To identify the setting of a story	6.10
M	To identify the plot of a story	6.11

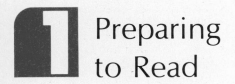

Preparing to Read

Summary

While Johanna was visiting her grandparents in Holland, World War II broke out and the German Army invaded Holland. Johanna's attic bedroom, which her father had used as a child, was taken by a German officer, Captain Braun. To make matters worse, the German Army ordered the wonderful lead figures on the church steeple, known as the little riders, melted down for German ammunition. At a secret meeting, the townspeople decided that the riders must be saved. In the middle of the night, Johanna and her grandparents moved the figures from the church to their house.

When the soldiers discovered that the riders were missing, Johanna's grandparents were taken away for questioning. Johanna knew that she must hide the riders to protect them and her grandparents. There was a hidden closet in the attic bedroom where they could be stored, but she had to work quickly while Captain Braun was away. Just when Johanna had moved the heavy figures to the attic, Captain Braun appeared. To

her surprise, the captain admired the beauty of the riders and helped Johanna hide them. When the German soldiers returned to search the house, nothing was found, and Johanna's grandparents were released. The family rejoiced at Johanna's success and Johanna came to regard Captain Braun as a friend, rather than as a member of the German Army.

Background

Margaretha Shemin was born in northern Holland in a small town much like the one she writes about in the story. She now lives in the United States.

"The Little Riders" is excerpted from a book by Ms. Shemin of the same title. The complete novel tells of the liberation of the town, the departure of the German soldiers, the arrival of Johanna's father, and the return of the little riders to the church tower.

The following book will provide you with additional background information on historical fiction.

Sutherland, Zena, and May Hill Arbuthnot. *Children and Books,* 6th ed. Chapter 12 deals with historical fiction.

Developing Vocabulary and Concepts

requisition: to make a formal request or demand, especially in writing
carillon: a set of bells on which a tune can be played
ordinance: an order, law, or decree, especially one made by a city government
plundered: robbed of goods or property by force
inaudible: incapable of being heard
liberating: setting free, releasing
tarpaulin: a piece of canvas or other material that has been made waterproof, used to cover exposed objects
defy: to resist openly and boldly
welled: rose up or poured forth
profusely: lavishly; liberally; abundantly
unceremoniously: not very courteously; abruptly or rudely
ajar: partly open, as a door

1. **a.** Read the following sentences aloud or write them on the board. If you read them aloud, write the underlined vocabulary on the board.

The soldier had come to <u>requisition</u> a room, and he handed Grandfather the written request signed by his commanding officer.
If you listen, you can hear the bells of the <u>carillon</u> playing a song.
The mayor's <u>ordinance</u> required all people to be home by 10 P.M.

The invaders <u>plundered</u> the townspeople's homes, stealing more than they could possibly use.

Grandfather could barely hear the whispering because it was almost <u>inaudible</u>.

The <u>liberating</u> armies set the people free.

The canvas <u>tarpaulin</u> was placed over the statue so that the statue wouldn't get wet in the rain.

If the soldiers <u>defy</u> the captain's orders, they will be punished.

Grandmother was very happy, and all her good feelings <u>welled</u> up in her.

The captain was very sorry and apologized <u>profusely</u>.

The soldier stormed into the room <u>unceremoniously</u>, without knocking on the door.

The door was <u>ajar</u>, so I peeked through the opening to see who was inside.

b. Ask students to give the meaning of each vocabulary word. Remind them to use the context clues in the sentences to help them.

2. Students will need to understand the situation at the beginning of the story. Tell them the following: The war in Europe discussed in the story is World War II (1939–45). At one time during the war, Holland was occupied by German soldiers. When a country is invaded and occupied, as Holland was, people cannot leave the country and sometimes cannot even leave the city where they live. The occupying forces can insist that people obey them. They might demand, for example, that people supply their soldiers with food or a room in which to live.

3. Ask students if any of them have ever seen a clock on a church or public building that, at a certain time each day, has figures that come out and dance, turn around, or march. (Most students will be familiar with the cuckoo clock, which, on a small scale, is something like such a mechanized clock.) Explain to students that the "little riders" in the story are lead figures on white lead horses that, at the stroke of each hour, come out of the doors on a church steeple.

 Use *Duplicating Masters 11,* pages 68 and 69.

Setting Purposes

Skills

Remind students that the author of "The Little Riders" actually grew up in a town in Holland much like the one in the story. Also remind them that Holland was occupied by German troops during World War II. Tell students to look for the actual historical events in the story as well as the fictional details that they think

The Little Riders

by MARGARETHA SHEMIN

In 1939, World War II began and the German Army invaded Holland. This story is about a fictional character named Johanna. In the story, Johanna could not return to her mother and father in America because of the war. She had to stay in Holland with her grandparents.

From the window of her room in Holland, Johanna could see the special clock under the church steeple. In the old clock were twelve statues of people on horseback. For hundreds of years, these little riders had ridden around the clock every hour when it chimed. Johanna's grandfather took care of the clock and the little riders. But then German soldiers came, and the little riders and the entire town were in danger.

were invented by the author to make the period of history more interesting to the reader.

Content

Have students read the lead-in to the story "The Little Riders." Tell students that they are going to read a story about a girl named Johanna who goes to Holland to visit her grandparents. Because of the outbreak of World War II, Johanna stays with her grandparents for four years. Ask students to notice as they read the story some of the ways in which Johanna grows and changes as the events of the story develop.

Reading and Discussing

Have students read the selection. Most students will be able to complete it in one sitting. If you prefer, the selection may be read in three parts, breaking before the last paragraph on page 536 and after the second paragraph on page 541.

NOTE: The questions that appear in the student's text at the end of the selection focus on comprehension of selection content and on understanding of historical fiction. Answers to these questions begin on page T466.

One day at dinner, Grandfather looked straight at Johanna, and his eyes were filled with pride and love. "There is bad news today, but nothing so bad that we can't bear it. A German soldier came to requisition a room in our house for a German officer, a certain Captain Braun. I explained to him that we used all the rooms and didn't have one room to spare. He never listened to me. He took your room," Grandfather continued. "There was nothing I could do about it, although I tried very hard for you."

It would be extremely dangerous, Johanna realized, to have a German soldier in the house. Johanna knew about the radio hidden in Grandfather's den and the weekly meetings Grandfather held upstairs. She knew there were many other dangerous secrets that Grandfather and Grandmother had never told her. All these secrets the house had kept within its walls, and the house had been the only safe place in a world full of enemies and danger. Now the house had been invaded too.

All afternoon, Johanna helped Grandmother. She took all her clothes out of the attic closet. Now that the closet was empty she could almost see the cubbyhole hiding all the way at the back of the closet. It had always been Johanna's secret hiding place. She opened the small door that was only big enough for her to crawl through. In the cubbyhole were some of her old toys, her teddy bear, which had traveled with her all the way from America to Holland, and some seashells her father had once brought back for her from a far country. She never played with them anymore, but she didn't want to leave them with Captain Braun.

When Captain Braun arrived, he clicked his heels and made a little bow in the direction of Grandmother and Johanna. Johanna turned her head away.

529

"I apologize to you," he said in broken Dutch. "I will try to cause no trouble to you. I wish you a good evening." Then he turned directly to Grandfather. "Would you be kind, sir, and show me the room?"

Grandfather didn't speak but led Captain Braun to the stairs and mounted them quickly. Captain Braun picked up his heavy sack and followed slowly. Johanna could hear the sack bump heavily on every step till it was carried all the way high up to her attic room. Then she heard the door close and Grandfather's footsteps coming downstairs.

Johanna went to bed early that night. She had felt tired, but now she couldn't fall asleep. She kept tossing in her new bed. There were strange, unfamiliar shadows on the wall. The big gray wall of the church seemed so near, ready to fall on top of the room. Faintly she heard the clock strike ten times. Then the door was opened

530

very softly, and Grandfather came into the room. He sat down in the chair next to Johanna's bed and took her hand in his own.

"Why don't you sleep, Johanna?" he asked. "You should try to sleep now. We have all had a hard day and so much has happened."

"I hate him," Johanna said, "and I hate this room too. From here I can see only the gray wall of the church. I can't see the riders, I can't even hear the carillon very clearly. How can I ever fall asleep without the little riders? I have always watched them just before I went to sleep. In the morning the carillon woke me up. Now a German soldier has my room that once was Father's room. He has no right to sit there and watch the riders and listen to the carillon."

Grandfather got up from the chair and walked over to the window. He looked up at the gray wall of the church.

"Captain Braun," he said, "will never see the little riders ride out on their horses and he will never hear the carillon. Today an ordinance came from the town commander. The riders are not allowed to ride anymore and the carillon may not play again. I just went to the church tower."

Grandfather turned away from the window and paced up and down the small room.

"All these years I have taken care of the riders so that they could ride when the clock struck the hour. But tonight I closed the little doors."

Johanna sat up in her bed, her arms around her thin knees. Her face looked small and white, her eyes big and dark.

"Why?" she asked Grandfather. "Why may the little riders not ride out anymore?"

531

"They didn't give us any reasons," Grandfather answered, "but we have seen this coming for a long time. This ordinance is only the beginning. The little riders are made of lead. The Germans need metal, and they may throw them into a melting pot to make munitions out of them for their armies. Everywhere the occupied countries are being plundered, their treasures taken away, and the bells of their churches melted down to be made into weapons. Grandmother and I have often talked of what to do if this ever threatened to happen to the little riders."

Grandfather patted Johanna's hand gently. "We will have to hide the riders, Johanna, if we want to keep them for the town. Go to sleep now, there is much to be done tomorrow."

Grandfather tucked the blanket around Johanna and left the room, but Johanna didn't want to sleep. She wanted to think about everything Grandfather had told her. The night was cool and quiet. From somewhere she heard the sound of a flute. She walked across the room and opened the door to the hall. The sound came from the top of the house. Barefoot, Johanna climbed silently up the attic stairs. Halfway up she could see her room.

Captain Braun had left the door open so that the cool night wind could blow through the warm room. He was sitting on Johanna's windowsill. His back was turned to the door, his long legs dangling out of the window. And he played his flute over the silent marketplace.

Johanna didn't watch him for long. She went downstairs without making a noise. She didn't close her door with a bang, but she closed it very firmly. When she was back in bed, she pulled the cover over her ears so that she couldn't hear a sound that could keep her awake. But it was a long time before she fell asleep.

532

The next day, everybody looked up at the church steeple, wondering what had happened. It was the first time in many hundreds of years that the little riders had not ridden out and the carillon had not played. Soon the town buzzed with the news of the ordinance from the town commander.

After a few days something happened—something of such tremendous importance that the Germans had suddenly much more urgent and grave matters on their minds than the twelve little riders high up on the church tower. Grandfather didn't think anymore about hiding them.

Johanna was sitting with Grandfather and Grandmother in the den, listening to the radio hidden behind the books in the bookcase. Then the big news came

crackling and almost inaudible, and none of them dared to believe it was true. Allied armies had landed in France. All morning long, Johanna and her grandparents kept the radio on. They had to hear over and over again the crackling voice that kept repeating the same bulletin.

Grandfather and Grandmother and Johanna spent much time upstairs in the den, listening to the radio. At first the liberating armies advanced fast. The south of Holland was free. Then the days became weeks and the weeks became months. The liberation of the north still seemed sure, but not so near anymore. Johanna still dreamed about her father, but she was afraid he would not come soon.

Life went on as it had in the four years before. Grandfather started to think again about a safe hiding place for the little riders, because now more than ever the Germans needed every scrap of metal for ammunition.

Now Johanna was almost used to the presence of Captain Braun in the house, but still she had never seen his face. In the morning she met him on the stairs, she going down for breakfast, he going up to his room after morning drill. In the evening she met him again, she going up to the den, he going down on his way out for dinner. He always said "Good morning" and "Good evening." Johanna always turned her head away from him and never answered. He walked softly in his heavy boots except when he had to ask Grandfather or Grandmother something. Then he stamped noisily with his boots so that they could hear him long before he knocked on the door. There was always time to hide the radio behind the books in the bookcase.

At night now Johanna sometimes forgot to close the door of her room, and she could hear the music of the

flute. When the summer nights were quiet, Captain Braun always played. But often now the air outside was filled with the droning sounds of heavy airplanes flying over. On such nights Johanna climbed out of her bed and leaned far out the window to see their lights high against the dark sky. She knew that many of them were American planes, and she imagined that her father might be in one of them. They were airplanes flying over Germany. On those nights Captain Braun did not play his flute.

One day when Captain Braun had gone out, Johanna went upstairs and looked at her old room. Her closet was full of coats and army caps with the German eagle on them.

On the wall, where once her pictures had hung, were now the pictures of Captain Braun's family. In one, an older lady and an older man were standing arm in arm in a garden full of flowers. In another, a young woman and a laughing boy were standing on skis in dazzling white snow. It was strange to see real Germans in a garden full of flowers and with skis on a sunny mountain slope.

Before Johanna left the room she sat down on her windowsill and looked at the church steeple. The little doors were closed now and the steeple looked old and gray, like any other church steeple.

"Don't worry, little riders," Johanna whispered to the closed doors. "It will be all right, the Germans will not get you." Tonight, Grandfather had told her, they would hide the little riders.

The night was loud with the sounds of the wind and the rain, but there were no overflying airplanes. Grandfather crossed the street first to open the door. Then came Grandmother and last Johanna.

Inside the tower it was completely dark. Grandfather had climbed the steps so often that he led the way. No one talked, and Johanna could not remember when the steps had ever seemed so long and steep. As they climbed higher, the sound of the wind and rain came louder and louder. Grandfather had already reached the top of the stairs, and now he handed the riders and the horses to Grandmother and Johanna.

The staircase was so narrow and steep they could take only one rider at a time. It was too dark for Johanna to see the little rider that she carried. She could only feel the cool metal against her hands. The rider was bigger than she had expected, reaching up almost to her waist. She started to carry him down. The rider, although made of lead, was hollow inside and not too heavy, but was clumsy to carry on the narrow, steep staircase. Each trip across the street and back up the church tower was harder than the one before. The last little rider seemed heaviest of all. Grandfather made one more trip to lock the door of the church tower.

In their own house they must be careful to make no noise that could waken Captain Braun, but here the stairs were wider and Grandfather and Grandmother could carry two riders at a time. Johanna felt weak and shaky when the last rider with his horse was finally carried safely into Grandfather's den.

The next morning after breakfast, Grandfather went to a nearby village where he had a friend who was a farmer. Dirk was one of the few farmers who had been allowed to keep his horse and wagon. Because he delivered eggs and fresh milk several times a week at the house of the German town commander, the German sentries who stood guard at the entrances of the town

never searched his wagon. Many times young men who were hiding from the Germans had left town in Dirk's wagon, hidden underneath the tarpaulin between the empty egg boxes and the rattling milk containers. Grandfather and Dirk had often worked together to take such young men to safer places in the country, and

537

Grandfather was sure Dirk would help hide the little riders. He knew they would stay hidden on Dirk's farm until they could return to the church steeple.

When Grandfather returned, it was still a few hours before dark. He and Johanna went upstairs to put the riders and their horses in the burlap sacks so that they could be taken away without delay when Dirk came. Johanna looked for the last time at the riders' faces. With her hands she covered their small hands that so many times had lifted the swords in proud salute to each other. The Germans will not get them, she thought. They will always ride over the town. Even a hundred years from now.

It was still light when Johanna and Grandfather finished and went downstairs. Except for the bark of a dog and the cooing of the doves that nested under the eaves of the church tower, it was quiet outside. Then, from the side street that led to the marketplace, came the sound of marching soldiers. It was unusual for a group of soldiers to be exercising at this late hour.

The doorbell rang loudly and insistently, and Grandfather went to open the door. Grandmother and Johanna

538

followed him into the hall. Nine soldiers were standing on the doorstep, and one of them was the spokesman.

"We are sent by the town commander to requisition from you the key to the church tower." As he spoke he looked around with his shiny little eyes. "We will take the statues of the riders with us tonight, and you can get the key back afterward at Headquarters. Hurry, we don't have all night," he concluded.

Grandfather reached up slowly for the big iron key that always hung on a peg near the stairs. He handed the key to the soldier. When they had gone, he closed the door and for a moment leaned heavily against it. Johanna saw small drops of perspiration under his nose and on his forehead.

"They will be back as soon as they have seen the riders are gone," Grandmother said. "We will have to hide them better."

"There is no time," Grandfather said. "They will be back in a few minutes, and where can we hide the riders? No, our only chance is somehow to keep them from going upstairs. If we can tell them something that will make them go away, even if it's only for a short time . . ."

539

Grandmother looked doubtful, Johanna thought, but Grandfather couldn't talk about it further. The soldiers were back. This time they didn't ring the doorbell. Instead they pounded the stocks of their rifles on the door. The spokesman was hot and red and angry.

"The old man and the old woman will come with us to Headquarters. The town commander can conduct the hearing himself. If he orders so, we will search the house later. We will not leave a thing unturned, and if those riders are hidden here," he said, shrugging his shoulders in disgust, "we will find them. And these people will learn what happens to those who dare defy an order given by a German officer." He looked at Johanna. "The child can stay," he said.

When the last soldier slammed the door behind him, Johanna found that her knees were shaking. She had to sit down on the bottom step of the staircase. The clock in the hall ticked, and the minutes passed by.

"If those riders are hidden here, these people will learn what happens to those who dare defy an order given by a German officer," the soldier had said.

540

They must be hidden more safely, Johanna knew, and she would have to do it. Dirk would certainly not come now. The neighbors must have seen what happened and they would have warned Dirk to stay far away from the house. Johanna looked out of the peephole in the door. One soldier was left standing on guard.

"We will not leave a thing unturned, and if those riders are hidden here, we will find them," the German had said.

The riders were big and there were twelve of them and the horses, too. What hiding place would be big enough? Sitting on the bottom step of the stairs, Johanna's mind wandered through the whole house, thinking of all the different closets, but not one was big enough to hide the riders safely. At last she thought of her attic room. Of course, her own secret hiding place was there. It was certainly big enough, but it was right in Captain Braun's room. But the more she thought about it now, the more she became convinced that it would also be the safest place to hide the riders. The Germans would certainly not think that the riders might be hidden in the room of a German officer, and they would probably not search his room. Captain Braun probably had not discovered the cubbyhole. Anyhow, it was the only place in the house where she could hide the riders. She would leave them in the burlap sacks and push them all the way deep in.

Tonight was Friday night and Captain Braun was not home. If she worked fast, the riders would be hidden before he came back. Johanna ran upstairs and started to carry the sacks to the attic room. She didn't put on the light for fear the soldier on guard would see it and come to investigate; instead, she took Grandfather's flashlight. She decided to do the heavy work fast and

541

carry everything upstairs. Putting the riders in the cubbyhole would be easier. She decided also to take the radio from behind the books and put it in the cubbyhole, too.

It wasn't easy. By the time the last horse and rider were in the attic room, Johanna was out of breath. Her hair was mussed and her skirt was torn in several places. It had also taken her much longer than she had expected, but if she worked fast there was still time enough before Captain Braun came home. In the closet, she pushed Captain Braun's uniforms aside and reached to open the bolt of the little door, but it had become stiff and rusty. She got down on her knees and tried again. The bolt didn't yield. Johanna felt warm and her hands started to tremble. Surely she would be able to open the bolt, it had never given her trouble before. But no matter how hard she tried, she could not open the bolt on the little door. She forgot everything around her, even the riders and Grandfather and Grandmother and the danger they were in at this moment. She thought only of one thing. The door must open. It must.

She was so busy she didn't hear the footsteps on the stairs nor the door of the attic room opening. She first saw Captain Braun when he was standing in the door of the big closet. He had to bend down a little not to hit his head against the low ceiling.

"What are you doing in the dark in my closet?" he asked.

He switched the light on so that Johanna's eyes were blinded by it, and she turned her head away. Around her on the floor were the sacks with the riders. The radio was right beside her and Johanna pushed it behind her back, but she couldn't hide the riders. Captain Braun kneeled down and opened one of the bags. There was nothing Johanna could do or say. He took out a white

542

horse with gentle black eyes and a fierce curly mane. Then he opened the other bags. The little riders and their horses were laying helpless on their backs on the floor of the closet. The legs of the horses were bent as if they wanted to get up and gallop away. The riders looked more brave and proud than ever, but Johanna knew that no matter how brave and proud they looked, they were forever lost and she could not save them anymore. Everything she had ever felt against the Germans welled up suddenly in her.

"I hate and I despise you," she burst out, "and so does every decent person and you'll never win the war. Grandfather says that you have already lost it." She talked so fast that she had to take a deep breath.

Then Johanna raised her eyes and looked at Captain Braun's face for the first time. He did not have a soldier's face. He had the face of a flute player.

"So these are the famous little riders," he said quietly. "I would like to look at them much longer, but it would be safer for them and for you to put them back in the sacks and hide them where they will not be found."

"But I can't," Johanna said. She wasn't feeling angry anymore, only very frightened. "The bolt of the door is rusty. I can't open it." She was surprised to hear that she was crying. "And they took Grandfather and Grandmother. They said, 'If we find the riders in this house, you will see what happens to people who disobey an order given by a German officer.'"

Captain Braun kneeled beside Johanna. His hands were strong and quick as he slipped aside the stiff bolt. He took the sacks and started to put the riders back in.

"What will you do to them?" Johanna asked.

"The little riders will be my guests for as long as they want to be," Captain Braun said. "I owe that to them.

544

They are the first Dutchmen who looked at me in a friendly way and did not turn their faces away when I spoke to them."

Johanna felt her face grow hot and red as he spoke. She bent down and started to help him put the riders and the horses back into the sacks.

In a few minutes the riders were hidden and the radio, too. At a moment when Captain Braun had his back turned, Johanna pushed it deep into the closet. One day when he was out she would come back and get it. Grandfather couldn't be without his radio.

"Go down now," Captain Braun said. "It's better for all of us if no one sees us together."

Johanna went downstairs and alone she waited in the dark living room. Outside, the soldier was still standing guard. She pushed Grandfather's big chair near the window and sat down, her tired arms leaning on the windowsill. From there, she saw them come across the marketplace.

Grandfather had his arm around Grandmother's shoulders as if to protect her from the soldiers who were all around them. This time, there were more than nine. As soon as Grandfather opened the door with his key, the soldiers swarmed over the room. The big, red-faced soldier was again in charge. At his command the others pushed aside the furniture and looked behind it. They ripped open the upholstery, although Johanna couldn't understand why. The riders and the horses were much too big to be hidden in the upholstery of a chair. When they left to search the upstairs, the room looked as if a tornado had passed through.

Grandfather and Grandmother went upstairs, too, but they were always surrounded by soldiers, so that Johanna could not speak one word to them.

545

The soldiers began with the desk in the den, taking out the drawers and dumping the contents in a heap on the floor. Then they got down on their knees and looked under the bed and knocked on the wooden floor.

The soldiers finally gave up. They had realized that there was nothing hidden in these rooms. Only the attic room was left. They climbed the last stairs. Johanna felt weak and shaky again. Even when they found Captain Braun, they might still decide to search the room. She was glad now that Grandfather and Grandmother had no idea where the riders were hidden. They walked confidently up the stairs, Grandmother winking again at Johanna behind the soldiers' backs.

The soldiers must not have know that the room was occupied by one of their own officers, because they were taken aback when they found Captain Braun with his legs on the table, writing in his music book. He rose from his chair. The soldiers apologized profusely, and

546

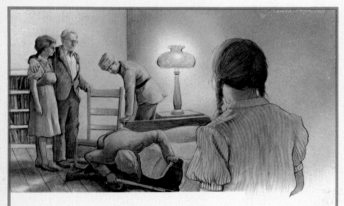

the red-faced man especially seemed extremely upset at having intruded so unceremoniously on the room of a German officer. Captain Braun put all of them at ease with a few friendly words, and he must have made a joke, for they laughed. For one terrible moment, Johanna thought that, after all, Captain Braun's face looked no different from all the other soldiers. What he had done tonight could be a trap and he could betray them. But the soldiers now made ready to go, and they went without searching the room. Captain Braun took up his pencil and music book.

The attitude of the soldiers changed during their walk downstairs. When they came they had been sure they would find the riders. Now they seemed uncertain. The big red-faced soldier seemed to take it very much to heart that he had failed to find the riders. He and the other soldiers seemed suddenly to be in a terrible hurry and left the house without saying a word.

547

Grandfather picked up Johanna and swung her high in the air, as he had done when she had still been a little girl.

"Oh, Johanna, we are so proud of you, but where in this house did you hide the little riders?"

Grandmother hugged Johanna, but she wouldn't let her tell the secret until they were all sitting quietly with a warm drink.

"Will they ever come back?" Johanna asked.

"I don't think so," Grandfather said. "They are convinced that the riders are not hidden here, and they can't prove that we ever had anything to do with their disappearance."

Johanna lay in bed that night, thinking about everything that had happened during the long day. She could hear the airplanes flying over the house. Every night it sounded as if there were more planes than the night before. This time, Johanna didn't think of her father; instead she thought of Captain Braun. She put on her slippers and walked upstairs. The door of the room stood ajar. Johanna pushed it open. Captain Braun was sitting at the table with his face buried in his hands. He looked up when he heard Johanna.

"I cannot sleep," Johanna said. "If I leave my door open, would you, please, play the flute for me?"

548

Questions preceded by a bullet are additional questions and appear in the Teacher's Edition only. The other questions appear in the student's text after the selection.

Understanding What You've Read

1. *What real historical event prevented Johanna from returning to America?* (War had broken out in Europe and she was prevented from leaving Holland. page 528) CRITICAL Identifying historical events

- *How did Johanna feel about having a German soldier in the house?* (Johanna realized it would be extremely dangerous. She felt that her grandparents' house, which had been the only safe place in a world full of enemies and danger, had been invaded. Encourage students to recognize that Johanna was probably very frightened and angry. page 529) CRITICAL Interpreting characters' feelings

- *What do we learn about Captain Braun when he comes to stay at Johanna's grandparents' house? How do you think the author wants the reader to feel about him?* (Accept all reasonable answers. Encourage students to recognize that he apologized to the family and said that he would try not to cause trouble and that he tried speaking in broken

Dutch. These actions and words make Captain Braun likable because he seems polite and gentle even though he is an enemy soldier. page 530) CRITICAL Identifying author's techniques of characterization

- *What responsibility did Johanna's grandfather have for the little riders?* (For many years, Johanna's grandfather had taken care of the little riders so that they could ride when the clock struck the hour. page 531) LITERAL Recalling stated information

- *On page 532, what does Grandfather tell Johanna might happen to the little riders?* ("The little riders are made of lead. The Germans need metal, and they may throw them into a melting pot to make munitions out of them for their armies.") LITERAL Recalling specific details

2. *What historical facts are used as details on pages 534–535 of the story?* (The Allied armies landed in France; they liberated places occupied by German troops and they advanced quickly; they freed the south of Holland, but the liberation of the north was going to take a while longer; the Germans now more than ever needed every scrap of metal for ammunition.) CRITICAL Identifying historical facts

- *How did Johanna act around Captain Braun? Why do you think she behaved this way?* (She never looked at his face. When he spoke to her, she turned away and never answered him. Johanna probably acted this way to show her contempt for the German Army. page 534) LITERAL/CRITICAL Interpreting characters' feelings

- *On page 534, what does the author tell us about Captain Braun that shows that the captain is thoughtful?* (He always walked softly in his heavy boots except when he was coming to speak to Johanna's grandparents. Then he stamped loudly to let them know he was coming so that they could hide the radio they listened to.) CRITICAL Interpreting author's techniques of characterization

- *What did Johanna's grandfather plan to do with the little riders after he had taken them from the church? What happened to stop this plan from working?* (Johanna's grandfather planned to hide them on the farm of a friend. This plan was halted because a group of German soldiers discovered that the little riders were missing and took Johanna's grandparents away for questioning. pages 536–540) LITERAL Recalling stated information

- *What action did Johanna take to save the little riders? What problem did she run into?* (She tried to hide them in her old hiding place in what was now Captain Braun's room. But she could not open the bolt on the little door no matter how hard she tried.   pages 541–542) LITERAL   Recalling specific details

3. *Why did Johanna dislike Captain Braun when she first met him? Why did she change her mind at the end of the story?* (Accept all reasonable answers. Encourage students to realize that she disliked him at first because he had "invaded" their house and had taken over her room, and because he was a German soldier. She changed her mind because he understood how special the little riders were and how terrible it would be if they were melted down for ammunition. He helped her hide and save the little riders.   pages 542–544) CRITICAL   Interpreting characters' feelings

● *How do you think Captain Braun felt about living in Holland as a German soldier?* (Accept all reasonable answers.) CRITICAL   Interpreting characters' feelings

● *How do you think Johanna's grandparents felt when they returned to the house and the soldiers began to search for the little riders? What do you think they thought would happen?* (The grandparents were probably very frightened, as well as angry at the way the German soldiers were destroying their things as they searched for the little riders. The grandparents probably thought that the soldiers would find the little riders and that they would be punished.   pages 545–547) CRITICAL   Interpreting characters' feelings

4. *Why do you think Johanna asked Captain Braun to play the flute?* (Accept all reasonable answers. Johanna had changed her mind about Captain Braun, and by asking him to play the flute, which she knew he loved doing, she was telling him in a way that she now considered him a person and not just an enemy soldier.   page 548) CRITICAL   Drawing conclusions

● *Often in the plot of a story, the characters are faced with a problem, then the characters take steps to solve the problem, and finally there is a solution to the problem. How would you briefly explain the plot of "The Little Riders"?* (The problem was that the Germans wanted to take the little riders and melt them down for ammunition. Johanna acted to solve the problem, with the help of Captain Braun, by hiding them in the closet in her old room. The solution to the problem was that now the little riders were safe and one day could be put back up in the church.) CRITICAL   Identifying the plot of a story

● *What is the setting of "The Little Riders"? Why is the setting important to the plot of the story?* (Accept all reasonable answers. Students should recognize that the setting is a small town in Holland that is very old and has certain cherished objects, among them the little riders. This is critical for students to understand because it explains why people were willing to risk so much to save the riders.) CRITICAL   Identifying the setting of a story

● *What makes "The Little Riders" a story of historical fiction rather than a nonfiction piece?* (Accept all reasonable answers. Students should recognize that the story is based on actual historical events—World War II and the occupation of Holland—but the story itself is fiction. It is a story that helps us to understand this particular time in history.) CRITICAL   Identifying historical fiction

Writing

(Optional) Have students complete one or both of the *Writing* activities on page 549. Or ask students to do the writing activity under *Additional Writing Activity.*

1. *Finish these sentences with fictional details. Each sentence is about an important historical person or event. You may want to look up some more facts in an encyclopedia.*
   a. As President Washington shook my hand, I said, ". . . ."
   b. The Declaration of Independence was being signed as the boy . . .
   c. The Wright brothers' plane might fly, but . . .
   d. Benjamin Franklin took off his bifocals, and . . .
   Writing fictional details

Tell students to list or outline their ideas before they begin writing. If students need additional help with the *Writing* activity, suggest that they consider the following: (a) President Washington's visit to the building site of the Capitol, where Benjamin Banneker was working; (b) the excitement of the American people at the signing of the Declaration of Independence; (c) the Wright brothers' first trial flight; (d) one of Benjamin Franklin's inventions.

You may wish to write the following opening line on the board to help students get started.

As President Washington shook my hand, I said, "It is a great honor for me to work on the Capitol building."

Have students think of their lines or use the one from the board and begin writing.

2. *One lesson you can learn from history is that ordinary people can display special courage during wartime. Explain in a sentence or two how Johanna showed her courage.*   Writing a sentence

Tell students to list or outline their ideas before they begin writing. If students need help with the *Writing* activity, suggest that they include all the following information: (a) describe the part Johanna played in carrying the little riders from the tower to the house; (b) tell about her decision to hide the riders when her grandparents were taken by the German soldiers; (c) describe her reaction when she was found hiding the little riders in Captain Braun's room.

You may wish to write the following opening phrases on the board to help students get started.

It was so dark in the tower that Johanna . . .
She got down on her knees and tried to . . .
Looking at the helpless little riders and their horses, Johanna . . .

Have students write their own sentences or choose a phrase from the board and begin writing.

Additional Writing Activity (Optional)

● *Pretend that you are Captain Braun. Write a paragraph in your diary that tells how you feel about being in Holland as an enemy soldier living in Johanna's grandparents' house.*   Writing a diary entry

Tell students to list or outline their ideas before they begin writing. If students need help with the *Writing* activity, suggest that they include the following information: (a) describe Captain Braun's feelings about the German plunder of the treasures of occupied countries; (b) describe his feelings when Johanna did not acknowledge him; (c) describe his feelings when he discovered Johanna trying to put the little riders in the closet of his room; (d) describe his actions and feelings when the German soldiers came to the house to search for the little riders.

You may wish to write the following opening lines on the board to help students get started.

Today I moved into the room of a little girl, who doesn't seem to want me in the house. I was shocked at first, but I decided to help the little girl because I was impressed by her courage.

Have students write their own opening line or choose one from the board and begin writing.

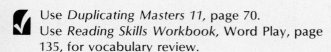

✔ Use *Duplicating Masters 11,* page 70.
Use *Reading Skills Workbook,* Word Play, page 135, for vocabulary review.

★ For additional resources and curriculum-related activities, see *Enrichment,* page T471.

More Historical Fiction

Courage to Adventure: Stories of Boys and Girls Growing Up with America selected by Child Study Association of America/Wel-Met. T. Y. Crowell, 1976. Here are nineteen stories about American children from many different ethnic heritages at many different times in our nation's history.

The Princess and the Lion by Elizabeth Coatsworth. Pantheon, 1963. About 200 years ago, an African princess, followed by her pet lion, sets out to free her brother who is held prisoner on a distant mountain.

Bears on Hemlock Mountain by Alice Dalgliesh. Scribner, 1952. There aren't supposed to be any bears on Hemlock Mountain—but there are. And Jonathan must find a way to escape from them.

The Strange Voyage of Neptune's Car by Joe Lasker. Viking, 1977. This story is based on the true adventures of Mary Patten, the first woman to command a clipper ship around Cape Horn.

Sarah Bishop by Scott O'Dell. Houghton Mifflin, 1980. Sarah must build a new life after her farm is destroyed during the Revolutionary War.

Boris by Jaap ter Haar. Delacorte, 1970. Boris's story reflects the true hardships that World War II meant for many European children.

Dragonwings by Laurence Yep. Harper & Row, 1975. Moon Shadow leaves China to make a new home in San Francisco shortly before the earthquake of 1906.

550

If students have not already read these books, you may wish to recommend them at this time. Bibliographic information about other books for students is given in the *Resource Center.*

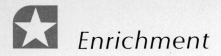

Enrichment

Hamilton Hill: September 18, 1784

Bibliography

The following books of historical fiction were also written by Jean Fritz.

Easy

Fritz, Jean. *Brendan the Navigator: A History Mystery About the Discovery of America.* The voyage of Saint Brendan of Ireland, who may have sighted the North American coast before the Vikings.

_____. *Can't You Make Them Behave, King George?* A biographical sketch of King George III of England at the time of the American Revolution.

Average

Fritz, Jean. *And Then What Happened, Paul Revere?* Details of Paul Revere's life and famous ride.

_____. *The Cabin Faced West.* A story of pioneer life in western Pennsylvania.

_____. *What's the Big Idea, Ben Franklin?* A brief biography of this eighteenth-century printer, inventor, and statesman.

_____. *Why Don't You Get a Horse, Sam Adams?* The true story of how Sam Adams learned to ride a horse.

Challenging

Fritz, Jean. *Brady.* A boy who discovers that his father works for the Underground Railroad.

_____. *Early Thunder.* A story set in Salem, Massachusetts, during the Revolutionary War.

_____. *I, Adam.* A vivid recreation of life in New England in the 1850's.

_____. *Stonewall.* The story of Stonewall Jackson and the emotional impact of the War Between the States on soldiers from both North and South.

_____. *Where Was Patrick Henry on the 29th of May?* A brief biography tracing Patrick Henry's progress from planter to statesman.

_____. *Will You Sign Here, John Hancock?* A biography of the first signer of the Declaration of Independence.

Records and/or Tapes

NOTE: Recordings may also be available on other labels.

Weston Woods. "And Then What Happened, Paul Revere?"; "Can't You Make Them Behave, King George?"; "What's the Big Idea, Ben Franklin?"; "Where Was Patrick Henry on the 29th of May?"; "Why Don't You Get a Horse, Sam Adams?"; "Will You Sign Here, John Hancock?" Jean Fritz narrates her portraits of historical figures from her book series.

Curriculum Coordination

Language Arts

1. Have students write letters to author Jean Fritz asking her how she goes about writing stories of historical fiction. Students may write to Ms. Fritz in care of one of her publishers. (See *Resource Center.*)

2. Invite a speaker from a local historical society to show slides about a particular person or event in history. Then have students write a piece of historical fiction about the person or event, adding fictional details and dialogue.

3. Plan a field trip to a historical site in your area. Have students imagine what it would have been like to live there during that particular historical period. Ask them to write a fictional diary entry as though they had lived back then. Encourage students to do extra research to give their entries a factual basis.

Social Studies

Have interested students find out more about the life of George Washington. Since many legends have been told about him, challenge students to do research to find out what is fact and what is fiction about our first president.

Art

Have students draw the sequence of events that took place in "Hamilton Hill." These drawings might be used to illustrate the story as it is read aloud to members of other classes.

The Temper of Tempe Wick

Bibliography

The following stories are based on real people or events in history.

Easy

Calhoun, Mary. *High Wind for Kansas.* An inventor tries to cross the Midwest in a wagon powered by sails.

Lasker, Joe. *The Strange Voyage of Neptune's Car.* Nineteen-year-old Mary Patten sails a clipper ship around the Cape of Good Hope.

Average

Levy, Harry. *Not Over Ten Inches High.* In eighteenth-century Boston, a boy fights to overcome a city ordinance that bans dogs over ten inches high.

Putnam, Alice. *The Spy Doll.* The story of a doll used to smuggle badly needed medicine during the Civil War.

Challenging

Baker, Betty. *Walk the World's Rim.* Chakoh, an American Indian in the sixteenth century, goes on a large expedition to Mexico and is one of four survivors who return.

Finlayson, Ann. *The Silver Bullet.* Real-life courier Lt. Daniel Taylor is the model for a fictional hero.

Smucker, Barbara. *Runaway to Freedom.* A story based on facts about the Underground Railroad.

The following books give information about the United States around the time of the American Revolution.

Easy

Colby, C. B. *Early American Crafts: Tools, Shops and Products.* A pictorial study of colonial life.

Average

Higgenbotham, Don, and Kenneth Nebenzahl. *Atlas of the American Revolution.* A series of maps drawn over 200 years ago show the battles of the Revolution that led to America's independence.

Lee, Susan, and John R. Lee. *Philadelphia.* The development of Philadelphia from its founding through the Revolution.

Challenging

Gorsline, Douglas. *What People Wore: A Visual History of Dress from Ancient Times to Twentieth-Century America.* Includes costumes relating to colonial times and the Revolutionary period.

Naden, Corinne J. *The Colony of New Jersey.* A history of New Jersey from its earliest settlement through 1787.

Films and Filmstrips

NOTE: For more information, see *Resource Center.*

Coronet Instructional Media. "Famous Patriots of the American Revolution: Molly Pitcher." Examines the roles of Molly Pitcher and other women in the American Revolution.

National Geographic. "Not Worth a Continental." An army corporal with a mandate to locate food for his starving troops must decide whether to demand supplies from a frightened family.

Pictura Films. "A Nation Is Born: Rugged Ragamuffins of the Continental Army." Depicts the beginning of the Revolutionary War, the struggles of the colonists, and the long hardships faced by the army.

Warren Schloat Productions. "Folk Songs of American History. Set I: Revolutionary War." Documentary photographs, engravings, and lithographs recounting episodes in American history from 1700 to 1864. Accompanied by traditional folk songs sung by Joan Baez, Glen Yarborough, and Peter, Paul, and Mary.

Records and/or Tapes

NOTE: Recordings may also be available on other labels.

Imperial. "Women in United States History: Women During the Revolutionary War Era." Discusses the contributions of women such as Mercy Warren, Abigail Adams, and Phillis Wheatley to the Revolution.

Miller-Brody Productions. "Oscar Brand's Songs of '76: A Folksinger's History of the Revolution." Songs from the Revolution, including "The Battle of Trenton" and "The Female Patriots."

Curriculum Coordination

Language Arts

1. Tempe's full name was Temperance Wick. Temperance means "the quality of being moderate; practicing or showing self-control." Ask if this name fits Tempe. Have students write a sentence telling why or why not.

2. Have a group of interested students prepare to read "The Temper of Tempe Wick" aloud. Ask that students divide the story into scenes so that everyone will have a chance to read a major part. Have some students read the conversations and others read the narrative parts.

3. Have students retell this story in the first person, as Tempe might have told it to a friend.

Social Studies

If possible, visit a museum, historical home, restored village, or other site from the Revolutionary period to give students more information about this time period in our history. If these resources are unavailable, have students research the Revolutionary War and prepare a short report to share with the class.

Art

Have students look closely at the details in the illustrations. Also have them check the books that have pictures of people from around 1780 listed in the bibliography. Students will see pictures of items that are no longer used and clothing styles that are no longer seen. Suggest that they draw pictures of those items that they think are typical of that era and make a bulletin-board display. Some students may wish to write sentences or short paragraphs explaining the function of some of the items.

The Little Riders

Bibliography

The following books contain stories of courage. Many of them are works of historical fiction.

Easy

Benchley, Nathaniel. *Sam the Minuteman.* Sam eagerly joins the fight for freedom and accompanies his father to battle.

Dodge, Nanabah Chee. *Morning Arrow.* How a Navajo boy earns the money to buy his grandmother a new shawl.

Duncan, Jane. *Brave Janet Reachfar.* Janet Reachfar rescues the sheep that have wandered off in a snowstorm.

Average

Anderson, Margaret J. *Searching for Shona.* Two girls, evacuated from Edinburgh during World War II, switch identities.

Blaine, Marge. *Dvora's Journey.* Life in Russia becomes increasingly difficult for Jews in 1904, and Dvora's parents decide to leave their homeland.

Child Study Association of America. *Courage to Adventure: Stories of Boys and Girls Growing Up with America.* A collection of nineteen stories about American children from many ethnic and cultural heritages.

Little, Jean. *Mine for Keeps.* Sarah expects special treatment when she returns home from a cerebral palsy center, but her family and classmates treat her as an able person, with no privileges, and Sarah must change her thinking.

Challenging

Coatsworth, Elizabeth. *The Princess and the Lion.* An Abyssinian princess sets out to free her brother.

Frank, Anne. *The Diary of a Young Girl.* The well-known story of the Frank family, who were hidden in an attic in Amsterdam during the Nazi occupation of Holland.

Haar, Jaap ter. *Boris.* Boris and his friend must go beyond the city limits to forage for potatoes during the German siege of Leningrad in World War II.

Kerr, Judith. *A Small Person Far Away.* Anna returns to Berlin to deal with survivors of the Nazi holocaust.

Knudson, R. *Fox Running.* A young Apache woman works hard to become an Olympic runner.

Krumgold, Joseph. *. . . And Now Miguel.* Miguel goes into the mountains to learn that the life of an adult—and a shepherd—requires courage. A Newbery Medal winner.

The following books are nonfiction and may be helpful to students who wish to make models of the little riders.

Average

Denzer, Ann Wiseman. *Making Things: The Hand Book of Creative Discovery.* Two books. A general guide to numerous crafts, containing instructions on making models from papier-mâché and working with clay.

Challenging

Color Crafts. *Papier-Mâché, Dyeing and Leatherwork.* Papier-mâché constructions colorfully presented.

Films and Filmstrips

NOTE: For more information, see *Resource Center.*

Films, Inc. "My Side of the Mountain." Twelve-year-old Sam leaves home and survives in the Canadian wilderness.

Miller-Brody Productions. "Call It Courage." The Newbery Medal-winning story of a Polynesian chief's young son, who conquers his fear of the sea and wins the respect of others.

_____. "The Perilous Road." The story of a boy's difficult transition from blind hatred to tolerance when he learns that his brother is an enemy Yankee.

_____. "The Upstairs Room." Courage, optimism, humor, and hope in a young girl's story of her days hiding on a farm in Holland during the German occupation.

Norwood Films. "Defense of Antwerp Against the V-1." Events in Antwerp, from the German occupation to the liberation by Allied forces.

Walt Disney Productions. "Treasure Island," Parts I and II. A classic tale of adventure, about a boy's growth into adulthood.

Records and/or Tapes

NOTE: Recordings may also be available on other labels.

Viking Press. "Transport." While escaping from Nazi Germany, a young girl helps others.

Curriculum Coordination

Language Arts

1. Encourage students to write their own endings to "The Little Riders." They know that the riders have been saved, that part of Holland has been liberated from the Germans, and that northern Holland expects to be liberated as well. Ask students what they think will happen to Johanna, to her grandparents, and to Captain Braun. Then have them write an ending to the story.

2. Johanna had gone to Holland to visit her grandparents and ended up staying four years. Her parents must have been very anxious about her safety. Imagine that you are Johanna. Select one event from the story and write a letter to Johanna's parents about it. Your letter may relate details about how Johanna felt and what she saw that were not actually included in the story.

3. Divide students into groups and have each group select one short scene from "The Little Riders" to dramatize. You might suggest that they pick the scene when Captain Braun first enters Johanna's grandparents' house or the scene when he discovers Johanna in his closet. Ask students to reread each scene they select and then act it out. Tell students that they may add scenes as long as the action and dialogue are consistent with the story.

4. Invite someone from your community who participated in World War II to speak to your class. Interested students might wish to write some historical fiction based on what they learn from the speaker.

Art

Have interested students make models of the little riders using clay or papier-mâché. The illustrations for the story can be used as a guide. Books listed in this *Enrichment* section give instructions for constructing figures.

Glossary

This glossary is a little dictionary. It contains the difficult words found in this book. The pronunciation, which tells you how to say the word, is given next to each word. That is followed by a word's meaning or meanings. Sometimes, a different form of the word follows the definition. It appears in boldfaced type.

The special symbols used to show the pronunciation are explained in the key that follows.

PRONUNCIATION KEY*

a	add, map	m	move, seem	u	up, done
ā	ace, rate	n	nice, tin	û(r)	urn, term
â(r)	care, air	ng	ring, song	yōō	use, few
ä	palm, father	o	odd, hot	v	vain, eve
b	bat, rub	ō	open, so	w	win, away
ch	check, catch	ô	order, jaw	y	yet, yearn
d	dog, rod	oi	oil, boy	z	zest, muse
e	end, pet	ou	out, now	zh	vision, pleasure
ē	even, tree	ōō	pool, food	ə	the schwa
f	fit, half	ŏŏ	took, full		an unstressed
g	go, log	p	pit, stop		vowel representing
h	hope, hate	r	run, poor		the sound spelled
i	it, give	s	see, pass		a in above
ī	ice, write	sh	sure, rush		e in sicken
j	joy, ledge	t	talk, sit		i in possible
k	cook, take	th	thin, both		o in melon
l	look, rule	ᵺ	this, bathe		u in circus

Foreign: N is used following a nasal sound: French *Jean* [zhäN].
    - indicates the [ny] sound: Spanish *señor* [sā·nyôr'].

In the pronunciations an accent mark (′) is used to show which syllable of a word receives the most stress. The word *bandage* [ban′dij], for example, is stressed on the first syllable. Sometimes there is also a lighter accent mark (′) that shows where there is a lighter stress, as in the word *combination* [kom′bə·nā′shən].

The following abbreviations are used throughout the glossary: *n.*, noun; *v.*, verb; *adj.*, adjective; *adv.*, adverb; *pl.*, plural; *sing.*, singular.

*The Pronunciation Key and the short form of the key that appears on the following right-hand pages are reprinted from *The HBJ School Dictionary*, copyright © 1977, 1972, 1968 by Harcourt Brace Jovanovich, Inc.

A

a·ban·don [ə·ban′dən] *v.* To leave; to fail to take care of. —**a·ban·doned**, *adj.*: an *abandoned* house.

a·bly [ā′blē] *adv.* With ability.

a·bun·dance [ə·bun′dəns] *n.* More than enough; an overflowing quantity.

ac·com·plish·ment [ə·kom′plish·mənt] *n.* Something done or completed; an achievement.

a·chieve·ment [ə·chēv′mənt] *n.* Something accomplished.

ac·tive [ak′tiv] *adj.* Busy or lively.

ac·tu·al [ak′chōō·əl] *adj.* Real.

ad·mit [ad·mit′] *v.* **ad·mit·ted** To accept as true.

ad·van·tage [ad·van′tij] *n.* Any circumstance that benefits someone or helps toward success.

af·fect [ə·fekt′] *v.* **af·fect·ed** To act on; have an effect on.

af·fec·tion [ə·fek′shən] *n.* A feeling of kindness, fondness, or love.

A·gi·ri·A·sa·sa [ä·gi′rē·ä·sä′sä] The wise man's name in "The Oba Asks for a Mountain."

air pock·et [âr′ pok′it] *n.* 1 A bubble of gas in the stomach. 2 A strong current of air that may cause an airplane to drop down sharply.

a·jar [ə·jär′] *adj., adv.* A little bit open, as a door.

al·ma·nac [ôl′mə·nak] *n.* A calendar in the form of a book or pamphlet that may state facts, predict the weather, or have wise little sayings or riddles.

Am·a·zon Riv·er [am′ə·zon riv′ər] *n.* A very large river which flows east across most of northern South America.

am·ne·sia [am·nē′zhə *or* am·nē′zhē·ə] *n.* Loss of memory. It can be caused by sickness, shock, or a hard hit on the head.

a·muse [ə·myōōz′] *v.* To entertain.

a·mus·ing [ə·myōō′zing] *adj.* Causing enjoyment, laughter, fun. —**a·muse**, *v.*

an·ces·tor [an′ses·tər] *n.* 1 A plant or animal of an earlier type from which later plants or animals have developed. 2 A person from whom one is descended, generally a person further back than a grandparent.

an·cient [ān′shənt] 1 *n.* A person who lived in early times. 2 *adj.* Very old.

an·tique [an·tēk′] *n.* Something very old, made a long time ago.

ap·pren·tice [ə·pren′tis] *n.* A person who works for another in order to learn that other person's trade or business.

arch [ärch] *n.* A curve at the top of a gate, doorway, or window: A stone *arch* is often used as a doorway.

ar·chae·ol·o·gist [är′kē·ol′ə·jist] *n.* A scientist who studies how people lived in the past, often by digging up their camps, tombs, cities, etc.

ar·chi·tect [är′kə·tekt] *n.* A person who draws plans for buildings or other structures.

as·cend [ə·send′] *v.* **as·cend·ing**, **as·cend·ed** 1 To succeed to; take over: *ascend* the throne (become king or queen). 2 To climb; rise.

as·sem·ble [ə·sem′bəl] *v.* **as·sem·bled** To bring together; collect.

at·om [at′əm] *n.* The smallest part of an element that can take part in a chemical reaction.

av·er·age [av′rij] *adj.* Usual, ordinary.

---

av·o·ca·do [av′ə·kä′dō] *n.* The green fruit of a tropical tree, eaten in salad and in other ways. It has one large pit.

awk·ward·ly [ôk′wərd·lē] *adv.* Being clumsy or embarrassing: walking *awkwardly* onto a stage.

B

bal·le·ri·na [bal′ə·rē′nə] *n.* A female ballet dancer.

bal·let [bal′ā *or* ba·lā′] *n.* A dance in which formal steps and movements are performed by costumed dancers. A ballet often tells a story.

bare·ly [bâr′lē] *adv.* 1 Only just; scarcely. 2 Plainly; openly.

bar·ter [bär′tər] *v.* To trade.

bate [bāt] **bat·ed** *v.* To eat or take nourishment—no longer used.

bea·gle [bē′gəl] *n.* A small dog with short legs and droopy ears.

Bell, Alexander Graham [bel, al′ig·zan′dər grā′əm] 1847–1922, the inventor of the telephone.

be·tray [bi·trā′] *v.* To give away a secret; to help an enemy.

bi·car·bon·ate of soda [bī·kär′bə·nit] *n.* A white powder that fizzes in water. Used in cooking or for an upset stomach. Also called *sodium bicarbonate*.

bind·er [bīn′dər] *n.* A notebook.

blow·hole [blō′hōl′] *n.* A nostril in the top of the head through which a dolphin, whale, etc. breathes.

bob [bob] 1 *v.* To move up and down or back and forth, with short, jerky motions. 2 *n.* A cork or float on a fishing line.

boom [bōōm] 1 *n.* A sudden increase in growth or riches: A *boom* usually does not last long. 2 *n.* The sound of an explosion. 3 *v.* To grow large and rich very quickly.

bore [bôr] *v.* **bored** 1 To make a hole in or through. 2 To make tired by being dull.

breath·tak·ing [breth′tā′king] *adj.* Taking one's breath away; very beautiful.

breed [brēd] 1 *v.* To produce young. 2 *n.* A particular kind of animal.

bur·den [bûr′dən] *n.* 1 A load. 2 Something difficult to carry or bear.

bur·lap [bûr′lap] *n.* A rough, loose cloth used for bags, sacks, etc.

bur·row [bûr′ō] 1 *n.* A hole or tunnel dug by an animal and used to live in, hide in, or escape through. 2 *v.* To make such a hole or tunnel.

bus·y·bod·y [biz′ē·bod′ē] *n.* A person or animal that interferes in the business of others. —**bus·y·bod·ies**, *pl.*

C

ca·boose [kə·bōōs′] *n.* The last car of a freight train.

car·a·van [kar′ə·van] *n.* A group of traders, pilgrims, or others who travel together, as across a desert.

add, āce, câre, pälm; end, ēqual; it, īce; odd, ōpen, ôrder; tōōk, pōōl; up, bûrn; ə = a in *above*, e in *sicken*, i in *possible*, o in *melon*, u in *circus*; yōō = u in *fuse*; oil; pout; check; ring; thin; ᵺis; zh in *vision*.

---

ca·reer [kə·rir′] *n.* The main work of a person's life.

car·il·lon [kar′ə·lon] *n.* A set of bells on which a tune can be played.

car·ri·on [kar′ē·ən] *n.* Dead and rotting flesh.

cas·u·al·ly [kazh′ōō·əl·ē] *adv.* In a cool manner, showing no emotion: He *casually* introduced himself to the famous writer.

cat·a·logue [kat′ə·lôg] *n.* 1 A list of things a store has for sale. 2 A card file showing the books in a library.

cell [sel] *n.* The basic unit of any living thing.

cen·sus [sen′səs] *n.* An official count of all the people in a country or city.

cen·ten·ni·al [sen·ten′ē·əl] *n.* The hundredth birthday of something: The Philadelphia *Centennial* Exposition was held one hundred years after the signing of the Declaration of Independence.

chal·lenge [chal′enj] 1 *n.* An invitation or dare to do something, usually dangerous or difficult. 2 *v.* To ask for a contest, duel, or fight.

char·ac·ter [kar′ik·tər] *n.* 1 A person, animal, etc., in a play, novel, story, etc. 2 All the qualities that make up the nature of a person. 3 Any letter, figure, or mark used in writing or printing.

charge [chärj] 1 *n.* An amount of stored electricity. 2 *v.* To fill with electricity. 3 *v.* To ask a price for. —**in charge** Having the care or control of.

Cher·o·kee [cher′ə·kē] *n.* A member of a tribe of American Indians. At first they lived in the southeastern U.S. Now many *Cherokees* live in Oklahoma.

cho·re·og·ra·pher [kôr′ē·og′rə·fər] *n.* A person who plans dancers' movements for performances.

cir·cu·la·to·ry [sûr′kyə·lə·tôr′ē] *adj.* Having to do with movement around or through something, as of the blood.

cit·a·del [sit′ə·dəl] *n.* A building that overlooks a city in order to protect it.

ci·vi·li·za·tion [siv′ə·lə·zā′shən] *n.* The art, skill, science, knowledge, and culture of a particular group of people at a particular time.

claim [klām] 1 *v.* To demand as one's own. 2 *n.* A demand for something as one's own.

clasp [klasp] 1 *n.* A fastening or hook to hold two parts together. 2 *v.* To fasten with a clasp. 3 *v.* To grasp or embrace.

clog [klog] *v.* To plug or fill up so nothing can move. —**clog·ged**, *adj.*

clum·sy [klum′zē] *adj.* Not smooth or easy; awkward.

clus·ter [klus′tər] *n.* A group or bunch of similar things close together.

cob·ble·stone [kob′əl·stōn′] *n.* A rounded stone that was used for paving streets.

coin·age [koi′nij] *n.* 1 Money. 2 The right to make coins.

col·league [kol′ēg] *n.* A fellow worker in a profession or organization; associate.

co·lo·ni·al [kə·lō′nē·əl] 1 *n.* A person who lives in a land separate from the country that controls it. 2 *adj.* Having to do with a colony or colonies.

com·mis·sion·er [kə·mish′ən·ər] *n.* A person chosen or elected to be head of a government department or assignment.

com·mit·ment [kə·mit′mənt] *n.* The state of being bound to a promise.

com·mu·ni·ty [kə·myōō′nə·tē] *n.* 1 A group of people living together in one area. 2 A group of people living together who share the same interests.

com·mu·ni·ty re·la·tions [kə·myōō′nə·tē ri·lā′shənz] *n.* The dealings between a business or organization and the public in general.
com·pan·ion [kəm·pan′yən] *n.* A person who spends time with another, sharing what the other person is doing.
com·pa·ny [kum′pə·nē] *n.* **1** A group of dancers, actors, or singers gathered to perform together. **2** A group of people who have come together because of some common interest or purpose. — **com·pa·nies,** *pl.*
com·pel [kəm·pel′] *v.* **com·pelled** To force.
com·plex [kəm·pleks′ *or* kom′pleks] *adj.* Made up of many parts.
con·cern [kən·sûrn′] **1** *v.* To relate to; involve. **2** *n.* An interest or worry.
con·cer·ti·na [kon′sər·tē′nə] *n.* A small musical instrument like an accordion.

con·di·tion [kən·dish′ən] *n.* **1** Physical fitness; state of being healthy. **2** The state of being of a person or thing.
cone [kōn] *n.* The dry fruit of certain trees, mostly evergreens.
cone-bear·ing [kōn′bâr′ing] *adj.* Producing a dry fruit that holds seeds: Pines and many other trees are *cone-bearing.*
con·sid·er·a·ble [kən·sid′ər·ə·bəl] *adj.* Rather large; worth noticing.
con·stant [kon′stənt] *adj.* **1** Happening over and over, without end. **2** Faithful.
con·tact [kon′takt] **1** *n.* A coming together, meeting; the relation of touching or being in touch with. **2** *v.* To get in touch with.
con·tract [kən·trakt′] *v.* To become smaller; pull together into a smaller space.
con·trar·y *adj.* **1** [kən·trâr′ē] Determined to disagree: He was *contrary* in choosing a movie. **2** [kon′trer·ē] Totally different: *contrary* beliefs.
cor·al [kôr′əl] **1** *n.* A stony substance formed by many, many skeletons of tiny sea animals. **2** *n.* The animal whose skeleton forms coral. **3** *n., adj.* A pinkish or yellowish red color.

cor·ner·stone [kôr′nər·stōn′] *n.* A stone set into the corner of a building: The date the building was started is often carved in the *cornerstone.*
count·less [kount′lis] *adj.* Too many to be counted.
count·y seat [koun′tē sēt′] *n.* The place where the members of the county government meet and have their offices.
cove [kōv] *n.* A small, sheltered bay along a shoreline.
coy [koi] *adj.* **1** Shy. **2** Pretending to be shy in order to flirt.
craft [kraft] *n.* A skill, especially one done with the hands.
craft shop [kraft′ shop′] *n.* A place to buy supplies for practicing a craft.
cray·fish [krā′fish′] *n.* A small, freshwater shellfish like a lobster. Also called *crawfish.*

add, āce, câre, pälm; end, ēqual; it, īce; odd, ōpen, ôrder; tŏŏk, pōōl; up, bûrn;
ə = a in *above,* e in *sicken,* i in *possible,* o in *melon,* u in *circus;* yōō = u in *fuse;* oil; pout;
check; ring; thin; this; zh in *vision.*

cres·cent [kres′ənt] *adj.* Curved like a quarter moon.

crib [krib] *n.* **1** A cage for storing corn. **2** A baby's bed with railings on the sides.
crim·son [krim′zən] *n., adj.* Deep red.
crit·ic [krit′ik] *n.* A person who judges the value of music, books, plays, etc., and writes about his or her judgments.
crouch [krouch] **1** *n.* The position of crouching. **2** *v.* To stoop down with the knees bent, as an animal about to spring. — **crouch·es.**
cru·sade [krōō·sād′] **1** *v.* To fight for a cause or against an evil. **2** *n.* A vigorous struggle against evil or for a cause.
crush [krush] *v.* To press or squeeze as to break or injure. — **crush·ing** *adj.* Overwhelming, overpowering.
crys·tal [kris′təl] **1** *n.* A body formed when something turns to a solid: A *crystal* has flat surfaces and angles in a regular pattern: salt *crystals,* ice *crystals.* **2** *adj.* Colorless, transparent.

A salt crystal

cu·bic inch [kyōō′bik inch′] *n.* A unit for measuring volume, equaling one inch wide by one inch high by one inch deep.

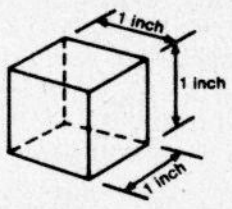

cue [kyōō] *n.* A word, action, etc., used in a play as a signal to another actor.
cul·ti·vate [kul′tə·vāt] *v.* **cul·ti·vat·ed** To prepare (land) for growing plants by loosening the soil.
cu·ri·os·i·ty [kyŏŏr′ē·os′ə·tē] *n.* **1** A desire to find out. **2** Something strange or unusual. — **cu·ri·os·i·ties,** *pl.*
cu·ri·ous [kyŏŏr′ē·əs] *adj.* Eager to know.
cur·rent [kûr′ənt] *n.* The part of a body of water or air that flows in a certain direction.
cur·ry [kûr′ē] *n.* A sauce or powder made of finely ground spices, used in cooking, especially in India and the Mideast.
curt·sy [kûrt′sē] **1** *n.* A bow made by bending the knees and leaning the upper body forward; used by females. **2** *v.* To make such a bow.
cy·cle [sī′kəl] *n.* **1** A series of stages in the growth of an animal or plant. **2** The time needed for these stages to take place. **3** A series of events that always happen in the same order and end back at the starting point.

D

darn [därn] **1** *v.* To mend cloth by stitching the hole with thread. **2** *n.* A place mended by darning. — **darn·ing** *adj.:* a *darning* needle.
da Vin·ci, Le·o·nar·do [də vin′chē, lā′ə·när′dō] 1452–1519, Italian painter, sculptor, engineer, and scientist.
dec·o·ra·tion [dek′ə·rā′shən] *n.* Something used to make something else more fancy or attractive; an ornament.
de·crease [di·krēs′] *v.* To get smaller.
ded·i·ca·tion [ded′ə·kā′shən] *n.* A giving over of one's life and/or time to a special purpose.
de·duc·tion [di·duk′shən] *n.* **1** A conclusion based on reasoning. **2** A subtraction: a thirty-dollar *deduction.*
de·fy [di·fī′] *v.* To refuse to follow (orders); resist openly.

de·mon [dē′mən] *n.* **1** A person having great energy or skill: a speed *demon.* **2** An evil spirit, devil.
de·part·ment [di·pärt′mənt] *n.* A separate part or division, as of a company, store, government, etc.
de·pend [di·pend′] *v.* **1** To be affected, influenced, or controlled by. **2** To trust; rely. — **de·pend·a·ble** [di·pen′də·bəl] *adj.* Worthy of trust; reliable.
de·scent [di·sent′] *n.* The act of going down to a lower point.
de·scrip·tive [di·skrip′tiv] *adj.* Telling what a person or thing is like.
de·sign [di·zīn′] *v.* **de·signed** To plan for a certain purpose.
de·sign·er [di·zī′nər] *n.* A person who plans the arrangement of the parts or features of something.
des·per·ate·ly [des′pər·it·lē] *adv.* Recklessly, carelessly — almost without hope.
de·vel·op·ment [di·vel′əp·mənt] *n.* **1** A growing larger or better. **2** The result of growing larger or better.
de·vice [di·vīs′] *n.* Something built for a specific purpose.
dig·ni·fied [dig′nə·fīd] *adj.* Having pride; calm and stately.
di·rec·tor [dī·rek′tər *or* di·rek′tər] *n.* A person who controls or manages, as in the production of a dance, movie, etc.
dis·ap·point [dis·ə·point′] *v.* **dis·ap·point·ed** To fail to meet the hopes of: Don't *disappoint* me.
dis·as·ter [di·zas′tər] *n.* An event causing great distress or ruin, as a fire, flood, etc.
dis·charge **1** [dis′chärj] *n.* The removal of an electrical charge. **2** [dis·chärj′ *or* dis′chärj] *v.* To set off or send forth an electrical charge.
dis·cour·age·ment [dis·kûr′ij·mənt] *n.* A feeling of being without hope or confidence.
Dis·ney, Walt [diz′nē, wôlt] 1901–1966, movie producer, especially known for animated cartoons *Mickey Mouse* and *Donald Duck.*
dis·tinct·ly [dis·tingkt′lē] *adv.* Very clearly.
dis·turb [dis·tûrb′] *v.* **dis·turbed** To break in upon with noise or change; upset.
dog·pad·dle [dog′pad′əl] *v.* **dog·pad·dling** To swim by paddling with each arm and kicking with each leg, as a dog does.
dol·ly [dol′ē] *n.* **1** A tool shaped like a small wooden stool on the end of a stick: The *dolly* was used to wash clothes by turning and pounding them in the water. **2** A flat frame set on wheels, used to move heavy objects. **3** A child's term for a doll.

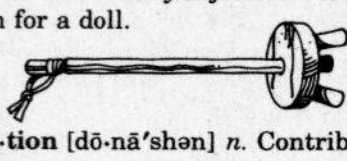

do·na·tion [dō·nā′shən] *n.* Contribution, gift.
draw [drô] *v.* **1** To pull or drag. **2** To make a picture, cartoon, or likeness of with lines.
drib·ble [drib′əl] *v.* **drib·bling** **1** To bounce or kick a ball very quickly. **2** Let fall in drops; drip or drool.
drift [drift] **1** *n.* Something piled up by wind or water: The snow piled in a *drift.* **2** *v.* To move or float in a current of water or air.
drift·wood [drift′wŏŏd′] *n.* Wood that is drifting in water or has washed up on shore.

add, āce, câre, pälm; end, ēqual; it, īce; odd, ōpen, ôrder; tŏŏk, pōōl; up, bûrn;
ə = a in *above,* e in *sicken,* i in *possible,* o in *melon,* u in *circus;* yōō = u in *fuse;* oil; pout;
check; ring; thin; this; zh in *vision.*

drive [drīv] **1** *n.* The moving of cattle or sheep. **2** *n.* Ambition. **3** *v.* To direct and control the movements of.
drop·let [drop′lit] *n.* A little drop.
drought [drout] *n.* A long time without rainfall during which the ground becomes very dry.
dwin·dle [dwin′dəl] *v.* To grow steadily smaller.

E

East·ern Wood·land In·di·ans [ēs′tərn wŏŏd′land′ in′dē·ənz] *n., pl.* Those American Indians who lived mostly on land thickly covered with trees in eastern North America.
e·clipse [i·klips′] *n.* A complete or partial hiding of the sun or moon: An *eclipse* occurs when the moon passes between Earth and the sun or when the moon passes through Earth's shadow.
e·di·tion [i·dish′ən] *n.* All the copies of a book or paper printed at one time and without differences.
ef·fect [i·fekt′] **1** *n.* Influence; the ability to cause something to change. **2** *v.* To bring about or cause.
em·bel·lish·ment [im·bel′ish·mənt] *n.* Something added to make attractive; decoration.
en·a·ble [in·ā′bəl] *v.* **en·a·bled** To make able; give the ability to: Tennis lessons will *enable* me to play better.
en·chant·er [in·chan′tər] *n.* A magician; sorcerer.
en·tire·ly [in·tīr′lē] *adv.* Totally.
en·vi·ron·ment [in·vī′rən·mənt] *n.* The conditions and surroundings that have an effect on the development of a person, animal, or plant.
e·qua·tion [i·kwā′zhən] *n.* A statement that two or more quantities are equal, as $5 \times 5 = 25$.
e·qua·tor [i·kwā′tər] *n.* An imaginary line that circles the Earth halfway between the North and South Poles.

es·tab·lish [ə·stab′lish] *v.* **es·tab·lished** To set up on a firm or lasting basis.
e·val·u·a·tion [i·val′yōō·ā′shən] *n.* An examination, check-up, test.
e·ven·tu·al·ly [i·ven′chōō·ə·lē] *adv.* In the end; finally.
ex·as·per·ate [ig·zas′pə·rāt] *v.* To annoy almost to the point of anger.
ex·cerpt [ek′sûrpt] *n.* A passage or section taken from a piece of writing.
ex·ec·u·tive [ig·zek′yə·tiv] *n.* One of the persons who is in charge of a business.
ex·pand [ik·spand′] *v.* To make or become larger.
ex·pose [ik·spōz′] *v.* **ex·pos·ing** To uncover; reveal.
ex·pos·i·tion [eks′pə·zish′ən] *n.* A showing; a display of things.

F

face [fās] **1** *n.* An outer level or flat surface, as of a crystal or a cliff. **2** *n.* The front of the head extending from forehead to chin and ear to ear. **3** *v.* To meet with courage.
fac·tu·al [fak′chōō·əl] *adj.* Made up of, or relying on, things known to be true.
faith [fāth] *n.* A religion or belief.
fa·mil·iar [fə·mil′yər] *adj.* Well known as through experience, study, or because often encountered.
far·sight·ed [fär′sī′tid] *adj.* **1** Showing good judgment in looking and planning ahead. **2** Able to see things at a distance more clearly than things that are near.

fas·ci·nat·ing [fas′ə·nāt·ing] *adj.* Very interesting.

fas·ci·na·tion [fas′ə·nā′shən] *n.* Great interest or attraction.

fear·some [fir′səm] *adj.* Frightening.

fea·ture [fē′chər] *n.* 1 A special article, story, or column, as in a newspaper. 2 Part of the face, as eyes, nose, or mouth.

feed [fēd] 1 *n.* Food for animals. 2 *v.* To give food to.

feld·spar [feld′spär] *n.* A hard mineral containing aluminum and other elements.

fid·dle·back chair [fid′(ə)l·bak′] *n.* A straight-back chair with no arms and a center piece down the back that is shaped like a fiddle (a violin).

field [fēld] 1 *n.* A large stretch of land. 2 *v.* To catch, as a ball. —**field·ed.**

fier·y [fīr′ē or fī′ər·ē] *adj.* Flaming; containing fire.

fife [fīf] 1 *n.* A small, shrill flute. 2 *v.* To play a fife. —**fifed.**

file [fīl] 1 *v.* To have something put on an official record. 2 *n.* A cabinet, drawer, or box in which papers are arranged according to a system. 3 *v.* To arrange and put in a file.

flash [flash] 1 *n.* A sudden blaze of light. 2 *v.* To shine brightly. 3 *v.* To move quickly. —**flashed.**

flus·tered [flus′tərd] *adj.* Confused; embarrassed; upset.

for·ty-nin·er [fôr′tē·nī′nər] *n.* Someone who went to California in 1849 to find gold.

Fo·rum [fôr′əm] *n.* The center for meetings, business, and courts in the ancient city of Rome.

fos·sil [fos′əl] *n.* The remains or impressions of an animal or plant of a past age, hardened and preserved in rock.

fossil

foul shot [foul′ shot′] *n.* In basketball, a free throw given to a player after an opponent makes physical contact, a foul, with that player.

frail [frāl] *adj.* Weak; easily damaged.

frame·work [frām′wûrk′] *n.* The inner structure around which something is built.

free·way [frē′wā′] *n.* A highway for fast traffic; expressway.

fre·quen·cy [frē′kwən·sē] *n.* Station or tuning on a radio receiver.

frus·tra·tion [frus·trā′shən] *n.* Defeat and disappointment.

fu·gi·tive [fyoo′jə·tiv] *n.* A person who is running from danger or arrest.

fu·ri·ous [fyoor′ē·əs] *adj.* 1 Very great: at a *furious* speed. 2 Very angry.

fuss·budg·et [fus′buj·it] *n.* A fussy, hard-to-please person.

G

gai·ter [gā′tər] *n.* A covering, as of cloth or leather, for the lower leg or ankle.

gale [gāl] *n.* A very strong wind.

gasp [gasp] *v.* **gasped** To struggle for breath with the mouth open.

add, āce, câre, pälm; end, ēqual; it, īce; odd, ōpen, ôrder; took, pool; up, bûrn; ə = a in *above*, e in *sicken*, i in *possible*, o in *melon*, u in *circus*; yoo = u in *fuse*; oil; pout; check; ring; thin; this; zh in *vision*.

---

gen·er·a·tion [jen′ə·rā′shən] *n.* One step or stage in the history of a family: My father is of a different *generation* than I.

ge·ol·o·gy [jē·ol′ə·jē] *n.* The study of the history and structure of the Earth's crust, especially as recorded in rocks.

gi·bral·tar [ji·brôl′tər] *n.* 1 A hard white candy, usually peppermint or lemon flavored. 2 With a capital letter, *Gibraltar* is the name of a place at the southern tip of Spain.

glare [glâr] *v.* To stare with a fierce and angry look.

gleam [glēm] 1 *n.* A ray or beam of light that is faint or shines for only a short time. 2 *v.* To shine with a gleam. —**gleam·ing.**

gloss·y [glôs′ē] *adj.* Smooth and shiny.

glow-worm [glō′wurm′] *n.* A firefly, or its larva, that glows in the dark.

Go·bi Des·ert [gō′bē dez′ərt] *n.* A rough, rocky desert about three times the size of California, in east central Asia.

gog·gles [gog′əlz] *n., pl.* Large glasses that protect the eyes from wind, dust, and sparks.

gold rush [gōld′rush′] *n.* The hurrying of settlers to a place where they think they can find gold: In 1849 there was a *gold rush* to California.

gran·ite [gran′it] *n.* A hard igneous rock that will take a high polish. It is often used as a building material.

graze [grāz] *v.* To feed on growing grass.

Greek [grēk] 1 *adj.* Having to do with an ancient people of southern Europe, their lands, or their language. 2 *n.* A person from Greece.

grit [grit] *n.* Bits of stone; gravel: Chickens, which have no teeth, need *grit* in their stomachs to grind their food.

grot·to [grot′ō] *n.* A cave. —**grot·toes,** *pl.*

gruff [gruf] *adj.* Rough; rude.

guard [gärd] 1 *n.* A device, attachment, etc., that makes something safe to use or keeps it from being lost. 2 *v.* To watch with care.

H

haugh·ti·ly [hô′tə·lē] *adv.* Proudly and scornfully.

haz·y [hā′zē] *adj.* Unclear, misty.

he·li·um [hē′lē·əm] *n.* A gas that is lighter than air and does not burn.

hemp [hemp] *n.* A tall plant of Asia, grown for its tough fiber, which is made into cloth, rope, etc.

her·ald [her′əld] 1 *n.* A bearer of important news; messenger. 2 *v.* To announce or foretell.

hinge [hinj] *n.* A joint on which something turns.

hol·low [hol′ō] 1 *n.* Valley. 2 *adj.* Empty on the inside, not solid.

Ho·mer [hō′mər] A Greek poet who lived almost 3,000 years ago; the author of the *Odyssey*.

home-spun [hōm′spun′] 1 *adj.* Made at home. 2 *n.* Cloth made of yarn spun at home. 3 *adj.* Plain; simple.

home·stead [hōm′sted] *n.* 1 A piece of land given to a settler by the U.S. government to farm, improve, and eventually own. 2 A person's land and house.

Home·stead Act [hōm′sted akt′] *n.* One of several Homestead Acts—laws that allowed settlers to buy land in the West with their work plus a very small amount of money.

---

home·stead·er [hōm′sted′ər] *n.* A settler who farmed land in order to buy it.

ho·ri·zon [hə·rī′zən] *n.* The line where the Earth and sky seem to meet.

horn of am·mon [hôrn′ uv am′ən] *n.* A sea shell that curls like the horn of a male sheep. Statues of an Egyptian god, Ammon, showed him with a sheep's curling horns.

horse·car [hôrs′kär] *n.* A trolley or "bus" drawn by horses along a track.

house 1 [houz] *v.* To give shelter to or lodge. 2 [hous] *n.* A building that people live in.

hurl [hûrl] *v.* **hurled** To throw with a great force.

husk·y [hus′kē] *n.* A large, strong dog used to pull sleds through snow.

Hwei Ming [hwā′ ming′] *n.* A Chinese female's name which means "clever." The word *ming* can also mean "light."

hy·dro·gen [hī′drə·jən] *n.* The lightest of all gases; it burns easily and has no smell or color: *Hydrogen* combines with oxygen to make water.

I

i·den·ti·fi·ca·tion [ī·den′tə·fə·kā′shən] *n.* The action of identifying, describing, or recognizing.

ig·ne·ous rocks [ig′nē·əs] *n.* Rocks formed at very high temperatures, as by a volcano.

I·le·sha [ē·lā′shä] *n.* A city in southwest Nigeria.

im·ag·i·na·tive·ly [i·maj′ə·nə·tiv·lē] *adv.* In a creative way.

im·mense [i·mens′] *adj.* Very large; huge.

im·press [im·pres′] *v.* **im·pressed** To affect the mind or feelings of, usually favorably.

im·pres·sion [im·presh′ən] *n.* 1 The pressing of paper on type; printing. 2 An effect on the mind or feelings.

im·prove·ment [im·proov′mənt] *n.* 1 The act of making better. 2 The result of becoming better.

in·au·di·ble [in·ô′də·bəl] *adj.* Incapable of being heard.

in·can·ta·tion [in′kan·tā′shən] *n.* The speaking of words or syllables that are supposed to have magical results: The wizard's *incantation* made a rabbit appear in the hat.

in·cor·po·rate [in·kôr′pə·rāt] *v.* To combine, bring together; to include as part of something else.

in·crease [in·krēs′] *v.* To get bigger.

in·de·pen·dence [in′di·pen′dens] *n.* Not having to depend or rely on someone or something; the condition of being independent.

in·de·pen·dent [in′di·pen′dənt] *adj.* Self-supporting; not subject to the authority or direction of others.

add, āce, câre, pälm; end, ēqual; it, īce; odd, ōpen, ôrder; took, pool; up, bûrn; ə = a in *above*, e in *sicken*, i in *possible*, o in *melon*, u in *circus*; yoo = u in *fuse*; oil; pout; check; ring; thin; this; zh in *vision*.

In·dies [in′dēz] *n., pl.* 1 Refers to southern and northern Asia and the islands nearby. 2 The East Indies. 3 The West Indies.

in·di·vid·u·al·ist [in′də·vij′oo·əl·ist] *n.* A person who believes in or lives in his or her own way, no matter what other people think.

in·dus·try [in′dəs·trē] *n.* A business; branch of manufacturing or business. —**in·dus·tries,** *pl.*

in·flu·ence [in′floo·əns] *n.* 1 A person with power to affect another person. 2 The power of a person or thing to have an effect on others.

inn·keep·er [in′kē′pər] *n.* A person who owns or operates an inn. An inn is a hotel or restaurant.

in·oc·u·late [in·ok′yə·lāt] *v.* To put a vaccine into a person's or animal's body to protect it against a certain disease.

in·sig·nif·i·cant [in′sig·nif′ə·kənt] *adj.* Lacking importance, meaning, size, or worth: an *insignificant* difference.

in·stance [in′stəns] *n.* An example or illustration.

in·tel·lec·tu·al·ly [in′tə·lek′choo·ə·lē] *adv.* Mentally; in a way having to do with intelligence.

in·tense [in·tens′] *adj.* Very strong, great, or deep: *intense* cold.

in·tent·ly [in·tent′lē] *adv.* With great attention.

in·trud·er [in·troo′dər] *n.* One who enters without permission or welcome.

in·ves·ti·gate [in·ves′tə·gāt] *v.* **in·ves·ti·gat·ing** To look into, find out about.

in·vest·ment [in·vest′mənt] *n.* The use to which money or time is put in order to gain something.

i·o·ta [ī·ō′tə] *n.* 1 The ninth letter of the Greek alphabet. 2 A small amount.

ir·ri·gate [ir′ə·gāt] *v.* **ir·ri·gat·ed** To furnish (land) with water by using pipes, ditches, or canals.

ir·ri·ga·tion [ir′ə·gā′shən] *n.* The supplying of land with water by artificial means such as through pipes, ditches, or canals.

i·tem [ī′təm] *n.* Any one thing in a group of things.

J

jade [jād] *n.* A type of stone, usually green but sometimes white, used in jewelry or carving.

jet stream [jet′ strēm′] *n.* A current of strong winds, 9,000 to 13,500 meters above Earth, blowing from the west at speeds of often more than 400 kilometers per hour.

John·ny Ap·ple·seed [jon′ē ap′əl·sēd′] Nickname of *John Chapman,* 1775–1845, American pioneer who planted apple trees all over the Midwest.

K

kil·ler whale [kil′ər (h)wāl′] *n.* A fierce, mostly black whale which hunts in packs. Generally, the whale does not attack humans.

L

lack [lak] *n.* A state of being without.

la·crosse [lə·krôs′] *n.* A game first played by North American Indians, using rackets or sticks and a small ball.

land bridge [land′ brij′] *n.* A narrow strip of land serving as a passage, or bridge, between two bodies of land.

Lat·in [lat′ən] *n.* The language of ancient Rome.

launch [lônch] *v.* 1 To hurl or fling into the air. 2 To move or push into the water.

lead·ing [lē′ding] *adj.* 1 Most important. 2 At the front; first.

leaf [lēf] 1 *v.* To turn the pages. 2 *n.* One of the pieces of paper making up a book. A page is really one side of a *leaf.* 3 *n.* One of the flat, thin, usually green parts of a plant or tree.

leop·ard seal [lep′ərd sēl′] *n.* A spotted seal found near Antarctica.

lib·er·ate [lib′ə·rāt] *v.* **lib·er·at·ing** To set free.

lieu·ten·ant [lōō·ten′ənt] *n.* A military rank below captain but above sergeant.

life·like [līf′līk′] *adj.* 1 Accurately representing real events: a *lifelike* movie. 2 Looking like a person or thing that is or was alive.

lime·stone [līm′stōn′] *n.* A common kind of rock made of the same substance as chalk.

lin·en [lin′ən] 1 *n.* Thread or cloth made from flax fibers. 2 *adj.* Made of linen.

link [lingk] 1 *n.* Connection. 2 *v.* To join, connect.

lla·ma [lä′mə] *n.* A South American animal related to the camel but smaller and with no hump.

lo·cal [lō′kəl] *adj.* In the nearby area.

lo·ca·tion [lō·kā′shən] *n.* The place where something is.

lock [lok] *n.* 1 An enclosed section of a canal in which ships can be raised or lowered by letting water in or out. 2 A device for fastening a door, safe, etc.

lo·cust [lō′kəst] *n.* An insect like a grasshopper that often moves in large groups and destroys crops.

loot [lōōt] 1 *v.* To rob by force. 2 *n.* Slang for money.

lu·na·tic [lōō′nə·tik] *n.* A person who is mentally ill.

Lyme Re·gis [līm′ rē′jis] *n.* A seaside town in southwest England, on the English Channel.

M

mag·ni·fy [mag′nə·fī] *v.* **mag·ni·fied** To make something look bigger.— **mag·ni·fied,** *adj.*

mam·mal [mam′əl] *n.* Any of the animals that have backbones and whose young are fed with milk from their mothers' bodies.

man·sion [man′shən] *n.* A large, impressive house, as of a wealthy person.

man·tle [man′təl] *n.* 1 One of the layers inside the Earth. 2 A loose-fitting, usually sleeveless garment worn over other clothing; a cloak.

mark·ing [mär′king] *n.* (*often plural*) The color pattern of an animal's fur, a bird's feathers, etc.

mat·ter [mat′ər] *n.* 1 Anything that has weight and takes up space. 2 A particular kind or form of substance: volcanic *matter.* 3 The ideas, facts, or meaning of a book, speech, etc.

mel·o·dy [mel′ə·dē] *n.* A succession of single tones in music; tune.

mem·o·ra·ble [mem′ər·ə·bəl] *adj.* Worthy of being remembered; easily remembered as being important.

men·ace [men′əs] *n.* Threat, danger.

---

mer·chan·dise [mûr′chən·dīz *or* mûr′chən·dīs] *n.* Goods bought and sold for profit.

met·ro·pol·i·tan [met′rə·pol′ə·tən] *adj.* Having to do with a large city and its surrounding suburbs.

mi·cro·or·gan·ism [mī′krō·ôr′gən·iz′əm] *n.* A tiny living thing visible only through a microscope, as a bacterium.

mim·ic [mim′ik] *n.* A person who imitates others.

min·er·al [min′ər·əl] *n.* A natural substance, neither vegetable nor animal, that is important for nutrition in living things.

min·now [min′ō] *n.* A small fish commonly used for bait.

mis·chief [mis′chif] *n.* 1 A person or animal that teases or plays tricks. 2 Tricks or teasing.

mis·sion [mish′ən] *n.* 1 A calling; one's chief purpose. 2 The task or duty that a person or group is sent to do.

mis·un·der·stand·ing [mis′un·dər·stand′ing] 1 *v.* Not understanding or understanding wrongly. 2 *n.* A disagreement.

mo·bile 1 [mō′bēl] *n.* A sculpture made of movable parts and hung in balance so that any breeze moves or turns it. 2 [mō′bəl] *adj.* Easily moved.

mol·lusk [mol′əsk] *n.* A member of a group of animals with soft bodies that are not divided into segments; it is usually protected by a hard shell. Snails and clams are mollusks.

moor·ing [mōōr′ing] *n.* The line, cable, anchor, etc., that holds a ship in place.

more·o·ver [môr·ō′vər] *adv.* Besides.

mouth [mouth] *n.* 1 The place where a river meets the sea. 2 The opening through which food is taken into the body and sounds are uttered.

mu·ni·tions [myōō·nish′ənz] *n.* (*usually pl.*) Materials and supplies used in war; guns, cannons, bullets, and shells.

mus·ket [mus′kit] *n.* An old type of firearm, now replaced by the rifle.

mu·tin·y [myōō′tə·nē] 1 *n.* A rebellion against authority, as by a group of soldiers against their commander. 2 *v.* To take part in a mutiny.

N

name·less [nām′lis] *adj.* 1 Having no name. 2 Not known by name. 3 Not fit to be spoken of: *nameless* terror.

na·tion·al [nash′ən·əl] *adj.* Having to do with the nation as a whole.

na·tion·al·i·ty [nash′ən·al′ə·tē] *n.* A group of people who come from a certain country.

na·tive [nā′tiv] *adj.* Born, grown, or living naturally in a particular area. 2 *n.* A plant or animal living in an area.

na·ture [nā′chər] *n.* 1 One's own combination of characteristics. 2 The world, except for things made by people.

nav·i·ga·tion [nav′ə·gā′shən] *n.* The art of charting the position and route of a ship, aircraft, etc.

nav·i·ga·tor [nav′ə·gā′tər] *n.* A person who charts the position and route of a ship, aircraft, etc.

net·ting [net′ing] *n.* Material made with strips woven together leaving holes between.

nev·er·the·less [nev′ər·thə·les′] *conj.* But, however.

New Am·ster·dam [n(y)ōō′am′stər·dam] *n.* Early Dutch settlement on the site of what is now New York City. In 1664 the British renamed it New York.

New Zea·land [n(y)ōō·zē′lənd] *n.* An island nation in the southern Pacific, southeast of Australia. It is a member of the British Commonwealth.

Norse [nôrs] *n., pl.* The early people who lived in northern Europe.

nudge [nuj] 1 *n.* A gentle push, as with the elbow. 2 *v.* To touch or push gently so as to attract attention.

O

O·ba [ō′bä] Powerful chief in the land of the Yoruba.

ob·ser·va·tion [ob′zər·vā′shən] *n.* The act of looking at something scientifically and making notes on it.

ob·serve [əb·zûrv′] *v.* To see or notice.

ob·ses·sion [əb·sesh′ən] *n.* An idea, thought, or feeling that fills the mind and cannot be driven out.

oc·ca·sion·al [ə·kā′zhən·əl] *adj.* 1 Happening now and then. 2 Made or suitable for a special occasion.

O·ke-U·mo [ō′kā·ōō′mō] *n.* A mountain in Nigeria.

o·me·ga [ō·mē′gə, ō·meg′ə, *or* ō·mā′gə] *n.* 1 The last letter in the Greek alphabet —symbol ω. 2 The end; the last.

or·di·nance [ôr′də·nəns] *n.* An order, or law, made by the government of a city or town.

or·gan·ism [ôr′gən·iz′əm] *n.* A plant or animal thought of as something built of parts and organs.

o·rig·i·nal [ə·rij′ə·nəl] 1 *n.* The first form of a piece of writing. 2 *adj.* Belonging to the beginning of something; first.

o·ver·pro·tect [ō′vər·prə·tekt′] *v.* **o·ver·pro·tect·ed** To protect (a child) too much and keep (the child) from normal experiences.

ox·y·gen [ok′sə·jin] *n.* A colorless, tasteless, odorless gas making up about a fifth of the Earth's atmosphere.

P

pains·tak·ing·ly [pānz′tā′king·lē] *adv.* Very, very carefully.

par·chee·si [pär·chē′zē] *n.* A game played on a cross-shaped board. *Parcheesi* is a trademark. The original game, called *pachisi,* is a very old game of India.

pat·ent [pat′(ə)nt] *n.* A government document giving an inventor the sole right to make and sell an invention or use a new process for a set number of years.

pa·trol [pə·trōl′] *n.* A person or group guarding an area.

pay dirt [pā′ dûrt] *n.* Earth in which something valuable, such as gold or silver, is found.

peer [pir] 1 *v.* To look closely in order to see clearly. 2 *n.* An equal, as in rank, talent, etc.: an artist without *peer.*

Pe·king [pē′king′] *n.* The capital of China.

Pe·nob·scot Bay [pə·nob′skot bā′] *n.* A bay in the state of Maine.

perch [pûrch] 1 *n.* A resting place for a bird. 2 *v.* To sit or place (something) on.—**perched.**

per·il [per′əl] *n.* Danger.

---

per·ma·nent [pûr′mən·ənt] *adj.* Continuing without change, lasting.— **per·ma·nent·ly,** *adv.*

per·plexed [pər·plekst′] *adj.* Puzzled; bewildered.

phi·lan·thro·pist [fi·lan′thrə·pist] *n.* A person who gives a great deal of time or money to helping others.

Pied Piper of Hamelin [pīd′ pī′pər uv ham′lin] A musician in a German folk story who led the rats out of the city of Hamelin by playing his pipe—a small flute or whistle. In revenge for not being paid he led the children of the city away also. *Pied* means having or wearing two or more colors in patches.

pier [pir] *n.* A structure built on pillars and jutting out over water, used as a landing place or walk.

pike [pīk] *n.* Road; turnpike.

pil·grim [pil′grim] *n.* A wanderer or traveler.

pix·ie *or* **pix·y** [pik′sē] 1 *n.* A fairy or elf. 2 *v.* To cast a magic spell over.— **pix·ied.**

plaque [plak] *n.* A flat metal plate with words or pictures pressed into it.

play out [plā′ out′] *v.* **played out** To use up, finish.

plun·der [plun′dər] *v.* **plun·dered** To rob of property or goods by force.

point [point] *n.* 1 A narrow piece of land extending out into water; cape. 2 The sharp end of something.

pol·i·cy [pol′ə·sē] *n.* A plan or method of action or conduct.

por·poise [pôr′pəs] *n.* A sea mammal similar to a small whale, mostly blackish with a blunt snout.

port·fo·li·o [pôrt·fō′lē·ō] *n.* A flat case for carrying papers or drawings.

po·si·tion [pə·zish′ən] *n.* 1 The place where someone or something is, especially in relation to other things or people. 2 A job.

po·tion [pō′shən] *n.* A liquid that is supposed to have medicinal, poisonous, or magical qualities.

prac·ti·cal [prak′ti·kəl] *adj.* Useful.

prai·rie [prâr′ē] *n.* A large area of level grassy land having few or no trees.

praise [prāz] *v.* **praised** To give a high opinion of something; show approval.

pre·dict [pri·dikt′] *v.* To say what is going to happen before it happens.

pre·dic·tion [pri·dik′shən] *n.* The act of saying what is going to happen before it happens: The weather forecaster's *prediction* is rain for Friday.

pre·fer [pri·fûr′] *v.* To like better.

pres·ent-day [prez′ənt·dā′] *adj.* As of now; modern.

pres·to [pres′tō] 1 *interj.* Before you know it; quickly, suddenly: "*Presto!*" is what a magician says when pulling a rabbit out of a hat. 2 *adj.* In music, very quick.

pre·vail·ing wes·ter·lies [pri·vā′ling wes′tər·lēz] *n., pl.* The west winds that are common in middle latitudes both north and south of the equator.

prey [prā] *n.* Any animal seized by another for food.

prick·ly [prik′lē] *adj.* 1 Having small, sharp points, as a cactus. 2 Stinging: a *prickly* feeling.

prin·ci·pal [prin′sə·pəl] 1 *n.* The head of an elementary school or high school. 2 *adj.* First in rank or importance; chief.

prin·ci·ple [prin′sə·pəl] *n.* 1 Good moral standards; honesty; fairness: The judge is a woman of *principle.* 2 A general truth or rule on which other truths are based: the *principle* of democracy.

proc·ess [pros′es] *n.* A way of making or doing something.

---

pro·ces·sion [prə·sesh′ən] *n.* A formal and serious parade.
pro·claim [prō·klām′] *v.* To make known; announce to the public.
pro·fes·sion [prə·fesh′ən] *n.* An occupation requiring a good education and mental—rather than physical—labor.
pro·fes·sion·al [prə·fesh′ən·əl] *adj.* 1 Describing a sport with players who are paid to play and practice under a manager's control. 2 Of or working in a profession.
prof·it [prof′it] *n.* The amount of money gained in a business deal after deducting all expenses.
pro·fuse·ly [prə·fyo͞os′lē] *adv.* In a generous way; abundantly.
proj·ect 1 [proj′ekt] *n.* A problem or task. 2 [prə·jekt′] *v.* To jut. 3 [prə·jekt′] *v.* To throw forward.
pro·nounce [prə·nouns′] *v.* To declare; to announce that something is so.
prop [prop] *n.* Any movable object needed on the stage for a play, except costumes and scenery.
pro·pose [prə·pōz′] *v.* **pro·posed** To put forward as a suggestion to be considered.
pros·per·i·ty [pros·per′ə·tē] *n.* The state of having more than enough on which to live.
pros·per·ous [pros′pər·əs] *adj.* Successful; thriving; wealthy and comfortable.
Pueb·lo [pweb′lō] 1 *adj.* Pertaining to a group of American Indian tribes in the Southwest. These tribes lived in towns with houses made of brick or stone. The Spanish word for "town" is *pueblo,* so the Spaniards called them the Pueblo people. 2 *n.* A member of a Pueblo tribe.
Puer·to Ri·co [pwer′tō rē′kō] *n.* An island in the West Indies that is a self-governing possession of the United States.
puf·fin [puf′in] *n.* A sea bird of the North Atlantic with a short neck and a triangular bill.

punc·ture [pungk′chər] *v.* To pierce with something sharp.

Q

quar·ry [kwôr′ē] *n.* An open place from which stone is removed for various uses.
quartz [kwôrtz] *n.* A hard glasslike mineral, sometimes found in colored forms.
ques·tion·naire [kwes′chən·âr′] *n.* A list of questions, usually printed, used to get information from a person.

R

raft [raft] *n.* A floating platform made of logs fastened together.

ram [ram] *n.* A male sheep.
rare [râr] *adj.* 1 Very unusual. 2 Hard to find. 3 Undercooked: *rare* meat.

add, āce, câre, pälm; end, ēqual; it, īce; odd, ōpen, ôrder; to͝ok, po͞ol; up, bûrn; ə = a in *above,* e in *sicken,* i in *possible,* o in *melon,* u in *circus;* yo͞o = u in *fuse;* oil; pout; check; ring; thin; this; zh in *vision.*

ra·vine [rə·vēn′] *n.* A long, narrow gorge or depression in the earth, usually cut out by a flow of water.

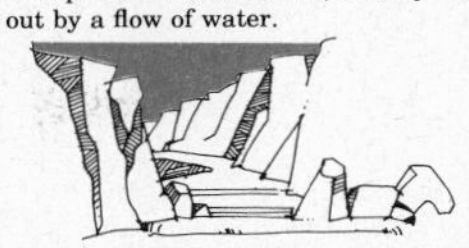

raw [rô] *adj.* 1 Not cooked. 2 Not processed: *raw* sugar. 3 Damp and chilling: *raw* weather.
ray [rā] *n.* 1 In mathematics, a part of a line that begins at a given point on the line and extends in only one direction. 2 A beam of light.
re·ac·tion [rē·ak′shən] *n.* 1 The action of two or more chemicals on one another; chemical change. 2 An action in response to something.
read·y-made [red′ē·mād′] *adj.* Clothing that you buy in a store. *Ready-made* clothes fit people of various sizes.
re·al·i·ty [rē·al′ə·tē] *n.* An actual person, thing, or fact.
re·al·ize [rē′əl·īz] *v.* To understand fully.
rear ad·mi·ral [rir′ ad′mə·rəl] *n.* A rank in the U.S. Navy above captain.
re·cep·tion [ri·sep′shən] *n.* 1 A receiving or welcoming. 2 A party at which hosts greet their guests.
rec·og·ni·tion [rek′əg·nish′ən] *n.* Notice and approval.
rec·og·nize [rek′əg·nīz] *v.* To identify, know.
rec·re·a·tion [rek′rē·ā′shən] *n.* Play, amusement, or relaxation.
re·gion [rē′jən] *n.* An area of land, usually large; a district.
re·hears·al [ri·hûr′səl] *n.* A practice session or performance to prepare for a public performance.
re·jec·tion [ri·jek′shən] *n.* The act of refusing to accept something.
re·la·tion [ri·lā′shən] *n.* 1 A connection between people and groups brought about by business or other contacts. 2 A connection between people by family or marriage.
re·lease [ri·lēs′] *v.* **re·leased** 1 To make available to the public; put on sale. 2 To set free.
re·mark·a·ble [ri·mär′kə·bəl] *adj.* Extraordinary, unusual, worthy of notice.
re·pro·duc·tion [rē′prə·duk′shən] *n.* The process by which animals or plants produce new life.
rep·tile [rep′til *or* rep′tīl] *n.* A cold-blooded animal that crawls on its belly or creeps on very short legs. Snakes, lizards, and crocodiles are reptiles.
req·ui·si·tion [rek′wə·zish′ən] *n.* A formal request or demand.
re·sist [ri·zist′] *v.* To refuse to give in to; to oppose.
re·solve [ri·zolv′] *v.* **re·solved** To decide firmly.
re·spect·ed [ri·spek′tid] *adj.* Honored; highly regarded.—**re·spect,** *v.*
re·spect·ful·ly [ri·spekt′fə·lē] *adv.* Politely.
res·pi·ra·to·ry [res′pə·rə·tôr′ē *or* ri·spīr′ə·tôr′ē] *adj.* Having to do with breathing.
re·spon·si·bil·i·ty [ri·spon′sə·bil′ə·tē] *n.* Duty or obligation.
re·stric·tion [ri·strik′shən] *n.* Something that limits something else.
re·view [ri·vyo͞o′] 1 *n.* An article that tells about and judges new books, plays, etc. 2 *v.* To go over again.
rib [rib] *n.* 1 One of the long, curving bones enclosing a person's or animal's chest. 2 A thing like a rib in use or shape, as the curved pieces in the framework of a boat.

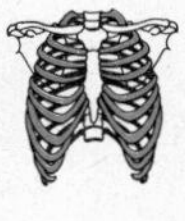

ridged [rijd] *adj.* Having a number of raised strips.
rif·fle [rif′əl] *v.* **rif·fling** To turn pages impatiently.
riled [rīld] *adj. informal* Angry.
Rip Van Win·kle [rip′ van′ wing′kəl] In Washington Irving's story, the hero who wakes after sleeping twenty years and finds the world changed.
ri·val [rī′vəl] *n.* Someone who wants the same thing that another person wants; a competitor: One team is a *rival* of another team.
rol·ling [rō′ling] *adj.* Hilly; swaying.
rough [ruf] *adj.* 1 Done quickly without worrying about small things. 2 Not smooth; bumpy.

S

sac [sak] *n.* A baglike part in an animal or plant. It usually contains a fluid.
Sac·a·ja·we·a [sä′kə·jə·wē′ə] 1787?–1884, an American Indian woman who helped the explorers Lewis and Clark.
sac·ri·fice [sak′rə·fīs] 1 *n.* The giving up of something. 2 *v.* To give up something.
sage·brush [sāj′brush′] *n.* A small shrub with white or yellow flowers found on the dry plains of the western U.S.
sand·bar [sand′bär′] *n.* A ridge of sand built by flowing water, as in a river.
scat·ter·ing [skat′ər·ing] *n.* 1 The breaking up and spreading of a beam of light by something that bends it in many directions. 2 A small number or amount of something spread all around.
schol·ar [skol′ər] *n.* A person who has learned a great deal through study.
schol·ar·ship [skol′ər·ship] *n.* Money that is awarded to a student to help pay for his or her education.
schoon·er [sko͞o′nər] *n.* A ship having two or more masts.

scoff [skof] *v.* **scoffed** To show disbelief; laugh at.
scull [skul] *n.* 1 A long oar worked from side to side over the rear of a boat. 2 A light, short oar, used in pairs by one person.
sec·tion [sek′shən] *n.* 1 A separate part or division. 2 A part of a city or community; district, area.
sen·si·tive [sen′sə·tiv] *adj.* Able to feel and recognize things easily and rapidly.
Se·quoi·a Na·tion·al Park [si·kwoi′ə nash′ən·əl pärk′] *n.* A national park in central California. It includes groves of giant sequoia trees and the highest mountain in the continental United States.
set [set] 1 *n.* All the scenery needed for one or more scenes of a play or movie. 2 *v.* To put in a certain position; place.
set·tee [se·tē′] *n.* A long bench or sofa with a back and arms, usually for two or three people.

add, āce, câre, pälm; end, ēqual; it, īce; odd, ōpen, ôrder; to͝ok, po͞ol; up, bûrn; ə = a in *above,* e in *sicken,* i in *possible,* o in *melon,* u in *circus;* yo͞o = u in *fuse;* oil; pout; check; ring; thin; this; zh in *vision.*

set·ting [set′ing] *n.* 1 Surroundings; environment. 2 The time and place of a work of literature.
shal·low [shal′ō] 1 *adj.* Not deep. 2 *n.* (*usually plural*) A shallow place in a body of water.
shan·ty [shan′tē] *n.* A roughly made, hastily built shack or cabin.
Sho·sho·ne [shō·shō′nē] 1 *adj.* Coming from a group of American Indian tribes that spoke the Shoshone language. These tribes used to live in the land that is now California and the northwestern states. 2 *n.* A member of a Shoshone tribe.
shrill [shril] *v.* **shrilled** To say or ask in high, piercing tones.
shuf·fle [shuf′əl] *v.* 1 To drag (the feet) in walking or dancing. 2 To push about or mix together without order.
si·lo [sī′lō] *n.* A tower for storing grain.
Sin·bad the Sail·or [sin′bad] In the *Arabian Nights,* a merchant who has adventures when he goes on a voyage.
sin·is·ter [sin′is·tər] *adj.* Threatening evil, trouble, or bad luck.
skull [skul] *n.* The bony framework or skeleton of the head.
slash [slash] *v.* **slashed** To cut through quickly, as with a knife.
slosh [slosh] *v.* **slosh·ing** To move, wade, or plod through water or mud.
smoke·shed [smōk′shed′] *n.* A building or room filled with smoke for treating or curing meat, fish, or cheese.
smug·gle [smug′əl] *v.* To bring in or take out secretly.
snake [snāk] *v.* **snaked** To move, wind, or crawl like a snake.
sod [sod] *n.* The top layer of earth held together by twisted roots of grass.
so·lar [sō′lər] *adj.* Relating to the sun.
so·lo [sō′lō] *adj.* Done by one person.
soothe [so͞oth] *v.* 1 To calm. 2 To soften or relieve: to *soothe* someone's grief.
source [sôrs] *n.* The thing, place, or person from which something comes.
span [span] *v.* **spanned** To extend across.
spe·cies [spē′shēz] *n., pl.* A group of living things that are alike and able to breed with one another.
spec·u·late [spek′yə·lāt] *v.* To form theories; to imagine possible reasons or answers for something.
spell·bound [spel′bound′] *adj.* 1 Not able to move, as if tied down by magic. 2 Under a magic spell.
spiral [spī′rəl] 1 *adj.* Winding or curving like a cone-shaped coil. 2 *n.* A curve. 3 *v.* To move in a curving path.
sprang [sprang] *v.* Moved suddenly and rapidly; leaped.—past tense of **spring.**
spun [spun] *v.* Twisted into thread; made into (yarn) by spinning.—past tense and past participle of **spin.**
squawk [skwôk] 1 *n.* A harsh, shrill cry. 2 *v.* To make a harsh, shrill cry.—**squawked.**
squid [skwid] *n.* A sea animal with ten arms. It has a long thin body, tail fins, and two arms that are longer than the other eight.
stage name [stāj′ nām′] *n.* The name a professional performer uses instead of the name given at birth.
stan·dard [stan′dərd] *adj.* 1 Made just like the model. 2 Widely accepted; regularly used.
Stan·dard Time [stan′dərd tīm′] *n.* A system for having all the clocks in a large area set at the same time.
steed [stēd] *n.* A horse, especially a spirited war horse.
stee·ple [stē′pəl] *n.* A tall structure that narrows to a point at its top, rising above a church tower.
stock [stok] *n.* 1 Farm animals. 2 A supply of something kept for use or sale. 3 The wooden part of a rifle that serves as a handle or support.

strag·gle [strag′əl] v. **strag·gled** To lag behind those one is traveling with.

stretch [strech] 1 n. A large area. 2 v. To extend beyond normal size.

stride [strīd] n. A long, sweeping step.

strike [strīk] 1 n. Discovery. 2 v. To make contact with; hit.

strode [strōd] v. Walked with long, sweeping steps.—past tense of **stride**.

style [stīl] n. 1 An individual manner of singing, playing an instrument, writing, etc. 2 The way in which something is done, built, etc.: a Greek *style* of architecture.

su·per·sti·tion [sōō′pər·stish′ən] n. The fear or belief, without reason, that certain things or actions will cause good or bad luck.

surf [sûrf] n. The waves of the sea as they break on a beach or reef.

surge [sûrj] 1 n. A rush; a sudden swelling or flow. 2 v. To move with a strong rush or wave.

sur·vey [sər·vā′] v. To measure exactly.

sur·vey·or [sər·vā′ər] n. A person who measures land.

sur·vive [sər·vīv′] v. To live through; remain alive.

swell [swel] 1 n. The long, continuous body of a rolling wave. 2 To increase or cause to increase.

T

tack·le [tak′əl] 1 n. Equipment or gear for a certain use. 2 v. To grab or attack.

tap [tap] 1 v. To release liquid from (something) by drilling a hole. 2 n. A light blow. 3 n. A faucet that controls the flow of liquids: a water *tap*.

tar·pau·lin [tär·pô′lin or tär′pə·lin] n. A piece of canvas or other material that has been made waterproof, used to cover exposed objects.

tech·ni·cal [tek′ni·kəl] adj. Having to do with mechanical or industrial skills.

tech·ni·cian [tek·nish′ən] n. A person who can adjust and handle electrical or other equipment, such as that used in staging a play.

the·a·ter [thē′ə·tər] n. 1 The arts involved in putting on plays. 2 A place built for the presentation of plays, films, and other performances.

thick·et [thik′it] n. A thick, dense growth, as of trees and bushes.

Thor [thôr] The god of thunder, war, and strength worshipped in northern Europe in early times.

tire·some [tīr′səm] adj. Boring; time-consuming.

ti·tle [tīt′əl] 1 n. A descriptive name given to show rank or honor. 2 n. The name of a book, story, play, etc. 3 v. To give a name.—**ti·tled**.

tongue [tung] n. 1 A language or dialect: the Greek *tongue*. 2 The movable muscular organ in the mouth used in eating or speaking.

tor·rent [tôr′ənt] n. A rapid flow.

trace [trās] 1 n. A very small amount of something. 2 n. A mark or sign left by some person or thing. 3 v. To follow the course or development of.

tramp [tramp] v. **tramp·ing** To hike.

trans·fer [trans′fər or trans·fûr′] v. **trans·ferred** To move from one person or place to another.

trans·lu·cent [trans·lōō′sənt] adj. Allowing some light to pass through but blocking a view of objects.

add, āce, câre, pälm;   end, ēqual;   it, īce;   odd, ōpen, ôrder;   tŏŏk, pōōl;   up, bûrn;
ə = a in *above*, e in *sicken*, i in *possible*, o in *melon*, u in *circus*;   yōō = u in *fuse*;   oil;   pout;
check;   ring;   thin;   ʇhis;   zh in *vision*.

571

---

trans·par·ent [trans·pâr′ənt] adj. So clear that objects on the far side can be easily seen.

tri·an·gu·lar [trī·ang′gyə·lər] adj. Having to do with, or shaped like, a triangle; having three sides.

trib·al [trī′bəl] adj. Having to do with a tribe or tribes.

trib·ute [trib′yōōt] n. 1 Money or other payment given by one group of people to another on demand, often as the price of peace and protection. 2 A speech, compliment, gift, etc., given to another with admiration, gratitude, or respect.

trig·ger [trig′ər] n. 1 Something that starts an action. 2 The small lever that fires a gun.

trill [tril] n. The rapid alternating of two tones that are nearly alike.

trol·ley [trol′ē] n. A kind of bus that runs on tracks through a city.

trough [trôf] n. A long, narrow, open box that holds food or water for animals.

tune [t(y)ōōn] 1 v. To adjust the strings of, to make the tones correct. 2 n. A melody, usually simple and easy to remember. 3 n. The condition of being at the proper musical pitch.

tu·tor [t(y)ōō′tər] n. A person who teaches another, usually privately.

tweez·ers [twē′zerz] n., pl. A small instrument used for grasping and holding small objects.

Twin Cit·ies [twin′ sit′ēz] n. St. Paul, the capital of Minnesota, and nearby Minneapolis, the state's biggest city.

twine [twīn] n. A heavy string made up of two or more strands twisted together.

twit·ter [twit′ər] v. **twit·tered** To utter light, high, chirping sounds like a bird.

typ·i·cal [tip′i·kəl] adj. Having the qualities or features of a whole group.

U

U·lys·ses [yōō·lis′ēz] The Latin name for *Odysseus*, the Greek hero of Homer's *Odyssey*.

un·cer·e·mo·ni·ous·ly [un′ser·ə·mō′nē·əs·lē] adv. In an informal, sometimes rude, way.

un·furl [un·fûrl′] v. **un·furl·ing** To spread out or open; uncurl or unroll.

un·paved [un·pāvd′] adj. Not paved; said of a surface that is not covered with concrete or other material.

ur·ban [ûr′bən] adj. Of, in, or having to do with a city.

V

valve [valv] n. 1 Half of the shell of a clam, oyster, etc. 2 A device in a musical instrument that opens and closes an air passage and so changes the pitch of a tone. 3 Any device that controls the flow of liquid, as through a pipe. *Valve* comes from the Latin word *valva*, meaning "the leaf of a door."

---

vane [vān] n. A device that shows the wind's direction. A fin at the rear end turns a pointer toward the wind.

vast [vast] adj. Huge; of very large size.

ven·i·son [ven′ə·sən] n. The flesh of deer, used as food.

vice·roy [vīs′roi] n. A person appointed to rule a country, colony, etc., as the personal agent of the king or emperor.

vic·to·ry [vik′tər·ē] n. Success; the overcoming of an enemy or of difficulty.

vir·tue [vûr′chōō] n. Good quality; moral excellence.

vis·i·ble [viz′ə·bəl] adj. Capable of being seen.

vo·cal cords [vō′kəl kôrdz′] n., pl. Either of two pairs of folds of membrane that stick out into the throat. The lower pair can be made to move back and forth and produce voice sounds when air from the lungs passes between them.

W

wake [wāk] 1 n. The track of disturbed water left behind by a moving ship. 2 v. To stop sleeping.

wal·lop [wol′əp] 1 n. *informal* A hard hit. 2 v. To strike with a wallop; beat soundly.—**wal·lop·ing**, adj. Large, impressive.

wal·low [wol′ō] 1 v. To roll or tumble about; to flounder, as in mud or water. 2 n. A muddy area used by animals for wallowing.

war·ble [wôr′bəl] v. **war·bling** To whistle or sing with trills, as some birds do.

ward·robe [wôrd′rōb′] n. 1 A collection of costumes, as in the theater. 2 A collection of clothing.

wash·board [wäsh′bôrd′ or wôsh′bôrd′] n. A board with a rippled metal surface: Sudsy clothes are rubbed on a *washboard* to squeeze the dirt out.

wea·ry [wir′ē] adj. Tired.

weath·er [weth′ər] v. **weath·ered** To change in looks and color by rain, wind, cold, etc.: The white house had *weathered* and was now gray.

weath·er·ing [weth′ər·ing] n. The process of breaking down rock by the weather's action.

well [wel] v. **welled** To rise up or flow, as water from a spring.

West [west] n. 1 North America, South America, and Europe. 2 The western part of the United States, especially west of the Mississippi River.

West In·dies [west′ in′dēz] n. A chain of islands extending eastward from southern Mexico past Puerto Rico, then bending south to South America.

wet·land [wet′land′] n. Swamps and marshes.

whol·ly [hō′lē] adv. Fully, completely.

win·dow box [win′dō boks′] n. A long box in which flowers can be planted. The *window box* may be either hung outside a window or set on a porch.

wink [wingk] v. **wink·ing** 1 To give off light in short flashes; twinkle. 2 To close and open the eye rapidly, often as a sign or hint.

World's Fair [wûrldz′ fâr′] A large fair in which a number of nations exhibit their goods, inventions, art, etc.

wring [ring] v. 1 To squeeze or twist, usually to get water out of. 2 To get by force, violence, or threats: to *wring* an answer out of someone.

add, āce, câre, pälm;   end, ēqual;   it, īce;   odd, ōpen, ôrder;   tŏŏk, pōōl;   up, bûrn;
ə = a in *above*, e in *sicken*, i in *possible*, o in *melon*, u in *circus*;   yōō = u in *fuse*;   oil;   pout;
check;   ring;   thin;   ʇhis;   zh in *vision*.

573

Y

yam [yam] n. A kind of sweet potato.

yelp [yelp] v. **yelped** To cry or bark sharply.

Yo·ru·ba [yō·rōō′bə] n. West African tribe from what is now Nigeria.

Z

Zeus [zōōs] The chief and most powerful of the ancient Greek gods.

zo·ol·o·gy [zō·ol′ə·gē] n. The science that has to do with animals, their classification, structure, development, etc.

add, āce, câre, pälm;   end, ēqual;   it, īce;   odd, ōpen, ôrder;   tŏŏk, pōōl;   up, bûrn;
ə = a in *above*, e in *sicken*, i in *possible*, o in *melon*, u in *circus*;   yōō = u in *fuse*;   oil;   pout;
check;   ring;   thin;   ʇhis;   zh in *vision*.

574

Index of Titles and Authors

575

576

B
C 3
D 4
E 5
F 6
G 7
H 8
I 9
J 0

Name _____

Context Clues

A. Decide the meaning of each underlined word. Use context clues to help you. Then fill in the circle next to the correct answer.

1. The sailors raised the **jib** before any of the other sails.

ⓐ a kind of dance   **ⓑ** a sail on a boat

ⓒ a kind of boat

2. I used to live in a city, but now I live in a **rural** area.

ⓐ crowded   **ⓑ** having to do with the country   ⓒ noisy

3. That was only a little **tiff.** Tom and I don't really fight.

ⓐ an unimportant quarrel   **ⓑ** a lie   ⓒ a hint

4. We looked up at the **tiers** of seats rising above us.

ⓐ rows of things placed one above the other

ⓑ kinds of theaters   ⓒ kinds of decorations

5. The wide brim of the **sombrero** shades the face of the wearer.

ⓐ an umbrella   **ⓑ** a kind of tree   ⓒ a kind of hat

6. Jenny, June, Maggie, and Sue live on Prairie Street. People call them the neighborhood **quartet.**

ⓐ a group of four   **ⓑ** neighbors   ⓒ a theater group

B. Complete each sentence below with an underlined word from part A.

1. The _____ started with a slight disagreement.

2. I belong to a musical _____. The four of us sing every week.

3. Many artists like to paint _____ scenes of barns and rolling hills.

4. The sailor mended a tear in the _____.

5. In Mexico, I bought a _____ to keep the sun out of my eyes.

6. Isabel's beautiful skirt had many _____ of lace.

Name _____

Clues to Word Meaning

A. How many word parts does each word have? Write the answer next to each word.

penniless _____   reread _____   replacement _____

traveler _____   bygone _____   hopeful _____

unworkable _____   gingerbread _____   misjudge _____

unimportant _____   disobey _____   gearshift _____

B. Choose one of the words from part *A* to complete each sentence below. Use the kind of word that is called for in parentheses.

1. (a root word with a suffix)

My mother is a cheery and _____ person.

2. (a compound word)

Many people enjoy remembering _____ years.

3. (a word with three word parts)

We will need a _____ for the part that is lost.

4. (a word with a prefix meaning "wrong")

I didn't want to _____ Jennifer's behavior. So I thought

about what I would do if I were Jennifer.

5. (a root word whose spelling is changed when a suffix is added)

After I spent all my savings, I was _____ .

6. (a word with three word parts)

Joe tried to do the puzzle, but without the missing pieces it was _____ .

7. (a word with the prefix meaning "again")

Isabel had to _____ the directions carefully to find the store.

8. (a compound word)

The _____ cookies that Father baked were delicious.

Name _____

The Dictionary

A. Write the letter of each word next to the dictionary respelling that it matches. Use the pronunciation key if necessary.

1. rep′ri·zent′ _____   **a.** cope

2. kōp _____   **b.** legion

3. kən·fyōo′zhən _____   **c.** represent

4. lē′jən _____   **d.** confusion

5. rə·pid′ə·tē _____   **e.** dolphins

6. sangk′chōo·er′ē _____   **f.** sanctuary

7. i·lā′tid _____   **g.** rapidity

8. dol′finz _____   **h.** elated

*add, āce, câre, pälm; end, ēqual; it, īce; odd, ōpen, ôrder; tŏŏk, pōol; up, bûrn;
ə = a in *above*, e in *sicken*, i in *possible*, o in *melon*, u in *circus;* yōo = u in *fuse;* oil; pout;
check; ring; thin; this; zh in *vision*.

B. Underline the words in part *A* that have more than one accented syllable.

C. Read the following sentences. Use the dictionary entry for *dash*. Choose the meaning that fits each sentence, and write the number of the definition on the line.

*dash [dash] **1** *v.* To throw violently so as to break or shatter: Angrily he *dashed* the vase to pieces. **2** *v.* To strike; hit: Waves *dashed* against the rocks. **3** *n.* A striking against; blow: the *dash* of rain on a windowpane. **4** *v.* To splash or sprinkle: After she fainted, we *dashed* water on her face. **5** *v.* To destroy; ruin: to *dash* hopes. **6** *v.* To rush: The children *dashed* out onto the playground. **7** *n.* A short race; sprint: a 50-yard *dash*. **8** *n.* A small bit: a *dash* of salt. **9** *n.* Spirit; zest: The Johnsons always add *dash* to a party. **10** *n.* A horizontal line (—) used as a punctuation mark, usually to show a pause or break in a sentence.

1. Wendy won the 20-meter **dash**. _____

2. Add a **dash** of pepper to the soup. _____

3. The definition followed a **dash** in the sentence. _____

4. If you want to be on time, you'll have to **dash**. _____

5. The news will **dash** her hopes of winning the prize. _____

6. The red scarf added **dash** to her appearance. _____

D. Now study the following entries for *mint*. Which entry gives the meaning used in each of the sentences below? Fill in the circle of the correct answer.

*mint¹ [mint] *n.* **1** Any of several sweet-smelling plants whose leaves are used for flavoring, especially peppermint and spearmint. **2** A candy flavored with mint.
mint² [mint] **1 *n.* A place where coins are lawfully made. **2** *v.* To make (coins). **3** *n.* A large amount: a *mint* of money. **4** *adj.* In original condition; brand-new; unused.

1. Miki found an old book in mint condition. ① ②

2. Chris took a piece of mint from the salad. ① ②

Name _____

Cause-and-Effect Relationships

A. Find the cause-and-effect relationships in the sentences below. Underline the words that express the cause. Draw two lines under the words that tell the effect.

1. Janice was hungry, so she made herself a big sandwich.

2. The camel's long eyelashes are important because they help shade its eyes from the bright desert sun.

3. Suddenly, it began to rain. The crowd ran for shelter.

4. The store had a sale, and so it was crowded all day long.

5. As a result of the successful sale, the store had only a few items left.

6. Jet planes make a great deal of noise. Therefore, many people dislike living near an airport.

7. The citizens believed the election was an important event. They turned out in great numbers to vote.

8. The sun was very hot. We all got bad sunburns.

9. It was −10°C. I was freezing in my light coat.

10. John got exactly what he wanted for his birthday. He was very pleased.

B. In the sentences in part A, circle the connecting words that signal the cause-and-effect relationship. (Not all the sentences have connecting words.)

C. Write the connecting word or words you could use to show the cause-and-effect relationship in the following sentences from part A.

1. sentence 3 _____   3. sentence 8 _____

2. sentence 7 _____   4. sentence 9 _____

Name _____

The Parts of a Book

A. Suppose that the examples below were in a book. In what part of the book would you find each one? Choose your answer from the following boldfaced words, and write it on the line after each example.

index   table of contents   glossary
introduction   bibliography

1. *Saved by a Princess*, by H. H. Higgins. American History

   Company. An exciting account of early settlers' lives. _____

2. Wampanoag [wam'pən•ō'ag] A Native American tribe. _____

3. Chapter 10. The Lost Colony . . . . . 215 _____

4. The stories in this book are true. They are based on

   the author's childhood in South Carolina. _____

5. Dare, Virginia, 219–221, 239 _____

B. Write *yes* or *no* on the line following each question.

1. Can an index tell you on how many pages a topic is

   mentioned in a book?   _____

2. Can you always find page numbers in a glossary?   _____

3. Do all books have an introduction?   _____

4. Does a table of contents show the parts of the book? _____

5. Could you use a bibliography to find the title of a book

   you might like to read?   _____

6. Can you find a list of books in an index?   _____

7. Does a glossary appear at the beginning of a book?   _____

8. Does a table of contents show topics in alphabetical

   order?   _____

Name _____

Topical Organization

A. Read the first paragraph of the article below. Underline the words that suggest topics you think will be covered in the article. Then finish reading the article.

① What's your favorite time of year? Is it the spring? Is it summer? Do you like autumn best, or winter?

② All the earth renews itself in the spring. What a lovely time it is! After a long winter, the new leaves and buds and flowers are very welcome. So is the change in the air. There is a softness in the air of spring that seems to make everyone happy.

③ It's no wonder that children like the summertime. It's vacation time, and there are long daylight hours for play. The days may be hot, but the children have fun.

④ But wait! How can anyone who lives where the seasons change resist the fall? The air is crisp and the trees wear their brightest dress. Many artists love the fall.

⑤ Fall brings us Halloween, Thanksgiving, pumpkin pies, football games, country fairs, and fallen leaves to play in.

⑥ Skaters and skiers love the winter. Even where the winter months do not bring snow, there are enjoyable changes on the earth. There are lovely winter holidays, too.

⑦ Indeed, there is surely something for everyone as each season rolls around.

B. How are the topics in this article related? Fill in the circle next to the correct answer.

① They are all about fun.　　③ They are all about things to do.

② They are all about seasons.　　④ They are all about holidays.

C. Read the beginning part of each sentence below. Fill in the circle next to the word that best completes the sentence.

1. Paragraph 2 is about　ⓐ spring　ⓑ summer　ⓒ fall　ⓓ winter.

2. Paragraph 3 is about　ⓐ spring　ⓑ summer　ⓒ fall　ⓓ winter.

3. Paragraph 4 is about　ⓐ spring　ⓑ summer　ⓒ fall　ⓓ winter.

4. Paragraph 5 is about　ⓐ spring　ⓑ summer　ⓒ fall　ⓓ winter.

5. Paragraph 6 is about　ⓐ spring　ⓑ summer　ⓒ fall　ⓓ winter.

D. Which paragraph introduces all the topics? Paragraph _____

Outlining

A. Complete the following framework for an outline. Write *major topic* **or** *subtopic* **on the line where it belongs.**

            Title

  I. Major topic

     A. Subtopic

     B. _____

 II. _____

     A. _____

     B. Subtopic

III. _____

B. Read the following paragraph. Write the details from the paragraph in outline form on the lines at the bottom of the page. Remember to use Roman numerals and capital letters and to give your outline a title.

My visit to the West included three states. In Texas I stayed two days in San Antonio. I also visited the Houston Space Center. In Arizona I saw the "Old West" town of Tombstone and, of course, the Grand Canyon. I drove home by way of Santa Fe, New Mexico.

_____

___ _____

    ___ _____

    ___ _____

___ _____

    ___ _____

    ___ _____

___ _____

Name _____

The Library

A. Which reference books would you use to find the answers to questions 1 through 8 below? Next to each question, write the letter that stands for the book you would use. For some questions, there is more than one book in which you could find the answer.

a. atlas   **c.** encyclopedia   **e.** rhyming dictionary

b. almanac   **d.** foreign language dictionary   **f.** biographical dictionary

1. Is there a rhyme for *minute*? _____

2. What is the longest river in Europe? _____

3. What was the first telegraph message? _____

4. How do you say "thank you" in German? _____

5. When was Beethoven born? _____

6. What is the capital of India? _____

7. Who invented the bicycle? _____

8. Who climbed Mt. Everest in 1980? _____

B. Study the catalogue card below. Then write your answers to the questions below the card.

```
J           SEASONS
500.9
A     Allison, Linda
            The Reasons for Seasons
               Little, Brown © 1975

         124 pp.
```

1. Is this an author card, a title card, or a subject card? _____

2. What is the book's title? _____

3. Where would you find this book? Fill in the circle next to the correct answer.

ⓐ with adult nonfiction   ⓒ with children's nonfiction

ⓑ with children's fiction   ⓓ with adult fiction

4. How many pages does the book have? _____

Name _____

The Topic and Main Idea of a Paragraph

A. Read each paragraph. What is the topic of each paragraph? Fill in the circle next to the correct answer.

1. The moth differs from the butterfly in several ways. The moth has featherlike antennae. The ends of a butterfly's antennae are knobbed. Most butterflies fly during the daytime. Most moths fly at night. Butterflies are helpful insects. They carry pollen from flower to flower. Except for the silk moth, most moths are harmful. They attack crops and trees. The "clothes moth" eats feathers and wool clothing.

(a) the clothes moth

(b) the silk moth

(c) butterflies and moths

(d) how moths fly

2. Three conditions combine to cause storms or tornadoes. One condition is a thick layer of warm, moist air near the earth's surface. The next condition is a layer of cold, heavy air above the warm air. Finally, if there are also strong winds about five miles above the earth, there may be a storm or tornado.

(a) causes of tornadoes and storms

(b) warm air

(c) strong winds

(d) earth's surface

3. There are many kinds of cactus plants. They vary widely in shape and size. Some cactus plants look like low bushes. Others grow like vines with roots exposed to the air. Some are short and bushy, while others grow as tall as trees. Some cactus plants provide a useful source of food, while others bear beautiful flowers that bloom in the night.

(a) bushes and trees

(b) roots that are exposed to the air

(c) shapes and sizes of plants

(d) cactus plants

4. The Golden Gate Bridge in the San Francisco area of California is one of the greatest suspension bridges in the world. Its overall length is nearly 9,000 feet. The bridge is made of steel and is supported from two towers by very thick cables that are over three feet in diameter. The bridge was completed in 1937.

(a) suspension bridges of the world

(b) towers

(c) steel and cables

(d) the Golden Gate Bridge

B. Which sentence in each paragraph in part *A* states the main idea? Underline that sentence in each paragraph.

Name _____

Unstated Main Ideas and Details

Read each paragraph below. Then answer the questions.

A. Rushing rivers have slowly carved out great canyons in the earth. Over a million years, high mountain peaks have been worn down into hills by the wind and weather. Ocean waves have changed rock cliffs into tiny grains of sand. The glaciers of ice that once covered the earth have helped to make the soil we have today.

1. What is the unstated main idea? Fill in the circle next to the correct answer.

(a) Over time, the earth's surface has been changing.

(b) Ocean waves changed rock cliffs.

(c) The earth was once covered by glaciers.

2. What details from the paragraph help explain the main idea? List the details below.

_____

_____

_____

B. Many businesses and factories have been moving away from the big cities. Many city-dwellers are leaving, too. More and more housing is being built in rural areas. Studies show that the population of most large cities is decreasing. At the same time, smaller towns are growing.

1. What is the unstated main idea? Fill in the circle next to the correct answer.

(a) Many houses have been built in the country.

(b) More Americans seem to be moving to cities.

(c) Many Americans are becoming interested in rural living.

2. Underline the details in the paragraph that help explain the unstated main idea.

Name _____

Pictures and Diagrams

Study the graphic aids and the caption. Write the word *picture*, *diagram*, or *caption* to complete each sentence.

Hurricane winds blow with terrible force. They reach speeds far above 150 miles an hour and do much damage. Oddly, however, the center, or "eye," of the storm is calm.

Wind Direction in a Hurricane

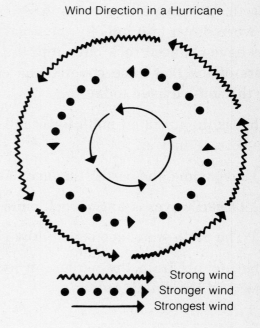

〰〰〰➤ Strong wind
●●●●●➤ Stronger wind
————➤ Strongest wind

1. The graphic aid on the right is called a _____.

2. The graphic aid on the left is called a _____.

3. The _____ tells about the picture.

4. The _____ gives information about the speeds reached by hurricane winds.

5. The words below the picture are called a _____.

6. An example of what can happen in a hurricane is clear from the _____.

7. Details of wind direction can be learned only from the _____.

8. From the _____, you can learn that the eye of a hurricane is calm.

9. The _____ tells you it is hard for a person to walk against a hurricane's wind.

Name _____

Maps and Graphs

Study the subway map below.

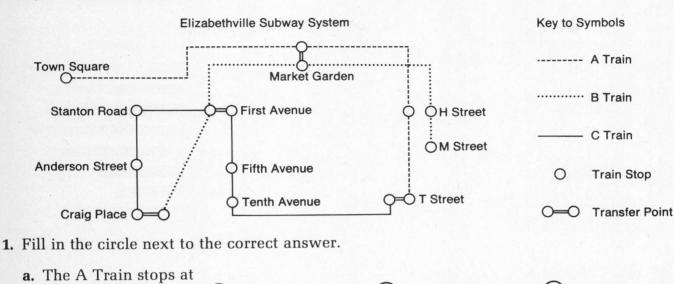

1. Fill in the circle next to the correct answer.

   a. The A Train stops at
   ① First Avenue   ② Craig Place   ③ Town Square   ④ Anderson Street.

   b. The B Train Stops at
   ① Stanton Road   ② T Street   ③ Market Garden   ④ Fifth Avenue.

   c. The C Train stops at
   ① M Street   ② Tenth Avenue   ③ Town Square   ④ Market Garden.

2. Judy lives at Craig Place and wants to go to Stanton Road. Which train should she take?   _____

3. Sally wants to go from First Avenue to H Street.

   a. At how many stations will she stop if she takes the B Train all the way?   _____

   b. If she takes the C Train, at what station must she transfer to the A Train?   _____

   c. If she takes the C Train and transfers to the A Train, at how many stations will she stop?   _____

4. Cliff lives on Fifth Avenue. He wants to go to Town Square. There are several different routes he can take. With your pen or pencil, trace the route Cliff must take on the map above if he wants to pass the fewest stops. (Count each transfer point as one stop.)

Name _____

Maps and Graphs

Study the three graphs below.

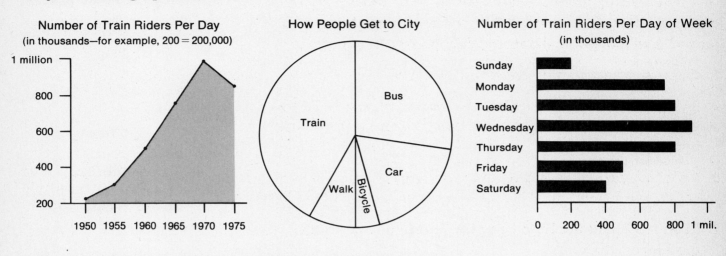

A. Read the beginning part of each sentence. Fill in the circle next to the correct answer.

1. The train had the greatest number of riders in (**a**) 1950 (**b**) 1955 (**c**) 1960 (**d**) 1970.

2. The train had the fewest riders in (**a**) 1950 (**b**) 1960 (**c**) 1970 (**d**) 1975.

3. The smallest number of people get to the city by (**a**) bicycle (**b**) train (**c**) bus (**d**) car.

4. The most people use the train on (**a**) Sunday (**b**) Wednesday (**c**) Monday (**d**) Friday.

B. Write *circle, line,* or *bar* on the line after each sentence to show which graph is related to the sentence.

1. Few people use their cars to get to work in the city. Trains and buses can get to the city faster than cars during rush hour.

   _____

2. Many businesses have four-day work-weeks. Many people also take long weekends. Therefore, there are more people going to work during the middle of the week than on Friday or Monday.

   _____

3. Many companies moved from the city in the 1970's. Few new businesses moved to the city. So there were fewer workers coming to the city in 1975 than in 1970.

   _____

Name _____

Facts and Fictional Details

A. Write *fact* or *fictional detail* on the line after each sentence to show what it is. A fact is something that can be proved, and a fictional detail is something made-up.

1. The first wheel was invented long, long ago. _____

2. A boy named Iago invented the bow and arrow 50,000 years ago when he shot his spear from a bent tree branch. _____

3. My dictionary says a hurricane is "a storm with strong winds and heavy rain." _____

4. "You see," said the little Princess Elizabeth, "my father is the King of England." _____

5. Long after Columbus's time, some people still believed that the earth was flat. _____

B. Read the following paragraphs. Then underline the sentences below each paragraph that are facts on which the story might be based.

1. Young Abe Lincoln was stretched out by the fireplace reading. The flames made lights shine in his dark hair. After an hour he got up and poked the fire to make more light. "You just keep burning bright awhile," he said, "so I can finish this book tonight." He knew he could not read the next day. He had to work hard all day on his father's farm.

a. Paintings and photographs show that Abe Lincoln had dark hair.

b. In Lincoln's time, many people read by firelight.

c. Lincoln was the sixteenth President of the United States.

d. Historical records show that Lincoln read a great deal.

2. "I would like our capital to be the most beautiful city in the world," said Benjamin to Andrew. The two friends were standing near the site of the future capital of the United States on the Potomac River. "It will take us many years of hard work, but it will be done," replied Andrew.

a. Benjamin Banneker was a land surveyor.

b. Historical records show that Banneker played an important part in building Washington, D.C.

c. Benjamin Banneker and Andrew Ellicott had a lasting friendship.

d. Benjamin wrote almanacs.

Drawing Conclusions

A. Read the paragraphs below. Study the conclusions that follow each one. Underline *two* conclusions that can be drawn from each paragraph.

1. The captain watched the radar screen closely as the ship moved ahead. She knew there were icebergs in this region. Suddenly she exclaimed softly. Then she ordered the ship to change direction.

a. The captain thought something was wrong with the ship's engine.

b. The radar had picked up something dangerous nearby.

c. The captain didn't want the ship to hit an iceberg.

d. The captain ordered the ship to stop.

2. When Terry looked out the window, she clapped her hands. Then she called to her sister. "Beth, look outside!" Beaming, the two children raced to the hall closet and eagerly dragged out their sleds.

a. It was summer.

b. It was winter.

c. There was snow on the ground.

d. It was raining hard.

3. The Lee family was delighted that it turned out to be a sunny day. As soon as they arrived at the site, the family pitched their tent. When the tent was up, Mr. and Mrs. Lee started to gather wood for the fire and the boys and girls started changing into their swimming clothes.

a. The Lee family went fishing.

b. The Lee family was near water.

c. The Lee family went home.

d. The Lee family went camping.

4. Sam saw the lions pace back and forth in their cages. In the arena were two monkeys in colorful costumes, balancing themselves on a barrel. Then he saw the trapeze artists flying from one swing to another, trying to perfect their act.

a. Sam went to a circus rehearsal.

b. Sam went to the zoo.

c. Sam went to the new circus movie.

d. Sam went to the museum.

B. Look at the dictionary entry and picture at the right. Study the conclusions listed below. Underline the one conclusion you can draw.

* **cow·catch·er** [kou′kach′ər] *n.* An iron frame on the front of a locomotive or streetcar to clear off anything on the track.

Cowcatcher

1. The cowcatcher pushes only cows off a track.

2. Cowhands use cowcatchers to round up cattle.

3. It is easier to push something off the tracks with a cowcatcher than with the bare front of a locomotive.

4. Cowcatchers were invented before the first trains were invented.

5. Cowcatchers are not used on modern trains.

Name _____

Generalizing

A. Write *valid* next to each generalization that is valid. A valid generalization should cover more than one or two specific cases. In each false generalization, circle the word that makes the statement false. Then write *false* on the line.

1. Everybody likes red and yellow. _____

2. It is never warm in the winter. _____

3. Many good writers read a great deal. _____

4. All artists are painters. _____

5. Cats and dogs are always enemies. _____

6. Most birds can fly. _____

7. Hurricanes sometimes do a lot of damage. _____

8. No one can lift that bag of sand. _____

B. Choose the one valid generalization that can be made based on the facts in each of the following paragraphs. Fill in the circle next to the correct answer.

1. The pioneers worked from sunrise to sundown. The men did most of the heavy work out-of-doors, felling trees and building cabins. Women worked hard both indoors and out, often working in the fields with the men. The children had work to do, too. Most pioneers had very little time to play. But when they did have time, it is said, they *really* played.

ⓐ Only men worked in pioneer days.

ⓑ Most pioneers had a hard and busy life.

ⓒ The pioneers worked hard all the time.

ⓓ The pioneers led a comfortable life.

2. Maria spends most of her free time reading. She likes reading biographies of famous people. She often stays up late into the night reading novels and plays. Maria also enjoys reading the magazines that come to her house every month. Every morning before she goes to school she likes to read about current events in the newspaper.

ⓐ Maria reads nothing but magazines.

ⓑ Maria enjoys all kinds of reading.

ⓒ Maria likes to read only biographies.

ⓓ Maria does not like reading at all.

Name _____

Comparison and Contrast

**A. Write either *comparison* or *contrast* on the line to show
what each sentence or sentence pair is. For any sentence or
pair of sentences that shows both comparison and contrast,
write *both* on the line.**

1. The little white clouds look like sheep in the sky.   _____

2. Giraffes, leopards, and some big snakes are alike in one
   way—they are all spotted.   _____

3. Leopards and snakes are meat-eaters. However, giraffes
   are plant-eaters.   _____

4. Once, much of the American farmer's work was done by
   hand. But today machines do the work.   _____

5. Tom's bike had three gear-speeds and a coaster brake.
   But Jim's was a ten-speed racer.   _____

6. The two bikes were the same color, and they had the
   same kind of seat.   _____

7. Pianos and flutes look very different and are played in
   different ways, but they both make a beautiful sound.   _____

**B. Underline the word clues to comparison and contrast in
the sentences above.**

C. Fill in the circle next to the correct answer.

1. What is being compared in sentence 1 in part *A*?

   (a) clouds and sheep   (b) sheep and sky

2. What is being compared in sentence 2?

   (a) the food of some animals   (b) the appearance of some animals

3. What is contrasted in sentence 5?

   (a) gears and brakes   (b) two bikes

4. What is being contrasted in sentence 4?

   (a) different kinds of farm work   (b) farm work at different times

Answers to Worksheets

Worksheet 1, Page T480
A. **1.** b **2.** b **3.** a **4.** a **5.** c **6.** a
B. **1.** tiff **2.** quartet **3.** rural **4.** jib **5.** sombrero
   6. tiers

Worksheet 2, Page T481
A. penniless, 2   reread, 2   replacement, 3
   traveler, 2   bygone, 2   hopeful, 2
   unworkable, 3   gingerbread, 2   misjudge, 2
   unimportant, 2   disobey, 2   gearshift, 2
B. **1.** hopeful **2.** bygone **3.** replacement **4.** misjudge
   5. penniless **6.** unworkable **7.** reread **8.** gingerbread

Worksheet 3, Page T482
A. **1.** c **2.** a **3.** d **4.** b **5.** g **6.** f **7.** h **8.** e
B. represent, sanctuary
C. **1.** 7 **2.** 8 **3.** 10 **4.** 6 **5.** 5 **6.** 9
D. **1.** 2 **2.** 1

Worksheet 4, Page T483
A. **1.** Cause: Janice was hungry
      Effect: she made herself a big sandwich
   2. Cause: they help shade its eyes from the bright
      desert sun
      Effect: The camel's long eyelashes are important
   3. Cause: Suddenly, it began to rain
      Effect: The crowd ran for shelter
   4. Cause: The store had a sale
      Effect: it was crowded all day long
   5. Cause: the successful sale
      Effect: the store had only a few items left
   6. Cause: Jet planes make a great deal of noise
      Effect: many people dislike living near an airport
   7. Cause: The citizens believed the election was an
      important event
      Effect: They turned out in great numbers to vote
   8. Cause: The sun was very hot
      Effect: We all got bad sunburns
   9. Cause: It was −10°C
      Effect: I was freezing in my light coat
   10. Cause: John got exactly what he wanted for his
      birthday
      Effect: He was very pleased
B. **1.** so **2.** because **3.** — **4.** and so **5.** As a result
   6. Therefore **7.** — **8.** — **9.** — **10.** —
C. **1.** So, Therefore, That is why, For this reason
   2. So, Therefore, That is why, For this reason
   3. So, Therefore, That is why, As a result
   4. So, Therefore, That is why, As a result

Worksheet 5, Page T484
A. **1.** bibliography **2.** glossary **3.** table of contents
   4. introduction (or bibliography) **5.** index
B. **1.** yes **2.** no **3.** no **4.** yes **5.** yes **6.** no **7.** no
   8. no

Worksheet 6, Page T485
A. time of year *or* spring, summer, autumn, winter
B. 2
C. **1.** a **2.** b **3.** c **4.** c **5.** d
D. 1

Worksheet 7, Page T486
A. Additions are in boldface.
   Title
   I. Major topic
      A. Subtopic
      B. **Subtopic**
   II. **Major topic**
      A. **Subtopic**
      B. Subtopic
   III. **Major topic**
B. My Visit to the West
   I. Texas
      A. San Antonio
      B. Houston Space Center
   II. Arizona
      A. Tombstone
      B. Grand Canyon
   III. Santa Fe, New Mexico

Worksheet 8, Page T487
A. **1.** e **2.** a, b, c **3.** c **4.** d **5.** c, f **6.** a, b, c **7.** b,
   c **8.** b, c
B. **1.** subject **2.** *The Reasons for Seasons* **3.** c
   4. 124

Worksheet 9, Page T488
A. **1.** c **2.** a **3.** d **4.** d
B. **1.** The moth differs from the butterfly in several
      ways.
   2. Three conditions combine to cause storms or tor-
      nadoes.
   3. There are many kinds of cactus plants.
   4. The Golden Gate Bridge in the San Francisco
      area of California is one of the greatest suspen-
      sion bridges in the world.

Worksheet 10, Page T489
A. **1.** a
   2. Rivers carved canyons. Wind and weather wore
      down mountains. Ocean waves wore down cliffs.
      Glaciers helped make soil.
B. **1.** c
   2. Many businesses and factories have been moving
      away from the big cities.
      Many city-dwellers are leaving, too. More housing
      is being built in rural areas.
      Population of most large cities is decreasing.
      Smaller towns are growing.

Worksheet 11, Page T490
1. diagram
2. picture
3. caption
4. caption
5. caption
6. picture
7. diagram
8. caption
9. picture

Worksheet 12 (part I), Page T491
1. **a.** 3 **b.** 3 **c.** 2
2. C Train
3. **a.** two **b.** T Street **c.** four
4. C Train from Fifth Avenue to First Avenue, B Train to Market Garden, A Train to Town Square

Worksheet 12 (part II), Page T492
A. 1. d **2.** a **3.** a **4.** b
B. 1. circle **2.** bar **3.** line

Worksheet 13, Page T493
A. 1. fact **2.** fictional detail **3.** fact **4.** fictional detail
   5. fact
B. 1. sentences a, b, d **2.** sentences a, b, c

Worksheet 14, Page T494
A. 1. b, c **2.** b, c **3.** b, d **4.** a, c
B. sentence 3

Worksheet 15, Page T495
A. 1. false, Everybody **2.** false, never **3.** valid
   4. false, All **5.** false, always **6.** valid **7.** valid
   8. false, No one
B. 1. b **2.** b

Worksheet 16, Page T496
A. 1. comparison **2.** comparison **3.** both **4.** contrast
   5. contrast **6.** comparison **7.** both
B. 1. like **2.** alike **3.** and (comparison); However
   (contrast) **4.** But **5.** But **6.** same, same **7.** different,
   different (contrast); but, both (comparison)
C. 1. a **2.** b **3.** b **4.** b

Skills Index

This Skills Index locates the pages in this Teacher's Edition on which each listed skill is taught. The numbers preceding the items in the index correspond to those that follow objectives in the teaching plans and are part of the HBJ Skills Code. The code may be used to locate materials related to a skill throughout all components and levels of the HBJ BOOKMARK READING PROGRAM, EAGLE EDITION. It can also serve as a basis for correlating the HBJ BOOKMARK READING PROGRAM, EAGLE EDITION with the management system or curriculum guide used in a school district. The code may be used to facilitate correlation of skills in the HBJ BOOKMARK READING PROGRAM, EAGLE EDITION with other new language arts and reading programs published by the School Department of Harcourt Brace Jovanovich. Teachers who wish to cross-reference these programs may do so by referring to these same numbers in each of the HBJ School Department programs in which they appear.

Boldfaced abbreviations identify a page from the *Reading Skills* book (**RS**) or *Duplicating Masters* (**DM**), or a *Worksheet* (**W**) from the back of this Teacher's Edition. Other page numbers, preceded by a T, refer to this Teacher's Edition.

Code Number	Skill	Pages
	Word Service/Decoding	
2.1; 2.2	to identify sound-letter relationships	T26–T29, T31
2.6	to identify the number of syllables in a word	T26–T29, **RS 3**/T29, T31, **DM 4**/T35, **DM 6**/T39, **W 2**, T140, T400
2.7;	to develop vocabulary words and concepts;	T15, **DM 1**/T15, T31, **DM 3**/T31, T36,
2.7; 3.0.1	to develop vocabulary words and concepts using context clues	**DM 5**/T36, T53, **DM 7**/T54, T69, **DM 9**/T69, T74, **DM 11**/T74, T93, **DM 13A**/T93, T99, **DM 13B**/T100, T110, **DM 14–15**/T111, T135, **DM 17**/T135, T140, **DM 19**/T140, T155, **DM 21**/T156, T174, **DM 23**/T174, T190, **DM 25**/T191, **DM 27**/T197, T215, **DM 29A**/T215, T220, **DM 29B**/T220, T225, **DM 30**/T225, T244, **DM 32**/T245, T249, **DM 34**/T250, T264, **DM 36**/T265, T269, **DM 38**/T270, T285, **DM 40**/T285, T290, **DM 42**/T291, T308, **DM 44**/T309, T314, **DM 46**/T315, T332, **DM 48**/T333, T337, **DM 49**/T338, T343, **DM 50**/T344, T364, **DM 52**/T365, T380, **DM 54**/T381, T385, **DM 56**/T386, T400, **DM 58**/T400, T405, **DM 60**/T406, T421, **DM 62**/T422, T426, **DM 64**/T427, T446, **DM 66**/T447, T452, **DM 67**/T453, T459, **DM 68–69**/T460
	Comprehension Skills	
3.0	to identify definitions in context	T10–T13, T15, T21–T23, T174
3.0.2	to identify and use context clues to determine word meaning	T10–T13, **RS 1**/T13, T15, **DM 2**/T20, T21–T23, **W 1**, T140, T173, **RS 16**/T173, T420, **RS 39**/T420

	Skill	Pages
Code Number	**Comprehension Skills, continued**	
3.1.2	to identify clues to time-order relationships	T190, **RS 19**/T195, T196, **RS 19**/T200, T421
3.2.1	to classify stated details by identifying groups to which they belong	T290, T308, T337
3.3.1; 3.3.3.8	to identify details that support the stated main idea of a paragraph	T36, T260–T262, **DM 37**/T268, **DM 39**/T269
3.3.1; 3.4.7	to use details to determine the unstated main idea of a paragraph	T260–T262, **RS 24**/T262, T264, T269, T274–T275, **W 10**, T405
3.3.3	to identify cause-and-effect relationships	T64–T67, **RS 7**/T67, T69, **DM 10**/T73, T74, **DM 12**/T77, T79–T81, **W 4**, T196, T249, T385
3.3.3.1	to identify words that signal cause-and-effect relationships	T64–T67, T69, T74, T79–T81
3.3.7.4	to determine the correct sequence for a set of events	T15, T53, T190, T196, T380, T405, T421
3.3.8	to identify the topic and the stated main idea of a paragraph	T36, T74, T239–T242, **RS 21**/T242, T244, **DM 33**/T247, T249, **DM 35**/T252, T254–T255, **W 9**, T260–T262, T264, T269, T274–T275, T380, T405
3.3.8.5	to identify comparisons and contrasts	T417–T419, **RS 38**/T419, T421, **DM 63**/T425, T426, **DM 65**/T429, T431–T434, **W 16**
3.4	to make inferences	T452
3.4.1	to draw conclusions based on given information and personal knowledge	T31, T190, T376–T378, **RS 34**/T378, T380, **DM 55**/T384, T385, **DM 57**/T389, T390–T392, **W 14**
3.4.2	to predict outcomes based on given information and personal knowledge	T69, T308, **RS 30**/T313
3.4.3	to make generalizations based on given information	T396–T398, **RS 36**/T398, **DM 59**/T404, T405, **DM 61**/T409, **W 15**
3.5.1	to distinguish between homophones	T52, **RS 6**/T52, T379, **RS 35**/T379
3.5.3; 3.0	to identify and use antonyms as context clues	T10–T13, T15, T134, **RS 11**/T134, T363, **RS 33**/T363
3.5.4; 3.0	to identify and use synonyms as context clues	T10–T13, T15, T68, **RS 8**/T68, T243, **RS 22**/T243
3.5.5; 3.0.2	to use context clues to determine the meanings of multiple-meaning words	T14, **RS 2**/T14, T189, **RS 18**/T189
3.6.1	to identify faulty conclusions; to distinguish valid from faulty generalizations	T376–T378, T385, T390–T392, T396–T398, T400, T405, T410–T412
3.6.3	to distinguish between fact and opinion	T15, T140, T244, **RS 23**/T248
3.6.4	to identify an author's purpose	T53, T426, **RS 40**/T430
3.6.7	to distinguish between facts and fictional details	T359–T362, **RS 32**/T362, T364, T368, **DM 53**/T369, T371–T372, **W 13,** T446, T452, T459
3.6.8	to identify information on which stated conclusions are based	T376–T378, T380, T385, T390–T392
3.6.9	to identify facts on which fictional accounts may be based	T359–T362, T364, T371–T373

Code Number	Skill	Pages
	Comprehension Skills, continued	
3.7	to recognize humor in illustrations	I110
	Language Skills	
4.1	to identify word parts: root words, prefixes, and suffixes	T26–T29, T31, T36, T41–T43, T155, T174, T263, **RS 25**/T263, T284, **RS 27**/T284, T399, **RS 37**/T399, T426
4.2.1	to identify base words in compound words	T26–T29, T30, **RS 4**/T30, T36, T41–T43, T135, T155, T264, T307, **RS 29**/T307, T314
4.4.1	to use etymologies to determine word meaning	T154, **RS 13**/T154
4.6.2	to identify antecedents of pronouns	T385
	Study Skills	
5.3.1	to follow a set of written directions	T155, **RS 14**/T160
5.4	to identify types of graphic aids	T302–T306, T308, T319–T321
5.4.1	to interpret information from a bar graph	T302–T306, T308, T314, T319–T321, T364
5.4.3	to interpret information from a map	T74, T302–T306, T308, T314, T319–T321, T364
5.4.3; 5.4.1	getting information from maps and graphs	**RS 28**/T305, **DM 45**/T313, **DM 47**/T318, **W 12**
5.4.4	to interpret information from a diagram	T280–T283, T295–T297
5.4.5	to interpret information from a picture	T69, T280–T283, T285, T290, T295–T297
5.4.7	to compare information obtained from graphic aids to textual information	T280–T283, **RS 26**/T283, T285, **DM 41**/T288, T290, **DM 43**/T294, **W 11,** T302–T306, T308, T319–T321, T400
5.5	to identify parts of a book where specific information may be found	T130–T133, **RS 10**/T133, T135, **DM 18**/T138, T140, **DM 20**/T142, **W 5**
5.5.1	to describe the purpose of an introduction	T130–T133
5.5.3	to use a table of contents	T130–T133, T144–T145, T249
5.5.6	to use a bibliography	T130–T133
5.5.8	to use an index	T130–T133, T144–T145, T290
5.6.3	to use guide words in a dictionary	T380
5.6.4	to use a dictionary to find word meaning	**RS 5**/T51, T53, **DM 8**/T58, **W 3**, T174, T269, T285
5.6.4; 5.6.6	to locate dictionary and glossary entries	T48–T51, T53, T60–T61
5.6.5	to use a dictionary pronunciation key	T48–T51
5.6.6	to use a glossary to find pronunciation and meaning	T130–T133
5.9	to scan a selection for specific information	T36, T135, T421
5.10.1	to identify topical organization	T150–T153, **RS 12**/T153, T155, **DM 22**/T159, T161–T164, **W 6**, T269, T290
5.10.2	to identify introductory paragraphs	T150–T153, T155
5.10.3	to identify summary paragraphs	T150–T153, T155
5.11	to identify reference materials in which specific information may be found	T31, T184–T188, T190, T196, T201–T203, T285

Code Number	Skill	Pages
	Study Skills, continued	
5.11.1	to use an encyclopedia	T244
5.11.2	to locate and use library catalogue cards	T184–T188, **RS 17**/T188, T190, **DM 26**/T195, T196, **DM 28**/T200, T201–T203, **W 8**, T244
	Literature Appreciation	
6.2.2	to recognize lyric poetry	T220
6.2.3	to recognize narrative poetry	T225
6.4.7	to identify historical fiction	T442–T445, **RS 41**/T445, T446, T452, T459, **DM 70**/T468
6.4.7.1	to identify historical events and real people in historical fiction	T442–T445, T446, T452, T459
6.4.7.2	to identify fictional details in historical fiction	T442–T445, T446, T452
6.6.1; 6.6.2	to recognize rhyme and stanzas in poetry	T220, T225
6.6.5	to recognize elements of humor	T89–T92, **RS 9**/T92, T93, T99, T110, **DM 16**/T120, T343
6.6.5.1	to recognize surprise endings or the unexpected in humor	T89–T92, T99, T110
6.6.6.3	to recognize sensory imagery in poetry	T211–T214, **RS 20**/T214, T215, **DM 31**/T229
6.6.6.4	to identify simile	T211–T214, T215, T220, T225
6.6.6.5	to identify metaphor	T211–T214, T215, T225
6.6.6.6	to recognize exaggeration as an element in humor	T89–T92, T93
6.6.6.7	to recognize word play as an element in humor	T89–T92, T99, T110
6.6.6.8	to identify personification	T211–T214, T215, T220
6.9.1	to identify theme in a story	T332
6.9.2	to compare and contrast story characters	T332
6.9.3	to recognize author's techniques of characterization	T343, T446, T459
6.9.3.3	to identify techniques of characterization: characters' words and actions	T93
6.9.4	to interpret characters' feelings and traits	T332, T337, T343, T446, T459
6.10	to identify the setting of a story	T459
6.11	to identify the plot of a story	T459
6.11.1	to recognize elements of plot	T332
6.12	to identify theme in a story	T329–T331, **RS 31**/T331, T332, T337, T343, **DM 51**/T349
6.12.1	to identify story details that relate to theme	T329–T331, T337, T343
	Writing	
7.1.5.1	to write a topical outline	T167–T172, **RS 15**/T171, T174, **DM 24**/T178, T179–T181, **W 7**, T264, T314
7.1.5.1.1	to write a title for a topical outline	T167–T172, T174

Scope and Sequence
of Continuous Skills Development
for Levels 10 through 12

The following symbols are used in the chart:

   I indicates the level at which a skill is introduced for the first time.
   M indicates the levels at which a skill is maintained.
   ❶ indicates the levels at which a skill is taught for mastery and tested in
      HBJ BOOKMARK, EAGLE EDITION management and evaluation components.

The Skills Index on page T499 contains references to specific pages in this
Teacher's Edition, the *Reading Skills Workbook,* the *Duplicating Masters,* and
the *Worksheets* for each skills objective identified for Level 11.

Levels

Word Service/Decoding		10	11	12
to build vocabulary		Vocabulary concepts are reinforced in all units at every level.		
to recognize or contrast sounds represented by single consonants and variant spellings		**M❶**	**M**	**M**
to recognize or contrast sounds represented by consonant digraphs		**M❶**	**M**	**M**
to recognize or contrast sounds of consonant digraphs represented by variant spellings		**M❶**	**M**	**M**
to recognize or contrast sounds represented by consonant clusters		**M❶**	**M**	**M**
to identify words using context and knowledge of initial and final consonants		**M**	**M**	**M**
to use context clues to identify words		**M❶**	**M❶**	**M**
to identify words using context and knowledge of phonics		**M❶**	**M❶**	**M**
to recognize or contrast short vowel sounds represented by variant vowel letters and variant spellings (See also phonograms.)	/a/	**M❶**	**M**	**M**
	/e/	**M❶**	**M**	**M**
	/i/	**M❶**	**M**	**M**
	/o/	**M❶**	**M**	**M**
	/u/	**M❶**	**M**	**M**
to recognize or contrast long vowel sounds represented by variant vowel letters and variant spellings (See also phonograms.)	/ā/	**M❶**	**M**	**M**
	/ē/	**M❶**	**M**	**M**
	/ī/	**M❶**	**M**	**M**
	/ō/	**M❶**	**M**	**M**
	/ū/	**M❶**	**M**	**M**

Word Service/Decoding, continued	Levels		
	10	11	12
to recognize other vowel sounds /ou/	M⊕	M	M
/oi/	M	M	M
/ô/	M⊕	M	M
/o͝o/	M⊕	M	M
/o͞o/	M⊕	M	M
/yo͞o/	M⊕	M	M
/ə/	M	M	M
to recognize syllables and accents	M⊕	M⊕	M

Comprehension (See also Literature Appreciation.)	10	11	12
to relate reading to illustrations	M	M	M
to classify words and sentences by association and function	M		
to recognize and understand word groups, phrases, and sentences	M	M	
to relate word order to sentence meaning	M⊕	M	M
to recognize punctuation as a clue to meaning	M	M	M
to use literal comprehension skills	M⊕	M⊕	M⊕
to use inferential comprehension skills	M⊕	M⊕	M⊕
to use critical comprehension skills	M	M	M
to recognize cause-and-effect relationships	M⊕	M⊕	M⊕
to infer: drawing conclusions	M⊕	M⊕	M⊕
to infer: predicting outcomes	M⊕	M	M⊕
to recognize a sequence of events	M⊕	M	M
to recognize the same idea stated in different words	M	M	M⊕
to recognize multiple ideas in sentences	M	M⊕	M⊕
to recognize multiple meanings of words	M⊕	M⊕	M
to recognize and understand questions	M	M	M
to recognize synonyms and antonyms	M⊕	M⊕	M
to use context clues to meaning	M⊕	M⊕	M
to identify words that signal fact and opinion	M⊕	M	M
to identify words that signal cause-and-effect relationships	M⊕	M⊕	M⊕
to identify pronouns and their antecedents	M⊕	M	M
to follow written directions	M⊕	M	M⊕
to recognize time order	M⊕	M	M
to recognize and recall details	M	M	M

Comprehension, continued	10	11	12
to recognize the main idea	M⊕	M⊕	M⊕
to distinguish between main idea and details	M⊕	M⊕	M⊕
to identify details that support the main idea	M⊕	M⊕	M⊕
to make an analogy	M	M	M
to make judgments	M	M	M
to summarize and paraphrase information	M	M	M
to distinguish between fact and opinion	M⊕	M⊕	M⊕
to recognize the author's purpose	M	M	M⊕
to identify the unstated main idea of a paragraph or selection	M	M⊕	M
to identify the topic of a paragraph or selection	M⊕	M⊕	M⊕
to distinguish between topic and main idea	M⊕	M⊕	M⊕
to identify conclusions, predictions, and speculations made by the author		I⊕	M⊕
to identify comparisons and contrasts in a selection	I	M⊕	M
to make generalizations		I⊕	M
to identify and judge the validity of the author's generalizations		I⊕	M
to identify different kinds of paragraphs		I⊕	M
to distinguish between facts and fictional details		I⊕	M
to distinguish between important and unimportant details in a paragraph			I⊕
to identify and distinguish between examples of slanted and objective writing			I⊕
to identify definitions in context		M⊕	

Language Skills	10	11	12
to extend language experience	M	M	M
to recognize and understand word groups, phrases, and sentences	M	M	
to relate word order to sentence meaning	M⊕	M	M
to recognize and understand questions	M	M	M
to recognize punctuation as a clue to meaning	M	M	M
to identify pronouns and their antecedents	M⊕	M	M
to recognize possessive forms	M		
to recognize typographical signals	M	M	M
to recognize contractions	M	M	
to recognize compound words and base words	M⊕	M⊕	M
to recognize homographs and homophones	M	M⊕	M
to identify inflected forms: nouns with -s, -es	M		

Language Skills, continued	10	11	12
to recognize inflected forms: spelling changes	M	M (T)	
to recognize irregular plural nouns	M	M	M
to identify root words	M (T)	M (T)	M
to recognize prefixes	M (T)	M (T)	M
to recognize suffixes	M (T)	M (T)	M
to identify Greek and Latin word parts	M	M	M
to recognize syllables and accents	M (T)	M (T)	M

Study Skills	10	11	12
to use the table of contents	M	M (T)	M
to recognize titles and subtitles	M	M (T)	M
to follow oral or written directions	M (T)	M	M (T)
to alphabetize	M (T)	M	
to use an index	M	M (T)	M
to compare information from graphic aids to textual information	M	M (T)	M
to use dictionary skills: entry words, guide words, pronunciation key	M (T)	M (T)	M
to skim and scan a selection	M	M	M (T)
to adjust reading speed to purpose			I (T)
to get information from an illustration	M (T)	M (T)	M (T)
to get information from a map	M (T)	M (T)	M
to get information from a diagram	M (T)	M (T)	M
to get information from a chart or table			M
to interpret captions	M (T)	M (T)	M (T)
to get information from a graph or time line	M (T)	M (T)	M
to use a dictionary or glossary to find pronunciation and meaning	M (T)	M (T)	M
to compare dictionary and glossary	M	M	M
to use an encyclopedia	M	M (T)	M (T)
to compare encyclopedia and dictionary	M	M (T)	M (T)
to use library skills to get specific information from books and other media	I	M (T)	M (T)
to use library skills: card catalogue	I	M (T)	M
to use an index	I	M (T)	M
to use a bibliography		I (T)	M
to summarize and paraphrase information	M	M	M
to identify topical organization		I (T)	M (T)
to write a topical outline		I (T)	M (T)

Study Skills, continued

	10	11	12
to identify useful study habits			I⊕
to take notes on a selection			I⊕
to identify and use parts of a newspaper and magazine			I⊕
to recognize metric terms	M	M	M
to identify reference materials in which specific information may be found		M⊕	

Literature Appreciation

	10	11	12
(An asterisk * identifies the level at which a literature appreciation skill is formally introduced in an Intermediate teaching unit, although students have had prior instruction in the skill at the Primary levels.)			
to develop skill in oral and choral reading	Oral reading activities occur in every teaching unit at every level. A choral reading selection and plays are introduced at Level 4.		
to compare and contrast selections	M	M	M
to recognize elements of characterization	M	M	M
to interpret characters' feelings and actions	M	M	M
to recognize techniques of characterization: author's description, other characters' descriptions, characters' words and actions	I	M	M
to create a story or story ending	M	M	M
to recognize and distinguish between forms of writing: realistic fiction and fantasy		M	M
to distinguish between narrative and expository writing	M	M	M
to recognize forms of writing: poetry	M	M	M
to recognize lyric, humorous, and narrative poetry	I	M	M
to recognize forms of writing: play	M	M	M
to recognize various forms of folk literature: folktales, fairy tales, fables, myths, hero tales, and tall tales	M	M	M
to identify theme		I	
to recognize plot sequence and development	M	M *	M
to recognize setting	M	M *	M
to identify elements of setting: explicit and implicit clues to time and place, changes in setting	I	M	M
to distinguish between nonfiction and fiction	M	M	M
to interpret figurative language	M	M	M
to identify simile and metaphor		I	M
to identify alliteration and onomatopoeia			I

Literature Appreciation, continued	10	11	12
to recognize forms of writing: biography and autobiography	M	M	M
to recognize various forms of humor	M	M	M
to recognize nonsense words and other imaginative uses of language	M	M	M
to recognize irony, exaggeration, satire, and personification	M	M	M
to recognize elements of poetry: rhyme, meter, form, and stanzas	M	M	M
to recognize imagery and consise expression in poetry		I	M
to recognize new views of familiar things in poetry	I	M	M
to interpret mood	M	M	M
to identify point of view in stories			M
to recognize differences in authors' and poets' styles	I	M	M
to recognize the relationship between an author's or poet's life and work	I	M	M
to recognize forms of writing: historical fiction		I	
to recognize surprise endings or the unexpected in humor		I	

Writing	10	11	12
to write a sentence	I	M	M
to write a paragraph	I	M	M
to write a recipe	I		M
to write an outline		I	M
to write a letter	I	M	M
to write a diary or journal	M	M	M
to write an essay	I	M	M
to write a report	M	M	M
to write a story	M	M	M
to write a fable	I		
to write a poem	M	M	M
to write a play	M	M	M
to write a myth			I

Index of Curriculum Coordination Activities

Selection	Language Arts	Science	Social Studies	Mathematics	Health/Physical Education	Music	Art	Career Education
A Boy and a Raccoon (p. T25)	✓	✓						✓
Penguin Paradise (p. T46)	✓	✓	✓				✓	✓
Living Lights in Our World (p. T47)	✓	✓	✓				✓	✓
Dolphin Days (p. T63)	✓	✓						✓
Giants in the Earth (p. T83)	✓	✓	✓				✓	
The Ship of the Desert (p. T84)	✓	✓	✓				✓	
The Toothpaste Millionaire (p. T121)	✓	✓	✓					✓
The Book That Saved the Earth (p. T122)	✓	✓	✓				✓	✓
Nothing New Under the Sun (Hardly) (p. T124)	✓	✓	✓		✓	✓		✓
A Street of Games (p. T148)	✓	✓	✓			✓	✓	
Feliciano! (p. T149)	✓	✓	✓				✓	✓
Shell Treasures (p. T166)	✓	✓	✓			✓		✓
Start Your Own Theater (p. T183)	✓	✓	✓		✓		✓	✓
Life with the Li'l Folks (p. T205)	✓	✓	✓				✓	✓
Truly a Ballerina (p. T206)	✓		✓			✓	✓	✓
Poetry: Group 1 (p. T231)	✓		✓			✓	✓	
Poetry: Group 2 (p. T232)	✓					✓	✓	
Poetry: Group 3 (p. T233)	✓	✓					✓	✓
Journey of the Tejas Woman (p. T258)	✓		✓				✓	
Lady Moody's Dream (p. T259)	✓		✓				✓	✓
The Peddler's Pack (p. T278)	✓		✓	✓				✓
The Secret of the Sea (p. T279)	✓		✓			✓	✓	✓
Golden Ghosts (p. T300)	✓	✓	✓			✓		✓
"Modern" America in the 1800's (p. T301)	✓	✓					✓	
Sod-Shanty Pioneers (p. T323)	✓		✓	✓			✓	
Whatever Happened to Main Street? (p. T324)	✓		✓				✓	
The Oba Asks for a Mountain: A Nigerian Tale (p. T350)	✓		✓					✓
The Seeing Stick (p. T352)	✓							✓
Petronella (p. T353)	✓						✓	
The Wind Watchers (p. T375)	✓	✓	✓			✓		✓
Curiosities from the Cliffs (p. T394)	✓	✓	✓	✓				✓
Ben Franklin Changes the World (p. T395)	✓	✓	✓	✓				✓
Little Things You Use Every Day (p. T415)	✓	✓			✓		✓	
Gifts from China (p. T416)	✓	✓	✓				✓	✓
He Reached for the Stars (p. T436)	✓	✓	✓				✓	
Daniel Villanueva: The Idea Is to Care (p. T437)	✓	✓					✓	✓
Hamilton Hill: September 18, 1784 (p. T469)	✓		✓					
The Temper of Tempe Wick (p. T470)	✓		✓				✓	
The Little Riders (p. T472)	✓						✓	